ADVANCED
ARTIFICIAL
INTELLIGENCE

Series on Intelligence Science

Series Editor: Zhongzhi Shi *(Chinese Academy of Sciences, China)*

Vol. 1   Advanced Artificial Intelligence
        by Zhongzhi Shi (Chinese Academy of Sciences, China)

ADVANCED ARTIFICIAL INTELLIGENCE

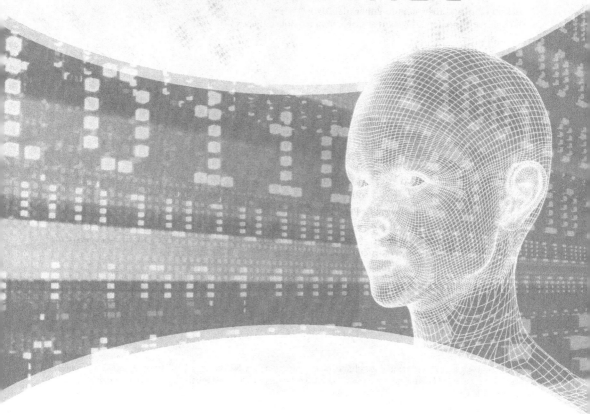

Zhongzhi SHI

World Scientific

NEW JERSEY · LONDON · SINGAPORE · BEIJING · SHANGHAI · HONG KONG · TAIPEI · CHENNAI

Published by

World Scientific Publishing Co. Pte. Ltd.

5 Toh Tuck Link, Singapore 596224

USA office: 27 Warren Street, Suite 401-402, Hackensack, NJ 07601

UK office: 57 Shelton Street, Covent Garden, London WC2H 9HE

British Library Cataloguing-in-Publication Data
A catalogue record for this book is available from the British Library.

ADVANCED ARTIFICIAL INTELLIGENCE
Series on Intelligence Science — Vol. 1

ISBN-13 978-981-4291-34-7
ISBN-10 981-4291-34-X

Printed in Singapore.

Preface

Artificial Intelligence's long-term goal is to build the human level of artificial intelligence. AI was born 50 years ago, in the bumpy road has made encouraging progress, in particular, machine learning, data mining, computer vision, expert systems, natural language processing, planning, robotics and related applications have brought good economic benefits and social benefits. Widespread use of the Internet is also exploring application of knowledge representation and reasoning, to build the semantic Web, improve the effectiveness of the rate of Internet information. The inevitable trend of information technology is intelligent. The intelligence revolution with the goal of replacing work performed by human brain work with machine intelligence will open up the history of human post-civilization. If the steam engine created the industrial society, then the intelligent machine must also be able to magically create a intelligent society to realize the social production automation and intelligence which promote the great development of knowledge-intensive economy.

Artificial intelligence is a branch of computer science, is a discipline to study of machine intelligence, that is to use artificial methods and techniques, developing intelligent machines or intelligent systems to emulate, extension and expansion of human intelligence, realize intelligent behavior. Artificial Intelligence in general can be divided into symbolic intelligence and computational intelligence. Symbolic intelligence is the traditional symbolic artificial intelligence, it is the basis of physical symbol system to study the knowledge representation, acquisition, reasoning process. Use of knowledge to solve problems is basic, the most important features of the current symbol intelligence, so people often put the current stage of artificial intelligence known as knowledge engineering. Knowledge Engineering research emphasis on knowledge information processing methods and technologies, and promote the development of artificial intelligence.

Computational intelligence, including neural computation, fuzzy systems, genetic algorithms, evolutionary planning and so on. To achieve intelligence revolution, we must better understand the human brain. Completely reveal the mysteries of the human brain is one of the biggest challenges facing the natural sciences. The early 21st century, the U.S. National Science Foundation (NSF) and the U.S. Department of Commerce (DOC) jointly funded an ambitious program —Convergent Technology for Improving Human Performance, which view the nano-technology, biotechnology, information technology and cognitive science as the four cutting-edge technology of the 21st century. Cognitive science as a top priority areas for development, advocating the development of these four technology integration, and described the prospects for such a science: cognitive science as the guide of convergent technology, because once we are able to on how, why, where, when to understand the four levels of thinking, we can use nanotechnology to make it with biotechnology and biomedicine to achieve it, and finally the use of information technology to manipulate and control it, make it work. This is a tremendous impact on human society.

On the surface, symbolic intelligence and neural computing is a completely different research methods, the former based on knowledge, The latter based on the data; the former use of reasoning, the latter mapping. In 1996, The invited presentation on "Computers, Emotions and Common Sense" given by Minsky at the fourth Pacific Region International Conference on Artificial Intelligence in the view that neural computation and symbolic computation can be combined and neural network is the foundation of symbolic system. Hybrid System is committed to the people, it is from this combination, which is consistent with our proposed hierarchical model of the human mind.

Agents interact with the environment to achieve intelligent behavior. Agent perception of information received from the environment, to work together to perform a variety of intelligent behavior. Since the 1990s, multi-agent systems become one of the core of artificial intelligence research.

Artificial life refers to the generation or construction of simulation system or model system with behavior characteristics of natural living systems by computers or precision machinery. Artificial life is the formation of new information processing system, a strong impetus to study biology and become a particularly useful tool. The study of artificial life may be combine information science and life science to form life information science which is a new ways of artificial intelligence research.

This book is separated into 15 chapters. The Chapter 1 is the introduction, starts from the cognitive questions of artificial intelligence, describing the guiding ideology of writing this book, an overview of the hot topics for current artificial intelligence research. Chapter 2 discusses logics for artificial intelligence with more systematic discussion of non-monotonic logic, and agent-related logic systems. Chapter 3 provides the constraint reasoning, introduced a number of practical constraints reasoning. Chapter 4 describes the qualitative reasoning, focusing on several important qualitative reasoning. Over the years author and his colleagues have been engaged in case-based reasoning research, and its main results constitute the Chapter 5. Probabilistic reasoning is an important uncertainty reasoning, given by Chapter 6 focuses on. Machine learning is the core of the current artificial intelligence research, but also knowledge discovery, data mining and other fields important basis for the book with the Chapter 7 for discussion, reflecting the latest progress of the study. Chapter 8 discusses support vector machine. Chapter 9 is related to explanation-based learning. Chapter 10 presents reinforcement learning. Chapter 11 describes rough set theory. Chapter 12 focuses on association rules. The evolutionary computation is discussed in Chapter 13, focusing on the genetic algorithm. In recent years, significant progress in the distribution of intelligence, combined with the results of our study, Chapter 14 presents the main theories and key technologies for multi-agent systems. The final chapter addresses artificial life, an overview of artificial life research and progress made.

Author set up the Advanced Artificial Intelligence courses for Ph.D and master students at the Graduate University of Chinese Academy of Sciences in 1994. Based on the lecture notes Science Press published the first edition book in 1998. The second edition book published in 2006. The book is defined as a key textbook for the regular higher education and widely used in China.

This book can serve as a textbook for artificial intelligence course in relevant professional post-graduate colleges and universities and senior undergraduate. It is also available in artificial intelligence, intelligent information processing, pattern recognition, intelligent control research and application of scientific and technical personnel to read reference.

Since author had limited ability, coupled with artificial intelligence developed rapidly and extensive research area, inappropriate and wrong with the book are bound. I sincerely appeal to scholars and readers for comments and help without hesitation.

Zhongzhi Shi
20.09.2009

Acknowledgement

I would like to take this opportunity to thank my family, particular my wife, Zhihua Yu and my children, Jing Shi and Jun Shi, for their support in the course of the book. I would also like to thank my organization, Institute of Computing Technology, Chinese Academy of Sciences, for providing good condition to do research on artificial intelligence.

In Intelligence Science Laboratory there are 6 post-doctors, 46 Ph. D. candidates, more than 100 master students have made contributions to the book. Thanks for their valuable works. In particular, Rui Huang, Liang Chang, Wenjia Niu, Dapeng Zhang, Limin Chen, Zhiwei Shi, Zhixin Li, Qiuge Liu，Huifang Ma, Fen Lin, Zheng Zheng, Hui Peng, Zuqiang Meng, Jiwen Luo, Xi Liu, Zhihua Cui have given assistance in English version of the book.

The book collects research efforts supported by National Basic Research Priorities Programme (No. 2007CB311004, No. 2003CB317004), National Science Foundation of China (No. 60775035, 60933004, 60970088), 863 National High-Tech Program (No. 2007AA01Z132), National Science and Technology Support Plan (No. 2006BAC08B06), Beijing Natural Science Foundation, the Knowledge Innovation Program of Chinese Academy of Sciences and other funding. I am very grateful to their financial supports.

My special thanks to Science Press for their publishing the book in Chinese version 1 and 2 in 1998, 2006 respectively. I am most grateful to the editorial staff and artist from World Scientific Publishing who provided all the support and help in the course of my writing this book.

Contents

Chapter 1

Introduction

1.1 Brief History of AI

Artificial Intelligence (AI) is usually defined as the science and engineering of imitating, extending and augmenting human intelligence through artificial means and techniques to make intelligent machines. In 2005, John McCarthy pointed out that the long-term goal of AI is human-level AI (McCarthy, 2005).

In the history of human development, it is a never-ending pursuit to free people from both manual and mental labor with machines. The industrial revolutions enable machines to perform heavy manual labor instead of people, and thus lead to a considerable economic and social progress. To make machines help relieve mental labor, a long cherished aspiration is to create and make use of intelligent machines like human beings.

In ancient China, many mechanical devices and tools have been invented to help accomplish mental tasks. The abacus was the most widely used classical calculator. The Water-powered Armillary Sphere and Celestial Globe Tower is used for astronomical observation and stellar analysis. The Houfeng Seismograph is an ancient seismometer to detect and record tremors and earthquakes. The traditional Chinese theory of Yin and Yang reveals the philosophy of opposition, interrelation and transformation, having an important impact on modern logics.

In the world, Aristotle (384-322, BC) proposed the first formal deductive reasoning system, syllogistic logic, in the Organon. Francis Bacon (1561-1626) established the inductive method in the Novum Organun (or "New Organon"). Gottfried Leibniz (1646-1716) constructed the first mechanical calculator capable of multiplication and division. He also enunciated the concepts of "characteristica universalis" and "calculus ratiocinator" to treat the operations of formal logic in a symbolic or algebraic way, which can be viewed as the sprout of the "thinking machine".

Since the 19th century, advancement of sciences and technologies such as Mathematical Logic, Automata Theory, Cybernetics, Information Theory, Computer Science and Psychology laid the ideological, theoretical and material foundation for the development of AI research. In the book "An Investigation of the Laws of Thought", George Boole (1815-1864) developed the Boolean algebra, a form of symbolic logic to represent some basic rules for reasoning in the thinking activities. Kurt Gödel (1906-1978) proved the incompleteness theorems. Alan Turing (1912-1954) introduced the Turing Machine, a model of the ideal intelligent computer, and initiated the automata theory. In 1943, Warren McCulloch (1899-1969) and Walter Pitts (1923-1969) developed the MP neuron, a pioneer work of Artificial Neural Networks research. In 1946, John Mauchly (1907-1980). and John Eckert (1919-1995) invented the ENIAC (Electronic Numerical Integrator And Computer), the first electronic computer. In 1948, Norbert Wiener (1894-1964) published a popular book of "Cybernetics", and Claude Shannon (1916-2001) proposed the Information Theory.

In a real world, quite a number of problems are complex ones, most of the times without any algorithm to adopt; or even if there are calculation methods, they are still NP problems. Researchers might introduce heuristic knowledge to solve such problem-solving to simplify complex problems and find solutions in the vast search space. Usually, the introduction of domain-specific empirical knowledge will produce satisfactory solutions, though they might not be the mathematically optimal solutions. This kind of problem solving with its own remarkable characteristics led to the birth of AI. In 1956, the term "Artificial Intelligence" was coined, and the Dartmouth Summer Research Project on Artificial Intelligence, proposed by John McCarthy, Marvin Minsky, etc., was carried on at Dartmouth College with several American scientists of psychology, mathematics, computer science and information theory. This well-known Dartmouth conference marked the beginning of the real sense of AI as a research field. Through dozens of years of research and development, great progress has been made in the discipline of AI. Many artificial intelligence expert systems have been developed and applied successfully. In domains such as Natural Language Processing, Machine Translation, Pattern Recognition, Robotics and Image Processing, a lot of achievements have been made, and the applications span various areas to promote their development.

In the 1950's, AI research mainly focused on game playing. In 1956, Arthur Samuel wrote the first heuristic game-playing program with learning ability. In the same year, Alan Newell, Herbert Simon etc. invented a heuristic program called the Logic Theorist, which proved correct 38 of the first 52 theorems from the "Principia Mathematica". Their work heralded the beginning of research on cognitive psychology with computers. Noam Chomsky proposed the Syntactics, the pioneer work of Formal Language research. In 1958, John McCarthy invented the Lisp language, an important tool for AI research which can process not only numerical values but also symbols.

In the early 1960's, AI research mainly focused on search algorithms and general problem solving (GPS). Allen Newell etc. published the General Problem Solver, a more powerful and universal heuristic program than other programs at that time. In 1961, Marvin Minsky published the seminal paper "Steps Towards Artificial Intelligence" established a fairly unified terminology for AI research and established the subject as a well- defined scientific enterprise. In 1965, Edward Feigenbaum etc. began work on the DENDRAL chemical-analysis expert system, a milestone for AI applications, and initiated the shift from computer algorithms to knowledge representation as the focus of AI research. In 1965, Alan Robinson proposed the Resolution Principle. In 1968, Ross Quillian introduced the Semantic Network for knowledge representation. In 1969, IJCAI (International Joint Conferences on Artificial Intelligence) was founded, and since then, the International Joint Conference on Artificial Intelligence (also shorted as IJCAI) was held biannually in odd-numbered years. Artificial Intelligence, an international journal edited by IJCAI, commenced publication in 1970.

In the early 1970's, AI research mainly focused on Natural Language Understanding and Knowledge Representation. In 1972, Terry Winograd published details of the SHRDLU program for understanding natural language. Alain Colmerauer developed Prolog language for AI programming at the University of Marseilles in France. In 1973, Roger Schank proposed the Conceptual Dependency Theory for Natural Language Understanding. In 1974, Marvin Minsky published the frame system theory, an important theory of Knowledge Representation. In 1977, Edward Feigenbaum published the well-known paper "The art of artificial intelligence: Themes and case studies in knowledge engineering" in the 5th IJCAI. He stated that Knowledge Engineering is the art of bringing the principles and tools of AI research to bear on difficult applications problems requiring expert knowledge for their solution. The technical issues of acquiring this knowledge, representing it, and using it appropriately to construct and explain lines-of-reasoning, are important problems in the design of knowledge-based systems.

In the 1980's, AI research developed prosperously. Expert systems were more and more widely used, development tools for expert systems appeared, and industrial AI thrived. Especially in 1982, the Japan's Ministry of International Trade and Industry initiated the Fifth Generation Computer Systems project, which dramatically promoted the development of AI. Many countries also made similar plans for research in AI and intelligent computers. China also started the research of intelligent computer systems as an 863 National High-Tech Program.

During the past more than 50 years, great progress has been made of AI research. Theories of Heuristic Searching Strategies, Non-monotonic Reasoning, Machine Learning, etc. have been proposed. Applications of AI, especially Expert Systems, Intelligent Decision Making, Intelligent Robots, Natural Language Understandings, etc. also promoted the research of AI. Presently, Knowledge Engineering based on knowledge and information processing is a remarkable characteristic of AI.

However, just as the development of any other discipline, there are also obstacles in the history of AI research. Even from the beginning, AI researchers had been criticized for their being too optimistic. In the early years of AI research, Herbert Simon and Allen Newell, two of the AI pioneers, optimistically predicted that:

• Within ten years, a digital computer will be the world's chess champion, unless the rules bar it from competition.
• Within ten years, a digital computer will discover and prove an important new mathematical theorem.
• Within ten years, a digital computer will write music that will be accepted by critics as processing as possessing considerable aesthetic value.
• Within ten years, most theories in psychology will take the form of computer programs, or of qualitative statements about the characteristics of computer programs.

These expectations haven't been completely realized even till today. 3 year old little child can easily figure out a tree in a picture, while a most powerful super computer only reaches middle level as children in tree recognition. It is also very difficult to automatically understand even stories written for little children.

Some essential theories of AI still need improvements. No breakthrough progresses have been made for some key technologies such as Machine Learning, Non-monotonic Reasoning, Common Sense Knowledge Representation and Uncertain Reasoning. It is also very difficult for global judgment, fuzzy information processing, multi-granular visual information processing, etc

Conclusively, AI research is still in the first stage of Intelligence Science, an indispensable cross discipline which dedicates to joint research on basic theories and technologies of intelligence by Brain Science, Cognitive Science, Artificial Intelligence and others. Brain Science explores the essence of brain and investigates the principles and models of natural intelligence in molecular, cellular and behavioral level. Cognitive Science studies human mental activities, such as perception, learning, memory, thinking and consciousness. AI research aims at imitating, extending and augmenting human intelligence through artificial means and techniques, and finally achieving machine intelligence. These three disciplines work together to explore new concepts, new theories and new methodologies for Intelligence Science, opening up prospects for a successful and brilliant future in the 21st century (Shi, 2006a).

1.2 Cognitive Issues of AI

Cognition is generally referred to as the process of knowing or understanding relative to affection, motivation or volition. Definitions of cognition can be briefly summarized into 5 main categorizes according to American psychologist Houston etc:

(1) Cognition is the process of information processing;
(2) Cognition involves symbol processing in psychology;
(3) Cognition deals with problem solving;
(4) Cognition studies mind and intelligence;
(5) Cognition consists of a series of activities, such as perception, memory, thinking, judgment, reasoning, problem solving, learning, imagination, concept forming, language using, etc.

Cognitive psychologist David H. Dodd etc. held that cognition involves three aspects of adaptation, structure and process, i.e., cognition is the process of information processing in certain mental structures for certain objectives.

Cognitive Science is the science about human perceptions and mental information processing, spanning from perceptual input to complex problem solving, including intellectual activities from individuals to the whole society, and investigating characteristics of both human intelligence and machine intelligence (Shi, 1990). As an important theoretical foundation for AI, Cognitive Science is an interdisciplinary field developed from Modern Psychology, Information Science, Neuroscience, Mathematics, Scientific Linguistics, Anthropology, Natural Philosophy, etc.

The blooming and development of Cognitive Science marked a new stage of research on human-centered cognitive and intelligent activities. Research on Cognitive Science will enable self understanding and self control, and lift human knowledge and intelligence to an unprecedented level. Moreover, it will lay theoretical foundations for the intelligence revolution, knowledge revolution and information revolution, as well as provide new concepts, new ideas and new methodologies for the development of intelligent computer systems.

Promoted by works of Allen Newell and Herbert Simon, research related to cognitive science originated in the late 1950's (Simon, 1986). Cognitive scientists proposed better models for mind and thinking than the simplified model about human developed by behaviorism scientists. Cognitive Science research aims at illustrating and explaining how information is processed during cognitive activities. It involves varieties of problems including perception, language, learning, memory, thinking, problem solving, creativity, attention, as well as the impact of environment and social culture on cognition.

In 1991, the representative journal "Artificial Intelligence" published a special issue on the foundation of AI in its 47th volume, in which trends about AI research are discussed. In this special issue, David Kirsh discussed five foundational questions for AI research (Kirsh, 1991):

(1) Pre-eminence of knowledge and conceptualization: Intelligence that transcends insect-level intelligence requires declarative knowledge and some form of reasoning-like computation-call this cognition. Core Al is the study of the conceptualizations of the world presupposed and used by intelligent systems during cognition.
(2) Disembodiment: Cognition and the knowledge it presupposes can be studied largely in abstraction from the details of perception and motor control.

(3) Kinematics of cognition are language-like: It is possible to describe the trajectory of knowledge states or informational states created during cognition using a vocabulary very much like English or some regimented logic-mathematical version of English.

(4) Learning can be added later: The kinematics of cognition and the domain knowledge needed for cognition can be studied separately from the study of concept learning, psychological development, and evolutionary change.

(5) Uniform architecture: There is a single architecture underlying virtually all cognition.

All these questions are cognitive problems critical to AI research, which should be discussed from the perspective of fundamental theories of Cognitive Science. These questions have become the watershed for different academic schools of AI research, as different academic schools usually have different answers to them.

1.3 Hierarchical Model of Thought

Thought is the reflection of the objective realities, i.e. the conscious, indirect and general reflection in a conscious human brain on the essential attributes and internal laws about the objective realities. Currently, we are in a stage emphasizing self knowledge and self recognition with the development of the Cognitive Science. In 1984, Professor Xuesen Qian advocated the Noetic Science research (Qian, 1986).

Human thought mainly involves perceptual thought, imagery thought, abstract thought and inspirational thought. Perceptual thought is the primary level of thought. When people begin to understand the world, perceptual materials are simply organized to form self-consistent information, thus only phenomena are understood. The form of thought based on this process is perceptual thought. Perceptual thought about the surface phenomena of all kinds of things can be obtained in practice via direct contact with the objective environment through sensories such as eyes, ears, noses, tongues and bodies, thus its sources and contents are objective and substantial.

Imagery thought mainly relies on generalization through methods of typification and the introduction of imagery materials in thinking. It is common to all higher organisms. Imagery thought corresponds to the connection theories of neural mechanisms. AI topics related to imagery thought include Pattern Recognition, Image Processing, Visual Information Processing, etc.

Abstract thought is a form of thought based on abstract concepts, through thinking with symbol information processing. Only with the emergence of language is abstract thought possible: language and thought boost each other and promote each other. Thus, physical symbol system can be viewed as the basis of abstract thought.

Little research has been done on inspirational thought. Some researchers hold that inspirational thought is the extension of imagery thought to sub-consciousness, during which a person does not realize that part of his brain is processing information. While some others argue that inspirational thought is sudden enlightenment. Despite all these disagreements, inspirational thought is very important to creative thinking, and need further research.

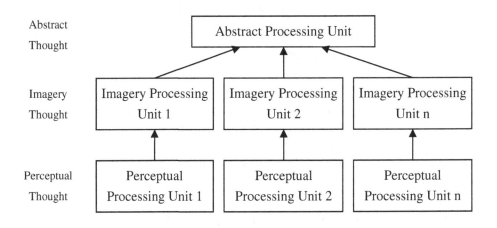

External Signals

Fig. 1.1. Hierarchical model of thought

In the process of human thinking, attention plays an important role. Attention sets certain orientation and concentration for noetic activities to ensure that one can promptly respond to the changes of the objective realities and be better accustomed to the environment. Attention limits the number of parallel thinking. Thus for most conscious activities, the brain works serially, with an exception of parallel looking and listening.

Based on the above analysis, we propose a hierarchical model of human thought, as shown in Fig. 1.1 (Shi, 1990a; Shi 1992; Shi 1994). In the figure, perceptual thought is the simplest form of thought, which is constructed from the surface phenomena through sensories such as eyes, ears, noses, tongues and bodies. Imagery thought is based on the connection theories of neural networks for highly parallel processing. Abstract thought is based on the theory of physical symbol system in which abstract concepts are represented with languages. With the effect of attention, different forms of thought are processed serially most of the time.

The model of thought studies the interrelationships among these three forms of thought, as well as the micro processes of transformation from one form to be other. Presently, much progress has been made. For example, attractors of neural networks can be used to represent problems such as associative memory and image recognition. Yet there is still a long way to go for a thorough understanding and application of the whole model. For example, further research is needed on the micro-process from imagery thought to logical thought.

1.4 Symbolic Intelligence

What is intelligence? Intelligence involves purposeful actions, reasonable thinking, as well as comprehensive capabilities to effectively adapt to the environment. Generally speaking, intelligence is one's capabilities to understand the objective world and apply knowledge to solve problems. Intelligence of an individual consists of comprehensive capabilities, such as: capability to perceive and understand objective things, the objective world and oneself; capability to gain experience and acquire knowledge through learning; capability to comprehend knowledge and apply knowledge and experience for problem analysis and problem solving; capabilities of association, reasoning, judgment and decision making; capability of linguistic abstraction and generalization; capabilities of discovery, invention, creativity and innovation; capability to timely, promptly and reasonably cope with the complex environments; capability for predictions of and insights into the development and changes of things. People live in the society, thus their intelligence is interrelated with the social environments. With the continuous development of human society, concepts of intelligence also evolve gradually.

AI (Artificial Intelligence), compared with natural intelligence of human, aims at imitating, extending and augmenting human intelligence through artificial means and techniques to achieve certain machine intelligence. The science of AI focuses on computational models of intelligent behaviors, develops computer systems for noetic activities such as perception, reasoning, learning, association, decision making, etc., and solves complex problems that only human experts can solve.

In the history of AI research, different levels of thought are studied from different views of Symbolicism, Connectionism and Behaviorism.

Symbolicism is also known as traditional AI. It is based on the physical symbol system hypothesis proposed by Alan Newell and Herbert Simon, which states that a physical symbol system has the necessary and sufficient means for general intelligent action. A physical symbol system consists of a set of entities, called symbols, which are physical patterns that can occur as components of another type of entity called an expression (or symbol structure). The system also contains a collection of processes that operate on expressions to produce other expressions: processes of creation, modification, reproduction and destruction.

Connectionism, also known as neural computing, focuses on the essentials and capabilities for non-programmatical, adaptive and brain-like information processing. The research field is rapidly developing in recent years, with a great number of neural network mechanisms, models and algorithms emerged continuously. Neural network systems are open neural network environments providing typical and practically valuable neural network models. The open system enables convenient adding of new network models to the existing system, so that new network algorithms can be debugged and modified with the friendly user interfaces and varieties of tools provided by the system. Moreover, it is also convenient to improve existing network models, thus the system provides excellent environment to develop new algorithms.

Neural computing investigates the brain functionalities based on the nervous system of human brains, and studies the dynamic actions and collaborative information processing capabilities of large numbers of simple neurons. The research focuses on the simulation and imitation of human cognition, including processes of perception and consciousness, imagery thought, distributed memory, self-learning and self-organization. Neural computing is particularly competent in parallel search, associative memory, self-organization of spatio-temporal data statistical descriptions, and automatic knowledge acquisition through interrelated activities. It is generally considered that neural networks better fitted low level pattern processing.

Basic characteristics of neural networks include: a. distributed information storage, b. parallel information processing, c. capabilities of self-organization and self-learning (Shi, 1993). Owing to these characteristics, neural networks provide a new means for information processing with computers. With more and more applications and in depth research of artificial neural networks, the researchers have found many problems of existing models and algorithms, and even met with some difficulties of the nonlinear theories or approximation theory. Despite these problems and difficulties, we believe that with the in-depth and extensive applications, neural networks will continue to develop and promote current techniques. The theory of neural field we proposed is such a new kind of attempt.

Currently, integration of symbol processing systems and neural network models is an important research direction. Fuzzy neural networks integrate fuzzy logic and neural networks, taking each other's advantages in theory, methodology and application, to develop systems with certain learning and dynamic knowledge acquisition capabilities.

Behaviorism, also known as behavior-based AI, in many respects reflects the behavior physiological views in AI. Rodney Brooks brought forward theories of intelligence without representation (Brooks, 1991a) and intelligence without reasoning (Brooks, 1991b), and stated that intelligence is determined by the dynamics of interaction with the world.

These three research genres investigate different aspects of human natural intelligence corresponding to different layers in the model of human thought. Roughly categorizing, it can be taken that Symbolism focuses on abstract thought, Connectionism focuses on imagery thought, while Behaviorism focuses on perceptual thought. The comparisons of Symbolism, Connectionism and Behaviorism is shown in Table 1.1

Table 1.1 Comparisons of Symbolism, Connectionism and Behaviorism.

	Symbolism	Connectionism	Behaviorism
Perceptual Level	Discrete	Continuous	Continuous
Representation Level	Symbolic	Continuous	Behavioral
Problem Solving Level	Top-down	Bottom-up	Bottom-up
Processing Level	Serial	Parallel	Parallel
Operational Level	Reasoning	Connection	Interaction
System Level	Local	Distributed	Distributed
Basic Level	Logic	Simulant	Intuitional Judgment

Some researchers classify AI research into two categories: symbolic intelligence and computational intelligence. Symbolic intelligence, also known as traditional AI, solves problems through reasoning based on knowledge. Computational intelligence solves problems based on connections trained from example data. Artificial Neural Networks, Genetic Algorithms, Fuzzy Systems, Evolutionary Programming, Artificial Life, etc. are included in computational intelligence.

Presently, traditional AI mainly focuses on knowledge based problem solving. In the practical point of view, AI is the science of knowledge engineering: taking knowledge as the object and investigating knowledge representation, acquisition and application. This book mainly introduces and discusses traditional AI. For computational intelligence, please refer to the book "Neural Networks" by Zhongzhi Shi (Shi, 2009).

1.5 Research Approaches of Artificial Intelligence

During the development of AI since the 1950's, many academic schools have been formed, each holding its specific research methodologies, academic views and research focuses. This section introduces some research methodologies of AI, focusing mainly on the cognitive school, logical school, and behavioral school.

1.5.1 Cognitive School

Cognitive school, with representative researchers such as Herbert Simon, Marvin Minsky and Allen Newell, focuses on functional simulation with computers based on human noetic activities. In the 1950's, Newell and Simon advocated the "heuristic program" together, and worked out the "Logic Theorist" computer program to simulate the thinking process of mathematical theorem proving. Then in the early 1960's, they developed the "General Problem Solver (GPS)", which simulates the common principles of human problem solving with three steps: first, set the initial problem solving plan; then, apply axioms, theorems and rules to solve the problems according to the plan; continually proceed with the means-end analysis, and modify the problem solving until the goal is achieved. Thus the GPS possesses certain universality.

In 1976, Newell and Simon proposed physical symbol system premise, and stated that a physical symbol system has the necessary and sufficient means for general intelligent action. Thus, an information processing system can be viewed as a concrete physical system, such as human neural system, computer construction system, etc. Each physical pattern is a symbol, as long as it can be distinguished from other patterns. For example, different English characters are different symbols. To operate on symbols relies on comparison among different symbols, i.e. distinguishing which symbols are the same and which ones are different. Thus fundamental task and functionality of a physical symbol system is to identify same characters and distinguish different ones.

In the 1980's, Newell etc. focused on the SOAR system, a symbolic cognitive architecture for general problem solving, based on the Chunking mechanism for learning and rule-based memory for representation of operators, search control, etc.

Minsky took the view of psychics, holding that in daily activities, people apply plenty of knowledge acquired and collected from previous experiences. Such knowledge is stored in the brain in a structure similar to frame. Thus, he proposed the frame knowledge representation structure in the 1970's. In the 1980's, Minsky believed that there is no unified theory for human intelligence. In the famous book "Society of Mind" he published in 1985, Minsky pointed out that the society of mind is a vast society of individually simple agents with certain thinking capabilities.

1.5.2 *Logical School*

Logical school, with representative researchers such as John McCarthy and Nils Nilsson, holds the logical perspective for AI research, i.e. describe the objective world through formalization. This academic school believes that:

- Intelligent machines will have knowledge of their environment.
- The most versatile intelligent machines will represent much of their knowledge about their environment declaratively.
- For the most versatile machines, the language in which declarative knowledge is represented must be at least as expressive as first order predicate calculus.

Logical school focuses on conceptual knowledge representation, model theoretic semantics, deductive reasoning, etc. in AI research. McCarthy claimed that everything can be represented with the unified frame of logics, and common sense reasoning will be difficult without some form of non-monotonic reasoning.

1.5.3 *Behavioral School*

Most AI research is based on too abstract and simple models for the real world. Rodney Brooks argued that it is necessary to go beyond this ivory tower of abstract models, and take the complex real world as the background instead, so that AI theories and technologies can be tested in real world problem solving, and improved in these tests.

In 1991 Brooks brought forward theories of intelligence without representation and intelligence without reason, and stated that intelligence is determined by the dynamics of interaction with the world. He simply called this work as "robots" or "behavior-based robots". There are a number of key aspects characterizing this style of work as follows (Brooks, 1991b):

- Situatedness: The robots are situated in the world and the world directly influences the behavior of the system.
- Embodiment: The robots have bodies and experience the world directly.
- Intelligence: The source of intelligence is not limited to just the computational engine. It also come from the situation in the world.
- Emergence: The intelligence of the system emerges from the system's interactions with the world and sometimes indirect interactions between its components.

Based on these ideas, Brooks programmed autonomous mobile robots, based on layered, asynchronous and distributed networks of augmented finite-state machines, each one being a comparatively independent unit for functionalities of advance, balance, prowl, etc. The robot walked successfully, and thus initiated a new approach to Robotics.

Different academic schools of AI research have different answers to the five foundational cognitive questions introduced in section 1.2. The logical school (represented by Nils Nilsson) holds positive answers to questions 1-4, and neutral answer to question 5; the cognitive school (represented by Allen Newell) holds positive answers to questions 1, 3 and 5; while the behavioral school (represented by Rodney Brooks) holds negative answers to all question of 1-5.

1.6 Automated Reasoning

Reasoning is the cognitive process of logically inferring a new judgment (conclusion) from one or more already known judgments (precondition). It is the reflection of the objective relationships in mind. People usually solve problems based on prior knowledge and make conclusions through reasoning. Theories and technologies of automated reasoning are important bases for research fields of program derivation, proof of program correctness, expert systems, intelligent robots, etc.

Early works of automated reasoning focused on automated theorem proving. Pioneer work includes the Logic Theorist developed by Herbert Simon and Allen Newell. In 1956, Alan Robinson proposed the Resolution Principle, making a great progress in research on automated reasoning. The resolution principle is easily applicable and logically complete, thus it becomes the computing model for the logic programming language Prolog. Though some methods outperforming the Resolution Principle in some aspects appeared later, e.g. natural deductive reasoning and term rewriting systems, yet they are limited due to the combination problem and the computational intractability essentially.

For a practical system, there always exist some non deductive cases. Thus, various reasoning algorithms have been proposed, which even weakens the attempt of finding a universal fundamental principle for AI. From the practical perspective of view, each reasoning algorithm conforms to its specific, domain related strategies based on different knowledge representation techniques. On the other hand, it is undoubtedly useful to find a universal reasoning theory. In fact, an important impetus for AI theoretical research is to find more general and universal reasoning algorithms.

An important achievement of automated reasoning research is nonmonotonic reasoning, a pseudo induction system. The so called nonmonotonic reasoning is the reasoning process in which adding new positive axioms to the system may invalidate some already proved theorems. Obviously, nonmonotonic reasoning is more complex than monotonic reasoning. In nonmonotonic reasoning, first hypotheses are made; then standard logical reasoning is carried out; if inconsistence appeared, then backtrack to eliminate inconsistence, and establish new hypothesis.

Raymond Reiter first set forth the closed world assumption (CWA) for nonmonotonic reasoning in 1978 (Reiter, 1978), and proposed the Default Reasoning (Reiter, 1980). In 1979, Jon Doyle developed the truth maintenance system (TMS) (Doyle, 1979). In 1980, John McCarthy formalized the theory of Circumscription (McCarthy, 1980). Circumscription of a predict P means to exclude most models based on P, and select only a minimum set of models in which P is assigned to true. Different circumscription criteria will produce different minimizations of predicates.

Quantitative simulation with computers is commonly applied for scientific computing. Yet people often predict or explain system behaviors without detailed calculation data. Such problem solving can not be achieved simply through deduction, thus qualitative reasoning is proposed in AI for representation and reasoning without precise quantitative information. In qualitative reasoning, physical systems or procedures can be decomposed into subsystems or model fragments, each with structuralized specifications of the subsystem itself and its interrelationships with other subsystems. Through approaches such as causal ordering and compositional modeling, functionalities and behaviors of the real physical systems can be qualitatively represented. Typical qualitative reasoning techniques include: QDE (qualitative differential equation) based modeling and reasoning by Johan de Kleer, process-centered modeling and reasoning by Kenneth Forbus, and constraint-centered qualitative simulation by Benjamin Kuipers. Combined approaches of quantitative and qualitative reasoning will make great impact to scientific decision making of expert systems.

Uncertainty is ubiquitous to real world problems, which results from the deviation of people's subjective cognition from the objective realities. Various causes may reflect such deviation and bring about uncertainty, such as randomicity of things, incompleteness, unreliability, imprecision and inconsistency of human knowledge, and vagueness and ambiguousness of natural language. With respect to different causes of uncertainty, different theories and reasoning methodologies have been proposed. In AI and knowledge engineering, representative approaches of uncertainty theories and reasoning methodologies are introduced in the following.

Probability theory is widely used to process randomicity and uncertainty of human knowledge. Bayesian theory has been successfully applied in the PROSPECTOR expert system, yet it relies on assigned prior probabilities. The MYCIN model based certainty factors, adopting some assumptions and principles for conjunction of hypothesis, is a simple and effective method, though it lacks well established theoretical foundations.

Dempster-Shafer theory of evidence introduces the concept of belief function to extend classical probabilities, and defines that belief function satisfies a set of axioms weaker than probability axioms, thus belief function can be viewed as a superset of existing probability functions. With belief function, even without precise probabilities, constrains on probability distributions can be set based on prior domain knowledge. The theory has well established theoretical foundations, yet its definition and computation is comparatively complex. In recent years, this theory of evidence has gained more and more research focuses, and many research achievements and application systems have been developed. For example, Lotfi Zadeh illustrated how the Dempster-Shafer theory can be viewed as an instance of inference from second-order relations, and applied in a relational database.

In 1965, Lotfi Zadeh proposed the Fuzzy Set, based on which a series of research have been made, including fuzzy logic, fuzzy decision making, probability theory, etc. For reasoning with natural language, Zadeh introduced fuzzy quantization to represent fuzzy propositions in natural language, defined concepts of linguistic variable, linguistic value and probability distribution, developed possibility theory and approximate reasoning. His work has attracted much research focuses. Fuzzy mathematics has been widely applied to expert systems and intelligent controllers, as well as for the research of fuzzy computer. Chinese researchers have done a lot in theoretical research and practical applications, drawing much attention from the international academics. However, many theoretical problems still remain to be solved in this domain. There are also some different views and disputes, such as, what is the basis for fuzzy logic? What about the problem of consistency and completeness of fuzzy logic? In the future, research focuses of uncertain reasoning may be centralized on the following three aspects: first, to solve existing problems of current uncertainty theories; second, to study the efficient and effective discrimination capabilities and judgment mechanisms of human beings for new theories and new methodologies to deal with uncertainties; and third, to explore methods and technologies to synthetically process varieties of uncertainties.

Theorem proving is a kind of specific intelligent behavior of human, which not only relies on logic deductions based on premises, but also requires certain intuitive skills. Automated theorem proving adopts a suit of symbol systems to formalize the process of human theorem proving into symbol calculation that can be automatically implemented by computers, i.e., to mechanize the intelligence process of reasoning and deduction. The mechanical theorem proving in elementary geometry and differential geometry proposed by Professor Wenjun Wu of Chinese Academy of Sciences is highly valued all over the world.

1.7 Machine Learning

Knowledge, knowledge representation and knowledge based reasoning algorithms are always considered at the heart of AI, while machine learning can be viewed as a most critical problem. For hundreds of years, the psychologists and philosophers held that the basic mechanism of learning is trying to transfer successful behaviors in one practice to other similar practices. Learning is the process of acquiring knowledge, gaining experience, improving performance, discovering rules and adapted to environments. Fig. 1.2 illustrates a simple model of learning with four basic elements of a learning system. The environment provides external information, similar to a supervisor. The learning unit processes information provided by the environment, corresponding to various learning algorithms. The knowledge base stores knowledge in certain knowledge representation formalisms. The performing unit accomplishes certain tasks based on the knowledge in the knowledge base, and sends the execution results to the learning unit through feedbacks. The system can be gradually improved through learning. Research on machine learning not only enables machines to automatically acquire knowledge and obtain intelligence, but also uncovers principles and secrets of human thinking and learning, and even helps to improve the efficiency of human learning. Research on machine learning also has a great impact on memory storage patterns, information input methods and computer architectures.

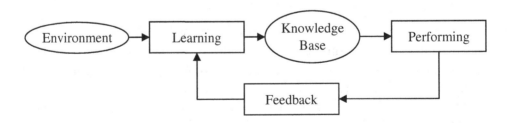

Fig. 1.2. Simple model of learning(Simon, 1983)

Research in machine learning roughly experienced four stages. The first and initial stage is learning without knowledge, focusing on neural models and self adaptative and self organization systems based on decision theories. However, as neural models and decision theories were fairly restricted and only achieved limited success, the research passion gradually depressed. The second stage in the 1960's is the low tide, focusing mainly on symbolic concept acquisition. Then in the third stage, interest in machine learning rejuvenated and many distinctive algorithms appeared since Patrick Winston's important paper of "Learning Structural Descriptions from Examples" in 1975. More importantly, it was then popularly recognized that a learning system would not learn high level concepts without background knowledge. Thus, great amount of knowledge were introduced to learning systems as background knowledge, bringing about a new era and new prospects for machine learning research. Due to the mass applications of expert systems and problem solving systems, knowledge acquisition has become the key bottleneck, to solve which heavily relies on the advances of machine learning research. There comes the fourth stage and another climax of machine learning research.

Main paradigms of machine learning include inductive learning, analytical learning, discovery learning, genetic learning, connection learning, etc. (Shi 1992b). Inductive learning has been most extensively studied in the past, focused mainly on general concept description and concept clustering, and proposed algorithms such as the AQ algorithms, version space algorithm, and ID3 algorithm. Analogical learning analyzes similarities of the target problem with previously known source problems, and then applies the solutions from the source problems to the target problem. Analytical learning, e.g. explanation-based learning, chunking, etc., learns from training examples guided by domain knowledge. Explanation-based learning extracts general principles from a concrete problems solving process which can be applied to other similar problems. As learned knowledge is stored in the knowledge base, intermediate explanations can be skipped to improve the efficiency of future problem solving. Discovery learning is the method to discover new principles from existing experimental data or models. In recent years, knowledge discovery in databases (KDD, also known as data mining, DM) has attracted great research focuses, which is considered to be a very practically useful research discipline by AI and database researchers. KDD mainly discovers classification rules, characteristic rules, association rules, differentiation rules, evolution rules, exceptional rules, etc. through methods of statistical analysis, machine learning, neural networks, multidimensional database, etc. Genetic learning based on the classic genetic algorithm is designed to simulate biological evolution via reproduction and variation and Darwin's natural selection paradigm. It takes each variant of a concept as an individual of the species, and evaluates different mutations and recombinations based on objective fitness functions, so as to select the fittest offsprings for survival. Connection learning recognizes different input patterns through training the neural networks with typical example instances.

Machine learning research is still in its primary stage, and needs extensive research efforts. Progress in machine learning research will enable breakthroughs in AI and knowledge engineering research. In the future, research focuses of machine learning will include cognitive models for the learning process, computational learning theories, new learning algorithms, machine learning systems integrating multiple learning strategies, etc.

1.8 Distributed Artificial Intelligence

Studies of human intellectual behaviors show that most human activities involve social groups consisting of multiple individuals, and large-scale complex problem solving also involves cooperation of several professionals or organizations. "Cooperation" is a major aspect of human intelligence pervasive in the human society, and thus the motivation for research in Distributed Artificial Intelligence (DAI).

With the development of computer network, computer communication and concurrent programming technologies since the 1980's, DAI is gradually becoming a new research focus in the field of AI. DAI is a subfield of AI investigating how logically and physically distributed agents cooperate with each other to perform intelligent behaviors. It enables collaborated and coordinated knowledge, skills and planning, solves single-objective and multi-objective problems, and provides an effective means for the design and construction of large-scale complex intelligent systems or computers to support cooperation.

The term DAI was coined by American researchers, and the first International Workshop on Distributed Artificial Intelligence was held at MIT in Boston, U.S.A. in 1980. From then on, all kinds of conferences on DAI or DAI related topics have been held continually all over the world, which greatly promotes the development and popularization of DAI technologies, and gradually deepens and broadens the research and applications of the science of DAI. With the increase in scale, scope and complexity of new computer based information systems, decision support systems and knowledge based systems, as well as the requirement to encode more complex knowledge in these systems, applications and development of DAI technologies is becoming increasingly important to these systems.

Research of DAI can be generally categorized into two domains: Distributed Problem Solving (DPS) and Multi-Agent System (MAS), both sharing the same research paradigm yet adopting different problem solving means. The goal of DPS is to establish large-granularity cooperative clusters to accomplish the common problem solving objectives. In a pure DPS system, problems are resolved into sub tasks, specific task executors are designed to solve the corresponding sub tasks, and all interaction strategies are incorporated as an integral part of the system. Such systems feature top-down design, since the whole system is established to solve the predefined objectives at the top end.

On the opposite side, a pure MAS system generally comprises pre-existing autonomous and heterogeneous agents without a common objective. Research on MAS involves coordinations and cooperations in knowledge, plan and behavior among groups of autonomous intelligent agents, so that they can jointly take actions or solve problems. Though the agent here is also a task executor, it is "open" to other peer agents, and can deal with both single objective and multiple objectives.

Nowadays, applications of computers are becoming more and more extensive, and problems to be solved are becoming more and more complex, which makes centralized control of the problem solving process and centralized processing of data, information and knowledge more and more difficult. Such distributed and concurrent processing of data and knowledge hails great potentials along with many pending difficulties to the development of AI. The spatial distribution, temporal concurrency and logical dependant relationships of multiple agents make the problem solving more complex in multi-agent systems than in single-agent systems.

Despite such difficulties, research on DAI is feasible, desirable and important for the following reasons:

(1) Technical foundations — Advances in technologies such as hardware architecture of the processors and communication between the processors make it possible to interconnect great amount of asynchronous processors. Such connection might be tightly coupled systems based on shared or distributed memory, or loosely coupled systems based on local networks, or even very loosely connected systems based on geographically distributed communication networks.

(2) Distributed problem solving — Many AI applications are distributed in nature. They might be spatially distributed, such as the explanation and

integration of spatially distributed sensors, or the control of robots cooperated in a factory. They might also be functionally distributed, such as the integration of several professional medical diagnosis systems to solve complex cases. They might even be scheduling distributed, for example in a factory, the production line is composed of several working procedures, each scheduled by an expert system.

(3) System integration — DAI systems well support modular design and implementation. A complex system can be resolved into several comparatively simple and task specific sub-modules, in order that the system can be easily constructed, debugged and maintained. It is more flexible to handle errors of decomposed sub-modules than a single integral module. On the other side, great economic and social benefit will be gained if the many existing centralized AI application systems can be used to construct distributed AI systems with minor modifications. For example, it will be extremely time-saving and practically effective if existing independent systems of liver diagnosis system, stomach diagnosis system, intestines diagnose system, etc. can be slightly modified to construct a complex expert system to diagnose digestive tract diseases. The plug-in approach we proposed for agent construction is an effective means to integrate existing AI systems.

(4) New approach to intelligent behavior — Implement intelligent behavior with intelligent agents. To become societies of mind, AI systems should have functions for interaction with the environment, as well as capabilities to cooperate and coordinate with each other.

(5) Meanings in cognitive science — DAI can be used for research and verification of the problems and theories in sociology, psychology, management, etc. Cooperative MAS based on belief, knowledge, hope, intention, promise, attention, object, cooperation, etc. provide effective means to understand and simulate the cognitive problems.

Therefore, no matter technically or socially, the emergence and development of DAI systems is imperative. It is also natural to apply DAI technologies to solve large-scale martial problems. Presently, research in this domain has made certain achievements in China.

MAS is a branch of DAI research. In a multi-agent system, an agent is an autonomous entity which continuously interacts with the environment and co-exists with other peer agents in the same environment. In other words, agent is an entity whose mental states consist of components such as belief, desire and intention. In a multi-agent system, the agents can be either homogeneous or heterogeneous, and the relationships among them can be either cooperative or competitive. A common characteristic of DAI and MAS is distributed behaviors of entities or agents. Multi-agent systems feature bottom-up design, because impractical, the distributed automatic individual agents are defined first, and then problem solving is accomplished with one or more agents. Both single objective and multiple objectives can be achieved. Research on MAS is dedicated to analysis and design of large-scale complex cooperative intelligent systems such as large-scale knowledge and information systems and intelligent robots, based on theories of problem solving through concurrent computing and mutual cooperation among logically or physically distributed multiple agents.

At present, MAS is a very active research direction, which aims at simulation of human rational behaviors for applications in domains such as real world and society simulation, robotics, intelligent machines, etc. An agent is characterized with features of autonomy, interaction with the environment, cooperation, communication, longevity, adaptability, real-time, etc. In order to survive and work in the constantly changing environment of the real world, agents should not only react to emergencies promptly, but also make middle or short term plans based on certain tactics, and then predict the future state through modeling and analysis of the world and other agents, as well as and cooperate or negotiate with other agents using the communication language.

To achieve these features, agent architecture should be studied, because architectures and functions of agents are closely related to each other: improper architecture may greatly limit the functions, while appropriate architecture may well support high level intelligence of agents. We proposed a compound architecture for an agent, which systematically integrates multiple parallel and comparatively independent yet interactional forms of mind, including reaction, planning, modeling, communication, decision making, etc. A Multi-Agent Environment (MAGE) is implemented through the agent kernel based plug-in approach we proposed for agent construction (Shi, 2003). With MAGE and the plug-in approach, compound agents can be conveniently constructed and debugged.

1.9 Artificial Thought Model

Development of computers can be roughly divided into two stages. In the first stage, the Von Neumann architecture is applied for numerical computation, document processing, and database management and query. All these applications have specific algorithms, though somewhat difficult in programming. The second stage focuses on symbolic and logical processing, in which knowledge and information processing mainly bases on reasoning. How to choose effective algorithm is the key problem to this stage of research. All these applications are well defined and explicitly represented problems of the ideal world. However, many real-world problems are ill-structured, such as pattern recognition, problem solving and learning from incomplete information, etc. These problems are in the category of intuitive information processing.

For intuitive information processing, theories and technologies of flexible information processing should be studied. Flexibility in real world has the following characteristics:

• Integrate varieties of complex and intricately related information containing ambiguity or uncertainty information;
• Actively acquire necessary information and knowledge, and learn general knowledge inductively from examples;
• Automatically adapt to users and changing environment;
• Self-organization based on the object for processing;
• Error tolerant information processing.

Actually, human neural networks capable of large-scale parallel and distributed information processing inherently support flexible information processing. Thus, we proposed the artificial thought model in Fig. 1.3.

The artificial thought model in Fig. 1.3 clearly illustrates that artificial thought bases on open autonomous systems, takes fully advantages of varieties of information processing patterns to achieve collective intelligence, then proceeds with flexible information processing, and finally solves real-world problems.

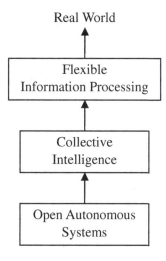

Real World

Flexible
Information Processing

Collective
Intelligence

Open Autonomous
Systems

Fig. 1.3. Artificial thought model

1.10 Knowledge Based Systems

An important impetus for AI research is to construct knowledge based systems to automatically solve difficult problems. Ever since the 1980's, knowledge engineering has become the most remarkable characteristic of AI applications. Knowledge based systems (KBS) include expert system, knowledge base system, intelligent decision support system, etc. In 1965, DENDRAL, which was designed to illustrate organic chemistry structures, developed to a series of expert system programs. Such systems mainly include two parts: one is the knowledge base, which represents and stores the set of task-related specific domain knowledge, including not only facts about the related domain, but also heuristic knowledge in expert level; the other is the inference engine, which includes series of inference methodologies to retrieve the reasoning path, and thus to form premises, satisfy objectives, solve problems, etc. As different mechanisms and concepts can be adopted, the inference engines have multiple patterns.

In knowledge based systems knowledge will be stored in the computer in defined structure for knowledge management, problem solving and knowledge sharing. Projects and softwares of "Knowledge Based Management System (KBMS)" have been initiated and developed all over the world, such as in America, in Japan (the NTT Company), as well as in China. Remarkable characteristic of KBMS is the integration of inference and query, which improves the maintenance of the knowledge base, and provides useful development environment for specific domain knowledge based systems.

Decision Support System (DSS) is evolved from the Management Information System (MIS), with its concept initiated in the early 1970's. It developed fast as an important tool to improve the competitiveness and productivity of companies, as well as to decide on the successfulness of a company. DSS has been adopted by various levels of decision makers in abroad, and attracted great focuses in China. Decision support techniques are critical to support scientific decision making. Early DSS is based on MIS and includes some standard models, such as the operational research model and the econometric model. In 1980, Ralph Sprague proposed a DSS structure based on data base, model base and dialog generation and management software, which has a great impact on later research and applications. In recent years, AI technologies have been gradually applied to DSS, and thus came in to being the intelligent decision support system (IDSS). In 1986, the author proposed the intelligent decision system composed of data base, model base, and knowledge base (Shi, 1988b), which improved the level of scientific management by providing an effective means to solve semi-structured and ill-structured decision problems. Characteristics of IDSS include the application of AI techniques to DSS, and the integration of database and information retrieval techniques with model based qualitative analysis techniques. In the 1990's, we developed the Group DSS (GDSS) based on MAS technologies, which attracted enormous research interests.

Building intelligent systems can imitate, extend and augment human intelligence to achieve certain "machine intelligence", which has great theoretical meanings and practical values. Intelligent systems can be roughly classified into four categories according to the knowledge contained and the paradigms processed: single-domain single-paradigm intelligent system, multi-domain single-paradigm intelligent system, single-domain multi-paradigm intelligent system, and multi-domain multi-paradigm intelligent system.

1. Single-domain single-paradigm intelligent system

Such systems contain knowledge about a single domain, and process only problems of a single paradigm. Examples of such systems include the first and second generation of expert systems, as well as the intelligent control system.

Expert systems apply domain-specific knowledge and reasoning methods to solve complex and specific problems usually settled only by human experts, so that to construct intelligent computer programs with similar problem solving capabilities as experts. They can make explanations about decision making procedure and learn to acquire related problem solving knowledge. The first generation of expert systems (such as DENDRAL, MACSYMA, etc.) had highly professional and specific problem solving capabilities, yet they lacked completeness and portability in architecture, and were weak in problem solving. The second generation of expert systems (such as MYCIN, CASNET, PROSPECTOR, HEARSAY, etc.) was subject-specific professional application system. They were complete in architecture with better portability, and were improved in aspects such as human-machine interface, explanation mechanisms, knowledge acquisition, uncertain reasoning, enhanced expert system knowledge representation, heuristics and generality of reasoning, etc.

2. Multi-domain single-paradigm intelligent system

Such systems contain knowledge about multiple domains, yet only process problems of a certain paradigm. Examples include most distributed problem solving system and multi-expert system. Generally, expert system development tools and environments are used to construct such large-scale synthetical intelligent systems.

Since intelligent systems are widely applied to various domains such as engineering technology, social economics, national defense affairs and ecological environment, several requirements are put forward for intelligent systems. To solve the many real-world problems such as medical diagnosis, economic planning, military commanding, financial projects, crop planting and environment protection, expert knowledge and experience of multiple domains might be involved. Many existing expert systems are single-subject, specific micro expert systems, which might not satisfy the users' practical demands. To construct multi-domain single-paradigm intelligent systems might be an approach to meet the users' requirements in certain degrees. Characteristics of such systems include:

(1) solve the user's real-world complex problems;
(2) adopt knowledge and experience of multiple domains, disciplines and professionals for cooperative problem solving;

(3) based on distributed open software, hardware and network environment;

(4) constructed with expert system development tools and environments;

(5) achieve knowledge sharing and knowledge reuse.

3. Single-domain multi-paradigm intelligent system

Such systems contain knowledge of only a single domain, yet process problems of multiple paradigms. Examples include compound intelligent system. Generally, knowledge can be acquired through neural network training, and then transformed into production rules to be used in problem solving by inference engines.

Multiple mechanisms can be used to process a single problem in problem solving. Take an illness diagnosis system as an example, both symbolic reasoning and artificial neural networks can be used. Then, compare and integrate the results of different methods processing the same problem, through which correct results might be obtained and unilateralism can be avoided.

4. Multi-domain multi-paradigm intelligent system

Fig. 1.4 illustrates the sketch map of such systems, which contain knowledge of multiple domains and process problems of different paradigms. Collective intelligence in the figure means that when processing multiple paradigms, different processing mechanisms work separately, accomplish different duties, and cooperate with each other, so that to represent collective intelligent behaviors.

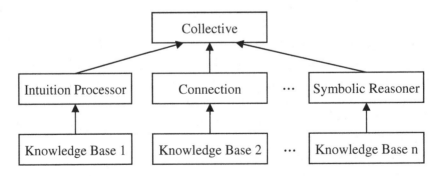

Fig. 1.4. Multi-domain multi-paradigm intelligent system

Synthetical DSS and KBS belong to this category of intelligent systems. In such systems, reasoning based abstract thought is based on symbolic processing, while imagery thought such as pattern recognition and image processing applies neural network computing.

Most intelligence problems are ill-structured and continuously changing, thus they are difficult to solve with a single specific algorithm. A plausible approach to solve such intelligence problems is to construct human-machine united open systems which interact with the environment. An open system is one which may always run into unexpected results during the system processing, and can receive external new information at any time.

Based on summarization and analysis of the design methods and implementation technologies of existing KBS, intelligent agent technologies are studied to construct large scale synthetical KBS with functionalities of multiple knowledge representation, synthetical knowledge base, self-organization and cooperation, automatic knowledge acquisition, continually improved intelligent behaviors, etc. Such systems are the primary means to construct multi-domain multi-paradigm intelligent system.

Exercises

1. What is Artificial Intelligence (AI)? What is the research objective of AI?
2. Please briefly introduce the main stages of development in the history of AI.
3. What are the five fundamental questions for AI research?
4. What is the physical symbol system? What is the physical symbol system assumption?
5. What is symbolic intelligence? What is computational intelligence?
6. Please describe the simple model of machine learning and its basic elements.
7. What is Distributed Artificial Intelligence (DAI)? What are the main research domains of DAI?
8. Please refer to relevant literature and discuss whether the following tasks can be solved by current computers:
   a) Defeat an international grandmaster in the world's chess competition;
   b) Defeat a 9 duan professional in a game of Go;
   c) Discover and prove a new mathematical theorem;
   d) Find bugs in the programs automatically.
9. How to classify knowledge based systems? How to achieve collective intelligence behaviors?

Chapter 2

Logic Foundation of Artificial Intelligence

2.1 Introduction

Logic as a formal science was founded by Aristotle. Leibniz reaffirmed Aristotle's logical developing direction of mathematics form and founded the mathematical logic. From the thirties of the last century, various mathematical methods were extensively introduced and used in the mathematical logic; with the result that mathematical logic becomes one branch of mathematics and is as important as algebra and geometry. Mathematical logic has spread out many branches such as model theory, set theory, recursion theory, and proof theory.

Logic is a primary tool in the study of computer science as well as in the study of artificial intelligence. It is widely used in many domains, such as the semasiology, the logic programming language, theory of software specification and validation, theory of data base, theory of knowledge base, intelligent system, and the study of robot. Objective of the computer science is essentially coincident with the goal of logic. On the one hand, the objective of the computer science is to simulate with the computer the function and behaviour of the human brain, and bring the computer to be an extension of the brain. Here the simulation of the function and behaviour of the human brain is infact to simulate the thinking process of persons. On the other hand, logic is a subject focused on the discipline and law of human's thinking. Therefore, the methods and results obtained in logic are naturally selected and put to use during the research of computer science. Furthermore, the intelligent behavior of human beings is largely expressed by language and character; therefore, simulation of human natural language is the point of departure for the simulation of human thinking process.

Language is the starting point for the study of human's thinking in the logic, as well as for the simulation of human's thinking in the computer science. Topics related to language are important issues that run through the domain of computer science. Many subjects of the computer science, such as programming languages and their formal semantics, knowledge representation and reasoning, and the natural language processing, are all related to language. Generally speaking, representation and reasoning are two basic topics in the computer science and the artificial intelligence. Majority of the intelligent behavior relies on a direct representation of knowledge, for which the formal logic provides an important approach.

Knowledge, especially the so-called common knowledge, is the foundation of intelligent behavior. Intelligent behavior such as analyzing, conjecturing, forecasting and deciding are all based on the utilization of knowledge. Accordingly, in order to simulate with computer the intelligent behavior, one should firstly make knowledge represented in the computer, and then enable the computer to utilize and reason about the knowledge. Representation and reasoning are two basic topics on knowledge in the study of artificial intelligence. They are entirely coincident with the two topics focused by the study of natural language, i.e., the accurate structure and reasoning of natural languages. Therefore, the methods and results obtained in logic are also useful for the study of knowledge in the artificial intelligence. The ability of representation and the performance of reasoning are a pair of contradictions for any logic system applied to intelligent systems. A trade-off between such a pair is often necessary.

The logic applied in majority of logic-based intelligent systems is first order logic or its extensions. The representation ability of first order logic is so strong that many experts believe that all the knowledge representation problems arising in the research of artificial intelligence can be carried out within the framework of first order logic. First order logic is suitable for representing knowledge with uncertainty. For example, the expression $\exists x\ P(x)$ states that there exists an object for which the property P holds, while it is not pointed out that which one is such an object. For another example, the expression $P \vee Q$ states that at least one of P and Q holds, but it is not determined whether P (or Q) really holds. Furthermore, first order logic is equipted with a complete axiom system, which can be treated as a standard of reference in the designing of strategies and algorithms on reasoning. Although first order logic is capable for representing majority of knowledge, it is not convenient and concise for many applications. Driven by various requirements, lots of logic systems have been proposed and studied; in the following we enumerate some typical examples.

(1) In order to represent knowledge on epistemic, such as believe, know, desire, intention, goal and commitment, various modal logics were proposed.

(2) In order to represent knowledge which is related to time, various temporal logics were proposed.

(3) In order to represent knowledge with uncertainty, the so-called fuzzy logic was proposed. As a system built upon the natural language directly, fuzzy logic adopts many elements from the natural language. According to Zadeh, the founder of fuzzy logic, fuzzy logic can be regarded as a computing system on words; in another words, fuzzy logic can be defined by the formula "fuzzy logic = computing with words".

(4) Knowledge of humans is closely interrelated to human activities. Accordingly, knowledge on behavior or action is important for intelligent systems. Compared with various static elements of logic, action is distinguished by the fact that the execution of actions will affect properties of intelligent systems. Representation and reasoning about actions are classical topics in the study of artificial intelligence; many problems, such as the frame problem and the qualification problem, were put forward and well studied. Many logic systems, such as the dynamic logic and the dynamic description logic, were also proposed.

(5) Computer-aided decision-making has become one of the important applications of computer. Persons always hold their predilections as while as they are making a decision. In order to represent the rule and simulate the behavior of people's decision-making process, it is inevitable to deal with the predilection. As a result, based on the management science, a family of so-called partial logics was proposed and studied.

(6) Time is one of the most important terms present in intelligent system. Some adverbs, such as occasionally, frequently and ofter, are used in the natural language to represent time. Knowledge about the time which is described by

these adverbs can not be represented with classical temporal logic. Therefore, an approach similar to the integral of mathematics was introduced into logic. With the resulted logic, time that described by various adverbs can be formally represented and operated.

2.2 Logic Programming

In this section we give a brief introduction to the logic programming language Prolog. Prolog was first developed by a group around Alain Colmerauer at the University of Marseilles, France, in the early 1970s. Prolog was one of the first logic programming languages, and it now the major Artificial Intelligence and Expert Systems programming language.

Prolog is declarative in style rather than procedural. Users just need to represent the facts and rules, over which the execution is triggered by running queries; the execution is then carried out according to find a resolution refutation of the negated query. In another words, users just need to tell the Prolog engine what to do but not how to do it. Furthermore, Prolog holds the following features.

(1) Prolog is a unification of data and program. Prolog provides a basic data structure named terms. Both data and programs of prolog can be constructed over terms. This property is fit for the intelligent program since the outputs of certain program can be executed as new generated programs.

(2) Prolog supports the automatic backtracking and pattern-matching, which are two of the most useful and basic mechanisms used in intelligent systems.

(3) Prolog uses recursion. Recursion is extensively used in the Prolog program and data structure, so that a data structure with big size can be manipulated by a short program. In general, the length of a program represented with Prolog is only ten percent of which written with the C++ language.

All of these features make Prolog suitable for encoding intelligent programs, and suitable for applications such as natural language processing, theorem proving and expert systems.

2.2.1 *Definitions of logic programming*

Firstly we introduce the Horn clause which is the constituent of logic programs.

A clause consists of two parts: the head and the body. As an IF-THEN rule, the condition portion of a clause is called the head and the conclusion portion of it is called the body.

Definition 2.1 A Horn clause is a clause that contains at most one literal (proposition / predicate) at the head.

Horn clauses in Prolog can be separated into three groups:

(1) Clauses without conditions (facts):   A.

(2) Clauses with conditions (rules):   A :- B_1, ..., B_n.

(3) Goal clauses (queries): ? :- B_1,...,B_n.

Semantics of above Horn clauses is informally described as follows:

(1) The clause A states that A is true for any assignments on variables.

(2) The clause A :- B_1,...,B_n states that for any assignments on variables: if B_1,..., and B_n are evaluated to be true, then A must also be true.

(3) The goal clause ? :- B_1,...,B_n represents a query that will be executed. Execution of a Prolog program is initiated by the user's posting of a query; the Prolog engine tries to find a resolution refutation of the negated query.

For example, here are two Horn clauses:

a) W(X,Y) :- P(X), Q(Y).

b) ?-R(X,Y),Q(Y).

The Horn clause indexed by i) is a rule, with P(X), Q(Y) the body and W(X,Y) the head. The Horn clause indexed by ii) is a query with R(X,Y),Q(Y) the body. The intuition of the query indexed by ii) is that whether R(X,Y) and Q(Y) hold and what are the value of X and Y in the case that R(X,Y)∧Q(Y) holds.

We are now to formally define Logic Programs.

Definition 2.2 A logic program is a collection of Horn clauses. In logic program clauses with same predicate symbol are called the definition of the predicate.

For example, the following two rules forms a logic program:

    Father(X,Y) :- Child(Y,X), Male(X).

    Son(Y,X) :- Child(Y,X), Male(Y).

This program can also be extended with the following facts:

    Child(xiao-li, lao-li).

    Male(xiao-li).

    Male(lao-li).

Taken these rules and facts as inputs of the Prolog engine, we can compile and execute it. Then the following queries can be carried out:

(1) query: ?- Father(X,Y), we will get the result Father(lao-li, xiao-li);

(2) query: ?- Son(Y,X), we will get the result Son(xiao-li, lao-li).

2.2.2 *Data structure and recursion in Prolog*

An important and powerful tool in problem solving and programming, recursion is extensively used in data structures and programs of Prolog.

Term is a basic data structure in Prolog. Everything including program and data is expressed in form of term. Terms of Prolog are defined recursively by the following BNF rule:

    <term> ::= <constant> | <variable> | <structure> | （<term>）

where structures are also called compound terms, and are generated by the BNF rule:

<structure> ::= <function>（<term> {, <term>}）

<function> ::= <atom>

List is an important data structure supported by Prolog. A list can be represented as a binary function cons(X, Y), with X the head of the list and Y the tail. The tail Y of a list cons(X, Y) is also a list which can be generated by deleting the element X from cons(X, Y). Elements of a list can be atoms, structures, terms and lists. Table 2.1 shows some notations on lists that be used in Prolog.

Table 2.1 Prolog list structure

[ ] or nil	empty table
[a]	cons(a,nil)
[a, b]	cons(a,cons(b,nil))
[a, b, c]	cons(a,cons(b,cons(c,nil))
[X I Y]	cons(X,Y)
[a, b I c]	cons(a,cons(b,c))

Finally we present an example on which recursion is used in programs of Prolog. Consider a simple predicate that checks if an element is a member of a list. It has the two clauses listed below:

member(X, [X I_]).

member(X,[_IY]) :- member(X,Y).

In this example, the predicate member is recursively defined, with the first Horn clause be the boundary condition and the second the recursive case.

2.2.3 SLD resolution

SLD resolution is the basic inference rule used in logic programming. It is also the primary computation procedure used in PROLOG. Here the name SLD is an abbreviation of "Linear resolution with Selection function for Definite clauses". Firstly we introduce definitions on definite clause.

Definition 2.3   A Definite clause is a clause of the form

$$A :- B_1,B_2,\ldots,B_n$$

where the head is a positive literal; the body is composed of zero, one or more literals.

Definition 2.4   A definite program is a collection of definite clauses.

Definition 2.5   A definite goal is a clause of the form

$$? :- B_1,B_2,\ldots,B_n$$

where the head is empty.

Let P and G be a program and a goal respectively, then the solving process for the corresponding logic program is to seek a SLD resolution for P∪{G}. Two rules should be decided for the resolution process: one is the computation rule on how to select the sub-goal; the other is the search strategy on how to go through the program. Theoretically, any search strategy used in artificial intelligence can be adopted. However, in practice, strategies should be selected according to their efficiency. Following is the standard SLD resolution process.

(1) Sub-goals are selected with a "left then right" strategy;

(2) The program is gone through with a strategy based on the depth-first search and the backtracking method;

(3) Clauses of the program P are selected with the same priority of their appearance in the program;

(4) The occur-check is omitted from the unification algorithm.

There are some characteristics for such a resolution process.

1. There exists simple and efficient method for the realization of depth-first search strategy.

The depth-first search strategy can be realized with just a goal stack. A goal stack for the SLD tree consists of branches which are going through. Correspondingly, the searching process is composed of the pop and push operators on the stack. In the case that the sub-goal on the top of the stack is unified with the head of some clause of the program P, the corresponding resolvent will be put into stack. While in the case that no clause could be unified, a backtracking operator will be triggered with the result that an element was poped from the stack; in this case, the resulted stack should be inspected for unification.

Example 2.1 Consider the following program:

$$p(X, Z) :- q(X,Y), p(Y,Z).$$

$$p(X,X).$$

$$q(a, b).$$

Let "?-p(X ,b)" be the goal. Then the evolvement of the goal stack is as follows.

Table 2.2. Prolog goal stack

?-p(X ,b).				G is put into stack
?-p(X ,b).	?- q(X,Y), p(Y,b).			A resolvent is put into stack
?-p(X ,b).	?- q(X,Y), p(Y,b).	?- p(b, b).		A resolvent is put into stack
?-p(X ,b).	?- q(X,Y), p(Y,b).	?- p(b, b).	?-q(b,W), p(W,b)	A resolvent is put into stack
?-p(X ,b).	?- q(X,Y), p(Y,b).	?- p(b, b).	□	An element is poped, then the resolvent □ is put into stack
?-p(X ,b).				The pop operation is triggered for three times
□				the resolvent □ is put into stack
				□ is poped

2. Completeness of SLD resolution proces is destroyed by the depth-first search strategy.

This problem can be partially solved according to change the order of sub-goals and the order of clauses of the program. For example, consider the following program:

(1) p(f(X)):- p(X).

(2) p(a).

Let "?-p(Y)" be the goal. Then it is obvious that the SLD resolution process will fall into an endless loop. However, if we exchange the order of clause (1) and clause (2), then we will get the result Y=a, Y=f(a), ….

Consider another program:

(1) q(f(X)) :- q(X).

(2) q(a).

(3) r(a).

Let "G: ?-q(Y), r(Y)" be the goal. Then the SLD resolution process will fall into an endless loop. However, if we exchange the order of sub-goals contained in G and get the goal "G: ?- r(Y),q(Y)", then we will get the result Y=a after the SLD resolution process.

In order to guarantee the completeness of the SLD resolution process, the width-first search strategy must be embodied in search rules of Prolog. Howerev, as a result, both the time and space efficiency of the process will be decreased, as while as the complexity of the process is increased. A trade-off is to maintain the depth-first seach strategy that is used in Prolog, and supplement it with some programs which embody other search strategies and are written with the Prolog language.

3. Soundness of SLD resolution is not guaranteed without occur-check.

Occur-check is a time-consuming operation in the unification algorithm. In the case that occur-check is called, the time needed for every unification process is linear to the size of the table, consequently the time needed for the append operation on predications is $O(n_2)$; here n is the length of the table. Since little unification process in the Prolog program use occur-check, the occur-check operator is omitted form unification algorithms of most Prolog systems.

In fact, without the occur check we no longer have soundness of SLD resolution. A sub-goal might can not be unified with a clause in the case that some variables occurring in the term. However, since the occur-check is omitted, the unification will still be executed and reach a wrong result. For example, let "p(Y, f(Y))" and "?-p(X, X)" be the program and the goal respectively. Then the unification algorithm will generate a replacement $\theta=\{Y/X,\ f(Y)/Y\}$ for the pair {p(X,X), p(Y, f(Y))}. Such a mistake will be covered if the variable Y is not used in the SLD resolution anymore. However, once the variable Y is used again, the resolution process will fall into an endless loop.

2.2.4 Non-logic components: CUT

Program is the embodiment of algorithm. Algorithm in the logic programming is characterized with the following formula:

$$algorithm = logic + control$$

Where the logic component determines the function of the algorithm; the control component determines the strategy which will be used to realize the function. Theoretically, a programmer just needs to specify the logic component, and then the corresponding control component can be automatically determined by the logic programming system. Howerev, most Prolog systems in practice can not reach such automation. As set forth, in order to guarantee a valid execution of the program, a programmer have to take the order of clauses into consideration. Another problem is the fact that an endless branch might be generated during the SLD resolution, according to the depth-first search strategy adopted by Prolog. In such a situation, the goal stack used in the resolution algorithm will be overflowed and bring the resolution process into an error state. The "CUT" component is introduced to solve this problem.

From the point of declarative semantics, CUT is a non-logical control component. Represented as the character "!", CUT can be treated as an atomic component and be inserted into clauses of the program or the order. Declarative semantics of a program is not affected by any "!" which appeared in the program or in the order.

From the point of operational semantics, some control information is carried by the CUT component. For example, let G be the following goal:

$$?- A_1,...,A_{m-1}, A_m, A_{m+1},...,A_k$$

Let the following, which is denoted by C, be one of the clauses of the program:

$$A:- B_1,..., B_i, ! , B_{i+1}, ..., B_q$$

Consider the state that sub-goals $A_1,...,A_{m-1}$ have been solved, and let G' be the current goal. Suppose A_m can be unified with A. After the unification operation, the body of the clause C is added into the goal G'. Now a cut "!" is contained in the current goal G'. We call Am a cut point and call the current goal G' as the father-goal of "!". Now it is the turn to solve sub-goals B1,…, Bi, ! , Bi+1, …, Bq one by one. As a typical sub-goal, "!" is valid and can be jumped over. Suppose a backtracking is triggered by the fact that some sub-goals behind "!" can not be unified, then the goal stack will be tracked back to Am-1, the sub-goal prior to the cut point Am. From the point of SLD tree, all the nodes which are rooted by the father-goal of "!" and are accessed still will be cut out.

For example, let P be the following program:

(1)   p(a).

(2)   p(b).

(3)   q(b).

(4)   r(X):- p(X), q(X).

(5)   r(c).

Let G be the sub-goal "?-r(X)". Then the SLD tree generated during the process of SLD resolutionis is presented as figure 2.1. However, if a cut is inserted into the clause (4) of program P, .i.e., the clause (4) of program P is changed as follows:

(4)' r(X):- p(X), !, q(X).

Then the corresponding SLD tree should become that presented in figure 2.2. In the later case, no solution will be generated since a critical part is cut out from this SLD tree.

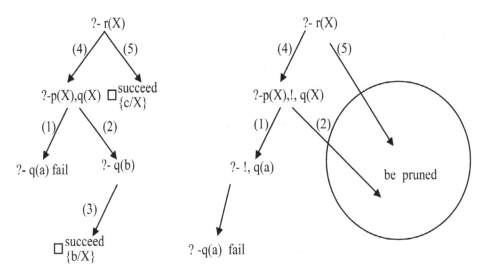

Figure 2.1. A SLD tree without !   Figure 2.2. A SLD tree with !

According to the example, soundness of SLD resolution might be destroyed by the CUT mechanism. Furthermore, incorporation of the CUT mechanism will cause the inconsistency between the declarative semantics and the operational semantics of logic programming. For example, let P be the following program which is designed to calculate the maximum value of two data.

$$\max(X, Y, Y) :- X =< Y.$$

$$\max(X, Y, X) :- X > Y.$$

We can check that declarative semantics and operational semantics of P are consistent. Now, we insert a CUT predication into P and get the following program P1:

$$\max(X, Y, Y) :- X =< Y, !.$$

$$\max(X, Y, X) :- X > Y.$$

Efficiency of the program is obviously increased; although both the declarative semantics and the operational semantics of P1 are not changed with respect to those of P. Efficiency of the program can be further increased if we replace P1 with the following program P2:

$$\max(X, Y, Y) :- X =< Y, !.$$

$$\max(X, Y, X).$$

However, althouth the operational semantics of P2 is still the same as that of P1, the declarative semantics of P2 is changed as follows: the maximum value of X and Y is always X, it can also be Y in the case of X≤Y. Obviously, the semantics of P2 is different from our original intention.

The "fail" is another predication used by Prolog. Acting as a sub-goal, the predication "fail" can not be solved at all and therefore will give rise to a backtracking. The predication CUT can be placed prior to the predication "fail" and forms the so-called cut-fail composition. During the SLD resolution process, in the case that a clause which contains a cut-fail composition is examined for resolution, resolution of the father-goal of the CUT predication will be finished directly. Therefore, efficiency of search will be increased.

For example, consider the following program P:

(1)   strong(X):- heart_disease(X), fail.

(2)   strong(X):- tuberculosis(X), fail.

(3)   strong(X):- nearsight(X), fail.

(4)   strong(X).

(5)   heart_disease(Zhang).

Let "?- strong(Zhang)" be the goal. According to the first clause of program P, the goal "strong(Zhang)" can be first unified with a resolvent "heart_disease(Zhang), fail"; then a backtracking will be triggered by the "fail" after the unification of "heart_disease(Zhang)". In the following steps, sub-goals "tuberculosis(Zhang)" (or "nearsight(Zhang)") which are generated according to the second clause (resp., the third clause) can not be unified. Finally, the goal "strong(Zhang)" will be unified according to the forth clause of P and produce a positive result. Backtracking is triggered with three times in this example. We can reduce the backtracking according to place a CUT prior to the "fail" occurring in the P. For example, the first three clauses of P can be changed as follows:

(1)   strong(X):- heart_disease(X), !, fail.

(2)   strong(X):- tuberculosis(X),!, fail.

(3)   strong(X):- nearsight(X), !, fail.

Then, according to first clause of the program, a backtracking will be triggered by the "fail" after the unification of the goal "strong(Zhang)" and unification of the new generated sub-goal "heart_disease(Zhang)". Since "strong(Zhang)" is the father-goal of the CUT that contained in the first clause of P, it will be poped from the goal stack also. Therefore, the SLD resolution will be finished right away and return a negative result.

Since first-order logic is undecidable, there is no terminable algorithm to decide whether G is a logic inference of P, for G and P any program and any goal respectively. Certainly, SLD resolution algorithm will return a corresponding result if G is a logic inference of P. However, in the case that G is not a logic inference of P, the SLD resolution process (or any other algorithm) will fall into endless loop. In order to solve this problem, the rule "negation as failure" is introduced into logic programming. For any clause G, if it can not be proved, then the rule will enable the result that ¬G is reasonable.

Based on the "negation as failure" rule, the predication "not" is defined in Prolog as follows:

       not(A) :- call(A), !, fail.

       not(A).

Here "call" is a system predication and "call(A)" will trigger the system to solve the sub-goal "A". If the answer of the sub-goal "A" is positive, then a backtracking will be triggered by the "fail" occurring in the first clause, and the SLD resolution will be finished right away; in this case, result for the clause "not(A)" is negative. However, if the answer of the sub-goal "A" is negative, then a backtracking will be triggered right away so that the "fail" occurring in the first clause will not be visited; in this case, result for the clause "not(A)" is positive according to the second clause.

2.3 Nonmonotonic Logic

Driven by the development of the intelligence science, various non-classical logics were preposed and studied since the eighties of the last century. Nonmonotonic is one of these logics (McDermott,1980).

The human understanding of the world is a dialectical developing process which obeys the negation-of-negation law. During the cognitive process, man's understanding of the objective world is always uncertain and incomplete; it will be negatived or completed as while as some new knowledge is acquired. As pointed by Karl Popper, the process of scientific discovery is a process of falsification. Under certain condition and environment, every theory always has its historical limitations. Along with the increase of human understands of the world and along with the development of scientific research, old theories will not meet the new needs and will be overthrew by the new discovery; upon that, old theories are negated and new theories are born. In this sense, the growth of human knowledge is in fact a nonmonotonic development process.

Classical logics such as the formal logic and the deductive logic are all monotonic in their dealing with the human cognitive process. With these logics, new knowledge acquired according to rigorous logic inference must be consistent with the old knowledge. In another word, if there is a knowledge base A and it is known that A implies the knowledge B, i.e. A→B, then the knowledge B can be inferenced by these logics. However, as stated above, human cognitive process is in fact nonmonotonic and is not consistent with such a process at all.

Nonmonotonic reasoning is characterized by the fact that the theorem set of an inference system is not monotonic increased along with the progress of inference. Formally, let F be the set of knowledge holded by humans at some stage of the cognitive process, and let $F(t)$ be the corresponding function on time t. Then the set $F(t)$ is not monotonic increased along with the progress of time. In another word, $F(t_1) \subseteq F(t_2)$ is not always holds for any $t_1 < t_2$. At the same time, human understanding of the world is in fact enhanced. A basic reason for such a phenomenon is the incomplete knowledge base used in the reasoning process. Nonmonotonic logic is a family of tools for the processing of incomplete knowledge.

Inference rules used in monotonic logics are monotonic. Let Γ be the set of inference rules of a monotonic logic, then the language $Th(\Gamma) = \{A \mid \Gamma \to A\}$ determined by these rules holds the following monotonicity:

(1) $\Gamma \in Th(\Gamma)$

(2)   if $\Gamma_1 \subseteq \Gamma_2$, then $Th(\Gamma_1) \subseteq Th(\Gamma_2)$

(3) $Th(Th(\Gamma)) = Th(\Gamma)$ (idempotence)

Where (3) is also called as fixed point. A marked feature of monotonic inference rules is that the language determined by them is a bounded least fixed point, i.e., $Th(\Gamma_1) = \cap \{s \mid \Gamma_1 \rightarrow S \text{ and } Th(S) = \Gamma_2\}$.

In order to deal with the property of nonmonotonic, the following inference rule is introduced:

(4)   if $\Gamma \neg \not\vdash \neg P$, then $\Gamma \mid\sim MP$

Here M is a modal operator. The rule states that if $\neg P$ can not be deduced from Γ, then P is in default treated as true.

It is obvious that a fixed point $Th(\Gamma) = \Gamma$ can not be guaranteed any more as while as the inference rule (4) is incorporated into monotonic inference systems. In order to solve this problem, we can first introduce an operator NM as follows: for any first-order theory Γ and any formula set $S \subseteq L$, set

(5) $NM\Gamma(S) = Th(\Gamma \cup AS\Gamma(S))$

Where $AS\Gamma(S)$ is a default set of S and is defined as follows:

(6) $AS\Gamma(S) = \{MP \mid P \in L \wedge P \in S\} - Th(\Gamma)$

Then, $Th(\Gamma)$ can be defined as the set of theorems that can be deduced from Γ nonmonotonically, i.e.,

(7) $Th(\Gamma) =$ the least fixed point of $NM\Gamma$

Rule (7) is designed to blend the inference rule (4) into the first-order theory Γ so that reasoning can be carried out with a closed style. However, since the definition of $Th(\Gamma)$ is too strong, not only the calculation but also the existence of $Th(\Gamma)$ can not be guaranteed. Therefore, definition of $Th(\Gamma)$ is revised as follows:

(8) $Th(\Gamma) = \cap(\{L\} \cup \{S \mid NM\Gamma(S) = S\})$

Now, let L be the language determined by these rules, then L must be a fixed point according to $NM\Gamma(L) = L$.

Furthermore, according to these rules, Γ is inconsistent if $Th(\Gamma)$ does not exist. The definition of $Th(\Gamma)$ presented in (8) can also be rewrited as follows:

(9) $Th(\Gamma) = \{P \mid \Gamma \quad \mid\sim P\}$

where $\Gamma \mid\sim P$ represent $P \in Th(\Gamma)$. We also use $FP(\Gamma)$ to denote the set $\{S \mid NM\Gamma(S)=S \}$ and call each element of this set as a fixed point of the theory Γ.

There are three major schools on nonmonotonic reasoning: the circumscription theory proposed by McCarthy, the default logic proposed by Reiter, and the autoepistemic logic proposed by Moore. In the circumscription theory, a formula S is true with respect to a limited range if and only if S cannot be proved to be true w.r.t. a bigger range. In the default logic, "a formula S is true in default" means that "S is true if there is no evidence to prove the false of S". In the autoepistemic logic, S is true if S is not believed and there are no facts which are inconsistent with S.

Various nonmonotonic logic systems have beed proposed by embracing the nonmonotonic reasoning into formal logics. These nonmonotonic logics can be roughly divided into two categories: nonmonotonic logics based on minimization, and nonmonotonic logics based on fixed point. Nonmonotonic logics based on minimization can again be devided into two groups: one is these based on the minimization of model, such as the logic with the closed world assumption and the circumscription proposed by McCarthy, and the other is these based on the minimization of knowledge model, such as the ignorance proposed by Konolige. Nonmonotonic logics based on fixed point can be devided into default logics and autoepistemic logics. The nonmonotonic logic NML proposed by McDermott and Doyle is a general default logic and was used for study the general foundation of nonmonotonic logics, and the default logic proposed by Reiter is a first-order formalization of default rules. Autoepistemic logic was firstly proposed by Moore to solve the so-called Hanks-McDermott problem on nonmonotinic logics.

2.4 Closed World Assumption

With respect to any base set KB of beliefs, the closed world assumption (CWA) provides an approach to complete the theory T(KB) which is defined by KB.

Here, a theory T(KB) is complete if either every ground atom in the language or its negation is in the theory. The basic idea of the CWA is that everything about the world is known (i.e., the world is closed); therefore, if a ground atom P can not be proved according to the theory, then P will be considered to be negative. The CWA completes the theory by including the negation of a ground atom in the completed theory whenever that ground atom does not logically follows from KB.

One of the important applications of the CWA is to complete the database system. For example, let KB be the following database which contains information about contiguities of countries:

$$\text{Neighbor(China, Russia)}.$$

$$\text{Neighbor(China, Mongolia)}.$$

$$\forall x \forall y \; (\text{Neighbor}(x, y) \leftrightarrow \text{Neighbor}(y, x))$$

Then, it is obvious that T(KB) is incomplete since neither Neighbor(Russia, Mongolia) nor ¬Neighbor(Russia, Mongolia) can be logically inferred from KB. According to the CWA, the database KB can be completed by adding the assertion ¬Neighbor(Russia, Mongolia) into it. It is obvious that the CWA is nonmonotonic because the set of augmented beliefs would shrink if we added a new positive ground literal to KB.

Let KBasm be the set of all of the assertions added into KB during the completing process. According to the CWA, it is obvious that for any ground atom P:

$$\neg P \in \text{KB}_{asm} \text{ if and only if } P \notin T(KB)$$

For example, with respect to the database KB presented in the previous example, we have KBasm = {¬neighbor(Russia, Mongolia)}.

Let CWA(KB)be the CWA-augmented theory,i.e., CWA(KB)=T(KB∪KBasm). It is obvious that CWA(KB) is more powerful compared with T(KB), since many results that can not be deduced from KB can now be derived from KB∪ KBasm.

The augmented theory CWA(KB) might be inconsistent. For example, let KB={P(A)∨P(B)}, then it is KBasm={¬P(A), ¬P(B)} since neither P(A) nor P(B) can be derived from KB, therefore the set KB∪KBasm is inconsistent. Inconsistency of the CWA-augmented theory is an important problem that needs to be solved.

Theorem 2.1 *CWA(KB) is consistent if and only if, for every* *positive-ground-literal clause $P_1 \vee P_2 \vee \ldots \vee P_n$ that follows from KB, there is at least one ground literal P_i which is entailed by KB.*

In other words, CWA(KB) is inconsistent if and only if there are positive ground literals P_1, P_2, ..., P_n such that KB $\models P_1 \vee P_2 \vee \ldots \vee P_n$ and KB$\not\models P_i$ for each $1 \leq i \leq n$.

Example 2.2 Let KB = { P(A)$\vee$P(B) }. It is obvious that CWA(KB) is inconsistent.

Example 2.3   Let KB = $\{\forall x(P(x)\vee Q(x)), P(A), Q(B)\}$. With respect to the atom A and B, KB will be augmented with ¬P(B) and ¬Q(A), and will resulted in a consistent theory. However, if there is an atom C, then the resulted theory is inconsistent since it is both (P(x)$\vee$Q(x)) $\not\models$ P(C) and (P(x)$\vee$Q(x))$\not\models$Q(C).

Generally speaking, theory augmented by the CWA might be inconsistent. However, if the knowledge base KB is composed of Horn clauses and is consistent, then the augmented theory CWA(KB) is also consistent. I.e., we have the following theorm:

Theorem 2.2 *If the clause form of KB is Horn and consistent, then the CWA augmentation CWA(KB) is consistent.*

The condition that KB be Horn is too strong for many applications. In fact, according to Theorem 2.1, such a condition is not absolutely necessary for the CWA augmentation of KB to be consistent. An attempt of weakening this condition leads to the idea of the CWA with respect to a predicate P. Under that convention, if KB is Horn in some predicate P and P is not provable from KB, then we can just add the negation of P into the set KBasm. Here, we say that a set of clauses is Horn in a predict P if there is at most one positive occurrence of P in each clause.

For example, suppose KB is {P(A)$\vee$Q(A), P(A)$\vee$R(A)}. It is obvious that KB is Horn in the predicate P, even though both P(A)$\vee$Q(A) and P(A)$\vee$R(A) are not Horn clauses. Set KBasm = {¬P(A)}, then we have KB$\cup$KBasm$\models$Q(A) and KB$\cup$KBasm$\models$R(A), and thereby get a consistent augmented theory CWA' (KB) with respect to the predicate P.

But in fact, respect to some predicate, consistency of the augmented theory can not be guaranteed still. For example, let KB={P(A)∨Q, P(B)∨¬Q}, and let P be the particular predicate; then we have KBasm ={¬P(A), ¬P(B)}. Since KB|=P(A)∨P(B), the augmented theory CWA'(KB) with respect to the predicate P is inconsistent.

2.5 Default Logic

Default reasoning is a family of plausible reasoning. The intuition of various forms of default reasoning is to derive conclusions based upon patterns of inference of the following form:

In the ordinary situation A holds,

In the typical situation A holds,

Then it is a default assumption that A holds.

A typical example of default reasoning is about the statement "birds fly". As we know, the statement "birds fly" is different from the statement "All birds will fly", since there are many exceptions suth as the penguins, ostriches and Maltese falson. Given a particular bird we will conclude that it flies according to the following plausible proposition:

In the ordinary situation birds can fly, or

In the typical situation birds can fly, or

If x is a bird, then it is a default assumption that x can flies.

However, if we know that this bird is an ostrich according to the subsequent discovery, we will revise our conclusion with a new result that this bird can not fly. Therefore, it is obvious that what reflected in this example is a process of plausible reasoning instead of deductive reasoning.

Based on the study of reasoning about incompletely specified worlds, a logic system named default logic was proposed by Reiter in 1980 (Reiter, 1980).

"By default" is an ordinary technology used in computer program designing. For example, let P be a program, let Q be a procedure specified in P, and let x be a variable that occurs in both P and Q. Then, the type of x which occurring in P will by default be the type of x which occurring in Q, unless the type of x is redeclared in Q. In another word, with the "by default" technology, operations of the system will be carried out according to predetermined rules, unless other requirements are explicitly specified by the programmer.

The idea of "by default" is introduced into logic by Reiter and forms the so-called default logic. In classical logics, new facts about a world are deduced from the known facts; all the facts that can be deduced are determined by facts contained in the knowledge base. In the default logic, knowledge base can be expanded with default knowledge so that more facts can be deduced; in spite that these default knowledges maybe are unreliable.

Default rules used in default logic is of the following form:

$$\frac{\alpha(\overline{x}) : M\ \beta_1(\overline{x}),\ldots, M\ \beta_m(\overline{x})}{W(\overline{x})} \qquad (2.1)$$

It can also be represented as follows:

$$\alpha(\overline{x}) : M\ \beta_1(\overline{x}),\ldots, M\ \beta_m(\overline{x}) \rightarrow W(\overline{x}) \qquad (2.2)$$

Here $\overline{x}$ is a parameter vector, $\alpha(\overline{x})$ is called the prerequisite of the default rule, $W(\overline{x})$ is the consequent, $\beta_i(\overline{x})$ is the default condition, and M is the default operator. The default rule is to be read as "If the prerequisite $\alpha(\overline{x})$ holds and it is concictent to assume $\beta_1(\overline{x}),\ldots,\beta_m(\overline{x})$, then infer that the consequent holds." For example, consider the following default rule:

$$\frac{bird(x) : M\ flies(x)}{flies(x)}$$

It states that if x is a bird and it is consistent to assume that x can fly, then infer that x can fly.

A default rule is closed if and only if none of $\alpha, \beta_1,\ldots, \beta_m, W$ contains a free variable.

Definition 2.7 *A default theory is a pair (D,W), where D is a set of default rules and W a set of closed formulas.*

A default theory (D,W) is closed iff every default rule contained in D is closed. Default theory is nonmonotonic. For example, suppose T=<W, D> is a default theory with D={$\frac{:MA}{B}$} and W=∅, then the formula B can be derived from T. However, if we add the knowledge ¬A into W and get the default theory T'=<D, W'>, where W'={¬A}, then the formula B can not be derived from T' any more, despite that T' is an extension of T together with W'⊇W.

Example 2.4 Suppose W = {*bird(tweety)*, ∀*x(ostrich(x)→ ¬flies(x))* }, and

$$D = \{ \quad \frac{bird \ (x) : M \ flies \ (x)}{flies \ (x)} \quad \}.$$

Then the formula flies(tweety) can be deduced from the default theory. However, if we add the knowledge ostrich(tweety) into W, then flies(tweety) can not be deduced any more.

Example 2.5 Suppose W = { *feathers(tweety)* }, and

$$D = \{ \quad \frac{bird \ (x) : M \ flies(x)}{flies(x)} , \ \frac{feathers(x) : M \ bird(x)}{bird(x)} \quad \}.$$

Then the formula flies(tweety) can be deduced from the default theory. However, it can not be deduced any more if we add the following knowledge into W:

$$ostrich(tweety),$$
$$\forall x(ostrich(x)→ ¬ flies(x))$$
$$\forall x(ostrich(x)→ feathers(x)).$$

Definition 2.8 *Let Δ=<D, W> be a closed default theory. Γ is an operator defined w.r.t. Δ such that, for any set S of closed formulas, Γ(S) is the smallest set satisfying the following three properties:*

(1) W⊆ Γ(S);

(2) Γ(S) is deductively closed, i.e., Th(Γ(S))= Γ(S);

(3) For any default rule $\alpha : M \beta_1,..., M \beta_m \rightarrow w$ contained in D: if $\alpha \in \Gamma(S)$

and ¬β_1, ..., ¬$\beta_m \notin$ S, then it must be w∈ Γ(S).

Definition 2.9 *A set E of closed formulas is an extension for Δ=<D, W> iff E is a fixed point of the operator Γ w.r.t. Δ, i.e., iff Γ(E) = E.*

Definition 2.10 *A formula F can be deduced from a default theory Δ=<D, W>, in symbols Δ|~F, iff F is contained in the extension of Δ.*

Example 2.6 Suppose D={ $\dfrac{:MA}{\neg A}$ } and W=∅. Then the default theory Δ=<D, W> has no extension.

The result of this example can be demonstrated as follows. Suppose there is a fixed point E of the operator Γ w.r.t. Δ, then: (a) If ¬A∉E, we will get ¬A∈E according to the third property of Definition 5.2 and arrive in a contradiction. (b) If ¬A∈E, then the default rule of D must has been applied in such a way that ¬A was added into E, therefore it must be ¬A∉E otherwise the rule can not be applied. So, we arrive in a contradiction again. As a result, there is no fixed point of the operator Γ w.r.t. Δ, i.e., the default theory Δ=<D, W> has no extension.

Example 2.7 Suppose D={ $\dfrac{:MA}{\neg B}, \dfrac{:MB}{\neg C}, \dfrac{:MC}{\neg F}$ }, W=∅. Then the default theory Δ=<D,W> has a unique extension E=Th({¬B, ¬F}).

For this example, it is easy to demonstrate that E is a fixed point of the operator Γ w.r.t. Δ. However, for any set S ⊆ {¬B, ¬C, ¬F} except {¬B, ¬F}, we can demonstrate that Th(S) is not a fixed point of Γ w.r.t. Δ.

Example 2.8 Suppose D={ $\dfrac{:MA}{A}, \dfrac{B:MC}{C}, \dfrac{F\vee A:ME}{E}, \dfrac{C\wedge E:M\neg A}{G}, \dfrac{M(F\vee A)}{}$ },

W = {B, C→F∨A, A∧C→¬E}. Then there are three extensions for the default theory Δ=<D,W>:

$$E1=Th(W \cup\{A,C\})$$

$$E2=Th(W \cup\{A,E\}),$$

$$E3=Th(W \cup\{C,E,G\}).$$

According to the above example, we can see that not all default theories have their extensions; at the same time, the number of extensions for a default theory is not limited to be one. Effective default reasoning on a default theory is based on the existence of extensions. Therefore, it is important to study and discuss the conditions about the existence of extension.

Theorem 2.3 *Let E be a set of closed formulas, and let $\Delta=<D, W>$ be a closed default theory. Define E0 $=W$ and for $i>0$ it is*

$$E_{i+1}=Th(E_i)\cup\{w \quad | \quad (\alpha \ : \ M\beta_1,...,M\beta_m\rightarrow w) \quad \in \quad D, \quad \alpha\in E_i,$$
$$\neg\beta_1,...,\neg\beta_m\notin E \},$$

Then E is an extension for Δ iff $E = \overset{\infty}{\underset{i=0}{\cup}} E_i$.

With this theorem, the three extensions of Example 2.8.can be examined to be right.

There is a special default rule $\dfrac{:M\neg A}{\neg A}$. A natural question about it is that whether the extension of a default theory determined by this default rule is the same of the corresponding CWA-augmented theory. Answer for this question is negative. For example, suppose W={P∨Q} and D={$\dfrac{:M\neg P}{\neg P}$, $\dfrac{:M\neg Q}{\neg Q}$}. Then is obvious that CWA(Δ) is inconsitent, but the set { P∨Q, ¬P} and { P∨Q, ¬Q } are all consistent extensions for Δ.

Example 2.9 Suppose D={$\dfrac{:MA}{\neg A}$}, W={A, ¬A}. Then the extension for $\Delta=<D,$ W> is E = Th(W).

This example is surprising since the extension for Δ is inconsistent. In fact, some conclusions on the inconsistency of extensions have been summed up:

(1) A closed default theory <D, W> has an inconsistent extension if and only if the formula set W is inconsistent.

Let E be an extension for <D, W>. The result can be demonstrated as follows. On the one hand, if W is inconsistent, then the extension E is also inconsistent since W⊆E. On the other hand, if E is inconsistent, then any default rule of D can be applied since any formula can be deduced from E; therefore, according to Theorem 2.3, we will get the result that $E=T_h(W)$. So, W is also inconsistent.

(2) If a closed default theory has an inconsistent extension then this is the unique extension for this default theory.

In the case that there are more then one extension for a default theory, some conclusions on the relationship between these extensions have been summed up also:

(3) If E and F are extensions for a closed normal default theory and if E⊆F, then E=F.

(4) Suppose Δ_1=<D_1,W_1> and Δ_2=<D_2,W_2> are two different default theories, and that W_1⊆W_2. Suppose further that extensions of Δ_2 is consistent. Then extensions of Δ_1 is also consistent.

Definition 2.11 *A default rule is normal iff it has the following form:*

$$\frac{A \; : \; MB}{B} \qquad (2.3)$$

where A and B are any formulas. A default theory Δ=<D,W> is normal iff every default rule of D is normal.

Normal default theories hold the following properties:

(1) Every closed normal default theory has an extension.

(2) Suppose E and F are distinct extensions for a closed normal default theory, then E∪F must be inconsistent.

(3) Suppose Δ=<D,W> is a closed normal default theory, and that D'⊆D. Suppose further that E'1 and E'2 are distinct extensions of <D',W>. Then Δ

has distinct extensions E1 and E2 such that E'1$\subseteq$ E1 and E'2$\subseteq$ E2.

2.6 Circumscription Logic

Circumscription logic (CIRC) is proposed by McCarthy for nonmonotonic reasoning. The basic idea of circumscription logic is that "the objects that can be shown to have a certain property P by reasoning from certain facts A are all the objects that satisfy P" (McCarthy, 1980). During the process of human informal reasoning, the objects that have been shown to have a certain property P are often treated as all the objects that satisfy P; such a treatment will be used in the further reasoning and will not be revised until other objects are discoveried to have the property P. For example, it is ever guessed by the famous mathematician Erdos that the mathematical equation xxyy = zz has only two trivial solution: x=1, y=z and y=1, x=z. But later it was proved by Chinese mathematical Zhao He that this mathematical equation has infinite number of trivial solutions and therefore overthrew Erdos's guess.

Circumscription logic is based on minimization. In the following, starting with a propositional circumscription which is based on minimal model, we first introduce basic definitions of circumscription. Then we will introduce some basic results on predicate cirsumscription.

Definition 2.12 *Let p_1, p_2 be two satisfying truth assignments for a propositional language L_0. Then p_1 is called smaller than p_2, written as $p_1 \succeq p_2$, if and only if $p_2(x)=l$ for any proposition x which holds $p_1(x)=l$.*

Definition 2.13 *Let p be a satisfying truth assignment of a formula A. We say that p is a minimal satisfying assignment of A if and only if there is no other satisfying truth assignment p' of A such that $p' \succeq p$.*

Definition 2.14 *A formula B is called a minimal entailment of a foumula A, written as $A \models M B$, if and only if B is true with respect to any minimal model of A.*

Minimal model is nonmonotonic. The following example reflect the property of minimal model:

$$p \models_M \neg q$$

$$p \vee q \models_M \neg p \vee \neg q$$

$$p, \ q, \ p \vee q \models_M p \wedge q$$

Definition 2.15 *Let* $Z = \{z_1, z_2, ..., z_n\}$ *be all the propositions occurring in a formula A. Then, a satisfying truth assignment P is called a* $\succeq^{Z}$ *minimal satisfying assignment of A if and only if there is no other satisfying truth assignment P' of A such that* $P \succeq^{Z} P'$. *Where,* $P \succeq^{Z} P'$ *if and only if* $P'(z)=1$ *for any proposition z which holds* $z \in Z$ *and* $P(z)=1$.

Definition 2.16 *Let* $P = \{p_1, p_2, ..., p_n\}$ *be all the propositions occurring in a formula A. Then, a formula* φ *is entailed by the propositional circumscription of P in A, written as* $A \models_P \varphi$, *if and only if* φ *is true with respect to any* $\succeq^{Z}$ *minimal satisfying assignment of A.*

The propositional circumscription CIRC(A, P) is defined as the following formual:

$$A(P) \wedge \forall P'(A(P') \wedge P' \rightarrow P)) \rightarrow (P \rightarrow P') \qquad (2.5)$$

Where A(P') is the result of replacing all occurrence of P in A by P'. If we use $P' \succ P$ to replace $P' \rightarrow P$, then CIRC(A,P) can also be rewrited as:

$$A(P) \wedge \neg \exists P'(A(P') \wedge P' \succ P) \qquad (2.6)$$

Therefore, logical inferences in the propositional circumscription can be represented as schemas of the form $A \models_P \varphi$ or CIRC(A,P) $\models \varphi$. The following theorem on the soundness and completeness has been proved:

Theorem 2.4 $A \vdash_P \varphi$ *if and only if* $A \models_P \varphi$.

In the following we advance the idea of propositional circumscription into predicate circumscription.

Definition 2.17 *Let T be a formula of a first-order language L, and let ρ be a set of predicates contained in T. Let M[T] and M*[T] be two models of T. Then, M* [T] is called smaller then M[T], written as M*[T] $\succeq$ M[T], if and only if:*

(1) M and M* have the same domain;

(2) all the relations and functions occurring in T, except these contained in ρ, have the same interpretation in M and M*;

(3) the extension of ρ in the M* is a subset of ρ in the M.

A model M of T is called $\succeq$ P- minimal if and only if there is no other model M' of T such that M $\succeq$ ₚM'.

Definition 2.18 M_m *is a minimal model of ρ if and only if $M=M_m$ for any model M such that M $\succeq$ ₚM_m.*

For example, let the domain be D={1, 2},

$T = \forall x \; \exists y (P(y) \wedge Q(x, y))$

$= [(P(1) \wedge Q(1, 1)) \vee (P(2) \wedge Q(1, 2))] \wedge [(P(1) \wedge Q(2, 1)) \vee (P(2) \wedge Q(2, 2))]$

Let M and M* be the following models:

M:	P(1)	P(2)	Q(1, 1)	Q(1, 2)	Q(2, 1)	Q(2, 2)
	True	True	False	True	False	True
M*:	P(1)	P(2)	Q(1, 1)	Q(1, 2)	Q(2, 1)	Q(2, 2)
	False	True	False	True	False	True

Then, model M and model M* has the same true assignments on Q. At the same time, P is true in both (1) and (2) of model M; however, for model M*, P is true in just (2). Therefore, we have M* $\succeq_P$ M. Furthermore, since M* $\neq$ M, we have M* $\succ_P$ M.

Let T be a set of beliefs, and let P be a predicate occurs in T. During the extension process, we should seek formula φ_P such that for any model M of T$\wedge\varphi_P$ there is no model M* of T which satisfies

$$M^* \succ_P M$$

The formula T$\wedge\varphi_P$ which satisfies such a principle of minimization is called circumscription of P on T.

Let P* be a predicate constant which has the same number of variables of that of P. Then, it can be demonstrated that any model of the following formula is a minimal model of P on T:

$$(\forall x\, P^*(x) \to P(x)) \wedge \neg(\forall x\, P(x) \to P^*(x)) \wedge T(P^*)$$

Therefore, any model of the following formula is a minimal model of P on T:

$$\neg((\forall x\, P^*(x)) \to P(x)) \wedge \neg(\forall x\, P(x) \to P^*(x)) \wedge T(P^*))$$

As a result, the following is a circumscription formula of P on T:

$$\varphi_P = \forall P^* \neg((\forall x\, P^*(x) \to P(x)) \wedge \neg(\forall x\, P(x) \to P^*(x)) \wedge T(P^*))$$

Definition 2.19 A formula φ is entailed by the predicate circumscription of P in A, written as T $\models_P \varphi$ or CIRC(T, P) $\models\varphi$, if and only if φ is true with respect to all the $\succeq^P$-minimal model of P.

The predicate circumscription CIRC(T,P) of P in T is defined as:

$$\begin{aligned} \text{CIRC(T, P)} = T \wedge\ &\forall P^* \neg((\forall x)(P^*(x) \to P(x)) \wedge \neg(\forall x)(P(x) \\ &\to P^*(x)) \wedge T(P^*)) \end{aligned} \tag{2.7}$$

It can also be rewrited as:

$$\begin{aligned} \text{CIRC(T, P)} = T \wedge \forall P^*\ &((T(P^*) \wedge (\forall x)(P^*(x) \to P(x))) \\ &\to(\forall x)(P(x) \to P^*(x))) \end{aligned} \tag{2.8}$$

Since it is a formula of high-order logic, we can rewrite it as:

$$\varphi_P = \forall P^*((T(P^*) \wedge (\forall x)(P^*(x) \to P(x))) \to (\forall x)(P(x) \to P^*(x))) \tag{2.9}$$

It states that if there is a P* such that T(P*) and $\forall x\ (P^*(x) \to P(X))$, then $\forall x\ (P(x) \to P^*(x))$ can be deduced as a conclusion.

If we use $P \wedge P'$ to replace P^* (here P' is a predicate constant with the same number of variables of that of P), then CIRC(T, P) can be writed as:

$$\varphi_P = T(P \wedge P') \quad \forall x(P(x) \wedge P'(x) \rightarrow P(x)) \rightarrow \forall x)(P(x) \rightarrow P(x) \wedge P'(x)) \quad (2.10)$$

And therefore we get the following formula:

$$T(P \wedge P') \rightarrow (\forall x)(P(x) \rightarrow P'(x)) \quad (2.11)$$

If we replace $(\forall x)(P^*x) \rightarrow P(x)$ by $P^* \succeq P$, then:

$$P^* \succ P \text{ represent } (P^* \succeq P) \wedge \neg (P \succeq P^*), \text{ and}$$

$$P^* = P \text{ represent } (P^* \succeq P) \wedge (P \succeq P^*)$$

And therefore we get

$$\varphi_P = \forall P^* (T(P^*) \wedge (P^* \succeq P) \rightarrow (P \succeq P^*)) \quad (2.12)$$

I.e., $\varphi_P = \forall P^* (T(P^*) \rightarrow \neg (P^* \succ P))$

$$= \neg (\exists P^*)(T(P^*) \wedge (P^* \succ P)) \quad (2.13)$$

Theorem 2.5 *Let T be a formula of a first-order language, and let P be a predicate contained in T. Then, for any P' such that* $T(P) \vdash T(P') \wedge (P' \succeq P)$, *it must be*

$$CIRC(T, P) = T(P) \wedge (P = P') \quad (2.14)$$

According to this theorem, if $T(P') \wedge (P' \succeq P)$ can be deduced from T(P), then $P = P'$ is the circumscription formula of P in T.

2.7 Nonmonotonic Logic NML

The nonmonotonic logic NML proposed by McDermott and Doyle is a general default logic for the study of general foundation of nonmonotonic logics (McDermott,1980). McDermott and Doyle modify a standard first-ordet logic by introducing a modal operator $\lozenge$, which is called compatibility operator. For example, the following is a formula of NML:

$$\forall x \ (Bird(x) \wedge \lozenge \ Fly(x) \rightarrow Fly(x))$$

It states that if x is a bird and it is consistent to assert that x can fly, then x can fly.

According to the example, it is obvious that default assumptions of default theory can be represented in NML, and therefore default theory can be treated as a special case of NML. However, in nonmonotonic logic, $\lozenge A$ is treated as a proposition in the formation of formulas; but in default theory $\lozenge A$ can only appear in default rules. Therefore, there are many fundamental differences between NML and default theory.

In the following, starting with the compatibility operator $\lozenge$, we give an introduction to the nonmonotonic reasoning mechanisms.

Firstly, according to the intuitive sense of $\lozenge$, we might introduce the following rule from the point of syntax:

$$\text{if } \vdash\!/ \ \neg A, \text{ then } \vdash \lozenge A$$

It states that if the negation of A is not derivable, then A is compatible. We can see that rules like this are in fact unsuitable, since the negation of each formula which is not a theorem will be accepted as formula, and consequently the nonmonotonic is eliminated.

Therefore, McDermott and Doyle adopted a different form as follows:

$$\text{if } \vdash\!/ \ \neg A, \text{ then } \vdash\!\!\sim \lozenge A$$

Here the notation $\vdash\!\!\sim$ is introduced to represent nonmonotonic inference, just like that used in default theory.

We can also distinguish $\vdash\!\!\sim$ from the inference relation $\vdash$ of first order logic according to the following discussion. We know that in the monotonic first order logic it is:

$$T \subseteq S \rightarrow Th(T) \subseteq Th(S)$$

Suppose

$$T \vdash \text{fly(tweety)} \tag{2.15}$$

and

$$S = T \cup \{\neg \text{ fly(tweety)}\} \tag{2.16}$$

Then, since $T \vdash$ fly(tweety) and $T \subseteq S$, we will get

$$S \vdash \text{fly(tweety)} \tag{2.17}$$

At the same time, since $\neg$fly(tweety) $\in S$, we have

$$S \vdash \neg \text{fly(tweety)} \tag{2.18}$$

Therefore, it is obvious that $Th(T) \subseteq Th(S)$ does not hold. So, the notation $\vdash\!\!\sim$ is different from $\vdash$.

Let FC be a first order predicate calculus system with the compatibility operator $\Diamond$ embraced in, and let LFC be the set of all the formulas of FC. Then, for any set $\Gamma \subseteq$ LFC, Th(Γ) is defined as:

$$\text{Th}(\Gamma) = \{A \mid \Gamma \vdash_{FC} A\}$$

Th(Γ) can also be defined according to another approach. For any set S$\subseteq$LFC, a nonmonotonic operator NMΓ is firstly defined as:

$$\text{NM}_\Gamma(S) = \text{Th}(\Gamma \cup \text{ASM}_\Gamma(S))$$

Where ASMΓ (S) is the assumption set of S and is defined as:

$$\text{ASM}_\Gamma(S) = \{ \Diamond Q \mid Q \in L_{FC} \wedge \neg Q \notin S \}$$

Then, Th(Γ) can be defined as:

$$\text{Th}(\Gamma) = \cap (\{L_{FC}\} \cup \{S \mid \text{NM}_\Gamma(S) = S\})$$

According to this definition, we can see that Th(Γ) is the intersection of all fixed points of NMΓ, or the entire language if there are no fixed points.

Now, the nonmonotonic inference $\mid\sim$ can be defined as: $\Gamma\mid\sim$ P if and only if P$\in$ Th(Γ).

It should be noted that $\Gamma\mid\sim$P requires that P is contained in each fixed point of NMΓ in the case that there are fixed points. However, in default theory, what is needed for P to be provable in Δ is juat that P is contained in one of Δ's extension, i.e., P is contained in one of the fixed points.

Example 2.10   Suppose Γ is an axiom theory which contains $\Diamond$P$\rightarrow$ $\neg$Q and $\Diamond$Q$\rightarrow$ $\neg$P, i.e.:

$$\Gamma = \text{FC} \cup \{\Diamond P \rightarrow \neg Q, \Diamond Q \rightarrow \neg P\}$$

Then there are two fixed points for this theory: (P, $\neg$Q) and ($\neg$P, Q).

However, for another theory Γ = FC$\cup$\{$\Diamond$P$\rightarrow\neg$P\}, we can demonstrate that it has no fixed points. The demonstration is as follows. Suppose NMΓ (S)=S'. If $\neg$P$\notin$S then we will have $\Diamond$P$\in$ASMΓ (S) and consequently $\neg$P$\in$S'; On the contrary, if $\neg$P$\in$S then we will have $\Diamond$P$\notin$ASMΓ (S), and consequently $\neg$P $\notin$S'. Therefore, S will never be equal with S', i.e., there is no fixed point for NMΓ.

The aboving phenomenon can be further explained according to the following results:

$$\{\Diamond P \rightarrow \neg Q, \Diamond Q \rightarrow \neg P\} \mid\sim (\neg P \vee \neg Q)$$

$$\{\Diamond P \rightarrow \neg P\} \mid\sim \text{contradiction}$$

McDermott and Doyle pointed out the following two problems on the reasoning process of NML:

(1) ◊A can not be deduced from ◊(A∧B); and;

(2) What can be deduced from {◊P→ Q, ¬Q} is surprising.

In order to overcome these problems, McDermott and Doyle introduced another modal operator □ called necessity. The relationship between ◊ and □ is as follows:

$$\Box P \equiv \neg \Diamond \neg P$$

$$\Diamond P \equiv \neg \Box \neg P$$

Here the first definition states that P is necessary if and only if its negation is incompatible; the second definition states that P is compatible if and only if its negation is not necessary.

2.8 Autoepistemic Logic

2.8.1 *Moore System* $\mathcal{L}_B$

Autoepistemic logic was proposed by Moore as an approach to represent and reason about the knowledge and beliefs of agents (Moore, 1985). It can be treated as a modal logic with a modal operator **B** which is informally interpreted as "believe" or "know". Once the beliefs of agents are represented as logical formulas, then a basic task of autoepistemic logic is to describe the conditions which should be satisfied by these formulas. Intuitively, an agent should believe these facts that can be deduced from its current beliefs. Furthermore, is an agent believe or do not believe some fact, then the agent should believe that it believe or do not believe this fact.

An autoepistemic theory T is sound with respect to an initial set of premises A if and only if every autoepistemic interpretation of T in which all the formulas of A are true is an autoepistemic model of T. The beliefs of an ideally rational agent should satisfy the following conditions:

(1) if P_1, ⋯, $P_n \in$ T, and P_1, ⋯, $P_n \vdash Q$, then $Q \in$ T, (where $\vdash$ means ordinary tautological consequence).

(2) If P∈ T, then **B**P ∈ T.

(3) If P∉ T，then ¬**B**P ∈ T.

No further conditions could be drawn by an ideally rational agent in such a state; therefore, the state of belief characterized by such a theory is also described by Moore as stable autoepistemic theories. If a stable autoepistemic theory T is consistent, it will satisfy the following two consitions:

(4) If **B**P ∈ T, then P∈ T.

(5) If ¬**B**P ∈ T，then P∉ T.

An autoepistemic logic named $\mathcal{L}_B$ was proposed and studied by Moore. This logic is built up a countable set of propositional letters, the logical connectives ¬ and ∧, and a modal connective **B**.

2.8.2 O$\mathcal{L}$ Logic

Based on the autoepistemic logic $\mathcal{L}_B$, Levesque introduced another modal connective **O** and built the logic **O**$\mathcal{L}$. Therefore, there are two modal operators, **B** and **O**, where **B**φ is read as "φ is believed" and **O**φ is read as "φ is all that is believed" (Levesque, 1990). Formulas of $\mathcal{L}_B$ and **O**φ are formed as usual as that of ordinary logic. The objective formulas are those without any **B** and **O** operators; the subjective formulas are those where all nonlogical symbols occur within the scope of a **B** or **O**. Formulas without **O** operators are called basic.

Be similar to that of classical propositional logic, any formula of the autoepistemic logic **B**φ can be transformed into a (disjunctive or conjunctive) normal form.

Theorem 2.6 (*Theorem on Moore disjunctive normal form*) *Any formula $\psi \in \mathcal{L}_B$*

can be logical equivalently transformed into a formula of the form

$\psi_1 \vee \psi_2 \vee \ldots \vee \psi_k$, where each ψ_i ($1 \le i \le k$) is an objective formula with the form

$$\mathbf{B}\varphi_{i,1} \wedge \ldots \wedge \mathbf{B}\,\varphi_{i,mi} \wedge \neg\mathbf{B}\varphi_{i,1} \wedge \ldots \wedge \neg\mathbf{B}\varphi_{i,ni} \wedge \psi_{ii}$$

.

Let L be a countable set of propositional letters. Let 2^L be the set of all the functions from the elements of L to $\{0, 1\}$, i.e., 2^L is the set of all the assignments of L. Let W be a subset of 2^L and w be an element of 2^L. Then, the truth-relation W, $w \models \psi$ for any formula of the logic $\mathcal{L}_B$ or the logic $\mathbf{O}\mathcal{L}$ can be defined according to the following definitions.

Definition 2.20 *For any formula ψ of the logic $\mathcal{L}_B$, the truth-relation W,$w \models \psi$ is defined inductively as follows:*

(1) For any propositional letter p， W,$w \models p$ iff $w(p) = 1$;

(2) W,$w \models \neg\psi$ iff   W, $w \not\models \psi$;

(3) W,$w \models (\psi \wedge \varphi)$ iff   W,$w \models \psi$ and W,$w \models \varphi$;

(4) W,$w \models \mathbf{B}\psi$ iff   W,$w' \models \psi$ for every $w' \in$ W.

Definition 2.21 *For any formula ψ of the logic $\mathbf{O}\mathcal{L}$, W,$w \models \mathbf{O}\mathcal{L}$ iff   W,$w \models \mathbf{B}\varphi$ and for every w', if W,$w' \models \varphi$ then $w' \in$ W.*

Therefore, the rule for $\mathbf{O}$ is in fact a very simple modification of the rule for $\mathbf{B}$. This can also be seen by rewriting both rules as follows:

$$\text{W,}w \models \mathbf{B}\psi \quad \text{iff} \quad w' \in \text{W} \Rightarrow \text{W,}w' \models \psi \text{ for every } w';$$

$$\text{W,}w \models \mathbf{O}\psi \quad \text{iff} \quad w' \in \text{W} \Leftrightarrow \text{W,}w' \models \psi \text{ for every } w'.$$

The modal operator $\mathbf{O}$ is closely related to stable expansion. To a certain extent, the operator $\mathbf{O}$ can be used to describe stable expansions, as shown by the following theorem and corollary.

Theorem 2.7 *(Stable expansion) For any basic formula ψ and any maximal set of assignments W, $W \models O\psi$ iff the set {$\psi|\psi$ is a basic formula and $W \models B\psi$} is a stable expansion of {ψ}.*

Corollary 2.1 *A formula ψ has exactly as many stable expansions as there are masimal sets of assignments where $O\psi$ is true.*

2.8.3 Theorems on normal forms

Theorems on normal forms play important roles in the study of stable set and stable expansion. In the following we reinspect these theorems from the point of semantics.

Definition 2.22 *For any basic formula ψ, rank(ψ) is inductively defined as follows:*

(1) if ψ is an objective formula, then rank(ψ) = 0;

(2) if $\psi = \psi_1 \wedge \psi_2$, then rank($\psi$) = Max(rank($\psi_1$), rank($\psi_2$));

(3) if $\psi = \neg\, \varphi$, then rank(ψ) = rank(φ);

(4) if $\psi = B\varphi$, then rank(ψ) = rank(φ) + 1.

Lemma 2.1 *The modal operator B has the following properties:*
(1) $\models B(B(\psi)) \leftrightarrow B(\psi)$;
(2) $\models B(\neg B(\psi)) \leftrightarrow \neg B(\psi)$;
(3) $\models B(B(\psi) \wedge \varphi) \leftrightarrow B(\psi) \wedge B(\varphi)$;
(4) $\models B(\neg B(\psi) \wedge \varphi) \leftrightarrow \neg B(\psi) \wedge B(\varphi)$;
(5) $\models B(B)(\psi) \vee \varphi) \leftrightarrow B(\psi) \vee B(\varphi)$;
(6) $\models B(\neg B(\psi) \vee \varphi) \leftrightarrow \neg B(\psi) \vee B(\varphi)$.

Lemma 2.2 $\models B$ $(B(\psi_1)$ $\vee \cdots \vee B(\psi_s)$ $\vee \neg B(\varphi_1)$ $\vee \cdots \neg B(\varphi_t)$ $\vee \varphi)$ $\leftrightarrow$ $(B(\psi_1)$ $\vee \cdots \vee B(\psi_s)$ $\vee \neg B(\varphi_1)$ $\vee \cdots \neg B(\varphi_t)$ $\vee B(\varphi))$.

Theorem 2.8 *(Theorem on Conjunctive normal form) For any formula* $\psi \in \mathcal{L}_B$,

it is φ $\mathcal{L}$ *-equivalent with some formula of the form* $\psi_1 \wedge \psi_2 \wedge \cdots \wedge \psi_k$, *where*

each $\psi_i (1 \leqslant i \leqslant k)$ *is of the form* $B^\varphi i,1$ $\vee \cdots \vee B^\varphi_{i,mi}$ $\vee \neg B^\varphi_{i,1}$ $\vee \cdots \vee \neg B^\varphi_{i,ni}$ $\vee \varphi_{ii}$ *with* $\varphi_{i,j}$, $\varphi_{i,n}$ $(1 \leqslant i \leqslant k, 1 \leqslant j \leqslant m_i, 1 \leqslant n \leqslant n_i)$ *and* ψ_{ii} *objective formulas.*

Proof. By indunction on the value of rank(ψ). If rank(ψ) = 1, then the result is obvious according to Theorem 2.6.

Suppose rank(ψ)=N and suppose the result hods for any formula φ with rank(φ)<N. Then, according to Theorem 2.6 we have

$$\psi = \psi^1 \vee \psi^2 \vee \cdots \vee \psi^k,$$

where each ψi ($1 \leq i \leq k$) is of the form

$$B\varphi^i_1 \wedge \cdots \wedge B\varphi^i_{mi} \wedge \neg B\varphi^i_1 \wedge \cdots \wedge \neg B\varphi^i_{ni} \wedge \psi_{ii}.$$

According to the induction hypothesis we have

$$\text{rank}(\varphi^i_j) \leq N\text{-}1, \quad \text{rank}(\varphi^i_t) \leq N\text{-}1, \text{ and rank}(\psi^{ii}) = 0.$$

Therefore, both φ^i_j and φ^i_t can be equivalently transformed into formulas whose rank value are less or equivalent to 1. Without lose of generality we let φ^i_j be a formula of the form

$$\chi^1 \wedge \cdots \wedge \chi^d,$$

where each χ_h ($1 \leq h \leq d$) is of the form

$$B\chi_{h,1} \vee \cdots \vee B\chi_{h,uh} \vee \neg B\chi'_{h,1} \vee \cdots \vee \neg B\chi'_{h,vh} \vee \chi_{hh}$$

and $\chi_{h,j}$, $\chi'_{h,n}$ ($1 \leq h \leq d, 1 \leq j \leq u_h, 1 \leq n \leq v_h$), χ_{hh}, are all objective formulas.

According to the semantic definition, the formula $B\varphi^i_j$ is equivalent to

$$B(\chi_1) \wedge \cdots \wedge B(\chi_d) \tag{2.19}$$

Furthermore, according to Lemma 2.2, each $B(\chi_h)$ is equivalent to

$$\mathbf{B}\chi_{h,\,1} \vee \cdots \vee \mathbf{B}\chi_{h,uh} \vee \neg\mathbf{B}\chi'_{h,1} \vee \cdots \vee \neg\mathbf{B}\chi'_{h,vh} \vee \mathbf{B}\chi_{hh} \qquad (2.20)$$

Where $\chi_{h,j}$, $\chi'_{h,n}$ ($1 \leq h \leq d$, $1 \leq j \leq u_h$, $1 \leq n \leq v_h$) and χ_{hh}, are all objective formulas.

Now, use expressions of the form of (2.20) to replace each occurrence of $\mathbf{B}\chi h$, and use expressions of the form of (2.19) to replace each occurrence of φ^i_j, we will get a formula ψ' which is $\psi\mathcal{L}$-equivalent with ψ and satisfies rank(ψ')=rank(ψ)+1. Finally, the proof can be completed by transforming the formula ψ' into a conjunctive normal form.

We can also reach the following result according to the duality property:

Corollary 2.2 *(Theorem on Disjunctive normal form) For any formula* $\psi \in \mathcal{L}_B$, *it is* $\psi\mathcal{L}$-*equivalent with some formula of the form* $\psi_1 \vee \psi_2 \vee \cdots \vee \psi_k$, *where each* ψ_i *(*$1 \leq i \leq k$*) is of the form* $\mathbf{B}\varphi_{i,1} \wedge \cdots \wedge \mathbf{B}\varphi_{i,mi} \wedge \neg\mathbf{B}\varphi_{i,1} \wedge \cdots \wedge \neg\mathbf{B}\varphi_{i,ni}$ $\wedge \psi_{ii}$ *with* $\varphi_{i,j}$, $\varphi_{i,n}$, *(*$1 \leq i \leq k$*,* $1 \leq j \leq m_i$*,* $1 \leq n \leq n_i$*) and* ψ_{ii} *objective formulas.*

2.8.4 $\diamond$ mark and a kind of course of judging for stable expansion

Firstly we introduce the $\diamond$-mark. Let L be a countable set of propositional letters, and let 2^L be the set of all the assignments of L.

Definition 2.23 *(*$\diamond$-*mark) For any basic formula* ψ, *its* $\diamond$-*mark* $\diamond\psi$ *is inductively defined as follows:*

(1) For any propositional letter p, $\diamond p = \{ w \mid w \in 2^L$ and $w(p){=}1 \}$;

(2) If $\psi{=}\neg\varphi$, **then** $\diamond\neg\varphi = \sim\diamond\varphi = 2^L - \diamond\varphi$, where $\sim$ is the complementary operator on sets;

(3) If $\psi{=}\psi_1 \wedge \psi_2$, then $\diamond\psi_1 \wedge \psi_2 = \diamond\psi_1 \cap \diamond\psi_2$, where $\cap$ is the the intersection operator on sets;

(4) If $\psi= \mathbf{B}\varphi$, $\diamond\mathbf{B}\varphi = \diamond\varphi$.

Lemma 2.3 *Let* ψ *and* φ *be objective formulas, then*

(1) $\vdash \psi \rightarrow \varphi$ *if and only if* $\Diamond \psi \subseteq \Diamond \varphi$;

(2) $\{\psi, \varphi\}$ *is satisfiable if and only if* $\Diamond \psi \cap \Diamond \varphi \neq \varnothing$.

Now, from the point of set theory, we can redefine the semantics of autoepistemic logic according to the following theorem.

Theorem 2.9 *Let* ψ *and* φ *be objective formulas, and let* W,w *be a model with* $W \subseteq 2^L$ *and* $w \in 2^L$. *Then:*

(1) $W,w \models \psi$ *iff* $w \in \Diamond \psi$;

(2) $W,w \models \psi \wedge \varphi$ *iff* $W,w \models \psi$ *and* $W,w \models \varphi$;

(3) $W,w \models \neg \psi$ *iff* $W \not\subseteq \Diamond \psi$;

(4) $W,w \models B\psi$ *iff* $W \subseteq \Diamond \psi$.

Next we introduce the **O**-property.

Definition 2.24 *Let* ψ *be a basic formula which is represented in the disjunctive normal form* $\psi_1 \vee \psi_2 \vee \ldots \vee \psi_k$, *where each* ψ_i *(*$1 \leqslant i \leqslant k$*) is of the form* $B\varphi_{i,1} \wedge \cdots \wedge B\varphi_{i,mi} \wedge \neg B\varphi_{i,1} \wedge \cdots \wedge \neg B\varphi_{i,ni} \wedge \varphi_{ii}$ *with* ψ_{ii} *an objective formula. Let* J *be a subset of* $\{1, \cdots, k\}$. *We say that* J *has the* **O**-*property if and only if the following conditions hold:*

(1) $\cup j \in J \Diamond \psi_{jj} \models B\varphi_{r,1} \wedge \cdots \wedge B\varphi_{r,mr} \wedge \neg B\varphi_{r,1} \wedge \cdots \wedge \neg B\varphi_{rnr}$ for each $r \in J$, and

(2) $\cup j \in J \Diamond \psi_{jj} \not\models B\varphi_{t,1} \wedge \cdots \wedge B\varphi_{t,mt} \wedge \neg B\varphi_{t,1} \wedge \cdots \wedge \neg B\varphi_{t,nt}$ for each $t \notin J$.

The **O**-property of J can be decided according to the following two approaches:

Lemma 2.4 *(The set theory approach)* J *has the* **O**-*property if and only if the following conditions hold (here* $\Diamond J$ *is the abbreviation of* $\cup j \in J \Diamond \psi_{jj}$*):*

(1) $\Diamond J \subseteq \Diamond \varphi_{r,\,p1}$ and $\Diamond_J \not\subseteq \Diamond \varphi_{r,\,p2}$ for each $r \in J$, $1 \leq p_1 \leq m_r$ and $1 \leq p_2 \leq n_r$, and

(2) For each $t \notin J$, there must be a q_1 with $1 \leq q_1 \leq m_t$ or a q_2 with $1 \leq q_2 \leq n_t$ such that

$\Diamond J \not\subseteq \Diamond \varphi_{t,\,q1}$ or $\Diamond J \subseteq \Diamond \varphi_{t,\,q2}$.

Lemma 2.5 *(The semantic approach) J has the **O**-property if and only if the following formula set is satisfiable:*

$\{ \psi^J \to \varphi_{r,p1} \mid r \in J$ and $1 \leq p_1 \leq m_r \} \cup \{ \neg \varphi_{r,\,p2} \mid r \in J$ and $1 \leq p_2 \leq n_r \}$

$\cup \{ \psi^J \} \cup \{ \bigvee_{t \notin J,\ 1 \leq q1 \leq mt} \{ \psi^J \wedge \neg \varphi_{t,q1} \} \vee \bigvee_{t \notin J,\ 1 \leq q2 \leq nt} \{ \psi^J \to \varphi_{t,q2} \} \}.$

Here ψ^J is the abbreviation of $\bigvee_{j \in J} \psi_{jj}$.

According to theorems on normal forms and either Lemma 2.4 or Lemma 2.5, we can conclude that for any set $J \subseteq \{1, \ldots, k\}$ it is decidable to examine whether J has the **O**-property.

Theorem 2.10 *Let ψ be a basic formula which is represented in the disjunctive normal form $\psi_1 \vee \psi_2 \vee \cdots \vee \psi_k$, where each ψ_i ($1 \leq i \leq k$) is of the form $B\varphi_{i,1} \wedge \cdots \wedge B\varphi_{i,mi} \wedge \neg B\varphi_{i,1} \wedge \cdots \wedge \neg B\varphi_{i,ni} \wedge \varphi_{ii}$ with ψ_{ii} an objective formula. Then, for any set $J \subseteq \{1, \ldots, k\}$, there is a decision procedure to decide whether J has the **O**-property.*

Furthermore, according to Lemma 2.5 and the fact that SAT problem is NP-completed, we can conclude that it is also a NP-completed problem to decide whether any set $J \subseteq \{1, \cdots, k\}$ has the **O**-property.

With the help of $\Diamond$-mark and **O**-property, we can construct a procedure to decide the stable expansions of a basic formula.

Theorem 2.11 *Let ψ be a basic formula which is represented in the disjunctive normal form $\psi_1 \vee \psi_2 \vee \cdots \vee \psi_k$, where each ψ_i ($1 \leq i \leq k$) is of the form $B\varphi_{i,1} \wedge \cdots \wedge B\varphi_{i,mi} \wedge \neg B\varphi_{i,1} \wedge \cdots \wedge \neg B\varphi_{i,ni} \wedge \psi_{ii}$ with ψ_{ii} an objective formula, and let W,w be a model. Then, $W,w \models O\psi$ if and only if there exist a set $J \subseteq \{1, \cdots, k\}$ which has the **O**-property and satisfys $W = \cup_{j \in J} \Diamond \psi_{jj} = \Diamond \cup_{j \in J} \psi_{jj}$.*

Proof. Recalling the definition, $W,w \models \mathbf{O}\psi$ if and only if

(1) $W,w \models \mathbf{B}\psi$, and

(2) $w' \in W$ for any w' which satisfys $W,w' \models \psi$.

Now suppose $W,w \models \mathbf{O}\psi$. Then we can construct a set $J = \{j \mid W,w \models \mathbf{B}\varphi_{j,1} \wedge \cdots \wedge \mathbf{B}\varphi_{j,mj} \wedge \neg \mathbf{B}\varphi_{j,1} \wedge \cdots \wedge \neg \mathbf{B}\varphi_{j,mj}\}$. It is easy to demonstrate that J has the $\mathbf{O}$-property; furthermore, according to (1) we will get $W \subseteq \cup_{j \in J} \Diamond \psi_{jj}$, and according to (2) we will get $\cup_{j \in J} \Diamond \psi_{jj} \subseteq W$. Therefore we have $W = \cup_{j \in J} \Diamond \psi_{jj}$. The other direction can be similarly demonstrated.

Corollary 2.3 *The number of stable expansions of the basic formula ψ is equivalent with the number of sets which have the $\mathbf{O}$-property and are subsets of $\{1, \cdots, k\}$.*

Corollary 2.4 *The basic formula ψ has exactly one stable expansion if and only if there is only one subset of $\{1, \ldots, k\}$ that has the $\mathbf{O}$-property.*

In the following are some examples.

Example 2.11 Suppose ψ is $\mathbf{B}p$. Then ψ can be transformed as $\mathbf{B}p \wedge \neg \mathbf{B}(r \wedge \neg r) \wedge (q \vee \neg q)$. Therefore, there is no stable expansion for ψ, since $\Diamond(q \vee \neg q)$, i.e. 2^L, is the only maximal set for examine.

Example 2.12 Suppose ψ is p. Then ψ can be transformed as $\mathbf{B}(q \vee \neg q) \wedge \neg \mathbf{B}(r \wedge \neg r) \wedge p$. Therefore, there is just one stable expansion since $\Diamond p \subseteq \Diamond(q \vee \neg q) = 2^L$ and $\Diamond p \not\subseteq \Diamond(r \wedge \neg r) = \emptyset$.

Example 2.13 Suppose ψ is $(\neg \mathbf{B}p \rightarrow q) \wedge (\neg \mathbf{B}q \rightarrow p)$. Then ψ can be transformed as $(\mathbf{B}p \wedge \mathbf{B}q) \vee (\mathbf{B}p \wedge p) \vee (\mathbf{B}q \wedge q) \vee (p \wedge q)$. Therefore, there are four maximal sets, $\diamondsuit_p \wedge_q$, $\diamondsuit_p \vee_q$, $\diamondsuit_p$ and $\diamondsuit_q$, which might have the O-property. It can be easily examined that $\diamondsuit_p$ and $\diamondsuit_q$ are the only two sets that have the O-property. Therefore, there are just two stable expansions for ψ.

Finally, we can present a procedure to determine the stable expansions of basic formulas:

Inputs: a basic formula ψ.

Initial state: N=0.

Step 1: Transform ψ into a disjunctive normal form ψ' with rank(ψ')=1;

Let k be the number of disjunctive branches of ψ';

Set $2^K = 2^k$, where 2^k is a set that composed of all the subsets of the set $\{1, \cdots, k\}$.

Step 2: Repeat the following operation until $2^K = \emptyset$: take out an element J

form 2^K, if J has the **O**-property then set $N=N+1$.

Outputs: N (i.e., the number of stable expansions of ψ).

2.9 Truth Maintenance System

Truth Maintenance System (TMS) is a problem solver subsystem for recording and maintaining beliefs in knowledge base (Doyle,1979). The relationship between TMS and default inference is similar to the relationship between production system and first-order logic. A truth maintenance system is composed of two basic operations: a) Make assumptions according to incompleted and finite informations, and take these assumptions as a part of beliefs; and b) Revise the current set of beliefs when discoveries contradict these assumptions.

There are two basic data structures in TMS: nodes, which represent beliefs, and justifications, which represent reasons for beliefs. Some fundamental actions are supported by the TMS. Firstly, it can create a new node, to which some statements of a belief will be attached. Secondly, it can add (or retract) a new justification for a node, to represent a step of an argumrnt for the belief represented by the node. Finally, the TMS can mark a node as a contradiction, to represent the inconsistency of any set of beliefs which enter into an argument for the node. In this case, the TMS invokes the truth maintenance procedure to make any necessary revisions in the set of beliefs. The TMS locates the set of nodes to update by finding those nodes whose well-founded arguments depend on changed nodes. When this happens, another process of the TMS, dependency-directed backtracking, is also carried out to analyze the well-founded argument of the contradiction node; then the contradiction can be eliminated according to locate and delete the assumptions occurring in the argument.

The TMS provides two services: truch maintenance and dependency-directed backtracking. Both of these services are carried out on the basis of the representation of reasons for beliefs.

1. Representation of Reasons for Beliefs

A node may have several justifications, each justification representing a different reason for believing the node. A node is believed if and only if at least one of its justifications is valid, i.e., at least one of its justifications can be deduced from the current knowledge base (where these beliefs generated according to assumptions are also included in this knowledge base).

In the TMS, each proposition or each rule can all be represented as a node. Each node is of the following two types:

the IN-node which has at least one valid justification, and

the OUT-node which has no valid justifications.

Therefore, there are four states for the knowledge of each proposition p: an IN-node for p, an OUT-node for p, an IN-node for $\neg p$, and an OUT-node for $\neg p$.

Each node has its justifications. The TMS employs two forms for justifications, called support-list (SL) and conditional-proof (CP) justifications. The former is used to represent reasons for believing the node, while the later is used to record the reasons for contradiction.

Each SL justification is of the following form:

$$(SL (<IN\text{-}list>) (<OUT\text{-}list>)) \qquad (2.21)$$

A SL justification is valid if and only if each node in its IN-list is IN-node, and each node in its OUT-list is OUT-node.

For example, consider the following SL justifications:

(1) It is now summer.   (SL ( ) ( ))

(2) The weather is very humid.   (SL (1) ( ))

In this example, IN-list and OUT-list of the SL justification of node (1) are all empty, it meas that the justification of node (1) is always valid and therefore the node (1) will always be an IN-node. We call nodes of this type as premise. IN-list of the SL justification of node (2) is composed of node (1), it means that node (2) is believed if node (1) is a IN-node. According to this example, we can see that the inference of TMS is in fact similar to the inference of predicate logic. Difference between them is that premises in the TMS can be retracted and correspondingly the knowledge base can be revised.

Based on the above example, we add an item to the OUT-list of node (2) and get the following SL justifications:

(1) It is now summer.   (SL ( ) ( ))

(2) The weather is very humid.   (SL (1) (3))

(3) The weather is very dry.

In this case, the condition for node (2) to be believed is that node (1) is an IN-node and node (3) is an OUT-node. All of these SL justifications state that "if it is now summer and there is no evidence to prove that the weather is very dry, then it can be derived that the weather is very humid". We call nodes whose SL justification has a nonempty OUT-list as assumptions.

Each CP justification is of the following form:

$$(CP <consequent> <IN\text{-}hypotheses> <OUT\text{-}hypotheses>) \qquad (2.22)$$

A CP justification is valid if (1) the consequent node is an IN-node, (2) each node of the IN-hypotheses is IN-node, and (3) each node of the OUT-hypotheses is OUT-node.

The set of hypotheses must be divided into two disjoint subsets, since nodes may be derived both from some IN-nodes and some OUT-nodes.

2. Default Assumptions

Let $\{F_1, ..., F_n\}$ be the set of alternative default nodes, let G be a node which represents the reason for making an assumption to choose the default. To make Fi the default, justify it with the following SL justification:

$$(SL \quad (G) \quad (F_1, ..., F_{i-1}, F_{i+1}, ..., F_n)) \tag{2.23}$$

If no additional information about the value exists, none of the alternative nodes except F_i will have a valid justification, so F_i will be an IN-node and each F_j with $j{\neq}i$ will be OUT-node. However, if a valid justification is added to some other alternative node and cause that alternative to become an IN-node, then the aboving SL justification will be invalid and make F_i an OUT-node. Consider the case that F_i has been selected as default assumption and a contradiction is derived from F_i, then the dependency-directed backtracking mechanism will recognize F_i as an assumption because it depends on the other alternative nodes being OUT. The backtracker may then justify one of the other alternative nodes, say F_j, and make F_i an OUT-node. Where, the backtracker-produced justification for F_j will have the following form:

$$(SL \quad <\text{various nodes}> \quad <\text{remainder nodes}>) \tag{2.24}$$

where <remainder nodes> represent the set of nodes except F_i and F_j.

The aboving approach will not work in the case that the complete set of alternatives cannot be known in advance but must be discovered piecemeal. To solve this problem, we can use a slightly different set of justifications with which the set of alternatives can be gradually extended.

Retaining the above notation and let $\neg F_i$ be a node which represents the negation of F_i. Then, arrange F_i to be believed if $\neg F_i$ is an OUT-node, and set up justifications so that if F_j is distinct from F_i then F_j supports $\neg F_i$. I.e., F_i is justified with

$$(SL \quad (G) \quad (\neg F_i)) \tag{2.25}$$

and $\neg F_i$ is justified with

$$(SL \quad (F_j) \quad (j \neq i)) \tag{2.26}$$

where F_j is an alternative distinct from F_i.

According to these justifications, F_i will be assumed if no reasons exist for using any other alternative. However, if some contradiction is derived from F_i, then $\neg F_i$ will become an IN-node and correspondingly F_i become an OUT-node.

The dependency-directed backtracking mechanism will be uased to recognize the cause of the contradiction and construct a new default assumption.

3. Dependency-Directed Backtracking

When the TMS makes a contradiction node as IN-node, it will invoke the dependency -directed backtracking to find and remove at least one of the current assumptions in order to make the contradiction node as an OUT-node. Let C be the contradiction node. The dependency -directed backtracking is composed of the following three steps.

Step 1. Trace through the foundations of the contradiction node C to find the set $S=\{A_1, ...,A_n\}$ which is composed of maximal assumptions underlying C. Where A_i is called a maximal assumption underlying C if and only if A_i is in C's foundations and there is no other assumption B in the foundations of C such that A_i is in the foundations of B.

Step 2. Create a new node NG to represent the inconsistency of S. NG is also called as nogood node for representing the following formula:

$$A_1 \wedge ... \wedge A_n \rightarrow false$$

which is equivalent with

$$\neg(A_1 \wedge ... \wedge A_n) \tag{1}$$

Node NG has the following CP justification:

$$(CP \quad C \quad S \quad ( )) \tag{2}$$

Step 3. Select some maximal assumption A_i from S. Let $D_1,...,D_k$ be the OUT-nodes in the OUT-list of A_i's supporting justification. Select D_j from this set and justify it with

$$(SL \quad (NG\ A_1 ... A_{i-1}\ A_{i+1} ... A_n) \quad (D_1 ... D_{j-1}\ D_{j+1} ... D_k)) \tag{3}$$

If the TMS finds other argumrnts so that the contradiction node C is still IN-node after the addition of the new justification for Dj, repeat this backtracking procedure.

As an example, consider a program scheduling a meeting. Firstly, suppose the date for the meeting is Wednesday. The corresponding knowledge base is as follows:

(1) The date for the meeting is Wednesday   (SL   ()   (2))

(2) The date for the meeting is not Wednesday

Here, node (1) is an IN-node since there is no argumrnts for the statement "the date for the meeting is not Wednesday".

Next, suppose it can be deduced from beliefs represented in other nodes, the node (32), node (40) and node (61), suth that the time for the meeting is 14:00. Then the corresponding knowledge base of the TMS is as follows:

(1) The date for the meeting is Wednesday (SL   ()   (2))

(2) The date for the meeting is not Wednesday

(3) The time for the meeting is 14:00 (SL   (32, 40, 61)   ())

Now suppose a previously scheduled meeting rule out the combination of the data of Wednesday and the time of 14:00, by supporting a new node with node (1) and node (3) and then declaring this new node to be a contradiction:

(4) Contradiction (SL   (1, 3)   ())

Then the dependency-directed backtracking system will trace the foundations of node (4) to find two assumptions, (1) and (3), both maximal. Correspondingly the following nogood node is constructed to record the result.

(5) nogood (CP   4   (1, 3)   ())

The TMS arbitrarily select node (1) and justifies (1)'s only OUT antecedent (2), and correspondingly change node (2) as follows:

(2) The date for the meeting is not Wednesday (SL   (5)   ())

Now, node (2) and node (5) are IN-nodes, and consequently node (1) and node (4) are OUT-nodes. Therefore, the contradiction is eliminated.

De Kleer pointed out some limitations of TMS and correspondingly proposed an assumption-based TMS (ATMS) (de Kleer,1986). A typical characteristic of ATMS is the capability of working with multiple conreadictory assumptions as once.

The ATMS consists of two components: a problem solver and a TMS. The problem solver includes all domain knowledge and inference procedures. Every inference made is communicated to the TMS. The TMS's job is to determine what data are believed and disbelieved fiven the justifications records thus far.

An ATMS justification describes how a node is derivable from other nodes, and is of the following form:

$$A_1, A_2, ..., A_n \Rightarrow D$$

Where D is the node being justified and is called the consequent; A_1, A_2, ..., A_n is a list of nodes and is called the antecedents. The nonlogical notation " $\Rightarrow$ " is used here because the ATMS does not allow negated literals and treats implication unconventionally.

Limited to the space, detailed discussion of ATMS is omitted here. Readers may refer to the relevant literatures.

2.10 Situation Calculus

Action is a basic concept in many branches of computer science. For example, in the branch of database theory, delete, insert and update of data are frequently used operations (or actions). These operations play an important role in the database. Another example is the multiagent system of distributed artificial intelligence, where various behavior (or actions) of agents are the basis of the cooperation of agents. The knowledge and beliefs of agents is an important research topic for multiagent system, where the update and revise of knowledge and beliefs are also based on the study of action theory.

Situation calculus is the most commonly used formalism for the study and process of actions. With respect to the progress of a database, Fangzhen Lin and Reiter embed situation calculus into a many-sroted first-order logic framework **LR** and established a formal foundation for action (Lin, 1994). In the **LR** framework, individuals are divided into three sorts: state, action and object.

Based on these three sorts, to characterize ab action, they described the precondition (under which the action could be performed) and the effect (the change of the world after the execution of the action) by sentences of **LR**. In **LR**, system with actions was treated uniformly as a logic theory that which was called basic action theory. The **LR** framework and the corresponding basic action theory provide a theoretical foundation for the study of actions.

Based on the **LR** framkwork, we present a many-sroted logic for the representation and reasoning about actions (Tian, 1997). In this logic, actions are treated as functions rather than individual sorts. Such a treatment is more coincident with the intuitive understanding of actions and also has a clear semantics in model theory. In the logic, the so-called minimal action theory is introduced to characterize systems with actions; a model theory is correspondingly established to analysis the progression in minimal action theory; finally, some results on the definability of progression in minimal action theory are presented.

2.10.1 Many-sorted logic for situation calculus

LR is defined to be a many-sorted first order logic (Lin, 1994). In its signature $\mathcal{L}$, there are three sorts: sort s for state, sort o for object and sort a for action. The constant S_0 of sort s is used to denote the initial state. There is a distinguished binary function **do** of type $<a, s; s>$; $do(a, s)$ denotes the successor state to s resulting from performing the action a. The binary relation **Poss** of type $<a, s>$ is also introduced; $Poss(a, s)$ means that it is possible to perform the action a in the state s. Finally, a binary relation $<$ of type $<s, s>$ is introduced to denote the sequential relation between states.

A relation symbol is called to be state independent if all its parameters are of sort o. A function symbol is called to be state independent if all of its parameters as well as its function value are of sort o. A relation symbol is called to be a fluent if there is a parameter of sort s while the other parameters are of sort o. The number of state independent relations, state independent functions and fluents are all supposed to be limit in $\mathcal{L}$.

Term, atom formula, and formula of **LR** are defined in the usual way.

For any state term st, $\mathcal{L}_{st}$ is defined to be the subset of $\mathcal{L}$ that does not mention any other state terms except st, does not quantify over state variables, and does not mention Poss and $<$. Formally, $\mathcal{L}_{st}$ is the smallest set satisfying the following conditions:

(1) if $\psi \in \mathcal{L}$ and it does not mention any state term, then $\psi \in \mathcal{L}_{st}$;

(2) for every fluent $F(x_1,...,x_n, st) \in \mathcal{L}_s$, $F(x_1,...,x_n, st) \in \mathcal{L}_{st}$;

(3) if ψ, $\varphi \in \mathcal{L}_{st}$, then $\neg\psi$, $\psi \wedge \varphi$, $\psi \vee \varphi$, $\varphi \rightarrow \psi$, $\psi \leftrightarrow \varphi$, $(\forall x)\ \psi$, $(\exists x)\ \psi$, $(\forall a)\ \psi$, and $(\exists a)\ \psi$ are all in $\mathcal{L}_{st}$, where x and a are variables of sort o and sort a respectively.

$\mathcal{L}_{st}^2$ is defined to denote the second-order extension of $\mathcal{L}_{st}$ by n-ary predicate variables on domain of sort o, $n \geq 0$. Formally, $\mathcal{L}_{st}^2$ is the smallest set satisfying the following conditions:

(1) $\mathcal{L}_{st} \subseteq \mathcal{L}_{st}^2$;

(2) if p is an n-ary predicate variable on domain of sort o, and $x_1,...,x_n$ are terms of sort o, then $p(x_1,...,x_n) \in \mathcal{L}_{st}^2$;

(3) if $\psi, \varphi \in \mathcal{L}_{st}^2$, then $\neg\psi$, $\psi \wedge \varphi$, $\psi \vee \varphi$, $\varphi \rightarrow \psi$, $\psi \leftrightarrow \varphi$, $(\forall p)\ \psi$, $(\exists p)\ \psi$, $(\forall x)\ \psi$, $(\exists x)\ \psi$, $(\forall a)\ \psi$ and $(\exists a)\ \psi$ are all in $\mathcal{L}_{st}^2$, where x and a are variables of sort o and sort a respectively, and p is an n-ary predicate variable on domain of sort o.

2.10.2 Basic action theory in LR

A basic action theory D is of the following form:

$$\mathbf{D} = \Sigma \cup D_{ss} \cup D_{ap} \cup D_{una} \cup D_{s0} \tag{2.27}$$

where

(1) Σ is a set of logic formulas stating that the domain of sort s is a branching temporal structure, with S_0 the root and $\mathbf{do}$ the successive function. Formally it contains the following axioms:

$S_0 \neq do(a,s)$

$do(a_1,s_1) = do(a_2,s_2) \rightarrow (a_1=a_2 \wedge s_1=s_2)$

$\forall P[(P(S_0) \wedge \forall a,s(P(s) \rightarrow P(do(a,s)))) \rightarrow \forall s \, P(s)]$

$\neg (s < S_0);$

$s < do(a,s') \leftrightarrow (Poss(a,s') \wedge s \leq s').$

(2) D_{ss} is a set of logic sentences expressing the effect after an action is performed. Generally, each sentence is of the form

$$Poss(a,s) \rightarrow (F(\vec{x},do(a,s)) \rightarrow \psi_F(\vec{x},a,s)) \tag{2.28}$$

Where F is a fluent and ψ_F is a logic formula in $\mathcal{L}_s$.

(3) D_{ap} is a set of logic sentences expressing the precondition under which an action could be performed. Each sentence has the following general form

$$Poss(A(\vec{x},s)) \rightarrow \psi_A(\vec{x},s) \tag{2.29}$$

Where A is an action and ψ_A is a logic formula in $\mathcal{L}_s$.

(4) D_{una} is a set of logic formulas expressing that two actions performed on two groups of objects will not have the same effect unless these two actions as well as these two groups of objects are the same respectively. Generally, each pair of formulas is of the following forms:

$$A(\vec{x}) \neq A'(\vec{y})$$
$$A(\vec{x}) = A(\vec{y}) \rightarrow (\vec{x} = \vec{y})$$

(5) D_{s0} is a finite set of logic formulas in $\mathcal{L}_{s0}$, and is called the initial condition of the action theory.

2.11 Frame Problem

The frame problem, first described by McCarthy and Hayes, arises when we attempt to describe the effects of actions or events using logic. Using classical logic, if we describe what changes when a particular kind of action is performed or a particular kind of event occurs, we also have to describe what doea not change. Otherwise, we cannot use the description to draw any useful conclusions.

When we use the apparatus of first-order logic to describe the effects of actions, the description of what does not change is considerably large than the description of what does change. However, when we describe the effects of actions, we should be able to concentrate on what changes, and be able to take what does not change for granted. Therefore, the frame problem is the problem of constructing a formal framework that enables us to do just this (Shanahan 1997).

2.11.1 *Frame Axiom*

Firstly let's consider the Block World example and represent it with the situation calculus. Let Σ be the conjunction of the following formulas of the initial situation S_0.

$$Holds(On(C,Table), S_0)$$

$$Holds(On(B,C), S_0)$$

$$Holds(On(A,B), S_0)$$

$$Holds(On(D,Table), S_0)$$

$$Holds(Clear(A), S_0)$$

$$Holds(Clear(D), S_0)$$

$$Holds(Clear(Table), S_0)$$

Suppose there is a single action Move and this action is described by the following effect axioms:

$$Holds(On(x, y), Result(Move(x, y), s)) \leftarrow Holds(Clear(x), s) \wedge$$
$$Holds(Clear(y), s) \wedge x \neq y \wedge x \neq Table$$

$$Holds(Clear(z), Result(Move(x, y), s)) \leftarrow Holds(Clear(x), s) \wedge$$
$$Holds(Clear(y), s) \wedge Holds(On(x,z), s) \wedge x \neq y \wedge y \neq z$$

Let Δ be the conjunction of these formulas. Then, $\Delta \wedge \Sigma$ entails many of the conclusions we would expect. For example, we have

$$\Delta \wedge \Sigma \models \text{Holds(On(A, D), Result(Move(A, D), } S_0))$$

However, many conclusions we would like to be able to draw are absent. For example, although B is on C in S0, and moving A to D doesn't change this fact, we do not have

$$\Delta \wedge \Sigma \models \text{Holds(On(B, C), Result(Move(A, D), S0))}$$

In another words, although we have captured what does change as the result of an action, wehave failed to represent what doesn't change. In general, the effect of an action is limited to certain range, majority of fluents are unaffected by the action. We need to capture the persistence of fluents that are unaffected by an action. To do this, we have to add some frame axioms.

For example, the following is a frame axiom for the fluent "On":

$$\text{Holds(On(}v, w\text{), Result(Move(}x, y\text{), }s\text{))} \leftarrow \text{Holds(On(}v, w\text{), }s\text{)} \wedge x \neq v$$

It states that if v is on w in the situation s and v is not the block x which will be moved, then v is still on w as while as the action Move(x, y) is executed. Based on this axiom, the set Δ and Σ, the formula Holds(On(B,C), Result(Move(A,D), S0)) can now be deduced.

Similarly, we can add the following frame axiom for the fluent "Clear":

$$\text{Holds(Clear(}x\text{), Result(Move(}y, z\text{), }s\text{))} \leftarrow \text{Holds(Clear(}x\text{), }s\text{)} \wedge x \neq z$$

Next, we introduce a fluent "Color" and an action "Paint" for the Block World:

(1) Color(x, c): block x has color c.

(2) Paint(x, c): painting block x color c.

Paint(x, c) has no preconditions since painting is always successful; the effect of Paint(x, c) is that x has color c. Therefore, the following formula should be added into Δ:

$$\text{Holds(Color(}x, c\text{), Result(Paint(}x, c\text{), }s\text{))}$$

Correspondingly, suppose each block has the Red color in the initial situation S0 and therefore we add the following formula into Σ:

$$\text{Holds(Color}(x, \text{Red}), S_0)$$

In the real world we know that the color of a block will not be affected by moving it. However, based on the current representation of Σ and Δ, the following result can not be reached at all:

$$\Delta \wedge \Sigma \models \text{Holds(Color}(A, \text{Red}), \text{Result(Move}(A, D), S_0))$$

In order to get this result, we need to add the following frame axioms into Δ:

$$\text{Holds(Color}(x, c), \text{Result(Move}(y, z), s)) \leftarrow \text{Holds(Color}(x, c), s)$$

$$\text{Holds(Color}(x, c_1), \text{Result(Paint}(y, c_2), s)) \leftarrow \text{Holds(Color}(x, c_1), s)$$

$\wedge\, x \neq y$

These axioms state that the color of any block x will not be affected by moving it, and the color of x will not be affected by the painting of any other block.

Similarly, with respect to the action "Paint", we need to introduce the following frame axioms, which state that values of the fluent "On" and the fluent "Clear" will not be affected by the action "Paint":

$$\text{Holds(On}(x, y), \text{Result(Paint}(z, c), s)) \leftarrow \text{Holds(On}(x, y), s)$$

$$\text{Holds(Clear}(x), \text{Result(Paint}(y, c), s)) \leftarrow \text{Holds(Clear}(x), s)$$

In general, because most fluents are unaffected by most actions, every time we add a new fluent we are going to have to add roughly as many new frame axioms as there are actions in the domain, and every time we add a new action we are going to have to add roughly as many frame axioms as there are fluents in the domain. Therefore, if ther are n fluents and m actions for a domain, then the total number of frame axioms will be of the order of n×m (Shanahan, 1997).

In the following we consider a more succinct approach of expressing the information in the frame axioms. This approach is remaining in the realm of classical first-order logic and do not need to modify the situation calculus significantly. Firstly, note that all frame axioms have a similar form of the following:

$$\text{Holds}(f, \text{Result}(a, s)) \leftarrow \text{Holds}(f, s) \wedge \Pi$$

Where f is a fluent, a is an action, and Π is a conjunction. So, we can use the following frame axiom:

$$\text{Holds}(f, \text{Result}(a, s)) \leftarrow \text{Holds}(f, s) \wedge \neg\text{Affects}(a, f, s)$$

Furthermore, corresponding to each frame axiom, we need to introduce an axiom for the formula ¬Affects(a, f, s). For example, the following axioms should be introduced for the Block World example:

$$\neg \text{Affects}(\text{Move}(x, y), \text{On}(v, w), s) \Leftarrow x \neq v$$

$$\neg \text{Affects}(\text{Paint}(z, c), \text{On}(x, y), s)$$

$$\neg \text{Affects}(\text{Move}(y, z), \text{Clear}(x), s) \Leftarrow x \neq z$$

$$\neg \text{Affects}(\text{Paint}(y, c), \text{Clear}(x), s)$$

$$\neg \text{Affects}(\text{Move}(y, z), \text{Color}(x, c), s)$$

$$\neg \text{Affects}(\text{Paint}(y, c2), \text{Color}(x, c1), s) \Leftarrow x \neq v$$

With these frame axioms, we can draw exactly the same conclusions. If we employ an implication in place of the simple negation, the number of formuas can be further cut down and resulted in the following three formulas.

$$\text{Affects}(a, \text{On}(x, z), s) \rightarrow a = \text{Move}(x, y)$$

$$\text{Affects}(a, \text{Clear}(x), s) \rightarrow a = \text{Move}(x, y)$$

$$\text{Affects}(a, \text{Color}(x, c2), s) \rightarrow a = \text{Paint}(x, c1)$$

These formulas are known as explanation closure axioms. Explanation closure axioms are an effective substitute for frame axioms, and are much more succinct. They form the basis of a whole class of monotonic solutions to the frame problem.

2.11.2 Criteria for a solution to the frame problem

How can we represent the effects of actions in a formal, logical way without having to write out all the frame axioms? This is the frame problem. Various approaches have been proposed for the frame problem. This leads us to consider what the criteria are for an acceptable solution. Shanahan offered three criteria on a satisfactory solution (Shanahan, 1997):

Representational parsimony;

Expressive flexibility;

Elaboration tolerance.

The criterion of representational parsimony is the essence of the frame problem; it requires that representation of the effects of actions should be compact. It is difficult to quantify the compactness precisely. A reasonable guideline is that the size of the representation should be roughly proportional to the complexity of the domain, where a good indication of the complexity of the domain is the total number of actions plus the total number of fluents.

A compact solution of the frame problem should be carry over to more complicated domains. That is to say, we have to see that the solution meets the second criterion, that of expressive flexibility. What is meant by a more complicated domain is not simply one with a larger number of fluents and actions, but rather one with features that demand a little extra thought before they can be represented. Some features are listed as follows:

- Ramifications,
- Concurrent actions;
- Non-deterministic actions; and
- Continuous change.

An action will have ramifications beyond its immediate effects if we have to take into account domain constraints. A domain constraint (sometimes called a state constraint) is simply a constraint on what combinations of fluents may hold in the sane situation. For example, suppose three are three blocks which are on top of each other. Let Stack(x,y,z) be a fluent which denotes that blocks x, y, and z are a stack. Then we could write effect axioms for Stack like those previously written for On, Clear and Colour. However, taken into account the domain constraints, we write the effect axiom for Stack as follows:

$$\text{Holds(Stack}(x, y, z), s) \Leftarrow x \neq \text{Table} \wedge \text{Holds(On}(y, x), s) \wedge \text{Holds(On}(z, y), s)$$

In the Blocks World examples considered so far, no two actions are ever performed at the same time. But concurrent actions and events are ubiquitous in everyday life. For example, there are concurrent actions if a block is moved by more than one person.

Another feature of complicated domains that can trouble a potential solution is the presence of non-deterministic actions or actions whose effects are not completely known. For example, when we toss a coin, we known it will come down either heads or tails, but we cannot say which.

Finally, we have the issue of continuous change. Continuous change is also ubiquitous in everyday life, such as speeding cars, filling vessels, and so on. In the Blocks World examples considered so far, all change is discrete. This doesn't mean that the change being represented is discrete, but rather for the convenience of abstraction. However, such representations are not always appropriate, since the continuous variation of some quantity is the salient feature of the domain in question. Continuous change is particularly hard to represent in the situation calculus, and this is one of the motivations for study in the event calculus, in which continuous change can be represented without too much difficulty.

The final criterion in the list is elaboration tolerance. A representation is elaboration tolerant to the extent that the effort required to add new information to the representation is proportional to the complexity of that information. During the process that argument a situation calculus theory a new action, if there are n fluents which will be directly affected, then it might require the addition of roughly n new sentences. But it should not necessitate the complete reconstruction of the old theory; facts about the effects should be gracefully absorbed into the old theory.

When the domain includes actions with ramifications, it is not enough to simply expand the explanation closure axioms. It calls for reconstruction and bring a great improvement to the original system. Such a reconstruction is expensive for any monotonic mechanisms. The goal of elaboration tolerance seems to be impossible to achieve if we remain in the realm of monotonic mechanisms. To solve this problem, many nonmonotonic reasoning mechanisms were proposed by AI researchers, such as the circumscription proposed by McCarthy and the default logic proposed by Reiter. In fact, frame problem is one of the driving forces for the study of nonmonotonic reasoning. The core idea of nonmonotonic solution to the frame problem is to formalize the common sense law of inertia. One component of this law is as follows: normally, given any action and any fluent, the action doesn't affect the fluent.

More generally, we want to write down just the effect axioms, declare the default assumption that "nothing else changes", and then appeal to some nonmonotonic formalism to work out the consequences. Since the early Eighties of the last century, there have been several candidates for such a formalism. Two of the most common are default logic and circumscription. Logic programming's negation-as-failure is another candidate, so long as its semantic is properly defined.

2.11.3 *Nonmonotonic solving approach of the frame problem*

Nonmonotonic reasoning was firstly adopted by McCarthy to solve the frame problem. Circumscription was proposed by McCarthy and applied in a solution of the frame problem. Cirsumscription allows us to declare that the extensions of certain predicates are to be minimized. For example, consider a formula set Γ from which the formula P(A) can be deduced, but from which we cannot show either P(x) or ¬P(x) for any x other than A. It follows from the circumscription of Γ minimizing P, writted CIRC[Γ ; P], that P(x) is false for any x unless Γ demands that it is true. So, ¬P(B) will follow from CIRC[Γ; P].

The way to apply circumscription to the frame problem is to minimize the predicate Affects (McCarthy calls the predicate Ab rather than Affects). However, minimizing Affects in a naïve way will yield counter-intuitive results.

According to the viewpoint of McCarthy, Hayes and Sandewall, formalization of the common sense law of inertia is the pivot for a nonmonotonic solution to the frame problem. Here the common sense law of inertia states that inertia is normal and change is exceptional. One component of this common sense law is the following default rule: normally, given any action (or event type) and any fluent, the action does not affect the fluent.

Consider the following universal frame axiom:

F_1:   [Holds(f, Result(a, s)) ↔ Holds(f, s)] ← ¬Affects(a, f, s)   (2.30)

It says that the fluents that hold after an action takes place are the same as those that held beforehand, except for those the action affects. This leaves us the tricky job of specifying exactly which fluents are not affected by exactly which actions, which is the essence of the frame problem.

If we simply replace the Affects predicate by the predicate Ab proposed by McCarthy, then we will get axioms of the following form:

F_2:   [Holds(f, Result(a, s)) ↔ Holds(f, s)] ← ¬Ab(a, f, s)   (2.31)

Let Σ be the conjunction of effect axioms, domain constraints and observation sertences. Theobvious way to augment Σ with the common sense lae of inertia is to conjoint it with (F_2) and then circumscribe it, minimizing Ab and allowing Holds to vary. In other words, we consider CIRC[$\Sigma \wedge (F_2)$; Ab ; Holds].

The approach that minimising Ab and allowing Holds to vary seems a sound approach to solve the frame problem. However, as McDermott and Hanks showed in 1968, this approach fails to generate the conclusions we require even with extremely straightforward examples. They distilled the essence of the difficulty into a simple example, the so-called Yale shooting problem.

In the Yale shooting problem, someone is killed by a gunshot. The formalization is composed of:

(1) three actions: Load, Wait, and Shoot;

(2) two fluents: Alive and Loaded;

(3) two effect axioms: the Load action puts a bullet in the gun, and the victim dies after a Shoot action so long as the gun is loaded at the time, I.e.:

Y_1: Holds(Loaded, Result(Load, s)) (2.32)

Y_2: ¬Holds(Alive, Result(Shoot, s)) ← Holds(Loaded, s) (2.33)

(4) two observation sentences about the initial situation S0: the victim is alive in the initial situation, and the gun is unloaded, i.e.:

Y_3: Hold(Alive, S_0) (2.34)

Y_4: ¬Holds(Loaded, S_0) (2.35)

Finally, a predicate UNA is introduced to guarantee the nuiqueness of names of actions and fluents. Formally, UNA($f_1, f_2, ..., f_k$) is defined as:

$$f_i(x_1, x_2, .., x_m) \neq f_j(y_1, y_2, ..., y_n)$$

for all $i<j<k$, and

$$f_i(x_1, x_2, .., x_n) = f_i(y_1, y_2, ..., y_n) \rightarrow (x_1=y_1 \wedge x_2=y_2 \wedge ... \wedge x_n=y_n)$$

for all $i<k$. With the predicate UNA, the following formulas are added for the Yale shooting problem:

Y_5: UNA(Load, Wait, Shoot) (2.36)

Y_6: UNA(Alive, Loaded) (2.37)

Y_7: UNA(S_0, Result) (2.38)

Now, consider the situation that obtains after the sequence of actions: Load, Wait, Shoot, i.e., consider the situation Result(Shoot, Result(Wait, Result(Load, S0))). What fluents hold in this situation if the circumscription polic is applied to these formulas? Intuitively, the gun will be loaded after the Load action, it still to be Loaded after the Wait action, and the victim will be die after the Shoot action, therefore we expect the circumscription of (Y_1) to (Y_7) to have the following consequence:

$$\neg Holds(Alive, Result(Shoot, Result(Wait, Result(Load, S_0)))) \qquad (2.39)$$

However, (2.37) does not follow from the circumscription.

Proposition 2.1 *(The Hanks-McDermott problem) If Σ is the conjunction of (Y_1) to (Y_7) then,*

$$CIRC[\Sigma \wedge (F2); Ab ; Holds] \not\models$$

$$\neg Holds(Alive, Result(Shoot, Result(Wait, Result(Load, S_0))))$$

This proposition can be proved as follows:

Consider any model M of $\Sigma \wedge (F_2)$ that meets the following criteria:

$$M \models Holds(Loaded, Result(Load, S_0))$$

$$M \models \neg Holds(Loaded, Result(Wait, Result(Load, S_0)))$$

$$M \models Holds(Alive, Result(Shoot, Result(Wait, Result(Load, S_0))))$$

It is easy to see that such models exist, and they will have the following properties:

$$M \models Ab(Load, Loaded, S_0)$$

$$M \models Ab(Wait, Loaded, Result(Load, S_0))$$

$$M \models \neg Ab(Shoot, Alive, Result(Wait, Result(Load, S_0)))$$

Then, with respect to the predicate Ab and Holds, it is obvious that we cannot remove either of the above properties and still have a model. Therefore, some of those models are minimal. Furthermore, since in any of these models we have

$$M \models Holds(Alive, Result(Shoot, Result(Wait, Result(Load, S_0))))$$

We also have

$$CIRC[\Sigma \wedge (F_2); Ab ; Holds] \not\models \neg Holds(Alive, Result(Shoot, Result(Wait, Result(Load, S_0))))$$

The Hanks and McFermott problem arises from a failure to respect the directionality of time. This failure is most dramatically highlighted when default logic is used to address the frame problem.

Definition 2.24 A default theory is a pair <Δ, Σ>, where Δ is a set of default rules, and Σ is a sentence of first-order predicate calculus.

Σ encapsulates certain knowledge of the domain, from which we can draw deductively valid inferences, while Δ represents the default knowledge, from which we draw defeasible conclusions.

The default theory <Δ, Σ> considered here is:

$$\Delta = \left\{ \frac{: \neg Ab(a, f, s)}{\neg Ab(a, f, s)} \right\}$$

and Σ is the conjunction of (Y_1) to (Y_4) with (F_2).

Definition 2.25 *A set of well-formed formulas is an extension of a default theory* <Δ, Σ> *if it is a fixed point of the operator Γ. Here the operator is defined as follows. If S is a set of well-formed formulas with no free variables, then $\Gamma(S)$ is the smallest set such that:*

(1) $\Sigma \subseteq \Gamma(S)$;

(2) if ϕ is a logical consequence of $\Gamma(S)$, then $\phi \in \Gamma(S)$; and

(3) if Δ include the default rule

$$\frac{\phi_1(\bar{x}) : \phi_2(\bar{x})}{\phi_3(\bar{x})}$$

and $\phi_1(\tau_1 ... \tau_n) \in \Gamma(S)$ and $\neg \phi_2(\tau_1 ... \tau_n) \notin \Gamma(S)$, then $\phi_3(\tau_1 ... \tau_n) \in \Gamma(S)$, where each τ_i is a non-variable term.

Each extension of a default theory will represent an acceptable set of beliefs. The way to construct extensions is natural: start with a set containing just Σ and its logical consequences, then repeatedly choose an applicable default, add its consequence, and form the corresponding deductive closure, until nothing more can be added.

More precisely, given a default theory $<\Delta, \Sigma>$, the corresponding extensions can be constructed accordin to the following algorithm:

$S' := \{ \}$

$S := \Sigma \cup$ logical consequences of Σ

While $S \neq S'$

$S' := S$

Choose any ϕ_1, ϕ_2, ϕ_3 and $\tau_1, ..., \tau_n$ such that

$$\frac{\phi_1(\overline{x}) : \phi_2(\overline{x})}{\phi_3(\overline{x})} \text{ in } \Delta \text{ and } \phi_1(\tau_1...\tau_n) \in S \text{ and } \neg\phi_2(\tau_1...\tau_n) \notin S$$

$S := S \cup \phi_3(\tau_1...\tau_n)$

$S := S \cup$ logical consequences of S

End While

This algorithm will not terminate in many cases, since the default rules will be applicable aninfinite number of times. However, in such cases each intermediate S is a subset of some extension, so we can still use the algorithm to obtain useful information by executing the loop a finite number of times.

Now, we can apply this algorithm to the default theory representing the Yale shooting problem. We start with the set $S = \Sigma \cup$ the logical consequences of Σ. Then we might choose to add:

$\neg$Ab(Wait, Loaded, Result(Load, S_0))

The default rule permits this since it is consistent with S. Next we add in the logical consequences of the new addition: the following is added according to (F_2):

Holds(Loaded, Result(Wait, Result(Load, S_0)))

and correspondingly the following is added according to (Y_2):

$\neg$Holds(Alive, Result(Shoot, Result(Wait, Result(Load, S0)))).

We would need to iterate the algorithm forever to obtain an extension, but we have already shown that extensions exist that include the above intended consequence.

Now for anomalous extensions, which we get simply by making a different choice when we apply the default rule. Again we start with the set $S = \Sigma \cup$ the logical consequences of Σ. But in this time, appluing the default rules, let's choose to add:

$$\neg Ab(Shoot, Alive, Result(Wait, Result(Load, S_0)))$$

This sentence is consistent with S, so the default rule permits its addition. Now we add in the logical consequences of this new addition with the result that the following is added:

$$\neg Holds(Loaded, Result(Wait, Result(Load, S_0)))$$

Since we already had:

$$Holds(Loaded, Result(Load, S_0))$$

and taken together, these two sentences give us:

$$Ab(Wait, Loaded, Result(Load, S_0))$$

This gives us the undesired consequence:

$$Holds(Alive, Result(Shoot, Result(Wait, Result(Load, S_0)))).$$

Therefore, with respect to the Yale shooting problem, default logic will yield anomalous extension in just the same way that circumscription yields anomalous models. In another word, the Hanks-McDermott problem is not merely a problem for circumscription. The exercise of showing how it arises with default logic offers an insight into why the difficulty arises. The intended extension arises when the default rule is applied in chronological order (i.e., earliest abnormalities are considered first); The anomalous extension arises when the default rules is applied in reverse chronological order (i.e., later abnormalities are considered first). Therefore, the intended extension is the result of postponing change until as late as possible. Based on this result, a technique named chronological minimization was proposed.

The Hanks-McDermott problem can be solved by the chronological minimization approach. But the Yale shooting problem is just one example. There are still other examples where chronological minimization supplies counter-intuitive conclusions. The best know of these is the stolen car problem.

The stolen car problem is a family of explanation problem. In an explanation problem, we know that certain fluents hold in some situations other then the initial situation, and we want to know the cause for holding of these fluents. In the stolen car scenario, a person parks the car in the morning and goes to work. According to the common sense law of inertia it can be inferred by default that the car is still in the car park at lunch time. However, when this person return to the car park in the evening he finds that the car has gone. Now the problem is to reason backward in time to the causes of the car's disappearance. In this case, the only reasonable explanation is that the car was stolen some time between morning and evening. Therefore, the default assumption that the car was still in the car park at lunch time is open to question.

The stolen car problem can be represented by the following three sentences. Here two successive Wait actions are used to represent the interval between morning and evening implicitly; the fluent Stolen represent that the car is not in the car park.

SC1: $\neg Holds(Stolen, S_0)$ (2.40)

SC2: $S_2 = Result(Wait, Result(Wait, S_0))$ (2.41)

SC3: $Holds(Stolen, S_2)$ (2.42)

Furthermore, let (Arb1) and (Arb2) be the following axioms:

Arb1: $Result(a1, s1) = Result(a2, s2) \rightarrow a1 = a2 \wedge s1 = s2$ (2.43)

Arb2: $S_0 \neq Result(a, s)$ (2.44)

Then, with chronological minimization, it will be manifested that the car disappeared during the second Wait, i.e.,

$$Ab(Wait, Stolen, Result(Wait, S_0)) \wedge \neg Ab(Wait, Stolen, S_0)$$

But in fact, the car could equally well have disappeared during the first Wait, and we would like the formalization of the common sense law of inertia to respect this possibility. In another word, what we would like is to be able to manifest the following result

$$Ab(Wait, Stolen, Result(Wait, S_0)) \vee Ab(Wait, Stolen, S_0)$$

and also that there exist two models M1 and M2 such that

$$M1 \models Ab(Wait, Stolen, Result(Wait, S_0))$$

and

$$M2 \models Ab(Wait, Stolen, S_0).$$

2.12 Dynamic Description Logic

2.12.1 *Description Logic*

Description logic is a kind of formalization of knowledge representation based on object, and it is also called concept representation language or terminological logic. Description logic is a decidable subclass of first-order logic. It has well-defined semantics and possesses strong expression capability. One description logic system consists of four parts: constructors which represent concept and role, TBox subsumption assertion, ABox instance assertion, and reasoning mechanism of TBox and ABox. The representation capability and reasoning capability of description logic system lie on aforementioned four elements and different hypothesis (Baader, 2003).

There are two essential elements, i.e. concept and role, in description logic. Concept is interpreted as subclass of domain. Role represents interrelation between individuals, and it is a kind of binary relation of domain set.

In certain domain, a knowledge base K = <T, A> consists of two parts: TBox T and ABox A. TBox is a finite set of subsumption assertions, and it is also called terminological axiom set. The general format of subsumption assertion is $C \subseteq D$, where C and D are concepts. ABox is a finite set of instance assertions. Its format is C(a), where a is individual name; or its format is P(a,b), where P is a primitive role, a and b are two individual names.

In general, TBox is an axiom set which describes domain structure, and it has two functions: one is to introduce concept name, the other is to declare subsumption relationship of concepts. The process of introducing concept name is expressed by A≐Cor $A \subseteq C$, where A is the concept which is introduced. The format of subsumption assertion of concepts is $C \subseteq D$. As to concept definition and subsumption relation definition, the following conclusion comes into existence:

$$C \doteq D \Leftrightarrow C \sqsubseteq D \text{ and } C \sqsubseteq D.$$

ABox is an instance assertions set, and its function is to declare attribute of individual or relationship of individuals. There are two kinds of format: one is to declare the relationship of individual and concept, the other is to declare the relationship of two individuals. In ABox, as to arbitrary individual a and concept C, the assertion which decides whether individual a is member of concept C is called concept instance assertion, i.e. concept assertion. $a \in C$ is denoted as $C(a)$; $a \notin C$ is denoted as $\neg C(a)$.

Given two individuals *a, b* and a role *R*, if individual *a* and individual *b* satisfy role *R*, then *aRb* is role instance assertion, and it is denoted as $R(a, b)$.

In general, according to the constructor provided, description logic may construct complex concept and role based on simple concept and role. Description logic includes the following constructors at least: intersection ($\cap$), union($\cup$), negation($\neg$), existential quantification($\exists$), and value restriction($\forall$). The description logic which possesses these constructors is called ALC. Base on ALC, different constructors may be added to it, so that different description logics may be formed. For example, if number restrictions "$\leq$" and "$\geq$" are added to the description logic ALC, then a new kind of description logic ALCN is formed. Table 2.3 shows the syntax and semantics of description logic ALC.

An interpretation $I = (\Delta^I, \cdot^I)$ consists of a domain Δ^I and an interpretation function $\cdot I$, where interpretation function $\cdot I$ maps each primitive concept to subset of domain Δ^I, and maps each primitive role to subset of domain $\Delta^I \times \Delta^I$. With respect to an interpretation, concept of ALC is interpreted as a domain subset, and role is interpreted as binary relation.

(1) An interpretation I is a model of subsumption assertion $C \subseteq D$, if and only if $C^I \subseteq D^I$;

(2) An interpretation I is a model of C(a), if and only if $a \in C^I$; an interpretation I is a model of P(a, b), if and only if $(a, b) \in P^I$;

(3) An interpretation I is a model of knowledge base K, if and only if I is a model of each subsumption assertion and instance assertion of knowledge base K;

(4) If knowledge base K has a mode l, then K is satisfiable;

(5) As to each model of knowledge base K, if assertion δ is satisfiable, then we say that knowledge base K logically implicate δ, and it is denoted as $K \models \delta$.

(6) As to concept C, if knowledge base K has a model I, and $C^I \neq \phi$, then concept C is satisfiable. The concept C of knowledge base K is satisfiable if and only if $K \not\models C \subseteq \perp$.

Table 2.3 Syntax and semantics of ALC

Constructor	Syntax	Semantics	Example
Primitive concept	A	$A^I \forall \Delta^I$	Human
Primitive concept	P	$P^I \subseteq \Delta^I \times \Delta^I$	has-child
top	$\perp$	Δ^I	True
Bottom	$\perp$	Φ	False
intersection	C∩D	$C^I \cap D^I$	Human∩Male
Union	C∪D	$C^I \cup D^I$	Doctor ∪Lawyer
Negation	¬C	$\Delta^I - C^I$	¬Male
Existential quantification	∃R.C	$\{x \mid \exists y, (x, y) \in R^I \wedge y \in C^I\}$	∃has-child.Male
Value restriction	∀R.C	$\{x \mid \forall y, (x, y) \in R^I \Rightarrow y \in C^I\}$	∀has-child.Male

The basic reasoning problems of description logic include concept satisfiability, concept subsumption relation, instance checking, consistency checking and so on, where the concept satisfiability is the most basic reasoning problem, other reasoning problem may be reduced to concept satisfiability problem.

In description logic, reasoning problem may be reduced to concept satisfiability problem through the following properties. As to concept C, D, there exists the following proposition:

(1) $C \subseteq D \Leftrightarrow C \cap \neg D$ is unsatisfiable;

(2) $C \doteq D$ (concept C and D are equivalent) $\Leftrightarrow$ both $(C \cap \neg D)$ and $(D \cap \neg C)$ are unsatisfiable;

(3) C and D are disjoint $\Leftrightarrow C \cap D$ is unsatisfiable.

2.12.2 *Syntax of dynamic description logic*

Dynamic description logic DDL is formed through extending traditional description logic (Shi, et al. 2005), while traditional description logic has many species. The dynamic description logic DDL studied here is based on description logic ALC.

Definition 2.27 The primitive symbols in DDL are:

- · concept names: $C_1, C_2, \ldots$;

- · role names: $R_1, R_2, \ldots$;

- · individual constant: $a, b, c, \ldots$;

- · individual variable: x, y, z, …;

- · concept operator: $\neg$, $\sqcap$, $\sqcup$ and quantifier $\exists$, $\forall$;

- · formula operator: $\neg$, $\wedge$, $\rightarrow$ and quantifier $\forall$;

- · action names: $A_1, A_2, \ldots$;

- · action constructs: ;(sequence), $\cup$(choice), *(iteration), ?(test);

- · action variable: $\alpha, \beta, \ldots$;

- · formula variable: $\varphi, \psi, \pi, \ldots$;

- · state variable: $u, v, w, \ldots$.

Definition 2.28 *Concepts in DDL are defined as follows:*

(1) Primitive concept P, top $\perp$ and bottom $\perp$ are concepts;

(2) If C and D are concepts, then $\neg$C, C $\cap$ D, and C $\cup$ D are concepts;

(3) If C is concept and R is role, then $\exists$ R.C and $\forall$ R.C are concepts;

(4) If C is concept and α is action, then $[\alpha]$C is action too.

Definition 2.29 *Formulas in DDL are defined as follows, where C is concept, R is role, a, b are individual constants, and x, y are individual variables:*

(1) $C(a)$ and $R(a, b)$ are called assertion formulas;

(2) $C(x)$ and $R(x, y)$ are called general formulas;

(3) Both assertion formulas and general formulas are all formulas;

(4) If φ and ψ are formulas, then $\neg\varphi$, $\varphi \wedge \psi$, $\varphi \rightarrow \psi$, and $\forall x\, \varphi$ are all formulas;

(5) If φ is formula, then$[\alpha]\varphi$ is also formula.

Definition 2.30 A finite set of $\{a_1/x_1, \ldots, a_n/x_n\}$ is an instance substitution, where $a_1, \ldots, a_n$ are instance constants which are called substitution items, $x_1, \ldots, x_n$ are variables which are called substitution bases, $x_i \neq x_j$ for each pair i, j i$_n$ $\{1, \ldots, n\}$ such that i $\neq$ j.

Definition 2.31 *Let φ be a formula, let $x_1, \ldots, x_n$ be all the variables occurring in φ, and let $a_1, \ldots, a_n$ be instance constants. If φ' is a substitution result of φ with$\{a_1/x_1, \ldots, a_n/x_n\}$, then φ' is called a instance formula of φ.*

Definition 2.32 *A condition in DDL is an expression of the form: $\forall C$, $C(p)$, $R(p, q)$, $p=q$ or $p \neq q$, where N_C is a set of individual constants, N_X is a set of individual variables, N_I is the union N_C and N_X, $p, q \in N_I$, C is concept of DDL, and R is role of DDL.*

Definition 2.33 *An action description is of the form $A(x_1, \ldots, x_n) \equiv (P_A, E_A)$, where,*

(1) A is the action name;

(2) x_1, ..., x_n are individual variables, which denote the objects on which the action operates;

(3) P_A is the set of *pre-conditions*, which must be satisfied before the action is executed, i.e. $P_A = \{\text{con} \mid \text{con} \in \text{condition}\}$;

(4) E_A is the set of post-conditions, which denotes the effects of the action; E_A is a set of pair *head/body*, where head$= \{\text{con} \mid \text{con} \in \text{condition}\}$, body is a condition.

Remark:

(1) Action defines the transition relation of state, i.e. an action A transits a state u to a state v, if action A can produce state v under state u. The transition relation depends on whether states u, v satisfy the pre-conditions and post-conditions of action A. The transition relation is denoted as u TA v.

(2) Because some states that happened before action A may influence post-condition of action A, there is some difference between pre-conditions and post-conditions. As to post-conditions head/body, if each condition of head can be satisfied in state u, then each condition of body can also be satisfied in state v.

Definition 2.34 *Let* $A(x_1,...,x_n) \equiv (P_A, E_A)$ *be a action description and let* $A(a_1, ..., a_n)$ *be the substitution of* $A(x_1, ..., x_n)$ *by* $\{a_1/x_1, ..., a_n/x_n\}$. *Then* $A(a_1, ..., a_n)$ *is called an action instance of* $A(x_1, ..., x_n)$. $A(a_1, ..., a_n)$*is called atom action,* $P_A(a_1, ..., a_n)$ *is the precondition of* $A(a_1, ..., a_n)$ *and* $E_A(a_1, ..., a_n)$ *is the result set of* $A(a_1, ..., a_n)$.

Definition 2.35 *Actions in DDL are defined as follows:*

(1) Atomic action $A(a_1, ..., a_n)$ is action;

(2) If α and β are actions, then $\alpha;\beta$, $\alpha \cup \beta$, and α^* are all actions;

(3) If φ is an assertion formula, then $\varphi?$ is action.

2.12.3 *Semantics of dynamic description logic*

The semantics of DDL can be illustrated by a structure composed of the following components:

(1) Non-empty set Δ, which is the set of all individuals discussed in a specified domain;

(2) The set of state W, which is the set of all state of the world in specified domain;

(3) An interpretation I which explains each individual, concept and role in DDL as follows:

① Each individual constant is interpreted as an element of Δ;

② Each concept is interpreted as a subset of Δ;

③ Each role is interpreted as a binary relation on Δ.

(4) Each action is mapped into a binary relation on W.

Next we will explain the semantics of DDL in detail. First, for a state u in DDL, an explanation $I(u) = (\Delta, \bullet^{I(u)})$ in u is composed of two components, written as $I(u) = (\Delta, \bullet^{I(u)})$, where explanation function $\bullet^{I(u)}$ maps each concept into a subset of Δ and maps each role into a binary relations on $\Delta \times \Delta$.

$\cdot \top^{I(u)} = \Delta$;

$\cdot \perp^{I(u)} = \varnothing$;

$\cdot C^{I(u)} \subseteq \Delta$;

$\cdot R^{I(u)} \subseteq \Delta \times \Delta$;

$\cdot (\neg C)^{I(u)} = \Delta - C^{I(u)}$;

$\cdot (\neg R)^{I(u)} = \Delta \times \Delta - R^{I(u)}$;

$\cdot (C \sqcap D)^{I(u)} = C^{I(u)} \cap D^{I(u)}$;

$\cdot (C \sqcup D)^{I(u)} = C^{I(u)} \cup D^{I(u)}$;

$\cdot (\exists R.C)^{I(u)} = \{x \mid \exists y.((x, y) \in R^{I(u)} \wedge y \in C^{I(u)})\}$;

$\cdot (\forall R.C)^{I(u)} = \{x \mid \forall y.((x, y) \in R^{I(u)} \Rightarrow y \in C^{I(u)})\}$;

$\cdot ([\alpha]C)^{I(u)} = \{x \mid uT_\alpha v \wedge x \in (C)^{I(v)}\}$.

Since the interpretation of the objects name does not depend on the particular world, we use the rigid designator and assume that each name of individual is uniform and does not change with state changing. Usually we write aI(u) as a for short.

Given action $A(x_1,...,x_n) \equiv (P_A, E_A)$, N_X^A is all variable set which happened in action A, I = $(\Delta^I, \cdot I)$ is an interpretation, and map $\gamma: N_X^A \rightarrow \Delta^I$ is an variable evaluation which happened in action A. As to individual constant $a \in N^C$ of ABox of DDL, $\cdot^I$ interprets a as an element of Δ^I, i.e. $aI \in \Delta^I$. As to individual variable or individual constant $p \in N^I$, their interpretation is given in the following:

$$p^{I,\gamma} = \begin{cases} \gamma(p), & \text{if } p \in N_X \\ p^I, & \text{if } p \in N_C \end{cases},$$

then the condition interpretations of DDL are as follows:

$\cdot$ If $C^I = \Delta^I$, then I and γ satisfy condition $\forall C$;

$\cdot$ If $a^{I,\gamma} \in C^I$, then I and γ satisfy condition $C(a)$;

$\cdot$ If $a^{I,\gamma} = b^{I,\gamma}$, then I and γ satisfy condition $a = b$;

$\cdot$ If $a^{I,\gamma} \neq b^{I,\gamma}$, then I and γ satisfy condition $a \# b$;

$\cdot$ If $<a^{I,\gamma}, b^{I,\gamma}> \in R^I$, then I and γ satisfy condition $R(a,b)$.

In each state u, assertion formulas connect individual constants to concepts and roles. So there are two kinds of assertion formulas, concept assertions with the form of C(a) and role assertions with the form of R(a_1, a_2). As to concept assertions, they declare the relation of individual constant and concept, i.e. the relation of element and set. Semantics of concept assertion can be interpreted as follows:

$\cdot\ u \models C(a)$ iff $a \in C^{I(u)}$;

$\cdot\ u \models \neg C(a)$ iff $a \notin C^{I(u)}$.

For example, under certain state, individual constant a denotes a block, and this means individual constant a belongs to the concept of block, and it is denoted as Block(a); individual constant b is a button, and it is denoted as Button(b).

Role assertions declare the relation of two individual objects or the attribute of individual object. It is a binary relation, and its semantics can be explained as the following:

$\cdot\ u \models R(a_1, a_2)$ iff $(a_1, a_2) \in R^{I(u)}$;

$\cdot\ u \models \neg R(a_1, a_2)$ iff $(a_1, a_2) \notin R^{I(u)}$.

For example, under certain state, agent a1 and agent a_2 are acquaintance, and it is denoted as $hasAquaintance(a_1, a_2)$, Object a presses on object b, and it is denoted as $On(a, b)$. Role assertions may also declare some attributes of individual object. For example, Button b_1 is in o pen state, and it is denoted as $hasState(b_1, O_N)$; the length of object a is 10,and it is denoted as $hasLength(a, 10)$.

Analogously, for a particular state u, those formulas that are composed of assertion formulas can be interpreted as follows, where φ and ψ are assertion formulas:

$\cdot\ u \models \neg\varphi$ iff $u \nvDash \varphi$;

$\cdot\ u \models \varphi \wedge \psi$ iff $u \models \varphi$ and $u \models \psi$;

$\cdot\ u \models \varphi \rightarrow \psi$ iff $u \models \varphi \Rightarrow u \models \psi$.

Action execution results in change of world state, so action also may be defined as a state transition relationship. But the process of action change is the process of individual attribute change or individual relation change in fact, so under certain state, all individual attribute, relation description and so on consists of the world state description. These individual attribute, relation descriptions may be defined based on action description (Definition 2.33). State in DDL corresponds to all condition interpretation of action description under corresponding state in fact, so action may be interpreted based on aforementioned condition interpretation and description logic interpretation.

Before action of DDL is defined, state transition (one state transits to other state under action) is defined first.

Definition 2.36 *Given two interpretations $I(u) = (\Delta, \bullet^{I(u)})$ and $I(v) = (\Delta, \bullet^{I(v)})$, under state u and v, an action $\alpha = (P\alpha, E\alpha)$ can produce state v when applied to state u (written $u \rightarrow_\alpha v$), if there exists an assignment map γ. $N_X^\alpha \rightarrow \Delta$, such that γ, I(u) and I(v) satisfy the following conditions:*

(1) I(u) and γ satisfy each condition of pre-conditions P_α;

(2) as to each pair head/body of post-conditions E_α, if I(u) and γ satisfy head, then I(v) and γ satisfy body.

In this case, we can say that action α can produce state v when applied to state u and assignment map γ, and it is denoted as $u \rightarrow_\alpha^\gamma v$.

The semantics of atomic and complex actions are defined as follows:

$\cdot \alpha = \{<u, v> \mid u, v \in W, u \rightarrow_\alpha^\gamma v \}$;

$\cdot \alpha;\beta = \{<u, v> \mid u, v, w \in W, u \rightarrow_\alpha^\gamma w \wedge w \rightarrow_\beta^\gamma v\}$;

$\cdot \alpha \cup \beta = \{<u, v> \mid u, v \in W, u \rightarrow_\alpha^\gamma v \vee u \rightarrow_\beta^\gamma v\}$;

$\cdot \alpha^* = \{<u, v> \mid u, v \in W, u \rightarrow_\alpha^\gamma v \vee u \rightarrow_{\alpha;\alpha}^\gamma v \vee u \rightarrow_{\alpha;\alpha;\alpha}^\gamma v \vee \ldots \}$;

$\cdot \varphi? = \{<u, u> \mid u \in W, u \vDash \varphi \}$.

Because aforementioned action interpretation is based on description logic, some new concepts about action may be given, and these new concepts supplement description logics.

Definition 2.37 *Given action α (primitive action or complex action), if there exist two interpretations $I(u) = (\Delta, \bullet^{I(u)})$ and $I(v) = (\Delta, \bullet^{I(v)})$ that satisfy $u \rightarrow_\alpha v$, then action α is realizable.*

Definition 2.38 *Given action α (primitive action or complex action), if there exists an interpretation $I(u) = (\Delta, \bullet^{I(u)})$ corresponding to ABox A, and an interpretation $I(v) = (\Delta, \bullet^{I(v)})$ corresponding to ABox A and TBox T, and $u \rightarrow_\alpha v$ is satisfied, then action a is realizable corresponding to ABox A.*

Definition 2.39 *Given two actions α and β (primitive action or complex action), as to arbitrary interpretations $I(u) = (\Delta, \bullet^{I(u)})$ and $I(v) = (\Delta, \bullet^{I(v)})$, the following condition is satisfied: if the existence of $u \rightarrow_\alpha v$ can make $u \rightarrow_\beta v$ come true, then action β subsumes action α, denoted as $\alpha \subseteq \beta$.*

Definition 2.40 *Given two actions α and β (primitive action or complex action), an arbitrary interpretation $I(u) = (\Delta, \bullet^{I(u)})$ corresponding to ABox A of DDL, and an arbitrary interpretation $I(v) = (\Delta, \bullet^{I(v)})$ corresponding to ABox A and TBox T, the following condition is satisfied: if the existence of $u \rightarrow_\alpha v$ can make $u \rightarrow_\beta v$ come true, then action β subsumes action α corresponding to ABox A, denoted as $\alpha \subseteq_A \beta$.*

Remark. Similar to Definition 2.38 and Definition 2.40, action realization or subsumption corresponding to TBox T may also be defined. In order to understand the action subsumption, the following is a simple example.

Given four action descriptions: $\alpha_1 = (\{A(a), \neg A(b)\}, \{\Phi/\neg A(a), \Phi/A(b)\})$, $\alpha_2 = (\{A(c), \neg A(d)\}, \{\Phi/\neg A(c), \Phi/A(d)\})$, $\alpha_3 = (\{A(x), \neg A(y)\}, \{\Phi/\neg A(x), \Phi/A(y)\})$ and $\alpha_4 = (\{A(y), \neg A(x)\}, \{\Phi/\neg A(y), \Phi/A(x)\})$, where a, b, c, d are individual constants, and x, y are individual variables, then we have $\alpha_1 \subseteq \alpha_3$, $\alpha_2 \subseteq \alpha_3$, $\alpha_1 \subseteq \alpha_4$, $\alpha_2 \subseteq \alpha_4$, $\alpha_3 \subseteq \alpha_4$ and $\alpha_4 \subseteq \alpha_3$, but there is no subsumption relation between α_1 and α_2.

Exercises

1. What is monotonic reasoning? What is nonmonotonic reasoning?
2. How is default rules represented in default theory? What representation forms does there exist?
3. A default theory is a pair T=<W, D>, with D a set of default rules and W a set of closed formulas. Please represent the following sentences with such a default theory.

(1) Some mollusks have shell.

(2) Cephalopods are mollusks.

(3) Not all cephalopods have shell.

4. Both the closed world assumption and the circumscription are formalisms for nonmonotonic reasoning. Please exposit these two formalisms and compare the difference between them.

5. Represent the following situations with the truth maintenance system:

(1) It is now summer.

(2) The weather is very humid.

(3) The weather is very dry.

6. How to maintain the consistence of a knowledge base by the truth maintenance system? Please illustrate it with an example.

7. Please represent the following monkey-and-bananas problem with situation calculus.

The world is composed of a monkey in a room, a bunch of bananas hanging from the ceiling, and a box that can be moved by the monkey. The bananas are out of the reach of the monkey; however, the box will enable the monkey to reach the bananas if the monkey climbs on it. The actions available to the monkey include *Go* from one place to another, *Push* an object from one place to another, *ClimbUp* onto or *ClimbDown* from an object, and *Grasp* or *Ungrasp* an object. Initially, the monkey is at A, the bananas at B, and the box at C. The question is how to get the bananas.

8. What are the basic elements of the description logic?

9. How are actions represented in the dynamic description logic?

Chapter 3

Constraint Reasoning

3.1 Introduction

A constraint usually refers to relational expressions which include several variables and is used to represent conditions which these variables must satisfy. Constraint representation has been widely applied to various field in artificial intelligence, including qualitative reasoning, model-based diagnosis, nature language understanding, scenery analysis, task scheduling, system dispose, scientific experiment planning, design and analysis of machinery and electronic apparatus, and so on. Design of constraint satisfaction system is a difficult and complex task because constraint satisfaction problem is generally a NP problem, which must be solved by using various strategies and heuristic information. From the view of knowledge representation, many important problems need studying, such as representing abstract, default reasoning and so on. Nonmonotonic reasoning has enough expressing ability, but it has low reasoning efficiency and even becomes non-calculated. Furthermore, it is inconvenient for nonmonotonic reasoning to express heuristic information and meta information. Semantic network can also represent abstract and default information, however, it does not have enough problem-solving ability. The constraint representation with abstract type can remedy deficiencies of both nonmonotonic reasoning and semantic network in expression. The study on constraint representation and default reasoning in type hierarchy is very meaningful.

In constraint reasoning, to solve the contradictions between narrowing search space and controlling reasoning cost, we proposed integrated search algorithm for constraint satisfaction, and designed appropriate forms of strategy such as intelligent backtracking, constraint propagation, variable instantiation ordering etc.. Through combining these strategies organically, the search space can be reduced effectively with reasonable calculation cost and the existing experimental result shows that this algorithm is superior to the other similar algorithms. In addition, some special relations have been realized, such as equality and inequality reasoning, unit sharing strategy of identical relation and the combination of inequality graph and interval reasoning. These realization combines evaluation of constraint expression and symbol relation together and strengthens symbolic deduction ability of constraint reasoning. In constraint languages, we designed SCL—an object-oriented constraint language. SCL realize an integrated constraint reasoning with default constraint representation and adopts certain-type control of regular language (e.g. condition structure), while confines the uncertain part to the data. As a result, constraint propagation with intelligent backtracking can be used to reduce uncertainty and narrow search space. At the same time, such regular structure also improves code readability and makes language studying easily. We have also realized constraint representation embedded in C++ so that constraint programming design fully utilizes the abundant computational resources of C++.

An constraint satisfaction problem(abbreviated as CSP) includes a set of variables and constraints between variables. In general, variables represent field parameter and each variable has a fixed value domain. One variable's value domain may be limited, for example, one Boolean domain only contains two values. The value domain may be dispersed and limitless(e.g. integer domain) and may be continuous as well(e.g. real number domain). Constraints can be used to describe field object's property, interrelation, task requirement, goal and so on. The goal of constrain satisfaction problem to find one or more assignments of all variables in order to satisfy all constraints.

Constraint representation is easy to understand, code and effective realize. Constraint representation has the following advantages:

(1) Constraint representation allows to represent domain knowledge in a declarative way and it has strong expressing ability. The application only needs to define goal conditions and data interrelation in a problem. Therefore constraint representation has the resembling characteristics of logic representation.

(2) Constraint representation allows variable domain to contain arbitrary values, while the proposition does only fetch true or false values. So constraint representation can keep some structural information of problem, such as variable domain size, variable interrelation etc. in order to offer heuristic

information for problem solving.

(3) Constraint representation is easy to be implemented in parallel, because information propagation in constraint network can be regarded running at the same time.

(4) Constraint representation is suitable for system of gradual increase. Constraint can be added to constraint network in gradual increase way.

(5) Constraint representation is easy to connect with problem solving models of field. Mathematical planning, equation solving and other techniques can be embedded into constraint system naturally.

Many constraint reasoning methods has been proposed in many years' study. According to data type of node in constraint network, constraint reasoning can be classified into following categories.

(1) Relation reasoning: New constraint relation reasoned out in reasoning process will be added into constraint network. Kuiper's ENV system, Simmon's Quantity Lattice system and Brooks' CMS system, are all belong to relation reasoning.

(2) Mark reasoning: Mark each node with a set of possible values, which will be limited by constraint in constraint propagation.

(3) Value reasoning: The node is marked with constant value. Constraints obtain values of unmarked nodes by using already marked nodes values. SKETCHPAD and THINGLAB both use value reasoning.

(4) Expression reasoning: It is a extension of value reasoning and the node might be marked with other node expressions. The different expressions of marked node should be equal and form result equations to be solved. CONSTRAINTS uses this kind of reasoning.

The value of constraint variable may be the number value, or not the number value, i.e. symbolic value. In general, the values of symbolic variable form a limited set. Therefore after constraint propagation stops, exhaust search can be used to decide the consistency of symbolic variable. While the number variable usually has limitless value domain, it is impossible to carry on the exhaustive search.

Above four kinds of constraint reasoning all have some shortcomings. For example, value reasoning can be not used in inequality constraint but in equation constraint. Relation reasoning and mark reasoning are difficult to control and prevent them to enter limitless circulation. In relation reasoning, it is difficult to decide whether new constraints are useful for solving given problem. The mark reasoning can be used in constraint with arbitrary form and thus be much better than other reasoning.

Existing constraint representation can be classified into several categories according to complexity, which are listed below:

- Unary predicate
- Order relation language, which only includes partial order relation of real variable
- Equations similar to " $x - y > c$" or " $x - y \geq c$"
- Linear equation and inequality of unit coefficient, that is all coefficients are - 1, 0, 1
- Linear equation and inequality of arbitrary coefficient
- Boolean combination of constraints
- Algebra and triangular equation

Compared with several important mark such as symbols, interval and real number, unary predicate is the most simple constraint.

The partial order relation appears in the systems which only cares about relations of the quantity. Some systems only care about event order without considering its time interval, such as NOAH system. In NOAH system, operations in each level of planning are appointed towards the partial order relation.

The inequality similar to $x - y \geq c$ is very useful for only knowing the differences between variables and these inequality constraints are widely used in TMM and a lot of task planning applications.

In the measure space of scalar multiplication, sometimes it is very useful to define quotient of two numbers. This kind of expression and difference definition are isomorphism and the isomorphism mapping is logarithm function. Allen and Kantz used the Boolean combination of quotient and order relation to implement the temporal reasoning.

The linear equation with unit coefficient is very useful for commonsense reasoning because this kind of relation is good enough to describe the conservation rule in qualitative. Conservation rule affirms the change of value is equal to the total increased deducts its total decreased values. If we are only interested in state change, then we can only take three variable value +, - and 0 and the equation coefficient is always unit coefficient.

The linear inequality is a kind of widely used constraint. Boolean combination of constraints is widely used in physical reasoning, circuit design and planning. Nonlinear equation and inequality are frequently involved in physical reasoning. In geometry reasoning, algebra and triangular equation are also involved frequently.

At present, research on constraint reasoning mainly concentrates on two aspects: constraint search and constraint languages. The main research of constraint search focuses on constraint satisfaction in definite domain. For definite domain, constraint satisfaction problem is generally a NP problem. At present, there are several following methods to solve CSP:

• Backtracking
• Constraint propagation
• Intelligent backtracking and truth maintainance
• Variable order instantiation
• Local revision

Constraint language is another main research aspect for constraint reasoning. The following is several typical constraint languages:

1. CONSTRAINTS

CONSTRAINTS is a circuit-based constraint representation languages. As a constraint representation language, CONSTRAINTS uses symbolic technology to solve mathematical equation. In CONSTRAITS, functions of physical parts and device structure are represented by constraints, which are generally linear equation and inequality, and condition expression. Constraint variables are usually the real variable of the physical quantity, and sometime assigned dispersed values as well, such as the state of the switch, working state of triode and so on. The system adopts the expression reasoning and value reasoning, and realizes dependence-directed backtracking.

One advantage of CONSTRAINTS is to represent constraints at type hierarchy and adopt constraint to represent function and structure of physical devices. One constraint's shortcoming is lack of methods which are similar to object-oriented language, and thus cannot define particular class concept. Meanwhile, constraint propagate method is monotonous. It lacks interval propagation mechanism on the real domain and domain propagation mechanism in the definite domain.

2. Bertrand

Bertrand is an advanced constraint language developed by Leler, whose computational model is a system based on enhanced term rewriting. On the whole, Bertrand adds the assignment function and type mechanism based on term rewriting system, which makes Bertrand can solve linear equation about real number and rational number. Bertrand also includes the function of abstracting data type. It has been already used for solving some problems in graphics and circuit.

Bertrand still cannot be regarded as real constraint language, but a generating tool for constraint satisfaction system. Basically it offers nothing mechanism to solve dispersed constraint and it doesn't offer propagation mechanism for interval propagation and order relation on real number domain. Bertrand can only offer value propagation.

3. Constraint logic programming language—CHIP

Main research on constraint language concentrates on constraint logic programming language, which aims to combine constraint satisfaction technology and logic programming. Such languages introduce constraint propagation (mainly arc consistency technology) on the basis of Prolog in order to improve search efficiency and strengthen expressing ability. CHIP(Constraint handling in Prolog) is such constraint logic programming language with great influence. The goal of CHIP is to solve a major kind of composition problems simply, conveniently, flexibly and effectively. CHIP strengthens the ability of logic programming through offering several kinds of new computational domain: definite domain, Boolean item and rational item. For all computational domain, CHIP offers effective constraint solving technology, including consistency technology of definite domain, unified technology for Boolean domain and pure type for rational domain and a general delay computing technology.

CHIP is mainly applied to two fields: operations research and hardware design. However, CHIP lacks the type mechanism which is extremely important for expressing the domain concept.

4. Constraint Hierarchy and HCLP

"Soft constraint" solving problem is a very interesting and important practical problem. In this research, the most influential work is from Borning et al.

(Freeman-Benson 1992). Borning presented the concept of constraint hierarchy in order to solve the "overly constrained" problem of graph design. The idea is that system can not only satisfy "Hard constraint", but also allow users to present as much "soft constraint" as possible. These soft constraints are divided into several priority grades, which is also called constraint hierarchy.

Constraint hierarchy is a definite set of marked constraints. Given a constraint level H, H_0 is a set of constraint that must be satisfied in H. H_1 is the strongest constraint of non-essential constraints and Hn is the weakest in which n denotes the grade of non-essential constraints.

The evaluation of constraint set is a function, which maps a free variable into an element of D domain. A solution of constraint hierarchy is a set of evaluation of free variable. Evaluation in solving set must at least satisfy essential constraint. In additional, the solving set should also satisfy the constraints of other evaluation. Among evaluation that satisfies essential constraint, there does not exist more evaluations that satisfies non-essential constraint than evaluations in the solving set. There are a variety of methods to compare satisfying degree which evaluation satisfies constraint. To adopt which method depends on specific application.

At the beginning, the evaluation of constraint hierarchy uses some methods to make constraint hierarchy be satisfied to the greatest extent. But these methods does not have declarative advantage of constraint representation system. Therefore Wilson, Borning, et al. designed hierarchical constraint logic programming language HCLP on the basis of constraint logic programming, which embeds constraint hierarchy into Prolog and makes hierarchical constraint system built totally on declarative representation. The minimal model theory of nonmonotonic theory is used to define the semantics of HCLP model. HCLP firstly utilizes backtracking method of common logic programming to obtain a necessary solution, which may include limited variable domain rather than variable value. Meanwhile, it also generates all constraints of current instantiations(constraint hierarchy), and then gradually limits the necessary solution by the generated constraint from stronger constraint to weaker constraint until inconsistent situations appear. As to the constraints in the same hierarchy, different orders of using constraints will cause different solutions.

The solution of constraint hierarchy is simple and swift, but incomplete, because the generated solution may not correspond to the minimal model of whole logic programming but a minimum model of reasoning path.

5. Object-oriented Constraint Language COPS

COPS system, developed by intelligent information processing laboratory of Institute of Computing Technology(ICT),Chinese Academy of Sciences, which utilizes object-oriented technology and combine declarative constraint representation and constraint hierarchy together. COPS absorbs regular language(mainly object-oriented programming language)in form. The solution inside COPS is realized by using constraint reasoning mechanism, which combines declarative constraint representation and constraint hierarchy to realize structured encapsulation of knowledge. By fully taking advantages of constraint representation and hierarchy, COPS tries to become a constraint satisfaction system with strong expressing ability and high solving efficiency. Design of COPS considers requirement of software engineering and try to determine uncertain problems: to realize iterative computation, COPS does not utilize only iterate statements but allow both the selection and iteration statements; Through overload of class methods, a constraint may have multiple implementation, which can improve the execution efficiency of program. COPS system is also an open system of gradual increment, in which users can realize the new data type and constraint relation through hierarchy definition. The constrain representation language COPS, has a lot of characteristics of artificial intelligence programming languages, such as constraint propagation, target-oriented and data-driven problem solving, limited backtracking, inheritance of object hierarchy and so on.

6. ILOG

ILOG Company established in 1987, whose general headquarter lies in Paris of France and California of U.S.A., is the world's leading provider of software component suite in optimization, visualization and business rule management fields, and applies the optimize algorithms to business software. The products of ILOG are widely used in telecommunications, traffic, national defense, electricity and the delivery etc.. ILOG Solver represents constraints by using modeling language.

3.2 Backtracking

Generate-and-test method is simplest and most direct to solve constraint satisfaction problem. Each possible combination of the variables is generated and then tested until a successful tested combination is found. This method is obviously less effective. Backtracking is a direct improvement for generate-and-test method. In backtracking, the variables are instantiated as a fixed order. When a new variable violates former instantiated variable, backtracking is performed to try other instantiated variable until all values of domain are tried. When all values are tried in failure, it backtracks the most recently instantiated variable and assigns it again.

Suppose the solution of CSP is made up of vectors with uncertain length, i.e.$(x_1, x_2, \ldots)$, which satisfies all constraints. X_i is the value domain of variable x_i, then the feasible solution space of CSP is $X_1 \times X_2 \times \ldots X_n$, where n is the number of variables.

At the beginning of backtracking, partial solution is a null vector. Then choose a variable x_1 from variable set and add it into partial solution. Usually x_1 takes the minimum element of X_1. The candidates of x_1 chosen under various constraints will form a subset S_1 of X_1. The constraints can be used to find out candidates from partial solution $(x_1, x_2, \ldots, x_{k-1})$ to $(x_1, x_2, \ldots, x_{k-1}, x_k)$. If $(x_1, x_2, \cdots, x_{k-1}, x_k)$ does not allow x_k to take any value, then $S_k = \phi$. On this condition, backtracking is done and assign a new permission value for x_{k-1}. If x_{k-1} does not have new permission value, further backtracking to x_{k-2} is done and so on. Suppose $T(x_1, x_2, \cdots, x_{k-1})$ denotes all fetching values of x_k. If partial solution $(x_1, x_2, \cdots, x_k)$ does not allow to have new expansion node, then bounding function $BT_k(x_1, x_2, \cdots, x_k)$ is false, otherwise true. The backtracking algorithm with only one solution is shown as follows:

Algorithm 3.1 Backtracking Algorithm

    Input: A CSP problem
      Output: Complete solution or return no solution
      procedure BACKTRACK
          begin
          k =1;
              while k>0 do
                  If x_k has unchecked value to make
                      $x_k \in T(x_1, x_2, \ldots, x_{k-1})$ and
                      $BT_k(x_1, x_2, , x_k)$ =true
                  then if$(x_1, x_2, \ldots, x_k)$ satisfy all constraints
                      then return(0) ; /* return one solution */
                      else k=k+1;
                  end if;
                  else k=k-1;
              endwhile

        return(1) ; /*Return no solution */
    end BACKTRACK

Although backtracking is better than the generate-and-test method, it still has low efficiency for nontrivial problems, that is because search in different paths of the space keeps failing for the same reasons. Some researchers think that the thrashing is caused by so-called local inconsistency. The simplest cause of thrashing concerns the so-called node inconsistency. If a variable vi contains a value a that does not satisfy the unary constraint on v_i, then the instantiation of v_i to a always results in inconsistency. Another possible source of thrashing is so-called arc inconsistency which is illustrated by the following example: Suppose the variables are instantiated in the order v_1, v_2,··· ,v_i, ···,v_j, ···, v_n. Suppose also that the binary constraint between v_i and v_j is such that for $v_i=a$, there is no value for v_j would satisfy such constraint. The search will fail while instantiation is tried with v_j and the failure will be repeated for each possible combination that the variables $v_r(i<r<j)$ can take.

Thrashing because of node inconsistency can be eliminated by removing those values from the domains of each variable that does not satisfy unary constraint. And the thrashing because of arc inconsistency can be eliminated by arc consistency algorithm. In the next section, the formal definition of arc consistency and corresponding algorithm will be presented.

3.3 Constraint Propagation

If for every value x in the current domain of v_i, there is some value y in the domain of v_j such that $v_i=x$ and $v_j=y$, which are permitted by the constraint between v_i and v_j, then arc(v_i,v_j) is arc consistent. The concept of arc consistency is directional, that is, if an arc(v_i,v_j) is consistent then it does not automatically mean that arc(v_j,v_i) is consistent. For example, if the current domain of v_1 is {a}, the current domain of v_2 is {a, b} and the constraint between v_1 and v_2 is unequal, then arc(v_1,v_2) is consistent but arc(v_2,v_1) is not consistent. Because there does not exist any value of v_1 to satisfy the unequal constraint for $v_2=b$. Obviously, an arc(v_i, v_j) can be make consistent by deleting those values which do not satisfy constraints. Furthermore, deletions of such values do not affect any solution of original CSP. The following algorithm realizes such deletion operation.

Algorithm 3.2 Revised Constraint Propagation Algorithm[Mackworth 1977]

procedure REVISE(V_i, V_j)
DELETE←false;
for each $x \in D_i$ do
       if there is no such $V_j \in D_j$
       such that (x, V_j) is consistent,
       then
           delete x from D_i;
           DELETE←true;
    endif
endfor
return DELETE;
end REVISE

To make every arc of constraint network consistent, it is not sufficient to execute REVISE for each arc just once. Once REVISE reduces the variable v_i, then each previously revised arc(v_i, v_j) has to be revised again because the domain of v_i might become smaller than before. The following algorithm obtains arc consistency for the whole constraint network.

Algorithm 3.3 Constraint Propagation Algorithm AC-1 [Mackworth 1977]
    procedure AC-1
    $Q \leftarrow \{(V_i, V_j) \in \text{arcs}(G), i \neq j\}$;
    repeat
      CHANGE ←false;
      for each $(V_i, V_j) \in Q$ do
         CHANGE ←REVISE(V_i, V_j)∨CHANGE;
      endfor;
    until not(CHANGE) ;
    end AC-1

The main shortcoming of AC-1 is that a successful revision will force all arcs to be revised in the next iteration, although only a small number of arcs are affected . AC-3 performs re-revision only for those arcs that are possibly affected by a previous revision, which improves AC-1 algorithm.

Algorithm 3.4 Constraint Propagation Algorithm AC-3 [Mackworth 1977]
    procedure AC-3
    $Q \leftarrow \{(V_i, V_j) \in \text{arcs}(G), i \neq j\}$;
    while Q not empty

select and delete any arc(V_k, V_m) from Q;
   if (REVISE(V_k, V_m)) then
      Q ←{(V_i, V_k) such that (V_i, V_k) ∈ arcs(G) ,$i{\neq}k, i{\neq}m$ }
   End if;
 End while;
end AC-3

The famous algorithm of Waltz(Waltz, 1975) is a special case of this algorithm and equivalent to another algorithm AC-2 proposed by Mackworth. Suppose that the domain size for each variable is d, and the total number of constraints network is e. The complexity of arc-consistency algorithm proposed by Mackworth is O(ed^3). Mohr and Henderson proposed another arc-consistency algorithm(Mohr, 1986), whose complexity is O(ed^2). Therefore, Mohr and Henderson's algorithm is optimal considering worst-case complexity.

Given an arc-consistent constraint network, is there an instantiation of the variable from current domains make the variable become a solution to CSP? If the domain size of each variable becomes one after obtaining arc consistency, then the network has exactly one solution. Otherwise, the answer is no in general. Nevertheless, arc-consistent algorithms reduce the search space of backtracking.

Since arc-consistency algorithm has not enough ability to replace backtracking, can another stronger consistent algorithm eliminate the search need in backtracking? The notion of K consistency captures different degrees of consistency for different values of K. A constraint network is K consistent if the following is true: Choose values of any K-1 variables that satisfy all the constraints among these variables, then choose any Kth variable. A value for this variable exists that satisfies all the constraints among these K variables. The exactly formal description is as following:

Suppose that the variables x_1, x_2,...,x_{k-1} are instantiated by value a_1, a_2, ... , a_{k-1} separately. If each value of a_1, a_2, ... , a_{k-1} satisfy all the constraints among x_1, x_2,...,x_{k-1},x_k, then for variable x_k, there is a value a_k to make value of a_1, a_2, ... , a_{k-1} , a_k satisfy all the constraints among x_1, x_2,...,x_{k-1},x_k .

A constraint network is strong K consistent if it is J consistent for all $J{\leq}K$. Node consistency is equivalent to strong 1 consistency. Arc consistency is equivalent to strong 2 consistency. Algorithms exist to make a constraint network strong K consistent for $K > 2$ (Cooper 1989). If a n-node constraint network is strong n consistent, then a solution to CSP can be found without any search. However, the worst-case complexity of the algorithm for obtaining n consistency in a n-node constraint network is also exponential.

However, the algorithm exists multinomial complexity for constraint network with special structure. The simplest case is that, arc-consistent algorithm can be used to solve the tree-structured constraint network within linear time complexity.

3.4 Constraint Propagation in Tree Search

Two different methods for solving CSP are discussed above: backtracking and constraint propagation. In the first method, different combinations of variable assignments are tested until a complete solution is found. This approach suffers from thrashing. In the second method, constraints between different variables are propagated to derive a simpler problem. Although any CSP can always be solved by achieving n consistency, the efficiency of this approach is usually lower than backtracking's. Furthermore, the k-consistency(k<n) algorithm does not ensure achieving global consistent solution. A integrated method is to embed constraint propagation inside a backtracking algorithm, as follows:

At first, a root node is created to solve original CSP. When a node is visited, a constraint propagation algorithm is used to achieve a desired consistency. If at a node, the domain of each variable contains only one value, and corresponding CSP is arc consistent, then the node represents a solution. If in the process of constraint propagation at a node, the domain of any variable becomes null, then the node is pruned. Otherwise select one variable (whose domain size >1), and new CSP node is created for each possible assignment of this variable. Each new CSP node is depicted as a successor node of the node representing current CSP. All these nodes are visited by a depth-first backtracking algorithm.

The problem now is how constraints propagate to what extent at each node. If no constraint propagation is done, then the method reverts to backtracking. If m-consistency algorithm is used to achieve m consistency for m CSP nodes which are unassigned would completely eliminate backtracking, and result in poor efficiency. Experience indicates that limited constraint propagation whose consistency is generally not stronger than arc consistency, can achieve the best efficiency.

3.5 Intelligent Backtracking and Truth Maintenance

Another method to overcome drawbacks of standard backtracking is intelligent backtracking in which backtracking is done directly to the variable that caused the failure. To see how intelligent backtracking works, consider the following example.

Suppose that variables v_1, v_2, and v_3 have been assigned values a_1, b_3, and c_2, respectively. Suppose that none of the values of v_3 were found compatible with the values b_1 and b_2 of v_2. Now suppose that all possible values of v_4 conflict with the choice of $v_1 = a_1$. The conflict is caused by the inappropriate choice of v_1, so the intelligent backtracking method will perform backtracking to v_1 and also undo the assignments of v_2 and v_3.

Although this kind of method can find correct backtracking node according to the failed source, it has not totally avoided the redundant path. Dependency-directed backtracking is a method to eliminate the drawback and widely used in truth maintenance system(TMS) developed by Doyle.

A TMS-based problem solver consists of two components: an inference engine and a TMS. The inference engine is used to derive new facts form old ones, while TMS is records the justifications of the derivations. New joining of fact might make some existing assumptions not true. Therefore the maintenance of justifications can abolish those assumptions not true any more. The method used for CSP is described as follows.

When a variable is assigned some value, a justification for this value is created. Then similarly, a default value is assigned to some other variable and is justified. At this time, the system checks whether the current assignments violate any constraint. If they do, then a new node is created that denotes that the pair of values for the two variables are contradictory. This node is also used to justify other value assignment. This process continues until a consistent assignment is found for all the variables. Such a system never performs redundant backtracking and never repeats any computation.

Although the amount of search performed by such a system is minimal, the cost of determining the source of constraint violation is high. Because reasoning steps are exponential increasing, the time and space complexity for storing and search are exponential. Hence, overall the method can take more time than even simple backtracking for a variety of problems.

Assumption-based truth maintenance system(ATMS) is another relevant work developed by de Kleer. The ATMS evolves from the TMS. TMS can be regarded as constraint propagation and ATMS is the expansion of TMS. TMS only maintains single context, while ATMS attempts to search for multiple contexts at the same time. Therefore, each fact derived is corresponding to assumptions that make the fact true. A conclusion may be true in multiple contexts. The assumptions differ form the justifications in the fact that they are believed unless there is evidence to the contradiction and can thus prove false. The advantage of ATMS lies in some temporary assumptions are shared and not need to create separately. The number of temporary assumptions is usually exponential increasing, therefore the procedure of assumption creation has exponential complexity. The ATMS has the following shortcomings:

- It is designed for complete solutions, for one solution unnecessary search is always done;
- It costs a lot of time and space for maintaining all contexts;
- It is difficult to correct mistake.

It is very difficult for this method to estimate storage requirement, and all deriving and assumptions should be recorded, which makes the method difficult to apply to large-scale system. Thus de Kleer and Williams proposed to use backtracking in order to control ATMS again, which is also similar to an intelligent backtracking method.

3.6 Variable Instantiation Ordering and Assignment Ordering

Another improvement for standard backtracking is variables instantiation ordering. Experiments show that this ordering can have substantial impact on the efficiency of backtrack search. Several heuristics have been developed for selecting variable ordering. One method is selecting the variable with the fewest value of domain for instantiation. Thus the order of variable instantiation is, in general, determined dynamically, which is different in different branches of search tree. Purdom and Brown extensively studied the heuristic, as well as its variants(Purdom, 1983), and the results show that they are substantial improvements over the standard backtracking method.

Another heuristic is to instantiate those variables first that participate in the highest number of constraints. This approach tries to ensure that the unsuccessful branches of search tree are pruned early.

Recall that the tree-structured constraint network can be solved without backtracking. Any given constraint network can be made a tree after deleting certain vertices. This set of vertices is called the *cycle cutset*. If a small cycle cutset can be found, then a good heuristic is to first instantiate all the variables in the cycle cutset and then solve the resulting tree-structured CSPs.

3.7 Local Revision Search

At present, most algorithms are constructive methods based on the tree search. But another method to solve combination problem draws people's attention for its surprising experimental results recently, that is so-called , "local revision"(Gu, 1992). Firstly, this method produces a global but may not inconsistent variable assignment, and then modifies some variable value according to the contradiction appeared in order to reduce the assignments that violates constraints, and repeats the process again until achieving a consistent assignment. This method follows a simple rule: Find a variable which causes the contradiction, then select a new assignment to it, such that assignments can reduce contradictions to the least. The basic idea of this method is as follows.

Given a set of variable, a set of binary constraint, and an assignment of each variable. If two variable values violate a constraint, then the two variables are contradictory.

The Process is to select a contradictory variable, and assign a new value to it in order to reduce contradictions to the least.

Local revision search is very effective, and the main reason is that, more information are provided by variable assignments, thus the next transforming state will reduce the contradictions tremendously.

Local revision search has shortcomings as well. First, the strategy is incomplete. When the solution of problem does not exist, the search may not stop. When the density of solution is low, the search efficiency is very low too. We compared revision search and tree search on graph coloring problem, the results show that when there are less edges in graph, revision search is better and otherwise, tree search has higher efficiency. If the problem has no solution, however, revision search will not stop.

At present, a new research direction of constraint search is studying the difficulty distribution of CSP. Although CSP is generally a NP problem, a large amount of CSPs can be solved during the tolerated time. The real intractable problems account for a small number.

3.8 Graph-based Backjumping

Graph-based backjumping is a kind dependency-directed method, in which dependency information comes from graph structure of constraint network. A constraint graph consists of vertex that denotes variable and edge that denotes constraint(binary constraint). The edge between two vertexes denotes that there exists binary constraint between these two variables denoted by vertexes. In graph-based backjumping, whenever a failure come out at some variable X, the algorithm always goes back to recent assigned variable connected to X in graph. The graph-based backjumping is described as follows.

Algorithm 3.5 Forward Propagation Algorithm

    Forward($x_1, \dots ,x_i, P$)
    begin
        if $i=n$ then Exit and Return current assignment;
            $C_{i+1} \leftarrow$computeCandidates($x_1, \dots ,x_i, x_{i+1}$) ;
            if C_{i+1} not null, then
            $x_{i+1}\leftarrow$The first element in C_{i+1};
             Delete x_{i+1} from C_{i+1}
             Forward ($x_1, \dots ,x_i, x_{i+1}$,P);
          else
            Jumpback($x_1, \dots ,x_i, P$);
        endif
    end

Where, P is a set of variables which will be backtracked.

Algorithm 3.6 Jumpback Algorithm

    Jumpback($x_1,\cdots , x_i, x_{i+1}, P$)
    begin
      if $i=0$,then Exit without solution;
          PARENTS$\leftarrow$Parents(x_{i+1});
          $P\leftarrow P\cup$PARENTS;
          $P\leftarrow P-x_j$; j is the biggest serial number of variables in P,
    If $C_j\neq\phi$,then
             x_j =first in C_j ;
             Delete x_j from C_j;
        Forward ($x_1,\dots ,x_j, P$);
      else
            Jumpback ($x_1,\dots ,x_{j-1}, x_j, P$);
      endif;
    end

3.9 Influence-based Backjumping

We improved graph-based backjumping to form a new influence-based backjumping. First of all, our goal is not only to utilize static connection relation, but also dynamic relevant information. The key problem is how to limit the cost of computing resources that caused by introducing dynamic information within reasonable scope. Through exquisite design of the algorithm and data structure, we succeeded in solving this problem.

Influence-based backjumping—IBMD (Influence-based-Backjumping, Most-constrained-first, Domain-filtering)integrates three strategies: most-constrained-first, domain filtering and backjumping. Most constrained first refers to selecting the variable with minimum "degree of freedom"to assign each time. The "degree of freedom" is mainly measured by the current domain of variable, because it is the most important and easiest quantity to calculate. The calculation can be also measured with help of connection degree of variable in constraint network. The most-constrained-first strategy is a very effective improvement for fixed variable instantiation ordering.

Domain filtering refers to deleting the value inconsistent with assigned variable values from variable domain. This is a constraint propagation technology with small cost. When a new variable is assigned, all those unassigned variable values which are inconsistent with this assignment will be deleted. The assignment is tentative, so deleted values must be stored. When some assignment is revoked, all deleted values caused by this assignment must be recovered.

Backjumping we designed is different from traditional dependency-directed backtracking, including graph-based backjumping. The traditional dependency-directed backtracking records explicitly assumption sets on which reasoning will rely. Once one-step backtrack is done, assumption set of revoked variable will be merged into the assumption set of recent assigned variables, which causes a lot of time cost and space cost. In order to avoid such cost, our backjumping does not backjump according to recorded assumption set. In fact, we do not need these records at all. Our backjumping method backjumps according to actual influence from one assignment to variable in filtering process. One assignment has influence on the variable vi, if and only if as least a value of current domain has been deleted in the filtering process caused by that assignment. Obviously the influence is calculated more accurately than the connection relation of network. Because connection relation is a possible data relevance, while influence relation is actual data dependence. Therefore, perhaps some two variables are connected in constraint graph, but do not influence each other under current context. The space cost of Influence-based backjumping has less space cost than graph-based backjumping. Furthermore, influence-based backjumping produces less time cost as well.

In IBMD, each instantiated variable stores a set of influenced variables. Given a IBMD's context(all assignments of instantiated variables), a variable v_i is influenced by v_j if and only if the instantiations of v_j reduces current domain of v_i to some extent.

IBMD includes forward instantiation and backward backtracking. In forward instantiation, select the variable whose current domain is minimal to assign at first. After the variable v_i assigned, domain filtering will be carried on. For all unassigned variable v_j, delete those values in its domain D_j, which are contradicting with assignment of v_i. If D_j becomes null, means that the assignment of v_i contradicts with previous variable assignment, therefore backtracking begins. Backtracking firstly recover values which have been deleted because of variable v_i instantiation. If all values of v_i have been tried, then backtracking continues going to previous variable v_h. If v_h has no influence on v_j or other variables whose all values have been tried, or v_h has been already tried all values, then make v_h as previous instantiation variable and repeat backtracking. Suppose that the procedure stops at variable v_g and the latest variable that influences v_g is v_f, then delete the instantiation value of v_g from D_g and record v_g and its instantiation value into influence set of v_f. And then assign v_g with new value again, thus back to forward instantiation backtracking. The algorithm written in C is as follows.

Algorithm 3.7 Influence-based Backjumpiing Algorithm(Liao, 1994)

```
IBMD()
{
  int var, failvar;
  while (uninstantiated ! =nil ) {
    var =mostConstrained() ;
        /*Choose a variable to instantiate */
  a[var] =domain[var][ 0];   /* Assign a value. */
      while ((failvar =propagate(var) )! =SUCCESS) {
        /*While inconsistent */
          if ((var =backjump(failvar) ==nil) return(0) ;
          /*If back up to top, exit */
```

```
        a[var] =domain[var][0]; /*Else reinstantiate var */
        }
    }
    return(1) ;
    }
```

Algorithm 3.8 Backjumping Algorithm (Liao, 1994)

```
    backjump (failvar)
    int failvar;
        {
        int assignedVar, sourceVar;
        failedVarSet =makeVariableSet() ;
        addVariableSet(failvar, failedVarSet) ;
            /*Initialize the set of failed variables */
        while ( (assignedVar =lastAssigned[ASSIGNEDHEAD]) ! =TOP)
        {/*Until go back to top */
                retract(assignedVar) ; {/*Retract the influences of the variable */
                if (relevant) /*The instantiation influence failedVarSet */
                    if (! exhausted(assignedVar) )break;
                else addVariableSet(assignedVar, failedVarSet) ;
                }
            }
        if (assignedVar ==TOP)   return(nil) ;
        for(sourceVar =lastAssigned[assignedVar];
            sourceVar ! =TOP && ! isCulpit(sourceVar) ;
            sourceVar =lastAssigned[sourceVar]) ;
            /*Find last variable that is relevant to the failure */
                domainfilter(sourceVar, assignedVar, a[assignedVar]) ;
            /*Filter the current value and record the influence */
        return(assignedVar) ;
        }
```

In the program, function mostConstrained() selects the minimum variable of current domain, and moves this variable form unassigned variable table uninstantiated to already assigned variable table instantiated. Propagate() is used for domain filtering. If some variable domain is null after domain filtering, then return this variable, otherwise return 0. Function retract() carries on backjumping and return the backjumped variable. If backjumping goes to the top, then return nil value. Array a[] is used for storing assigned values of each variable. Two dimension array domain[][] is used to record state of each assigned value of each variable: belonging to current domain or has been deleted by some instantiated variable. The values which belong to current domain are chained together with the suffix, as well as those values have been deleted by the same variable instantiation.

The algorithm implements exhaustive search, thus has exponential time complexity. The space complexity is $O(n(n+d))$, where n is the number of variable, d is the size of variable domain(suppose all variables have equal domain size).

IBMD has been used to test a series of examples and compared with some other algorithms, which includes backtracking(BT), conflict-based backtracking(CBJ), the algorithm only adopting most-constrained-first method(MCF) and the algorithm only adopting most-constrained-first and domain filtering methods(MD). The experimental results show that IBMD is superior to these algorithms to some extent. For example, N queen's problem is solved with IBMD on the workstation sparc-1. For N =100, IBMD algorithm takes less 2 seconds. On the same machine, BT algorithm takes more than 10 seconds for 2 queen's problem. For N $\geq$ 30, BT algorithm takes several hours at least. For N=50 MCF algorithm takes more than 10 seconds and takes several hours for N$\geq$60. For N queen's problem, MD algorithm and IBMD algorithm nearly have the same performance and IBMD is slightly superior to MD. There are several reasons here. First of all, in N queen's problem, there is little one-step backtracking. Domain filtering strategy can reduce much "out-layer" inconsistency. However "deep-layer" inconsistency involves many other variables. Secondly the extra cost of IBMD are less than MD. Table 3.1 shows the execution time of different algorithms operating on N queen's problem.

We have also tested the graph-coloring case. When the connection degree of vertexes is small($\leq$7), backtracking is hardly used and the IBMD performance is equivalent to MD performance. When increasing connection degree, IBMD performance is obviously superior to MD.

Compare the IBMD algorithm with other similar algorithms as follows.

(1) Compared with backjumping(BJ)

BJ can only backjump to latest variable caused by inconsistent variables. But if the latest variable has already tried all values, backtracking is to be the same as common backtracking. Therefore BJ is very limited in improvement of performance. However, IBMD can backtrack continuously until find a variable, which is correlated with the inconsistency and not all values have been tried.

(2) Compared with graph-based backjumping

The topology connection of constraint network is an approximation of actual data dependence. Under particular context, two graph-relevant variables probably will not influence each other. And what IBMD utilized is actual influence.

(3) Compared with conflict-based backjumping

Prosser,et al. proposed some improvement of backjumping on IJCAI conference in 1993, such as CBJ (Conflict-based BackJumping). The starting points of IBMD and CBJ are similar, but in realizing they differ a lot. CBJ has a drawback. Each variable has a dependence variable set. When backjumping is done once, the merge of sets should be carried on, therefore CBJ causes very large time cost. However, this problem does not exist in IBMD algorithm.

A aspect that IBMD is superior to all other algorithms described above is that IBMD combines the most-constrained-first and domain filtering strategies together.

Table 3.1 Execution time of running N queen's problem(unit :sec)

n	BT	CBJ	IBMD	n	BT	CBJ	IBMD
8	0.0	0.0	0.0	26	324.0	323.6	0.0
9	0.0	0.0	0.0	27	389.4	389.5	0.0
10	0.0	0.0	0.0	28	2810.2	2799.0	0.0
11	0.0	0.0	0.0	29	1511.1	1517.2	0.0
12	0.1	0.0	0.0	30	*	*	0.1
13	0.0	0.1	0.0	40	*	*	0.3
14	0.5	0.5	0.0	50	*	*	1.8
15	0.4	0.5	0.0	60	*	*	0.7
16	3.3	3.7	0.0	70	*	*	1.4
17	1.9	2.2	0.0	80	*	*	1.0
18	16.9	17.9	0.0	90	*	*	1155.7
19	1.1	1.3	0.0	100	*	*	1.8
20	101.6	105.5	0.0	110	*	*	158.9
21	4.6	4.7	0.0	120	*	*	*
22	1068.1	1048.4	0.0	130	*	*	11.5
23	16.2	16.2	0.0	140	*	*	*
24	290.5	289.6	0.0	160	*	*	7.1
25	35.8	35.9	0.0	200	*	*	14.0

note: "*" represents the time ≥2 hours

3.10 Constraint Relation Processing

3.10.1 *Unit Sharing Strategy for Identical Relation*

In constraint reasoning, if two variables always take the same value, then the relation of these two variables is identical relation, which is a kind of important constraint relations. For instance, two devices are connected in series in the circuit, which means that the electric current through one device is equal to the other device. A square can be defined as a rectangle whose length and width are equal. Although identical relation can be processed by common constraint relation, it is necessary to carry on special processing for its popularity and special semantic. As a result, it can avoid the low efficiency of common CSP solver, more importantly it can directly reduce the computing scale of CSP. Because the two equal variable should take the same value, they can be regarded as the same variable in computing. This is the basic idea of unit sharing strategy.

A simple method to realize unit sharing strategy is that replacing equal variables with a new variable, however, this will lead to global variable replacement of constraint network. Meanwhile, consider that some equal relations are defined after making some assignment assumptions, therefore original variable information before equated must be kept. So we use binary tree to represent variable information. For equation $x=y$, if x and y have been already assigned, then determine whether they are equal and return Boolean value. If x is assigned but y is not, then determine whether the values of x are belong to the domain of y. If the condition is not true, then return "inconsistence" information(failure information). Otherwise, assign the value of x to y. If x and y are not assigned yet, then create a new variable node $com(x,y)$ which is called common node of x and y and its two branch nodes are x and y respectively. The domain of $com(x,y)$ is the intersection set of domains of x and y. If the intersection set is null, then return "inconsistent" information(fail information). Constraint connections between x or y and other nodes, are all merged into $com(x,y)$. All operations on x or y later will be implemented by operating on $com(x,y)$.

In general, when a variable involves a lot of equation constraints, such as the equation set $\{x=y, y=z, x=u\}$, our method will form a big binary tree.

The root node of binary tree gather all information of all branch nodes. It becomes an agent for all leaf nodes of binary tree. And the node set of current visited variable is all root node set of such binary tree(including isolation node). For tree search, it is necessary to consider that equation is made after assumption assignment. After assumption assignment is revoked, the equivalent relation of assertions is no longer tenable, which should be revoked as well. The method is to revoke its corresponding common node. The equation reasoner offers to inquiry equal relation of any two variables with the same type, even they are not assigned. This strategy has the following advantages, which certainly may be interrelated.

(1) The complexity of constraint search is mainly depend on the number of constraint variable. The unit sharing strategy merges two or more variables with identical relation into one variable. Therefore the strategy can be used to reduce search space.

(2) Make the constraint reasoner can find inconsistencies relevant to identical relation before variables are not assigned. For example, for constraints $\{x=y, y=z, x\neq z \}$, even x, y and z are not assigned yet, system can check out inconsistency of constraints.

(3) Make constraint propagation run. The unit sharing strategy of identical relation reduces the number of unknown variables and reduce the number of unknown variables of one constraint relation as well. In general, only when the number of unknown variable in one constraint relation is less enough, constraint propagation can be carried on. Constraint propagation at early time is equivalent to pruning branches close to root node of search tree ahead of time, therefore can reduce search space greatly.

For example, for the constraint $r(x,y,z)$ which includes three enumerated variables x, y and z, after x is instantiated, if y and z are different variables, in general we can do consistency refinement for domain of y or z. If there exists one constraint $y=z$, then means that unassigned variable is only one. Therefore constraint propagation can be carried on.

(4) Make constraint language have ability of pattern matching in symbol processing.

In order to explain the advantage of such strategy, we consider taking qualitative add operation of qualitative physic implemented by COPE language as example. One physical quantity that varies in real domain can be characterized by qualitative variable for its positive and negative aspects. One qualitative variable can take three values: position , negation , zero:

enum qualitative {pos, neg, zero };

Qualitative add operation can be defined as following:

```
qualsum (x,y,z)
enum qualitative x,y,z;
{
    if (x=y) z=x;
    if (x=zero) z=y;
    if (y=zero) z=x;
}
```

If we have constraint program

```
main
{
    enum qualitative u, v, w;
    w =zero;
    qualsum(u, w, v) ;
    qualsum(u, v, w) ;
}
```

We do no need take any tentative search to achieve the only solution, which is $\{u =zero, v =zero, w =zero \}$. By qualsum($u, w, v$) and $w =zero$, we have $u=v$, which make qualsum(u, v, w) reason out $u=w =zero$; Thus $v =u =zero$.

3.10.2 Interval Propagation

In addition to equality relation, the most common relation is the inequality relation. Especially for the analysis and design of electronic apparatus, the use of inequality is particularly important. The most basic reasoning of inequality representation is to test variable value. That is, variable value is known already, then calculate and check whether variable value satisfies the inequality. Simply this kind of calculation can only be used for generate-and-test strategy, which has the lowest efficiency. We have realized stronger inequality reasoning.

A common used inequality reasoning is interval reasoning, i.e. the interval propagation in constraint network. Given interval limit of some variables, other variables' interval limit can be reasoned out by ordering relation among variables. For example, suppose that constraint $x > y$ and the interval of variable x and y are

$[l_x, g_x]$ and $[l_y, g_y]$ respectively, then after constraints propagate, the interval of variable x and y are

$$[max(l_x, l_y), g_x]$$
$$[l_y, min(g_x, g_y)]$$

If $g_x < l_y$, then it means the contradiction.

This reasoning can be promoted to more complicated equation or inequality as well. Consider equation $x + y = z$, and current interval of variable x, y and z are $[l_x, g_x]$, $[l_y, g_y]$ and $[l_z, g_z]$ respectively. if $l_x + l_y > g_z$ or $g_x + g_y < l_z$, it means the contradiction. Otherwise the z's new interval values of $[l'_z, g'_z]$ are

$$l'_z = max(l_x + l_y, l_z)$$
$$g'_z = min(g_x + g_y, g_z)$$

x's new interval values of $[l'_x, g'_x]$ are

$$l'_x = max(l_z - g_y, l_x)$$
$$g'_x = min(g_z - l_y, g_x)$$

y's new interval values of $[l'_y, g'_y]$ are

$$l'_y = max(l_z - g_x, l_y)$$
$$g'_y = min(g_z - l_x, g_y)$$

3.10.3 Inequality Graph

In many AI applications such as qualitative reasoning, temporal reasoning and activity planning, what they care about is the relative relation among variables. Therefore the reasoning of ordering relation is very important. This is actually reasoning on axioms of inequality, such as identical relation, partial order relation etc..

All inequalities which are similar to $x \leq y$ and $x \neq y$ are used to made up an inequality graph. Relation $x \geq y$ is represented as $y \leq x$, and $x < y$ is represented as $x \leq y$ and $x \neq y$, and $x > y$ is represented as $y \leq x$ with $x \neq y$ (identical relation has been implemented by unit sharing strategy).

Definition 3.1 *Positive Cycle. A inequality graph is a marked graph <V, E>, in which V is a set of nodes and E is a set of xry relations, where $x, y \in V$ and r denotes $\leq$ or $\neq$ relation. A positive path in graph is a node series $v_1, v_2, ..., v_b$, such that for i ($i = 2, ..., l$),$(v_{i-1} \leq v_i)$ is a edge in the graph. If $v_1 = v_b$, then the path is called positive cycle.*

Obviously, the inequality graph has the following properties:

Property 3.1 *In a positive cycle, if ≠ relation does not exist between any two nodes, then all nodes denotes the same variables in this cycle.*

Property 3.2 *There exists a positive cycle in a inequality graph, if there exists ≠ relation between any two nodes in the cycle, then inequality graph contains inconsistency.*

Property 3.1 can be used to carry on equivalent transformation on inequality graph to make it exclude positive cycle. The method is merging all nodes of positive cycle into one single node according to unit sharing strategy for all positive cycle of graph. Result graph obtained is called reduced inequality graph.

Property 3.2 can be used to define inconsistency of inequality graph.

Definition 3.2 *One inequality graph is inconsistent, if and only if in this graph there exists a edgee, in which some two variable nodes have "≠"relation.*

Theorem 3.1 *One inequality graph is inconsistent, if and only if in its reduced graph , there exist one edge with"≠"relation from one variable node to itself.*

Base on these two facts, the inequality reasoner carries on graph traversal. If a positive cycle is found out, then use unit sharing strategy to merge the cycle into one variable node. If one variable's domain is null or one variable has one ≠ relation pointed to itself, then report the inconsistency. It is easy to prove the completeness of operations described above for partial order relation and identical relation. Given a set *W* including identical relation, inequality relation and partial order relation, and the set *G* of axiom about identical relation and partial order relation, then *W*∪*G* is inconsistent if and only if inequality graph corresponding to *W* is inconsistent.

Compared with deductive method, graph operation method is much more effective. Because the graph traversal has linear complexity.

3.10.4 *Inequality Reasoning*

The inequality graph reflects structural characteristic of inequality. When the variable node in the inequality graph is limited by interval, besides operation of inequality graph, constraints propagate in the inequality graph. All these operations are caused after inequality graph receives an outside input. The outside inputs include adding a relation expression *x* r *y* into the network, where *x* and *y* are variables or constants, but at least one variable; r is one of relations =, ≠, <, ≤, >, ≥.

For r is =, If variable x and y are both not assigned, then merge them into one variable node according to unit sharing strategy, check whether positive cycle generates, and possibly simplify and check the consistency of inequality graph. If the new node domain is smaller to some extent than the domain of x or y, then propagate the interval along inequality graph. If x and y are both assigned variables or constants, then decide whether their values are equal; If there exists only one unassigned variable and the value of another variable drops on this unassigned variable domain, then assign the value to the unassigned variable and propagate constraints; Otherwise, report the inconsistency.

For r is $\leq$, if variable x and y are already assigned, then decide whether $\leq$ relation is tenable; Otherwise, carry on consistency limit to the interval of x and y. If the limited interval of the x or y is smaller to some extent, then propagate the interval along inequality graph. If these two variables are both not unassigned, then add an edge with relation $\neq$ into this inequality graph, check whether positive cycle generates, and possibly simplify and check the consistency of inequality graph.

For r is $\neq$, if variable x and y are both already assigned, then decide whether $\neq$ relation is tenable.

For $x<y$, $x>y$ and $x \geq y$, their equivalent transformation are $(x \leq y) \wedge (x \neq y)$,$(y \leq x) \wedge (x \neq y)$,$y \leq x$ respectively.

Inequality reasoner offers inquiry of inequality relation between any two variables with the same type, even they are not assignment. The method which combines symbol reasoning and interval propagation, is not only to regard inequality as the internal predicate to reduce the reasoning cost, but also eliminate the redundancy and reduce the solution scale of problem. Furthermore, as a general inequality reasoner, it can carry on symbol reasoning before the situation that variable is not assigned or even added interval limit. For example, system can check the inequality set and find out $\{x \leq y,\ y \leq z,\ x > z\}$ contains inconsistent. Inequality reasoning makes system have a function of propagating partial relation. The function has been used widely in qualitative reasoning. By realizing operations of equality and inequality reasoning, system increases the reasoning depth, avoids more generated tests and thus reduces search space.

3.11 Constraint Reasoning System COPS

A main function of constraint reasoning system to offer common and effective constraint reasoning mechanism for user. This reasoning mechanism should overcome the search problem caused by uncertainty. Constraint propagation is also a technology to reduce uncertainty. From language representation view, we think that uncertain part should be explicitly marked out and limited to data part. By this way, the data relevance can be identified, and the data domain can be operated, which thus make constraint propagation and intelligent backtracking used to reduce uncertainty and search space. Meantime, such regular structure improves the readability of the code and make language studying easy so that special search technology such as constraint propagation and intelligent backtracking can be used. The logic programming language Prolog takes inductive proof method of Horn clause, a technology of tentative solving, as unified computing mechanism. Although Prolog is simple, it is very difficult to use.

In constraint reasoning system COPS, constraint programming language COPS combines object-oriented technology, logic programming, production system and constraint representation together. COPS absorbs basic forms of object-oriented programming language, applies constraint propagation and heuristic mechanism into solving, combines declarative constraint representation and type hierarchy together and realizes structural knowledge encapsulation(Shi 1996). COPS language has the following characteristics:
- Combine type hierarchy and constraint representation together;
- Realize default constraint reasoning;
- Realize conditional constraint and other part of regular programming;
- Realize effective constraint reasoning.

1. Constraint and Rule

A constraint is a predicate expression:
$$P(t_1,\ldots,t_n)$$
Where, $t_1, \ldots, t_n$ are items ,which typically includes variable; P is a predicate symbol and predicate can be internal function such as sum, times, eq (equal) ,neq(not equal) ,ge(great than or equal to) ,gt(great than) ,which can also be defined by users.

Conditional constraint has the following forms:

```
if {
condition₁: constraint₁;
        . . .
conditionₙ: constraintₙ
}
```

Where,condition$_1$,…,condition$_n$ are Boolean expression. Constraint$_1$,…
,constraint$_n$ is a constraint or a constraint table having{ }.

The rule is used for defining new function, method, predicate, or adding constraint to object. The form of rule is

RULE [class: :]Predicate (variable or constant) (Boolean expression)
{
constraint$_1$;
$\cdots$
constraint$_n$;
CASE
Boolean expression$_1$: constraint$_1$;
$\cdots$
Boolean expression$_m$: constraint$_m$;
}
For example:
RULE multiple(INTEGER: *x, INTEGER: y, INTEGER: z) (neq(y, 0))
{
equal(x, divide(z, y));
}

which defines constraint relation among three variables x, y and z :$x = z \div y$.

2. Class Definition

In COPS system, entity of problem field is defined as class, and entity's internal attributes and relations are encapsulated in class. Multiple entities with certain relation can be encapsulated in high-level class. The definition of class in COPS is similar to class definition in C++:

CLASS [class name] [: super class name]
{
　　//Attribute definition
　　Data type: Attribute name;
　　 $\cdots$
　　//Rule definition
　　Rule name;
　　 $\cdots$
　　//Function definition
　　Function name;
　　 $\cdots$
　　//Method definition
　　Method name;
　 …
}

The whole COPS program is made up of class definition and rule. COPS language keeps the style of relational declarative language, meanwhile offers class and method of object-oriented language. By this way, COPS not only strengthens the regulatory and flexibility of programming but also improves readability and usage. COPS language can make user focus on the problem description and not care about solution in detail. Because COPS language is very similar to object-oriented language (C++), its description is clear and easy to use and it can fully utilize the encapsulation and inheritance mechanism to expand and reuse. COPS system has already been carried on the simulation of circuit successfully.

3. Constraint Reasoning in COPS

In COPS system, constraint reasoning mainly depends on production composition and constraint propagation, which has the heuristic characteristics of ranked conditional term-rewriting system, utilizing state information of problem solution, default rule, assumption reasoning, and propagation in different areas etc.. The key algorithm of COPS system is as following.

Algorithm 3.9 Main-COPS which is a core algorithm in COPS.
1. procedure main _ COPS
2. {
3.   Invoke yacc program, generate internal structure;
4.   Initialize;
5.   Set up COPS constant trueNode;
6.   Allocate memory for global variable;
7.   Interpreter the program with internal structure;
8.   Construct constraint network for unsolved constraint and variable;
9.   While trigger the constraint of constraint network
10.   Interpreter triggered constraint
11. }

Yacc (Yet Another Compiler Compiler) is a another compiler of compiler. It transforms context-free grammar into a table set of simple auto-machine, which carries on a LR grammar analysis program. The output file y.tab.c must be compiled by C compiler and produces the program yyparse, which must be installed together with lexical analyzer yylex, main program and error handler yyerror.

The interpreter of the algorithm is as follows:

```
Interpreter:
{
  switch (constraint type)
  case Constant:
              return Constant:
  case global variable:
     interprete global variable:
  case local variable or argument:
              interprete local variable or argument:
  case object-attribute pair:
              interprete object-attribute pair:
  case function call:
              interprete function call:
    case method call:
              interprete method call:
  case CASE expression:
              interprete CASE expression:

     ...
        default:
         report error
}
```

COPS system fully utilizes the encapsulation and inheritance mechanism to expand and reuse. Through overloading member function, COPS realizes constraint solution efficiently and flexibly. We can also design new solution class and add a lot methods of constraint solution to improve the weakness that original system only has single strategy. At present, the main problem to solve is that message passing across different classes, value propagation for sharing variables and composition exploding in consistency maintenance. In the future, we plan to apply constraint technology to multi-agent system in order to solve cooperation and negation problem and apply constraint reasoning to solve multi-goals problem in intelligent decision support system.

3.12 ILOG Solver

Constraint program is a computing system about constraints. Its input is a group of constraints and problems to solve and output is the solution scheme. The algorithms to solve the problem are all basic functions of constraint programming language. What programmer has to face is how to describe problem as a model consisting of constraints, and the description language can be very close to natural language. If the problem is regarded as a kind of constraint, then the solution is to achieve one or several constraints, each of which is sufficient condition of given constraints, that is, the obtained constraints should satisfy the given constraints. Then, constraint programming can be called constraint-oriented programming method.

ILOG Company established in 1987 and is the French leading provider of software component suite in optimization, visualization and business rule management areas. During the past time, ILOG Company was carrying on development and innovation of enterprise software package and service constantly and made customers optimize the flexibility of business treatment, and improved the operation efficiency of these companies. There are more than 1000 global companies and 300 software suppliers using ILOG. With the development of China's economy, ILOG Company has seen the broad development prospect of Chinese market and sets up representative office in Beijing in August of 2002, which commands the market of Greater China region including Hong Kong, Macao, Taiwan.

Constraint planning is program in computer system based on constraint rule. The idea of constraint planning is to describe constraints of problem to solve problem and finally find our a scheme which satisfies all constraints. The key of realizing planning and scheduling is resource scheduling based on constraint rule and constraint, and optimizing the plan to reach the goal that you need. ILOG Solver is used to solve the complicated processes like multiple operations, multiple resources etc for dispersed manufacturing; solve ordering problem such as optimizing ordering(Flowshop scheduling) for the manufacturing of repeating type or procedure type . ILOG Solver is a constraint programming language which embeds the process-oriented language. It combines object-oriented programming and constraint logic programming together, includes logic variable and solves problem through increment-type constraint satisfaction and backtracking. The main language components are as follows in ILOG Solver:

```
variables : C ++ object            //variable
    integer variable CtIntVar
```

```
        floating variable CtFloatVar
        boolean variable CtBoolVar
    Memory Management                        // memory management
        new:
        delete:
    Constraints                              // constraint
        CtTell(x == (y + z) );
        Basic constraints: =,¡Ü,¡Ý,<>,+, -,*,/,subset, superset, union,
                intersection, member, boolean or, boolean and, boolean not,
                boolean xor,
        CtTell((x ==0) | | (y ==0));
        CtIfThen (x < 100, x = x+1) ;
        Search                               // search
            CTGOALn: how to execute   CTGOAL1(CtInstantiate, CtIntVar*
x)
            {
            CtInt a = x->chooseValue() ;
            CtOr(Constraint(x == a),
            CtAnd(Constraint(x ! =a),
            CtInstantiate(x) ));
            }
    Schedule                                 // schedule
        CtSchedule class
            Global object: time original ···tineMin
                        time horizon ···timeMax
    Resources                                // resource
            CtResource
            CtDiscreteResource
            CtUnaryResource
            CtDiscreteEnergy
            CtStateResource
    Activities                               // operation
            CtActivity class
            CtIntervalActivity
```

Activity is defined as the start time, end time, time span, operation requiring, providing, consuming and resource production.

Constraint planning has already drawn the high attention of experts of each field, because it is able to solve very difficult problem in reality. No matter we use the advanced genetic algorithm, or use the simulation method of human-computer interaction, we need further study on complex constraint of the manufacturing industry, multi-goals optimization, extensive search and the uncertainty problem of workshop production. Event-based scheduling method is adopted here, in which at least one resource is idle. Two or more operations can use this resource, and OSR (Operation Selection Rule) decides which operation is loaded. OSR is the key factor to determine the quality of planning. Independent operation selection rules are shown in detail as follows:

(1) Early finish date: select early finished operation(maybe order finish date)
(2) Highest priority first: select operation with highest priority(minimum value)
(3) Lowest priority first: select operation with lowest priority(maximum value)
(4) Highest order attribute field: select operation with highest(maximum) attribute field of order
(5) Lowest order attribute field: select operation with lowest(minimum) attribute field of order
(6) Dynamic highest attribute field of order: select operation with dynamic highest(maximum) attribute field of order
(7) Dynamic lowest attribute field of order: select operation with dynamic lowest(minimum) attribute field of order
(8) Planning record order: select operation that first come first served in order
(9) Key rate: select operation with the minimum key rate
  Key rate = planning working time left / (finish date - current date)
(10) Real key rate: select operation with the minimum real key rate
  Real key rate =real working time left / (finish date - current date)
(11) Least remain operation(static): select operation with least remain operation time
(12) Longest waiting time: select operation with the longest waiting time
(13) Shortest waiting time: select operation with the shortest waiting time
(14) Maximum process time: select operation with maximum process time
(15) Minimum process time: select operation with minimum process time
(16) Minimum operation idle time: select operation with minimum idle time idle time of the order =remain finish time - remain working time idle time of operation = idle time of task / remain operation number
(17) Minimum operation idle time: select operation with minimum idle time of order
(18) Minimum remain time of work: select operation with minimum remain work time of order

RSR (Resource Selection Rule) is to select operation to be loaded in which resource of resource group.

(1) Early ending time: select resource first used to finish operation
(2) Early start time: select resource first used to start operation
(3) Latest ending time: select resource last used to finish operation
(4) Same to previous operation: select resource used in previous operation
(5) No-bottleneck early start time: select resource no-bottleneck first used to start operation

Relevant selection rule refers to when an operation selection rule is selected , then corresponding resource selection rules are automatically selected.

(1) Serial circulation order: select operation with the same or the next maximum(minimum) serial value. When there is no operation with maximum serial value, the order will be opposite and select the minimum operation.
(2) Serial decreasing order: select operation with the same or the next minimum serial value
(3) Serial increasing order: select operation with the same or the next maximum serial value
(4) Minimum preparing series: select operation with minimum preparing time and recent serial value
(5) Minimum preparing time: select operation with minimum preparing or changing time
(6) Serial circulation order of time zone: select operation with the same or the next maximum(minimum) serial value. And only consider the operation of the order finished date in the particular time zone. When there is no operation with maximum serial value, the order will be opposite and select the minimum operation.
(7) Serial decreasing order of time zone: select operation with the same or the next minimum serial value . And only consider the operation of the order finished date in the particular time zone.
(8) Serial increasing order of time zone: select operation with the same or the next maximum serial value. And only consider the operation of the order finished date in the particular time zone.
(9) Minimum preparing series of time zone: select operation with minimum preparing time and recent serial value. And only consider the operation of the order finished date in the particular time zone.

(10) Minimum preparing time of time zone: select operation with minimum preparing time or changing time. And only consider the operation of the order finished date in the particular time zone.

The following takes house decoration as an example(see Figure3.1), in which ILOG Scheduler is used to provide the planning scheme in order to describe the solving principles of CSP. Suppose that the start task costs 1000 Yuan each day, and total fund is 20000 Yuan. When the project goes on the 15th day, fund can increase by 9000 Yuan.

Adopt ILOG Scheduler to schedule, the constraint program is as follows:

```
CtSchedule* schedule = new CtSchedule(0, horizon);
// To create an operation with given duration.
CtIntervalActivity* act = new  CtIntervalActivity(schedule, duration);

//To define constraint between act1 and act2.
act2->startsAfterEnd(act1,0);

//To create a total budget of limited funds (here 29000).
CtDiscreteResource* res =
```

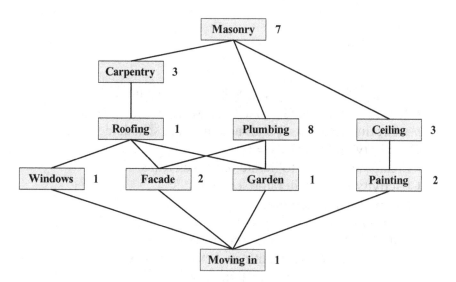

Fig. 3.1. House Decoration Operation

```
new CtDiscreteResource(schedule, CtRequiredResource,capacity);
// To state that only 20000 is available in first 15 days
res->setCapacityMax(0,date,cap);
// To state that an operation act consumes c units of resources.
act->consumes(res, c);

CtBoolean  IsUnScheduled(CtActivity* act){
  // Return true if operation does not have a fixed start time.
  if (act->getStartVariable()->isBound())
     return CtFalse;
  else
     return CtTrue;
}

CtBoolean IsMoreUrgent(CtActivity* act1,
          CtActivity* act2){
  // Returns true if act1 is more urgent than act2.
  // Returns true if act2 is not limited (==0)
  if (act2 == 0)
     return CtTrue;
  else if (act1->getStartMax() < act2->getStartMax())
     return CtTrue;
   else
     return CtFalse;
}

CtActivity* SelectActivity(CtSchedule* schedule){
  // Returns the unscheduled activity with the smallest latest
  // statrt time. Returns 0 if all activities are scheduled.
  CtActivity* bestActivity = 0;
  //Creates an iterator to iterate on all activities.
  CtActivityIterator* iterator(schedule);
  CtActivity* newActivity;
  while(iterator.next(newactivity))
     if((IsUnScheduled(newActivity))
        && (IsMoreUgent(newActivity, bestActivity)))
        bestactivity = newActivity;
  return bestActivity;
}
```

```
void SolveProblem(CtSchedule* schedule){
    // Solve the problem assuming constraints have been posted.
    CtActivity* act = SelectActivity(schedule);
    while (act !=0) {
        act->setStartTime(act->getStartMin());
        act = SelectActivity(schedule);
    }
}
```

ILOG Scheduler solves the above problem, the planning of decoration process is illustrated in Figure 3.2.

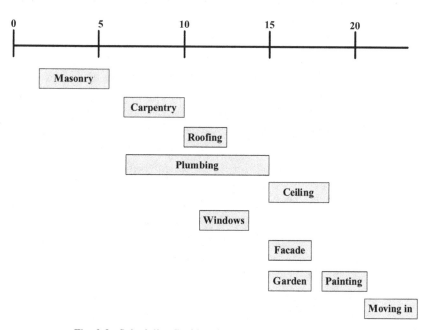

Fig. 3.2. Scheduling Problem in House Decoration

Exercise

1. What is constraint satisfaction problem? What categories can constraint reasoning be divided into?
2. What is arc consistency? Illustrate its asymmetry with examples.
3. Please write constraint propagation AC-1 and AC-3 algorithm, compare the similarities and differences between them.
4. Try to write influence-based backjumping algorithm IBMD using programming language, and test it through N queen's question. Compare it with other constraint algorithms.
5. How make constraint reasoning system COPS can solve symbolic reasoning problem and also do numeric analysis?
6. Write a scheduling system of a workshop with ILOG Solver language.

Chapter 4

Qualitative Reasoning

Qualitative reasoning starting from description of the physical system structure and life system structure, deduces the behavior description in order to predict the systematic behavior and provide the reason. It explains the systematic behavior through local structural rules among the systematic parts, i.e. the transition of behavior of part state only relates to directly adjacent part.

4.1 Introduction

The qualitative reasoning theory in artificial intelligence originates from the study on physical phenomenon. The early works are usually focused on some physical course, such as dynamics, hydrodynamics, thermal current et al. In 1952, Simmons proposed the causality of qualitative analysis. In 1977, Rieger published the paper (Rieger,1977) on simulation of causality. In 1984, Vol. 24 of "Artificial Intelligence" magazine published a special edition of qualitative reasoning, which included the laying foundation papers of de Kleer, Forbus and Kuipers. This indicated that the qualitative reasoning was becoming mature. In 1986, Iwasaki and Simon published paper titled "Causality in Device Behavior"(Iwasaki & Simon,1986). Over the past ten years, these basic approaches have played an important role in the research and application of qualitative reasoning, and make it become one of the most fruitful fields in artificial intelligence. In 1993, Vol. 59 of "Artificial Intelligence" magazine published a group of papers, reviewing these laying foundation works

Different qualitative reasoning approaches have been proposed according to the different structural description of physical systems. Common approaches are qualitative model approach by de Kleer (de Kleer,1984), qualitative process approach by Forbus(Forbus,1984) and qualitative simulation approach by

147

Kuipers(Kuipers,1984). Physical systems involved in De Kleer's qualitative model approach are composed of devices such as the tubes, valves and containers, etc. Constraint conditions (qualitative equations) reflect at the junctions of these devices, giving qualitative explanation according to qualitative equations. In Forbus's qualitative process approach, the change of a physical system is caused by processes and a physical course is described by some processes. Kuipers directly uses the parameters of the part as the state variables to describe the physical structure. Qualitative restraint is generated by the physical law directly. One parameter's changing with time is regarded as the qualitative state array. Solution algorithm proceeds from initial state, produces the follow-up states of different possibility, and then repeats this course through the filtration of consistency until no new state to appear.

Besides above three kinds of basic approaches, there are other research works. Davis has proposed a fault diagnosis approach from the structure description. Reiler has proposed a fault diagnosis approach from basic principle. Williams has built a mixed algebra system Q1, which combines qualitative operation and qualitative reasoning, and has discussed algebra property of it. He has also realized designing qualitative reasoning with qualitative equation. Iwasaki and Simmons have applied causality formalized characteristic and comparatively static approach used in economics and thermodynamics to qualitative causality analysis, and have given a formalized definition to causality. Weld has designed the qualitative simulation program in molecular biology, has found out the circulation appearing repeatedly with cluster approach, and has also discussed the situation of non-continuous quantity through confirming the last state of the system by the analysis of circulation.

4.2 Basic approaches in qualitative reasoning

Human's description or explanation towards physical world usually proceeds with certain intuitive qualitative way. Differential equation and concrete number value are seldom involved. For example, to avoid people's falling down or colliding when riding a bicycle, the motion equations are not necessary. Only intuitive but roughly accurate description according to the changing trend of several main parameters is enough.

Generally, the standard course to analyze the behaviors in motion system can be divided into three steps:

(1) Determine parameters to describe the characters of the target system.

(2) Express the relationship between the parameters with equations.

(3) Analyze these equations and get the number value.

When solving these kinds of behavior problems in motion system with computer, the following three questions will be faced:

(1) Quite a lot of knowledge is required in Step (1) and (2), and corresponding algorithms are also required.

(2) Properties in some target systems are difficult to express in mathematics formulae.

(3) Step (3) can get number value, but the behavior of target system is not distinct.

In order to solve the question (2) and (3), qualitative reasoning usually adopts following analysis steps:

(1) Structure recognition: dividing target system into parts.

(2) Causality analyses: analyzing how target system spreads when input varies.

(3) Behavior reasoning: analyzing how the internal state changes in target system when input varies with time.

(4) Function explanation: The result of behavior reasoning indicates the behaviors of target system, which can explain the function of target system.

On the whole, the idea of qualitative reasoning can understood as:

(1) Grasp the main factor of the described target and neglect the secondary factor in order to simplify the description of the problem.

(2) Disperse the parameter $x(t)$ which varies continuously with time into qualitative value set. Usually the qualitative value $[x]$ of variable x is defined as:

$$[x] = \begin{cases} -, & if \quad x < 0 \\ 0, & if \quad x = 0 \\ +, & if \quad x > 0 \end{cases}$$

(3) Convert the differential equation into qualitative (algebra) equation according to the physical law, or directly build qualitative simulation or qualitative process description according to the physical law.

(4) Provide the qualitative explanation finally.

4.3 Qualitative Model

de Kleer has noticed that symbolic computation and reasoning are the most ideal tool to understand the physical world around people. In 1974, de Kleer participated in the half a year long confusion seminar. A series of familiar but confusing problems were discussed in this seminar, such as rebound, pulley, pendulum and spring, etc. The purpose of this seminar was to study the process of people's thinking and reasoning. While de Kleer left the seminar with totally different subjects. He has found that traditional mathematic and physical equations are useless or necessary in most of the cases. Simple qualitative reasoning can bring satisfying solutions to lots of confusing problems with one or two extremely simple equations at most.

In order to solve classic physical problems, de Kleer has studied what kinds of knowledge are required and how to build up problem solving systems with them. Physical systems involved in his qualitative model approach are composed of devices such as tubes, valves and containers, etc. Constraint conditions (qualitative equations) reflect at the junctions of these devices, giving qualitative explanation according to qualitative equations.

Firstly, variable's qualitative value set and corresponding qualitative operation need to be defined in order to create qualitative algebra equations and differential equations.

The qualitative value set is a discrete set. Its elements are gained by the division of the number axis. Usually number axis $(-\infty,\infty)$ are divided into three sections: $(-\infty,0)$, 0 and $(0, \infty)$. It is stipulated that qualitative value set is $\{-,0,+\}$, and the qualitative value of variable x is defined as following:

$$[x] = \begin{cases} -, & if \quad x < 0 \\ 0, & if \quad x = 0 \\ +, & if \quad x > 0 \end{cases}$$

Besides, ∂x is used to express the qualitative value of dx/dt:

$$\partial x = \left[\frac{dx}{dt} \right]$$

The plus and multiply operations are expressed by $\oplus$ and $\otimes$, which is defined as:

y \ x	-	0	+
-	-	-	?
0	-	0	+
+	?	+	+

$$[x] \oplus [y]$$

Y \ X	-	0	+
-	+	0	-
0	0	0	0
+	-	0	+

$$[x] \otimes [y]$$

Among above definitions, symbol ? denotes uncertain or undefined. Assuming e_1, e_2 are equations, the following gives the operation rules of $\oplus$ and $\otimes$:

$$[0] \oplus [e_1] \Rightarrow [e_1]$$

$$[0] \otimes [e_1] \Rightarrow [0]$$

$$[+] \otimes [e_1] \Rightarrow [e_1]$$

$$[-] \otimes [e_1] \Rightarrow -[e_1]$$

Operator + and × can be converted into $\oplus$ and $\otimes$, using the following rules:

$$[e_1 + e_2] \Rightarrow [e_1] \oplus [e_2]$$

$$[e_1 \times e_2] \Rightarrow [e_1] \otimes [e_2]$$

It is easy to convert common algebra equations and differential equations into qualitative equations. The process of qualitative reasoning is to give explanation with qualitative equations. Now we take the qualitative analysis of the pressure regulator as example to explain the approach of qualitative model reasoning.

The pressure regulator controls the flow valve through spring, so as to make the flow value a certain settled value, and not influenced by the influent flow and the change of load. According to the physics:

$$Q = CA\sqrt{2\frac{P}{\rho}} \qquad P > 0$$

$$\frac{dQ}{dt} C\sqrt{2\frac{P}{\rho}}\frac{dA}{dt} + \frac{CA}{\rho}\sqrt{\frac{\rho}{2P}}\frac{dP}{dt}$$

Among them Q denotes the flow value through the valve, P denotes the pressure, A denotes the area that the valve opens, C is constant coefficient, and ρ denotes quality density of fluid. Qualitative equations are gained according to the operation and convert rules:

$$[Q] = [P]$$
$$\partial Q = \partial A + \partial P \qquad (\text{if } A > 0)$$

We can also build up related qualitative equations according to the physical rules such as consistency and continuity, etc. Then we can get qualitative explanation by these qualitative equations. The regulator is described with three special states: OPEN state, WORKING state and CLOSE state:

OPEN state	A = Amax	Qualitative equation	[P] = 0	$\partial P = 0$
WORKING state	0<A<Amax	Qualitative equation	[P] = [Q]	$\partial P + \partial A = \partial Q$
CLOSED state	A = 0	Qualitative equation	[Q] = 0	$\partial Q = 0$

Besides discussing the qualitative analyses of each state, we can also discuss the qualitative analyses of states variation. De Kleer has built ENVSION system using constraint propagation and producing testing approach for qualitative equations solution.

4.4 Qualitative Process

The qualitative process reasoning proposed by Forbus describes physical phenomenon as some related processes. Each process is described as a set of individuals, preconditions, quantity conditions, parameter relations and influences. Reasoning process sequentially chooses some useful processes from the known process table to describe a physical phenomenon. Following is the key idea about qualitative physics in qualitative process theory:

(1) The organizational principle is the physical process. Ontology plays an important role in the organization of knowledge. The physical process is very intuitive when people carry out reasoning on physical system. So it is sound to organize the theory in physical field with it.
(2) Express number value with the sequence relation. The important property difference often comes from comparing. For example, flowing is produced when the pressure and temperature are different, phase transformation occurs when temperature reaches a certain critical value, etc. Under many circumstances, it is more natural to express number value with a set of ordinal relations.
(3) The single assumption mechanism. The physical process is regarded as the mechanism to produce variation. So any variation must be interpreted as the direct or indirect influence of some physical processes. Process ontology has laid the foundation in the causality of the qualitative physical theory.
(4) Combined qualitative mathematics. When people carry out reasoning on complicated systems, part of information is used and combined up.
(5) Clear expression and reasoning on model assumption. Clearly expressing the applicable condition of some particular knowledge and modeling particular system from field theory have become the central tasks of qualitative physics.

The variation of a physical system is caused by process. A physical process is described with some processes. That is the basic idea of qualitative process reasoning approach. Following introduces the description of quantity space and process in qualitative process reasoning.

1. Quantity Space

(1) Time is expressed by intervals. The relations between intervals are before, after and equal. Two intervals can be joined. Moment is regarded as extremely short, whose duration is zero.

(2) The object parameter is called Quantity, which is composed of its amount and derivative.

①A_m expresses the amount value of the quantity, A_s expresses the symbol of the quantity.

②D_m expresses the derivative value of the quantity, D_s expresses the symbol of the quantity derivative.

③(MQ_t) expresses the value of quantity Q at the moment t.

④HAS-Quantity is a predicate, which means some object has some parameter.

(3) All the possible values of a quantity compose the quantity space, and there are semi-order relations among the elements of the quantity space.

If $Q_1 = f(Q_2)$ increases monotonically, Q_1 and Q_2 are qualitatively in direct proportion, which is denoted by $Q_1 \propto Q_+ Q_2$. If $Q_1 = f(Q_2)$ decreases monotonically, Q_1 and Q_2 are qualitatively in inversely proportion, which is denoted by $Q_1 \propto Q_- Q_2$.

2. Process

A physical process are composed of a set of individuals, a set of preconditions, a set of quantity conditions, a set of parameter relations and a set of influences. A specific instance of a process is called process instance, which is denoted by PI.

Influence refers to those which can cause the parameter variation. Influence can be classified into direct influence and indirect influence. If a process influences quantity Q at certain moment, say Q is influenced directly. If count n influences Q directly and influence is positive, or negative, or zero, we denote it with $1+(Q, n)$, or $1-(Q, n)$, or $1\pm(Q, n)$. When quantity Q is the function of other quantity, say Q is influenced indirectly, such as qualitative proportional $\propto Q$. Process table refers to all the possible processes in one field.

In the approach of process reasoning, a physical course can be described with some processes. Following explains the working principle of this approach, taking process of heat flow as example:

Process heat-flow.	// process of heat flow
Individuals:	//a set of individuals
src an object, Has-Quantity(src, heat)	//src is heat source
dst an object, Has-Quantity(dst, heat)	// dst is the object being heated
path a heat-path,	//path is heat flow path
Heat-connection(path, src, dst)	//connect src with dst

Preconditions: //a set of preconditions
   Heat-Aligned(path)   //align heat flow path
Quantity Conditions: //a set of quantity conditions
   A[temperature(src)]>A[temperature(dst)] //src'temperature>dst's temperature
Relations: //a set of relations
   Let flow-rate be a quantity   //flow-rate is a quantity
   A[flow-rate] > ZERO.   //flow-rate >0
   flow-rate $\propto Q+$ (temperature(src) -temperature(dst))
      //flow-rate is proportional with the difference of src and dst
Influences: //a set of influences
   1-(heat(src), A[flow-rate])   //flow-rate's negative influence on heat(src)
   1+(heat (dst), A[flow-rate])   // flow-rate's positive influence on heat(dst)

3. Deduction process

Following is the deduction process in qualitative process reasoning:

(1) Select the process. For a set of known individuals, find out the possible process instance PI in the process table according to the individual illustration of each process.

(2) Confirm the activated PI. Confirm the state of each PI in accordance with the precondition, quantity condition. Those which meet these conditions are activated PI. Activated PI is called the process structure.

(3) Confirm the variation of quantity. The individual's variation is expressed by Ds value of corresponding quantity. The variation of quantity can be influenced directly by the process, and can also be influenced indirectly by $\propto Q$.

(4) Confirm the structural variation of process. Variation of quantity will cause the variation of process structure. Confirming this kind of variation is also called restraint analyses. Then the description of a physical process steps from the PI built in (1) into next PI.

   Repeat steps (1)—(4) then a series of process description of a physical process is obtained.

   Restraint analyses is to confirm the quantity variation in the quantity space according to Ds value. Firstly find the neighbor of the current quantity in the quantity space. If it is a restraint one, some processes will be stopped and some will begin. All the possible variations of the semi-order relations concerned with the restraint quantity confirm the variation path of the current activated process.

Here we explain the deduction course of process approach, taking the process description of boiler heating process as example. Boiler has a container full of water. The cover of the boiler is sealed when heating. Fire is the heat source. The boiler will explode when the pressure in the container exceeds p-burst(CAN), assuming that the temperature of the heat source does not changed.

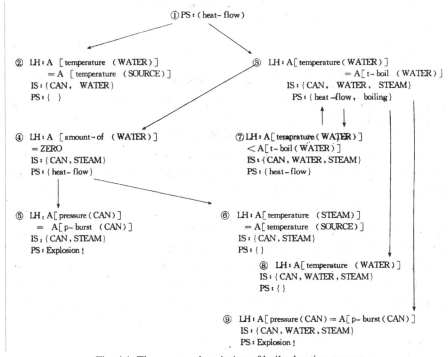

Fig. 4.1. The process description of boiler heating process

Fig 4.1 gives the process description of boiler heating process, among which PS is the process structure, LH is the restraint assumption, IS is the individual. Following is the process explanation of the boiler heating process.

When begins from ①, process structure only contains hear-flow, which ② and ③ can be derived from. In ②, the temperature of water equals to the temperature of heat source, then the process of heat-flow ends. In ③, water begins to boil, which can be described by processes of heat-flow and boiling. Then ④, ⑦, ⑧, ⑨ can occur. In ④, water dries out, which can derive the explosion process in ⑤ or the end when the steam temperature reaches the heat source temperature in ⑥. In ⑦, water boils which makes the pressure rise and the boiling point improve. The process returns to ③ because the water temperature is lower than the boiling point. In ⑧, the process ends because the water temperature reaches the heat source temperature. In ⑨, the pressure in the container is too high, which is described by process p-burst(CAN), and explosion occurs.

4.5 Qualitative Simulation Reasoning

Kuipers published thesis titled "Common sense reasoning about causality: deriving behavior from structure" in 1984. In this paper, a framework of qualitative simulation reasoning is built, the qualitative structure and the qualitative behavior express approach, which are abstracted from ordinary differential equation, are briefly proposed. Subsequently, his thesis titled "Qualitative Simulation" was published in AI magazine in 1986. In this paper, the abstract relation is definite and a QSIM algorithm used for qualitative simulation is proposed. The validity and incompleteness of the algorithm are proved by abstract relation. These two papers have established the foundation of qualitative simulation.

Qualitative simulation derives the behavior description from the qualitative description of the structure. It directly uses the parameters of the part as state variables to describe the physical structure. Qualitative constraints are obtained directly from the physical law. The variation of a parameter with time is regarded as the qualitative state sequence. The solving algorithm proceeds from the initial state, generates each possible subsequent state, and then repeats this process with consistent filtration until no new state appears.

The structure description of qualitative simulation is composed of systematic state parameters and constraint relations. Parameters are regarded as the differentiable function of time. Constraints are the binary or multi- relations. For example, the derivative of speed is acceleration, which is expressed by DERIV(Vel,acc). f = ma is expressed by MULT(m,a,f). The monotone increasing of f with g is expressed by $M^+(f,g)$. The monotone decreasing of f with g is expressed by $M^-(f,g)$.

Behavior description cares about the variation of parameters. Assuming parameter f(t) is a differentiable function from [a, b] to $[-\infty, \infty]$, the landmark value of f is a finite set, which at least contains f(a) and f(b), and the element in set {t|t ∈ [a,b] ∧ f(t) is landmark value} is called differentiated point.lj

Definition 4.1   *Assuming $l_1<l_2<\cdots<l_k$ are the landmark values of $f: [a,b] \rightarrow[-\infty, \infty]$, for any $t \in [a,b]$, the qualitative state QS(f,t) of f in t is regulated as ordered pare, which is defined as following:*

$$qval = \begin{cases} l_j, & f_t = l_j \\ (l_j, l_{j+1}), & f_t \in (l_j, l_{j+1}) \end{cases}$$

$$qdir = \begin{cases} inc, & f'(t) > 0 \\ std, & f'(t) = 0 \\ dec, & f'(t) < 0 \end{cases}$$

Definition 4.2   *Assuming t_i, t_{i+1} are adjacent differentiating points, the qualitative state QS(f, t_i, t_{i+1}) of f in (t_i,t_i+1) is regulated as*

$$QS(f,t), \qquad t\in(t_i,t_{i+1}) \tag{4.1}$$

Definition 4.3   Assuming the qualitative behaviors of f in [a,b] are qualitative states sequence QS(f,t_0), QS(f,t_0,t_1), QS(f, t_1), $\cdots$,QS(f, t_n), among them t_i(i=0,1,$\cdots$,n) indicate all the differentiating points and $t_i < t_{i+1}$, if F = {$f_1, \cdots, f_n$}, the qualitative behaviors of F are

$$QS(F,t_i) = \{ QS(f_1,t_i), \cdots, QS(f_n,t_i)\} \tag{4.2}$$
$$QS(F,t_i,t_{i+1}) = \{ QS(f_1,t_i,t_{i+1}), \cdots, QS(f_n,t_i,t_{i+1})\} \tag{4.3}$$

Among them ti are the elements of the union of $f_1, \cdots, f_k$.

4.5.1 *Qualitative state transformation*

Qualitative state transformation often occurs in qualitative simulation. Assuming *f* is a differentiable function, it must obey the intermediate value theorem and mean value theorem when transforming from one qualitative state to another qualitative state. There are two kinds of qualitative state transformation: one is P transformation, which transforms from time point to time interval, another is I transformation, which transforms from time interval to time point. Following gives the transformation table:

P transformation	$QS(f,t_i)$	$\Rightarrow$	$QS(f,t_i,t_{i+1})$
P_1	$<l_j,std>$	$\Rightarrow$	$<l_j,std>$
P_2	$<l_j,std>$	$\Rightarrow$	$<(l_j,l_{j+1}),inc>$
P_3	$<l_j,std>$	$\Rightarrow$	$<(l_{j-1},l_j),dec>$
P_4	$<l_j,inc>$	$\Rightarrow$	$<(l_j,l_{j+1}),inc>$
P_5	$<(l_j,l_{j+1}),inc>$	$\Rightarrow$	$<(l_j,l_{j+1}),inc>$
P_6	$<l_j,dec>$	$\Rightarrow$	$<(l_{j-1},l_j),dec>$
P_7	$<(l_j,l_{j+1}),dec>$	$\Rightarrow$	$<(l_j,l_{j-1}),dec>$

I transformation	$QS(f,t_i,t_{i+1})$	$\Rightarrow$	$QS(f,t_{i+1})$
I_1	$<l_j,std>$	$\Rightarrow$	$<l_j,std>$
I_2	$<(l_j,l_{j+1}),inc>$	$\Rightarrow$	$<l_{j+1},std>$
I_3	$<(l_j,l_{j+1}),inc>$	$\Rightarrow$	$<l_{j+1},inc>$
I_4	$<(l_j,l_{j+1}),inc>$	$\Rightarrow$	$<(l_j,l_{j+1}),inc>$
I_5	$<(l_j,l_{j+1}),dec>$	$\Rightarrow$	$<l_j,std>$
I_6	$<(l_j,l_{j+1}),dec>$	$\Rightarrow$	$<l_j,dec>$
I_7	$<(l_j,l_{j+1}),dec>$	$\Rightarrow$	$<(l_j,l_{j+1}),dec>$
I_8	$<(l_j,l_{j+1}),inc>$	$\Rightarrow$	$<l^*,std>$
I_9	$<(l_j,l_{j+1}),dec>$	$\Rightarrow$	$<l^*,std>$

Among them l^* is the new landmark value, $l_j <l^*< l_{j+1}$.

4.5.2 QSIM algorithm

QSIM algorithm can simulate the system behaviors. Send the initial state into ACTIVE table at first, then repeat (1)—(6) until ACTIVE table is empty.

Algorithm 4.1 QSIM algorithm

1. Choose one state from ACTIVE table.

2. For each parameter, find all possible transformation according to the transformation table.

3. Create set of binary group and ternary group according to the constraint variable transformation and make consistent filtering according to constraint relationship.

4. Combine tuples according to the public variable constraint, then make consistent filtering to the combined tuples.

5. Generate all the possible public explanation from the residual tuples. Each explanation generates a new state as the subsequent state of the current state.

6. Make public filtering to the new states, then send the residual states to the ACTIVE table.

Following states are excluded by public filtering:

- No change state: such as I_1, I_4, I_7

- Cycle state: new state is same to a former state

- Divergent state: one parameter value is ∞, which means the current time point is the finish point.

Here we take the qualitative simulation of process of throwing ball up as example to explain QSIM algorithm, Assuming that the height of the ball is Y, speed is V and acceleration is A .

Known constraint relationship are:

$$DERIV(Y,V)$$
$$DERIV(V,A)$$
$$A(t)=g<0$$

Ball moves up in initial state(t_0,t_1):

$$QS(A,t_0,t_1)=<g, std>$$
$$QS(V,t_0,t_1)=<(0,\infty),dec>$$
$$QS(Y,t_0,t_1)=<(0,\infty),inc>$$

Make all possible transformation to each parameter. I transformation is needed because it is in the time interval now:

A	I_1	<g, std>	⇒	<g, std>
V	I_5	<(0,∞),dec>	⇒	<0,std>
	I_6	<(0,∞),dec>	⇒	<0,dec>
	I_7	<(0,∞),dec>	⇒	<(0,∞),dec>
	I_9	<(0,∞),dec>	⇒	$<l^*,std>$
Y	I_4	<(0,∞),inc>	⇒	<(0,∞),inc>
	I_8	<(0,∞),inc>	⇒	$<l^*,std>$

Following creates tuple set according to constraint. Make consistent filtering to single constraint at first. Those filtered here are denoted by C. Then combine the tuples and make consistent filtering to them. Those filtered here are denoted by W.

According to DERIV(Y,V):

(I_4,I_5)	C	(I_8,I_5)	W
(I_4,I_6)	C	(I_8,I_6)	
(I_4,I_7)		(I_8,I_7)	C
(I_4,I_9)	W	(I_8,I_9)	C

According to DERIV(V,A):

(I_5,I_1)	C	(I_7,I_1)	
(I_6,I_1)		(I_9,I_1)	C

Among that, in tuple(I_4,I_5), I_4 makes the qualitative state of Y transit to $<(0,\infty),inc>$, while I_5 makes the qualitative state of V transit to $<0,std>$, which is not consistent with constraint(Y,V). So (I_4,I_5) is filtered out. The I_9 in tuple (I_4,I_9) and (I_9,I_1) are both the transitions to V . As (I_9,I_1) has already been filtered out, (I_4,I_9) is also filtered out.

The left tuples have formed two global explanations as following:

Y	V	A
I_4	I_7	I_1
I_8	I_6	I_1

The first explanation has no transition and is filtered out. The second explanation is the only subsequent state. Now:

$$QS(A,t_1)=<g, std>$$
$$QS(V,t_1)=<0,dec>$$
$$QS(Y,t_1)=<Y_{max},std>$$

Among that, Y_{max} is the new landmark value.

4.6 Algebra Approach

Williams has built a mixed algebra combined qualitative with quantitative and realized the corresponding symbol algebra program MINIMA, which is the qualitative simulation of MACSYMA , providing a tool for simplifying, decomposing and combining qualitative equations(Williams, 1988). The design of one kind of physical problems can be handled by this algebra system.

This algebra system is defined upon real number R and symbol S' = {+,-,0,?}, allowing quantitative operations in R and qualitative operations in S', such as +, -, × and / operations in R ; $\oplus$, $\Downarrow$, $\otimes$ and $\oslash$ operations in S' and qualitative operator [] . Commutative law, associative law and distributive law are all tenable , except that $\oplus$ has no inverse element in [S', $\oplus$, $\otimes$] . So:

$$s \oplus u = t \oplus u \quad \not\Rightarrow \quad s = t$$
$$s \oplus t = u \quad \not\Rightarrow \quad s = u \Downarrow t$$

This system can be used for designing. For example, there are an auto loaded drinking bottle and a drinking storage container. A device is required to change the liquid height of the bottle and the container. So when the liquid height H of the bottle drops, the bottle can get drinking supply from the container. This design process can be assumed directly as that:

The rise or drop of the liquid height H_b is decided by the drinking flux Q_b. The pressure P of container bottom is in proportion to the drinking density, namely, pressure is decided by height. It is required that when the pressure of the bottle decreases in relation to the pressure of the container. Drinking flows to the bottle from the container. Obviously, the required device can be implemented by a pipe between the bottle and the container. The reasoning process of this design involves not only the value and qualitative symbol but also the accurate relationship in some place.

The mentioned mixed algebra can be used to describe and this problem. MINIMA system can automatically deal with this problem.

Object $H_v - H_b = [\dfrac{d}{dt} H_b]$

$H_b \times A_b = V_b$ //container model, the drinking volume is the product of sectional area and height

$H_b = V_b / A_b$

$H_v - H_b = [\dfrac{d}{dt}(\dfrac{V_b}{A_b})]$

$H_v - H_b = [(\dfrac{d}{dt} V_b)/ A_b]$

$H_v - H_b = [(\dfrac{d}{dt} V_b)] \oslash [A_b]$

$[A_b] = [+]$ //container model

$[H_v - H_b] = [\dfrac{d}{dt}V_b]$

$Q_b = \dfrac{d}{dt}V_b$ //container model

$[H_v - H_b] = [Q_b]$

$P_v = d \times g \times H_v$ //container model, the pressure is the product of density, gravity acceleration and height

$H_v = P_v /(d \times g)$

$[P_v /(d \times g) - H_b] = [Q_b]$

$P_b = d \times g \times H_b$ //container model

$H_b = P_b /(d \times g)$

$[P_v /(d \times g)- P_b /(d \times g)] = [Q_b]$

$[P_v - P_b] \oslash ([d] \times [g]) = [Q_b]$

$[d] = [+]$ drinking property

$[g] = [+]$ gravity property

$[P_v - P_b] \oslash ([+]\otimes [+]) = [Q_b]$

$[P_v - P_b] = [Q_b]$

The last expression is exactly the relationship of the pressure of both ends of a pipe and flow. So, only one pipe is required to link the bottle and the container.

4.7 Spatial Geometric Qualitative Reasoning

Spatial qualitative reasoning is to carry out qualitative reasoning with geometric shape or movement property. First it is needed to qualitatively express the spatial location and movement style, and then carry out reasoning research and predicted analyse about geometric shape and movement property, finally give the logical explanation. Spatial qualitative reasoning is carried out through defining a group of space and looking for their relationship. Major research at present is to develop explanation theory focused on spatial qualitative modeling approach, spatial shape, qualitative express of relationship and qualitative technologies formalization, etc. But it is still far from solving engineer problems in general. Now express logic of space, time and continuous movement has been built up combining Allen's temporal logic (Allen,1984) with Randall's spatial logic(Randall,1992).

Besides, the spatial planning theory derived from spatial qualitative reasoning can be used in distributed design which looks for a group of satisfying constraints for a group of geometric objects. Related approaches are mainly used in the fields of automatic design and qualitative modeling, etc. Some results that are of practical significance have been gained in this field, such as solving theory of constraint satisfaction problems (CSP). In fact, lots of spatial qualitative planning are geometric constraint satisfaction problems.

4.7.1 *Spatial logic*

The main task to carry out geometric simulation about spatial geometric object and its movement is to produce envisionment about its possible states. Envisionment is to model the system and generate spanning tree of its possible states. There are two kinds of envisionment, total envisionment and attainable envisionment. Attainable envisionment is to build the possible state spanning tree from some special states for the modeling system. While total envisionment can generate all the possible states of the system (Cui,1992).

In 1992, Randell, etc, have built up RCC spatial temporal logic in order to carry out stainable envisionment about spatial problem, which has been realized. Similar to QSIM approach of Kuipers, the simulation algorithm based on RCC logic begins with structural description of the system. Initial state is considered as the root node of spanning tree. Possible behaviors are the paths from the root node to the leaf node in the tree.

The foundation of spatial logic is to assume a primitive binary relation C(x,y). Among that, x and y indicate two regions and predicate C indicates sharing more than one public point, which means touching each other and is of reflexivity and symmetry.

1. The definitions of eight basic relations

With relation $C(x,y)$, a group of basic binary relation can be defined as:

(1) DC(x,y): indicating the two regions don't have touch with each other.
(2) EC(x,y): indicating the two regions have external touch with each other.
(3) PO(x,y): indicating the tow regions partly cover with each other.
(4) = (x,y):   indicating the tow regions are totally the same.
(5) TPP(x,y): indicating x is a strict part of y and they are tangent(inside).
(6) NTPP(x,y): indicating x is a strict part of y but they don't touch each other.

(7) $TPP^{-1}(x,y)$:   indicating y is a strict part of x and they are tangent.

(8) $NTPP^{-1}(x,y)$: indicating y is a strict part of x and they don't touch each other.

The definition of these eight relation can be constructed by $C(x,y)$ and some assistant description functions, which have used some transitional state predicates such as $P(x,y)$ (partly belong to), $PP(x,y)$(strictly partly belong to), $O(x,y)$(cover), etc.

2. The connections between the basic relations

This spatial logic is similar to the Allen's logic, which also expresses the possible connections between binary relations with the pre-calculated transitivity table. With any relation $R_3(a,c)$ in the table, all the possible binary relations $R_1(a,b)$ and $R_2(b,c)$ can be found out. This table is useful to qualitative simulation. While recent research hasn't given the building algorithm of the transitivity table. But Randell has mentioned that his simulation program has used this table to verify the consistency of state description during envisionment process.

Besides, the relation between geometric object and geometric area is expressed by function space(x,t). It denotes that the geometric area occupied by geometric object x at the moment of t is space(x,t). t can be ignored regardless of time. Usually, in order to simplify operation, variable x is directly used to express the geometric area occupied by geometric object x if there is no different meanings.

3. The transition between the basic relations

According to the shapes of the two regions, the eight basic relations mentioned above can be divided into six subsets:

(1)   DC   EC   PO   =
(2)   DC   EC   PO   TPP
(3)   DC   EC   PO TPP^{-1}
(4)   DC   EC   PO   TPP   NTPP
(5)   DC   EC   PO TPP^{-1} $NTPP^{-1}$
(6)   DC   EC   PO

The division of the six subsets can be understood as: If the shapes of two geometric areas are totally the same, the way they exist in the space can only be the four situations listed in subset (1). If there are a sphere and a hemisphere with same radius, their relations can only be the situations listed in subset (2). The relations between a disk with radius R and a column with radius R/2 can only be the three situations listed in subset (6).

It is worth notice that subset (3) and (5) are respectively the reverse set of subset (4) and (5). That is if x and y are two space area, their shapes determine that the set composed of their possible relations $R(x,y)$ is subset (2). Then when we take into account the relation $R(y,x)$, the result set is subset (3). So we can believe that from (1) to (2), (3), then (4), (5), finally (6) reflects the relation of shapes of the two geometric areas from specialization to common.

Then we can make two shape-changeless areas move in the space and change their relations. The change is only restricted to the following four sequences:

(1)   DC $\leftrightarrow$ EC $\leftrightarrow$ PO $\leftrightarrow$ =
(2)   DC $\leftrightarrow$ EC $\leftrightarrow$ PO $\leftrightarrow$ TPP(TPP^{-1})
(3)   DC $\leftrightarrow$ EC $\leftrightarrow$ PO $\leftrightarrow$ TPP(TPP^{-1}) $\leftrightarrow$ NTPP(NTPP^{-1})
(4)   DC $\leftrightarrow$ EC $\leftrightarrow$ PO

4.7.2 Temporal spatial relation

1. Position state and motion state

The eight RCC relations are classified into position state and motion state by Galton. He has given the classification definition with some logical forms about temporal relation by Allen. First we introduce the concepts, predicates, and functions used by Calton.

(1) The described time is divided into interval and moment.
(2) The described predicate of state exists:
    Holds-on(s,i) indicates state s exists on interval i.
Holds-at(s,t) indicates state s exists at moment t.
(3) Predicate Div(t,i) indicates moment t is in interval i.
(4) Function inf(i) indicates the beginning moment of interval i.
(5) Function sup(i) indicates the ending moment of interval i.

Definition 4.4   *Position state: if state s satisfies*

$$\forall i \, (\text{Holds-on}(s,i)) \rightarrow \text{Holds-at}(s,\inf(i)) \wedge \text{Holds-at}(s,\sup(i))$$

That is, if state s exists on interval i, the state exists at both the beginning moment and the ending moment of this interval. State with this property is called position state.

Definition 4.5 *Motion state: if state s satisfies*

$$\forall t\,(\text{Holds-at}(s,t) \rightarrow \exists i\,(\text{Div}(t,i) \wedge \text{Holds-on}(s,i)))$$

That is, if state s exists at moment t, there must be an interval containing this moment which s exists on. State with this property is called motion state.

Then the above eight basic relations can be classified into:

Position state: EC, =, TPP, TPP^{-1}

Motion state: DC, PO, NTPP, NTPP^{-1}

The two kinds of states can be distinguished by their performance: Position state is critical and motion state is steady.

2. Perturbation principle

Galton has proposed the perturbation principle according to this classification, which is an axiom system describing how spatial states transit on the temporal interval.

Definition 4.6 *Perturbation: if RCC relation R and R' satisfies*

$$\exists\,t(\text{Holds-at}(R(a,b),t) \wedge (\exists\,i(\text{Holds-on}(R'(a,b),i)) \wedge (\inf(i)=t) \vee (\sup(i)=t)))))$$

That is, if there are a state R at moment t and an interval i which begins or ends at t. R' is the state on i. Then R and R' are the perturbations of each other.

Perturbation principle: Each RCC relation is the perturbation of itself. And one static state can only have one motive state that they are the perturbation of each other, vice versa (Only rigid body is involved).

Assuming R is a RCC state, $R_1, R_2, ..., R_n$ are the all perturbations of R. There are six axioms according to perturbation principle.

(A1) $\text{Holds-on}(R(a,b),i) \rightarrow \vee_{i=1}^{n} \text{Holds-at}(R_i(a,b),\sup(i))$;

(A2) $\text{Holds-on}(R(a,b),i) \rightarrow \vee_{i=1}^{n} \text{Holds-at}(R_i(a,b),\inf(i))$;

(A3) $\text{Holds-at}(R(a,b),t) \rightarrow \exists t' \vee_{i=1}^{n} \text{Holds-on}(R_i(a,b),(t,t'))$;

(A4) $\text{Holds-at}(R(a,b),t) \rightarrow \exists t' \vee_{i=1}^{n} \text{Holds-on}(Ri(a,b),(t',t))$;

(A5) $\text{Holds-on}(s,(t_1,t_2)) \wedge \neg\text{Holds-at}(s,t_3) \wedge t_2 < t_3 \rightarrow \exists t\,\text{Holds-on}(s,(t_1,t)) \wedge$

$\forall t'$ $(t < t' \rightarrow \neg$Holds-on$(s,(t,t'))))$;

(A6) Holds-on$(s,(t_2,t_3)) \wedge \neg$Holds-at$(s,t_1)$ $\wedge t_1 <t_2 \rightarrow \exists t$ Holds-on$(s,(t_1,t_2)) \wedge \forall t'$ $(t < t' \rightarrow \neg$Holds-on$(s,(t',t_2))))$.

Axioms (A1) and (A2) indicate that if there is a relation R on the interval i, there must be a perturbation relation of R , which exists at the beginning moment or the ending moment of this interval.

Axioms (A3) and (A4) indicate that if there is a relation R at the moment t, there must be moment t'_1 and moment t'_2, which makes the perturbation relation of R respectively exists on (t'_1,t) and (t,t'_2).

Axioms (A5) and (A6) indicate that if there is a state s on the interval (t_1,t_2) and it no longer exists at moment t_3, there must be a moment t in $(t_2,t_3)(t_3 > t_2)$ or $(t_3,t_1)(t_3 < t_1)$ at which the state of s transits.

4.7.3. Applications of temporal and spatial logic

The above axioms system can be used in the reasoning about the relations of spatial objects. For example, if it is known that DC(a,b) exists at moment t_1 , PO(a,b) exists at moment t_2 and $t_1 < t_2$, it must be a moment t in (t_1,t_2), at which EC(a,b) exists. That is:

$$\text{Holds-at(DC}(a,b),t_1) \wedge \text{Holds-at(PO}(a,b),t_2) \wedge t_1 < t_2 \rightarrow$$
$$t(\text{div}(t,(t_1,t_2))) \wedge \text{Holds-at(EC}(a,b),t))$$

These theories can also be used to description and reasoning about events. Predicates are introduced:

Occurs-at (T,t) indicates event T occurred at tieme t.

Occurs-on (T,i) indicates event T occurred on interval i.

Function Trans(R_1,R_2) indicates the event that state R_1 transits to state R_2.

The two predicates connect event with time. Function Trans builds mapping relations between state and event. Galton has classified event into seven kinds:

(1) R_1 is position state, R_2 is motion state, R_2 is the perturbation of R_1 .
(2) R_1 is motion state, R_2 is position state, R_2 is the perturbation of R_1 .
(3) R_1 and R_2 which have same perturbation R_3 are motion states.
(4) R_1 and R_2 which have no same perturbation are motion states.
(5) R_1 and R_2 are all position states.
(6) R_1 is position state, R_2 is motion state, but they are not the perturbation of each other.

(7) R_1 is motion state, R_2 is position state, but they are not the perturbation of each other.

The occurring situation of each event can be described with above logic. In fact, (1) and (2) can only be instantaneous. That is, it occurs at one moment. (4),(5),(6) and (7) can only be continuous. That is, it occurs on one interval. (3) can be instantaneous or continuous. The event occurring and condition have been discussed in (Galton,1993) in detail.

4.7.4. Randell algorithm

Randell's simulation program begins with initial state, generates all the possible state spanning trees according to the constraints and rules, then gives the behavior description, prediction, and explanation (Cui,1992). This approach is similar to the QSIM of Kuipers. Constraints can be classified into two classes: interstate and interstate. For example, an amoeba has eaten food. The food has been part of the amoeba. So this state will keep on. This is a constraint between states. The constraints between states, expressed directly by clause Φ, have the following form:

$$\Phi(R_o \Rightarrow (R_1 \vee R_2 \cdots \vee R_n))$$

or

$$\Phi(R_o \Rightarrow (R_1 \vee R_2 \cdots \vee R_n))$$

The above two expressions respectively indicate that if state Ro occurs, the subsequent state must be $(R_1 \vee R_2 \cdots \vee R_n)$,or the subsequent state must not be $(R_1 \vee R_2 \cdots \vee R_n)$.

Randell has also introduced adding rule and deleting rule in the simulation program. Adding rule is that system will import one object in the next state, and deleting rule conversely. For example, once amoeba eats food, a vacuole will be added. Once vacuole is full of waste and rejected, it will be deleted.

(1) The express approach to add rule is:

add $O_1,O_2, \cdots ,O_n$ with ψ_1 when ψ_2,
That is when ψ_2 is established,$O_1,O_2,...,O_n$ are added to the system and ψ_1 is founded.
(2) The express approach to delete rule is:
delete $O_1,O_2, \cdots ,O_n$ when ψ_2,

That is when $\psi 2$ is established, delete $O_1, O_2, \cdots, O_n$.

Algorithm 4.2 Randell algorithm. Assuming initial state S_0 has been put into states set S :

1. stop if S is empty;
2. choose state S_i from S and remove it;
3. go to step 2 if S_i is an inconsistent state;
4. apply state constraint and choose usable transition rule;
5. generate next possible states set with selected rules;
6. apply adding and deleting rules;
7. check constraint between states;
8. add the left states to S and go to step 1.

Exercises

1. What is the meaning of qualitative, what is qualitative reasoning?
2. Simply describe some basic qualitative reasoning approaches.
3. What kind of problem is to be solved by qualitative reasoning approach, describe its analyse steps.
4. Please describe the boiler heating process with qualitative process.
5. Qualitative simulation reasoning is a relatively important qualitative reasoning architecture, please simply describe its basic approach.
6. Try to compare the qualitative reasoning based on algebra and geometry.
7. Qualitative reasoning has been actually implemented in economy analysis and prediction, please consulting data and study a qualitative reasoning system.

Chapter 5

Case-Based Reasoning

5.1 Overview

In order to solve a new problem, we often recall and search in memory to find similar problems that have been successfully solved, and reuse the knowledge required in these problems' solving to solve the new problems. For example, a doctor treats a patient by recalling another person who exhibited similar symptoms.

The new problem at hand is termed as target case, while the previous problems and their solutions in memory are base cases. Briefly speaking, case-based reasoning (CBR for short) solves new problems by adapting previously successful solutions to similar problems.

A case is a contextualized piece of knowledge representing an experience. It contains the past lesson that is the content of the case and the context in which the lesson can be used (Kolodner,1993). Specifically speaking, a case should have the following characteristics:

(1) A case contains implicitly some concrete knowledge related to a certain context; this kind of knowledge is usually concerned with how to do something.
(2) Cases can be of all kinds, in different forms, and with different granularities. They can contain time slices large or small, effects of the application of solution.
(3) Useful experiences are coded in cases. These experiences are helpful for the reasoners to reach the goal more easily, or predicate the possibility of failure.

Case-Based Reasoning (CBR) is a relatively developed branch in Artificial Intelligence. It is a kind of reasoning based on previously practical experiences. From traditional point of view, reasoning is a process of conclusion drawing by "cause-effect" chains, which has been used by many expert systems. CBR is a quiet different view, in which knowledge is implicitly contained in cases, not in the form of rules explicitly. These cases record all sorts of relevant contexts in the past. CBR solves new problems by adapting previously successful solutions to similar problems, rather than by a reasoning chain. For a new problem, CBR retrieves the most relevant case from memory or in the case base, and then does some revision to the case to produce a suitable solution to the present problem.

CBR is rational because there are two characteristics in the reality: regulation and repetition. Wholly speaking, there are certain regulations exist in the world, and actions happening under similar conditions will produce the similar results. As it goes, "reality takes shape in the memory alone", and the past experiences may carry some hints to the future.

The researches on CBR originate from the investigations on the mechanism of reasoning and learning from a cognitive perspective. From the children's simple activity to experts' cautious decision, human affairs are usually accomplished with the help of people's recollection unconsciously or consciously. The mankind often acts according to experiences, and people are intelligent systems in some sense, so it is intuitive to applying such kind of reasoning based on experiences to researches and applications of Artificial Intelligence. Generally speaking, CBR has made the following contributions to Artificial Intelligence:

(1) knowledge acquisition: This is a difficult process, often referred to as the *knowledge acquisition bottleneck* in knowledge-based systems. The most challenges to implement knowledge-based systems are the elicitation of an explicit model of the domain and the implementation of knowledge often in the form of rules, which require teamwork between domain experts and knowledge engineers. Sometimes creating an explicit model of the domain knowledge is extremely difficult. CBR does not require an explicit domain model, and the need for knowledge acquisition in CBR can be limited to establishing how to characterize cases.

(2) knowledge maintenance : Knowledge update is necessary due to the incompleteness of the initial system knowledge. The newly-generated knowledge may be conflict with what systems already know, thus a process of conflict elimination is necessary to maintain the consistency of the knowledge base. Knowledge maintenance in knowledge-bases systems is hard and expensive, while CBR systems learn by acquiring new knowledge as cases thus making maintenance easier.

(3) Improvement in problem solving efficiency: Problem solving in CBR can reuse the previous solutions, and is not from the scratch as that in classic inferences. Particularly, the previous records can help in advance the solutions doomed to failure.

(4) Improvement in problem solving quality: The records of previous failure help in the current attempt to avoid failure in advance.

(5) Improve user acceptance degree: Users are ready to accept a conclusion only when they are shown how it is reached. CBR systems draw conclusions on the basis of historical facts. Facts speak louder than words; conclusions in CBR systems are more convincing.

The Key Laboratory of Institute of Intelligent Information Processing, Institute of Computing Technology, Chinese Academy of Sciences has carried out a series of research in CBR. Z. Shi et al. propose a memory network model and case-based search algorithm (Shi, 1992) in 1991. H. Zhou develops EOFDS, a CBL-based design system for internal-combustion engine oil product (Zhou, 1993). In 1994, H. Xu develops a CBR-based weather forecast system, while two years later, J. Wang develops FOREZ, a CBR-based predication and deployment system for Wang's Dam in Huanghe River. S. Ye designs and implements a CBR-based system for fishing ground predication. (Ye, 2001)

5.2 Basic Notations

Analogical problem solving is the process of finding the solution to a new problem by applying an analogy between the recalled similar old problems and the new problem, and by the analogy, new knowledge is generated through reasoning to help problem solving. The solution to the new problem can also be generated on the analysis of, and adjust to the previous problem solutions. So in addition to the ability to record the solutions to similar old problems, an computation model should also have learning skills, I.e., the skill of adjust the solutions based on past useful experiences. When people can't obtain the solution to the problem after retrieval and revision to the existing solutions to similar problems, some weak methods should be employed. So, analogy learning is a kind of learning based on knowledge (or experience). The general model of analogical problem solving is shown in Fig. 5.1.

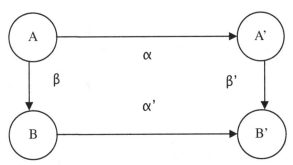

Fig. 5.1. The general model of analogical problem solving

Analogical problem solving can be formulized as: Suppose B is the solution the problem A, given a new problem A' that is similar to A by some predefined criteria, how to gent its solution B'? As shown in Fig. 5.1, β represents the dependence between B and A, and is called causality. α is the similarity of source domain A and the target domain A'. β', the dependence between B' and A' can be computed on the basis of β and α. The following are some definitions about analogy learning.

Definition 5.1 (*Similarity*) *Suppose P_1 and P_2 are finite sets of predicates. If $q_1 \in P_1$, and $q_2 \in P_2$ are the same, then ordered pair $<q_1,q_2> \in P_1 \times P_2$ is similar.*

Definition 5.2 (*Partial Match*) *Suppose s and t are finite sets of literals with shared constants. For $s \in S$, $t \in T$, as for Q, if $Q^\theta \subseteq s \subseteq s \times t$, and there is an one-to-one mapping between Q^θ and $v(Q)^\theta$, then (Q, θ) is a general partial match of s and t.*

Definition 5.3 (*Intensity*) *Suppose (Q, θ) and (Q', θ') are two partial matches of $s \times t$. If there is a substitution ξ such that $Q'\xi \subseteq Q$, and for any $W \in v(Q')$*

$W \theta' = W \xi \theta$, *then* (Q, θ) *is more intensive than* (Q', θ'), *written as* (Q, θ) $\geq (Q', \theta')$.

Definition 5.4 *(Maximal Partial Match)* (Q, θ) *is a maximal partial match of* $s \times t$ *if for any partial match of* $s \times t$, (Q', θ') *such that* $(Q, \theta) \geq (Q', \theta')$.

Definition 5.5 *(Analogical Learning) Suppose* $s_1, s_2 \in S$, $t_1 \in T$, $\beta \in S \times S$, $s_1 \times s_2 \in \beta$, *and m is a maximal partial match of* $s_1 \times t_1$. *Analogical learning is the process of finding a* t_2 *such that* $t_2 \in T$ *on the basis of facts* $t_1 \times t_2 \in \beta$ *and that m is a maximal partial match of* $s_2 \times t_2$.

5.3 Process Model

CBR is a kind of analogical reasoning. When a new problem is encountered, a set of similar cases are retrieved from memory according to some properties of the target case. But the result is coarse, might not be correct, we must verify their similarities, which makes us further explore more details of the target and potential base cases. Actually, some analogical mapping has already been carried out locally and tentatively at this stage. After this process, the potential base cases have already been arranged in an partial order according to the similarity with the target cases. We enter the stage of analogical mapping. We choose the most similar base case from the potential base case set, and construct a one-to-one mapping between them. In the next step, we get a complete (or partial) solution to the new problem by utilizing this mapping and the solution of the base case. If the solution is a partial one, then add it to the initial descriptions of the target case and restart a new round of the whole analogy course. In the case that the suggested solution is not a valid solution to the target case, an explanation on the reason why it fails is given and the system will evoke the mending module to revise the suggested solution to get an confirmed one, which provides an opportunity to learn from failure. The system should record reasons to fail, in order to avoid the same mistakes in future. Finally, the evaluation on the validity of the analogical reasoning should be given. The whole analogy course is carried on in an accumulative manner. Fig. 5.2 sketches the general structure of CBR.

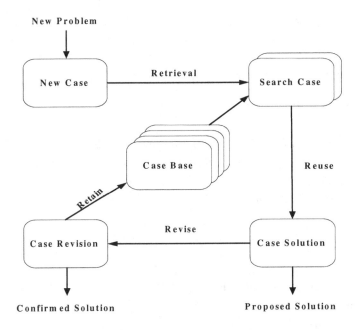

Fig. 5.2. Structure of CBR

CBR can be identified into two types: problem-solving CBR and interpretive CBR. The former solves new problems by adapting solutions that were used to solve old problems; the latter utilizes previous cases as evidences for what it pleads. A CBR process is shown in Fig. 5.3. The subjects that matter in CBR include:

(1) *Case Representation*: Efficiency is closely linked to case representation in CBR systems. Case representation involves: what should be contained in a case; how to choose the storage structure of a case; and how to organize and index the cases to facilitate the retrieval of potentially useful cases. The organization and indexing aspects are especially important when the system handles thousands of complex cases.

(2) *Analysis Model*: Analysis models are used to analyze the target case, identify and elicit the information used to find the best match.

(3) *Case Retrieval*: It is the process of finding the potentially useful cases and choosing the best match utilizing the search information. It is the very similar ways the mankind solve problems on the basis of previous experiences. When a new problem is encountered, people resort to

previous cases and get the best match case related to the problem. Due to the fact that whether the retrieved case helps in the following phases mainly depends on the case quality got in this phase, case retrieval is very crucial. Generally speaking, it is by no means an accurate match, and can only be a partial or approximate match. So, the criterion of similarity evaluation is demanding and of great importance. A well definition of the similarity is critical to find a useful base case.

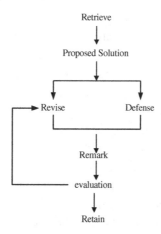

Fig. 5.3. A CBR process

(4) *Analogical Mapping*: Construct the corresponding between the target case and the base one.

(5) *Analogical Transformation*: Transform the information in the base case in the form easy use in problem solving in the target case. The adaptation of the solution in the base case is involved in this process, which aims to construct the solution in the new situation. The consideration in this adaptation process includes the differences between the target case and the base one, the decision on which part in the base case can be reused in the target case. As to the simple classification question, we only need to apply the classification result of the base cases to the target base directly. There is no need to consider their differences in that the above process of case retrieval has already fulfilled the job. As for problem solving, the system needs to revise the solution of base case according to differences between the target case and base case.

The case reuse can be classified into two types in terms of the information reused: result reuse and method reuse. To the former, when the solution in the base case needs an adaptation, the system looks for prominent differences between the base case and the target one and then applies a set of adaptation rules to suggest a solution. The method reuse cares little about the solution stored in the retrieved case, and reuses the algorithms, or rules employed in the problem solving in the base cases to produce a new solution to the target case. In this process, information useful in the base case, such as the can operation of the operator, consideration of the sub goal, search route of success or failure, etc., are reconsidered and reinstanced in the target case, which is also referred to as Derivational adaptation.

(6) *Explanation*: Explain the failure in the transformation from solution in the base case to the generation of new solutions to the target case; provide the cause-and-effect analysis report. Make explanations in successful cases sometimes. Explanation-based indexing techniques, which determine relevant features for each case, analyze each case to find which of their features are predictive. Cases are then indexed by those features. Indexing based on explanations an important method too.

(7) *Case revise: Some revises* are similar to analogical transformation. The input data for the revise process comprise a proposed solution and a failure report; sometimes an explanation might also be included. The revise process is to adapt the input solution to preclude the factors leading to failures.

Case revise happens when the proposed solution is regarded as not good, so the first step in case revise is the evaluation on the proposed solution. Only in the cases that the solution is evaluated to be not good, a revise process is evoked.

The evaluation on a proposed solution can fulfilled on the basis of feedbacks after the solution's application, or by consulting domain experts. It takes some time to wait a feedback, e.g., patient's therapeutic effects. The method of simulation temporal environment is usually employed in solution evaluations due to the above consideration.

The mistake revise generally involves the mistake finding and the reason diagnosis. Looking for the reason is for explaining and analyzing the mistake, in order to find out the reason and suit the remedy to the case, revising the reason to make the mistake makes it not recur. Certainly, revising can use the knowledge model of the field to go on mending, can be input and finished by users too.

(8) Analogy Verification: prove the validation of the analogy mapping between the

base cases and the target one.

(9) Case Retainion: Once the solution to the new problem has been generated, it may be useful in the future problems of the situation similar to it. It is necessary to add it into the current case base. The retainion of newly-generated solution is also a process of knowledge acquisition, or in other words, LEARNING. Case retainion involves the choice of information that should be kept, the way to integrate the new case to the case base organically, and the work to revise and refine the base cases, such as generalization and abstraction.

The determination on what should be kept involves the following several considerations generally: description of the features involved, the result of the current problem solving, and the explanations on success or failure.

Additional indices should be assigned to the newly-added cases to facilitate their retrieval. Indices should be constructed in such a way that the cases only be retrieved in the related cases. For this reason, adjustments on the index contents, even the structure of case base should be done, such as changes on the intensity of the indices or the weights of feature concerned.

5.4 Case Representation

The brain's memory mechanism for knowledge is still an open problem now. A great range of knowledge representation methods, such as production rules, semantic network, frame, object-oriented representation, have been employed in the present knowledge-based system, but it seems that they are unsuitable in learning systems, especially in the analogically learning system. The reason is that the knowledge in memory should be not only structural and well-organized, but also easy to retrieval, retainion, and learning.

Many researches on memory have been launched extensively in the fields of physiology, psychology, etc. Psychological researchers focus on the general theory of memory, and have proposed many conceptual models for memory. Some typical ones are episodic memory, semantic memory, associative memory, and Schank's dynamic memory theory.

Knowledge has some structure in nature. Experts adapt semantic memory in their fulfill some tasks to store information involved in problem solving. This kind of information memory methods has the following advantages:

(1) facilitate the information retrieval;
(2) organize the content easily into the tree-like level or network;
(3) confine the effects of knowledge change to a part and make it easy for information management;
(4) facilitate to the sharing of knowledge.

In Schank's dynamic memory theory(Schank,1982), knowledge is stored in structures of the following four types: Memory Organization Packet (MOP), Scene, Script, and Thematic Organization Packet (TOP). A MOP can contain some scenes, while each scene can contain many scripts. Meanwhile, Meta-MOPs may be contained in upper levels of MOP. Those structures form a network according to some predefined organizational principles, and can be searched by indices.

5.4.1 *Semantic Memory Unit*

Semantic Memory Unit (SMU) refers to those concepts, modes, and themes that are involved in the courses of knowledge's study, analysis, understanding, and memory, and the conceptual knowledge acquired in the courses. In other words, SMUs are acquired by the system through "calculation" to elicit the factors that reflect the characteristics of knowledge and that are well organized to linked knowledge together.

The knowledge in our memory is a real memory and serves for the future use well only when it is constructed on the basis of processing to some degree. SUM is not only the generation of a certain respect of concrete problem and concrete knowledge, but the essential understanding of them. Using SMUs as centers, those concrete knowledge and concrete problems can be linked in a well-organized manner in terms of the relationship between SMUs.

A critical question arises here: which factors of knowledge should be chosen as SMUs? Each kind of knowledge has its one's own inherent characteristics, and the choice tactics vary according to the characteristics of knowledge. As for some new knowledge, we generally regard concepts contained in the knowledge as primary memory targets. As the knowledge accumulates, the system acquires the analytical capacity of the concrete problem, which can be used for analyzing themes of the concrete problem. Finally, some abstract conceptual understandings are summarized. For example, in astronomy, the fact that celestial bodies rotate around is a general understanding of the relation among the celestial bodies. The binary relation "rotate around" can be abstracted as a SMU. Through this vocabulary, we can associate it with not only concrete knowledge, but also the concrete image. Another point in choice tactics is the consideration to abstract those important modes involved in knowledge as a SMU. These modes are not expressed in characters, but a special kind of expression methods made up of some special symbols.

5.4.2 *Memory Network*

The knowledge we remembered is not isolated, but is linked closely or loosely into a unified system in terms of a certain factor. We use the notation of memory network to summarize this aspect of knowledge (Shi, 1992). A memory network is a network of SMUs constructed according to the relations among the component SUMs. Every node in a memory network represents a SMU, which can be described as the following structure:

SMU   =

  {

    SMU_NAME slot

    Constraint slots

    Taxonomy slots

    Causality slots

    Similarity slots

    Partonomy slots

    Case slots

    Theory slots

  }

(1) SMU_NAME slot: SUM slot for short, is the conceptual description of the SMU, usually a word or a phrase.

(2) Constraint slots: CON slots for short, are the restraints on the SMU. Usually, they are just restraints on the description of the SMU and not in a structural manner. In addition, each constraint includes a CAS facet linked to a THY facet.

(3) Taxonomy slots: TAX slots for short, define some parents and sons of this SMU in its involved taxonomy systems. So, they describe the classification among the nodes in the memory network.

(4) Causality slots: CAU slots for short, define the cause and effect connections to other SMUs. The SUM may be other SMU's cause, or the effect of other SMUs. So, they describe the cause and effect connection among the nodes in the memory network.

(5) Similarity slots: SIM slots for short, define the SUMs similar to the SUM and describe the similarity among the nodes in the memory network.

(6) Partonomy slots: PAR slots for short, define the SUMs with whole-part relation to the SUM.

(7) Case slots: CAS slots for short, define the set of cases relevant to the SUM.

(8) Theory slots: THY slots for short, define the theory about the SUM.

The above eight kinds of slots can be divided into three classes. The first is about the inter-SMU relations, including TAX slots, CAU slots, SIM slots, and PAR slots; the second type is about the content and characteristics of the SUM's own, including SMU slot and THY slots; the last type is about the information of cases related to the SMU, including CAS slots and CON slots. As for similar SMUs, we introduce a special kind of nodes, i.e., the intension nodes MMU to express the fact that the SMUs linked to the SMU have similar intension with the SMU. Knowledge more special can be stored near the SMU by adding additional restraints to the SMU and hence a lot of knowledge can be retrieved through the corresponding SMU. This makes memory of knowledge layered into levels. PAR slots do not influence the retrieval of knowledge in our model, yet they play an important role in the recall of knowledge. Through the whole-part connections, we can recall the knowledge of a certain theme or a certain field. The memory in THY slots is about the theories about SMU, e.g., the knowledge of "resource conflict". The knowledge can be represented by any ripe representation methods, such as production rules, frames, and object-oriented formalisms. In some cases, this makes knowledge processing can be done locally. In the memory network, the semantic relations among nodes guarantee the easy retrieval of knowledge relevant to a certain SMU.

It easy to see that the memory network is quite complicated, yet it can really reflected the intricate inner relations among all kinds of knowledge. The complexity of the network makes the construction of the memory network and its learning process very complex too. For people, the memory network is the result of long-term accumulation of studying and thinking. In this process, new nodes and knowledge are increasing constantly; meanwhile, the knowledge about a certain node not used for a long time is forgotten. It means that the construction process of the memory network is a learning process of knowledge in fact.

The memory network can account for the forgetfulness of knowledge in some sense. Some concrete contents of the nearly-unused knowledge are generally totally forgotten unconsciously, yet some roughly impressions about this kind of knowledge can be left in memory. It means that the memory network is a long-time memory, while the memory of slots is short-term and will die away gradually or vanish. We can describe the above phenomenon with the notation of memory intensity. In general, the memory intensity is a function of time and recall. As time elapses, the memory intensity will be weakened, and after a recall, the memory intensity of the knowledge increases to some extent.

The memory network has some resemblance to the semantic network. It is a kind of model developed on the basis of the semantic network; and they both code information in networks: nodes to express information, arcs between nodes to express the semantic relations. Yet there are many differences between them. The most primary difference is in the expression of information. The information expression power of the semantic network are confined to the network itself, namely knowledge can only be represented by nodes and the connections among nodes. But the expression power of the memory network is far beyond the semantic network:

(1) Store and use the theory and concrete cases represented in other representation methods;
(2) Store special knowledge by adding restraints to the nodes;
(3) Organize similar knowledge by intension nodes.

(4) Have an agent as a memory unit that can finish certain tasks independently.

Serials of reasoning can be taken on the basis of memory network. The following is some examples:

(1) Knowledge can be inherited among nodes through the semantic relations. This point is similar to inheritance reasoning in semantic networks.

(2) Restraints satisfiability refers to the intra process of acquirement of special knowledge by adding additional restraints to the node's intension

(3) As for the knowledge stored in THY slots, reasoning methods, i.e., forward- and backward reasoning, information transmission, can be adapted according to the representation methods.

(4) CAS slots are about cases, so CBR methods can be adopted. Hence, case-based abstraction and generalization are operations that can be implemented in the memory network.

5.5 Case Indexing

The organization of cases includes two parts: the content of cases, which should be useful to problem solving; and the indices of cases, which reflect the differences among cases and are involved in the structure and the retrieval of cases.

Typically a case comprises the following three main components: the *problem* or *scene* that describes problem to be solved and the states of world when the case occurred; the *solution* which states the solution to that problem; and/or the *result* that describes the new state of the world after the case occurred. The first two parts are the must-contained parts in any CBR systems, while the *result* is optional.

(1) The *problem* or *scene* is the description of problems to be solved or the states of world to be understood. They generally include the following contents: The goal of the system when the case occurred, the tasks involved in the fulfillment of the goal, and all the characteristics of the world states or environments related to the possible solutions.

(2) The content of the *solution* is how the problem is solved under a particular situation. It may be just a simple solution to the problem, or the process to reach this answer.

(3) The *result* records whether the solution has been implemented successfully and the situation after the solution's implementation. With the results, CBR can provide the cases that once worked successfully while providing proposed solutions; meanwhile, potential problems can be avoided with the records of previous failures. When a sufficient understanding of the problem is absent, CBR works better through the result parts.

Case indexing is an important aspect in retrieving and recalling the useful cases relevant to the new problem. Case indexing involves assigning indices to cases with an aim to facilitate their retrievals. Given a new case, the system can retrieve the relevant cases by their indices that characterize the cases in the case base, if any.

The following are three principles for case indexing:

(1) The indices should be relevant to the concrete domain. The indices in the database is general enough to divide the database averagely, thus the retrieval in database can be faster. While in CBR systems, indices should be predicative and concrete enough to simplify the access and retrieval of relevant cases.
(2) The indices should be predicative and abstract enough to allow for widening the future use of the case base.
(3) The indices should be concrete enough to be recognized in future. Too abstract indices will efface the differences among the cases.

5.6 Case Retrieval

Case retrieval is the process of find the best match in the case base to the current problem. The knowledge in CBR systems is a history of solved problems in the past (i.e., cases), rather in the form of rules as that in other experts systems. A case in the case base contains the description of the problem and the situation when the case occurred. When a new case is added to the base, indices on its primary characteristics are also constructed. When a new problem is encountered, the system utilizes the knowledge of similarities and indices to retrieve the most similar cases to the current problem or situation. This retrieval process plays an important role in CBR in that the cases retrieved influence the quality of the current problem solving. The process can be divided into three phases: feature identification, tentative matching, and final selection.

Feature Identification is to identify the relevant features on the analysis of the problem. The features can be obtained by the following method: (1) extract the features of the question directly from its description. For example, the system can extract some keywords from the problem description that is in natural languages. The extracted keywords can be viewed as features of the problem. (2) elicit the features after a understanding of the problem, such as the feature elicitation in image analyzing and processing. (3) obtain the feature from users by the human-machine interaction according to the requirements of context or knowledge model. The system utilizes users' answers heuristics to constrain and direct the search and make the retrieved case more accurate.

Tentative Matching means to find a group of candidate from the case base to the current problem. It relies on the indices of the features fixed in Feature Identification. Retrieval of cases from the case base must be equipped with the ability to perform partial matches and construct a partial order on the similarities among cases, since in general there is no existing case that exactly matches the new case. The similarities can be computed in terms of syntax structures without the utilization of domain knowledge, or be estimated on the basis of a deep analysis and thorough understand. Some well-known concrete methods are: nearest neighbor, induction, knowledge guided induction and template retrieval; we can also give weights to the features reflecting their importance.

Final Selection is to choose one or several cases with the most similarity to the target case from the tentative matches. It is closely related to the domain knowledge. First, explanations can be made by the knowledge engineers, or be computed based on the knowledge model. Then the system evaluates the explanations, and arranges the candidates into a queue according to some criterion. The one that receives the highest rating becomes the best match, for example the most relevant one or the one with the most rational explanations.

A normal course of case retrieval is sketched by the left picture of Fig. 5.4. The input is the target case, i.e., the present case. It comprises the current scene and reasoning goal. The scene is refined after an analysis on it. If there are cases similar to the target case in the case base, then the indices of the target case related to those similar cases can be calculated out. The retrieval algorithms rely on the indices and the target case to search in the case base to find potentially useful cases. The algorithms need the ability to perform partial matches between the target case and cases in the base. Then the system retains a group of partial matches with potential use. Finally the system ranks these partial matches and chooses the most useful case.

There are three key points in the case retrieval: The retrieval algorithms, matching function, and situation assessment. The following discussion focuses on the retrieval algorithms. Algorithms are closely linked to the data structures that they process. So we can not isolate our discussion on the retrieval algorithms to the organization of case bases. Bases with different organization should be searched by different algorithms accordingly. Different organizational forms have both pros and cons, and the choice of them should be determined by the application in use.

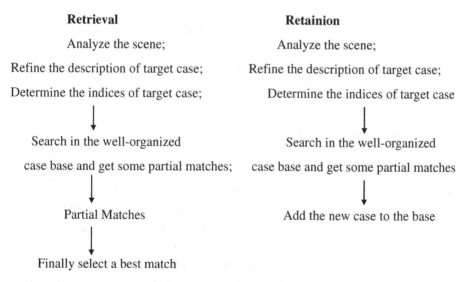

Retrieval

Analyze the scene;

Refine the description of target case;

Determine the indices of target case;

↓

Search in the well-organized

case base and get some partial matches;

↓

Partial Matches

↓

Finally select a best match

Retainion

Analyze the scene;

Refine the description of target case;

Determine the indices of target case

↓

Search in the well-organized

case base and get some partial matches

↓

Add the new case to the base

Fig. 5.4. The process of retrieval and retainion

There have been formed a series of methods for cases' organization and retrieval in CBR: the serial or parallel ones; the flat or layered ones; the ones with indices on the small or the great granularities to distinguish different examples. The mostly-used methods are of based on the inverted index, which can search in the case base serially or parallelly. The application system constructed by Kitano can already deal with more than 25,000 cases. Among the frequently-used methods for case retrieval are: nearest neighbor, induction, and template retrieval.

(1) Nearest neighbor: This approach assesses the similarity between stored cases and the new input case based on matching a weighted sum of features. The key point here is to determine the weights of the features. One limitation of this approach is the time complexity increases with the case number of case base linearly. Therefore this approach is more effective when the case base is relatively small.

(2) Induction: Induction algorithms determine which features do the best job in discriminating cases, and generate a decision tree to organize the cases in memory effectively. This approach is useful when a single case feature is required as a solution, and where that case feature is dependent upon others.

(3) Template retrieval: It is similar to SQL-like queries, and returns all cases that fit within certain parameters. This technique searches all examples   that can return within the range of certain parameter value and is often   used before other techniques, such as nearest neighbor, to limit the search space to a relevant section of the case base.

5.7 Similarity Relations in CBR

The process of retrieving the most similar cases to the current problem or situation is especially critical in that the successful retrieval of cases with high quality is the prerequisite of successful applications. Due to the fact that case retrieval is carried on the basis of similarity, the successful retrieval of similar cases is totally determined by the definition of "similarity". We can not get useful cases using an inappropriate similarity measure assessment among the cases, let alone successful applications. Similarity is a core concept in case-based reasoning.

As indicated by case representation, a case comprises many attributes, and the similar degrees among the cases are defined in terms of the similarity degrees among the component attributes. Among well known similarities are: semantic similarity, structural similarity, goal similarity, and individual similarity.

5.7.1 *Semantic similarity*

If one case is analogical to another, then there must be some similarity among their semantics. One foundation in CBR is how to assess the similarity between cases in order to retrieve appropriate base cases. The analogies between two cases can be identified into the following three types: positive analogy, negative analogy, and uncertain analogy. The positive analogy is the analogy determined by some similar aspects among cases, the negative analogy is the one that determined by the dissimilar aspects, and the uncertain analogy is the analogy other than the above types. One of the conditions for two analogical cases is: the essential property and causality of the model is not a part of negative analogy. The uncertain analogy makes the analogy have a certain predicative aspects, which are not necessarily true. To solve a problem analogically, there must be some similarity between the essential features of the base case and the target case, which is the foundation for the analogy.

Still some scholars define two types of similarity: surface similarity and structural similarity. The surface similarity is defined as the similar aspects that are not the essential ones in the process of adapting past experiences to the new case. On the contrary, the ones that affect the adaptationion process are structural similarities. A less strict definition for structural similarly is the semantic overlap of the relations. The two types of similarities play different roles in the analogy process. The surface one helps in the tentative analogy and individual identifications; while the structural one not only facilitates the analogical search, but also plays a very great role in the construction of analogical mapping.

5.7.2 *Structural similarity*

If there is a certain mapping between two structures, and this kind of corresponding relation can reserve structural consistency, then the structures are isomorphic. Structural consistency requires that the one-one mapping between two isomorphic structures guarantees the involved individuals and the component mappings are one-one relations too, and such mappings respect the previous corresponding relations among the individuals. Isomorphism carries great effects on the validity of analogical reasoning.

The meaning of structural similarities is great to similarity-based retrievals. First, as we have found, analogy is still possible in the cases with dissimilar surface similarities when the cases' structures are similar. The atom and the solar system are totally different entities in different fields. At the first sight, there are not any essential connections between them. However, deep researches can reveal their highly similar space structures. Second, the isomorphism or similarities among substructures can free us from the complex overall consideration, and make us focus on the interesting parts locally. This is particularly important in the cases there are some local similarities between two cases that dissimilar as a whole. For example, in the aspects of story understanding, stories are general far from each other; however, there may be surprising similarities at a certain plot, or a certain personality, etc. In planning, we should not merely consider the usability of the whole solution to the base case; moreover, we should also put attention in the sub solutions in the cases the whole solution is not appropriate. It is unwise to totally discard the proposed solution when it is proved to be not sufficient.

The concept of isomorphism and structural similarity plays a very important role in our analogical retrieval model. The structure similarity facilitates the tentative retrieval of base cases, while isomorphism reminds us to give much higher priorities to those base cases with isomorphism or sub-isomorphism relations to the target case.

5.7.3 Goal's features

The final purpose of problem solving is to fulfill the goal posed by the problem itself, and the goal directs people's during the process of problem solving. In a set of cases similar to the current one, those with potential usefulness to the goal achievement should gain higher priority for consideration over the cases whose implicated goals are irrelevant to that of the target case.

Given a structure, when we add information about its goals to it, the resulted structure will gain more semantic similarity and structural consistency. In other words, the goal features will increase the dependability of our choice on the best match. Meanwhile, it can also constrain the search for the base case to a limited part. Keane's analogical retrieval model search the base cases based on the analysis on the goals features (Keane 1988). Keane names the goal features as structural index in analogical retrieval.

However, can we ignore those base cases without any goal relevance? In fact, goal features is just an important additional restraint. If we emphasize goal features too much, we might lose the potential useful cases with similar sub structures by the filter of goal features, which is unwise.

5.7.4 Individual similarity

Another emphasis in our model is the restraints posed by the classification information about individuals. Informally speaking, if two individuals have some similarities, then they belong to the same classification. In the concept clustering, we cluster the concept set in terms of the relevance or closeness among them. Relevance refers to the average of similar degrees between the features of the concepts. But here, we still cluster electric wires and rope into the same class, because they both can be used to tie up things.

Sometimes, some individuals in a case play the primary role in the problem solving. In those situations, this kind of cases should be used as the primary retrieval information to search the case base tentatively. After the finish of tentative retrieval, we should pay more attention to the cases within the same class as the target case or having whole-part relations with the target case. The analogy among individuals helps us to identify them. The partial solutions to the case can help to find the whole solution.

5.7.5 Similarity assessment

(1) The similarity among numeric features.

$$Sim(V_i, V_j) = 1 - d(V_i, V_j) = 1 - d_{ij}$$

$$\text{or} \quad Sim(V_i, V_j) = \frac{1}{1 + d(V_i, V_j)} = \frac{1}{1 + d_{ij}}$$

$$d_{ij} = \left| V_i - V_j \right|$$

$$\text{or} \quad d_{ij} = \frac{|V_i - V_j|}{\max\{V_i, V_j\}} \tag{5.1}$$

where V_i, V_j are two possible values for feature V.

(2) The similarity among categorical features.

The similar degree for categorical features is generally identified into two types: the simple method is to compare the corresponding values of the features. If the two are identical, the similar degree between the features is 0; otherwise, is considered to be 1. Other methods may incorporate some differential ranking into the definitions of similarity according to the detailed relations among the feature values, rather than the simple 0-or-1 division. The former is actually similarity in quality, i.e. the division between to be or not to be, while the latter is similarity in quantity, the further discrimination among the features. Generally speaking, the former is common and suitable for all kinds of situations; the latter is needed to be predefined and related to domain knowledge, thus serves special purpose. The above two kinds of similarity assessment methods have different application domains of their own.

(3) The similarity among ordered features.

Ordered features are the features lying between the numeric and the categorical ones, thus the similarity degrees for them lie between the quality and quantity assessments too. When the values for a feature are in order, we can assign different similarity degrees to different segments of the whole line of possible values. Compared with categorical features, the ordered features have more regular similarity assessment rules. Suppose the whole line of values can be divided into n segments, then the similarity between feature values in segments i and j can be defined as $1 - \frac{|i-j|}{n}$.

Features of different types can be transformed into each other. A feature can be delineated by a set of numbers sometimes or by ordered values too. For example, students' examination marks can be reflected by natural numbers from 0 to 100, or by different classes A, B, and C.

When we calculate the similar degrees among cases, we should consider a weighted sum of similar degrees of all features. The similar degrees among cases are often defined as distances. Typical distances are:

(1) Manhattan distance:

$$d_{ij} = \sum_{k=1}^{N} \left| V_{ik} - V_{jk} \right| \tag{5.2}$$

where V_{ik} and V_{jk} are the values of the k_{th} feature of case i and j, respectively.

(2) Euclidean distance:

$$d_{ij} = \sqrt{\sum_{k=1}^{N} (V_{ik} - V_{jk})^2} \tag{5.3}$$

(3) Minkowski distance

$$d_{ij} = \left[\sum_{k=1}^{N} \left| V_{ik} - V_{jk} \right|^q \right]^{1/q}, \qquad q>0 \tag{5.4}$$

The above definitions are normal in that every feature influences the similarity among two cases equally. Actually each feature contributes differently the similar degrees, therefore we still need to add weights to features reflecting their importance. The above definitions can be rewritten as:

$$d_{ij} = \sum_{k=1}^{N} w_k d(V_{ik}, V_{jk}) \tag{5.5}$$

where w_k is the weights of kth features of the cases, and normally $\sum_{k=1}^{N} w_k = 1$;

and $d(V_{ik}, V_{jk})$ is the distance between the ith case and the jth one on the dimension of kth feature, which can be computed by the classical definitions, or other definitions.

The similar degree between two cases can be defined in terms of the above definition of distances:

$$SIM_{ij} = 1 - d_{ik} \quad \text{if} \quad d_{ij} \in [0,1]$$

$$\text{or:} \quad SIM_{ij} = \frac{1}{1+d_{ij}} \quad \text{if } d_{ij} \in [0, \infty) \tag{5.6}$$

In addition, ReMind system developed by Cognitive System Company employ the following definition to calculate similar degrees among cases:

$$\sum_{i=1}^{n} w_i \times \text{Sim}(f_i^I, f_i^R) / \sum_{i=1}^{n} w_i \tag{5.7}$$

where w_i is the weight of i-th feature of the case, Sim is the similarity function, and f_{Ii}, f_{Ri} are the values of i-t_h feature of the target case and the potential base cases in case base.

5.8 Case Reuse

The case reuse can be classified into two types in terms of the information reused: result reuse and method reuse. To the former, the adaptation is applied directly to the solution stored in cases. The system looks for prominent differences between the base case and the target one and then applies a set of adaptation rules to suggest a solution. Instead of the solutions stored, the method reuse reuses the algorithms, or rules employed in the problem solving in the base cases to produce a new solution to the target case, while the choice of adaptation methods are dependent on the concrete problems.

Case revise happens when the proposed solution is regarded as not good, so the first step in case revise is the evaluation on the proposed solution. Only in the cases that the solution is evaluated to be not good, a revise process is evoked. The evaluation on a proposed solution can fulfilled on the basis of feedbacks after the solution's application, or by consulting domain experts. It takes some time to wait a feedback, e.g., patient's therapeutic effects, while some kinds of real-time feedbacks are required in some situations.

Generally speaking, there is no existing case that exactly matches the new case, so in problem solving CBR systems, it is necessary to transform or adapt the solutions to the retrieved cases to the new problem. The revise process use the description of the current problem and a suggested solution gotten in the reuse process to output a better solution.

The revision may be just simple replacement to some components of the suggested solution, or very complex to revise the whole structure of the suggested solution. Revision can take place in the process that the suggested solution forms, or be postponed until some exceptions arise during the execution of the suggested solution. Revision is generally fulfilled by adding new content to or deleting some content from the suggested solutions, and replacement or retransformation of some parts of the suggested solution.

The revise methods can be classified into four types: substitution, transformation, special-purpose adaptation and repair, and derivational replay.

1. Substitution

Substitution is a class of structural adaptation techniques that get the suggested solution by appropriate component substitutions. It includes:

(1) Reinstantiation, is used to instantiate features of an old solution with new features. For example, CHEF can reinstantiate chicken and snow peas in a Chinese recipe with beef and *broccoli* thereby creating a new recipe.

(2) Parameter adjustment, a structural adaptation technique that compares specified parameters of the retrieved and current case to modify the solution in an appropriate direction. It is a heuristics method for parameters with numeric values, and depends on the concrete models of input and output.

(3) Local search, is the method using additional knowledge as heuristics to find replacement values. For example, in pastry design, in the absence of oranges, we can use this method to search some fruit similar to oranges (such as apples) as a second choice with the help of knowledge about fruit.

(4) Query, obtains the substitution content by the conditional queries to case base or additional knowledge base.

(5) Specialized search, searches the case base and knowledge base at the same time, and use the knowledge base as heuristics to direct its search in the case bases.

(6) Case-based substitution, uses other cases to propose a substitution.

2. Transformation

Transformation includes: (1) common-sense transformation, which replaces, deletes or increases some components to the old solution by basic and easy-understood commonsense. The typical transformation method is "to delete the secondary components". (2) model-guided repair, which uses a causal model to guide adaptation and often used in diagnosis systems.

3. Special-purpose adaptation and repair

This kind of method is used mainly in the domain-dependent and structural adaptations. Various heuristics are used to index the potential useful cases.

Generally the heuristics in this method serves by giving evaluations on approximate solutions and is controlled by rule-based production systems.

4. Derivational replay

The above three kinds of revise methods are based on adaptations on the solutions to the base cases. Derivational replay cares how the solutions driven, and use the method of deriving an old solution or solution piece to derive a solution in the new situation. Compared with the case-based substitution methods mentioned above, derivational replay is a kind of case-based revise methods.

5.9 Case Retainion

The process of case retainion is similar to that of case retrieval. The word "remember" has two kinds of meanings: storage and retrieval. Incorporating the problem and solution to the case base as a new case involves the index-mechanism to assign indices to the cases to facilitate its future retrieval, and the insertion algorithms to store the new case in the appropriate place in the case base. Generally speaking, the search performed in case retainion is the same as that in case retrieval. The insertion algorithms aim to find a place for the new case, while retrieval algorithms are to return the most similar cases. Arrangement on cases begins when potential useful cases are returned, and the systems need to reorganize the case base after the insertion of new cases.

If the new problem has been solved successfully, the problem and solution should be stored as a new case for future use. Case retainion is the process of learning and knowledge acquisition, which involves deciding what information to retain and in what form to retain it; how to index the case for future retrieval; how to integrate the new case into the case base, and how to organize and manage the case base.

Deciding what information to retain includes the following considerations: Feature descriptions involved in the problem; the solution to the problem; and explanations on the success.

Additional indices should be assigned to the newly-added cases to facilitate their retrieval. Indices should be constructed in such a way that the cases only be retrieved in the related cases. For this reason, adjustments to the index contents, even the structure of case base should be done, such as changes on the intensity of the indices or the weights of feature concerned.

As time goes by, the case base becomes larger and larger. This will cause great waste of the memory space and retrieval time. In this light, the system should perform effective organization and management on the case base.

Retrieval, reuse, revise and retainion are four main processes in a CBR cycle, and the reasoning process of CBR is also named as Four- R process.

5.10 Instance-Based Learning

Instance-based learning (IBL for short), is a family of inductive learning methods closely linked to case-based learning (Aha,1991). The learning algorithms in IBL simply store the already classified instances, and when a new query instance is encountered, classify the instance into the same class as the most similar related instance retrieved from the instance base. Rather than complex index mechanisms, IBL uses the feature-value pairs as the primary representation method. This approach also does no revisions on instances, yet it is proved to be very useful.

In the researches of learning from examples or supervised learning, a variety range of concept representation formalisms have been put forward, including rules, decision tree, connectionist networks, etc. All these methods predict the new instance based on the abstraction and generalization of the training instances. Instance-based learning can be viewed as an extension of the nearest neighbor method in that it uses the typical instances to denote the corresponding concepts directly, rather than generalizing a set of abstractions of the training instances. Its prediction about the new query is estimated under the similarity assumption, i.e., the classification results on similar instances are similar too. IBL retrieves a set of instances similar to the new instance, and returns a result for the new query based on a systemic analysis of the retrieved results. The nearest neighbor learning is incremental, and gains the best prediction accuracy for instances whose feature values are continuous, compared with other learning methods (Biberman,1994).

The k-nearest neighbor algorithm (k-NN for short) is the general form of nearest neighbor method, where k is the number of most nearest neighbors. Two key points in the application of k-NN are: How to retrieve some instances similar to the instance form the instance base; and how to assess the retrieved results to form the prediction value for the present example. The former includes how to define the similarities among instances and the criteria for the choice of k. Weiss et al. provide better solutions in the cases where feature values are symbols or discrete ones(Weiss, 1991). Aha gives a method, named as cross validation, to determine the value of k (Aha,1997).

5.10.1 *Learning tasks of IBL*

In IBL, an instance is described as a set of feature-value pairs. Each instance contains several features, and missing feature values are tolerated. All instances are described by the same n features, which define an n-dimensional instance space. Exactly one of there features corresponds to the category feature; while the other n-1 features are referred to as predictor features. IBL algorithms can learn a lot of overlapping concepts, yet in general the learning only involves exactly one category feature and the categories are disjoint does not overlap and its outputs are basically simple.

Generally speaking, an output of IBL algorithms is a concept description, which is a function mapping from instances to categories: Given an instance in the instance space, the function gives a classification, i.e., a predication on this instance's category attribute. An instances-based concept description includes a set of stored instances, and possibly information about their performances in the past classification processes. This set of instance can change after each query instance is processed.

Classification function: It receives as the input the similarity function's results and the classification performance records for instances, and outputs a classification for i. *Concept description updater*: It maintains records on classification performance, and determines which instances should be incorporated in the concept description. IBL assumes that similar instances have similar classifications, thus it classifies the new instances according to their most similar neighbors' classifications. Meanwhile, when prior knowledge is absent, IBL assumes that all features' contributions to classification are equal, i.e. feature weights reflecting their importance are identical in the similar function. This bias requires normalizations of each features' value domain.

Different from most other supervised learning algorithms, no explicit abstractions such as decision trees or decision inductions are needed in IBL algorithms. Most learning algorithms maintain a set of generalizations of instances to form their abstract representations, and adopt simple matching to classify the represented instances. However, IBL algorithms do little in representation phase in that they do not store explicit generalizations, yet there is more calculation on similarities among cases in the classification phase when a new instance is encountered.

The performance of IBL algorithms are generally be assessed in terms of the following respects:

(1) Generalization capability: the ability to determine which concepts can be describable and the learning power of the algorithms. IBL algorithms can PAC-learn any concept whose boundary is a union of a finite set of closed hyper-curves of finite size.
(2) Classification accuracy.
(3) Learning rate.
(4) Incorporation costs: the overhead involved in updating the concept descriptions of a training instance, including classification costs.
(5) Storage requirement: the size of the concept descriptions which for IBL algorithms, is defined as the number of saved instances used for classification decisions.

5.10.2 *Algorithm IB1*

The key idea of the IB1 algorithm is quite simple: Given an instance, it assumes that the instance is in the same category as its nearest neighbor. Yet, it is must be acknowledged that IB1 will fails in the cases that the given attributes are logically inadequate for the description of the target concept.

Algorithm 5.1: IB1 algorithm

1. $CD \leftarrow \emptyset$ //CD=Concept description
2. For each $x \in$ Training Set do
3.   for each $y \in CD$ do
4. $sim[y] \leftarrow$ similarity(x,y).
5. $y_{max} \leftarrow$ some $y \in CD$ with maximal $sim[y]$
6.   if class(x)=class (y_{max})
7.   then classification $\leftarrow$ correct
8.   else classification $\leftarrow$ incorrect
9. $CD \leftarrow CD \cup \{x\}$

It is a fact that under general statistical assumptions, the nearest neighbor decision policy has a misclassification rate at most twice the optimal Bayes in the worst cases. This result is relatively weak in that it is gotten in the cases that the number of samples is unbounded.

5.10.3 *Reducing storage requirements*

In IB1 algorithm, only the instances that lie between the ε-neighborhood and the ε-core of C are used in the production of an accurate approximation of the target concept. The other instances have no contribution to the determination of the concept boundary. So, only keeping those useful instances will save a large number of memory spaces. However, without the whole knowledge about the concept boundary, this set is not known. But it can be approximated by the set of misclassified instances. This is the key idea of the algorithm IB2.

Algorithm 5.2: IB2 algorithm.

1. $CD \leftarrow \varnothing$ //CD=Concept description
2. For each $x \in$ Training Set do
3.   For each $y \in CD$ do
4. $sim[y] \leftarrow$ similarity (x,y)
5. $y_{max} \leftarrow$ some $y \in CD$ with maximal $sim[y]$.
6.   if class(x)=class (y)
7.   then classification $\leftarrow$ correct
8.   else
9.   classification $\leftarrow$ incorrect
10. $CD \leftarrow CD \cup \{x\}$.

Different from IB1, the IB2 algorithm only saves misclassified instances, most of which lies between the ε-neighborhood and th ε-core of C(for some rationally small positive number ε), and is close to the boundary. In the cases where the instances vary greatly in their distance from the concept boundary, the reduction of storage requirements is significantly small in IB2.

The classification accuracy decreases more dramatically than that of IB1 does as the level of noise increases in that those noisy instances are almost always misclassified. Since IB2 saves only a small part of the non-noisy training instances, its saved noisy instances have more chances to be used to generate poor classifications.

IB3 is the improvement of IB2 that employs a "selective utilization filter" to determine which of the saved instances should be used to make classification decisions in such a way that IB3 is insensitive to noise.

Algorithm 5.3: IB3

   1. $CD \leftarrow \emptyset$ //CD=Concept description

   2.   for each $x \in$ Training Set do

   3.   for each $y \in CD$ do

   4. $sim[y] \leftarrow similarity(x,y)$

   5.   if $\exists\{y \in CD|acceptable\ (y)\}$ then

   6. $y_{max} \leftarrow$ some acceptable $y \in CD$ with maximal $sim[y]$

   7.   else

   8. $i \leftarrow$ a randomly-selected value in $[1,|CD|]$

   9. $y_{max} \leftarrow$ some $y \in CD$ that is the i-th most similar instance to x

  10.   if $class(x) \neq class(y_{max})$

  11.   then

  12.   classification$\leftarrow$correct

  13.   else

  14.   classification$\leftarrow$incorrect

  15. $CD \leftarrow CD \cup \{x\}$

  16.   for each $y \in CD$ do

  17.   if $sim\ [y] \geq sim[y_{max}]$

  18.   then

  19.   update y's classification record

  20.   if y's record is significantly poor

  21.   then $CD \leftarrow C\text{-}\{y\}$.

The IB3 algorithm maintains a classification record, e.g., the number of correct and in correct classification attempts, with each saved instance. A classification record is a summary of an instance's classification performance on the current training instances and hints the performance in the future. Meanwhile, IB3 employs a significance test to determine which instances are good classifiers and which ones are noisy. The noisy instances are discarded from the concept description. For each training instance i, all classification records are updated for instances that are at least as similar as i's most similar acceptable neighbor.

When no instance in storage is acceptable, we adopt a policy that assumes that at least one instance is acceptable. If none of the saved instances are acceptable, a random number γ will be generated from $[1, n]$, where n is the number of saved instances. Then the γ most similar saved instances' classification records are updated. If there is at least one acceptable instance, say i, then the instances whose classification records need updating are those that are in the hyper-sphere, centered on i with radius equal to the normalized distance between i and its nearest neighbor.

IB3 employs the notion of confidence interval of proportions test to determine whether an instance is acceptable, mediocre, or noisy. Confidence intervals are determined by both the instance's current classification accuracy and the observed relative frequency of the class it belongs to. The instance is acceptable in the cases where its accuracy interval's lower endpoint is greater than the class frequency interval's higher endpoint. Similarly, instances are noisy when their accuracy interval's higher endpoint is less than their class frequency interval's lower endpoint. If the two intervals overlap, then it is mediocre and a further decision process will be employed to decide whether the instance is to be accepted or discarded.

The learning performance IB3 is highly sensitive to the number of irrelevant features employed in instance descriptions. Meanwhile, with increasing dimensionality, its storage requirements increase exponentially, yet learning rate decreases exponentially. IB3 cannot represent overlapping concepts and respects the assumption that every instance is a member of exactly one concept. Fortunately, this can be solved by learning a separate description for each concept.

IBL has the following advantages. The approach is simple, relatively robust; and its algorithms have a relatively relaxed concept bias. They learn piecewise-linear approximations of concepts incrementally with faster learning rate than other algorithms when their bias is not satisfied by target concepts, especially when the boundary of the target concept is not parallel to the feature dimensions. Finally, the updating costs in IBL algorithms are relatively low. IBL updating costs includes classification costs, which requires $O(|N|*|A|)$ feature examinations, where $|N|$ is the number of saved instances and $|A|$ is the number of features used in instance descriptions. C4.5 requires $O(|I|*|A|^2)$ feature examinations, where $|I|$ is the size of the training set. Meanwhile, parallel processing methods and index strategies can be employed to further reduce the computation complexity for IBL.

5.11 Forecast System for Central Fishing Ground

As indicated by psychological researches, mankind is good at making decisions based on its past experiences. The restrictions posed by human memory capacity make it difficult for people to recall the appropriate cases correctly, especially when the number of cases is daunting big.. Compared with people, computers have the advantages in terms of "memory", i.e., computers can store a large number of cases and retrieve relevant ones fast. It is exactly the scope of case-based decision aiding to combine the merits of people and machine together to help decision making.

It has attracted extensive attentions of the countries all over the world to employ the modern science and technology to develop the marine resources, maintain and manage marine fishery resources well, and realize the sustainable development of sea fishery. The utilization of computer, remote sensing, automation, geographical information system can not only offer macroscopic decision information for developing and managing in the sea fishery, but also direct the microcosmic concretely for the use of marine fishery resources.

Under the support of 863 Program, we launched researches on remote sensing information and resource assessment system for sea fishery, and the concerning system integration and case illustration for the better utilization of resources and development of fishery of the sea areas in our country. It serves to strengthen the new and high technology to the support function of maintaining, utilizing and administrative skill of fishery resources of marine exclusive economic zone in the future. We use China East Sea (north latitude 25 degree to 34 degree, 130 of east longitude with west sea area) as the demonstration area for fishing ground prediction and lay a good foundation for the utilization and development of fishery resources in open seas and oceans. The fishing ground prediction utilizes technologies such as data mining, CBL, expert system, and analysis technology in the fishery of remote sensing, sea fishery serve under the support of the geographical technology of information system, and together with the knowledge and experiences domain experts, implements Learning and Decision-support System for fishing ground analysis and prediction.

5.11.1 *Problem Analysis and Case Representation*

In addition to make assessment on fishery resources (medium and long-term predictions), the important function of the system is to make the short-term prediction (the fishing ground centre) . The fishing ground refers to the ocean areas with intensive fish or other economic marine animals in certain season that are worth developing and utilizing. The central fishing ground is the fishing ground with higher average net product and gross total product. Accurate predictions can directly improve the product and efficiency of the fishery production and brings great economic benefits.

The migration of fish and formation of central fishing ground have been influenced by the following factors: temperature of sea water (including marine surface temperature, the temperature of marine ground floor), data about platform, such as the salt degree of sea water, salt gradient ion, the flow rate of Changjiang River, wind directions and velocities, and marine chlorophyll density. However, the migration of the fish is influenced by a lot of factors and is too complicated to be described by traditional mathematics method and model. Furthermore, the knowledge of experts about the fishing ground is inaccuracy, and incomplete in some sense. Fortunately, we have already collected the data about fishery conditions in China East Sea for 20 years. These materials are very valuable in that a lot of useful information and knowledge can be elicited out from them, which can be used to predict the trend of the fishing ground. The system has been adopted CBR in that CBR is very suitable in situations where there is little domain knowledge and many exceptions for the general rules, but only a large number of historical data are available, domains are described in terms of cases, and the problems are not totally understood.

According to the fact that information about sea states is usually collected weekly and for the sake of easy computation, we simplify the demand according to the actual conditions and make a week as the predication cycle. In this way, the problem can be formulated as how to predicate the central fishing ground in next week according to the information of aquatic products in this week (the position, the output and size). Even so, the problem is quite difficult too, in that the position and size of fishing ground are space data. Meanwhile, the information of sea state involves about 600 pieces of space and un-space attributes, methods such as the decision tree, regression, etc. are not very suitable. On the basis of the above consideration, we adopt CBR, a kind of Lazy Learning (Aha, 1997).

A rational, consistent case representation is essential in the process of case library building. A prominent question in a CBR system is how to combine situation, solution and outcome to form a case representation. In our system, we employ the Object Orientated Technologies to express the sea state and fishing condition, and every instance of a class is captured by a record in database and created dynamically during the system evolvement.

Through the proper pre-treatment, the initial data are turned into forms suitable for machine learning. The primitive records take the form of time, place, output, manner, etc. (records from some fishery company even have no output records), upon which we must compute the central fishing grounds. Meanwhile, for simplicity, we neglect fishing grounds' form and only take their sizes into consideration. We classify these primitive records into groups in terms of time and manner, and can do some reduction in some clustering ways to find central fishing grounds, which can be revised in the following phase through human-computer interaction:

(1) Combine the adjacent central fishing grounds around until there are no adjacent ones;

(2) Eliminate the central fishing ground with output lower than a preset threshold;

(3) If the number of central fishing grounds is still big after the above processes, eliminate the fishing grounds with smaller size and modest output;

(4) Combine the remaining fishing grounds to form the central fishing ground: the position of the central fishing ground is their geometric centre, its size is the number of the component fishing grounds and the output is their accumulation.

(5) alize the result of Step 4, and users do some revision according to the specific situations;

(6) the result in database.

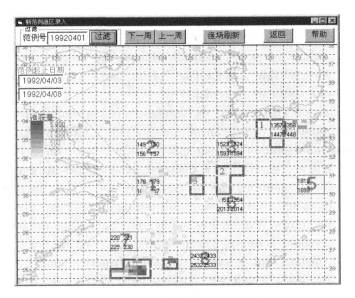

Fig. 5.6. Central fishing grounds after clustering and human revision

With the help of tools we have developed, domain experts can classify the historical data in a short period of time.

5.11.2 *Similarity Measurement*

A key point is CBR is how to retrieve the "best" similar cases. Case retrieval is based on the similarity compares, and totally determined by their definition of "similarity". It is hardly the case that we can find satisfactory cases with an un-proper definition of similarity. So the similarity definition carries a great weight in CBR systems. However, similarity is a notion that is always coarse, incomplete, and ever-changing. The optimum choice of cases usually follows the following rules: Compute the semantic, structure, target, and individual similarities using the corresponding algorithms to assess the overall similarities between cases; then calculate the whole similarity according to the importance of these similarities in the question, it is similar to the total dynamic weighting.

In our system, we employ the following three methods to measure the similarities:

·Similarity in terms of position

$$\text{sim1} = \sum(w_i * \text{distance}(\text{pos}(\text{goal}) - \text{pos}(\text{source}))) / \sum w_i \qquad (5.8)$$

·Similarity in terms of temperature

$$\text{sim2} = \sum(w_i * \text{difference}(\text{temp}(\text{goal}) - \text{temp}(\text{source}))) / \sum w_i \qquad (5.9)$$

·Similarity in terms of temperature gradient

$$\text{sim3} = \sum(w_i * \text{difference}(\text{delta}(\text{goal}) - \text{delta}(\text{source}))) / \sum w_i \qquad (5.10)$$

where w_i is the weight. The closer temperature test spot to the central fishing ground (d_i), the w_i is greater. Suppose d_{max} is the diameter of the marine area, $w_i=1$ when $d_i=0$, and $d_i= d_{max}$, w_i is a preset value w_0(can be modified by users), otherwise

$$w_i = 1 - \frac{d_i(1-w_0)}{d_{max}} \qquad (5.11)$$

5.11.3 *Indexing and Retrieval*

Case reuse is the process of choosing the best matching case from stored ones and adapting its solutions to solve the new problem. The process can be divided into analogy mapping and analogy conversion. A precondition of the adaptation of base case to problem solving in the target case is a one-to-one mapping between the features of the target and base cases, and choice of relations and structures can used in the target case. So, in the analogy mapping, two primary problems are: the identification and mapping of features, and choice of mapping relations and structures.

Case indexing involves assigning indices to cases to facilitate their retrieval. The main indexing methods include near neighbor, induction, knowledge guide, or their combinations. The main difficulty in our system lies in the fact that the information of sea state and fishing condition is related to space and time. For clarity, we do the following simplification. Suppose C_{t1} is the sea state at time t_1, which is a precondition (condition attribute) of fishing grounds; and G_{t1} is the fishing ground at t_1, including output, size, and decision attributes. Case at t_1 $I_{t1}= (C_{t1}, G_{t1})$ is a vector with high dimension. $I_{t1-tn}=\{I_{t1}, I_{t2}, ...,I_{tn}\}=\{(C_{t1}, G_{t1}), (C_{t2}, G_{t2}), ..., (C_{tn}, G_{tn})\}$ is a case sequence, where t_{i+1} is the next week of t_i, and $\Box G_t=G_{ti+1}-G_{ti}$ is the change of the fishing ground in a week.

Suppose $\Gamma_{s'1\text{-}s'k}$ and $\Gamma_{t'1\text{-}t'k}$ are subset of $I_{s1\text{-}sm}$, $I_{t1\text{-}tn}$ with k-elements and total order, and that sim(.) is the similarity measurement function. If $\forall I_{s'i} \in \Gamma_{s'1\text{-}s'k}, \forall I_{t'i} \in \Gamma_{t'1\text{-}t'k}$, $\mathrm{sim}(I_{s'i}, I_{t'i}) \geq \delta_{(1\leq i \leq k)}$, written as $\Gamma_{s'1\text{-}s'k} \approx \Gamma_{t'1\text{-}t'k}$, then $I_{s1\text{-}sm}$ and $I_{t1\text{-}tn}$ are k-δ totally similar, where δ is the predefined threshold value between 0 and 1. Obviously, the bigger k and δ are, the bigger degree of the similarity between $I_{s1\text{-}sm}$ and $I_{t1\text{-}tn}$.

Suppose $C`_{s'1\text{-}s'k}$ and $C`_{t'1\text{-}t'k}$ are k-elements subsets of condition sequences $C_{s1\text{-}sm}=\{C_{s1},...,C_{sm}\}$ and $C_{t1\text{-}tn}=\{C_{t1},...,C_{tm}\}$. If $\forall C_{s'i} \in C'_{s'1\text{-}s'k}, \forall C_{t'i} \in C'_{t'1\text{-}t'k}$, $\mathrm{sim}(C_{s'i}, C_{t'i}) \geq \delta_{(1\leq i \leq k)}$, written as $C_{s'1\text{-}s'k} \approx C_{t'1\text{-}t'k}$, then $I_{s1\text{-}sm}$ and $I_{t1\text{-}tn}$ are k-δ conditional similar, where δ is the predefined threshold value between 0 and 1.

Suppose $I_{u\text{-}cur}=\{I_u, I_{u+1},...,I_{cur}\}$ is a fishing ground sequence of length cur-u+1 from time u to time cur, and $I_{u\text{-}cur+1}=\{I_u, I_{u+1},...,I_{cur}, I_{cur+1}\}=\{I_{u\text{-}cur}, I_{cur+1}\}$ represents the evolvement of fishing grounds from time u to the time cur+1, where $I_{cur+1}=(C_{cur+1}, G_{cur+1})$, C_{cur+1} can be gathered accurately in the way that the meteorological phenomena is analyzed, and G_{cur+1} is the fishing ground in next week needed to be predicted. Suppose $\Gamma_{u'1\text{-}u'k}$ is a total order subset of $I_{u\text{-}cur+1}$ with elements I_{cur} and I_{cur+1}. Our task is to find a history sequence $I_{v\text{-}w}$ with sub-sequence $\Gamma_{v'1\text{-}v'k}$ k-δ totally similar to $\Gamma_{u'\text{-}u'k}$. $\Gamma_{u'1\text{-}u'k} \approx \Gamma_{v'1\text{-}v'k}$ implies $C'_{u'1\text{-}u'k} \approx C'_{v'1\text{-}v'k}$, which implies in turn $G_{cur+1} = G_{u'k} \approx G_{v'k}$. Finally, we can fix the position of G_{cur+1} by $G_{v'k}$.

As demonstrated by experiments, the condition for totally similar is very strong. The notion of conditional similarity serves well. Suppose $C'_{u'1\text{-}u'k}$ is a total order subset of $C_{u\text{-}cur+1}$ with elements C_{cur} and C_{cur+1}. Our task is to find a history sequence $C_{v\text{-}w}$ with sub-sequence $C`_{v'1\text{-}v'k}$ $k$-$\delta$ conditionally similar to $C`_{u'1\text{-}u'k}$. $C'_{u'1\text{-}u'k} \approx C'_{v'1\text{-}v'k}$ implies $G_{cur+1} = G_{u'k} \approx G_{v'k}$, then $G_{cur+1}=G_{cur}+\triangle G$ and $\triangle G=G_{v'k}-G_{v'k\text{-}1}$ are the changes fishing grounds of this week takes to form fishing grounds next week. This it is the very reason we introduce several similarity measurements in previous section.

Due to the fact that it is difficult to set the value of, we adopt k- nearest neighbor method to retrieve k nearest neighbors, based on which the central fishing ground of next week can be calculated with great robustness and no value of δ.

5.11.4 *Revision with Frame*

Frame, as a knowledge representation method, is suggested by Marvin Minsky for recognition, natural language dialog, and other complex actions in 1975 (Minsky, 1975). A frame is a data-structure for representing a stereotyped entity, such as a situation, a concept, or an event. As for a new situation, we can get an instance of the entity by filling the values to the structure. The frame structure also offers a way to prediction for a particular entity under a concrete context where we can find the needed information. Slots are the places in frame structures where predication information stored. A frame comprises a number of slots, and each slot has its own name and the values that go into it. The values in the slot describe the attributes of the entity the frame represents. Usually, the slots are complex structures that have facets describing the properties of them, and every facet describes the characteristic of the slot from one viewpoint. Each facet takes one or more value, which is described by a concept or some concepts. Frame theory is a important knowledge representation technology and gains extensive application in that it organize knowledge in a human-like and concise manner. But the existing frame systems still lack the way to deal with conflicts in prediction and uncertain knowledge.

According to the prediction and study on marine fishery resources, we defined a frame system KBIF with a power to express uncertain knowledge with different importance. The main characteristics of KBIF includes: Weight – the influence degree of every slot on the frame, trust factor – the degree of every slot can be believed, and preference factor - the inclination degree in inheritance from parent frames.

The fish migration is influenced by a lot of factors and is too complicated to be described by traditional mathematics method and model. The prediction algorithm in CBR can only make predication based on some factors accumulated through a large number of historical data, while the expert knowledge of the fishing grounds is inaccuracy and incomplete. The key point in prediction accuracy is how to revise the prediction results about the central fishing grounds effectively. The knowledge representation in *KBIF* adopts three kinds of knowledge processing models: frame model, blackboard structure, fuzzy reasoning, and accordingly expert revision systems are divide into three parts: atom set, rule set, and conclusion set. The application of three models confers *KBIF* with a great expansibility and flexibility in rule definition.

Model One: Frame Model *KBIF*. The knowledge (mainly many kinds of restriction factors) in *KBIF* is coded in terms of rules and the domain experts can define the impact factors flexibly. These factors form a consistent system through inter-factor communications and reach the goal collaboratively.

The atom set is constructed as follows: First of all, collect the restricting factors in the formation of central fishing grounds, and divide them as the primitive elements of prediction rules. Each element is an atom of prediction rules, while all these elements form the atom set, i.e. the frame. The atom set utilizes knowledge representation principle of *KBIF* to express all influence factors that can be expressed in the prediction algorithm, and every factor can be treated as a slot in the frame. The frame is named as "The rule set of revision system" and layered into the following three layers: The station data, flow rate of the Changjiang River, and flow divisions. The station data include: Wind speed, wind direction, precipitation, temperature, atmospheric pressure, time, water temperature, salt degree, name of station, etc. The flow rate comprises time, month average. The flow divisions include: surface temperature, surface temperature gradient, surface salt degree, surface salt gradient, vertical water temperature gradient, vertical salt gradient, ground floor salt degree, ground floor salt d gradient, time, water temperature of ground floor and water temperature of ground floor. Atom set can be extended along with the enhancement of domain experts' understanding and meet the expanding requirement on prediction of central fishing grounds.

Model Two: Blackboard structure. We have developed the subsystem of blackboard in a broad sense on the basis of *KBIF*, which plays an important role in the decision process. With this subsystem, the users can divide the solution space into sub-structures, i.e., rule sets by homogeneity and heterogeneity cut arbitrarily.

We have defined the notion of virtual blackboard, which can be instanced to blackboard systems in accordance with the predication characteristics of fishery resources. It combines the knowledge sources, i.e., atom sets, rule generation set, and concrete application of fuzzy reasoning. The architecture of KBIF is a miniature blackboard, including a group of atom sets, a miniature blackboard and a controller for rule production. The architecture offers an effective combination of a knowledge layer and an experience reasoning layer. Atom sets are coded in the system implicitly, corresponding to the frame model, and can be expanded if needed. The controller for rule production combine the atom sets according to the requirements of experts, then it fills the blackboard with these combinations and offers two kinds of functions(blocking and enumerating) to promote the inference efficiency, finally produces the particular rules. This manner offers the ability of rule production gradually, lighten the inference load of expertise reasoning, and avoid the omission of knowledge while keeping focus on the internal structure of knowledge. The visual interface that the system used to express such structure enhances the knowledge expression method and offers effective inference ability.

Model Three: Fuzzy reasoning. We use fuzzy methods to choose the rules to be used in the revision of prediction results and thus more accurate results can be generated. In the rule set of prediction and revision system, the positions, sizes, outputs of central fishing grounds(X axle, Y axle) are defined fuzzily, and new predication results can be reached by revising the results generated by CBR reasoning. After the whole predication process, we can revise the conclusion sets through a learning process on the sequence of conclusions ordered by some pre-defined credibility degrees. In this manner, we can approach constantly and gradually to a believed solution.

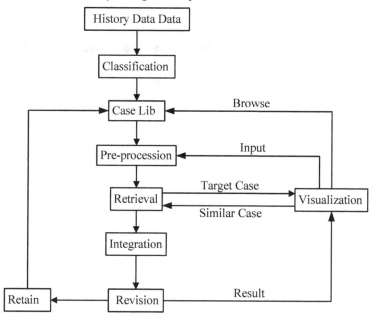

Fig. 5.7. System architecture

5.11.5 *Experiments*

The system architecture is sketched in Fig. 5.6. The historical data are stored in the case library, after a series of pretreatments such as appropriate clustering, variation. In order to improve the predication precision, we employ multi-strategy retrieval and utilize different similar computing technologies to find out the array of neighboring similar fishing grounds. Then the prediction results will be revised in accordance to the rules already stored in the system. The joint employment of machine learning and expertise will further improve the predication precision and system robustness.

While predicting the fishing grounds in winter, the historical data in summer are not considered, and due to the fact that remote fishing grounds have little effects on the formation of central fishing grounds, we only choose those sea situations closer to central fishing grounds. In our experiments, we choose 150 out of 600 pieces of sea situations dynamically. In this way, calculation can be reduced greatly through filtrations in terms of time and position while keeping prediction precision to a certain degree; the system respond time is less than 7 seconds. Visual human-computer interaction module offers friendly interface for input, output, inspection, and revision (see Fig. 5.7).

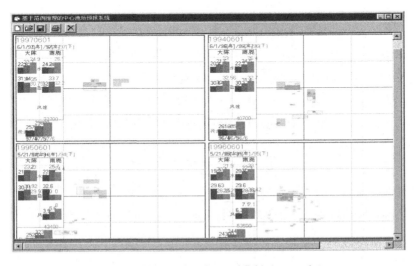

Fig. 5.8. The sea situation and fishing grounds

We measure the predication results in terms of the following two factors: completeness, that is the rate of predication fishing grounds over the actual ones; precession refers to the difference between prediction fishing grounds and actual fishing grounds. The fishery experts thinks that the precision is up to 80% once the difference is less than a fishing district. The experiments indicate the average prediction precision of the system is up to 78%, and our system has the value to be popularized(see Fig. 5.8). We have already finished the demonstration test, and now are cooperating with Shanghai Fishery Politics Bureau to apply the system to production.

Exercises

1. Explain what CBR is in your own words and describe several CBR systems briefly.
2. Describe the representation forms of cases and the basic thought underlying CBR.
3. Illustrate some applicable occasions for CBR ; and sketch the general process of CBR in terms of the flow diagram
4. What is the advantage of CBR over Rule-Based Learning (RBR)? Where are the abilities of CBR（CBL）systems.
5. List some kinds of similarities between the target cases and base ones; and try to compare the characteristics of some mainly-used methods for similarity measurement.
6. Refer to relevant materials and introduce an application system based on CBR; then discuss key challenges posed by CBR systems and how to overcome them.
7. Demonstrate the differences by examples between CBR systems and expert systems.

Chapter 6

Probabilistic Reasoning

6.1 Introduction

Bayesian Network is a graphic model for describing the connection probabilities among variables. It provides a natural representation of casual relationship and is often used to explore potential relationships among data. In the network, nodes represent variables and directed links represent dependant relationships between variables. With firm mathematical foundation, Bayesian Theory offers method for brief function calculation, and describes the coincidence of brief and evidence, and possesses the incremental learning property that brief varies along with the variation of evidence. In data mining, Bayesian networks can deal with incomplete or noisy data set. It describes correlations among data with probabilistic measurement, and thereby solves the problem of data inconsistency. It describes correlations among data with graphical method, which has clear semantic meaning and understandable representation. It also makes prediction and analysis with casual relationships among data. Bayesian network is becoming one of the most remarkable data mining methods due to its nice properties, including unique knowledge representation of uncertain information, capability for handling probability, and incremental learning with prior knowledge.

6.1.1 *History of Bayesian theory*

The foundational work of Bayesian School is Reverend Thomas Bayes' (1702-1761) "An Essay towards solving a Problem in the Doctrine of Chances". Maybe he felt the work was not perfect enough, this work was published not in his lifetime, but posthumously by his friend. As famous mathematician Laplace P. S. educed Law of Succession based on Bayesian method, Bayesian method and theory began to be recognized. In 19th century, because the problem of motivating and constructing prior probabilities was not adequately answered, Bayesian theory was not well accepted at that time. Early in 20th century, B. de Finetti and Jeffreys H. made significant contribution to Bayesian theory. After World War II, Wald A. proposed statistical decision theory. In this theory, Bayesian method played an important role. Besides, the development of information science also contributed to the reincarnation of Bayesian theory. In 1958, Bayes' paper was republished by Biometrika, the most historical statistical magazine in Britain. In 1950s, Robbins H. suggested to combine empirical Bayesian approach and conventional statistical method. The novel approach caused the attention of statistical research field, and soon showed its merits, and became an active research direction.

With the development of artificial intelligence, especially after the rise of machine learning and data mining, Bayesian theory gained much more development and applications. Its connotation has also varied greatly from its origination. In 1980s, Bayesian networks were used for knowledge representation in expert systems. In 1990s, Bayesian networks were applied to data mining and machine learning. Recently, more and more papers concerning Bayesian theory were published, which covered most fields of artificial intelligence, including casual reasoning, uncertain knowledge representation, pattern recognition, clustering analysis and so on. There appears an organization and a journal, ISBA, which focus especially on the progress on Bayesian theory.

6.1.2 Basic concepts of Bayesian method

In Bayesian theory, all kinds of uncertainties are represented with probabilities. Learning and reasoning are implemented via probabilistic rules. The Bayesian learning results are distributions of random variables, which show the briefs to various possible results. The foundations of Bayesian School are Bayesian theorem and Bayesian assumption. Bayesian theorem connects prior probabilities of events with their posterior probabilities. Assume the joint probability density of random vector x and θ is p(x, θ), and p(x) and p(θ) give the marginal densities of x and θ respectively. In common cases, x is an observation vector and θ is an unknown parameter vector. The estimation of parameter θ can be obtained with the observation vector via Bayesian theorem. The Bayesian theorem is as follows:

$$p(\theta \mid x) = \frac{\pi(\theta) p(x \mid \theta)}{p(x)} = \frac{\pi(\theta) p(x \mid \theta)}{\int \pi(\theta) p(x \mid \theta) d\theta} \ (\pi(\theta) \text{ is the prior of } \theta) \qquad (6.1)$$

From the formula above, we see that in Bayesian method the estimation of a parameter needs the prior information of the parameter and the information from evidence. In contrast, traditional statistical method, e.g. maximum likelihood, only utilizes the information from evidence. The general process to estimate parameter vector via Bayesian method is described as follows:

(1) Regard unknown parameters as random vector. This is the fundamental difference between Bayesian method and traditional statistical approach.
(2) Defined the prior $\pi(\theta)$ based on previous knowledge of parameter θ. This step is a controversial step, and is attacked by conventional statistical scientists.
(3) Calculate posterior density and make estimation of parameters according to the posterior distribution.

In the second step, if there is no previous knowledge to determine the prior $\pi(\theta)$ of a parameter, Bayes suggested to assume uniform distribution to be its distribution. This is called Bayesian assumption. Intuitionally, Bayesian assumption is well accepted. Yet, it encounters problem when no information about prior distribution is available, especially when parameter is infinite. Empirical Bayes (EB) Estimator combines conventional statistical method and Bayesian method, so that it applies conventional method to gain the marginal density $p(x)$, and then ascertains prior $\pi(\theta)$ with the following formula.

$$p(x) = \int_{-\infty}^{+\infty} \pi(\theta) p(x \,|\, \theta) d\theta$$

6.1.3 Applications of Bayesian network in data mining

1. Bayesian method in classification and regression analysis

Classification is to classify an object based on its feature vector and some constrains. In data mining, we mainly study how to learn classification rules from data or experiences. For classification, sometimes each feature vector correspond to one class label (determinate classification); sometimes different classes can overlap, where samples from different classes are very similar and we can only tell the probabilities of a sample in all classes and choose a class for the sample according to the probabilities. Bayesian School provides two methods to handle this situation: one is selecting the class with maximum posterior probability; the other is selecting the class with maximum utility function or minimum lost function. Let feature vector be $X = (x_1, x_2, ..., x_m)$, and class vector be $C = (c_1, c_2, ..., c_l)$. Classification is to assign a class c_i ($i \in (1, ..., l)$) to a feature vector X.

In the first method, the class c_i with maximum posterior probability will be selected, viz. $P(c_i|x) \geq P(c_j|x)$ $j \in (1 \cdots l)$. In this case the decision function is $r_i(x) = p(c_i|x)$. It has been proved that in this method the minimum classification error can be guaranteed.

The second method is often used in decision theory. It utilizes average benefit to evaluate decision risk, which has close relationship with degrees of uncertainty. Let $L_{ij}(X)$ be the loss of misclassifying a feature vector X of class c_i to class c_j. The class with minimum loss of X is $\underset{i}{Minimize} \{\sum_{j=1}^{l} L_{ij}(x) \cdot P(c_j | x)\}$. In this case, the decision function is $r_i(x) = \sum_{j=1}^{l} L_{ij}(x) \cdot P(c_j | x)$. If diagonal elements of $L_{ij}(X)$ are all 0 and non-diagonal elements of $L_{ij}(X)$ are all 1, viz. correct classification makes no loss and misclassification has same loss, the first method and the second method are equal.

In data mining, the research on Bayesian classification mainly focuses on how to learn the distribution of feature vectors and the correlation among feature vectors from data so that to find the best P(c_i|x) and $L_{ij}(X)$). By now successful models have been proposed, including Naïve Bayesian, Bayesian Network and Bayesian Neural Network. Bayesian classification method has been successfully applied to many fields, such as text classification, alphabet recognition, and economic prediction.

2. Bayesian method in casual reasoning and uncertain knowledge representation

Bayesian network is a graph to describe probabilistic relations of random variables. These years, Bayesian network has been the primary method of uncertain knowledge representation in expert system. Many algorithms have been proposed to learn Bayesian network from data. These techniques have gained reasonable success in data modeling, uncertainty reasoning and so on.

Compared to other knowledge representation method in data mining, such as rule representation, decision tree, artificial neural networks, Bayesian network possesses the following merits in knowledge representation (Cooper, 1992):

(1) Bayesian network can conveniently handle incomplete data. For example, when we face the classification or regression problem with multiple correlative variables, the correlation among variables is not the key element for standard supervised learning algorithms. As a result, missing values will cause large predictive bias. Yet Bayesian network can handle incomplete data with the

probabilistic correlation of variables.

(2) Bayesian network can learn the casual relation of variables. Casual relation is a very important pattern in data mining, mainly because: in data analysis, casual relation is helpful for field knowledge understanding; it can also easily lead to precise prediction even under much interference. For example, some sale analyzers wonder whether advertisement increasing will cause sales increasing. To get the answer, the analyzer must know whether advertisement increasing is the causation of sale increasing. For Bayesian network, this question can be easily answered even without experimental data, because the causal relation has been encoded in the Bayesian network.

(3) The combination of Bayesian network and Bayesian statistics can take full advantage of field knowledge and information from data. Everyone with modeling experiences knows that prior information or field knowledge is very important to modeling, especially when sample data are sparse or hardly to obtain. Some commercial expert system, which is constructed purely based on field expert knowledge, is a perfect example. Bayesian network, which expresses dependent relation with directed edge and uses probabilistic distribution to describe the strength of dependence, can integrate the prior knowledge and sample information well.

(4) The combination of Bayesian network and other models can effectively avoid over-fitting problem.

3. Bayesian method in clustering and pattern discovery

Generally, clustering is a special case of model selection. Each clustering pattern can be viewed as a model. The task of clustering is to find a pattern, which best fits the nature of data, from many models based on analysis and some other strategies. Bayesian method integrates prior knowledge and characteristics of current data to select the best model.

With Bayesian analysis Vaithyanathan et al. proposed a model based hierarchical clustering method (Vaithyanathan,1998). By partitioning feature set, they organized data to a hierarchical structure. The features either have unique distribution in different classes or have same distribution in some classes. They also give the method to determine the model structure with marginal likelihood, including how to automatically determine the number of classes, depth of the model tree, and the feature subset of each class.

AutoClass is a typical system that implements clustering with Bayesian method. This system automatically determines the number of classes and complexity of model by searching all possible classifications in the model space. It allows that features in certain classes have correlation and successive relation existing among classes (in the hierarchical structure of classes, some classes can share some model parameters). Detailed information about AutoClass can be found in the Website http://ic-www.arc.nasa.gov/ic/projects/bayes-group/autoclass.

Above, we only list some typical applications of Bayesian method. The applications of Bayesian method in data mining are far more to from these. The Bayesian neural network, which combines Bayesian method and neural network, and the Bayes Point Machine, which combines Bayesian method and statistical learning, are all interesting examples of applications of Bayesian method. Interested readers can find more in book (Amari, 1985).

6.2 Foundation of Bayesian Probability

6.2.1 *Foundation of probability theory*

Probability is a branch of mathematics, which focuses on the regularity of random phenomena. Random phenomena are phenomena that different results appear under same conditions. Random phenomena include individual random phenomena and substantive random phenomena. The regularity from the observation of substantive random phenomena is called statistical regularity.

Statistically, we conventionally call an observation, a registration or an experiment about phenomenon a trial. A random trial is an observation on a random phenomenon. Under same condition, random trials may lead to different results. But the sphere of all the possible results is estimable. The result of a random trial is both uncertain and predictable. Statistically, the result of a random trial is called random event, shortly by event.

Random event is the result that will appear or not appear in a random trial. In random phenomenon, the frequency of a mark is the total number that the mark appears in all trials.

Example 6.1 To study the product quality of a factory, we make some random samplings. In each sampling, the number of samples is different. The result of sampling is recoded and presented in Table 6.1.

Table 6.1 The result of sampling of product quality

Number of products examined	5	10	50	100	300	600	1000	5000	10000
Number of qualified products	5	8	44	91	272	542	899	4510	8999
Frequency of qualification	1	0.8	0.88	0.91	0.907	0.892	0.899	0.902	0.8997

In the Table, the number of products examined is the total number of products examined in one sample. The number of qualified products is the total number of qualified products in the examination. The frequency of qualification is the proportion of qualified products in all the products examined in one sample. From the Table, we can easily see that the relation of the number of a mark and the frequency of a mark. We can also find a statistical regularity. That is, as the number of products examined increases, the frequency of qualification inclines to 0.9 stably. Or the frequency of qualification wavers around a fixed number $p = 0.9$. So p is the statistical stable center of this series of trials. It represents the possibility of qualification of an examined product. The possibility is called probability.

Definition 6.1 *Statistical Probability: if in numbers of repeated trials the frequency of event A inclines to a constant p stably, it represents the possibility of appearance of event A, and we call this constant p the probability of event A, shortly by P(A).*

$$p = P(A)$$

So a probability is the stable center of a frequency. A probability of any event A is a nonnegative real number that is not bigger than 1.

$$0 \leq P(A) \leq 1$$

The statistical definition of probability has close relation with frequency and is easily understood. But it is a tough problem to find the probability of an arbitrary event with experiments. Sometimes it is even impossible. So we often calculate probability with classical probabilistic method or geometrical probabilistic method.

Definition 6.2 *Classical Probability: Let a trial have and only have finite N possible results, or N basic events. If event A contains K possible results, we call K/N the probability of event A, shortly P(A)*

$$P(A) = K/N \tag{6.2}$$

To calculate a classical probability, we need to know the number of all the basic events. So classical probability is restricted to the cases of finite population. In the case of infinite population or the total number of basic events unknown, geometrical probability model is used to calculate probability. Besides, geometrical probability also gives a general definition of probability.

Geometrical random trial: Assume Ω is a bounded domain of M-dimensional space, and $L(\Omega)$ is the volume of Ω. We consider the random trial that we throw a random point into Ω evenly and assume: (1) Random point may fall in any domain of Ω, but cannot fall outside of Ω. (2) The distribution of random point in Ω is even, viz. the possibility that random point falls into a domain is proportional to the volume of the domain, and is independent of the position or the shape of the domain in Ω. Under the restrictions above, we call a trial a geometrical random trial, where Ω is basic event space.

Event in geometrical random trial: Assume that Ω is the basic event space of geometrical random trial, and A is a subset of Ω that can be measured with volume, where L(A) is the M-dimensional volume of A. Then the event of "random point falls in domain A" is represented with A. In Ω, a subset that can be measured with volume is called a measurable set. Each measurable set can be viewed as an event. The set of all measurable subsets is represented by F.

Definition 6.3 *Geometrical Probability: Assume Ω is a basic event space of a geometrical random trial, and F is the set of all measurable subsets of Ω. Then the probability of any event A in F is the ratio between the volume of A and that of Ω.*

$$P(A) = V(A)/V(\Omega) \tag{6.3}$$

Definition 6.4 *Conditional Probability: The probability of event A under the condition that event B has happened is denoted by P(A|B). We call it the conditional probability of event A under condition B. P(A) is called unconditional probability.*

Example 6.2 There are two white balls and one black ball in a bag. Now we take out two balls in turn. Questions: (1) How much is the probability of the event that a white ball is picked in the first time? (2) How much is the probability of the event that a white ball is picked in the second time when a white ball has been picked in the first time?

Solution: Assume *A* is the event that a white ball is picked in the first time, and *B* is the event that a white ball is picked in the second time. Then {*B|A*} is the event that a white ball is picked in the second time when a white ball has been picked in the first time. According to Definition 6.4 we have:

(1) No matter under repeated sampling or non-repeated sampling, $P(A)=2/3$
(2) When sampling is non-repeated, $P(B|A)=1/2$; When sampling is repeated, $P(B|A) = P(B) = 2/3$. The conditional probability equals to non-conditional probability.

If the appearance of any of event *A* or *B* will not affect the probability of the other event, viz. $P(A) = P(A|B)$ or $P(B) = P(B|A)$. We call event *A* and *B* independent events.

Theorem 6.1 *(Addition Theorem) The probability of the sum of two mutually exclusive events equals to the sum of the probabilities of the two events. That is*

$$P(A+B) = P(A)+P(B)$$

The sum of probabilities of two mutually inverse events is 1. In another word, if $A+A^{-1} = \Omega$, and A and A^{-1} are mutually inverse, then P(A)+ P(A^{-1})=1, or P(A)=1-P(A^{-1})

If A and B are two arbitrary events, then

$$P(A+B)=P(A)+P(B)-P(AB)$$

holds. This theorem can be generalized to the case that involves more than three events.

$$P(A+B+C)=P(A)+P(B)+P(C)-P(AB)-P(BC)-P(CA)+P(ABC)$$

Theorem 6.2 *(Multiplication Theorem) Assume A and B are two mutually independent non-zero events, then the probability of the multiple event equals to the multiplication of probabilities of event A and B, that is:*

$$P(A \cdot B)=P(A) \cdot P(B) \text{ or } P(A \cdot B)=P(B) \cdot P(A)$$

Assume A and B are two arbitrary non-zero events, then the probability of the multiple event equals to the multiplication of the probability of event A (or B) and the conditional probability of event B (or A) under condition A (or B).

$$P(A \cdot B)=P(A) \cdot P(B|A) \text{ or } P(A \cdot B)=P(B) \cdot P(A|B)$$

This theorem can be generalized to the case that involves more than three events. When the probability of multiple event $P(A_1A_2...A_{n-1})>0$, we have:

$$P(A_1A_2...A_n)=P(A_1) \cdot P(A_2|A_1) \cdot P(A_3|A_1A_2) ...P(A_n|A_1A_2A_{n-1})$$

If all the events are pairwise independent, we have:

$$P(A_1A_2...A_n)=P(A_1) \cdot P(A_2) \cdot P(A_3) ...P(A_n)$$

6.2.2 Bayesian probability

(1) Prior Probability. A prior probability is the probability of an event that is gained from historical materials or subjective judgments. It is not verified and is estimated in the absence of evidence. So it is called prior probability. There are two kinds of prior probabilities. One is objective prior probability, which is calculated according to historical materials; the other is subjective prior probability, which is estimated purely based on the subjective experience when historical material is absent or incomplete.

(2) Posterior Probability. A posterior probability is the probability that is computed according to the prior probability and additional information from investigation via Bayesian Formula.

(3) Joint Probability. The joint probability of two events is the probability of the

intersection of the two events. It is also called multiplication formula.

(4) Total Probability Formula. Assume all the influence factors of event A are B_1, B_2, ..., and they satisfy $B_i \cdot B_j = \varnothing$, $(i \neq j)$ and $P(\cup B_i) = 1$, $P(B_i) > 0$, $i = 1, 2, ...,$ then we have:

$$P(A) = \sum P(B_i) P(A|B_i) \tag{6.4}$$

(5) Bayesian Formula. Bayesian formula, which is also called posterior probability formula or inverse probability formula, has wide application.

Assume $P(B_i)$ is prior probability, and $P(A_j|B_i)$ is new information gained from investigation, where $i=1, 2, ..., n$, and $j=1, 2, ..., m$. Then the posterior probability calculated with Bayesian Formula is:

$$P(B_i \mid A_j) = \frac{P(B_i)P(A_j \mid B_i)}{\sum_{k=1}^{m} P(B_k)P(A_j \mid B_k)} \tag{6.5}$$

Example 6.3 One kind of product is made in a factory. Three work teams (A_1, A_2, and A_3) are in charge of two specifications (B_1 and B_2) of the product. Their daily outputs are listed in Table 6.2

Table 6.2 Daily outputs of three teams

	B1	B2	Total
Team A1	2 000	1 000	3 000
Team A2	1 500	500	2 000
Team A3	500	500	1 000
Total	4 000	2 000	6 000

Now we randomly pick out one from the 6000 products. Please answer the following questions.

1. Calculate the following probabilities with Classical Probability

(1) Calculate the probabilities that the picked product comes from the outputs of A_1, A_2 or A_3 respectively.

Solution: $P(A_1)=3000/6000=1/2$

$P(A_2)=2000/6000=1/3$

$P(A_3)=1000/6000=1/6$

Calculate the probabilities that the picked product belongs to B_1 or B_2 respectively

Solution: $P(B_1)=4000/6000=2/3$

$P(B_2)=2000/6000=1/3$

(2) Calculate the probability that the pick product is B_1 and come from A_1

Solution: $P(A_1 \cdot B_1) = 2000/6000 = 1/3$

(3) If that the product comes from A_1 is known, how much is the probability that it belongs to B_1?

Solution: $P(B_1|A_1) = 2000/3000 = 2/3$

(4) If the product belongs to B_2, how much is the probability that it comes from A_1, A_2, or A_3 respectively?

Solution: $P(A_1|B_2) = 1000/2000 = 1/2$

$\quad\quad\quad P(A_2|B_2) = 500/2000 = 1/4$

$\quad\quad\quad P(A_3|B_2) = 500/2000 = 1/4$

2. Calculate the following probabilities with Conditional Probability

(1) If a product comes from A_1, how much is the probability that it belongs to B_1?

Solution: $P(B_1|A_1) = (1/3)/(1/2) = 2/3$

(2) If a product belongs to B_2, how much is the probability that it comes from A_1, A_2, or A_3 respectively?

Solution: $P(A_1|B_2) = (1/6)/(1/3) = 1/2$

$\quad\quad\quad P(A_2|B_2) = (1/12)/(1/3) = 1/4$

$\quad\quad\quad P(A_3|B_2) = (1/12)/(1/3) = 1/4$

3. Calculate the following probabilities with Bayesian Formula.

(1) Known: $P(B_1) = 4000/6000 = 2/3$

$\quad\quad\quad P(B_2) = 2000/6000 = 1/3$

$\quad\quad\quad P(A_1|B_1) = 1/2$

$\quad\quad\quad P(A_1|B_2) = 1/2$

Question: If a product comes from A_1, how much is the probability that it belongs to B_2?

Solution: Calculate Joint Probabilities:

$\quad\quad\quad P(B_1)P(A_1|B_1) = (2/3)(1/2) = 1/3$

$\quad\quad\quad P(B_2)P(A_1|B_2) = (1/3)(1/2) = 1/6$

Calculate Total Probability:

$\quad\quad\quad P(A_1) = (1/3) + (1/6) = 1/2$

Calculate posterior probability according to Bayesian Formula:

$\quad\quad\quad P(B_2|A_1) = (1/6) \div (1/2) = 1/3$

(2) Known: $P(A_1) = 3000/6\,000 = 1/2$

$\quad\quad\quad P(A_2) = 2000/6\,000 = 1/3$

$\quad\quad\quad P(A_3) = 1000/6\,000 = 1/6$

$\quad\quad\quad P(B_2|A_1) = 1000/3\,000 = 1/3$

$P(B_2|A_2)=500/2\ 000=1/4$

$P(B_2|A_3)=500/1\ 000=1/2$

Question: If a product belongs to B_2, how much is the probability that it comes from A_1, A_2, or A_3?

Solution: Calculate Joint Probabilities:

$P(A_1)P(B_2|A_1)=(1/2)(1/3)=1/6$

$P(A_2)P(B_2|A_2)=(1/3)(1/4)=1/12$

$P(A_3)P(B_2|A_3)=(1/6)(1/2)=1/12$

Calculate Total Probability P(B2):

$P(B_2)=\sum P(A_i)P(B_2\mid A_i)$

$=(1/2)(1/3)+(1/3)(1/4)+(1/6)(1/2)=1/3$

Calculate posterior probability according to Bayesian Formula:

$P(A_1|B_2)=(1/6)\div(1/3)=1/2$

$P(A_2|B_2)=(1/12)\div(1/3)=1/4$

$P(A_3|B_2)=(1/12)\div(1/3)=1/4$

6.3 Bayesian Problem Solving

Bayesian learning theory utilizes prior information and sample data to estimate unknown data. Probabilities (joint probabilities and conditional probabilities) are the representation of prior information and sample data in Bayesian learning theory. How to get the estimation of these probabilities (also called probabilistic density estimation) is much controversy in Bayesian learning theory. Bayesian density estimation focuses on how to gain the estimation of distribution of unknown variables (vectors) and its parameters based on sample data and prior knowledge from human experts. It includes two steps. One is to determine prior distributions of unknown variables; the other is to get the parameters of these distributions. If we know nothing about previous information, the distribution is called non-informative prior distribution. If we know the distribution and seek its proper parameters, the distribution is called informative prior distribution. Because learning from data is the most elementary characteristic of data mining, non-informative prior distribution is the main subject of Bayesian learning theory research.

The first step of Bayesian problem solving is to select Bayesian prior distribution. This is a key step. There are two common methods to select prior distribution, namely subjective method and objective method. The former makes use of human experience and expert knowledge to assign prior distribution. The latter is analyzing characters of data to get statistical features of data. It requires sufficient data to get the true distribution of data. In practice, these two methods are often combined. Several common methods for prior distribution selection are listed in the following. Before we discuss these methods, we give some definitions first.

Let θ be the parameter of a model, $X = (x_1, x_2, ..., x_n)$ be observed data, $\pi(\theta)$ be the prior distribution of θ. $\pi(\theta)$ represents the brief of parameter θ when no evidence exists. $l(x_1, x_2, ..., x_n|\theta) \propto p(x_1, x_2, ..., x_n|\theta)$ is likelihood function. It represents the brief of unknown data when parameter θ is known. $h(\theta|x_1, x_2, ..., x_n) \propto p(\theta|x_1, x_2, ..., x_n)$ is the brief of parameter θ after new evidence appears. Bayesian theorem describes the relation of them

$$h(\theta \mid x_1, x_2, \cdots x_n) = \frac{\pi(\theta)\, p(x_1, x_2, \cdots x_n \mid \theta)}{\int \pi(\theta)\, p(x_1, x_2, \cdots x_n \mid \theta)\, d\theta} \propto \pi(\theta) l(x_1, x_2, \cdots x_n \mid \theta)$$

(6.6)

Definition 6.5 *Kernel of Distribution Density: If f(x), the distribution density of random variable z, can be decomposed as f(x), = cg(x), where c is a constant independent of x, we call g(x) the kernel of f(x), shortly f(x) $\propto$ g(x). If we know the kernel of distribution density, we can determine corresponding constant according to the fact that the integral of distribution density in the whole space is 1. Therefore, the key of solving distribution density of a random variable is to solve the kernel of its distribution density.*

Definition 6.6 *Sufficient Statistic: To parameter θ, the statistic t(x_1, x_2, ..., x_n) is sufficient if the posterior distribution of θ, h(θ|x_1, x_2, ..., x_n), is always a function of θ and t(x_1, x_2, ..., x_n) in spite of its prior distribution.*
This definition clearly states that the information of θ in data can be represented by its sufficient statistics. Sufficient statistics are connections between posterior distribution and data. Below, we give out a theorem to judge whether a statistic is sufficient.

Theorem 6.3 The Neyman-Fisher Factorization Theorem: Let $f\theta$ (x) be the density or mass function for the random vector x, parametrized by the vector θ. The statistic t = T(x) is sufficient for θ if and only if there exist functions a(x) (not depending on θ) and $b\theta$ (t) such that $f\theta$ (x) = a(x) $b\theta$ (t) for all possible values of x.

6.3.1 Common methods for prior distribution selection

1. Conjugate family of distributions

Raiffa and Schaifeer suggested using conjugate distributions as prior distributions, where the posterior distribution and the corresponding prior distribution are the same kind of distribution. The general description of conjugate distribution is as follows:

Definition 6.7 *Let the conditional distribution of samples x_1, x_2, ..., x_n under parameters θ is $p(x_1, x_2, ..., x_n|\theta)$. If the prior density function $\pi(\theta)$ and its resulting posterior density function $\pi(\theta|x)$ are in the same family, the prior density function $\pi(\theta)$ is said to be conjugate to the conditional distribution $p(x|\theta)$.*

Definition 6.8 *Let $P = \{p(x|\theta): \theta \in \Theta\}$ be the density function family with parameters θ. $H = \pi(\theta)$ is the prior distribution family of θ. If for any given $p \in P$ and $\pi \in H$, the resulting posterior distribution $\pi(\theta|x)$ is always in family H, H is said to be the conjugate family to P*

When the density functions of data distribution and its prior are all exponential functions, the resulting function of their multiplication is the sample kind of exponential function. The only difference is a factor of proportionality. So we have:

Theorem 6.4 *If for random variable Z, the kernel of its density function $f(x)$ is exponential function, the density function belongs to conjugate family.*

All the distributions with exponential kernel function compose exponential family, which includes binary distribution, multinomial distribution, normal distribution, Gamma distribution, Poisson distribution and Dirichlet distribution.

Conjugate distributions can provide a reasonable synthesis of historical trials and a reasonable precondition for future trials. The computation of non-conjugate distribution is rather difficult. In contrast, the computation of conjugate distribution is easy, where only multiplication with prior is required. So, in fact, the conjugate family makes firm foundation for practical application of Bayesian learning.

2. Principle of maximum entropy

Entropy is used to quantify the uncertainty of event in information theory. If a random variable x takes two different possible value, namely a and b, comparing the following two case:

(1) $p(x=a) = 0.98$, $p(x=b) = 0.02$,

(2) $p(x=a) = 0.45$, $p(x=b) = 0.55$,

Obviously, the uncertainty of case 1 is much less than that of case 2. Intuitively, we can see that the uncertainty will reach maximum when the probabilities of two values are equal.

Definition 6.9 Let x be a discrete random variable. It takes at most countable values a_1, a_2, ..., a_k, ..., and $p(x=a_i) = p_i$ $i = 1, 2, ...$ The entropy of x is $H(x) = -\sum_i p_i \ln p_i$. For continuous random variable x, if the integral $H(x) = -\int p(x) \ln p(x)$ is meaningful, where p(x) is the density of variable x, the integral is called the entropy of a continuous random variable.

According to the definition, when two random variables have same distribution, they have equal entropy. So entropy is only related to distribution.
Principle of maximum entropy: For non-information data, the best prior distribution is the distribution, which makes the entropy maximum under parameters θ.

It can be proved that the entropy of a random variable, or vector, reaches maximum if and only if its distribution is uniform. Hence, the Bayesian assumption, which assumes non-information prior to be uniform, fits the principle of maximum entropy. It makes the entropy of a random variable, or vector, maximum. Below is the proof of the case of limited valued random variable.

Theorem 6.5 *Let random variable x take limited values a_1, a_2 , ..., a_n. The corresponding probabilities are p_1, p_2, ..., p_n. The entropy H(x) is maximum if and only if $p_1 = p_2 = ... = p_n = 1/n$.*

Proof   Consider $G(p_1, p_2, ..., p_n) = -\sum_{i=1}^{n} p_i \ln p_i + \lambda(\sum_{i=1}^{n} p_i - 1)$. To find its maximum, we let partial derivative of G with respective to p_i to be 0, and get the equations:

$$0 = \frac{\partial G}{\partial p_i} = -\ln p_{i-1} + \lambda \qquad\qquad (i = 1, 2, ..., n)$$

Solve the equations, we get $p_1 = p_2 = ... = p_n$. Because $\sum_{i=1}^{n} p_i = 1$, we have $p_1 = $

$p_2 = \ldots = p_n = 1/n$. Here the corresponding entropy is $-\sum_{i=1}^{n}\dfrac{1}{n}\ln\dfrac{1}{n} = \ln n$.

For continuous random variable, the result is the same.

From above, when there is no information to determine prior distribution, the principle of maximum distribution is a reasonable choice for prior selection. There are many cases where no information is available to determine prior, so Bayesian assumption is very important in these cases.

3. Jeffrey's principle

Jeffrey had made significant contribution to prior distribution selection. He proposed an invariance principle, which well solved a conflict in Bayesian assumption and gave out an approach to find prior density. Jeffrey's principle is composed of two parts: one is a reasonable requirement to prior distribution; the other is giving out concrete approach to find a correct prior distribution fitting the requirement.

There is a conflict in Bayesian assumption: If we choose uniform as the distribution of parameter θ, once we take function $g(\theta)$ as parameter, it should also obey uniform distribution and vice versa. Yet the above precondition cannot lead to expected result. To solve the conflict, Jeffrey proposed an invariance request. That is, a reasonable principle for prior selection should have invariance.

If we choose $\pi(\theta)$ as the prior distribution of parameter θ, according to invariance principle, $\pi_g(g(\theta))$, the distribution of function $g(\theta)$ should satisfy the following:

$$\pi(\theta) = \pi_g(g(\theta))|\, g'(\theta)| \tag{6.7}$$

The key point is how to find a prior distribution $\pi(\theta)$ to satisfy the above condition. Jeffrey skillfully utilized the invariance of Fisher information matrix to find a required $\pi(\theta)$.

The distribution of parameter θ has the kernel of the square root of information matrix $I(\theta)$, viz. $\pi(\theta) \propto |\, I(\theta)|^{1/2}$, Where $I(\theta) = E(\dfrac{\partial \ln p(x_1,x_2,\cdots x_n;\theta)}{\partial \theta})(\dfrac{\partial \ln p(x_1,x_2,\cdots x_n;\theta)}{\partial \theta})'$. The concrete deriving process is not presented here. Interested readers can find them in related references. It is noted that Jeffrey's Principle is just a principle of finding reasonable prior, while using square root of information matrix as the kernel of prior is a concrete approach. They are different. In fact, we can seek other concrete approaches to embody the principle.

6.3.2 *Computational learning*

Learning is that a system can improve its behavior after running. Is the posterior distribution gained via Bayesian formula better than its corresponding prior? What is its learning mechanism? Here we analyze normal distribution as an example to study the effect of prior information and sample data by changing parameters.

Let $x_1, x_2, \ldots, x_n$ be a sample from normal distribution $N(\theta, \sigma_1^2)$, where σ_1^2 is known and θ is unknown. To seek $\tilde{\theta}$, the estimation of θ, we take another normal distribution as the prior of θ. That is

$$\pi(\theta) = N(\mu_0, \sigma_0^2).$$

The resulting posterior distribution of θ is also normal distribution:

$$h(\theta | \overline{x}_1) = N(\alpha_1, d_1^2)$$

where

$$\overline{x}_1 = \sum_{i=1}^{n} \frac{x_i}{n}, \quad \alpha_1 = (\frac{1}{\sigma_0^2}\mu_0 + \frac{n}{\sigma_1^2}\overline{x}_1)/(\frac{1}{\sigma_0^2} + \frac{n}{\sigma_1^2}), \quad d_1^2 = (\frac{1}{\sigma_0^2} + \frac{n}{\sigma_1^2})^{-1},$$

Take α_1, the expectation of the posterior $h(\theta | \overline{x})$ as the estimation of θ, we have:

$$\tilde{\theta} = E(\theta | \overline{x}_1) = (\frac{1}{\sigma_0^2}\mu_0 + \frac{n}{\sigma_1^2}\overline{x}_1) \cdot d_1^2 \tag{6.8}$$

Therefore, $\tilde{\theta}$, the estimation of θ, is the weighted average of μ_0, the expectation of prior, and $\overline{x}_1$, the sample mean. σ_0^2 is the variance of $N(\mu_0, \sigma_0^2)$, so its reciprocal, $1/\sigma_0^2$, is the precision of μ_0. Similarly, σ_1^2/n is the variance of sample mean $\overline{x}$, so its reciprocal is the precision of $\overline{x}_1$. Hence, we see that $\tilde{\theta}$ is the weighted average of μ_0 and $\overline{x}_1$, where the weights are their precisions respectively. The smaller the variance, the bigger the weight. Besides, the bigger the sample size n, the smaller the variance σ_1^2/n, or the bigger the weight of sample mean. This means that when n is quite large, the effect of prior mean will be very small. Above analysis illustrate that the posterior from Bayesian formula integrates the prior information and sample data. The result is more reasonable than that based on merely prior information or sample data. The learning mechanism is effective. The analysis based on other conjugate prior distribution leads to similar result.

According to previous discussion, with the conjugate prior, we can use the posterior information as the prior of next computation and seek the next posterior by integrating more sample information. If we repeat this process time after time, can we get posterior increasingly close to the reality? We study this problem in the following:

Let new sample x_1, x_2, ... , x_n is from normal distribution $N(\theta, \sigma_2^2)$, where σ_2^2 is known and θ is unknown. If we use previous posterior $h(\theta|\bar{x}_1) = N(\alpha_1, d_1^2)$ as the prior of next round computation, then the new posterior is $h_1(\theta|\bar{x}_2) = N(\alpha_2, d_2^2)$, where

$$\bar{x}_2 = \sum_{i=1}^{n} \frac{x_i}{n}, \quad \alpha_2 = (\frac{1}{d_1^2}\alpha_1 + \frac{n}{\sigma_2^2}\bar{x}_2)/(\frac{1}{d_1^2} + \frac{n}{\sigma_2^2}) \quad d_2^2 = (\frac{1}{d_1^2} + \frac{n}{\sigma_2^2})^{-1}.$$

We use $\alpha_2 = (\frac{1}{\sigma_0^2}\mu_0 + \frac{n}{\sigma_1^2}\bar{x})/(\frac{1}{\sigma_0^2} + \frac{n}{\sigma_1^2})$, the expectation of posterior

$h_1(\theta|\bar{x}_2)$ as the estimation of θ. Because $\alpha_1 = (\frac{1}{\sigma_0^2}\mu_0 + \frac{n}{\sigma_1^2}\bar{x}_1) \cdot d_1^2$, we have

$$\alpha_2 = (\frac{1}{d_1^2}\alpha_1 + \frac{n}{\sigma_2^2}\bar{x}_2) \cdot d_2^2 = (\frac{1}{\sigma_0^2}\mu_0 + \frac{n}{\sigma_1^2}\bar{x}_1 + \frac{n}{\sigma_2^2}\bar{x}_2) \cdot d_2^2$$

$$= (\frac{1}{\sigma_0^2}\mu_0 + \frac{n}{\sigma_1^2}\bar{x}_1) \cdot d_2^2 + \frac{n}{\sigma_2^2}\bar{x}_2 \cdot d_2^2 \tag{6.9}$$

and $\frac{n}{\sigma_2^2} > 0$, so $d_2^2 = (\frac{1}{d_1^2} + \frac{n}{\sigma_2^2})^{-1} = (\frac{1}{\sigma_0^2} + \frac{n}{\sigma_1^2} + \frac{n}{\sigma_2^2})^{-1} < d_1^2 = (\frac{1}{\sigma_0^2} + \frac{n}{\sigma_1^2})^{-1}$

In α_2, $(\frac{1}{\sigma_0^2}\mu_0 + \frac{n}{\sigma_1^2}\bar{x}_1) \cdot d_2^2 < \alpha_1$. It is clearly that because of the addition of new sample, the proportion of original prior and old sample declines. According to equation (6.9), with the continuous increase of new sample (here we assume the sample size keeps invariant), we have:

$$\alpha_m = (\frac{1}{\sigma_0^2}\mu_0 + \frac{n}{\sigma_1^2}\bar{x}_1 + \frac{n}{\sigma_2^2}\bar{x}_2 + ... + \frac{n}{\sigma_m^2}\bar{x}_m) \cdot d_m^2$$

$$= (\frac{1}{\sigma_0^2}\mu_0 + \sum_{k=1}^{m}\frac{n}{\sigma_k^2}\bar{x}_k) \cdot d_m^2 \quad (k = 1, 2, ... , m) \tag{6.10}$$

From equation (6.10), if the variance of new samples are same, they equal to a sample with the size of $m \times n$. The above process weighted all the sample means with their precisions. The higher the precision, the bigger the weight. If the prior distribution is estimated precisely, we can use less sample data and only need a little computation. This is especially useful in the situation where sample is hard to be collected. It is also the point that Bayesian approach outcomes other methods. Therefore, the determination of prior distribution in Bayesian learning is extremely important. If there is no prior information and we adopt non-information prior, with the increase of sample, the effect of sample will become more and more salient. If the noise of sample is small, the posterior will be increasingly close to its true value. The only matter is that large computation is required.

6.3.3 *Steps of Bayesian problem solving*

The steps of Bayesian problem solving can be summarized as follows:

(1) Define random variable. Set unknown parameters as random variable or vector, shortly by θ. The joint density $p(x_1, x_2, ..., x_n; \theta)$ of sample $x_1, x_2, ..., x_n$ is regarded as the conditional density of $x_1, x_2, ..., x_n$ with respect to θ, shortly by $p(x_1, x_2, ..., x_n | \theta)$ or p(D|θ).
(2) Determine prior distribution density $p(\theta)$. Use conjugate distribution. If there is no information about prior distribution, then use Bayesian assumption of non-information prior distribution.
(3) Calculate posterior distribution density via Bayesian theorem.
(4) Make inference of the problem with the resulting posterior distribution density.

Take the case of single variable and single parameter for example. Consider the problem of thumbtack throwing. If we throw a thumbtack up in the air, the thumbtack will fall down and reset at one of the two states: on its head or on its tail. Suppose we flip the thumbtack $N+1$ times. From the first N observations, how can we get the probability of the case head in the $N+1$th throwing?

Step 1 Define a random variable Θ. The value θ corresponds to the possible value of the real probability of head. The density function $p(\theta)$ represents the uncertainty of Θ. The variable of the ith result is X_i ($i=1,2,..., N+1$), and the set of observation is $D=\{X_1=x_1,..., X_n=x_n\}$. Our objective is to calculate $p(x_{N+1}|D)$.

Step 2 According to Bayesian theorem, we have $p(\theta|D)=\dfrac{p(\theta)p(D|\theta)}{p(D)}$, where

$p(D) = \int p(D|\theta)p(\theta)d\theta$, p(D|$\theta$) is the binary likelihood function of sample.

If θ, the value of Θ, is known; the observation value in D is independent; and the probability of head (tail) is θ, the probability of tail is $(1-\theta)$; then:

$$p(\theta|D) = \frac{p(\theta)\theta^h (1-\theta)^t}{p(D)} \tag{6.11}$$

Where h and t are the times of head and tail in the observation D respectively. They are sufficient statistics of sample binary distribution.

Step 3 Seek the mean of Θ as the probability of case head in the N+1th toss:

$$p(X_{N+1} = heads \,|\, D) = \int p(X_{N+1} = heads \,|\, \theta)p(\theta \,|\, D)d\theta$$

$$= \int \theta \cdot p(\theta \,|\, D)d\theta \equiv E_{p(\theta|D)}(\theta) \tag{6.12}$$

Where $E_{p(\theta|D)}(\theta)$ is the expectation of θ under the distribution $p(\theta|D)$

Step 4 Assign prior distribution and supper parameters for Θ.

Common method for prior assignment is to assume prior distribution first, and then to determine proper parameters. Here we assume the prior distribution is Beta distribution:

$$p(\theta) = Beta\left(\theta \,|\, \alpha_h, \alpha_t\right) \equiv \frac{\Gamma(\alpha)}{\Gamma(\alpha_h)\Gamma(\alpha_t)} \theta^{\alpha_h - 1}(1-\theta)^{\alpha_t - 1} \tag{6.13}$$

Where $\alpha_h > 0$ and $\alpha_t > 0$ are parameters of Beta distribution, and $\alpha = \alpha_h + \alpha_t$, and $\Gamma(\cdot)$ is Gamma function. To distinguish with parameter θ, σh and α_t are called "Supper Parameters". Because Beta distribution belongs to conjugate family, the resulting posterior is also Beta distribution.

$$p(\theta|D) = \frac{\Gamma(\alpha + N)}{\Gamma(\alpha_h + h)\Gamma(\alpha_t + t)} \theta^{\alpha_h + h - 1}(1-\theta)^{\alpha_t + t - 1}$$

$$= Beta\left(\theta \,|\, \alpha_h + h, \alpha_t + t\right) \tag{6.14}$$

To this distribution, its expectation of θ has a simple form:

$$\int \theta \cdot Beta(\theta \,|\, \alpha_h, \alpha_t)d\theta = \frac{\alpha_h}{\alpha} \tag{6.15}$$

Therefore, for a given Beta prior, we get the probability of head in the N+1th toss as follows:

$$p(X_{N+1} = heads \,|\, D) = \frac{\alpha_h + h}{\alpha + N} \tag{6.16}$$

There are many ways to determine the supper parameters of prior Beta distribution $p(\theta)$, such as imagined future data and equivalent samples. Other methods can be found in the works of Winkler, Chaloner and Duncan. In the method of imagined future data, two equations can be deduced from equation (6.16), and two supper parameters α_h and α_t can be solved accordingly.

In the case of single variable multiple parameters (a single variable with multiple possible states), commonly X is regarded as a continuous variable with Gaussian distribution. Assume its physical density is $p(x|\theta)$, then we have:

$$p(x \mid \theta) = (2\pi v)^{-1/2} e^{-(x-\mu)^2/2v^2}$$

where $\theta = \{\mu, v\}$.

Similar to previous approach on binary distribution, we firstly assign the prior of parameters and then solve the posterior with the data $D=\{X_1=x_1, X_2=x_2,\ldots, X_N=x_N\}$ via Bayesian theorem.

$$P(\theta|D)=p(D|\theta)p(\theta)/ p(D)$$

Next, we use the mean of Θ as the prediction:

$$p(x_{N+1} \mid D) = \int p(x_{N+1}|\theta)p(\theta \mid D)d\theta \tag{6.17}$$

For exponential family, the computation is effective and close. In the case of multisamples, if the observed value of X is discrete, Dirichlet distribution can be used as the prior distribution, which can simplify the computation.

The computational learning mechanism of Bayesian theorem is to get the weighted average of the expectation of prior distribution and the mean of sample, where the higher the precision, the bigger the weight. Under the precondition that the prior is conjugate distribution, posterior information can be used as the prior in the next round computation, so that it can be integrated with further obtained sample information. If this process is repeated time after time, the effect of sample will be increasingly prominent. Because Bayesian method integrates prior information and posterior information, it can both avoid the subjective bias when using only prior information and avoid numerous blind searching and computation when sample information is limited. Besides, it can also avoid the affect of noise when utilizing only posterior information. Therefore it is suitable for problems of data mining with statistical features and problems of knowledge discovery, especially the problems where sample is hard to collect or the cost of collecting sample is high. The key of effective learning with Bayesian method is determining prior reasonably and precisely. Currently, there are only some principles for prior determination, and there is no operable whole theory to determine priors. In many cases the reasonability and precision of prior distribution is hardly to evaluate. Further research is required to solve these problems.

6.4 Naïve Bayesian Learning Model

In naïve Bayesian learning models, training sample I is decomposed into feature vector X and decision class variable C. Here, it is assumed that all the weights in a feature vector are independently given the decision variable. In another word, each weight affects the decision variable independently. Although the assumption to some extent limits the sphere of naïve Bayesian model, in practical applications, naïve Bayesian model can both exponentially reduce the complexity for model construction and can express striking robustness and effectiveness even when the assumption is unsatisfied (Nigam, 1998). It has been successfully applied in many data mining tasks, such as classification, clustering, model selection and so on. Currently, many researchers are working to relax the limitation of independence among variables (Heckerman, 1997), so that the model can be applied more widely.

6.4.1 Naïve Bayesian learning model

Bayesian theorem tells us how to predict the class of incoming sample given training samples. The rule of classification is maximum posterior probability, which is given in the following equation:

$$P(C_i \mid A) = P(C_i) * P(A \mid C_i) \Big/ P(A)$$

(6.18)

Here A is a test sample to be classified, $P(Y|X)$ is the conditional probability of Y under the condition of X. The probabilities at the right side of the equation can be estimated from training data. Suppose that the sample is represented as a vector of features. If all features are independent for given classes, P(A|Ci) can be decomposed as a product of factors: $P(a_1 \mid C_i) \times P(a_2 \mid C_i) \times \cdots \times P(a_m \mid C_i)$, where ai is the ith feature of the test sample. Accordingly, the posterior computation equation can be rewritten as:

$$P(C_i \mid A) = \frac{P(C_i)}{P(A)} \prod_{j=1}^{m} P(a_j \mid C_i)$$

(6.19)

The entire process is called naïve Bayesian classification. In the common sense, only when the independent assumption holds, or when the correlation of features is very weak, the naïve Bayesian classifier can achieve the optimal or sub-optimal result. Yet the strong limited condition seems inconsistent with the fact that naïve Bayesian classifier gains striking performance in many fields, including some fields where there is obvious dependence among features. In 16 out of total 28 data sets of UCI, naïve Bayesian classifier outperforms the C4.5 algorithms and has similar performance with that of CN2 and PEBLS. Some research works report similar results(Clark & Niblett,1989; Dougherty Kohavi & Sahami,1995). In the same time, researchers have also successfully proposed some strategy to relax the limitation of independence among features (Nigam, 1998).

The conditional probability in formula (6.19) can be gained using maximum likelihood estimation:

$$P(v_j \mid C_i) = \frac{count(v_j \wedge c_i)}{count(c_i)} \tag{6.20}$$

To avoid zero probability, if the actual conditional probability is zero, it is assigned to be $0.5/N$, where N is the total number of examples.

Suppose that there are only two classes, namely class0 and class1, and a_1, ..., a_k represent features of test set. Let $b_0 = P(C = 0)$, $b_1 = P(C = 1) = 1 - b_0$, $p_{j0} = P(A_j = a_j \mid C = 0)$, $p_{j1} = P(A_j = a_j \mid C = 0)$, then:

$$p = P(C = 1 \mid A_1 = a_1 \wedge \cdots \wedge A_k = a_k) = (\prod_{j=1}^{k} p_{j1})b_1 / z \tag{6.21}$$

$$q = P(C = 0 \mid A_1 = a_1 \wedge \cdots \wedge A_k = a_k) = (\prod_{j=1}^{k} p_{j0})b_0 / z \tag{6.22}$$

where z is a constant. After taking logarithm on both sides of the above two equations, we subtract the second equation from the first one and get:

$$\log p - \log q = (\sum_{j=1}^{k} \log p_{j1} - \log p_{j0}) + \log b_1 - \log b_0 \tag{6.23}$$

Here, let $w_j = \log p_{j1} - \log p_{j0}$, $b = \log b_1 - \log b_0$, the above equation is written as:

$$\log (1 - p) / p = -\sum_{j=1}^{k} w_j - b \tag{6.24}$$

After taking exponential on both sides of equation (6.24) and rearranging, we have:

$$p = \frac{1}{1 + e^{-\sum_{j=1}^{k} w_j - b}} \tag{6.25}$$

To calculate this value, we assume that feature A_j has $v(j)$ possible values. Let

$$w_{jj'} = \log P(A_j = a_{jj'} \mid c = 1)$$

$$\log P(A_j = a_{jj'} \mid c = 0) \quad (1 \leq j' \leq v(j)) \tag{6.26}$$

We have:

$$P(C(x) = 1) = \frac{1}{1 + e^{-(\sum_{j=1}^{k} \sum_{j'}^{v(j)} I(A_j(x) = a_{jj'})w_{jj'} - b)}} \tag{6.27}$$

Where I is a characteristic function. if φ is true, then $I(\varphi)=1$; else $I(\varphi)=0$; In practical computation, equation (6.27) can be calculated similar to equation (6.20).

In fact, equation (6.27) is a perception function with a sigmoid activation function. The input of this function is the possible values of all features. So, to some extent, naïve Bayesian classifier is equal to a perception model. Further research demonstrated that naïve Bayesian classifier can be generalized to logical regression with numerical features.

Consider equation (6.20). If A_j takes discrete values, $count(A_j = a_j \wedge C = c_i)$ can be calculated directly from training samples. If A_j is continuous, it should be discretized. In unsupervised discretization, a feature is discretized into M equally wide sections, where $M=10$ commonly. We can also utilize more complicated discretization method, such as supervised discretization method.

Let each A_j be a numerical feature (discrete or continuous). The logical regression model is:

$$\log \frac{P(C=1 \mid A_1 = a_1, \cdots A_k = a_k)}{P(C=0 \mid A_1 = a_1, \cdots A_k = a_k)} = \sum_{j=1}^{k} b_j a_j + b_0 \qquad (6.28)$$

After transforming as that of equation (6.24), we have:

$$p = \frac{1}{1 + e^{-\sum_{j=1}^{k} b_j a_j - b_0}} \qquad (6.29)$$

Obviously, this is also a perception function with a sigmoid activation function. Its inputs are all the feature values. Using function $f_j(\varphi)$ to replace $b_j a_j$. If the sphere of A_j is divided into M parts and the ith part is $[c_{j(i-1)}, c_{ji}]$, the function $f_j(\varphi)$ is:

$$b_j a_j = f_j(a_j) = \sum_{i=1}^{M} b_{ji} I(c_{j(i-1)} < a_j \leq c_{ji}) \qquad (6.30)$$

where b_{ji} is a constant. According to equation (6.29) and (6.30), we have:

$$P(C(x)=1) = \frac{1}{1 + e^{-(\sum_{j=1}^{k} \sum_{i}^{M} b_{ji} I(c_{j(i-1)} < a_j \leq c_{ji})) - b_0}} \qquad (6.31)$$

This is the final regression function. So naïve Bayesian classifier is a non-parametric and non-linear extension of logical regression. By setting $b_{ji} = (c_{j(i-1)} + c_{ij})/(2b_j)$, we can get a standard logical regression formula.

6.4.2 *Boosting of naïve Bayesian model*

In boosting, a series of classifiers will be built, and in each classifier in series, examples misclassified by previous classifier will be given more attention. Concretely, after learning classifier k, the weights of training examples that are misclassified by classifier k will increase, and classifier $k+1$ will be learnt based on the newly weighted training examples. This process will be repeated T times. The final classifier is the synthesis of all the classifiers in series.

Initially, each training example is set with a weight. In the learning process, if some example is misclassified by one classifier, in the next learning round, the corresponding weight will be increased, so that the next classifier will pay more attention to it.

The boosting algorithm for binary classification problem is given out by Freund and Scbapire as the AdaBoost Algorithm (Freund, 1995).

Algorithm 6.1 AdaBoost Algorithm.

Input:

N training examples $< (x_1, y_1 >, \cdots (x_N, y_N) >$

Distribution of the N training examples, D: w, where w is the weight vector of training example.

T: the number of rounds for training.

1. Initialize:

2. Initial weight vector of training examples: $w_i = 1/N\ i = 1, \cdots, N$

3. for $t=1$ to T

4.   Given weights w_i^t, find a hypothesis $H^{(t)} : X \rightarrow [0, 1]$

5.   Estimation the general error of hypothesis $H^{(t)}$:

$$e^{(t)} = \sum_{i=1}^{N} w_i^{(t)} \mid y_i - h_i^{(t)}(x_i) \mid$$

6.   Calculate $\beta^{(t)} = e^{(t)} \Big/ (1 - e^{(t)})$

7.   Renew the next round weights of examples with

$$w_i^{(t+1)} = w_i^{(t)} (\beta^{(t)})^{1 - \mid y_i - h_i^{(t)}(x_i) \mid}$$

8.   Normalize $w_i^{(t+1)}$, so that they are summed up to 1

9. End for

10. Output

$$h(x) = \begin{cases} 1 & if\ \sum_{t=1}^{T} (\log \frac{i}{\beta^{(t)}}) h^{(t)}(x) \geq \frac{1}{2} \sum_{t=1}^{T} (\log \frac{i}{\beta^{(t)}}) \\ 0 & otherwize \end{cases}$$

Here we assume that all the classifiers are effective. In another word, for each classifier, the examples correctly classified are more than the ones misclassified, $e^t < 0.5$. Hence, $\beta^{(t)} < 1$. When $\mid y_i - h_i^{(t)}(x_i) \mid$ increases, $w_i^{(t+1)}$ will increase accordingly. The algorithm fulfills the idea of boosting.

Some notes to the algorithm:

(1) $h^{(t)}(x)$ is calculated via output formula, and the result is either 0 or 1.

(2) The calculation of conditional probability $P(A_j = a_{jj} \mid C = c)$ in formula (6.20). If we do not consider the weights, the computational basis for *count(condition)* is 1. For example, if there are k examples satisfied condition, then *count(condition)* = k. If we consider the weights, the computational basis for each example is its weight. For example if there are k examples satisfied condition, then $count(condition) = \sum_i^k w_i$. In this case, the adjustment of weights embodies the idea of boosting.

(3) The output of the algorithm means that for an incoming input x, according to Step 6 in the algorithm, we can use the result of learning to generate of output by voting.

The final combined hypothesis can be defined as:

$$H(x) = \frac{1}{1 + \prod_{t=1}^{T} (\beta^{(t)})^{2r(x)-1}}$$

where $r(x) = \dfrac{\sum_{t=1}^{T} (\log 1/\beta^t) H^{(t)}(x)}{\sum_{t=1}^{T} (\log 1/\beta^t)}$

Below we will demonstrate that after boosting the represent capability of combined naïve Bayesian classifier equals to that of multiple layered perception model with one hidden layer. Let $\alpha = \prod_{t=1}^{T} \beta^t$ and $v^{(t)} = \log \beta^{(t)} / \log \alpha$, then:

$$H(x) = \frac{1}{1 + \alpha^{2(\sum_{t=1}^{T} v^{(t)} H^{(t)}(x))-1}} = \frac{1}{1 + e^{\sum_{t=1}^{T} 2\log \beta^{(t)} H^{(t)}(x) - \sum_{t=1}^{T} \log \beta^{(t)}}}$$

The output of combined classifier is the output of a sigmoid function, which takes the outputs of single classifiers and their weights as its parameters. Since a naïve Bayesian classifier equals to a perception machine, the combined classifier equals to a perception network with a hidden layer.

The boosting naïve Bayesian method for multiple classification problems is as follows:

Algorithm 6.2 Multiple Classification AdaBoost Algorithm

    Input:

    N training examples $< (x_1, y_1 >, \cdots (x_N, y_N) >$

    Distribution of the N training examples, D: w, where w is the weight vector of training example.

    T: the number of rounds for training.

  1. Initialize:

      Initial weight vector of training examples $w_i = 1/N, \ i = (1...N)$

  2. *for* $t = 1$ *to* T

  3.   Given weights w_i^t , find a hypothesis $H^{(t)} : X \to Y$

  4.   Estimation the general error of hypothesis $H^{(t)}$:

$$e^{(t)} = \sum_{i=1}^{N} w_i^{(t)} I(y_i \neq h_i^{(t)}(x_i))$$

  5.   Calculate $\beta^{(t)} = e^{(t)} \big/ (1 - e^{(t)})$

  6.   Renew the next round weights of examples with

$$w_i^{(t+1)} = w_i^{(t)} (\beta^{(t)})^{1 - I(y_i = h_i^{(t)}(x_i))}$$

  7.   Normalize $w_i^{(t+1)}$, so that they are summed up to 1

  8. End for

  9. Output:

$$h(x) = \arg \max_{y \in Y} \sum_{t=1}^{T} (\log \frac{i}{\beta^{(t)}}) I(h^{(t)}(x) = y)$$

Where $I(\phi) = 1$ if $\phi = T$; $I(\phi) = 0$ otherwise.

6.4.3 *The computational complexity*

Suppose a sample in the sample space has f features, and each feature takes v values. The naïve Bayesian classifier deduced by formula (6.27) will have $fv+1$ parameters. These parameters are accumulatively learnt $2fv+2$ times. In each learning process, each feature value of each training example will improve the final precision. So the time complexity for n training examples is $O(nf)$, independent of v. Substantially, this time complexity is optimal. For boosting naïve Bayesian classifier, the time complexity of each round is $O(nf)$. T round training corresponds to $O(Tnf)$. Notice that T is a constant. So the entire time complexity is still $O(nf)$.

For naïve Bayesian classifier, the primary computation is counting. Training examples can be processed either sequentially or in batches from disk or tape. So this method is perfectly suit for knowledge discovery on large data set. Training set is not necessarily loaded to memory entirely, and part of it can be kept in the disks or tapes. Yet the boosting naïve Bayesian model also has the following problems.

(1) From the idea of boosting, when noise exists in training set, boosting method will take it as useful information and amplify its effect with large weight. This will reduce the performance of boosting. If there are many noise data, boosting will lead to worse result.

(2) Although theoretically boosting can achieve 0 error rate for training set, in its practical application of naïve Bayesian model, 0 classification error in training set is generally hardly guaranteed.

6.5 Construction of Bayesian Network

6.5.1 *Structure of Bayesian network and its construction*

In short, Bayesian network is a directed acyclic graph with probabilistic notes. The graphic model can be utilized to represent the (physical or Bayesian) joint distribution of large variable set. It can also be used to analyze correlations among numerous variables. With the capability of learning and statistical reasoning under Bayesian theorem, it can fulfill many data mining tasks, such as prediction, classification, clustering, casual analysis and so on.

Given a series of variables $X=\{x_1, x_2, \ldots, x_n\}$, a Bayesian network is composed of two components: one is network structure S, which represents the conditional independence among variables X; the other is local distribution set P, which is related to every variable. The two components define the joint probability of X. S is a directed acyclic graph. Nodes in S and variables in X are one to one correspondingly. Let x_i be a variable or node and Pa_i be the parent nodes of x_i in S. The absence of arc between nodes usually represents conditional independence. The joint probability of X is represented as:

$$p(X) = \prod_{i=1}^{n} p(x_i \mid Pa_i) \qquad (6.32)$$

where $p(x_i | Pa_i)(i = 1, 2, \ldots, n)$ is the local probabilistic distribution in formula (6.32). The pair (S, P) represents the joint probabilistic distribution $p(X)$. If Bayesian network is constructed merely based on prior information, the probabilistic distribution is Bayesian, or subjective. If Bayesian network is constructed purely based on data, the distribution is physical, or objective.

To construct Bayesian network, we should do the following work:

Step 1 Determine all the related variables and their explanations. To do so, we need: (1) Determine the objective of the model, or make a reasonable explanation of given problem; (2) Find as many as possible problem related observations, and determine a subset that is worth of constructing model; (3) Translate these observations into mutual exclusive and exhaustive state variables. The result of these operations is not unique.

Step 2 Construct a directed acyclic graph, which expresses conditional independent assertion. According to multiplication formula, we have:

$$p(X)= \prod_{i=1}^{n} p(x_i \mid x_1, x_2, \cdots, x_{i-1}).$$
$$= p(x_1) p(x_2 \mid x_1) p(x_3 \mid x_1, x_2) \cdots p(x_n \mid x_1, x_2, \cdots, x_{n-1}) \qquad (6.33)$$

For any variable X, if there is a subset $\pi_i \subseteq \{x_1, x_2, \cdots, x_{i-1}\}$, so that x_i and $\{x_1, x_2, \cdots, x_{i-1}\} \backslash \pi_i$ are conditional independent. That is, for any given X, the following equation holds.

$$p(x_i \mid x_1, x_2, \cdots, x_{i-1}) = p(x_i \mid \pi_i), \qquad (i=1,2,\cdots,n) \qquad (6.34)$$

According to formula (6.33) and (6.34) we have $p(x)= \prod_{i=1}^{n} p(x_i \mid \pi_i)$. The variable set $(\pi_1, \ldots, \pi_n)$ corresponds to the parent set $(Pa_1, \cdots, Pa_n)$. So the above equation can also be written as $p(X)= \prod_{i=1}^{n} p(x_i \mid Pa_i)$. To determine the structure of Bayesian network, we need to (1) sort variables $x_1, x_2, \cdots, x_i$; (2)determine variable set $(\pi_1, \cdots, \pi_n)$ that satisfies formula (6.34).

Theoretically, finding a proper conditional independent sequence from n variables is a combination explosion problem, for it will require comparison among n! different sequences. In practice, casual relation is often used to solve this problem. Generally, casual relation will correspond to conditional independent assertion. So we can find a proper sequence by adding arrowed arcs from reason variables to result variables.

Step 3 Assign local probabilistic distribution $p(x_i|Pa_i)$. In the discrete case, we need to assign a distribution for each variable on each state of its parent nodes. Obviously, the steps above may be intermingled but not purely performed in sequence.

6.5.2 *Probabilistic distribution of learning Bayesian network*

Consider the following problem: given the structure of a Bayesian network, how can we learn the probabilistic distribution, or how can we update its original prior, based on observed data? Here we use Bayesian approach, which integrates prior knowledge and data to improve existing knowledge. This technique can be applied to data mining. Assume that the physical joint distribution of variables $X=(x_1, x_2, \cdots, x_n)$ can be coded in some network structure S:

$$P(x|\boldsymbol{\theta}_s, \ S^h)=\prod_{i=1}^{n} p(x_i \mid \boldsymbol{Pa}_i, \boldsymbol{\theta}_i, S^h) \qquad (6.35)$$

where $\boldsymbol{\theta}_i$ is the parameter vector of distribution $p(x_i \mid \boldsymbol{Pa}_i, \boldsymbol{\theta}_i, S^h)$; $\boldsymbol{\theta}_s$ is the vector of parameter groups$(\boldsymbol{\theta}_1, \boldsymbol{\theta}_2, \cdots, \boldsymbol{\theta}_n)$; S^h is the hypothesis that physical joint distribution can be decomposed according with structure S. It is noted that the decomposition is not cross, or overlapped. For example, given $X=\{x_1, x_2\}$, any joint distribution of X can be decomposed to a no-arc network or a network with the only arc $x_1 \rightarrow x_2$. This is cross or overlapped. Besides, suppose we generate a random sample D=$\{x_1, \cdots, x_n\}$ based on the physical distribution of X. An element x_i of D represents an observed value of the sample, and is called a case. We define a vector valued variable Θ_S corresponding to parameter vector $\boldsymbol{\theta}_s$ and assign a prior density function $p(\boldsymbol{\theta}_s|S^h)$ to represent the uncertainty of Θ_S. Then the probability learning of Bayesian network is described as: given a random sample D, to calculated the posterior $p(\boldsymbol{\theta}_s| D,S^h)$.

Below we use unrestricted multinomial distribution to discuss the basic idea of probability learning. Assume that each variable $x_i \in X$ is discrete and has r_i possible values $x_i^1, x_i^2, \cdots, x_i^{r_i}$. Each local distribution function is a set of multinomial distributions, each of which corresponds to a composition of $\boldsymbol{Pa}_i$. That is to say, let

$p(x_i^k \mid pa_i^j, \boldsymbol{\theta}_i, \ S^h)=\theta_{ijk}>0$
$i=1,2, \cdots,n; \quad j=1,2, \cdots,q_i; \quad k=1,2, \cdots,r_i)$ $\qquad (6.36)$

where $pa_i^1, pa_i^2, \cdots, pa_i^{q_i}$ represent the composition of $\boldsymbol{Pa}_i$; $q_i=\prod_{Xi \in Pa_i} r_i$; θ_i

$=((\theta_{ijk})_{k=2}^{r_i})_{j=1}^{q_i}$ is parameter; θ_{ij1} is not included for $\theta_{ij1}=1-\sum_{k=2}^{r_i}\theta_{ijk}$ can be

calculated from other parameters. For convenience, we define parameter vector

$\theta_{ij}=(\theta_{ij2}, \theta_{ij3},..., \theta_{ijr_i}), \quad (i=1,2, \cdots, n; \quad j=1,2, \cdots, q_i)$

Given the local distribution functions above, we still require two assumptions to make the calculation of posterior $p(\theta_s \mid D,S^h)$ close:

(1) There is no missing data in sample D, or D is complete;

(2) Parameter   vectors   are   mutually   independent,   viz.

$$p(\theta_s \mid S^h) = \prod_{i=1}^{n} \prod_{j=1}^{q_i} p(\theta_{ij} \mid S^h).$$ This is called parameter independence.

Under the above assumptions, for given random sample D, parameters are independent:

$$p(\theta_s \mid D, S^h) = \prod_{i=1}^{n} \prod_{j=1}^{q_i} p(\theta_{ij} \mid D, S^h) \tag{6.37}$$

Then we can update each parameter vector θ_{ij} independently. Suppose each parameter θ_{ij} has the prior distribution of Dirichlet distribution $\mathrm{Dir}(\theta_{ij} \mid \alpha_{ij1}, \alpha_{ij2}, \cdots, \alpha_{ijr_i})$, we get the posterior distribution:

$$p(\theta_{ij} \mid D, S^h) = \mathrm{Dir}(\theta_{ij} \mid \alpha_{ij1} + N_{ij1}, \ \alpha_{ij2} + N_{ij2}, \ \cdots, \ \alpha_{ijr_i} + N_{ijr_i}) \tag{6.38}$$

where N_{ijk} is the number of cases in D that satisfy $X_i = x_i^k$ and $Pa_i = pa_i^j$.

Now we can make interested prediction by seeking the mean of possible θ_s.

For example, for the $N+1$th case, $p(x_{N+1} \mid D, S^h) = \underset{p(\theta_s \mid D, S^h)}{E} (\prod_{i=1}^{r_i} \theta_{ijk})$. According to the parameter independence given D, we can calculate the expectation:

$$p(x_{N+1} \mid D, S^h) = \int \prod_{i=1}^{n} \theta_{ijk} \cdot p(\theta_s \mid D, S^h) d\theta = \prod_{i=1}^{n} \int \theta_{ijk} \cdot p(\theta_{ij} \mid D, S^h) d\theta_{ij}$$

and finally get:

$$p(x_{N+1} \mid D, S^h) = \prod_{i=1}^{n} \frac{\alpha_{ijk} + N_{ijk}}{\alpha_{ij} + N_{ij}} \tag{6.39}$$

where $\alpha_{ij} = \sum_{k=1}^{r_i} \alpha_{ijk}$ and $N_{ij} = \sum_{k=1}^{r_i} N_{ijk}$. Because unrestricted multinomial distribution belongs to exponential family, the above computation is rather easy. A Bayesian network with respect to variables X represents the joint distribution of X. So, no matter a Bayesian network is constructed from prior knowledge, or data, or integration of them, in principle, it can be used to deduce any interested probability. Yet, the precise or even approximately precise reasoning on a Bayesian network with discrete variables is NP hard. Current solution is to simplify computation based on some conditional independence, or to construct simple network topology for some specific reasoning problem, or to simplify the network structure at the cost of less precision loss. Even though, it often requires considerable computation to construct a Bayesian network. For some problem, such as naïve Bayesian classification, using conditional independence can largely reduce computation without losing much precision.

When sample data are incomplete, except for some special cases, we need to borrow approximation method, such as Monte-Carlo method, Gaussian approximation, EM algorithm to find Maximum Likelihood (ML) or Maximum A Posteriori (MAP) and so on. Although these algorithms are mature, the computational cost is large.

6.5.3 *Structure of learning Bayesian network*

When the structure of a Bayesian network is undetermined, it is possible to learn both the network structure and the probabilities from data. Because, in data mining, there are huge amount of data, and it is hard to tell the relation among variables, the structure-learning problem is practically meaningful.

The network structure that represents the physical joint probability of X is improvable. According to Bayesian approach, we define a discrete variable to represent the uncertainty of network structure. The states of the variable correspond to all possible network structure hypotheses S^h. We set its prior as $p(S^h)$. For given random sample D, which comes from the physical distribution of X, we calculate the posterior probability $p(S^h|D)$ and $p(\theta_S \mid D,S^h)$, where θ_S is parameter vector. Then we use these posteriors to calculate interested expectations.

The computation of $p(\theta_S \mid D, S^h)$ is similar to that we illustrate in the previous section. The computation of $p(S^h|D)$ is theoretically easy. According to Bayesian theorem, we have:

$$p(S^h|D) = p(S^h,D)/ p(D) = p(S^h)p(D|S^h)/ p(D) \qquad (6.40)$$

where $p(D)$ is a structure independent normalizing constant, and $p(D|S^h)$ is marginal likelihood. To determine the posterior of network structure, we need only calculate marginal likelihood for each possible structure.

Under the precondition of unrestricted multinomial distribution, parameter independence, Dirichlet prior and complete data, the parameter vector θ_{ij} can be updated independently. The marginal likelihood of data is exactly the multiplication of marginal likelihoods of each i-j pair.

$$p(D|S^h) = \prod_{i=1}^{n} \prod_{j=1}^{q_i} \frac{\Gamma(\alpha_{ij})}{\Gamma(\alpha_{ij} + N_{ij})} \cdot \prod_{k=1}^{r_i} \frac{\Gamma(\alpha_{ijk} + N_{ijk})}{\Gamma(\alpha_{ijk})} \qquad (6.41)$$

This formula is originally proposed by Cooper and Herskovits in 1992(Cooper,1992).

In common cases, the number of possible Bayesian networks with n variable is larger than exponential in n. It is intractable to exclude these hypotheses. Two approaches can be used to handle this problem, namely model selection and selective model averaging. The former approach is to select a "good" model from all the possible models (structure hypotheses), and use it as the correct model.

The latter approach is to select a reasonable number of "good" models from all the possible models, and pretend that these models are exhaustive. The questions are: how to decide whether a model is "good" or not? How to search "good" models? Whether precise result can be yielded when these approaches are applied to Bayesian structure? There are some different definitions and corresponding computational methods about "good" model. The last two questions are hardly to be answered theoretically. Some research work had demonstrated that using greedy algorithm to select single good model often leads to precise prediction (Chickering,Heckerman, 1996). Applying Monte-Carlo method to perform selective model averaging is sometime effective as well. It may even result in better prediction. These results are somewhat largely responsible for the great deal of recent interest in learning with Bayesian network

In 1995, Heckerman pointed out that under the precondition of parameter independence, parameter modularity, likelihood equivalence, and so on, the methods for learning Bayesian non-casual network can be applied to learning casual network. In 1997, he suggested that under casual Markov condition, the casual relationship could be deduced from conditional independence and conditional correlation(Heckerman, 1997). This makes it possible that when interference appears, corresponding effect can be predicted.

Below is a case study that Heckerman et al. used Bayesian network to perform data mining and knowledge discovery. The data came from 10318 Wisconsin high school seniors (Sewell and Shah, 1968). Each student was described by the following variables and corresponding states

- Sex (SEX): male, female;
- Socioeconomic Status (SES): low, lower middle, upper middle, high;
- Intelligence Quotient (IQ): low, lower middle, upper middle, high;
- Parental Encouragement (PE): low, high;
- College Plans (CP): yes, no.

Table 6.3 Sufficient statistics

(male)	4	349	13	64	9	207	33	72	12	126	38	54	10	67	49	43
	2	232	27	84	7	201	64	95	12	115	93	92	17	79	119	59
	8	166	47	91	6	120	74	110	17	92	148	100	6	42	198	73
	4	48	39	57	5	47	132	90	9	41	224	65	8	17	414	54
(female)	5	454	9	44	5	312	14	47	8	216	20	35	13	96	28	24
	11	285	29	61	19	236	47	88	12	164	62	85	15	113	72	50
	7	163	36	72	13	193	75	90	12	174	91	100	20	81	142	77
	6	50	36	58	5	70	110	76	12	48	230	81	13	49	360	98

Our goal here is to discover the factors that affect the intention of high school seniors to attend college, or to understand the possibly causal relationships among these variables. Data are described by the sufficient statistics in Table 6.3. In this table, each entry represents a statistic of a state which cycles through all possible configurations. For example, the first entry indicates that the statistic for the configuration (SEX=male, SES=low, IQ=low, PE=low, CP=yes) is 4; the second entry states that the statistic for the configuration (SEX=male, SES=low, IQ=low, PE=low, CP=no) is 349. In the cycling of configuration of variables in the table, the last variable (CP) varies most quickly, and then PE, IQ, SES. SEX varies most slowly. Thus, the upper 4 lines are the statistics for male students and the lower 4 lines are that of female students.

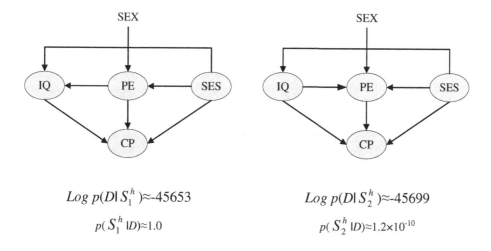

$$Log\ p(D| S_1^h)\approx -45653$$

$$p(S_1^h |D)\approx 1.0$$

$$Log\ p(D| S_2^h)\approx -45699$$

$$p(S_2^h |D)\approx 1.2\times 10^{-10}$$

Figure 6.1. Most likely network structures with no hidden variables

When analyzing data, we assume that there are no hidden variables. To generate priors for network parameters, we utilize an equivalent sample size of 5 and a prior network where $p(X| S_c^h)$ is uniform. Except that we exclude the structure where SEX and/or SES have parents and/or CP has children, we assume that all network structures are equally likely. Because the data set is complete, we use formula (6.40) and (6.41) to calculate the posterior of network structure. After searching all network structure exhaustively, we find two most likely networks, which are shown in Figure 6.1. Note that the posterior probabilities of the two most likely network structures are very close. If we adopt casual Markov assumption and assume that there are no hidden variables, the arcs in the two graphs can all be interpreted casually. Some of these results, such as the influence of socioeconomic status and IQ to the college plan, are not surprising. Some other results are very interesting: from both graphs, we can see that the influence of Sex to the College Plan is conveyed by the influence of Parental Encouragement. Besides, the only difference between the two graphs is the direction of arc between PE and IQ. Two different casual relationships seem both reasonable. The right network is selected by Sprites et al. in 1993 with non-Bayesian method.

The most questionable result is that socioeconomic status has direct influence to IQ. To verify the result, we consider a novel model, which replaces the direct influence in original model with a hidden variable pointing to SES and IQ. Besides, we also consider such models where hidden variable points to SES, IQ and PE and none or one or both of two links of SES-PE and PE-IQ are removed. For each structure, the number of hidden variables in these models varies from 2 to 6.

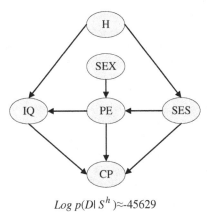

$Log \; p(D| S^h) \approx -45629$

Figure 6.2. The posteriori most likely network structure with a hidden variable

We use the Cheeseman-Stutz variant of Laplace Approximation to compute the posterior probabilities of these models. To find the MAP $\tilde{\theta}_s$, we use EM algorithm and take the largest local maximum from 100 runs with different random initial $\tilde{\theta}_s$. The model with the highest MAP is shown in Figure 6.2. This model is 2×10^{10} times more likely than the best model containing no hidden variables about. Another most likely model contains a hidden variable and has an additional arc from the hidden variable to PE. This model is only 5×10^{-9} times less likely than the best model. Suppose that no reasonable models are ignored, strong evidence suggests that there is a hidden variable influencing the SES and IQ. An examination of the probabilities in Figure 6.2 suggests that the hidden variable corresponds to some concept like "parent quality".

Using Bayesian method to learn the structure and probabilities of Bayesian network from prior information and sample information so that to construct a whole Bayesian network opens an avenue for applying Bayesian network to data mining and knowledge discovery. Compared with other data mining methods, such as rule-based method, decision tree and artificial neural network, Bayesian network has the following characteristics:

(1) It can integrate prior and posterior information, so as to avoid the subjective bias when using merely prior information, to avoid the large blind searching and computation when sample is lack, and to avoid the influence from noise when using only posterior information. As long as prior is determined properly, we can perform effective learning, especially when sample is hard or costly to gain.

(2) It can handle incomplete data set.

(3) It can explore casual relations in data.

(4) There are mature and effective algorithms. Although probabilistic reasoning is NP hard for any arbitrary Bayesian network, in many practical problems, these operations can be either simplified by adding some constrains or solved by some approximation methods.

Yet, the computation of Bayesian network is huge. The Bayesian network seems less efficient than some other methods if a problem is also be resolved by other efficient approaches. Although there are some methods for prior determination, which is extremely important when sample is hard to get, in practice, to find a reasonable prior involving many variables is still a hard problem. Besides, Bayesian network requires many assumptions as precondition. There are no ready rules to judge whether a practical problem satisfies the assumptions or not. These are problems deserve further study. Still, it can be predicted that in data mining and knowledge discovery, especially in data mining with probabilistic statistical features, Bayesian network will become a powerful tool.

6.6 Bayesian Latent Semantic Model

With the prevalence of Internet, Web information is increasing in exponential way. It has been a research focus of Web information processing that how to organize the information reasonably, so that to find expected target in massive web data, and how to effectively analyze the information so that to mine new and latently useful pattern in massive web data. The classification of Web information is an effective approach for improving searching effectiveness and efficiency. For example, when searching with Web search engine, if the class information of query is available, the searching sphere will be limited and the recall will be improved. Meanwhile, classification can provide good organization of information so that to help user to browse and filter information. Many big Websites adopt this kind of information organization. For example, Yahoo maintains its Web catalog structure manually; Google uses some sorting mechanism to let the most user-related pages ranked ahead, so as to make users' browse convenient. Deerwester et al. take the advantage of linear algebra and perform information filtering and latent semantic index (LSI) via singular value decomposition (SVD) (Deerwester, 1990). They project the high dimensional representation of documents in vector space model (VSM) to a low dimensional latent semantic space (LSS). This approach on the one hand reduces the scale of the problem, and on the other hand to some extent avoids the over sparse data. It gains preferable effects in many applications including language modeling, video retrieval, and protein database.

Clustering is one of main approaches in text mining. Its primary effects include: a) by clustering search results, Website can provide users required Web pages in terms of classes, so that users can quickly locate to their expected targets; b) generating catalog automatically; c) analyzing the commonness in web pages by clustering them. The typical clustering algorithm is K-means clustering. Besides, some new clustering algorithms, such as self-organizing map (SOM), clustering with neural networks, probability based hierarchical Bayesian clustering (HBC), also receive much study and many applications. Yet most clustering algorithms are unsupervised algorithms, which search the solution space somewhat blindly. Thus, the clustering results are often lack of semantic characters. Meanwhile, in high dimensional cases, selecting proper distance metric becomes very difficult.

Web classification is one kind of supervised learning. By analyzing training data, classifiers can predict the class labels for unseen Web pages. Currently, there are many effective algorithms to classify Web pages, such as naïve Bayesian method and SVM. It is a pity that obtaining a large amount of classified training samples, which are necessary for training high precise classifiers, are very costly. Besides, in practical, different classification architectures are often inconsistent. This makes daily maintaining of Web catalog difficult. Kamal Nigam et al. proposed a method that can utilize documents with class labels and those without class labels to train classifier. It only requires a small amount of labeled training samples, and can learn a Bayesian classifier by integrating knowledge in the unlabeled samples (Nigam, 1998).

Our basic idea for solving this problem is as follows. If some Web pages $D = \{d_1, d_2, \cdots, d_n\}$ consist a description of some latent class variables $Z = \{z_1, z_2, \cdots, z_k\}$, firstly, by introducing Bayesian latent semantic model, we assign documents containing latent class variables to corresponding class; then we utilize naïve Bayesian model to classify the documents containing no latent class variables with the knowledge in previous step. According to the characters of these two steps, we define two likelihood functions, and use EM algorithm to find the local optimal solution with the maximum likelihood. This approach on the one hand avoids blind search in the solution space like unsupervised learning; on the other hand it requires only some class variables but not large amount of labeled training samples. It will release website managers from fussy training document labeling and improve the efficiency of web page automatic classification. To distinguish with the supervised learning and unsupervised learning, this approach is named semi-supervised learning.

The basic idea of latent semantic analysis (LSA) is to project the documents in high dimensional vector space model (VSM) to a low dimensional latent semantic space. This projection is performed via singular value decomposition (SVD) on entry/document matrix $N_{m \times n}$. Concretely, according to linear algebra, any matrix Nm*n can be decomposed as follows:

$$N = U \sum V^T \tag{6.42}$$

where U, V are orthogonal matrixes ($UU^T = VV^T = I$); $\sum = diag(a_1, a_2, \cdots, a_k, \cdots, a_v)$ ($a_1, a_2, \cdots, a_v$ are singular values) is a diagonal matrix. In latent semantic analysis, the approximation is gained by keeping k biggest singular values and setting others to 0:

$$\tilde{N} = U \tilde{\sum} V^T \approx U \sum V^T = N \tag{6.43}$$

Because the similarity between two documents can be represented with $NN^T \approx \tilde{N}\tilde{N}^T = U \tilde{\sum}^2 U^T$, the coordinate of a document in the latent semantic space can be approximated by $U \tilde{\sum}$. After projecting the representation of a document from high dimensional space to low dimensional semantic space, the sparsity of data, which exists in high dimensional space, does not exist any more in the low dimensional latent semantic space. This also indicates that even if there is no common factor between two documents in high dimensional space, we may still find their meaningful connections in low dimensional semantic space.

After the SVD and projecting documents from high dimensional space to low dimensional latent semantic space, the scale of a problem is effectively reduced. LSA has been successfully applied to many fields, including information filtering, text indexing and video retrieval. Yet SVD is sensitive to variation of data, and seems stiff when prior information is lack. These shortcomings limit its application.

According to our experiences, description on any problem is developed centering on some theme. There are relative obvious boundaries between different themes. Because of differences in personal favors and interests, people's concerns on different themes vary. There is prior knowledge in different themes. Accordingly, we proposed the Bayesian latent semantic model for document generation.

Let document set be $D = \{d_1, d_2, ..., d_n\}$, and word set be $W = \{w_1, w_2, ..., w_m\}$. The generation model for document $d \in D$ can be expressed as follows:

(1) Choose document d at the probability of $P(d)$;

(2) Choose a latent theme z, which has the prior knowledge $p(z|\theta)$;

(3) Denote the probability that theme z contains document d by $p(z|d,\theta)$

(4) Denote the probability of word $w \in W$ under the theme z by $p(w|z,\theta)$

After above process, we get the observed pair (d, w). The latent theme z is omitted, and joint probability model is generated:

$$p(d,w) = p(d)p(w|d) \tag{6.44}$$

$$p(w|d) = \sum_{z \in Z} p(w|z,\theta)p(z|d,\theta) \tag{6.45}$$

This model is a hybrid probabilistic model under the following independence assumptions:

(1) The generation of each observed pair (d, w) is relative independent, and they are related via latent themes.

(2) The generation of word w is independent of any concrete document d. It only depends on latent theme variable z.

Formula (6.45) indicates that in some document d, the distribution of word w is the convex combination of latent themes. The weight of a theme in the combination is the probability, at which document d belongs to the theme. Figure 6.3 illustrates the relationships between factors in the model.

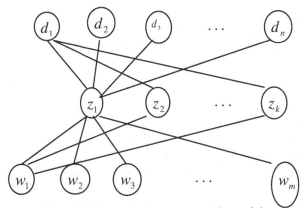

Figure 6.3. Bayesian latent semantic model.

According to Bayesian formula, we substitute formula (6.45) into formula (6.44) and get:

$$p(d,w) = \sum_{z \in Z} p(z \mid \theta) p(w \mid z, \theta) p(d \mid z, \theta) \tag{6.46}$$

Compared with LSA, Bayesian latent semantic model has firm statistical foundation and avoid the data sensibility in LSA. It also utilizes prior information of latent theme variables to avoid over stiff like the SVD. In Bayesian latent semantic model, formula (6.42) can be rewritten as:

$$U = \{p(d_i \mid z_k)\}_{n \times k}$$
$$V = \{p(w_i \mid z_k)\}_{m \times k}$$
$$\tilde{\Sigma} = diag(p(z_k), p(z_k), \cdots p(z_k))$$

So it has same representation form as that of SVD.

In LSA, the criterion for parameter selection is minimum least square loss. From the view point of Bayesian learning, in our model, we have two applicable criterions: maximum a posterior (MAP) and maximum likelihood (ML).

MAP estimation is applied to find the proper latent theme variable under the condition of document set D and word set W:

$$P(Z \mid D, W) = \prod_{z \in Z} \prod_{d \in D} \prod_{w \in W} p(z \mid d, w) \tag{6.47}$$

According to Bayesian formula, we have:

$$p(z \mid d, w) = \frac{p(z) p(w \mid z) p(d \mid z)}{\sum_{z \in Z} p(z) p(w \mid z) p(d \mid z)} \tag{6.48}$$

ML estimation is used to find a proper value of the following expression:

$$\prod_{d \in D} \prod_{w \in W} p(d, w)^{n(d,w)} \tag{6.49}$$

where $n(d, w)$ represents the count of word w in document d. In practice, we often take logarithm of the likelihood, shortly log-likelihood.

$$\sum_{d \in D} \sum_{w \in W} n(d, w) \log p(d, w) \tag{6.50}$$

A general approach to maximize the two estimations is expectation maximum (EM), which is discussed in detail in section 6.7.

6.7 Semi-supervised Text Mining Algorithms

6.7.1 *Web page clustering*

Presently there are many algorithms for text classification, and they can achieve satisfied precision and recall. Yet the cost for obtaining labeled training documents is very high. Nigam et al. proposed an approach, in which they used mix corpus including labeled and unlabeled documents to train classifier and gained good classification results, but they still need certain number of labeled documents (Nigam, 1998). Web clustering is to merge related web pages into one cluster with some similarity criterion. When dealing with high dimensional and massive data, conventional clustering methods can not achieve satisfied effectiveness and efficiency. The reason is: on the one hand, unsupervised search in solution space is to some extent blind; on the other hand, common similarity metric, e.g. Euclidean distance, does not work well in high dimensional space and it is hard to find proper similarity metric in this situation. Considering the characters of supervised learning and unsupervised learning, we proposed a semi-supervised learning algorithm. Under the framework of Bayesian latent semantic model, we can classify documents into different classes with some user provided latent class variables. In this process, no labeled training documents are required.

The general model is described as: given document set $D = \{d_1, d_2, ..., d_n\}$ and its word set $W = \{w_1, w_2, ..., w_m\}$, and a group of class variable $Z = \{z_1, z_2, ..., z_k\}$ with its prior information $\theta = \{\theta_1, \theta_2, ..., \theta_k\}$, try to seek a division D_j ($j \in (1, ..., k)$) of D, so that:

$$\bigcup_{j=1}^{k} D_j = D, \quad D_i \cap D_j = \phi \ (i \neq j)$$

Firstly, we divide D into two sets: $D = D_L \cup D_U$, where

$$D_L = \{d \mid \exists j, z_j \in d, j \in [1...k]\},$$

$$D_U = \{d \mid \forall j, z_j \notin d, j \in [1...k]\}$$

In our algorithm, the classification process includes two stages:

Stage 1 Utilize Bayesian latent semantic model with the parameters estimated based on EM algorithm to label the documents in D_L:

$$l(d) = z_j = \max_i \{p(d \mid z_i)\} \tag{6.51}$$

Stage 2 Train a naïve Bayesian classifier with the labeled documents in D_L, and label documents in D_U with this classifier. Then update parameters of Bayesian latent semantic models with EM algorithm.

6.7.2 Label documents with latent classification themes

Ideally, any document will not contain more than one latent class theme. In this case, we can easily label a document with it latent theme. In practice, however, the ideal status is hard to achieve. On the one hand, it is difficult to find such latent theme; on the other hand, there may be multiple themes in one document. For example, a document labeled with "economics" may contain words of other themes, e.g. "politics" and/or "culture". We handle these cased by labeling them with the most related theme. Under ML criterion, after some rounds of EM iterations, we finally determine the theme of test document according to formula (6.51).

EM algorithm is one of the primary parameter estimation approaches for sparse data. It performs E step and M step alternately, so that to find the most likely result. The general process of EM algorithm is described below:

(1) E step: calculate expectation based on the current parameters;
(2) M step: find the proper parameter with maximum likelihood based on the expectation in E step;
(3) Compute the likelihood with the renewed parameters. If the likelihood exceeds predefined threshold or number of iteration exceeds predefined value, stop. Otherwise, go to Step (1).

In our algorithm, we adopt following two steps to perform iteration

(1) In E step, we obtain the expectation via the following Bayesian formula:

$$P(z \mid d, w) = \frac{p(z)p(d \mid z)p(w \mid z)}{\sum_{z'} p(z')p(d \mid z')p(w \mid z')} \tag{6.52}$$

In terms of probabilistic semantics, the formula explains the probability of word w in document d with latent theme variable z.

(2) In M step, we use the expectation from the above step to estimate the density of parameters.

$$p(w \mid z) = \frac{\sum_d n(d, w)p(z \mid d, w)}{\sum_{d,w} n(d, w')p(z \mid d, w')} \tag{6.53a}$$

$$p(d \mid z) = \frac{\sum_w n(d, w)p(z \mid d, w)}{\sum_{d',w} n(d', w)p(z \mid d', w)} \tag{6.53b}$$

$$p(z) = \frac{\sum_{d,w} n(d, w)p(z \mid d, w)}{\sum_{d,w} n(d, w)} \tag{6.53c}$$

Compared with SVD in LSA, EM algorithm has linear convergence time. It is simple and easy to implement, and it results in local optimal of likelihood function. Figure 6.4 shows the relation of iteration times and corresponding maximum likelihood in our experiment.

6.7.3 *Learning labeled and unlabeled data based on naïve Bayesian model*

Conventional classification methods usually learn classifiers based on labeled training samples to classify unlabeled data. Yet obtaining large amount of labeled training samples is very costly and fussy. Kamal Nigam et al.'s research indicated that unlabeled data also contain useful information for learning classifiers. Accordingly, we use naïve Bayesian model as classifier; and label the unlabeled training samples with a special non-label status; then estimate these label with EM algorithm.

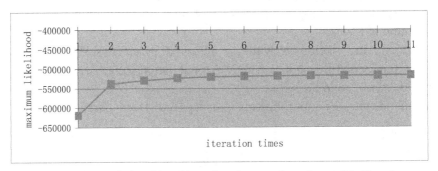

Figure 6.4. Relationship of iteration times and maximum likelihood

Here, we present the general description of text classification with naïve Bayesian classifier: given the training document set $D = \{d_1, d_2, ..., d_n\}$ and its word set $W = \{w_1, w_2, ..., w_m\}$, each training document is represented as a $m+1$ dimensional vector $d_i = <w_1, w_2, ..., w_m, c_i>$, where $c_i \in C = \{c_1, c_2, ..., c_k\}$ is a class variable. The classification task is to predict the class of unseen document $d = <w_1, w_2, ..., w_m>$:

$$c = \max_{j \in 1...k}\{p(c_j \mid \boldsymbol{d}, \theta)$$

where θ is parameter of model)

To calculate the above expression, we expend the factor in the expression and get:

$$p(d \mid c_j, \theta) = p(\mid d \mid)\prod_{k=1}^{\mid d \mid} p(w_k \mid c_j; \theta; w_q, q < k) \qquad (6.54)$$

When computing formula (6.54) with naïve Bayesian model, we need to introduce the following independence assumptions:

(1) The generation of words in documents is independent of the content. That is to say, same words at different position of a document are independent.
(2) Words in a document are independent of the class of the documents.

Based on the above independence assumption and Bayesian formula, equation (6.54) can be rewritten as:

$$p(c_j \mid d, \theta) = \frac{p(c_j \mid \theta) p(d \mid c_j, \theta)}{p(d \mid \theta)}$$

$$= \frac{p(c_j \mid \theta) \prod_{r=1}^{m} p(w_r \mid c_j, \theta)}{\sum_{i=1}^{k} p(c_i \mid \theta) \prod_{r=1}^{m} p(w_r \mid c_i, \theta)} \tag{6.55}$$

The learning task becomes to learn parameters of model from prior information in training data. Here we adopt multinomial distribution and Dirichlet conjugate distribution.

$$\theta_{c_j} = p(c_j \mid \theta) = \frac{\sum_{i=1}^{|D|} I(c(d_i) = c_j)}{|D|} \tag{6.56a}$$

$$\theta_{w_t \mid c_j} = p(w_t \mid c_j, \theta) = \frac{\alpha_{jt} + \sum_{i=1}^{|D|} n(d_i, w_t) I(c(d_i) = c_j)}{\alpha_{j0} + \sum_{k=1}^{m} \sum_{i=1}^{|D|} n(d_i, w_k) I(c(d_i) = c_j)} \tag{6.56b}$$

where $\alpha_{j0} = \sum_{i=1}^{k} \alpha_{ji}$ is the super-parameter of model; $c(\cdot)$ is the class labeling function $I(a = b)$ is characteristic function (if $a = b$, then $I(a = b)=1$; otherwise $I(a = b)=0$).

Although the applicable condition for naïve Bayesian model is somewhat harsh, numerous experiments demonstrate that even when independence assumption is unsatisfied, naïve Bayesian model can still work robustly. It has been one of the most popular methods for text classification.

Below we will classify unlabeled documents according to MAP criterion based on the knowledge in these unlabeled documents.

Consider the entire sample set $D = D_L \cup D_U$, where D_L is the set of documents that has been labeled in the first stage. Assume that the generation of all samples in D is mutually independent; then the following equation holds:

$$p(D \mid \theta) = \prod_{d_i \in D_U} \sum_{j=1}^{|C|} p(c_j \mid \theta) p(d_i \mid c_j, \theta) \cdot \prod_{d_i \in D_L} p(c(d_i) \mid \theta) p(d_i \mid c(d_i), \theta) \tag{6.57}$$

In the above equation, unlabeled documents are regarded as mix model. Our learning task is to gain the maximum estimation of model parameter θ with the sample set D. according to Bayesian theorem, we have:

$$p(\theta \mid D) = \frac{p(\theta) p(D \mid \theta)}{P(D)} \tag{6.58}$$

For fixed sample set, $p(\theta)$ and $p(D)$ are both constants. Take logarithm on the both sides of equation (6.58). We have:

$$l(\theta \mid D) = \log p(\theta \mid D)$$

$$= \log \frac{p(\theta)}{p(D)} + \sum_{d_i \in D_U} \log \sum_{j=1}^{|C|} p(c_j \mid \theta) p(\boldsymbol{d}_i \mid c_j, \theta) \qquad (6.59)$$

$$+ \sum_{d_i \in D_L} \log p(c(\boldsymbol{d}_i) \mid \theta) p(\boldsymbol{d}_i \mid c(\boldsymbol{d}_i), \theta)$$

To label the unlabeled documents, we need latent variables in LSA. Here we introduce k latent variables $Z = \{z_1, z_2, ..., z_k\}$, where each latent variable is a n-dimensional vector $z_i = <z_{i1}, z_{i2}, ..., z_{in}>$, and if $c(d_j) = c_i$ then $z_{ij} = 1$, otherwise $z_{ij} = 0$. So equation (6.59) can be rewritten as follows:

$$l(\theta \mid D) = \log \frac{p(\theta)}{p(D)} + \sum_{i=1}^{|D|} \sum_{j=1}^{|C|} z_{ji} \log p(c_j \mid \theta) p(\boldsymbol{d}_i \mid c_j, \theta_j) \qquad (6.60)$$

In equation (6.59), z_{ji} for labeled documents is known. The learning task is to maximize model parameters and to estimate z_{ji} of unlabeled documents.

Here we still apply EM algorithm to learn knowledge about unlabeled documents. Yet the process is somewhat different from the previous stage. In the kth iteration in the E step, we will use naïve Bayesian classifier to find the class label of unlabeled documents based on the current estimation of parameters.

$$p(d \mid c_j, \theta^k) = \frac{p(c_j \mid \theta^K) \prod_{r=1}^{m} p(w_r \mid c_j; \theta^k)}{\sum_{i=1}^{k} p(c_i \mid \theta^k) \prod_{r=1}^{m} p(w_r \mid c_i; \theta^k)}, \qquad j \in 1, \cdots, k$$

The class c_i corresponding to MAP is the expected label of the unlabeled documents:

$$z_{id} = 1, z_{jd} = 0 \ (j \neq i)$$

In the step M, we maximize the estimation of current parameters based on the expectation obtained from the just previous E step.

$$\theta_{c_j} = p(c_j \mid \theta) = \frac{\sum_{i=1}^{|D|} z_{ji}}{|D|} \qquad (6.61a)$$

$$\theta_{w_t \mid c_j} = p(w_t \mid c_j, \theta) = \frac{\alpha_j + \sum_{i=1}^{|D|} n(d_i, w_t) z_{ji}}{\alpha_0 + \sum_{k=1}^{m} \sum_{i=1}^{|D|} n(d_i, w_k) z_{ji}} \qquad (6.61b)$$

Organizing Web information into catalogs is an effective way to improve the effectiveness and efficiency of information retrieval. It can be achieved by learning classifiers with labeled documents and predicting class label of new

Web page with the leant classifiers. Yet the acquisition of labeled training data is often costly and fussy. Web page clustering, which can cluster documents according to some similarity metric, can help to improve the retrieval. The problem is that solution search of traditional clustering methods is somewhat blind and lacks semantic meaning. Thus the effect of clustering is usually unsatisfied. In this section, we proposed a semi-supervised learning algorithm. Under the framework of Bayesian latent semantic model, the new algorithm uses no labeled training data but only a few latent class/theme variables to assign documents to corresponding class/theme. The algorithm includes two stages. In the first stage, it applies Bayesian latent semantic analysis to label documents, which contain latent theme variable(s); in the second stage, it uses naïve Bayesian model label the documents without latent theme with the knowledge information in these documents. Experimental results demonstrate that the algorithm achieves high precision and recall. We will further investigate related issues, such as the influence of latent variable selection on the clustering result and how to implement word clustering under the framework of Bayesian latent semantic analysis.

Exercises

1. Please explain conditional probability, prior probability and posterior probability.
2. Please describe Bayesian Formula and explicate its significance thoroughly.
3. Please describe some criterions for prior distribution selection.
4. What does 'Naïve' mean in Naïve Bayesian classification? Please briefly state the main ideas for improving Naïve Bayesian classification.
5. Please describe the structure of Bayesian network and its construction, and exemplify the usage of Bayesian network.
6. What is semi-supervised text mining? Please describe some applications of Bayesian model in Web page clustering.
7. In recent years, with the development of Internet technology, Bayesian rules are widely applied. Please exemplify two concrete applications of the Bayesian rules and explain the results.

Chapter 7

Inductive Learning

7.1 Introduction

Inductive learning is one of the most extensive approaches in symbol learning. Its task is to induct a general conceptual description from a series of known positive and negative examples given about a concept. Through inductive learning, new concepts can be obtained, new rules created and new theories found. Generalization and specification are the general operations of inductive learning. Generalization is used to expand assumed semantic information so that it can include more positive examples and be applied in more situations. Specialization is an opposite operation of generalization. It is used to constrain application range of conceptual description.

Inductive learning program is the procedure to describe the content mentioned above by programming language. The language to write the inductive program is referred to as inductive programming language. The system which can execute inductive program and accomplish the specialized task of inductive learning is referred to as inductive learning system, which could be independent or embedded into another greater knowledge processing system. The input of general inductive program is the description of few observations in scientific experiments, while the output is the overall feature description of an object category or classification discriminative description of several object categories.

In contrast to deduction, the start premise of induction is concrete fact rather than general truth while the reasoning objective is likelihood general assertion to explain fact in form and predict new truth. Induction attempts to lead to complete and correct description from given phenomenon or part of its concrete observations. Induction has two aspects – generating likelihood assumption and its effectiveness (construction of truth value status). Only the former has preliminary significance of the research of inductive learning. The assumption effectiveness is secondary, because the assumption generated by hypothesis is discriminated by human experts and tested by known approaches of deductive reasoning and mathematical statistics.

Inductive learning can be classified into instance learning, observation and discovery learning. The task of instance learning, also referred to as concept acquisition, is determined by general concept description, which should explain all given positive instances and exclude all given negative instances. These positive and negative instances are provided by source of information. The source of information is very extensive. It can be natural phenomenon or experiment results. Instance learning which learns from classified examples according to supervisor is a supervised learning algorithm.

Observation and discovery learning is also referred to as description generation. This kind of learning will generate and explain the disciplines and rules of all or most observations without the help of supervisor. It includes concept clustering, construction classification, discovery theorems, expression theories. Observation and discovery learning which learn from observations without classification, or be discovered by functions itself, are unsupervised learning algorithms.

Since inductive reasoning leads to complete knowledge status from definite and incomplete knowledge status, it is a kind of non-monotonous reasoning. However, inductive reasoning cannot verify whether the knowledge is right, while non-monotonic logic provides theory foundation for us to handle non-monotonic generative knowledge.

The basic idea of inductive principle is to formulate a scientific theory through assumption on the basis of a great deal of observations. All observations are singular proposition, while a theory is usually a universal proposition in domain. There is not a logical inevitable implication relation between singular proposition and universal proposition. They are usually default held for facts cannot be observed. We use inductive assertion derived from inductive reasoning as knowledge from the database. Furthermore, they are used as default knowledge. When new proposition contract with them has been emerged, the original default knowledge derived from inductive reasoning would be thrown down so that the consistence of system knowledge can be kept.

A general definition of inductive learning from individual concept is as following:

(1) Given an instance space constructed by all instances, each instance has several attributes.

(2) Given a description language, the descriptive capability of the language includes describing every instance (realized by describing its attributes) and describing some instance sets, which is referred to as concept.

(3) When learning executes, some instances are extracted from instance space. The set constructed by these instances is referred to as positive instance set. Then, other instances are extracted from instance space, which is referred to as negative instance set.

(4) If a concept A, which includes positive instance set completely and whose intersection with negative instance set is empty set, can be found in limited steps, A is the individual concept for learning and learning is success, otherwise fail.

(5) If a definite algorithm exists so that learning is always successful for any given positive and negative instance set, the instance space is called acquisitive in the form of the language.

The representative approaches of inductive learning include version space, AQ11 algorithm, decision tree, etc. which will be discussed in this chapter respectively.

7.2 Logic Foundation of Inductive Learning

7.2.1 Inductive general paradigm

In order to depict conceptual inductive learning concretely, the general paradigm of inductive learning is given here (Michalski, 1983).

Given:

(1) premise statements (facts), F, it is knowledge related to individual object in an object category or partial features of an object.

(2) a tentative inductive asertion (which may be empty), it is generalization item or generalization description about objects.

(3) background knowledge that defines assumptions and constraints on observing statements and candidate inductive hypotheses, assertions generated by them, including any related general or domain specific knowledge.

Find:

an inductive assertion (hypothesis), H, that is tautology or weak implication observing statements which should meet background knowledge.

An hypothesis H tautological implicit fact F, which means that F is the logic reasoning of H, i.e. $H \Rightarrow F$ holds. That is, if expression $H \Rightarrow F$ is always true in any explanation, it can be represented as follows: $H \rhd F$, H is specialized to F or $F \lk H$. F is summed up or generalized to H.

Here, the procedure reasoning F from H is a tautological procedure. Since $H \Rightarrow F$ must hold according to patterns mentioned above, so if H is true, F must be true. On the contrary, the procedure reasoning H from fact F is a non-tautological procedure. That is, if fact F is false, H must be false.

Here H weak implicit F means that fact F is not a definitive conclusion H, but a reasonable or partial conclusion H. With the concept of weak implication, this pattern has possible and partial hypothesis which only needs to explain some facts of all facts. However, we still focus on the hypothesis of tautological implication facts.

Table 7.1 Basic symbols

Symbols	Significance
□	not
$\wedge$	conjunction（logic product）
$\vee$	disjunction（logic add）
□	implication
□	logic equivalence
$\leftrightarrow$	item rewrite
□	exclusive or
F	fact set
H	hypothesis
$\triangleright$	specialization
$\Bbbk$	generalization
□	reformalization
$\square v_i$	existentially quantified variable vi
$\square I v_i$	value existentially quantified variable v_i
$\square v_i$	universally quantified variable vi
D_i	concept description
K_i	judge predicate of name of an concept
::>	Implication conjunct concept description and concept name
e_i	an event（description of a situation）
E_i	predicate only if event is true for concept k_i
X_i	attribute
LEF	evaluation function
DOM(P)	domain of descriptor P

With regard to any given facts set, innumerable hypothesis implicit these facts could be generated. This needs background knowledge to provide constraints and optimal principles, so that innumerable hypothesis could be decreased to one or several optimal hypothesis.

In order to formalize logic foundation of conceptual inductive learning, basic symbols are given in Table 7.1, and the explanations to the simple are appended.

7.2.2 Conditions of concept acquisition

In concept acquisition observed statements facts F can be viewed as implications of the form:

$$F: \{e_{ik} ::> K_i\} \qquad\qquad i \in I \qquad\qquad (7.1)$$

where e_{ik}(training event of K_i) is symbol description of number k instance of concept K_i. Conceptual predicate K_i, i is suffix set of K_i. $e_{ik} ::> K_i$ means that "all events in accordance with description e_{ik} can be asserted to be instances of concept K_i ". The inductive hypothese H seeked out by learning program can be depicted by concept recognition rule set. Its form is as following:

$$H: \{D_i ::> K_i\} \qquad\qquad i \in I \qquad\qquad (7.2)$$

where D_i is the description of concept K_i, i.e. expression D_i is logic conclusion of events, which can be asserted as an instance of concept K_i.

Using E_i to represent all description of training events in concept K_i ($i \in I$), according to the definition of inductive assertion, it must hold $H \triangleright F$. In order to let D_i become the description of concept K_i, using expression (7.1) and (7.2) to replace H and F respectively, the following condition must hold:

$$\forall\, i \in I \quad (E_i \Rightarrow D_i) \qquad\qquad (7.3)$$

i.e. all training events of K_i must be in accordance with D_i. If every event only belongs to one concept, the following condition also holds:

$$\forall\, i,j \in I \quad (D_i \Rightarrow \sim E_i) \quad \text{if} \quad i \neq j \qquad\qquad (7.4)$$

it means training events of every concept K_i ($j \neq i$) are not in accordance with D_i. Condition (7.3) is referred to as integral condition. Condition (7.4) is referred to as consistence condition. As accepted by concept recognition rule, inductive assertion must meet these two conditions, so that the integral and consistence can be assured. Integral condition and consistence condition provide logical foundation for conceptual algorithm of instance learning.

Description of a kind of objects is a expression satisfying integral condition, or conjunction of these expressions. This kind of description judges given category from all possible categories. Difference description of an object category is a expression satisfying integral condition, or disjunction of these expressions. Its objective is to label given category in few other categories.

The main interest of knowledge acquisition lies in symbol description orirnted reasoning. This description should be easily understood, and easily applied when generating intelligence model which represents its information. Therefore, description generated by inductive reasoning should be similar to human knowledge representation.

In inductive learning classification, a guiding principle is choosing language type of inductive learning such as some kind of definitive form or similar concept of common predicate logic, decision tree, generative rule, semantic network, framework, multi value logic, modal logic.

On the basis of predicate logic, representative capability can be improved through modifying and expanding, adding some extra form and new concept. Michalski et al. proposed APC(Annotated Predicate Calculus), so that it is more proper for reasoning. Main differences between APC and common predicate calculus include: (1) every predicate, variable and function are endowed a label. Label is the set of background knowledge related to learning problem of the descriptor. Such as definition of concept descriptor represents, relation between the label and other concepts, effective range of descriptor, etc. (2) except for predicate, APC also includes compound predicate, whose arguments can be compound items. A compound item is combined with several common items, such as $P(t_1 \vee t_2, A)$. (3) relation predicate among expressions are represented as selective symbol relation, such as: $=, \neq, >, \geq, \leq, <$. (4) except for universal quantified and existential quantified, there is numeral quantified, which is used to represent numeral information of an object satisfied a expression.

7.2.3 Background knowledge of problems

With regard to a given observation statement set, innumerable inductive assertion implicate these statement could be constructed. Therefore, some additional information, i.e. background knowledge of problems, should be used to restrain possible range of inductive assertion, and decide one or some optimal inductive assertions. For example, in learning approach Star, background knowledge includes several parts: (1) descriptor information used in observation statement is added in every descriptor label; (2) form hypothesis about observation and inductive assertion; (3) select standard of attributes of list inductive assertion; (4) various reasoning rules, heuristic rules, specific subprogram, general and independent procedure, so that learning system generates logic conclusion and new descriptor of given assertion. Since descriptor choice in observation statement makes important influence on generating inductive assertion, descriptor choice should be considered firstly.

Main content of learning system input is an observation statement set. Descriptor in these statements is observable feature and useful test data. Deciding these descriptors is a main issue of inductive learning. Learning approaches can be depicted by initial descriptor and relation degree of learning problem. The relations include: (1) related completely, that is, all descriptors in observation statement set are directly related to learning task. Learning task is forming an inductive assertion relating these descriptors. (2) related partially, there are many useless or redundant descriptors. Some of them are related. Now learning task is to choose the most related descriptors, and construct rational inductive assertion based on these descriptors. (3) related indirectly, observation statement does not include descriptors directly related to problems. However, in initial description, some descriptors can be used to generate related descriptors. The task of learning is to generate these related descriptors directly, and get inductive assertion.

Descriptor labeling is background knowledge set related to descriptors and learning problems. It includes:

- Type description of definition domain and descriptors;
- Operator description related to descriptors;
- Constraints and relation description among descriptors;
- Significance and vary law of descriptors representing number in problems;
- Features of descriptors applicable to objects;
- Class including given descriptor, i.e. parent node of descriptor;
- Synonym that could replace the descriptor;
- Definition of descriptors;
- Typical example of given descriptors of objects.

Definition domain of descriptor is a set of values that descriptor can have. For example, human's body temperature is between 34°C and 44°C, then the value of descriptor "body temperature" can only be in this range. Descriptor type is decided by relation of elements in definition domain of descriptor. According to the structure of definition domain of descriptor, there are three basic types:

(1) Nominal descriptor. Definition domain of this descriptor is composed of independent symbol or name. That is, values in value set have not structural relation, such as fruit, people's name.

(2) Linear descriptor. Elements in value set of this kind of descriptors are in accordance with a totally ordered set. For example, funds, temperature, weight, product are all linear descriptors. Variables representing ordinal number, interval, ratio and absolute calibration are specific instances of linear descriptor. Functions which map a set to a totally ordered set are linear descriptors too.

(3) Structural descriptor. Its value set is a tree forming graphical structure, reflecting generative levels among values. In such structure, parent node represents more general concept than child node. For example, in value set "place name", "China" is parent of "Beijing", "Shanghai", "Jiangsu", "Guangdong", etc. Definition domain of structural descriptor is defined by a group of reasoning rules explained by background knowledge of problems. Structural descriptor can be further subdivided into ordered and unordered

structural descriptor. Descriptor type is very important to determine operation of applied descriptor.

In learning system Star, basic form of assertion is c-expression, which is defined as a conjunction normal form:

< quantifier form><conjunction of relation statement>   (6.5)

where < quantifier form > represent none or many quantifiers。 <relation statement> is specific form of predicate. Following is an example of c-expression:

$$\exists P_0, P_1([shape(P_0 \wedge P_1) = box][weight(P_0) > weight(P_1)])$$

i.e. shape of object P_0 and P_1 is box, and object P_0 is more weighty than object P_1. An important specific form of c-expression is a-expression, i.e. atomic expression, which does not include "inter disjunction". Inter conjunction and disjunction mean "and" and "or" of conjunction items respectively; outer conjunction and disjunction mean "and" and "or" of conjunction predicate, i.e. "and" and "or" in common sense.

7.2.4 Selective and constructive generalization rules

A generalization rule is to transform a description into a more general description. A more general description tautologically implicates the initial description. Since generalization rule is non- tautological, if $F \vdash H$, then for all facts that makes F to be false, they make H to be false ($\sim F \Rightarrow \sim H$).

In concept acquisition, if a rule $E::>K$ is transformed into a more general rule $D::>K$, it must hold $E \Rightarrow D$. So we can get generalization rules using tautological implication in formal logic. For example, formal logic holds $P \wedge Q \Rightarrow P$, then it can be transformed into generalization rule:

$$P \wedge Q \quad ::> \quad K \quad \vdash \quad P::> \quad K \tag{7.6}$$

If using labeling predicate calculus to rep resent these generalization rule, we should mainly consider transforming one or more statement into a single more general generalization rule:

$$\{D_i \quad ::> \quad K_i\} \quad i \in I \quad \vdash \quad D \quad ::> \quad K \tag{7.7}$$

Equals to:

$$D_1 \wedge D_2 \wedge \cdots \wedge D_n ::> \quad K \quad \vdash \quad D \quad ::> \quad K \tag{7.8}$$

The rule represents that if an event meets all description D_i ($i \in$ I), then it must meet a more general description D.

A basic characteristic of generalization transform is as following. What it gets is only a hypothesis, and must be tested using new data. Furthermore, generalization rule do not assure that the descriptor gotten from it is rational or useful. Generalization is divided into two categories: constructive and selective. If in generating concept description D, all descriptions used have been appeared in initial concept description D_i ($i \in$ I), then it is called selective generalization rule, otherwise constructive generalization rule.

1. Selective generalization rules

Assume CTX, CTX$_1$, CTX$_2$ represent arbitrary expression.

(1) Condition elimination rule

$$CTX \wedge S ::> K \quad \overline{\mathsf{k}} \quad CTX ::> K \qquad (7.9)$$

where S is a predicate or a logic expression.

(2) Add selective item rule

$$CTX_1 ::> K \quad \overline{\mathsf{k}} \quad CTX_1 \vee CTX_2 ::> K \qquad (7.10)$$

generalize concept description through adding selective item rule, such as:

$$CTX \wedge [color = red] ::> K \quad \overline{\mathsf{k}} \quad CTX \wedge [L = R_2] ::> K$$

(3) Enlarge quote range rule

$$CTX \wedge [L = R_1] ::> K \quad \overline{\mathsf{k}} \quad CTX \wedge [color: red \wedge blue] ::> K \qquad (7.11)$$

where $R_1 \subseteq R_2 \subseteq DOM(L)$, DOM(L) is domain of L, L is a item, R_i is a set of values L can have.

(4) Closed interval rule

$$\left. \begin{array}{l} CTX \wedge [L = a] ::> K \\ CTX \wedge [L = b] ::> K \end{array} \right| \overline{<} CTX \wedge [L = a \cdots b] ::> K \qquad (7.12)$$

where L is linear descriptor, a and b is specific value of L.

(5) Climbing generalization tree rule

$$\left. \begin{array}{l} CTX \wedge [L = a] ::> K \\ CTX \wedge [L = b] ::> K \\ \vdots \\ CTX \wedge [L = i] ::> K \end{array} \right| \overline{<} CTX \wedge [L = S] ::> K \qquad (7.13)$$

where L is structural descriptor, in the generalization tree domain of L, S represents the lowest parent node whose successors are $a, b, \cdots, i$.

(6) Rule transforming constant into variable

$$\left. \begin{array}{l} F[a] \\ F[b] \\ \vdots \\ F[i] \end{array} \right| \overline{<} \forall x F[x] \qquad (7.14)$$

where $F[x]$ is descriptor dependent with variable x, a, b, $\cdots$, i are constants. For descriptor $F[x]$, if some values of x (a,b, $\cdots$, i) make $F[x]$ hold, then we can get assumption: for all values of x, $F[x]$ holds.

(7) Rule transforming conjunction into disjunction

$$F_1 \wedge F_2 ::> K \quad \vdash F_1 \vee F_2 ::> K \tag{7.15}$$

where F_1, F_2 are arbitrary description.

(8) Rule enlarging quantifier range

$$\forall x F[x] ::> K \quad \vdash \exists x F[x] ::> K \tag{7.16}$$

$$\exists_{(i_1)} x F[x] ::> K \quad \vdash \exists_{(i_2)} x F[x] ::> K \tag{7.17}$$

where I_1, I_2 are domain of quantifiers (set of integer), and $I_1 \subseteq I_2$.

(9) Generalization decomposition rule

Used in concept acquisition:
$$\left. \begin{array}{c} P \wedge F_1 ::> K \\ \sim P \wedge F_2 ::> K \end{array} \right| \vdash F_1 \vee F_2 ::> K \tag{7.18}$$

Used in description generalization

$$P \wedge F_1 \vee \sim p \wedge F_2 \vdash F_1 \wedge F_2 \tag{7.19}$$

where P is predicate.

(10) Anti-enlarge rule

$$\left. \begin{array}{c} CTX_1 \wedge [L = R_1] : :> K \\ CTX_2 \wedge [L = R_2] : :> \sim K \end{array} \right| \vdash [L \neq R_2] ::> K \tag{7.20}$$

where R_1, R_2 are disjunction expression.

Given an object description which belongs to concept K (positive instance), and an object description does not belong to concept K (negative instance), the rule will generate a more general description which includes these two descriptions. This is the basic idea of learning difference description from instances.

2. Constructive generalization rule

Constructive generalization rule can generate some inductive assertion. Descriptors they used do not appear in initial observation statement, that is, these rules transform the initial representing space.

(1) General constructive rule

$$\left. \begin{array}{c} CTX \wedge F_1 ::> K \\ F_1 \Rightarrow F_2 \end{array} \right| \vdash CTX \wedge F_2 ::> K \tag{7.21}$$

the rule represents that if a concept description consists a part F_1, F_1 implicate another concept F_2, a more general description can be gotten by using F_2 to replace F_1.

(2) Computing variable rule

   Computing quantifier (CQ rule):

$$\exists_{V1,V2,\cdots,Vk}F[V_1,V_2,\cdots,V_k]$$

CQ rule will generate a new descriptor "#v-COND", representing number of v_i meeting a certain condition COND. For example, "#v_i-length—2..4" represents number of vi whose length is between 2 and 4.

   Computing number of predicate (CA rule): in description, descriptor is a relation which possesss several variables REL(v_1,v_2, $\cdots$), CA rule will compute the number of predicate which meets condition COND in relation REL.

(3) Generating link attribute rule

   In concept description, if variables in a concept description formulate a link because of the difference of transfer relation, the rule can generate descriptors of some particular objects in depicting link. This kind of object may be as follows:

- LST-object: "minimum object", or starting object of link
- MST-object: ending object of link
- MID-object: middle object of link
- Nth-object: the N-th object of link

(4) Rule detecting dependence relation of descriptors

   Assume that given an object set representing a concept, we use attribute description to depict features of object. The description defines attribute values of object, and do not depict structural features of object. Assume that in all fact descriptions, values of linear descriptor x are ascending ordered, while values of another linear descriptor y are ascending or descending ordered, then a 2-dimensional descriptor M(x,y) is generated, which represents that there is monotonic relation between x and y. Descriptor has value ↑ when value y is ascending, otherwise descriptor has value ↓.

7.3 Inductive Bias

Bias plays an important role in concept learning. Bias means all factors affecting assume selection in concept learning except for positive and negative example. These factors include: (a) language describing assumption. (b) assumption space considered by program. (c) assumption procedure according to what order. (d) admit definitive criterion, that is, research procedure with known assumption could be terminated, or proceed to select a better assumption. Employing bias approach, learning partial difference assumption will result in different inductive leaps. Bias has two features(Utgoff, 1986):

(1) A strong bias is one that focuses the concept learning on relatively small number of hypotheses. On the contrary, a weak bias is one that allows the concept learner to consider relatively large number of hypotheses.
(2) A correct bias is one that allows the concept learner to select the target concept. Conversely, an incorrect bias cannot select target concept.

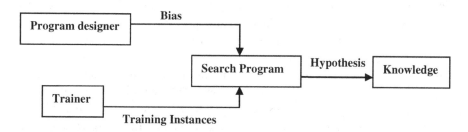

Figure 7.1. Role of bias in inductive learning

Figure 7.1 shows the role of bias in inductive learning. From the figure we can know that given any training examples with specific order, induction becomes an independent variable function. When bias is strong and correct, concept learning can select available objective concept. When bias is weak and incorrect, concept learning is difficult because no guide can select hypothesis. In order to transform a weaker bias, following algorithm could be employed:

(1) Recommend new concept descriptions to be added to the concept description language through heuristics;
(2) Translate the recommendations into new concept descriptions formally represented by concept description language;
(3) Assimilate newly formed concepts into the restricted space of hypotheses in a manner that maintains the organization of the hypothesis space.

In the algorithm mentioned above, step 1 determines a better bias. Machine executes transforming in step 2 and step 3, resulting in that new concept description language is better than former description language.

To realize inductive learning, it is necessary to study a good bias. As for fundamental problem of bias transform, it includes tasks about assimilate generating knowledge and question acquisition, computing initial bias, approaches of goal freedom and goal sensitivity, etc. It needs to be studied further.

7.4 Version Space

Version space takes the whole rule space as initial assumed rule set H. According to information of training examples, it makes generalization or specialization to set, increasingly reducing the set H. Finally H is converged into rules that only include quest. The term version space is used to refer to this set because it contains all plausible versions of the emerging concept.

In 1977 Mitchell pointed out that rules in rule space can build partial order according to their general degree. Figure 7.2 shows a partial order in a rule space, where TRUE means that there is no condition, and this is the most general concept. Concept $\exists x$: CLUBS(x) means that at least a club is more specific than the former. Concept $\exists x,y$:CLUBS(x) $\wedge$ HEARTS(y) means that at least a club and a heart exist and they are more specific than the former. Arrows in the figure point to more general concept from specific concept.

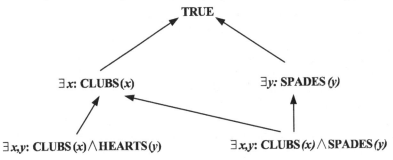

Figure 7.2. A partial order in rule space

Figure 7.3 is the sketch map after ordering the general rule space. The highest point in the figure is the most general rule (concept). It is a point without description, i.e. a point without condition. All examples are in accordance with the concept. Points on the lowest line are correspond concepts of positive training examples. Each point corresponds to a positive example. For example, every example shows suit and rank of a card C, such as:

$$\text{SUIT(C, clubs)} \wedge \text{RANK(C,7)}$$

This is a positive training example, at the same time it is the most specific concept. Concept RANK(C,7) are points at the middle of rule space. It is more specific than no description, and more general than positive training example.

When searching rule space, we use a possible rational set of hypothesis rule *H*. *H* is the subset of rule space. It is a segment of rule space. The subset composed of most general elements of *H* is referred to as set *G*; the subset composed of most specific elements of *H* is referred to as set *S*. In rule space, *H* is a segment between upper bound *G* and lower bound *S*. So set *H* can be represented by *G* and *S*.

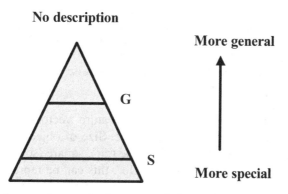

Figure 7.3. Sketch map of general rule space ordering

Initial set *G* of version space is the highest point (the most general concept); initial set *S* is points of the lowest line (positive training examples); initial set *H* is the whole rule space. In the search procedure, set *G* increasingly drops (specialization); set *S* increasingly rises (generalization); *H* increasingly reduces. Finally *H* is converged into a request concept. Several algorithms are introduced as follows.

7.4.1 Candidate-elimination algorithm

Mitchell proposed an algorithm named candidate-elimination algorithm. It represents set *H* using bound set *G* and *S*. Set *H* called version space. All concept description in *H* meet all positive examples provided, and do not meet any negative example provided.

At beginning, *H* is the whole rule space. After accepting positive training instances, the program is generalized. Through eliminating some specific concepts, set S rises. After accepting negative training instances, the program is specialized. Through eliminating some general concepts, set *G* drops. Both of them eliminate some candidate concepts. The procedure can be divided into four steps(Mitchell, 1977).

Algorithm 7.1 Candidate-elimination Algorithm.

1. Initialize the sets S and G respectively. At this time S includes all possible positive training instances (the most specific concept), and the scale of S is too great. Initial set S of the actual algorithm only includes the first positive training instance, and this kind of H is not whole space.

2. Accepting a new training instance. If it is positive instance, firstly eliminate the concept that does not cover new positive instance from G, then modify S to the most specific result generalized from new positive instances and original elements of S (that is, as less as possible modifying S, but S is required to cover the new positive instances). If it is negative instances,   firstly eliminate the concept that covers the new negative instance from S, then modify G to the most general result specialized from new negative instances and original elements of G (that is, as less as possible modifying G, but G is required not to cover the new negative examples).

3. If $G=S$ and it is single element set, go to step 4, otherwise go to step 2.

4. Output the concept in H (i.e. G and S).

The following is an example. We use feature vectors to describe object. Every object has two features: size and shape. Size of object could be large (lg) or small (sm). Shape of object could be circle (cir), square (squ) or triangular (tri). To let the program know the concept "circle", this can be represented as (x, cir), where x represents any size.

Initial set H is rule space. Set G and S are as follows respectively:

$G=\{(x,y)\}$

$S=\{(\text{sm squ}), (\text{sm cir}),(\text{sm tri}),(\text{lg squ}), (\text{lg cir}), (\text{lg tri})\}$

Initial version space H is shown at figure 7.4.

The first training example is positive example (sm cir), which means that a small circle is a circle. After modifying algorithm S we can get

$G =\{(x\ y)\}$

$S =\{(\text{sm cir})\}$

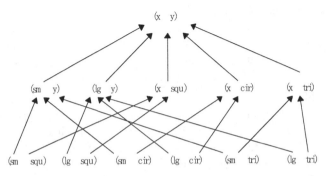

Figure 7.4. Initial version space

Figure 7.5 shows the version space after the first training instance. Four concepts linked by arrows construct version space. These concepts meet the first training instance, and no other concepts do. In actual algorithm this is taken as initial version space, not in Figure 7.4.

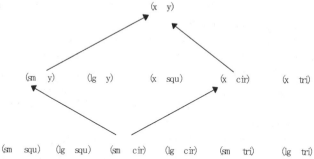

Figure 7.5. Version space after the first training example

The second training instance is negative example (lg tri), which means that a large triangle is not a circle. This step specializes the set G, and it can get:
$$G = \{(x\ cir), (sm\ y)\}$$
$$S = \{(sm\ cir)\}$$
Figure 7.6 shows the version space after the second training instance. At this time H only includes three concepts, which meet the previous concept, but do not meet all concepts of this negative instance.

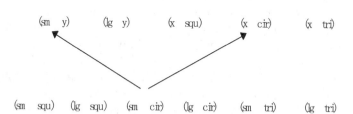

Figure 7.6. Version space after the second training example

The third training instance is positive instance (lg cir), which means that large circle is a circle. This step firstly eliminates the concepts that do not meet the positive instance, and then generalizes S and the positive instance. It gets:
$$G = \{(x\ cir)\}$$
$$S = \{(x\ cir)\}$$
The algorithm ends at this time, and outputs the concept $(x\ cir)$.

There are several supplement explanations about this algorithm:

1. Understanding the set G and S. As for new instances that meet required concepts, S is the set of sufficient conditions, and G is the set of necessary conditions. For example, after the first training instance, (sm cir) is sufficient condition. That is, small circle must meet the required concept, when program do not know whether the large circle meets. In addition, after the second training instance, (x cir) and (sm y) are necessary conditions. That is, the instance which meets the required concept is either circle or small. When algorithm ends, $G=S$, i.e. it meets the necessary and sufficient condition.

2. When learning the positive instances, S is generalized, and this often makes S enlarged. When learning the negative examples, G is specialized, and this often makes G enlarged. The scale of G 和 S is too large which will make the algorithm difficult to apply. Algorithm is breath-first search for the rule space under the guide of training examples. As for large rule space, the algorithm is too slow to accept.

7.4.2 Two improved algorithms

Basic learning algorithms of version space are very difficult to apply, so people proposed some improved algorithms. There are two improved algorithms among them only employ positive instance learning. They are similar to the procedure mentioned above to modify S.

The first algorithm is collision match algorithm. It is used to learn the concept represented by "parameterized structural representation". In the procedure mentioned above to modify S, it always do as less as possible generalization so that it can cover new positive example. If descriptive form is predicate expression, the procedure is equal to find the largest public sub-expression. This only needs to eliminate the least conjunction condition. For example, set S is as follows.

$S=\{BLOCK(x)\wedge BLOCK(y)\wedge SQUARE(y)\wedge RECTANGLE(x)\wedge ONTOP(x,y)\}$

Which means block x is rectangle, block y is square, and x is on y. If next positive training example I_1 is as follows.

$I_1 = \{BLOCK(w)\wedge BLOCK(v)\wedge SQUARE(w)\wedge RECTANGLE(v)\wedge ONTOP(w, v)\}$

Which means block w is square, block v is rectangle, and w is on v.

Through the procedure to modify S, following public subset will be generated

$S'=\{S_1, S_2\}$

Where

$S_1=BLOCK(a)\wedge BLOCK(b)\wedge SQUARE(a)\wedge RECTANGLE(b)$

$$S_2=BLOCK(c)\wedge BLOCK(d)\wedge ONTOP(c,d)$$

S_1 equals to assume that position ONTOP is not related to required concept. S_2 equals to assume that block shape is not related to required concept. It should be noticed that, when x correspond to w and y correspond to v, position relations between S and I_1 are matched while shape features are not matched. On the contrary, when x correspond to v and y correspond to w, shape features are matched while position relations between S and I_1 are not matched. This phenomenon is collision in match. In order to solve the collision, we use two elements in S' to consider these two sides respectively.

The second approach is to maximize unified generalization. This algorithm is used to find the maximum unified generalization of predicate expression. It is similar to collision match algorithm, but the representative language it uses allow many-to-one argument link in match.

Version space has two main shortages:

1. Lack anti-noise ability

All data-driven algorithms (include version space) are hard to handle training instances with noise. Since concepts gotten from algorithms should meet request of every training instance, a training instance would make a big influence. Sometimes wrong instances make program get wrong concepts, sometimes even no concepts. At this time H becomes empty set.

In order to solve the problem Mitchell proposed an approach to save multiple sets of G and S. For example, S_0 meets all positive instances, and S_1 meets all other positive instances except one, S_2 etc. are similar. If G_0 exceeds S_0, H_0 is empty set. This means that no concept meets all instances. So program finds G_1 and S_1, so that we can get H_1. If H_1 is empty too, it gets H_2.

2. Learn disjunction concept

Version space cannot discover disjunction concept. Some concepts are disjunction form. For example, PARENT maybe father or mother. This can be represented as PARENT(x)=FATHER(x) $\vee$ PARENT(x)=MOTHER(x). Since set G and S are conjunction form, above-mentioned algorithm cannot find disjunction concepts.

The first solution uses representation language without disjunction connective. It repeats many times to eliminate candidate elements so that it can find many conjunction descriptions covered all examples.

Algorithm 7.2 Algorithm to Learn Disjunction Concept

1. Set S is initialized to include one positive instance, and set G is initialized to include no description.
2. As for every negative instance, modify set G.

3. Select a description g in *G*, and take *g* as a conjunction term of solution set. *g* does not cover any negative instance, but it will cover part of positive instances. Then eliminate all positive instances specific than *g* from positive instance set (i.e. positive instances covered by g).

4. For residual positive instances and negative instances, repeat step1, 2 and 3 until all positive instances are covered. Disjunction of *g* gotten from each repeat is required concept.

The disjunction does not cover any negative instance, and every *g* does not cover any negative instance either. The disjunction covers all positive instances, and every g covers positive instances eliminated by it. Notice, since there is not a procedure to modify *S*, *g* does not cover all positive instances. However, *g* at least covers the positive instance at first step, so *g* should at least eliminate this positive instance.

The second solution is referred to as AQ algorithm(Michalski, 1975), which is similar to the former algorithm. But AQ algorithm uses heuristics to select a positive instance at the first step, requiring the positive instance is not covered by several past *g*. Larson improves AQ algorithm, and applies it to spread predicate calculus representation.

7.5 AQ Algorithm for Inductive Learning

In 1969, Michalski proposed AQ learning algorithm, which is an example-based learning algorithm. AQ algorithm generates disjunction of selected assumption, which covers all positive examples but does not cover any negative example. Its basic algorithm is:

Algorithm 7.3 Simple AQ Learning Algorithm

1. Randomly select one positive example as a seed.
2. Generate consistent generalization expression of the example (referred to as star).
3. According to bias standard, select the optimal generalization expression from star. If needed, it specialize the assumption.
4. If this hypothesis covers all positive examples, then go to step 2.

Michalski proposed AQ11 in 1978 (Michalski and Larson, 1978). AQ11 algorithm searches rule space, repeatedly eliminate candidate elements, and gets general rules. AQ11 algorithm turns problems of learning discriminative rules into a series of problems of learning single concept. In order to get rules of class C_i, it takes examples of class C_i as positive examples, and all examples of other classes as negative examples. It can get descriptions that cover all positive examples but do not cover any negative example, which can be taken as rules of

C_i. Discriminative rules found may overlap in unobserved region of example space.

In order to find classification rule set which does not overlap, AQ11 takes examples of class C_i as positive examples, and negative examples include all examples of other classes $C_j (j \neq i)$ and all examples in positive example region of various unhandled classes $C_k (1 \leq k \leq i)$. Then, class C_2 only covers parts that class C_1 does not cover. Parts that class C_3 covers are parts that neither class C_2 nor C_1 covers.

Discriminative rules gotten from AQ11 correspond to the most general description set meet training examples. That is, set G of various classes, such as G_1, G_2, etc. Sometimes the most specific description sets meet training examples which need to be used. That is, set S of various classes, such as S_1, S_2, etc.

Michalski et al. employed AQ11 program in learning diagnosed rules of soy sick. In program, 630 descriptions of plants with soy sick have been provided. Each description has 35 feature vectors. At the same time, expert diagnose conclusions have been pooled. Program of selecting examples selects 290 sample plants as training examples. Selective principle makes distance between examples as larger as possible. Other 340 plants take as test set for check the acquired rules.

7.6 Constructing Decision Trees

A particularly efficient method for exploring the space of concept descriptions is to generate a decision tree. Hunt,Marin and Stone have developed Concept Learning System(CLS) (Hunt, Marin and Stone, 1966). CLS uses a lookahead strategy similar to minimax. At each stage, CLS explores the space of possible decision trees to a fixed depth, chooses an action to minimize cost in this limited space, then moves one level down in the tree. It intends to solve single concept learning tasks and uses the learned concepts to classify new instances.

The main idea of CLS algorithm is as following. First, start from an empty decision tree, improve original decision tree by adding new discriminative node, until decision tree could correctly classify the training examples.

Algorithm 7.4 CLS Algorithm

1. Let initial status of decision tree T only includes a root (X, Q), where X is a set of all training examples, Q is a set of all test attributes;
2. If all leaf nodes (X', Q') , of T have following status: when all training examples of the first vector X' belong to same class, or the second vector Q' is

void, cease to execute the learning algorithm, learning result is T;

3. Otherwise, select a leaf node (X', Q') without the status mentioned in step 2;

4. As for Q', we select test attribute according to certain rules. Assume that X' was divided into m non-intersect subsets X_i', $1 \leq i \leq m$, by different values of b. sticking m branches from (X', Q'), each branch represents different value of b, then formulate m new leaf nodes $(X_i', Q'-\{b\})$, $1 \leq i \leq m$;

5. Go to step2.

It can be seen from description of CLS algorithm that the construct procedure is procedure of hypothesis specialization, so CLS algorithm can be seen as a learning algorithm with only one operator, which can be represented as: through adding a new discriminative condition (discriminative node), specialize current hypothesis. CLS algorithm recursively calls the operator, acting at every leaf node, and constructing a decision tree.

In the steps 2 of algorithm 7.4, if there does not exist contradiction among training set, which means there does not exist two examples without same attribute belong to same class, then if the second condition is met (i.e. Q' is empty), the first condition will be met too (i.e. all training examples of X' belong to same class). This means the cease condition should be chosen from one of them. However, as for existing contradiction training set, above-mentioned statement must not hold.

In the step 4, the algorithm should meet $m>1$ or classification is pointless. However, because there are contradiction training examples, it is difficult to assure $m>1$.

In the step4, the algorithm does not give selective standard of test attributes, so CLS has been improved through many ways.

7.7 ID3 Learning Algorithm

Algorithm 7.4 did not give how to select test attribute b, Hunt had proposed several selective standard. In various decision tree learning algorithms, the most influential is ID3 algorithm proposed by Quinlan in 1979 (Quinlan, 1979). ID3 algorithm takes the decline velocity of information entropy as selective standard of test attribute. Decline of information entropy is decline of information uncertainty.

7.7.1 *Introduction to information theory*

In 1948, Shannon proposed and developed information theory, studying information and mathematic measure, which measures the magnitude of information through eliminating the uncertain degree of various symbols in information source. A series of concepts has been proposed:

(1) Self-information. Before receive a_i, uncertainty of receiver send a_i to information source which is defined as self-information $I(a_i)$ of information symbol a_i. i.e. $I(a_i) = -\log p(a_i)$, where $p(a_i)$ represents probability of a_i sent by information source.

(2) Information entropy. Self-information reflects uncertainty of symbols, while information entropy can be used to measure uncertainty of the whole information source X. It is defined as follows

$$H(X) = p(a_1)I(a_1) + p(a_2)I(a_2) + \ldots\ldots p(a_r)I(a_r)$$

$$= -\sum_{i=1}^{r} p(a_i)\log p(a_i) \tag{7.22}$$

Where r represents all possible number of symbol of information source X. Information entropy is defined as average self-information content provided by information source when it sends a symbol. Here log is logarithm taking 2 as bottom.

(3) Condition entropy. Condition entropy $H(X/Y)$ is used to measure receiver receiving the random variable Y, random variable X still exists uncertainty when information source X and random variable Y are not mutual independent. Let X be correspondent to source symbol a_i, Y be correspondent to source symbol b_j, then $p(a_i/b_j)$ is probability, the condition entropy as follows:

(4) Average mutual information. It is used to represent the amount of information about X provided by signal Y, represented as $I(X,Y)$:

$$H(X/Y) = -\sum_{i=1}^{r}\sum_{j=1}^{s} p(a_i/b_j)\log p(a_i/b_j) \tag{7.23}$$

$$I(X,Y) = H(X) - H(X/Y) \tag{7.24}$$

7.7.2 Attribute selection

In algorithm 7.4, we only have one empty decision tree when learning starts, not knowing how to classify examples according to attributes. In terms of training set we should construct the decision tree to partition the whole example space based on attributes. Let training set be X and will be divided them into n classes. Assume that the number of training example belonging to the ith class is C_i, total number of training examples in X is $|X|$. If probability that a example belongs to the ith class is written as $P(C_i)$, then:

$$P(C_i) = \frac{C_i}{|X|} \tag{7.25}$$

At this time, uncertainty of decision tree partition C is:

$$H(X,C) = -\sum P(C_i)\log P(C_i) \tag{7.26}$$

In context without confusion, $H(X, C)$ is simply written as $H(X)$.

Decision tree learning procedure is a procedure that decision tree makes uncertainty of partition increasingly diminished. If we select attribute a to test, when we know $a = a_j$

$$H(X/a) = -\sum_i \sum_j p(Ci; a = a_j)\log p(Ci/a = a_j)$$

$$= -\sum_i \sum_j p(a = a_j)p(Ci/a = a_j)\log p(Ci/a = a_j)$$

$$= -\sum_j p(a = a_j)\sum_i p(Ci/a = a_j)\log p(Ci/a = a_j) \tag{7.27}$$

Assume that number of examples belonging to the ith class is C_{ij}, written as

$$P(Ci, a = a_j) = \frac{C_{ij}}{|X|}, \text{ i.e. } P(C_i, a=a_j) \text{ is probability belonging to the ith class}$$

when test attribute a is a_j. At this time, uncertainty degree of decision tree classification is condition entropy of training set to attribute X

$$H(X_j) = -\sum_i p(Ci/a = a_j)\log p(Ci/a = a_j) \tag{7.28}$$

After selecting test attribute a, for every leaf node X_j meets $a=a_j$, the information entropy about classification information is:

$$H(X/a) = \sum_j p(a = a_j)H(X_j) \tag{7.29}$$

The amount of information provided by classification of attribute a is $I(X ; a)$:

$$I(X, a) = H(X) - H(X / a) \tag{7.30}$$

The less the value of expression (7.29) is , the larger the value of expression (7.30) would be. This means the more information provided by test attribute a, the less uncertainty degree for classification after selecting a. Quinlan's ID3 algorithm selects the attribute which makes $I(X; a)$ maximum to be test attribute, i.e. selects attribute a which make expression (7.29) minimum.

7.7.3 ID3 algorithm

Except for using information measure as standard, ID3 algorithm introduces increment learning techniques. In CLS algorithm, since algorithm needs to know all training examples at beginning, when training example set is too large, examples cannot be immediately put into memory and have some problems. Quinlan introduces windows for increment learning to solve the problem. The following is ID3 algorithm(Quinlan, 1983).

Algorithm 7.5 ID3 Algorithm

1. Select random subset X1 with scale of W from the whole training example set X (W is window scale, and subset is referred to as window);
2. With the standard that makes the value of expression (7.29) minimum, select each test attribute to form current decision tree;
3. Scan all training examples sequentially, and find current exception of current decision tree, if there is not any exception, the algorithm ends.
4. Combine some examples of current window and some exceptions in step 3 to form new window, go to step 2.

In order to construct new window in step 4, Quinlan tried two different strategies: one is to retain all examples of window and add appointed exceptions get from step 3. This strategy will enlarge the window more large. The other strategy corresponds to retain a training example for each node of current decision tree, other examples are deleted from the window and replaced by exceptions. The experiments showed that both approaches work well, but if the concept is so complicated that windows with fixed scale W cannot be found, the second approach may be not converged.

7.7.4 Application example of ID3 algorithm

Table 7.2 gives a data set may have noise. There are four attributes: Outlook, Temperature, Humidity and Windy. It is divided into two classes: *P* and *N*, represent positive example and negative example respectively. What we should do is to construct decision tree and classify the data.

Since the number of examples belong to class P and N is 12 at beginning, entropy value is:

$$H \ (\ X \ ) \ = \ - \ \frac{12}{24} \log \ \frac{12}{24} \ - \ \frac{12}{24} \log \ \frac{12}{24} \ = \ 1$$

If Outlook is selected as test attribute, then according to formula (7.23), condition entropy is:

$$H \ (\ X \ / \ Outlook \ ) \ = \ \frac{9}{24} (- \frac{4}{9} \log \ \frac{4}{9} - \frac{5}{9} \log \ \frac{5}{9}) + \frac{8}{24} (- \frac{1}{8} \log \ \frac{1}{8} - \frac{7}{8} \log \ \frac{7}{8})$$

$$+ \ \frac{7}{24} (- \frac{1}{7} \log \ \frac{1}{7} - \frac{6}{7} \log \ \frac{6}{7}) \ = \ 0.5528$$

Table 7.2 Daily weather classification

Attribute	Outlook	Temperature	Humidity	Wind	Class
1	Overcast	Hot	High	Not	N
2	Overcast	Hot	High	Very	N
3	Overcast	Hot	High	Medium	N
4	Sunny	Hot	High	Not	P
5	Sunny	Hot	High	Medium	P
6	Rain	Mild	High	Not	N
7	Rain	Mild	High	Medium	N
8	Rain	Hot	Normal	Not	P
9	Rain	Cool	Normal	Medium	N
10	Rain	Hot	Normal	Very	N
11	Sunny	Cool	Normal	Very	P
12	Sunny	Cool	Normal	Medium	P
13	Overcast	Mild	High	Not	N
14	Overcast	Mild	High	Medium	N
15	Overcast	Cool	Normal	Not	P
16	Overcast	Cool	Normal	Medium	P
17	Rain	Mild	Normal	Not	N
18	Rain	Mild	Normal	Medium	N
19	Overcast	Mild	Normal	Medium	P
20	Overcast	Mild	Normal	Very	P
21	Sunny	Mild	High	Very	P
22	Sunny	Mild	High	Medium	P
23	Sunny	Hot	Normal	Not	P
24	Rain	Mild	High	Very	N

If Temperature is selected as test attribute, then:

$$H \ (\ X \ / \ Temp \ ) \ = \ \frac{8}{24} (- \frac{4}{8} \log \ \frac{4}{8} - \frac{4}{8} \log \ \frac{4}{8}) + \frac{11}{24} (- \frac{4}{11} \log \ \frac{4}{11} - \frac{7}{11} \log \ \frac{7}{11})$$

$$+ \ \frac{5}{24} (- \frac{4}{5} \log \ \frac{4}{5} - \frac{1}{5} \log \ \frac{1}{5}) \ = \ 0.6739$$

If Humidity is selected as test attribute, then:

$$H(X/Humid) = \frac{12}{24}(-\frac{4}{12}\log\frac{4}{12} - \frac{8}{12}\log\frac{8}{12})$$
$$+ \frac{12}{24}(-\frac{4}{12}\log\frac{4}{12} - \frac{8}{12}\log\frac{8}{12}) = 0.9183$$

If Windy is selected as test attribute, then:

$$H(X/Windy) = \frac{8}{24}(-\frac{4}{8}\log\frac{4}{8} - \frac{4}{8}\log\frac{4}{8}) + \frac{6}{24}(-\frac{3}{6}\log\frac{3}{6} - \frac{3}{6}\log\frac{3}{6})$$
$$+ \frac{10}{24}(-\frac{5}{10}\log\frac{5}{10} - \frac{5}{10}\log\frac{5}{10}) = 1$$

We can see that $H(X/Outlook)$ is minimum which means that information about Outlook provides great help for classification, providing largest amount of information, i.e. $I(X, Outlook)$ is maximum. Therefore, Outlook should be selected as test attribute. We can see $H(X) = H(X/Windy)$, i.e. $I(X, Windy) = 0$. Information about Windy cannot provide any information about classification. After select Outlook as test attribute, training example set is divided into three subsets, generating three leaf nodes. Using above procedure to each leaf node in order, we can get decision tree as shown in Figure 7.7.

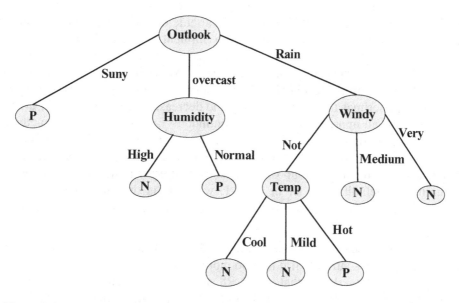

Figure 7.7. Decision tree generated by training table 7.2

ID3 algorithms have extensive application. The most famous is C4.5(Quinlan, 1993). New function of C4.5 is that it can transform decision tree into equivalent rule representation. In addition, C4.5 solve data learning problem of continuous value.

7.7.5 *Dispersing continuous attribute*

Decision tree is mainly used to learn the approach that take discrete variable as attribute type. To learn continuous variable, it must be dispersed. However, in some algorithm (such as C4.5), it is easier to select the dispersed continuous attribute than to select the discrete attribute. In these algorithms, for a continuous attribute, firstly order different values of stored training examples, then select each pair of neighbor central points as standard to differential attribute values. Since these dispersed attribute only represented by one example, continuous attribute will be selected in priority.

Dougherty employs an information entropy based procedure to disperse continuous attribute. They disperse continuous global variable before generating the decision tree, rather than disperse local variable based on examples of a node like C4.5. Since local data is less, it is easily influent by noise of the data. Based on information entropy, this approach recursively divides continuous value into many discrete attributes. In addition, it employ MDL standard. They find this approach do not drop the classification accuracy when used in C4.5. On the contrary, it sometimes raises the accuracy and decreases the size of trees in C4.5. Auer proposed an approach to disperse continuous variable using local method. His T2 algorithm divides continuous variable into many discrete variables but not binary continuous variable. It is not doing recursive divide as above, but doing complete search to find a group of intervals so that error in training example set is minimum. Default value of m is $C+1$, where C is the number of partition classes. Therefore, complexity of T2 is proportional to $C^6 f^2$. f is number of attribute.

In C4.5 Release8 (R8), Quinlan proposed a local, MDL based approach to penalize continuous attribute if it has too more values.

Experiment data shows that, C4.5 R8 approach has better performance in most situations, but Dougherty approach of global discretization has better performance in small data set. T2 works well when data is partitioned into less classes.

7.8 Bias Shift Based Decision Tree Algorithm

The key of constructing good decision tree is to select good attributes. In common, among a great deal of decision tree which can fit given training examples, the smaller size of the tree, the more predict capability of the tree. To construct as small as possible, the key is to select proper attributes. Since the problem of constructing minimum tree is a NP complete problem, a large amount of research can only employ heuristics to select good attributes. Attribute selecting dependents on impurity measures of various example subsets. Impurity measures include information gain, ratio of information gain, Gini-index, distance measures, J-measures, G-statistics, $\chi2$ statistics, P^0 zero-probability assumption, evidence weights, minimal description length(MDL), orthogonal approach measures, correlation degree and Relief, etc. Different measures have different effect, so difference between single-variant decision tree and multi-variant decision tree has emerged. The conclusions of deeply studying of these measures are not agreeable. No one algorithm is absolute predominance in solving problems of attribute select, data noise, data increasing, pre-pruning and post-pruning, pruning cease standard, etc. Empirical and intuitive feeling replaced strict and complete theory proof.

In fact, above problems are bias problems in decision tree learning. Bias plays an important role in concept learning. Utgoff points out that inductive learning does not exist without bias. Inductive bias means all factors except primitive training instances, including language describing hypothesis, program space considering hypothesis, order of hypothesis procedure, admitting definitive standard, etc. Bias has two features: one is that strong bias focus on concept learning in relative less hypotheses. On the contrary, weak bias focus on concept learning in relative more hypotheses; another feature is that correct bias permits concept learning selecting target concept, while incorrect bias cannot select target concept. When bias is strong and correct, concept can select useful target concept immediately; when bias is weak and incorrect, the task of concept learning is very difficult.

Bias can be divided into two categories: representation bias and procedure bias. Since family of ID3 algorithm lacks support of background knowledge, it is an inductive learning algorithm with support of relatively weak bias. We strengthen the bias of decision tree through shift of representation bias and procedure bias.

7.8.1 *Formalization of bias*

First of all, we define basic concepts of bias formally.

Definition 7.1 *S is a search space defined in <A，C，F，T，L>, where attribute vector A={a₁, ···,aₘ} has definite or infinite elements; classification vector C={c₁, ···,cₖ} has definite elements. For given A and C, F is set of all concepts; T is set of training examples with n tuples; L represents a learning algorithm family.*

Definition 7.2 *A learning algorithm l defines a map from T to F, that is:*

$$t\{t \in T\} \xrightarrow{l(t,f)} f\{f \in F\}, \quad l \in L \tag{7.31}$$

Definition 7.3 $D_{A \times C}$ *is a probability distribution on A ×C; t is n tuples which is defined on A ×C and suffice $D_{A \times C}$. Let D_C be a probability distribution on C, and identity of attribute set $IA(A_1, A_2)$ means probability that put a random attribute to same class given concepts f and D_C. That is:*

$$(T_0(A_1, f)) = l(T_0(A_2, f))), \quad l \in L \cap T_0 \subseteq T \cap A_1, A_2 \subseteq A \cap f \in F$$

Definition 7.4 *Let f_g be the target concept, correctness of bias CorrB can be defined as:*

$$CorrB = P_{D_A}(f_g(a) = f(a)), \quad f \in F \cap a \in A \tag{7.32}$$

Definition 7.5 *Let |S| be number of elements in S, then bias strength StrB can be defined as:*

$$StrB = \frac{1}{|S|} \tag{7.33}$$

Definition 7.6 *Let $State_0(S) = <A_0, C, f, T, l>$ and $State_1(S) = <A_1, C, f, T, l>$ be two states of search space, bias shift BSR is defined as:*

$$State_0(S) \xrightarrow{BS^R} State_1(S)$$

Definition 7.7 *Let D_A be a probability distribution on A, and identity of learning algorithm $IL(l_1, l_2)$ means probability that put a random training example t to same class given concepts f and D_A. That is:*

$$IL(l_1, l_2) = P_{D_A}(l_1(t, f) = l_2(t, f)), \quad t \in T \cap l_1, l_2 \in L \cap f \in F \tag{7.34}$$

Definition 7.8 *Predict accuracy PA of learning algorithm l is defined as:*

$$PA(l) = P_{D_{A \times C}}(f_{l(t)}(a) = c), \quad f \in F \cap t \in T \cap c \in C \tag{7.35}$$

Definition 7.9 *Let $State_0(S) = <A, C, f, T, l0>$ and $State_1(S)= <A, C, f, T, l1>$ be two states of search space, procedure bias shift BSP is defined as:*

$$State_0(S) \xrightarrow{BS^P} State_1(S)$$

Theorem 7.1 *Let l_1 and l_2 be learning algorithms, when $PA(l_1) \geqslant PA(l_2)$ holds, selecting $l1$ has more correct bias.*

Proof When $PA(l_1) \geqslant PA(l_2)$ holds, classifier generated by l_1 can classify more examples correctly. That is:

$$P_{D_{A \times C}}(f_{l_1(t)}(a) = c) \geq P_{D_{A \times C}}(f_{l_2(t)}(a) = c) \tag{7.36}$$

After we project bias correctness to distribution $D_{A \times C}$, we can get:

$$CorrB = P_{D_{A \times C}}(f_g(a) = c)$$

Since target concept is embodied to a large extent by classifier generated by learning algorithms, bias correctness can be adapted as:

Substituting algorithms l_1 and l_2 to above formula and combining with formula

$$CorrB = P_{D_{A \times C}}(f_{l(t)}(a) = c)$$

(7.36), we can get following:

$$CorrB_1 = P_{D_{A \times C}}(f_{l_1(t)}(a) = c) \geq CorrB_2 = P_{D_{A \times C}}(f_{l_2(t)}(a) = c)$$

Selecting l_1 has more correct bias. The Theorem 7.1 was proved.

7.8.2 Bias shift representation

Decision tree learning algorithm is actually efficient, but because of lacking support of background knowledge, it cannot handle various generalizations. As for inductive algorithms based on predicate logic (e.g. AQ11, INDUCE), this function is the most preliminary and inseparable from learning procedure. One result of lacking background knowledge is that procedure of constructing become complicated and not easily understood by domain experts.

Many systems attempt to solve this problem. Such as: algorithm PRISM of Cendrowska, INDUCT algorithm of Gaines, and other techniques introduced by Quinlan, Lavrac etc. which make decision tree easier and more precise. However, they only focus on information included in history data, attempt to mine more useful resource.

We propose a pre-processing algorithm which can make use of learning algorithm based on representation transform and can handle various generalizations. This approach firstly pre-processes the primitive training instances, calls generalization algorithm CGAOI, makes primitive training instances achieve appointed concept level, then pre-processes the primitive training instances again.

In order to realize the proposed algorithm, first concept level is introduced.

Definition 7.10 *A concept level is a mapping sequence from inferior concepts to superior concepts. These mapping sequences are organized in tree to generate a concept level tree.*

Definition 7.11 *A primitive training example set E^0 corresponds to a concept level forest $F = \{F_1, \cdots, F_i, \cdots, F_\varpi\}$, where F_i is a set of concept level tree corresponding to the ith attribute Ai, $1 \leqslant i \leqslant \varpi$. $F_i = \{T_1, \cdots, T_j, \cdots, T_\tau\}$, where T_j is the jth concept level tree of attribute A_i, $1 \leqslant j \leqslant \tau$.*

Definition 7.12 *When there is no concept level tree in attribute A_i, $F_i = NULL$.*

Definition 7.13 *A concept level database D is used to save history concept level trees.*

In all attributes of primitive training set, many attributes have their own fixed concept level. For example, if a commodity is made in Beijing, we can say it is made in China. Furthermore, we also can say it is made in Asia. This is a concept level of {Product Places : Beijing, China, Asia}.

Concept level is used to represent requested background knowledge to control procedure of generalization or specialization. Through organizing concepts of different level into a tree classification, concept space can be represented as partial order from specialization to generalization. The most general concept is description with empty meaning, which can be represented as "ANY"; the most specific concept is leaf in tree classification. Making use of concept level, we can represent found rules as form simpler, easier more special and more logical.

7.8.3 Algorithms

1. Classification guided attribute oriented inductive algorithm CGAOI

Classification guided attribute oriented inductive algorithm CGAOI can generalize original relation into appointed concept level. We proposed Classification guided attribute oriented inductive algorithm CGAOI. This approach is a supervised approach. As guide of classification learning task, it preprocesses primitive training instances, and softly outputs generalization relation of appointed level.

In the guide of classification feature of primitive training instances, the algorithm realizes basic operation oriented by attribute induction, such as attribute eliminating, concept refining, attribute threshold controlling and frequency propagating. At the same time, it realizes generalization consistency examination, data noise eliminating, automatic concept level generating, etc.

Algorithm 7.6 Classification guided attribute oriented inductive algorithm CGAOI

Input: Primitive training instance subset E^0, attribute set A^0, current attribute A; concept level tree T, appointed concept level tree L; appointed attribute controlling threshold Y; current concept level, current attribute controlling threshold Y^0.
Output: appointed concept level training example subset E, attribute set A, frequency C^T.
1. Call algorithm GCCC to generalize consistency check and noise elimination, return Ret1;
2. If generalization consistency check fails, then return failure;
3. Do concept improving operation under the control of Y and L;
4. Attribute elimination and frequency propagation;
5. Return success.

Theorem 7.2 *The representative bias shift will be stronger and more accurate through algorithm CGAOI processing.*

2. Preprocessing algorithm PPD

In the algorithm, we take specific attribute value of database as bound of generalization and specification. When attribute controlling threshold larger than current attribute value (or level lower than current level), it calls generalization procedure; on the contrary, it calls specialization procedure to reduce primitive training instances subset to corresponding concept level.

Algorithm 7.7 Preprocessing algorithm PPD

Input: Primitive training instance subset E^0; attribute set A^0; concept level forest F ; concept level database D; appointed concept level L; appoint attribute controlling threshold Y; current concept level; current attribute controlling threshold Y^0;
Output: Appointed concept level training example subset E; attribute set A;

1. Do operation to each attribute A_i in attribute set A^0;
2. Whether concept level tree F_i of A_i is empty;
3. if it is empty, then call algorithm AGCH to generate concept level tree F_i of A_i
   automatically, return Ret1;
4. Ret1= -1, go to step 1;   // A_i have no concept level tree
5. If ($Y = Y^0 \cap L = L^0$), then go to step 1;
6. If ($Y < Y^0 \cup L > L^0$), then call generalization algorithm CGAOI, return Ret2;
7. Ret2 = -1, go to step 1;   // if fail, then abandon generalization
8. Ret2 = 0, go to step 11;   // generalization success

9. If above conditions are not met, then go to step 1;

10. Call algorithm MEA to train example subset and maintain attribute set;

11. Call algorithm STCH to store concept level tree of A_i into concept level database D;

12. Go to step 1.

7.8.4 *Procedure bias shift*

Various decision tree learning algorithms have their own advantage, and the basic point of our proposed decision tree learning algorithm based on bias shift is employ their advantages. At the same time, learning algorithm has complicated relation with their learning task and attributes of training set, such as size, dimension, domain, etc. we cannot use simple controlling branch sentence to realize the selection of seek optimum algorithm. Therefore, we introduce the concept of two-level decision tree learning algorithm based on bias transform (see Figure 7.8).

The algorithm is designed based on the idea of two-level and multiple strategies. Two-level learning places the focus on: the first level is case-based reasoning used to select the most proper algorithm to solve primitive training example set from various decision tree learning algorithms with different evaluation standard, adaptive domain, size of training examples; the second learning task is used to construct classifier, that is, using selected decision tree algorithms, infer classification rules of decision tree representative form from cases without order and rule.

Case-based reasoning is a strategy that gets source case in memory from prompt of target case, and guides target case solving from source cases. Here, target cases are generated from classical case base of various decision tree algorithms. As for a given primitive training instance subset, we firstly extract its retrieval information tuple θ to retrieval in case base. Similarity in retrieval procedure meets optimal index ς in definition 7.24.

Multi-strategy learning is not constrained in one learning algorithm. It also provides mechanism to introduce new algorithms and classical examples. The mechanism provides a seamless link among original register algorithm, new classical case set and original register classical case set. The mechanism is realized by interface of human-machine interaction and classical case base maintain algorithm.

Definition 7.14 *Bias coefficient* $C^b = [\ C_1^b\ , \cdots,\ C_\varpi^b\ ]^T$ *represents relativity between various attributes of primitive training set and learning task, where ϖ is number of attribute of primitive training example set.*

Definition 7.15 *Cost coefficient* $C^c = [\, C_1^c , \cdots, C_\varpi^c \,]^T$ *represents cost to get every attribute of primitive training set, where ϖ is number of attribute of primitive training example set.*

Definition 7.16 *Primitive training example set E is objective learning task based set which is not constructed by BSDT algorithm.*

Definition 7.17 *An algorithm a is a decision tree learning algorithm which is registered in BSDT and certified feasible. The name of the algorithm is its unique sign. An algorithm set A is a set of all algorithms registered in BSDT.*

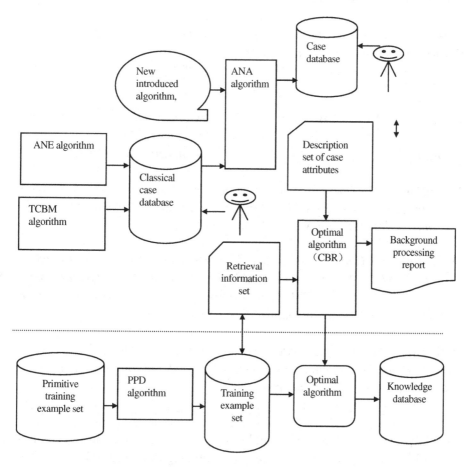

Figure 7.8. BSDT algorithm structure

Definition 7.18 *Algorithm index table AI is a set of names of all algorithm a registered in BSDT. Algorithm set A is corresponding to algorithm index table AI one-to-one.*

Definition 7.19 *Case attribute description set Θ is a six-element tuple < $\pi, S^e, S^d, S^t, \eta, N^a$> defined in classical case base, where π denotes domain name of classical training examples set E^t handled by algorithm δ; S^e represents size of E^t; S^d represents dimension of E^t; S^t represents time of generating decision tree which accords with E^t through algorithm δ; η represents error-classification ratio of decision tree; N^a represents name of algorithm δ. Here N^a is taken as a class sign of case base.*

Definition 7.20 *Retrieval information tuple θ is a three-element tuple <a_1, a_2, a_3> defined in primitive training example set, where a_1 represents domain name of given primitive training example set; a_2 represents size of E; a_3 represents dimension of E.*

Definition 7.21 *Case base CE is a set of cases generated by BSDT algorithm. Its six attributes are described by case attribute description set; category $N^a \in$ algorithm index table AP; example ce $\in$CE is generated by algorithm ANA.*

Definition 7.22 *Domain name $\pi \in$ domain name set Π. In BSDT, Π ={1-agriculture, 2-industry, 3-commence, 4-education, 5-electronics, 6-physics, 7-chemistry, 8-mathematics, 9-medicine, 10-others}.*

Definition 7.23 *Classical case base TEB = example index table EI $\cup$classical case table TET。Example index table EI is a set of all domain names π registered in algorithm BSDT; classical example table TET is a set of examples which get from a domain and named by a domain name π.*

Definition 7.24 *An optimal index ζ is a case retrieval standard decided by both case attribute description set Θ and retrieval information tuple θ. It is determined by following formula:*

$$\zeta = (a_1 = \pi) \wedge (|a_2 - S^e| < \lambda_1) \wedge (|a_3 - S^d| < \lambda_2) \wedge (S^t \bullet \eta < \lambda_3)$$

where λ_1, λ_2, λ_3 are tuple threshold, dimension threshold and tree controlling threshold respectively, and can be tuned in running time. In BSDT, default value of λ_1, λ_2, λ_3 are (where T_{in}, E_S, E_η are tuple interval, error-classification ratio and expectation of generating time respectively):

$$\lambda_1 = 0.1 \times T_{in}, \quad \lambda_2 = 2, \quad \lambda_3 = \frac{E_S \times E_\eta}{\sqrt{2}}$$

Definition 7.25 An algorithm is a optimum algorithm Γ if and only if it meets optimal index ζ and makes λ_3 minimum.

Definition 7.26 *The background handling report REP is a text file ErrRep.txt. when BSDT cannot find optimum algorithm Γ in appointed path, it will record error information, and inform manager to handle it.*

Definition 7.27 *In BSDT algorithm the register procedure should do following tasks:*

(1) Store name of an algorithm N^a into algorithm index table AI, and store algorithm itself in directory appointed by BSDT.
(2) Store name of an example set N^{es} into example index table EI, and store classical case table TET in classical case base.

7.8.5 Bias shift based decision tree learning algorithm BSDT

BSDT algorithm firstly call seek optimum algorithm SM to get optimum algorithm Γ. Then seek the algorithm in system directory and current working directory. If no algorithm is found, it should be eliminated from case base and algorithm index table, in case fail to find next time.

In fact, seek optimum algorithm SM is a procedure using case-based reasoning. As for a given primitive training set, we firstly extract its retrieval information tuple θ, then search optimum algorithm meet optimal index ζ in case base. When case base is empty or SM algorithm fails, take GSD as default selection of optimum algorithm.

Since inference in algorithm running should be decreased, BSDT journal can be taken as a means for manager to intervene system.

Algorithm 7.8 Bias Shift Based Decision Tree Learning Algorithm BSDT。

Input: primitive training example set;
Output: target knowledge base;

1. Call preprocessing algorithm PPD;
2. Call seek optimum algorithm SM to get optimum algorithm Γ ;
3. Search algorithm Γ in appointed path;
4. If algorithm exists,
5.   then Call Γ ;
6. Generate decision tree and/or production rule set;
7. Store learning result into target knowledge base;
8. If algorithm does not exist,
9.   then let $\rho =3$, call case base maintain algorithm CBM to delete Γ from case base and corresponding data structure;
10.   go to step 2;
11. Fill out the journal for BSDT.

7.8.6 Typical case base maintain algorithm TCBM

Algorithm TCBM realizes various operation to typical case base, such as adding new example set, example set version updating, deleting example set, deleting example set and adding or deleting examples of example base, etc. Only when add or delete new example or modify existing example subset, the algorithm can be activated. Because of employing hierarchical activating mode, after TCBM algorithm modify classical case base, it would automatically call each algorithm in algorithm index table to execute again to construct case base in accordance with the content of classical case base. Case base and modification of related data structure are selected to influence optimum algorithm directly.

Algorithm 7.9 Typical case base maintain algorithm TCBM
Input: Primitive case base, case index table, case set S_0, domain name π , maintain operator ρ
Output: Modified case base, case index table

1. IF $\rho <1$ and $\rho >5$ THEN return;
2. IF $\rho =1$, THEN   /* adding new case set */
Call ANE algorithm to add new case;
3. IF $\rho =2$, THEN   /* typical case base version updating */
4. examine whether example index table and domain name π exists;
5. IF exists
6. delete corresponding table from case base;
7. delete related items in case index table;
8. call algorithm ANE to introduce new case set;
9. IF $\rho =3$, THEN   /* deleting case set */

10. Examine whether example index table and domain name π exists, if not, return;
11. Delete corresponding table from base;
12. Delete domain name π from example index table;
13. IF $\rho = 4$, THEN   /* adding examples to example base */
14. IF domain name π is not in the index table
    call algorithm ANE to add new domain;
15. Check the appropriateness of record value and discard inappropriate record value; store training set S0 into corresponding table in order;
16. IF $\rho = 5$, THEN   /* deleting examples of example base */
17. IF domain name π is not in index table, then return;
18. Delete cases in table;
19. Extract(S_0, π);   /* generating case for typical case base */
20. Store cases;

7.8.7 Bias feature extracting algorithm

Features of candidate algorithms can help us to select optimum bias automatically using optimal algorithm. These features are organized according to the form of definition 7.19. The procedure will be activated when typical case base or algorithm index table varies,.

Algorithm 7.10 Bias feature extracting algorithm
Input: classical example base CEB, register algorithm RA, example set ES, example index table EI, algorithm index table AI, case base CB, operator OP
Output: modified CB

1. If op=1   // CB is empty
2.   then { If EI = NULL || AI = NULL }   return
3.   For i=1 to maxRA
4.   For j=1 to maxEI
5.   For k=1 to Interval do
6.   {using algorithm AI(i) to generate a classifier in example set EI(j)
7.   and generate a data iterm according to definition 7.19
8.   store data item into CB; }
9. Else if op=2   // adding a new algorithm
10.   then { For i=1 to maxEI
11.   For j=1 to Interval do
12.   {using algorithm RA to generate a classifier in example set EI(j)
13.   and generate a data term according to definition 7.19
14.   store data into CB; }
15. Else if op=3   // adding a new example set
16.   then{ For i=1 to maxRA

17.   For j=1 to Interval do
18.   {using algorithm AI(i) to generate a classifier in example set EI(j)
19.   and generate a data term according to definition 7.19
20.   store data into CB; }
21. Else if op=4   // deleting an old register algorithm
22   . thenDelete related item of RA from CB
23. Else if op=5   // deleting an old register example set
24.   then   Delete related item of ES from CB;
25. Else return failed;
26. Modify Interval according to the size of CEB

7.8.8 Improved decision tree generating algorithm GSD

We use cost coefficient C^c and bias coefficient C^b for constructing attribute selecting function ASF, and set their default value. Following gives constructing method of attribute selecting function ASF.

Definition 7.28 $E^0=\{e_1^0,...,e_v^0\}$ is a set of primitive training examples, $A^0=\{A_1^0,..., A_v^0\}$ is attribute set of E^0, where v is maximum number of primitive training examples, ϖ is maximum number of attribute of E^0; $A_i=\{V_1,..., V_v\}$ represents v different values of attribute i.

Definition 7.29 $E = \{e_1,..., e_n\}$, $A^T= A \cup A^X = \{A_1,..., A_m\} \cup A^X= \{A_1,..., A_m, A_{m+1}\}$, which are training example set and attribute set through preprocessing under introducing background knowledge and algorithm CGAOI, where $1 \leqslant n \leqslant v, 2 \leqslant m \leqslant \varpi$.

Definition 7.30 $A^X = C^T = [C_1^T,..., C_n^T]$ T is propagate frequency getting from algorithm CGAOI.

Definition 7.31 $C=\{C_1,...,C_k\}$ are k possible classes in primitive training example set E. Pi represents the probability of class C_i in E.

Definition 7.32 In procedure of generating decision tree, each attribute oriented test must make the value of attribute selecting function ASF maximum.

Definition 7.33 ASF function is defined as follow:
$$\text{ASF}(A_i) = \frac{f(A_i) \bullet g(A_i)}{h(A_i)}$$

where $f(A_i)$ indicates benefit of attribute i; $g(A_i)$ indicates bias of attribute i; $h(A_i)$ indicates cost of attribute I, $1 \leqslant i \leqslant k$.

(1) Following formula gives definition of $f(A_i)$, where U^I represents useful information; N^I represents useless information; T^I represents total information = $U^I + N^I$.

$$f(A_i) = \frac{U^I}{T^I} = 1 - \frac{N^I}{T^I}$$

Let:

$$\Delta I = H(T^I) - H(N^I)$$

$$-\Delta I = H(N^I) - H(T^I) = \log_2(N^I) - \log_2(T^I) = \log_2 \left[\frac{N^I}{T^I} \right]$$

$$2^{-\Delta I} = \left[\frac{N^I}{T^I} \right] = 1 - \left[\frac{U^I}{T^I} \right] = 1 - f()$$

$$f(A_i) = 1 - 2^{-\Delta I}$$

$$\Delta I = Gain(A_l, E) = I(E) - Ent(A_l, E)$$

$$I(E) = -\sum_{j=1}^{k} P_j \log_2 P_j, P_j = \frac{|E \cap C_j|}{|E|} \bullet CT_j$$

$$Ent(A_l, E) = \sum_{i=1}^{v} \frac{|E_i|}{|E|} I(E_i)$$

$$f(A_i) = 1 - 2^{-Gain()}$$

(2) $g(A_i)$ is defined as:

$$g(A_i) = C^b{}_i$$

(3) $h(A_i)$ is defined as:

$$h(A_i) = C^c{}_i + 1$$

From which we can get expression:

$$\text{ASF}(A_i) = \frac{(1 - 2^{-Gain()}) \bullet C^b}{C^c + 1}$$

Our decision tree generating algorithm GSD is a modified version of Quinlan's C4.5 algorithm. The modification is embodied in two aspects: input and attribute selecting. Input of GSD employs preprocess algorithm PPD to output appointed concept level training example subset. Furthermore, it uses attribute selecting function ASF to replace attribute selecting standard of C4.5.

Algorithm 7.11 Decision tree generating algorithm GSD
Input: Training set
Output: Decision tree, rule set

1. Select standard CR from Gain, Gain Ratio and ASF;
2. If all data items belong to one class, then decision tree is a leaf labeled with the class sign;
3. Else, use optimum test attribute to divide data items into subset;
4. Recursively call step 2、3 to generate a decision tree for each subset;
5. Generate decision tree and transform to rule set.

7.8.9 Experiment results

BSDT algorithm uses following dataset (Table 7.3).

Table 7.3 Experiment dataset

Dataset	#training example number	#attribute number	#class number	#example number of test set
anneal	898	38	5	-
breast-cancer	699	10	2	-
credit	490	15	2	200
genetics	3,190	60	3	-
glass	214	9	6	-
heart	1,395	16	2	-
hypo	2,514	29	5	1,258
letter	15,000	16	26	5,000
sonar	208	60	2	-
soybean	683	35	19	-
voting	300	16	2	135
diabetes	768	8	2	-

Parts of the dataset come from UCI test database (ftp://ics.uci.edu/pub/machine-learning-database). Following measure is used to test dataset.
Using random selecting approach to divide dataset DS without given dataset (such as: anneal, breast-cancer, etc) into test set TS and learning set LS, and let TS = DS×10%;

(1) Classifier C_0 is generated by using C4.5 algorithm and testifying 10 times in learning set LS, which has the predict accuracy P_0 after tested in TS;

Table 7.4 Predict accuracy comparison

Dataset	P0	P1	P2
Anneal	96.9±10.4	97.1±9.7	97.8±10.8
breast-cancer	95.7±2.1	96.2±1.7	97.2±2.5
credit	84.8±2.5	87.4±1.8	89.5±2.1
genetics	98.7±4.4	98.7±4.4	98.7±4.4
glass	68.9±9.2	75.2±6.5	75.2±6.5
heart	77.8±4.3	79.6±3.9	79.8±3.7
hypo	93.2±4.2	92.7±3.9	92.7±3.9
letter	88.4±9.8	93.7±8.7	93.7±8.7
sonar	65.4±7.1	74.7±12.1	74.7±12.1
soybean	78.9±5.9	84.8±6.5	84.8±6.5
voting	95.8±1.3	95.9±1.6	95.9±1.6
diabetes	74.3±3.0	76.1±3.1	77.2±2.3

(2) Classifier C_1 is generated by using algorithm BSDT and testifying 10 times in learning set LS, which has the predict accuracy P_1 after tested in TS;

(3) Classifier C_2 is generated by using algorithm BSDT with attribute selecting function ASF and testifying 10 times in learning set LS, which has the predict accuracy P_2 after tested in TS;

(4) For each algorithm we compute average value of 15 experiments, so that getting stable predict model;

(5) Compare results of P_0, P_1 and P_2 and predict accuracy are listed in Table 7.4.

It can be seen from Table 7.4 that after classified by decision tree classification predict model generated by algorithm BSDT, precisions of all dataset are improved. Predict precision of ASF function defined by cost coefficient and bias coefficient is obviously improved. Experiment results show that, ASF function and algorithm BSDT is effective.

We implement a method integrated various decision tree learning algorithms in algorithm BSDT. It is an effective approach to integrate various machine learning algorithms, and it assures optimum selection of representation bias and procedure bias, so it supports multiple strategy learning algorithm.

7.9 Computational Theories of Inductive Learning

Computational theories of learning mainly study sample and computation complexity of learning algorithm. This section focuses on Gold learning theory and Valiant learning theory.

Computational learning theory is very important for building a science of machine learning, otherwise, it is difficult to recognize the scope of applicability of a learning algorithm or analyze the learnability in different approaches. Convergence, feasibility, and approximation are essential issues which require computational learning theory to give a satisfying learning framework containing reasonable restrictions. In computational learning theory early efforts along these aspects are based primarily on Gold's framework (Gold, 1967). In context of formulization linguistic learning, Gold introduces concept of convergence, which handles the problem of learning from examples. Learning algorithm allows to propose many assumptions without knowing when they are correct, only determining the point where their computations are correct assumption. Because of high complexity of Gold algorithm, this style is not applied in practical learning.

Based on Gold's learning framework, Shapiro proposed model reasoning algorithm to study the relation between formal language and its explanation, that is, relation between grammar and semantics of formal language. Model theory takes formula, sentence theory and their explanation – model as mathematic object to study. Shapiro model reasoning algorithm can get a theory output only need to input definite fact (Shapiro, 1981).

In 1984, Valiant proposed a new learning framework (Valiant, 1984), which require high approximation with objective concept, and do not require accurate identification of object concept. Kearns, Li, Pitt and Valiant gave some new results to concept which can be represented as Boolean formula. Haussler applied Valiant framework to analyze problems of version space and inductive bias, and gave computing formula of computational complexity.

7.9.1 *Gold's learning theory*

The research of Gold's linguistic learning theory introduces two basic concepts, i.e., limit identification and enumeration identification, which plays an important role in early theory research of inductive reasoning (Gold, 1967).

Limit identification takes inductive reasoning as an infinitive procedure. Ultimate or limit act can be seen as its successful standard. Assume M is an inductive reasoning approach, which attempts to describe unknown rule R correctly. Assuming M runs repeatedly, example set of R becomes more and more large, forming an infinite sequence g_1, g_2, $\cdots$ speculated by M. If there exists a number m, they would make gm be the correct description of R,

$$g_m = g_{m+1} = g_{m+2} = \cdots,$$

Then the limit of the example sequence M can identify R correctly. As unknown rules are learned more and more, M can successfully modify the speculation about R. If M stops modifying its speculation after definite times, and the final speculation is the correct description of R, then M correctly identifies R at the limit of the example sequence. Notice, M cannot confirm whether it can converge into a correct assumption, because whether there exists a contradiction between new data and current speculation is unknown.

Enumeration identification is the first approach to speculate the abstraction of multinomial sequence, that is, it systematically searches possible rule space, until finds speculation in accordance with all data so far. Suppose that concrete domain of rule is prescribed, there is a enumeration, i.e. $d_1, d_2, d_3, \cdots$, so that each rule in enumeration has one or multiple description. Given an example set of a rule, through the table, enumeration identification will find the first description d_1, that is, if it is compatible with given example, then speculation is d_1. This approach cannot confirm whether it can achieve correct limit identification. If example representation and compatible relation meet following two conditions, enumeration approach assures limit identifying all rules of that domain:

(1) A correct assumption is always compatible with given examples.
(2) Any wrong assumption is not compatible with sets with examples large enough or all sets.

In order to compute enumeration approach, enumeration $d_1, d_2, d_3, \cdots$ must be computable, it must compute that given description is compatible with given example set.

Algorithm 7.12 Enumeration identification algorithm

Input:
• The set of a group of expressions $E = e_1, e_2, \cdots$
• Oracle TE to provide enough objective example set.
• Oracle LE of ordering information.
Output:
A series of hypotheses H_1, H_2, …, each hypothesis H_i is in E, and is consistent with the ith example.
Procedure:
1. Initialize: $i \leftarrow 1$;
2. examples $\leftarrow$ emptyset;
3. Loop:
4.   call TE(), add example to set examples;

5.   While   LE(e_i,+x) = no, for positive example set +x,or
6.   LE(e_i,-x) = yes, for negative example set -x,
7. $i \leftarrow i + 1$;
8. Output e_i.

7.9.2 Model inference

A model inference problem is an abstraction from scientific problems. In this abstraction we try to find some unknown model M which can explain some results. Shapiro gave the following definition of the model inference problem. Suppose that a first order language L and two subsets of it, an observational language Lo, a hypothesis language L_h, are given. In addition, an oracle for some unknown model M of L is given. The model inference problem is to find a finite Lo-complete axiomatization of M. In order to solve the model inference problem, Shapiro has developed a model inference algorithm in terms of Gold's theory (Shapiro, 1981).

L sentence is divided into two subsets: observable language Lo and hypothesis language L_h. Assuming that

$$\square \in L_o \subset L_h \subset L'$$

Where $\square$ is empty sentence. Then model inference problem can be defined as follows: given one-order language L and two subsets: observable language L_o and hypothesis language L_h. Further, given a handle mechanism oracle to unknown model M of L, model inference problem is to find a definite L_o of $M -$ completed axiomatization.

Algorithm to solve model inference problem is referred to as model inference algorithm. Enumeration of model M is an infinite sequence F_1, F_2, F_3, $\cdots$, where F_i is the fact about M, each sentence α of L_o is taken place at fact F_i = <α,V>,i > 0. Model reasoning algorithm reads a enumeration of observable language L_o once. A fact which generates definite set of sentences of hypothesis language L_h is referred to as speculation of algorithm. A kind of model inference algorithm is as follows:

Algorithm 7.13 An enumeration model inference algorithm (Shapiro, 1981).

1. Let h be a total recursive function
2. Set S_{false} to {$\square$}, S_{true} to {}, k to 0
3. Repeat
4.   read the next fact F_n =<α,V>
5.   add α to S_v

6.   while there is an $\alpha \in S_{\text{false}}$ such that $T_k \vdash_n \alpha$

7.   or there is an $\alpha_i \in S_{\text{true}}$ such that $T_k \neg \vdash_{n(i)} \alpha_i$ do

8. $k = k+1$

9.   output T_k

10. Forever

Where, α_1, α_2, α_3, $\cdots$ are a fixed effective enumeration of all sentences of L_o, T_1, T_2, T_3, $\cdots$ are a fixed effective enumeration of all finite sets of sentences of L_h, and M is a model for L. Symbol $T \vdash_n \alpha$ denotes that can derive α in n derivation steps or less, $T \neg \vdash_{n(i)} \alpha$ denotes that T can not derive α in n steps or less.

Algorithm 7.13 is not feasible because of its global nature. Whenever it finds that a set of sentences is not an axiomatization of the model it simply discards it and searches through all finite sets of sentences until it finds the next plausible conjecture. In order to overcome this problem, Shapiro developed an incremental inference algorithm which is called the contradiction backtracing algorithm, since it can trace a contradiction between a conjecture and the facts back to its source, which is a false hypothesis (Shapiro, 1981).

7.9.3 Valiant's learning theory

Valiant claims that a learning machine must have following properties (Valiant, 1984):

(1) Machine can learning concept of all classes. Furthermore, these classes can be characterized.
(2) Concept class is proper and uncommon for general knowledge.
(3) Computational procedure that Machine deducts expected program required in feasible steps.

Learning machine is composed of learning protocols and deduction procedure. Learning protocols prescribe the approach to get information from outer. Deduction procedure is a mechanism, and correct recognition algorithm of learning concept is deductive. From a general point of view, approach to study learning is to prescribe a possible learning protocol. Using this learning protocol to study concept class, recognition program can be deducted in multinomial time. Concrete protocol permits to provide two kind of information. The first is access to typical data, which are positive examples of concepts. To be precise, assume that these positive examples essentially have an arbitrary probability distribution, it calls subprogram EXAMPLES to generate positive examples whose relative probability distribution is definite. The second available information source is ORACLE. In basic version, when submitting data, it will tell whether learning the data is positive example of concept.

Assuming that X is an example space, a concept is a subset of X. If an example is in concept, it is a positive example; else it is a negative example. Concept representation is a concept description; concept class is a group of concept representation. Learning model has effective learnability of concept class. Valiant learning theory only requires that good approximation to objective concept has high probability. It permits concept description generated by learner and objective concept has a small bias, which is an argument of learning algorithm. In addition, probability permit learner fail is δ, which is also an input argument. Differences between two concepts employ probability distribution D in example space X to evaluate:

$$\text{diff}_D(c_1, c_2) = \sum_{x \in X, c_1(x) \neq c_2(x)} D(x) \tag{7.37}$$

According to protocol, a concept class C is learnable if and only if there exists an algorithm which use protocol to represent all objective concepts $c^* \in C$ and all distribution D:

(1) Executive time is multinomial related to $\dfrac{1}{\varepsilon}$, $\dfrac{1}{\delta}$, number of c^* and other arguments.

(2) Concept c in output C has probability 1-δ

$$\text{diff}_D(c, c^*) < \varepsilon$$

In Valiant's learning theory, there are two complexity measures. One is sample complexity, which is the number of random example, used to generate high probability and low error. Another computational complexity is performance complexity, which is defined as computing time needed to generate assumption with given numbers of samples in the worst case.

Assuming that L is learning algorithm, C is a kind of object concept in example space X. For any $0 < \varepsilon$, $\delta < 1$, $S_\varepsilon^L(\varepsilon, \delta)$ represents minimum number of sample m so that in any objective concept $c \in C$, any distribution in X, given m samples of c, L generates an assumption, whose probability is at least 1-δ, error is at most ε. $S_\varepsilon^L(\varepsilon, \delta)$ is referred to as L sample complexity of target class c.

Following we discuss sample complexity of two learning algorithms.

a) Classification algorithm of learning conjunction concept

The content of the algorithm is as follows:

(1) For given sample, find the minimum main atom of each attribute. These

atoms do conjunction to form assumption h.

(2) If h does not include negative examples, then returns h, else gets the result, and holds that sample is not in accordance with any pure conjunction concept.

Haussler analyzed this algorithm, and concluded that its sample complexity $S_c^L(\varepsilon,\delta)$ is(Haussler, 1988)

$$C_0(\log(\frac{1}{\delta})+n)/\varepsilon \leq S_c^L(\varepsilon,\delta) \leq C_1(\log(\frac{1}{\delta})+n\log(\frac{1}{\varepsilon}))/\varepsilon \quad (7.38)$$

where C_0, C_1 is positive constant.

b) Greedy algorithm of learning pure conjunction concept.

Algorithm 7.14 Greedy Algorithm of Learning Pure Conjunction Concept

1. As for given samples, finds the minimum main atom of each attribute.
2. At beginning, pure conjunction assumption h is empty, when there is negative examples in samples, do
3. In all attributes, find the minimum main atom, which delete most negative examples and add them to h. If no minimum main atom, then any negative example can be deleted. The loop ends.
4. Eliminate deleted negative examples from samples.
5. If there is no negative examples, then return h, else report samples are inconsistent with any pure conjunction concept.

Haussler discussed the problem of sample complexity of the algorithm in paper（Haussler, 1988）, and gave the following result:

$$C_0(\log(\frac{1}{\delta})+s\log(\frac{n}{s}))/\varepsilon \leq S_c^L(\varepsilon,\delta) \leq C_1(\log(\frac{1}{\delta})+s(\log(\frac{sn1}{\varepsilon}))^2)/\varepsilon \quad (7.39)$$

where C_0,C_1 are positive constants, s is the maximum number of atoms in pure conjunction concept.

We can see from above mentioned, Valiant's learning theory only requires assumption generated by learning algorithm can approach objective concept well with high probability, and do not require to identify target concept precisely. This kind of learning theory is "approximately correct" identification, sometimes simply called PAC(Probably Approximately Correct) Theory. Valiant's learning theory has more practical significance than Gold's learning theory.

Exercises

1. What is inductive learning? What are its main characteristics?
2. Through examples, explain the application of selective and constructive

generation rules.

3. What is the bias problem in decision tree learning? Simply describe several bias learning algorithms.

4. What is hypothesis space? Describe the relation among hypotheses in hypothesis space.

5. How are the inductive reasoning patterns which AQ learning approach comply with? Why we say procedure of AQ learning is procedure of searching hypothesis space?

6. Combining with figure of rule space ordering, describe the basic idea of version space.

7. Give the procedure that candidate deleting algorithm is used in following dataset:

    Positive example: a) object(red, round, apple)
                             b) object(green, round, mango)
    Negative example: a) object(red, large, banana)
                             b) object(green, round, guava)

8. Narrate decision tree learning approach and its applicable situation.

9. In procedure of constructing decision tree, what principle that selection of test attribute should be employed? How to realize it?

10. Narrate the basic idea and building steps of ID3 algorithm.

11. Given following data, answer the questions.

StudiedHard	HoursSelptBefore	Breakfast	GotA
No	5	Eggs	No
No	9	Eggs	No
Yes	6	Eggs	No
No	6	Bagel	No
Yes	9	Bagel	Yes
Yes	8	Eggs	Yes
Yes	8	Cereal	Yes
Yes	6	Cereal	Yes

(1) How much is the initial entropy of GotA?
(2) Which attribute that decision tree (ID3) will select as root node?
(3) Construct the decision tree.

12. In what aspects that C4.5 learning algorithm improved ID3 learning algorithm?

13. What is the sample complexity and computational complexity of learning algorithm?

14. Why Valiant's learning theory has more practical significance than Gold's learning theory?

Chapter 8

Support Vector Machine

Vapnik and his research group have studied machine learning based on finite samples since 1960s. A complete theory, Statistical Learning Theory, has been established until 1990s (Vapnik, 1995). Moreover a new universal learning algorithm Support Vector Machine(SVM) has been proposed. SVM minimizes the probability of classification error based on the structural risk minimization inductive principle. The main idea of SVM is mapping the nonlinear data to a higher-dimensional linear space where the data can be linearly classified by hyperplane (Vapnik et al., 1997). One advantage of SVM is the capacity of disposing linearity non-separable cases.

8.1 Statistical Learning Problem

8.1.1 *Empirical risk*

We consider the learning problem as a problem of finding a desired dependence between input and output (or supervisor's response) using a limited number of observations. Learning problems could generally be represented as to find uncertain dependency relationship between variables y and x where the joint probability distribution function $F(x, y)$ is unknown. The selection of the desired function is based on a training set of n independent and identically distributed observations:

$$(x_1, y_1), (x_2, y_2), \ldots, (x_n, y_n). \tag{8.1}$$

Given a set of functions $\{f(x, w)\}$, it aims at choosing a best function to approximate the supervisor's response $f(x, w_0)$, which makes the risk function

$$R(w) = \int L(y, f(x, w)) d\ F(x, y) \tag{8.2}$$

309

be minimal. Where $\{f(x,w)\}$ is the set of expected functions, w is functional general parameters. $L(y,f(x,w))$ measures the loss, or discrepancy between the response y of the supervisor to a given input x and the response $f(x, w)$ provided by the learning machine. Different type of learning problems have diverse formal loss function.

Empirical risk minimization inductive principle is used in the classical methods of learning problem. Empirical risk defined on the basis of the training set.

$$R_{emp}(w) = \frac{1}{l}\sum_{i=1}^{l} L(y_i, f(x_i, w)) \tag{8.3}$$

Machine learning designs learning algorithm for minimizing $R_{emp}(w)$.

8.1.2 VC Dimension

Statistical learning theory is inductive learning's theory on the basis of small sample size. One significant concept is VC Dimension (Vapnik-Chervonenkis Dimension) in pattern recognition. The VC dimension of a set of indicator functions $f(x,w)$ is equal to the largest number h of vectors that can be separated into different classes in all the 2^h possible ways using this set of functions (i.e., the VC dimension is the maximum number of vectors that can be shattered by the set of functions). The VC dimension is equal to infinity if there exists a set of vectors that any number of samples can be shattered by the functions $f(x,w)$. The VC dimensions of a set of bounded real functions is defined by transformed indicated functions with threshould.

The VC dimension of the set of functions (rather than the number of parameters) is responsible for the generalization ability of learning machine. Intuitively, learning machines with high VC dimensions are more complexity and power. At the moment there is no universal theory to calculate VC dimension of an arbitrary function set. In n dimensions real space Rn the VC dimension of linear classification and linear real function is $n+1$. However, The VC dimension of $f(x, \alpha)=\sin(\alpha x)$ are infinite. In statistical learning theory, it is still a problem that how to calculate VC dimension using theory and experimental method.

8.2 Consistency of Learning Processes

8.2.1 Classical definition of learning consistency

In order to construct algorithms for learning from a limited number of observations, we need an asymptotic theory (consistency is an asymptotic concept). We describe the conceptual model for learning processes that are based on the empirical risk minimization inductive principle. The goal of this part is to describe necessary and sufficient conditions for the consistency of learning processes that minimize the empirical risk.

Definition 8.1 The Empirical Risk Minimization Inductive Principle (Vapnik ,1995).

We say that the principle (method) of ERM is consistent for the set of functions $L(y,w)$ and for the probability distribution function $F(y)$ if the following two sequences converge in probability to the same limit (see the schematic Figure 8.1):

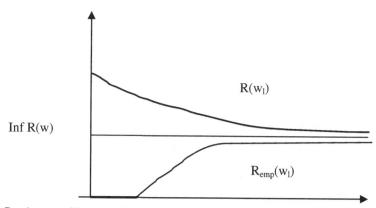

Figure 8.1 Consistency of Learning Process

$$R(w_l) \xrightarrow[l \to \infty]{P} \inf_{w \in \Lambda} R(w) \qquad (8.4)$$

$$R_{emp}(w_l) \xrightarrow[l \to \infty]{P} \inf_{w \in \Lambda} R(w) \qquad (8.5)$$

In other words, the ERM method is consistent if it provides a sequence of functions $L(y,w_l)$, $l = 1,2, \dots$, for which both expected risk and empirical risk converge to the minimal possible value of risk. Equation (8.4) asserts that the values of achieved risks converge to the best possibility, while Equation (8.5) asserts that one can estimate on the basis of the values of empirical risk the minimal possible value of the risk.

8.2.2 Key theorem of learning theory

In 1989 Vapnik and Chefvonenkis proposed the key theorem of learning theory as follows (Vapnik and Chefvonenkis, 1991).

Theorem 8.1 Let $L(y,w), w \in \Lambda$ be a set of functions that satisfy the condition

$$A \le \int L(y,w)dF(y) \le B \qquad (A \le R(w) \le B). \qquad (8.6)$$

Then for the ERM principle to be consistent in the following sense:

$$\lim_{l \to \infty} P\{\sup_{w \in \Lambda} R(w) - R_{emp}(w)) > \varepsilon\} = 0, \qquad \forall \varepsilon > 0. \qquad (8.7)$$

It is necessary and sufficient that the empirical risk $R_{emp}(w)$ converge uniformly to the actual risk $R(w)$ over the set $L(y,w), w \in \Lambda$. We call this type of uniform convergence uniform one-sided convergence.

8.2.3 VC entropy

Definition 8.2 Let $A \le L(y,w) \le B, \omega \in \Lambda$, be a set of bounded loss functions. Using this set of functions and the training set $z_1, \ldots z_l$, one can construct the following set of l-dimensional vectors:

$$q(w) = (L(z_1,w), \cdots, L(z_l,w)), \qquad w \in \Lambda. \qquad (8.8)$$

This set of vectors belong to the l-dimensional cube and has a finite minimal ε-net in the metric C (or in the metric L_p).

Let $N = N^{\wedge}(\varepsilon; z_1, \cdots, z_l)$ be the number of elements of the minimal ε-net of this set of vectors $q(w)$, $w \in \Lambda$. Note that $N^{\wedge}(\varepsilon; z_1, \cdots, z_l)$ is a random variable, since it is constructed using random Vectors $z_1,...,z_l$.The logarithm of the random value $N^{\wedge}(\varepsilon; z_1, \cdots, z_l)$, $H^{\wedge}(\varepsilon; z_1, \cdots, z_l) = \ln N^{\wedge}(\varepsilon; z_1, \cdots, z_l)$ is called the random VC entropy of the set offunctions $A \le L(y,w) \le B, w \in \Lambda$ on the sample $z_1,...,z_l$. The expectation of the random VC entropy

$$H^{\wedge}(\varepsilon; l) = EH^{\wedge}(\varepsilon; z_1, \cdots, z_l)$$

is called the VC entropy of the set of functions $A \le L(y, w) \le B, w \in \Lambda$ on samples of size 1. Here the expectation is taken with respect to the product measure $F(z_1, \cdots, z_l)$.

Theorem 8.2 For uniform two-sided convergence it is necessary and sufficient that the equality

$$\lim_{l \to \infty} \frac{H^\Lambda(\varepsilon, l)}{l} = 0, \quad \forall \varepsilon > 0 \tag{8.9}$$

be valid. In other words, the ratio of the VC entropy to the number of observations should decrease to zero with increasing numbers of observations.

Corollary 8.1 Under some conditions of measurability on the set of indicator functions $L(y, w), w \in \Lambda$, necessary and sufficient condition for uniform two-sided convergence is $\lim_{l \to \infty} \dfrac{H^\Lambda(l)}{l} = 0$, which is a particular case of equality (8.9).

Theorem 8.3 In order for uniform one-sided convergence of empirical means to their expectations to hold for the set of totally bounded functions $L(y, w), w \in \Lambda$, it is necessary and sufficient that for any positive δ, η and ε, there exist a set of functions $L^*(y, w^*), w^* \in \Lambda^*$ satisfying following

$$L(y, w) - L^*(y, w^*) \ge 0, \forall y,$$
$$\int (L(y, w) - L^*(y, w^*)) dF(y) \le \delta. \tag{8.10}$$

such that the following holds for the ε-entropy of the set $L^*(y, w^*), w^* \in \Lambda^*$, on samples of size l.

$$\lim_{l \to \infty} \frac{H^{\Lambda^*}(\varepsilon, l)}{l} < \eta.$$

According to these key theorems, we study learning theory. Moreover, we describe a sufficient condition for consistency of the ERM principle by using different methods and functions. On the basis of these functions three milestones of learning theory are constructed:

(1) We use VC entropy to define the following equation describing a sufficient condition for consistency of the ERM principle.

$$\lim_{l \to \infty} \frac{H^\Lambda(l)}{l} = 0 \tag{8.11}$$

(2) We use the annealed VC entropy to define the following equation describing a sufficient condition for consistency of the ERM principle.

$$\lim_{l \to \infty} \frac{H^\Lambda_{ann}(l)}{l} = 0 \tag{8.12}$$

where the annealed VC entropy
$H^\Lambda_{ann}(l) = \ln EN^\Lambda(z, \cdots, z_l)$.

(3) We use the growth function to define the following equation describing a sufficient condition for consistency of the ERM principle.

$$\lim_{l \to \infty} \frac{G^\Lambda(l)}{l} = 0 \tag{8.13}$$

where the growth function
$G^\Lambda(l) = \ln \sup_{z, \cdots, z_{l1}} N^\Lambda(z, \cdots, z_l)$.

8.3 Structural Risk Minimization Inductive Principle

Statistical learning theory systematically analyze relationship of inhomogeneous function set, empirical risk and actual risk, the bounds on the generalization ability of learning machines (Vapnik, 1995). Here we will only consider functions that correspond to the two-class pattern recognition case: For the set of indicator functions (including the function minimizing empirical risk.)，Now choose some η such that $0 \leqslant \eta \leqslant 1$. Then for losses taking empirical risk $R_{emp}(w)$ and actual risk $R(w)$ with probability 1-η, the following bound holds (Burges, 1998):

$$R(w) \leq R_{emp}(w) + \sqrt{\frac{h(\ln(2l/h)+1) - \ln(\eta/4)}{l}}$$

where h is a non-negative integer called the Vapnik Chervonenkis (VC) dimension. And l is the total of samples.

It follows that statistical learning's actual risk $R(w)$ have two parts: one is empirical risk $R_{emp}(w)$ defined to be just the measured mean error rate on the training set (for a fixed, finite number of observations); another is VC confidence. The confidence interval reflects the maximal difference of between actual risk and empirical risk. Meanwhile, it reflects risk bring structure complexity. There are some relations between the confidence interval, VC dimension h and sample number l. The inequality (8.14) could simply be expressed as:

$$R(w) \le R_{emp}(w) + \Phi(h/l) \tag{8.14}$$

According to the second term on the right-hand side of the inequality (8.14), $\Phi(h/l)$ increases while the VC dimension, h increases. Therefore, the confidence interval increases while learning machine's complexity and the VC dimension increase. Moreover, the difference between actual risk and empirical risk increase when learning machines use a small sample of training instances.

Note that the bound for the generalization ability of learning machines is a conclusion in the worst case. Furthermore, the bound is not tight in many cases, especially when VC dimension is higher. When $h/l > 0.37$, the bound is guaranteed not tight (Burges, 1998). When VC dimension is infinite, the bound does not exist.

To construct small sample size methods we use both the bounds for the generalization ability of learning machines with sets of totally bounded nonnegative functions, $0 \le L(z,w) \le B$, $w \in \Lambda$ (Λ is abstract parameters set), Each bound is valid with probability at least $1 - \eta$.

$$R(w_l) \le R_{emp}(w) + \frac{B\varepsilon}{2}(1 + \sqrt{1 + \frac{4R_{emp}(w_l)}{B\varepsilon}}), \tag{8.15}$$

and the bound for the generalization ability of learning machines with sets of unbounded functions,

$$R(w_l) \le \frac{R_{emp}(w_l)}{(1 - a(p)\tau\sqrt{\varepsilon})_+} \tag{8.16}$$

$$a(p) = \sqrt[p]{\frac{1}{2}(\frac{p-1}{p-2})^{p-1}}$$

where

$$\varepsilon = 2\frac{\ln N - \ln \eta}{l}$$

There are two methods to minimize the actual risk. One is to minimize the empirical risk. According to upper formula, the upper bound of actual risk decreases while the empirical risk decreases. The other is to minimize the second term on the right-hand side of the inequality (8.15). We have to make the VC dimension a controlling variable. Latter method conformances small sample size.

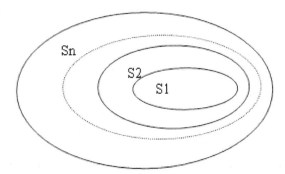

Figure 8.2. A structure on the set of functions is determined by the nested subsets of functions. (Picture from Vapnik , 1995).

Let the set S of functions L(z,w) be provided with a structure consisting of nested subsets of functions $S_k = \{L(z,w), w \in \Lambda_k\}$, such that (See Figure 8.2)

$$S_1 \subset S_2 \subset \cdots \subset S_n \qquad (8.17)$$

where the elements of the structure satisfy the following two properties:

(1) The VC dimension hk of each set S_k of functions is finite. Therefore,
$h_1 \leqslant h_2 \leqslant ,..., \leqslant h_n, \ldots$.
(2) Any element S_k of the structure contains either a set of totally bounded functions,$0 \leqslant L(z,w) \leqslant B_k$; $\alpha \in \Lambda_k$ or a set of functions satisfy the following inequality for some pair (p, τ_k).

$$\sup_{w \in \Lambda_k} \frac{(\int L^p(z,w)dF(z))^{\frac{1}{p}}}{\int L(z,w)dF(z)} \leq \tau_k \qquad p>2 \qquad (8.18)$$

We call this structure an admissible structure.

For a given set of observations $z_1,...,z_l$ the SRM principle chooses the function $L(z,w_{kl})$ minimizing the empirical risk in the subset S_k for which the guaranteed risk (determined by the right-hand side of inequality (8.15) or by the right-hand side of inequality (8.16) depending on the circumstances) is minimal.

The SRM principle defines a trade-off between the quality of the approximation of the given data and the complexity of the approximating function. As the subset index n increases, the minima of the empirical risks decrease. However, the term responsible for the confidence interval increases.

The SRM principle takes both factors into account by choosing the subset Sn for which minimizing the empirical risk yields the best bound on the actual risk.

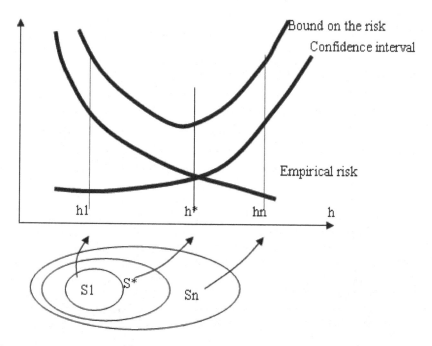

Figure 8.3. The bound on the structural risk is the sum of the empirical risk and the confidence interval. (Picture from Vapnik 1995).

8.4 Support Vector Machine

Support Vector Machine (SVM) is a new type of universal learning machine proposedrecently. SVM has extra advantages for pattern classification.

8.4.1 *Linearly separable case*

Suppose the training data (x_1, y_1) , ..., (x_l, y_l) , $x \in R_n$, $y \in \{+1, -1\}$, where l is the sample size, n is the dimension of input data. We can construct a hyperplane to absolutely separate two-class samples for the case where the training data are linearly separable. The hyperplane be described as:

$$(w \bullet x) + b = 0 \tag{8.19}$$

where • denote vector dot products. To describe the separating hyperplane let us use the following form:

$$w \bullet x_i + b \geq 0, \qquad \text{if } y_i=+1$$

$$w \bullet x_i + b < 0, \qquad \text{if } y_i=-1$$

where w denote hyperplane's normal direction, $\dfrac{w}{\|w\|}$ denote unit normal vector, and $\|w\|$ denote Euclid modular function.

We say that this set of vectors is separated by the optimal hyperplane (or the maximal margin hyperplane) if the training data is separated without error and the distance between the closest vector to the hyperplane is maximal (See Figure 8.4).

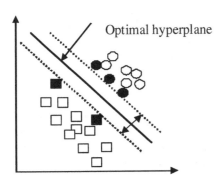 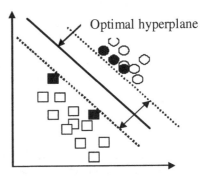

Figure 8.4. The optimal separating hyperplane

For linearly separable case, to find the optimal separating hyperplane is to solve the following quadratic programming problem. Given training samples, find a pair consisting of a vector w and a constant (threshold) b such that they minimize the function

$$\min \Phi(w) = \frac{1}{2}\|w\|^2 \qquad (8.20)$$

under the constraints of inequality type

$$y_i(w \bullet x_i + b) - 1 \geq 0, \qquad i = 1,2,\cdots,l \qquad (8.21)$$

optimize function $\Phi(w)$ is quadratic form, and the constraint condition is linear. Thus, it is a typical quadratic programming problem that can be solved by Lagrange multiplier method. Introduce Lagrange multipliers $\alpha_i \geq 0, i = 1, 2, \cdots, l$:

$$L(w, b, \alpha) = \frac{1}{2} \|w\|^2 - \sum_{i=1}^{l} \alpha_i \{y_i(x_i \bullet w + b) - 1\} \tag{8.22}$$

where, the extremum of L is the saddle point of equality (8.22) . To find the saddle point one has to minimize this function over w and b and to maximize it over the nonnegative Lagrange multipliers α. At the saddle point, the solutions w^*, b^*, and α^* should satisfy the conditions

$$\frac{\partial L}{\partial b} = \sum_{i=1}^{l} y_i \alpha_i = 0 \tag{8.23}$$

$$\frac{\partial L}{\partial w} = w - \sum_{i=1}^{l} y_i \alpha_i x_i = 0 \tag{8.24}$$

where, $\dfrac{\partial L}{\partial w} = \left(\dfrac{\partial L}{\partial w_1}, \dfrac{\partial L}{\partial w_2}, \cdots \dfrac{\partial L}{\partial w_l} \right)$.

Therefore, through solving quadratic programming problem, SVM attain corresponding α^* and w^* satisfying the following equality

$$w^* = \sum_{i=1}^{l} \alpha_i^* y_i x_i \tag{8.25}$$

and the optimal hyperplane (See Figure 8.4).

For transform linearly separable case, the original problem becomes the following problem.

$$\max_{\alpha} W(\alpha) = \sum_{i=1}^{l} \alpha_i - \frac{1}{2} \sum_{i=1}^{l} \sum_{j=1}^{l} \alpha_i \alpha_j y_i y_j x_i \bullet x_j = \boldsymbol{\Gamma} \bullet \boldsymbol{I} - \frac{1}{2} \boldsymbol{\Gamma} \bullet \boldsymbol{D} \boldsymbol{\Gamma} \tag{8.26}$$

satisfying the following constraints

$$\sum_{i=1}^{l} y_i \alpha_i = 0, \qquad \alpha_i \geq 0, \quad i = 1, 2, \cdots, l \tag{8.27}$$

where, $\boldsymbol{\Gamma} = (\alpha_1, \alpha_2, \cdots, \alpha_l)$, $\boldsymbol{I} = (1, 1, \cdots, 1)$, $\boldsymbol{D}$ is a $l \times l$ symmetric matrix, each element is as follow:

$$D_{ij} = y_i y_j x_i \bullet x_j \qquad (8.28)$$

This fact follows from the classical Karush-Kuhn-Tucker (KKT) theorem, according to which necessary and sufficient conditions for the optimal hyperplane are that the separating hyperplane satisfy the conditions:

$$\alpha_i \{ y_i (w \bullet x_i + b) - 1 \} = 0, \qquad i = 1,2,\cdots,l \qquad (8.29)$$

According to equality (8.25), only these samples satisfying $\alpha_i > 0$ determine classification result while those samples satisfying $\alpha_i = 0$ do not. We will call these samples satisfying $\alpha_i > 0$ support vectors.

We train samples to attain vectors α^* and w^*. Selecting a support vectors sample x_i, we attain b^* by the following equality:

$$b^* = y_i - w \bullet x_i \qquad (8.30)$$

For a test sample x, calculate the following equality

$$d(x) = x \bullet w^* + b^* = \sum_{i=1}^{l} y_i \alpha_i^* (x \bullet x_i) + b^* \qquad (8.31)$$

According to the sign of $d(x)$ to determine which class x belongs to.

8.4.2 Linearly non-separable case

In linearly separable case, decision function is constructed on the basis of Euclid distance, i.e. $K(x_i, x_j) = x_i \bullet x_j = x_i^T x_j$. In linearly non-separable case, SVM maps the input vectors x into a high-dimensional feature space H through some nonlinear mapping (see Figure 8.5). In this space, an optimal separating hyperplane is constructed. The nonlinear mapping $\Phi : R^d \rightarrow H$:

$$x \rightarrow \Phi(x) = (\phi_1(x), \phi_2(x), \cdots, \phi_{i(x)}, \cdots)^T \qquad (8.32)$$

where, $\phi_i(x)$ is a real function.

Feature vector $\Phi(x)$ substitutes input vector x, equality (8.28) and (8.31) are transformed as follows:

$$D_{ij} = y_i y_j \Phi(x_i) \bullet \Phi(x_j) \qquad (8.33)$$

$$d(x) = \Phi(x) \bullet w^* + b^* = \sum_{i=1}^{l} \alpha_i y_i \Phi(x_i) \bullet \Phi(x) + b^* \qquad (8.34)$$

The optimize function equality (8.26) and decision function equality (8.31) only refer inner product $x_i \bullet x_j$ of training samples. Therefore, we calculate inner product in high-dimensional space using inner product functions in input space. On the basis of relational theory, a kernel function $K(x_i \bullet x_j)$ is parallelism of inner product in a certain space if it satisfies Mercer's condition (Vapnik, 1995).

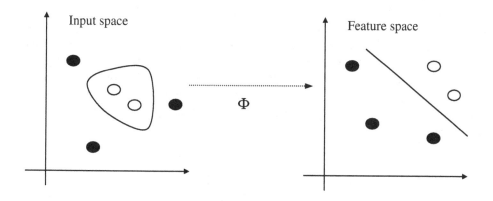

Figure 8.5. The SVM maps the input space into a feature space

Using some appropriate inner product function $K(x_i \bullet x_j)$, SVM maps the input space vectors into a feature space vectors through some nonlinear mapping. Moreover, the complexity of calculate does not increase. The object function equality (8.26) is transformed to the following equality

$$\max_{\alpha} W(\alpha) = \sum_{i=1}^{l} \alpha_i - \frac{1}{2} \sum_{i=1}^{l} \sum_{j=1}^{l} \alpha_i \alpha_j y_i y_j K(x_i, x_j) \qquad (8.35)$$

Thus, the corresponding classifying function becomes the following equality.

$$d(x) = \sum_{i=1}^{l} y_i \alpha_i^* K(x, x_i) + b^* \qquad (8.36)$$

It is called support vector machines (SVM).

For a given $K(x,y)$, the corresponding function $\Phi(x)$ exists under certain condition. It is necessary and sufficient that the condition as follow is satisfied.

Given an arbitrary function g(x), if $\int_a^b g(x)^2 dx$ is finite,

$$\int_a^b \int_a^b K(x,y)g(x)g(y)dxdy \ge 0 \tag{8.37}$$

is valid.

This decision condition is not feasible. It is well known that polynomial function satisfy Mercer's condition. Therefore, $K(x,y)$ satisfy Mercer's condition if it approaches some polynomial function.

The learning machines that construct decision functions of the type (8.36) are called support vector machines (SVM). In SVM the complexity of the construction depends on the number of support vectors rather than on the dimensionality of the feature space. The scheme of SVM is shown in Figure 8.6.

In nonlinear case, SVM maps the input space vectors into a high-dimensional feature space vectors through some nonlinear mapping defined inner product functions. Thus, SVM can find the generalized optimal separating hyperplane in feature space.

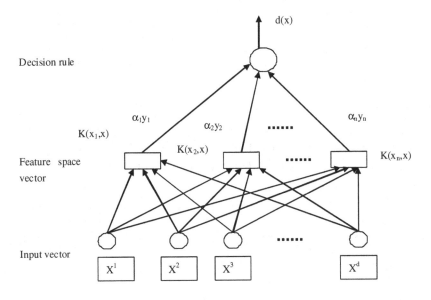

Figure 8.6. Support Vectors Machine (SVM)

8.5 Kernel Function

Using different functions for convolution of the inner products kernel function, one can construct learning machines with different types of nonlinear decision surfaces in input space. At present, prevalent kernel functions are polynomial kernel function, radial basis function, multi-layer perceptron and dynamic kernel function.

8.5.1 Polynomial kernel function

Polynomial kernel function:

$$K(x, x_i) = [(x, x_i) + 1]^d \tag{8.38}$$

We construct a d-dimensional polynomials decision function of the form

$$f(x, \alpha) = sign\left(\sum_{\substack{sup\ port\ vector}} y_i \alpha_i [x_i \bullet x) + 1]^d - b \right)$$

8.5.2 Radial Basis Function

Classical radial basis function (RBF) machines use the following set of decision rules:

$$f(x) = sign\left(\sum_{i=1}^{l} \alpha_i K_\gamma (|x - x_i|) - b \right) \tag{8.39}$$

where $K\gamma(|x - x_i|)$ depends on the distance $|x - x_i|$ between two vectors. For any fixed γ, the function $K\gamma(|x - x_i|)$ is a nonnegative monotonic function. It tends to zero as training sample's total goes to infinity. The most popular function of this type is

$$K_\gamma (|x - x_i|) = \exp\left\{ -\frac{|x - x_i|^2}{\sigma^2} \right\} \tag{8.40}$$

To construct the decision rule (8.39) one has to estimate

(1) the value of the parameter γ,
(2) the number N of the centers x_i,
(3) the vectors x_i, describing the centers,
(4) the value of the parameters α_i.

In contrast to classical RBF methods, each center denotes a support vector in this method. Furthermore, all four types of parameters are chosen to minimize the bound on the probability of test error.

8.5.3 *Multi-layer Perceptron*

Multi-layer perceptron define inner product kernel function using sigmoid function. The number N of hidden units (the number of support vectors) are found automatically. The sigmoid kernel satisfies Mercer conditions as follow

$$K(x_i, x_j) = \tanh(\gamma x_i^T x_j - \Theta) \tag{8.41}$$

Using this arithmetic we avoid local minima problem that puzzles neural network.

8.5.4 *Dynamic kernel function*

Amari and Wu proposed a method of modifying a kernel function to improve the performance of a support vector machine classifier (Amari, 1999). This is based on the structure of the Riemannian geometry induced by the kernel function. U denotes feature mapping $U = \Phi(x)$, then

$$dU = \sum_i \frac{\partial}{\partial x_i} \Phi(x) dx_i$$

$$\|dU\|^2 = \sum_{i,j} g_{ij}(x) dx_i dx_j$$

where $g_{ij}(x) = \left(\dfrac{\partial}{\partial x_i} \Phi(x) \right) \bullet \left(\dfrac{\partial}{\partial x_j} \Phi(x) \right)$. The $n \times n$ positive-definite matrix $(g_{ij}(x))$ is the Riemannian metric tensor induced in S. $ds^2 = \sum_{ij} g_{ij}(x) dx_i dx_j$ is Riemannian distance. The volume form in a Riemannian space is defined as

$$dv = \sqrt{g(x)} dx_1 \cdots dx_n$$

where $g(x) = \det(g_{ij}(x))$. The factor $g(x)$ represents how a local area is magnified in U under the mapping $\Phi(x)$. Therefore, we call it the magnification factor. Since $k(x, z) = (\Phi(x) \bullet \Phi(z))$ we can get

$$g_{ij}(x) = \frac{\partial}{\partial x_i \partial z_j} k(x,z)\Big|_{z=x}$$

In particular for the Gaussian kernel function $k(x,z) = \exp\{\frac{|x-z|^2}{2\sigma^2}\}$, we have

$$g_{ij}(x) = \frac{1}{\sigma^2}\delta_{ij}$$

In order to improve the performance of a SVM classifier, Amari and Wu proposed a method of modifying a kernel function. To increase the margin or separability of classes, we need to enlarge the spatial resolution around the boundary surface in U. Let $c(x)$ be a positive real differentiable function, $k(x,z)$ denote Gaussian kernel function, then

$$\tilde{k}(x,z) = c(x)k(x,z)c(z) \tag{8.42}$$

Also is a kernel function, and

$$\tilde{g}_{ij}(x) = c_i(x)c_j(x) + c^2(x)g_{ij}$$

Where, $c_i(x) = \frac{\partial}{\partial x_i}c(x)$. Amari and Wu defined $c(x)$ as

$$c(x) = \sum_{x_i \in SV} h_i e^{\frac{\|x-x_i\|^2}{2\tau^2}} \tag{8.43}$$

Where, τ is a positive number, hi denotes coefficient. Around the support vector x_i, we have

$$\sqrt{\tilde{g}(x)} \approx \frac{h_i}{\sigma^n} e^{\frac{nr^2}{2\gamma^2}} \sqrt{1 + \frac{\sigma^2}{\tau^4}\gamma^2}$$

Where $\tau = \|x - x_i\|$ is the Euclid distance between x and x_i. In order to make sure $\sqrt{\tilde{g}(x)}$ is larger near the support vector x_i and is smaller in other region, we need

$$\tau \approx \frac{\sigma}{\sqrt{n}} \tag{8.44}$$

In summary, the training process of the new method consists of the two steps:

(1) Train SVM with a primary kernel k (Gaussian kernel), then modify training result according to equalities (8.42), (8.43) and (8.44), we attain $\tilde{k}$.

(2) Train SVM with the modified kernel $\tilde{k}$.

When SVM use the new training method, the performance of the classifier is improved remarkably, and the number of support vectors decreases such that it improves the velocity of pattern recognition.

Exercises

1. Compare Empirical Risk Minimization (ERM) Inductive Principle and Structural Risk Minimization (SRM) Inductive Principle.
2. What is VC dimension's meaning? Why does VC dimension reflect function set's learning capacity?
3. What are three milestones of statistics learning theory's? What problem was resolved in each milestone?
4. Describe support vector machine's primitive idea and mathematical model.
5. Why does statistical learning theory be support vector machine's theory foundation, and in which area it represent?
6. Under linearly separable case, given a hyperplane defined as follows:

$$w^T x + b = 0$$

where, w denotes weight vector, b denotes bias, x denotes input vector. If a set of input pattern $\{x_i\}_{i=1}^N$ satisfy the following conditions

$$\min_{i=1,2,\cdots,N} | w^T x_i + b | = 1$$

(w,b) is called canonical pair of hyperplane. Prove it that conditions of canonical pair conduce distance between bounds of two classification is 2/||w||.

7. Briefly narrate the primitive concept that support vector machine solve nonlinearity separable problem.
8. Two layer perceptron's inner product kernel is defined as

$$K(x, x_i) = \tanh(\beta_0 x^T x_i + \beta_1)$$

under which values of β_0 and β_1, the kernel function does not satisfy Mercer's condition.

9. What is the advantage and limitations for support vector machine and radial basis function (RBF) network while they respectively solve the following assignments?

(1) pattern recognition

(2) nonlinear regression

10. In contrast to other classification method, what are support vector machine's significant advantages? Please explain theoretically.

Chapter 9

Explanation-Based Learning

Explanation based learning (abbreviated as EBL) is a kind of analytic learning. Under the guidance of domain theory, this learning method constructs the explanation structure of cause and effect of the solving process based on the analysis of only one single example solving and acquires control information which can be used for solving similar problems later.

9.1 Introduction

Explanation-based learning was originally proposed by DeJong from the University of Illinois in 1983. On the basis of empirical inductive learning, EBL takes advantage of domain theory to explain single problem solving. This is an inference analysis about cause and effect of knowledge and general control strategy can be generated.

In 1986 Mitchell, Keller and Kedar-Cabelli put forward a unified framework of explanation based generalization (abbreviated as EBG) and defined the EBL as the following two steps(Mitchell et al., 1986):

(1) Generate an explanation structure by means of analysis one problem solving.
(2) Generalize the explanation structure and obtain general control rules.

DeJong and Mooney proposed a more general terminology EBL and it became an independent branch of machine learning. As a kind of deductive learning essentially, EBL makes deductive inference, stores useful conclusions and constructs control information for future similar problem solving after knowledge refinement and compilation. Unlike empirically-based learning methods that require large numbers of examples, EBL always investigates one training instance (commonly positive instance) deeply to get an explanation structure. The analysis consists of three steps: first interprets why the training instance is an example one of the desired concepts (goal concepts) and then generalizes the explanation structure, making it suit a large scope of examples, and finally gets a general description from explanation structure and it is the general description of the generalization of the initial example.

EBL can be used in different application fields including control information acquirement, knowledge refinement, software reuse, computer aided design and computer aided instruction. In the traditional programs, the main function of explanation is to illustrate programs, offer hints and provide better readability. According to the characteristic of artificial program, explanation has been given new meaning and it works in:

(1) Making detailed explanation for the results of inference process and promoting the acceptability of the system;
(2) Tracking wrong decisions and discovering knowledge deficiency and wrong concepts in the knowledge base;
(3) Training the novice.

The way of explanation thus becomes simpler. The followings are the general adopted methods of explanation:

(1) Prepared text: make text preparation in English and insert it into programs;
(2) Traced execution: traverse the target tree, retrieve relevant rules by means of summarizing targets relevant to conclusions in order to show how to reach the conclusions;
(3) Strategic explanation: denote control knowledge explicitly, i.e. meta-knowledge is used for general description and rules are totally separated from domain theory. Explanations that afford solving methods are constructed from the general depiction of strategy.

EBL mainly adopts traces execution to explain the causation relationship among knowledge after traversing the target tree. Based on the analysis of cause and effect the control information is learned.

9.2 Model for EBL

R.M.Keller demonstrated that EBL relates to three different spaces: example space, concept space and concept description space(Keller,1987). Concept on one hand can be expressed as a set composed of a certain instances extensively and on the other hand it can also be denoted as the properties of instances in the example space intensively. Figure 9.1 illustrates the relationship among three spaces.

Concept space refers to the set composed of all concepts that a learning program can depict. Every point corresponds to a unique subset of example space. For instance, C_1 corresponds to I_1, I_2 and I_3. However, one point in the concept space corresponds to more points in concept description space, these points can be divided into two categories: operational and non-operational. Here, C_1 corresponds to D_1 (non-operational description) and D_2 (operational description). Two descriptions correspond to the same concept are called synonymy. A case in point is that D_1 and D_2 are synonymy. The task of EBL is to transfer the non-operational descriptions into operational descriptions.

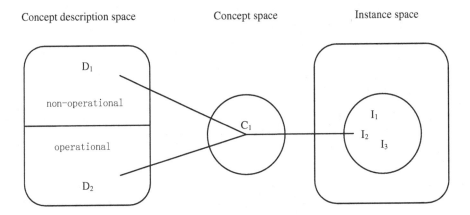

Figure 9.1. Space description of EBL

As shown in figure 9.1, D_1 is the initial and non-operational description submitted to the system and D_2 is the learned final, operational description. Therefore, D_1 can be regarded as the starting point for searching while D_2 is the solution point. The explanation is just transformation of space and operable is the criterion for halt of searching. Concept operational is defined as the transformation from D_1 to D_2 (Keller, 1987).

From the concept's point of view, each EBL system is made up of operational evaluation process, description of appraisal concept and generation of operational evaluation results. The three dimension characteristics generated from the evaluation process include variability, granularity and certainty. Table 9.1 shows the characteristics of operationality of several systems.

Table 9.1. Characterizing operationality assessment

System	Variability	Granularity	Certainty
GENESIS	Dynamic	Binary	No guarantee
LEX2	Dynamic	Binary	No guarantee
SOAR	Dynamic	Binary	No guarantee
PRODIGY	Static	Continual	No guarantee
Meta-LEX	Dynamic	Continual	Guarantee

A model of EBL can be established based upon the above space description. The EBL system mainly comprises of perform system PS, learning system EXL, and domain knowledge base KB (set of rule transformation of various descriptions). Let concept space be C, concept description space be CD and example space be I, the working process of the system is as follows: The input of EXL is description D_1 (usually inoperable) of concept C_1, description transformation of D_1 is pursued (this is a searching process) based on knowledge in KB. PS tests every transformed result, the learning process is over and D_2 is outputted until PS gets an operable description D_2. The model is illustrated in figure 9.2.

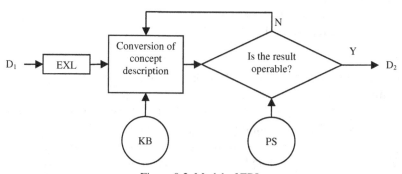

Figure 9.2. Model of EBL

9.3 Explanation-Based Generalization

9.3.1 *Basic principle*

In 1986 Mitchell, Keller and Kedar-Cabelli put forward a unified framework of explanation based generalization (abbreviated as EBG). The basic principle is to construct an explanation structure for a certain condition and generalize the explanation structure to make it fit more general circumstances. Generalization of EBL takes advantage of logical representation of knowledge and ways of deductive problem solving.

In order to define the generalization problem considered here, we first introduce some terminology. A concept is defined as a predicate over some universe of instances, and thus characterizes some subset of the instances. Each instance in this universe is described by a collection of ground literals that represent its features and their values. A concept definition describes the necessary and sufficient conditions for being an example of the concept, while a sufficient concept definition describes sufficient conditions for being an example of the concept. An instance that satisfies the concept definition is called an example, or positive example of that concept, whereas an instance that does not satisfy the concept definition is called a negative example of that concept. A generalization of an example is a concept definition which describes a set containing that example. An explanation of how an instance is an example of a concept is a proof that the example satisfies the concept definition. An explanation structure is the proof tree, modified by replacing each instantiated rule by the associated general rule.

A formal specification of Explanation-Based Generalization can be formally described as(Mitchell et al., 1986):
Given:

(1) Goal Concept: A concept definition describing the concept to be learned.
(2) Training Example: An example of the goal concept.
(3) Domain Theory: A set of rules and facts to be used in explaining how the training example is an example of the goal concept.
(4) Operationality Criterion: A predicate over concept definitions, specifying theform in which the learned concept definition must be expressed.

Determine:
• A generalization of the training example, and satisfies the two conditions:

(1) A sufficient concept definition for the goal concept.
(2) Satisfies the operationality criterion.

Explanation-Based Generalization can be divided into two steps: The first step is to explain: that is to construct an explanation tree in terms of the domain theory that proves how the training example satisfies the goal concept definition. This explanation must be constructed so that each branch of the explanation structure terminates in an expression that satisfies the operationality criterion. The second step is to generalize: determine a set of sufficient conditions under which the explanation structure holds, stated in terms that satisfy the operationality criterion. This is accomplished by regressing the goal concept through the explanation structure. Actually, the first step separates the relevant properties and irrelevant properties of instance apart, while the second step is to analysis the explanation structure.

(1) Generate explanation. After an instance is given, system begins to solve the problem. If the inference is executed backwardly from goal, relevant rules that match the consequents need to be searched from domain knowledge base. When these rules are found, goals are set to be consequence and rules become premise, and then the relationship is recorded. Premises of these rules are considered to be sub-goals, the inference goes on until the problem solving completes. Once the solution is acquired, the goal is proofed that it can be satisfied and the explanation structure of cause and effect is obtained.

There are generally two ways to construct explanation structure. The first one is to make a set of operators for every inference to construct action sequences to form explanation structure; the other one is traversing the structure of proof tree in top-down way. The former is general, leaving out description of some facts while the latter is more specific, every fact appears in the proof tree. The explanation can be constructed in the process of problem resolving and it can also be accomplished after the problem solving. These two methods are so called learn while study and learn after study.

(2) Generalize core event of the explanation structure. In this step, generally adopted way is to convert constants into variables, i.e. to change the concrete data into variable for these examples and omit some unimportant information; only preserve key information for solution. Production rules are created to obtain control knowledge for generalization.

To see how the EBG method works more concretely, considering the problem of learning the concept SAFE-TO-STACK (x, y). The task is to learn to recognize pairs of objects $<x, y>$ such that it is safe to stack x on top of y. The instance of SAFE-TO-STACK is as follows:

Given:
- Goal Concept: Pairs of objects $<x, y>$ such that SAFE-TO-STACK (x, y), where SAFE-TO-STACK$(x,y) \Leftrightarrow$ NOT(FRAGILE(y)) $\vee$ LIGHTER(x,y).
- Training Example:
  ON (OBJ1, OBJ2)
  ISA (OBJ1, BOX)
  ISA (OBJ2, ENDTABLE)
  COLOR (OBJ1, RED)
  COLOR (OBJ2, BLUE)

VOLUME (OBJ1, 1)
DENSITY (OBJ1, .1)

...

- Domain Theory:

VOLUME (p1, v1) $\wedge$ DENSITY (p1, d1) $\rightarrow$ WEIGHT (p1, v1*d1)
WEIGHT (p1, w1) $\wedge$ WEIGHT (p2, w2) $\wedge$ LESS (w1, w2) $\rightarrow$
LIGHTER (p1, p2)
ISA (p1, ENDTABLE) $\rightarrow$ WEIGHT (p1, 5) (default)
LESS (.1, 5)

...

- Operationality Criterion: The concept definition must be expressed in terms of predicates used to describe examples (e.g., VOLUME, COLOR, DENSITY) or other selected, easily evaluated predicates from the domain theory (e.g. LESS).

Determine:
- Generalization of training example is to give a sufficient concept definition for the goal concept and to satisfy operationality criterion.

EBG system constructs explanation tree in terms of the domain theory and makes the training example satisfy goal concept definition. Figure 9.3 shows an explanation tree of SAFE-TO-STACK (OBJ1, OBJ2).

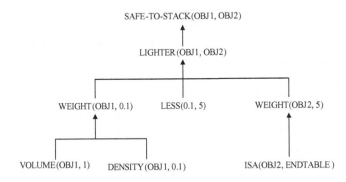

Figure 9.3. SAFE-TO-STACK (OBJ1, OBJ2) EXPLANATION STRUCTURE

Figure 9.4. Reveals generalization steps of SAFE-TO-STACK (OBJ1, OBJ2). In term of rules in the domain theory, the goal concept expression SAFE-TO-STACK (*x, y*) is regressed through the rule LIGHT(p1, p2)$\rightarrow$ SAFE-TO-STACK(p1, p2); similarly, regressing LIGHTER(*x, y*) through the rule WEIGHT (*x*, w1) $\wedge$ WEIGHT (*y*, w2) $\wedge$ LESS (w1, w2) and the yielded predicates are shown in the second layer. In the third layer, the conjunct WEIGHT(*x*, w1) is in turn regressed through the rule VOLUME(p1, v1)∧DENSITY(p1, d1)→ WEIGHT(p1, v1*d1) and therefore yields VOLUME(x, v1) ∧ DENSITY(x, d1). Regressing the conjunct WEIGHT (y, w2) through the rule ISA (p2, ENDTABLE) →WEIGHT (p2, 5) and yielding ISA(y, ENDTABLE). Finally, since no rule consequent can be unified with the conjunct LESS (w1, w2), this conjunct is simply added to the result expression. Therefore the concept description of SAFE-TO-STACK(x, y) is as follows:

VOLUME(x, v1) ∧DENSITY(x, d1) ∧LESS (v1*d1, 5) ∧ISA(y, ENDTABLE) →SAFE-TO-STACK (x, y)

This illustration satisfies operationality criterion.

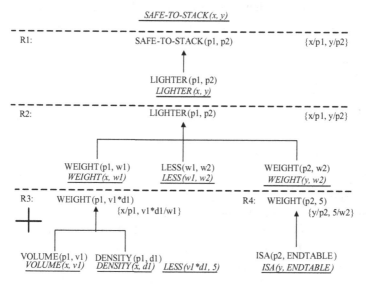

Figure 9.4. Generalizing from the explanation of SAFE-TO-STACK (OBJ1, OBJ2)

Explanation-based generalization does not lead to truly 'new' knowledge, but only enables the learner to reformulate what the learner already knows implicitly. EBG must understand the initial description of goal concept and even if the description is correct it is inoperable. Informally speaking, the learner can not improve its performance by means of effectively utilizing the description, that is to say, the concept description itself is different from whether the concept can be used. The task of EBG system is to narrow the difference according to transformation of initial description or to make the initial description operable.

9.3.2 Interchange with explanation and generalization

In 1987, Hirsh from the University of Stanford proposed a new Explanation based Generalization (Hirsh, 1987), which is making explanation and generalization by turns.

1. Logical description of problem

The learning system provides various ways for inference which include forward, backward and inductive reasoning. The logical representation makes the semantic of EBG clearer and provides more convenient language environment. For instance, suppose the learner needs to learn goal concept Safe-to-Stack (V1, V2), the domain theory can be represented as:

Fact knowledge：
 On (obj1, obj2)
 Isa (obj2, Endtable)
 Color (obj1, red)
 Color (obj2, blue)
 Volume (obj1, 1)
 Density (obj1, 0.1)
Domain rule:
 Not (Fragile(y)) →Safe-to-Stack(x,y)
 Lighter(x, y) →Safe-to-Stack(x,y)
 Volume (p1, v1) ∧Density (p1, d1) ∧X (v1, d1, w1) →Weight (p1, w1)
 Isa (p1, Endtable) →Weight (p1, 5)
 Weight(p1,w1)∧Weight(p2,w2)∧ <(w1,w2) →Lighter (p1,p2)

2. Generate explanation structure

In order to proof that the example above satisfies goal concept, the system begins to process backward inference that is to decompose the goal in terms of existing facts in knowledge base. Every time a rule is used, the rule is applied to the goal concept which is variable. In this way, the explanation structure of the example is yielded while at the same time the variable generalization explanation is produced as well.

3. Generate the control rule

 Conjunction of all the leaf nodes in the explanation structure is considered as antecedent and the goal concept in the vertex is taken as consequent, the intermediate composed of the explanation structure is omitted. Therefore the generalized production rule is created. The solving process is fast and the efficiency is high when this control rule is applied to resolve similar problems.

Nevertheless, it is too general to realize generalization by means of transformation from constant to variable, and the rule may fail in some special cases.

9.4 Explanation Generalization using Global Substitutions

DeJong and Mooney proposed Explanation Generalization using Global Substitutions (abbreviated as EGGS) (DeJong & Mooney, 1986) in 1986. In EBG, through goal concept regression of instance explanation structure, the disjunction is left out to realize generalization. The EGGS explains construction unit constructors and connects these units when explanation can be unified.

The robot planning STRIPS(Fikes, Hart and Nilsson, 1972) was the first to realize generalization explanation. It is a macro command system, which constructs and generalizes robot planning. When the goal is given, STRIPS executes search process, finds out a sequence of operators and transforms a given initial world model status into goal status. The initial model and goal are as follows:

Initial world model:
    INROOM(ROBOT,R1)
    INROOM(BOX1,R2)
    CONNECTS(D1,R1,R2)
    CONNECTS(D1,R2,R3)
    BOX (BOX1)
        $\vdots$
    $(\forall x, y, z) [CONNECTS(x, y, z) \Rightarrow CONNECTS(x, z, y)]$
The goal formula:
    $(\exists x)[BOX(x) \wedge INROOM(x, R1)]$
    The operators STRIPS adopted is as follows:
    GOTHRU(d,r_1,r_2)
    Precondition:INROOM(ROBOT,r1) $\wedge$ CONNECTS(d,r1,r2)
    Delete list:INROOM(ROBOT,r1)
    Add list: INROOM(ROBOT,r2)
PUSHTHRU (b, d, r_1, r_2)
    Precondition:INROOM(ROBOT,r_1)$\wedge$CONNECTS(D,r_1,r_2)$\wedge$INROOM(b,r_1)
    Delete list:INROOM(ROBOT,r_1) INROOM(b,r_1)
    Add list:INROOM(ROBOT,r_2) INROOM(b,r_2)

In STRIPS the triangle table is adopted to represent robot planning generalization and resolution proof is used for antecedent condition. Figure 9.5 shows the triangle table of description operator GOTHRU (d, r1, r2) and PUSHTHRU (b, d, r1, r2).

*INROOM (ROBOT, R1) *CONNECTS (D1, R1, R2)	GOTHRU(D1, R1, R2)	
*INROOM (BOX1, R2) *CONNECTS (D1, R1, R2) *CONNECTS (x, y, z) ⇒ *CONNECTS (x, z, y)	*INROOM (ROBOT, R2)	PUSHTHRU(BOX1, D1, R2, R1)
		INROOM (ROBOT, R1) INROOM (BOX1, R1)

Figure 9.5. Triangle Table

The triangle table is useful, which shows how the other operators and initial world models affect the antecedent of operators. The algorithm of STRIPS generalization is as follows:

For each equality between p_i and p_j in the explanation structure do
  Let θ be the MGU of p_i and p_j
  For each pattern p_k in the explanation structure do
    Replace p_k with $p_k\theta$

STRIPS employs the explanation based generalization algorithm of the triangle table to yield the generalization sequence of operators. In the first step, all the constants in the whole generalization table are substituted with variables. And secondly, in terms of two standard constraint tables, one is to hold the dependency relationship of operators and the other one is that antecedents of the operators in the generalization tables are provable. This is the same as in the previous proof of antecedents in the planning. Through generalization, a generalization table displayed in figure 9.6 is created by STRIPS.

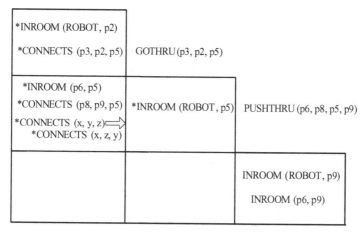

Figure 9.6. Generalize triangle table

The learning method DeJong et al. used is to learn schemata. The main idea of schemata is to arrange relevant knowledge into a group in order to attain a certain objective while constructing systematical knowledge. Schemata are a partial ordering set of operators, and the simple schemata relates to each other together. EGGS applies dynamic operationality criterion, when the system learns a general schema of a concept, this concept is operable. The problem of EGGS can be depicted as(DeJong and Mooney, 1986):

Given:
- · Domain Theory: Consists of three parts: a) a specification of types of objects in the world and their properties; b) a set of inference rules for inferring properties and relations from other properties and relations; c) a library of problem solving operators and already known general schemata. These schemata can be previously learned or hand-coded.
- · Goal: General specification of goal status.
- · Initial world status: A specification of the objects in the world and their properties.
- · Observed operator/state sequence (optional): An observed sequence of low-level operators, performed by an expert, which achieves an instance of the goal. In some situations, some operators may be missing, in which case they must be inferred from achieved state given in the input.

Determine:
- · A new schemata that achieves the goal status in a general way.

EGGS has always maintained two independent substitution tables SPECIFIC and GENERAL. Table SPECIFIC is used for substitution of explanation structure to receive the explanation of concrete instance, while table GENERAL substitute the generalized explanation. Let σ be the substitution of SPECIFIC, γ be the substitution of GENERAL, then the generalization is formally presented as:

for each equality between expression e_1 and e_2 in the explanation structure:

If e_1 is the antecedent of a domain rule and e_2 is the consequent of a domain rule

Then   let ϕ = the most general unifier of $e_1\sigma$ and $e_2\sigma$

let $\sigma = \sigma\phi$ // update SPECIFIC substitution

let δ = the most general unifier of $e_1\gamma$ and $e_2\gamma$

let $\gamma = \gamma\delta$ // update GENERAL substitution

Else let ϕ = the most general unifier of $e_1\sigma$ and $e_2\sigma$

let $\sigma = \sigma\phi$ // update SPECIFIC substitution

Based on the above illustration, Mooney and Bennett proposed an algorithm of Explanation Generalization using Global Substitutions EGGS, which is similar to abstract STRIPS.

Algorithm 9.1 Explanation Generalization using Global Substitutions (EGGS) (DeJong and Mooney, 1986)

1.   let γ be the null substitution {}.
2.   for each equality between p_i and p_j in the explanation structure do:
3.   let p_i' be the result of applying γ to p_i.
4.   let p_j' be the result of applying γ to p_j.
5.   let θ be the MGU of p_i' and p_j'.
6.   let γ be $\gamma\theta$.
7.   for each pattern p_k in the explanation structure do:
8.   replace p_k with $p_k\gamma$.

9.5 Explanation-Based Specialization

Minton and Carbonell from the university of Carnegie-Mellon proposed a learning method called Explanation-Based Specialization (abbreviated as EBS) (Minton, 1987) in 1987. A learning system PRODIGY is developed by means of EBS, which overcomes shortcomings in EBG. EBS learns from multi-object concept learning, the process of explanation is the detailed illustration of every goal concept. After the process of explanation, the description of goal concept is converted to a corresponding control rule, which can be used for selecting proper node, sub-goal, operators and constraints. The concrete method is as follows:

PRODIGY is a general problem solver combined with learning modules. The architecture is depicted in Figure 9.7. Based on problem solver of operator, a unified control structure for inference rule and operator search is exhibited. The problem solver comprises of a simple reason maintenance sub-system and stipulates the influential operators. The search of problem solver can be navigated by control rules.

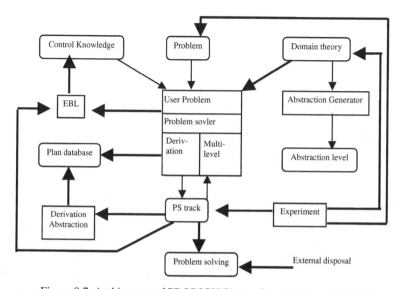

Figure 9.7. Architecture of PRODIGY(Picture from Minton et al.,1989)

The EBL module obtains control rule by tracking problem solver. The explanation is constructed from domain theory and problem solver, and then the result expression is converted into control rule for searching. The derived module is the derived analogy, which can recap the whole solution of previous similar problems. From figure 9.7, it is obvious that analogy and EBL are two independent mechanisms to get the control information for a concrete domain. The experimental learning module is to refine the incomplete or incorrect domain theory. When the plan execution controller detects that there is some difference between inner expectation and outer expectation, the experimental module is triggered. Abstraction generator and abstraction level model provides multi-level plan capability. Based upon the depth first analysis of certain domain knowledge, the domain theory is divided into several abstraction levels. The PRODIGY builds abstract results and makes refinement when a problem begins to solve.

PRODIGY can learn from four goal concepts: success, failure, the only choice and restriction of goals. Every time a goal and an example is given to a user, the system first decomposes the goal to the leaf node backwardly and gains the corresponding goal concepts and then analyzes the problem solving track to explain why the instance satisfies the goal concept.

For example, if a solution is obtained then control rule of the concept of success should be learned; while there is no solution, control rule of the concept of failure should be learned; if some option is unique then control rule of the selection concept should be learned and finally if the success of a certain goal must rely on other goals, then control rule of restriction of goals should be learned.

1. The process of explanation

The process of explanation is the detailed illustration in PRODIGY. Explanation is to search for proof in the knowledge base by means of using training examples. The process of explanation equals to a bottom-up proof tree with goal concept as its roof. Every step of explanation must choose a rule consistent with the given example from domain knowledge base and generate a node. Every rule is a particular description of node sub-goal. The algorithm of explanation is as follows:

1. If this concept is primitive, then there is no rule implies the concept, so return with no modification, else go to step 2.
2. Call the recognizer corresponds to the concept (that is the mapped function connecting goal concept and knowledge base), take out those rules consistent with training examples. Every non-negative atomic formula is a sub-concept. If the sub-concept has never been specialized, then specialize the sub-concept and rename the specialized variable and simplified the sub-concept with specialization substitution.
3. Return.

Here the goal concepts have become totally specialized concepts, apply these concepts mechanically with corresponding rule schema, a control rule can be thus obtained.

2. Learn the control rule

There are four static control rule schemas aimed to four goal concept in PRODIGY. The control rule can be found when a certain detailed description of goal concept matches rule schema. Preference rules can be learned from the concept of success, which indicates under what circumstances the choice is successful while rejections rules are learned from the concept of failure which shows a refusal option. If the other choices all fail, then the option is unique and the selection rules can therefore be learned.

The following takes concept of failure as an example to explain the explanation and the formation of control rules. This is a problem of action plan for domain background building block. For the learning of a certain failed plan action, the yielded explanation is:

(OPERATOR-FAILS op goal node) if
(AND (MATCHES op (PICKUP x))
(MATCHES goal (HOLDING x))
(KNOWN node (NOT (ONTABLE x))))

Here the lowercase characters are variables. The above expression is the result of generalizing the failed action by the formal knowledge in the domain knowledge base and it means that if the current node is not "ONTABLE x" and the current operator is "PICKUP x", then the operator "PICKUP x" is a failed operator. Thus the learned rejection rule from the failed concept is:

(REJECT OPERATOR (PICKUP x)) if
(AND (CURRENT-NODE node)
(CURRENT-GOAL node (HOLDING x))
(CANDIDATE-OPERATOR (PICKUP x))
(OPERATE-FAILS op goal node))

Here op= (PICKUP x), goal= (HOLDING x), node= (NOT (ONTABLE x)). The rules mean that if the current node is (NOT (ONTABLE x)), current goal is (HOLDING x), the candidate operator on the node is (PICKUP x) and the operator fails under this node and this objective, then operator (PICKUP x) should be refused.

By passing the control rule to four strategies which include node choose, sub-objective, operator and a group method of constraints, the capability of the problem solver can be dynamically improved. When dealing with similar problem solving, selection rules are used to choose proper sub-sets, and then rejection rules are taken to do the filter, at last preference rules are adopted to search for the best heuristic choice to reduce the amount of search.

3. Knowledge representation

The knowledge base of PRODIGY is composed of domain level axiom and construct level axiom. The former deals with domain rules and the latter contains inference rules in problem solving. Both of them are represented in declarative logical language to better extend the inference explicitly.

Though there is no distinct generalization in PRODIGY, its domain rules, inference rules of problem solving in particular, have actually contain generalization. They are not made up of primitive domain knowledge which makes them generalizable. On the other hand, PRODIGY generates the explanation by proof tree according to generalization, thereafter the results of the description acquired from the explanation is specialization of goal concept and generalization of example, which makes the result not too generalizable and can be used commonly.

9.6 Logic Program of Explanation-Based Generalization

As mentioned in previous sections, an explanation structure about the training examples should be established first in EBG. This is actually a theorem proving problem thus EBG can be regarded as the extension of resolution theory prove of Horn clauses and the generalization can be considered as the attachment of standard theorem proving.

9.6.1 *Operational principle*

The logic program design language, for example Prolog and so on are based on resolution principle. The main point of resolution principle is to check out whether the set of clauses contains null clause. Virtually, resolution principle is a kind of deductive rule by which the result clauses are created from the clauses set.

Resolution principle: Given initial clauses C_1 and C_2 and there is no common variables, L_1 and L_2 are two literals of C_1 and C_2 respectively. If there is a most general unifier of L_1 and $\neg L_2$, then clause $(C_1 - L_1) \vee (C_2 - L_2)$ is denoted as the resolvent of C_1 and C_2.

For a given goal, the detailed process of searching for clause match of Turbo Prolog is a unified process, which completes the parameter transmission in other programming language. The following is the unified algorithm:

Algorithm 9.2: The unification algorithm of Turbo Prolog

(1) Free variable can be unified with other tem arbitrarily. The free variable becomes the bounded unified term after unification.
(2) Constant can be unified with itself or free variables.
(3) If functor of two compound terms are the same and with same number of parameter, then the unification can be done under the condition that every sub-term can be unified correspondingly. The bounded variable should be substituted with unified bounded value.

The first thing EBG need to do is to create explanation structure of training examples, that is taking the training example as target, acquiring a proof of the training examples by searching and matching the domain theory (the domain theory has already been represented as rules and facts in Prolog). Therefore, unification algorithm should be used to create an explanation structure. Based on this, unification algorithm can be treated as the fundamental of realization of EBG and the generalization can be formed.

The domain theory is stored as the inner database when EBG is implemented based on Turbo Prolog. In terms of creating explanation structure of training examples, it is easier to retrieval the database (domain theory) and search for the matched rules like the way we use predicates.

Even if Prolog is based on unification algorithm, unification algorithm still needs to be explicitly executed when implementing EBG with Prolog. This means predicates of Turbo Prolog are required to finish the unification algorithm and this is actually primitive idea of program design. Predicates are defined to deal with term unification and term table unification. It is by means of unification algorithm the explanation is accomplished and the proof tree is set up.

The next step of generalization is to get proof tree according to goal concept regression. This regression involves substitution of constant with variables and new term unification and so on. It is hard to effectively substitute constant with variables, especially when the variable is not bounded. Though regression by predicate has been defined, more work still need be done as to the way of increasing its universality and treat with more variables not bounded.

Explanation and generalization are two steps of EBG. However it is easy to think of explanation first and then the proof structure can be transferred to generalization. Therefore, the two steps are executed consecutively and independently, the whole proof tree and every path need to be preserved. Here, we consider the two steps execute interchangeably. When the system attempts to proof that the training example is an example of goal concept, search begins from the goal concept backwardly until the training example gets a match. During this process, every time a rule is used it is used to the variable goal concept without example, thereafter the generalized explanation structure is constructed while at the same time the explanation of training instances is created, the two phases of EBG is combined together.

9.6.2 *Meta Explanation*

The simple Prolog meta explanation is as:
```
prolog(Leaf):-clause(Leaf,true).
prolog((Goal1,Goal2)):-
    prolog(Goal1),
    prolog(Goal2).
prolog(Goal):-
```

```
                clause(Goal,Clause),
                prolog(Clause).
```
The core of Prolog EBG is established, and the algorithm is as:
```
prolog_ebg(X_Goal,X_Gen,[X_Goal],[X_Gen]:-clause(X_Goal,true).
prolog_ebg((X_Goal,Y_Goal),(X_Gen,Y_gen),Proof,GenProof):-
        prolog_ebg(X_Goal,X_Gen,X_Proof,X_GenProof),
        prolog_ebg(Y_Goal,Y_Gen,Y_Proof,Y_GenProof),
        concat(X_Proof,Y_Proof,Proof),
        concat(X_GenProof,Y_GenProof,GenProof).
prolog_ebg(X_Goal,X_Gen,[Proof],[GenProof]):-
        clause(X_Gen,Y_Gen),
        copy((X_Gen:-Y_Gen),(X_Goal:-Y_Goal)),
        prolog_ebg(Y_Goal,Y_Gen,Y_Proof,Y_GenProof),
        concat([X_Goal],[Y_Proof],Proof),
        concat([X_Gen],[Y_GenProof],GenProof).
```

9.6.3 *An example*

A "suicide" example is given to illustrate how to implement EBG.
Input:

> Target concept： suicide(x).
> Domain theory： a group of clauses or rules
> > Suicide(x):- kill(x, x).
> > Kill (A, B):- hate (A, B),
> > > Possess (A, C),
> > > Weapon(C).
> > Hate (A, A):- depressed (A).
> > Possess (A, C):- buy (A, C).
> > Weapon (Z):- gun (Z).
> Training examples： a group of fact clauses
> > Depressed (john).
> > buy(john,gun1).
> > gun (gun1).
> > Suicide (john).
> Operational criterion: here only consider the simple static standard
> > Operational (depressed).
> > Operational (gun).
> > Operational (buy).

As shown in Figure 9.8 the explanation structure is established. We can see from the explanation mechanism of Prolog that the Top-Down strategy is adopted when creating the explanation structure. Every time a rule is exerted, this rule is varied then used for generalized explanation structure and thus gets the generalized explanation structure of suicide(x) while establishing the explanation structure of suicide (john). Figure 9.9 demonstrates this process.

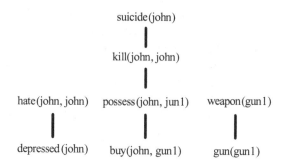

Figure 9.8. Explanation structure of suicide (john)

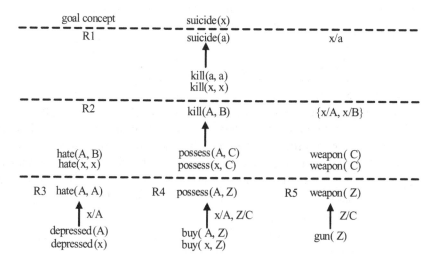

Figure 9.9. Generalization of rule suicide(x)

The generalization of Figure 9.9 is based on regression; the constants should be variable in the predicates.

Another way to implement EGB is on one hand creating the concrete proof structure of suicide (john) and on the other hand getting the generalized explanation structure from suicide (*x*). The connection is that rules concrete example selected are just those generalized explanation need. That is to say, problem space should be searched when establishing concrete example explanation in order to find the usable rules, while creating generalized explanation can do with searching using the rules that the training examples used.

9.7 SOAR Based on Memory Chunks

By the end of 1950s, a model of storage structure was invented by means of using one kind of signals to mark the other signals in neuron simulation. This is the earlier concept of chunks. The chess master kept memory chunks about experiences of playing chess under different circumstances in mind. In the early of 1980s, Newell and Rosenbloom proposed that the system performance can be improved by acquiring knowledge of model problem in task environment and memory chunks can be regarded as the simulation foundation of human action. By means of observing problem solving and acquiring experience memory chunk, the complex process of each sub-goal is substituted and thus ameliorates the speed of the problem solving of the system, thereafter laid a solid foundation for empirical learning.

In 1986, J.E. Laird from the University of Michigan,   Paul S. Rosenbloom from the University of Stanford and A. Newell from Carnegie Mellon University developed SOAR system(Laird et al., 1986), whose learning mechanism is to learn general control knowledge under the guidance of outside expert. The outer guidance can be direct, or an intuitionistic simple question. The system converts the high level information from outer expert into inner presentations and learns to search the memory chunk(Golding et al., 1987). Figure 9.10 presents the architecture of SOAR.

The processing configuration is composed of production memory and decision process. The production memory contains production rule, which can be used for searching control decision. The first step is detailed refinement; all the rules are referred to working memory in order to decide the priorities and which context should be changed and how to change. The second step is to decide the segment and goal that needs to be revised in the context stack.

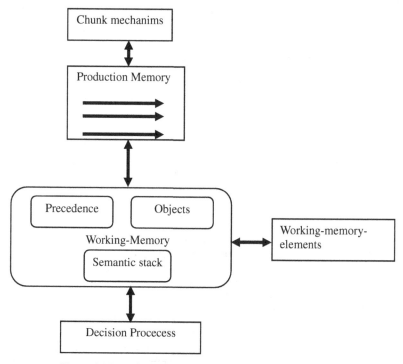

Figure 9.10. Architecture of SOAR(Picture from Laird et al.,1986)

Sometimes because of incompleteness of knowledge, impasse is reached for lack of unique decision. In order to solve this problem, sub-goal and new context are constructed automatically. The capability of problem solved by SOAR can eliminate impasse by choosing problem space, status and operator, create sub-goal for every impasse. We take eight-puzzle problem as an example, the initial status and goal status is revealed in Figure 9.11.

Initial status		
2	3	1
	8	4
7	6	5

Goal status		
1	2	3
8		4
7	6	5

Figure 9.11. Initial and goal status of eight-puzzle problem

The process of the problem solving is shown in Figure 9.12.

1. G_1 solve-eight puzzle
2. P_1 eight-puzzle sd
3. S_1

2	3	1
	8	4
7	6	5

4. O_1 place-blank
5. $=>G_2$ (resolve-no-change)
6. P_2 eight-puzzle
7. S_1
8. $=> G_3$ (resolve-tie-operator)
9. P_3 tie
10. S_2 (left, up, down)
11. O_5 evaluate-objects(O_2 (left))
12. $=>G_4$ (resolve-no-change)
13. P_2 (eight-puzzle)
14. S_1
15. O_2 left
16. S_3

2	3	1
8		4
7	6	5

17. O_2 left
18. S_4
19. S_4
20. O_n place-1

Figure 9.12. Trace of SOAR execution on eight-puzzle(Picture from Laird et al., 1986)

Whenever the problem solver can not solve a problem successfully, system enters into problem space to ask for guidance from experts. The experts supervise in two ways. The first one is to give direct instruction and the system begins to spread all the operators and current status, and experts appoint one operator relying on current conditions. This operator need to be assessed, which is to create a sub-goal and solve this problem by the operator. If there is a solution, the operator is workable and the system then takes the operator and tests why the solution by the operator is correct. The test process is summarized to learn a general condition from the experts, chunk in deed.

Another way is a simple and intuitionistic one. System decomposes the problem into inner presentations according to tree's structure grammatically and the initial statuses are attached, then to ask for help from experts. One simple and intuitionistic advice is given according to outer instruction from experts; they should be similar to the initial problems. Sub-goal is created to solve this problem and the sequences of operators are obtained. The learning mechanism learns the memory chunk based on each sub-goal solving therefore the system can solve the initial problem from memory chunk without asking for guidance.

The memory chunk, which uses working-memory-elements to collect conditions and constructs memory chunk in SOAR system, is the key for learning. When a sub-goal is created for solving a simple problem or assessing the advice from experts, the current statuses are stored into w-m-e. System gets initial statuses of sub-goal from w-m-e and deletes solution operators as the conclusion action after the sub-goal is solved. This generative production rule is memory chunk. If the sub-goal is similar to the sub-goal of the initial problem, memory chunk can be applied to initial problem and the learning strategy can apply what has already learned from one problem to another.

The formation of memory chunk depends on the explanation of sub-goal. The imparting learning is applied when converting the instructions of experts or simple problems into machine executable format. Lastly, experiences obtained from solving simple and intuitionistic problems can be applied to initial problems, which involve analogy learning. Therefore, the way of learning in SOAR system is a comprehensive combination of several learning methods.

9.8 Operationalization

Operationalization is a process of translating a non-operational expression into an operational one. The initial expression might represent a piece of advice or concept which arenonoperational with respect to an agent because they are not expressed in terms of data and actions available to the agent. An operationalizing program faces the task of reformulating the original expression in terms of data and actions that are available to the agent.Operationality criterion is one of the input requirements of EBG. As for operationality criterion, Mitchell, Keller and Kedar-Cabelli pointed out : "concept description should be represented as predicates of training examples and predicates selected from domain theory and easier to assess" (Mtchell et al., 1986). Obviously, this is intuitionistic and simple, only one predicate operational (pid) should be added into domain theory and explain what predicates are operable. However, this kind of processing is static which can not satisfy the demand of practical learning system. Therefore more importance has been attached to how to define the operationality criterion as dynamic, such as introducing theorem prover mechanism to define the operationality criterion dynamically, EBG can even be adopted to change operationality criterion. In this way, inference mechanism should be introduced instead of just enumerating the operable predicates. Rules and facts (premises) are needed to make inferences. This involves some techniques about meta-level programming and the system should be capable of treating with meta-rule. But Turbo Prolog does not support meta-level programming, if operationality criterion is defined as dynamic; some meta-level predicates should be implemented in the system which makes the system support meta-level knowledge. Thereafter we define the operationality criterion as static temporally and store some predefined predicates into inner database.

The aim of operationality criterion is that the learned concept is expected to improve the efficiency of system. Someone believes that if a concept description can be effectively applied to recognize corresponding instance, it will be operable. However the concept description can not only be applied to recognize instance but also space index and so on thus the above viewpoint is not perfect.

Keller defined operationality criterion as follows(Keller, 1987):
Given:

- A concept description
- A performance system that makes use of the description to improve performance
- Performace objectives specifying the type and extent of system improvement desired.

Then the concept description is operable if it satisfies the following conditions:

(1) Useable: the execution system can take advantage of the concept description.

(2) Effectiveness: when the concept description is adopted by the execution system, the execution of system can be improved according to the requirements.

Figure 9.13 illustrates a generalization explanation structure of Safe-to-Stack(x, y).

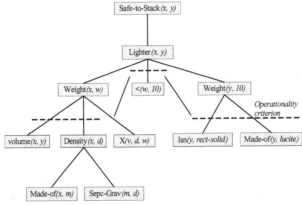

Figure 9.13. Prune of operationality criterion

All the leaf nodes in the explanation structure is operable, a case in point is Made-of(x,m) and Spec-Grav(m,d). Some intermediate nodes might be operable, in the above figure, Density(x,d) is operable. Therefore the operable boundary can be acquired in the figure. All the nodes below the dashed line are operable. As for the intermediate operable nodes, sub-explanation can be deleted from the explanation structure. In the above figure, Made-of(x,m) and Spec-Grav(m,d) should be deleted. This is called "Prune of operationality". The following rules are acquired after explanation in Figure 9.13:

Volume(x,v) $\wedge$ Density(x,d) $\wedge$ X(v,d,w)

$\wedge$ Isa(y,rect-solid) $\wedge$ Made-of(y,lucite)

$\wedge <$ (w,10) $\rightarrow$ Safe-to-Stack(x,y)

As for the disposal of operationality criterion, it is a little too complex. Only the confirmation of operationality criterion involves more aspects and this will affect the performance of the learning system directly, consequently it is a rather important problem.

There is no precise definition of operationality criterion among lots of systems. Many systems take it for granted that operationality criterion should be independent and static. The static standard proposed by DeJong & Mooney can not satisfy the requirements and the operationality criterion should be the function that can prove structure in terms of an example, that is to say, operationality criterion should be dynamic. For instance, predicate of end-point for the generalized explanation structure should be operable; the operationality can also be defined by a theorem prover mechanism. EBG can even be applied to decide operationality. Anyway, the operationality criterion must reflect the computation cost and benefit of learning, and make sure the computation cost ought not to higher than the benefit. However, the initial EBL leaves out this. It is generally believed that knowledge learned from EBL problem solver system can certainly improve performance of the system, but this is too optimistic and simply. Generally speaking, EBL often implements heuristic strategy, which can not guarantee the improvement under all circumstances. For instance, the learning of STRIPS MACROPS is actually deteriorates efficiency. If the accumulated time of testing premise of macro-operator exceeds the saving time by using macro-operator for searching, then the overall performance is lowered. Hence it is obvious that operationality is no doubt completely independent with system.

There is no doubt EBG proposed by Mitchell et.al is an intuitionist way to test the practically of explanation explicitly by operationality criterion. But as DeJong and Mooney pointed out the above operationality criterion only include a small portion of predicates and only the new knowledge can be assessed directly but not test its usefulness. As in the example of EBG, operationality criterion requires that explanation must go on until it's calculable directly or the properties can be observed directly. META-LEX considers the learning environment; making cost of testing a property change with the system knowledge thereafter operationality criterion becomes dynamic instead of static. PRODIGY further improves the definition of operationality criterion.

9.8.1 *Utility of PRODIGY*

PRODIGY gets knowledge from experience analysis and interaction with experts. Its learning aim is to obtain the goal concept with regard to problem solving such as to learn goal concepts of successful, unsuccessful, and preferred. The typical domain of problem solving is JSP (Job scheduling problem) which converts the raw material by LATHE, CLAMP, POLISH operations as to become products. The learning task for PRODIGY is to summarize under what circumstances a particular operation is successful or unsuccessful. One peculiarity of this system is that by adding some control rules, its efficiency is improved and the solution's quality is amended. Meanwhile, new search which can not be obtained without adding searching path considering efficiency can be found now. As for operationality, PRODIGY requires that the learned knowledge should be able to improve efficiency of problem solving and the control knowledge is not only feasible but also applicable. Hence, the operationality includes applicability: the learned control rule is not only feasible which means it can exert but also the rule is capable of improving system performance. The applicability is defined as:

$$\text{Utility} = (\text{AvrSavings} \times \text{ApplicFreq}) - \text{AvrMatchCost} \tag{9.1}$$

And :

AvrMatchCost = average cost for matching the rule

AvrSavings = average saved time while applying the rule

ApplicFreq = frequency of application of the rule

When a control rule is learned, PRODIGY will preserve the statistical information of its usage to decide its utility. If the utility value of the rule is negative, this rule needs giving up. The operationality is to a large extent represented by utility from this point of view. Therefore operationality can be quantified and it should not be predefined but the value should be determined dynamically during the system execution.

It is helpful for constructing general EBL and makes the evaluation of operationality more mature to ascribe utility into operationality. Most of the previous systems define operationality from the efficiency to recognize training examples which is far more from adequate as for a general definition. For one thing, the definition of operationality assumes concept description will be applied to recognize training examples. Actually the concept description can be useful in other ways, for instance the generalization of training examples. For another, most systems recognize training examples and assess operationality by execution time but virtually there are different aspects of efficiency to assess the performance, such as space efficiency. It is operable considering time efficiency while inoperable when considering space efficiency. Besides efficiency, there are cost, simpleness etc which may affect the operationality, are related to performance

9.8.2 Operationality of SOAR

SOAR, which is developed by Laird, Newell and Rosembloom, introduces a different way of defining operationality criterion. It is not developed as a single EBL system, but only attempts to implement a general cognitive structure by means of an independent learning mechanism chunking. The operation of chunking is to sum up the examined information when dealing with each sub-goal. This is very similar to EBL, and it seems that EBL can be implemented in SOAR by chunking. The input of chunking is the linear sequences or tree-like sequences of operators. The task of the system is to convert the operators into meta-operators or chunk. SOAR mainly uses chunking to obtain knowledge thereafter leave out the utility. On one hand it is supposed that chunking obtains knowledge automatically and on the other hand the performance of SOAR is measured according to the number of choices made when completing a task. Since chunking can reduce the amount of choices, it is worth while according to performance formula. In fact, each choice itself may be complicated; hence the amount of choice is not proportional to the execution time of mainframe without considering this.

9.8.3 Operationality of MRS-EBG

Hirsh implemented MRS-EBG in the logical programming system; the operationality criterion is provable based on meta-inference of MRS. In MRS, the proof strategy can be illustrated with meta-theory. For instance, meta-rule can be used to elaborate on this kind of rule: it is more possible to choose a proof path which takes advantage of arithmetic predicates. Predicates contained in MRS can show this property. Therefore it is easy to show the following operationality rule:

Arithmetic_Predicates $(pred(arg_1, arg_n))$-operational$(pred(arg_1, arg_5))$

Hirsh believed that the previous EBG generated the explanation structure of an example and the generalized explanation structure. However, there is no operationality inference when the explanation structure is created, the operationality should be determined and explanation structure can be changed in generalization. Operationality is used to delete explanation structure during generalization and the rules are formed from gained structure. Though most of generalization is achieved during explanation, there is still no combination of explanation and generalization

In MRS-EBG, operationality is determined during explanation. Once a branch is terminated due to lack of operationality, backtrack immediately, and search for another proof which can create an operationality concept definition of this branch. Therefore, the operationality of goal concept can be found eventually.

9.8.4 Operationality of META-LEX

In META-LEX, operationality considers factors of system performance. The basic idea is to assess the operationality by experience: system uses concept description and checks whether action of the system attains initial goals of the system. META-LEX learns a set of steps in problem solving forwardly, or the description of the set. If the performance does not attain the expected level, META-LEX can assess to what extent the description is executable, and it can also illustrate if the searching direction is right. This kind of assessing operationality is dynamic. It depends on the current status and the current goal of performance. What is more, this assessment can generate measurement and efficiency. But this cost much for the system must be tested once operationality is assessed.

The operationality is vital to EBL system. However, current methods to detect operationality depend on whether the performance hypothesis can be simplified (these hypothesis are easy to be broken). Though researchers from home and abroad are seeking for effective methods for dealing with simplification, most of the research only treats with theory application while in real applications it is hard to get a satisfied answer. There is still a long way to go for investigation.

9.9 EBL with imperfect domain theory

9.9.1 Imperfect domain theory

One of the most important problems in EBL is domain theory. As the premise of EBL, domain theory should be complete and correct. These demands are often hard to meet in real applications and in reality domain theory is always incomplete and incorrect. If the domain theory can not explain the training example, the existing EBG will be invalid.

The imperfect of domain theory may involve the following conditions:

(1) Incomplete: Lack of rules and knowledge in the domain theory thus no explanation of training example can be given.

(2) Incorrect: Some rules in the domain theory is unreasonable thus incorrect explanation might be created.

(3) Intractable: Domain theory is too complex; the existing resource can not afford to create an explanation tree for training examples.

In order to solve the problem of imperfect domain theory, we make some attempts in inverting resolution and deep knowledge based approach.

9.9.2 Inverting Resolution

Resolution theorem in first order logic is the foundation of machine theorem proving and the main way to construct explanation in EBL(Muggleton etal., 1988).

Resolution theorem: Let C_1, C_2 be two clauses without any common variables. L_1, L_2 are two literals of C_1 and C_2 respectively, if there is a most general unifier σ, then clause

$$C = (C_1 - \{L_1\}) \sigma \cup (C_2 - \{L_2\}) \sigma \qquad (9.2)$$

is the resolution clause of C_1 and C_2.

Inverting resolution deals with that given C and C_1 how to obtain C_2. In propositional logic, $\sigma = \Phi$, so the inverting clause (9.2) can be converted into:

$$C = (C_1 \cup C_2) - \{L_1, L_2\} \qquad (9.3)$$

From formula (9.3), the following formulas can be concluded:

(1) if $C_1 \cap C_2 = \varnothing$, then $C_2 = (C - C_1) \cup \{L_2\}$

(2) if $C_1 \cap C_2 \neq \varnothing$, C_2 needs to contain the arbitrary sub-set of $C_1 - \{L_1\}$, therefore, generally speaking:

$$C_{2i} = (C - C_1) \cup \{L_2\} \cup S_{1i} \qquad (9.4)$$

Here, $S_{1i} \in P (C_1 - \{L_1\}$, $P(x)$ represents the power set of set x.

It is obvious if there are n literals in C_1, the number of solution for C_2 is 2n-1.

In the first order logic, let $\sigma = \theta_1 \theta_2$, θ_1 and θ_2 satisfy:

(1) The variable domain of θ_1 and θ_2 is domain of C_1 and domain of C_2 respectively.

(2) $L_1 \theta_1 = L_2 \theta_2$

Therefore:

$$C_2 = (C - (C_1 - \{L_1\}) \theta_1) \theta_2^{-1} \cup \{\overline{L_1}\} \theta_1 \theta_2^{-1}$$

$$= ((C - (C_1 - \{\theta_1\}) \theta_1) \cup \{\overline{L_1}\} \theta_1)) \theta_2^{-1} \qquad (9.5)$$

C_1 is unit literal, that is when $C_1 = \{L_1\}$,

$$C_2 = (C \cup \{\overline{L_1}\}\theta_1)\theta_2^{-1} \qquad (9.6)$$

θ_2^{-1} is inverse substitution, which is the only inverse substitution θ^{-1} satisfied with $t\theta\theta^{-1} = t$ given term and literal t and substitution θ. What is more, if $\theta = \{v_1/t_1,\ldots,v_n/t_n\}$, then:

$$\theta^{-1} = \{(t_1,\{P_{1,1},\ldots P_{1,m1}\})/v_1,\ldots,(t_n,\{P_{n,1},\ldots,P_{n,mn}\}/v_n) \qquad (9.7)$$

Here, $P_{i,mj}$ is the position of variable v_i in t. Inverting resolution substitute all t_i on the position of of with v_i $\{P_{i,1},\ldots,P_{i,mi}\}$ in t.

EBL aims to construct an explanation tree with regard to training examples from the initial description of goal concept by taking advantages of domain theory (stored in the knowledge base). The whole process is generally based on goal-driven inference. When the learning fails caused by explanation can not continue lack of some particular rule, inverting resolution is used to overcome this problem(Haibo Ma, 1990).

Domain theory (knowledge base) is represented by production rule. Some pre-processing needs to be done to knowledge base to create a dependent tree describing the relationship of rules. Therefore, domain theory is made up of a group of generation rules and a dependent table.

The dependent table is the denotation of relationships among predicates based on rules of the knowledge base. The table includes rules and semantic information about predicates. A simple example is given to show the structure of dependent table.

Knowledge base:

Rule 1.Sentence (S_0, S):- noun-phrase (S_0, S_1),
verb-phrase (S_1,S).

Rule 2.noun-phrase (S_0, S):-determiner (S_0, S_1),
noun (S_1, S).

Rule 3.noun-phrase (S_0, S):-name (S_0, S).

Rule 4.verb-phrase (S_0, S):-intransitive-verb (S_0, S).

The dependent table is as following:

Table 9.2

Predicate symbol	Head	Body	Basic predicate
sentence	1		Intransitive-verb, name, determiner, noun
noun-phrase	2,3	1	Name, determiner, noun
verb-phrase	4	1	Intransitive-verb

The basic predicates are those that meet the need of operationality criterion. The first column is all inoperable predicates. We will not make further description in terms of constructing the dependent table. The followings are two algorithms which completes the EBL.

Algorithm 9.3 Algorithm of generation of explanation tree

1. Inference backwardly from goal concept, extend the explanation tree gradually, the tree is and/or tree.
2. Inverting resolution algorithm is called when a failed node is met.
3. Analyze the complete explanation tree and generalize to get a new description of goal concept.

Algorithm 9.4 Algorithm of Inverting Resolution

1. If the current failed node F is operable, then backtracking; if F is inoperable, go to step 2.
2. The predicate symbol of node P corresponds to node F is Pred , check out if there is other path for Pred based on dependent table, if there is no, go to step 4.
3. Check other paths or nodes of Pred in the dependent table whether their corresponding operable predicates (basic predicates) can be satisfied by the training example.
   ① If there is a path stratifies the training example, then choose this path, explanation tree is completed, end the algorithm.
   ② The corresponding operable predicates (basic property) of the rest of the path or node of Pred in the dependent tree collide with training example or the training example does not contain the path, go to step 4.
4. Infer all sub-nodes of node P except node F; go back to node F after dealing with all the sub-nodes.
5. Apply inverting resolution to unused training properties to get a pseudo rule between node F and the rest of properties, the creation of whole explanation tree is completed, end of algorithm.

The algorithm described here can complete the EBL without perfect domain theory, which is just short of very few rules. If the domain theory is so scatted that can not form a complete knowledge structure, this algorithm will fail and resort to ways of constructing knowledge base and tools, or to exert inductive learning or analogy learning.

Last but not the least, although this algorithm can do the EBL, it lacks some rules and thus introduces some inaccurate factors, the truth of the whole explanation tree might be influenced and the identical truth can not be held as for the explanation. If confidence can be added to the explanation tree, the distinction can be made from the learning based on perfect domain theory when consider the value and transmission of confidence.

9.9.3 *Deep knowledge based approach*

Domain theory of fault diagnosis is often imperfect. How to refine the knowledge base of fault diagnosis is an important problem. A learning model that used for malfunction diagnosis of distillation columns based on deep knowledge is proposed (Cuiying Lv,1994). The construction of the model can be divided into four steps: instance explanation, hypothesis generation, hypothesis confirmation and extension. The model can discover new fault which the existing knowledge can not find and pursue correct diagnosis. The process of learning based on deep knowledge can be generalized as:

1. An instance is presented by the environment.
2. Explanation of instances: explain the instance based on EBL. The explanation may succeed or not. Success means it is explainable according to domain knowledge of the system; otherwise it can not be explainable by means of domain knowledge. If successful, go to step 5 for extension, else go to step 3 to generate hypothesis. The explanation tree is created to explain. If successful there will be a perfect explanation tree otherwise the explanation tree is imperfect.
3. Hypothesis generation: System attempts to confirm the absence of knowledge based on current instance. When the knowledge absence is found, a hypothesis that can remedy the knowledge absence is created, the goal-end of the hypothesis is replaced with the absence-end and the data-end of the hypothesis is substituted with data-end of the input instance. Then go to step 4 hypothesis confirmation.
4. Hypothesis confirmation: Deep knowledge base is used. Search for the relationship between the goal-end of hypothesis and data-end in the deep knowledge base. That is attempting to confirm whether there are some common properties between he goal-end of hypothesis and data-end in the deep knowledge base. This could be successful or not. If it fails, return to step 3 hypothesis generation and get a new hypothesis, if it is successful, go to step 5 extension.
5. Extension: Extend the confirmed hypothesis. The consequence of extension is that some more generalized hypothesis can be acquired. The whole process of extension is made up of two phases: the first one is to vary constants of hypothesis maximumly while the second step is to extend the hypothesis to get one or more generalized concepts.

6. The extended hypothesis is delivered to execution units.

Exercises

1. What is Explanation-based learning? What are the advantage and disadvantage of EBL compared with inductive learning?
2. Briefly illustrate three different spaces involved in EBL and the relationship among them.
3. Illustrate the generalization process of EBL, and elaborate on the function of goal concept, training example, domain theory and operationality criterion in learning.
4. Compare the basic idea of EBG and EBS.
5. Construct domain theory for EBL based on problems you selected. Apply these theories to some training instances and explain the EBL.
6. Illustrate the definition of operationality criterion and the way to make operationality criterion dynamically.
7. Illustrate the solving strategy of EBL in incomplete domain theory.
8. Suppose C=Son (Bob, Ram), C1=Daughter (Bob, Ram), determine C2 according to inductive logical programming.

Chapter 10

Reinforcement Learning

10.1 Introduction

People often learn by interacting with outside environment. Reinforcement learning (RL) is a computational approach to the study of learning from interaction. RL is the learning of a mapping from situations to actions so as to maximize a scalar reward of reinforcement signal. The learner does not need to be directly told which actions to take, as in most forms of machine learning, but instead discover which actions yield the most reward by trying them. In the most interesting and challenging cases, an action may affect not only the immediate reward, but also the next situation, and consequently all subsequent rewards. These two characteristics— trial-and-error and delayed reinforcement—are the two most important distinguishing characteristics of RL.

Reinforcement learning is not defined by characterizing learning methods, but by characterizing a learning problem. Any method that is well suited to solving that problem, we consider to be a reinforcement learning method. RL addresses the question of how an autonomous agent that senses and acts in its environment can learn to choose optimal actions to achieve its goals. RL is very different from supervised learning, the kind of learning studied in almost all current research in machine learning, statistical pattern recognition, and artificial neural networks. Supervised learning is learning under the tutelage of a knowledgeable supervisor, or "teacher", which explicitly tells the learning agent how it should respond to training inputs. RL concerns a family of problems in which an agent evolves while analyzing consequences of its actions, with a simple scalar signal (the reinforcement) given out by the environment.

The study of RL develops into an unusually multi-disciplinary field; it includes researches specializing in artificial intelligence, psychology, control engineering, statistical research, and so on. RL has particularly rich roots in the psychology of animal learning, from which it takes its name. A number of impressive applications of RL have also been developed. RL has attracted much research in the past decade. Its incremental nature and adaptive capabilities make it suitable for use in various domains, such as automatic control, mobile robotics and multi-agent system. Particularly with the breakthrough of the mathematical basis of reinforcement learning, the application of RL increasingly conducted, as one of the hot spots of the current research in the field of machine learning.

The history of reinforcement learning had two main threads, both long and rich, which were pursued independently before intertwining into modern reinforcement learning. One thread concerned learning by trial and error and started in the psychology of animal learning. This thread run through some of the earliest work in artificial intelligence and led to the revival of reinforcement learning in the early 1980s. The other thread concerned the problem of optimal control and its solution using value functions and dynamic programming. For the most part, this thread did not involve learning. Although the two threads were largely independent, the exceptions revolve around a third, less distinct thread concerning temporal-difference methods. All three threads came together in the late 1980s to produce the modern field of reinforcement learning.

In early artificial intelligence, before it was distinct from other branches of engineering, several researchers began to explore trial-and-error learning as an engineering principle. The earliest computational investigations of trial-and-error learning were perhaps by Minsky and Farley and Clark, both in 1954. In his Ph.D. dissertation, Minsky discussed computational models of reinforcement learning and described his construction of an analog machine; composed of components he called SNARCs (Stochastic Neural-Analog Reinforcement Calculators). Farley and Clark described another neural-network learning machine designed to learn by trial-and-error. In the 1960s one finds the terms "reinforcement" and "reinforcement learning" being widely used in the engineering literature for the first time. Particularly influential was Minsky's paper "Steps Toward Artificial Intelligence"(Minsky,1961), which discussed several issues relevant to reinforcment learning, including what he called the credit-assignment problem: how do you distribute credit for success among the many decisions that may have been involved in producing it? In 1969 Minsky got Turing Award in computer due to above contribution.

In 1994 and 1995 the interests of Farley and Clark shifted from trial-and-error learning to generalization and pattern recognition, that is, from reinforcement learning to supervised learning. This began a pattern of confusion about the relationship between these types of learning. Many researchers seemed to believe that they were studying reinforcement learning when they were actually studying supervised learning. For example, neural-network pioneers such as Rosenblatt (1958) and Widrow and Hoff (1960) were clearly motivated by reinforcement learning---they used the language of rewards and punishments---but the systems they studied were supervised learning systems suitable for pattern recognition and perceptual learning. Even today, researchers and textbooks often minimize or blur the distinction between these types of learning. Some modern neural-network textbooks use the term trial-and-error to describe networks that learn from training examples because they use error information to update connection weights. This is an understandable confusion, but it substantially misses the essential optional character of trial-and-error learning.

The term "optimal control" came into use in the late 1950s to describe the problem of designing a controller to minimize a measure of a dynamical system's behavior over time. One of the approaches to this problem was developed in the mid-1950s by Richard Bellman and colleagues by extending a 19th century theory of Hamilton and Jacobi. This approach uses the concept of a dynamical system's state and a value function, or "optimal return function" to define a functional equation, now often called the Bellman equation. The class of methods for solving optimal control problems by solving this equation came to be known as dynamic programming (Bellman,1957). Bellman also introduced the discrete stochastic version of the optimal control problem known as Markovian decision processes (MDPs), and Ron Howard devised the policy iteration method for MDPs in 1960. All of these are essential elements underlying the theory and algorithms of modern reinforcement learning.

Finally, the temporal-difference and optimal control threads were fully brought together in 1989 with Chris Watkins's development of Q-learning (Watkins et al.,1989) This work extended and integrated prior work in all three threads of reinforcement learning research. By the time of Watkins's work there had been tremendous growth in reinforcement learning research, primarily in the machine learning subfield of artificial intelligence, but also in neural networks and artificial intelligence more broadly. In 1992, the remarkable success of Gerry Tesauro's backgammon playing program, TD-Gammon(Tesauro, 1992), brought additional attention to the field. Other important contributions made in the recent history of reinforcement learning were too numerous to mention in this brief account; we cite these at the end of the individual chapters in which they arise.

10.2 Reinforcement Learning Model

The reinforcement learning problem is meant a straightforward framing of the problem of learning from interaction to achieve a goal. The learner or decision-maker is called the agent. The thing it interacts with, comprising everything outside the agent, is called the environment. These interact continually, the agent selecting actions and the environment responding to those actions and presenting new situations to the agent. The model of RL is illustrated in Figure 10.1.

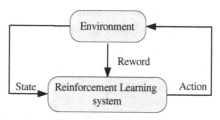

Fig. 10.1. Reinforcement learning model

More specifically, the agent exists in an environment described by some set of possible state S .It can perform any of a set of possible action A. Each time it performs an action at in some sate st the agent receives a real-valued reward r_t that indicates the immediate value of this state-action transition. This produces a sequence of states s_i, actions ai and immediate rewards r_i. The task of the agent is to learn a control policy $\pi:S \rightarrow A$, that maximizes the expected sum of these rewards, with future rewards discounted exponentially by their delay. The agent's goal, roughly speaking, is to maximize the total amount of reward it receives over the long run, as shown in Formula 10.1. In learning, the principle of RL is: if the reward is positive, strengthen the action later, otherwise, weaken the action.

$$\sum_{i=0}^{\infty} \gamma^i r_{t+i} \qquad 0 < \gamma \leq 1 \qquad (10.1)$$

A reinforcement learning task that satisfies the Markov property is called a Markov decision process, or MDP. If the state and action spaces are finite, then it is called a finite Markov decision process (finite MDP). Finite MDPs are particularly important to the theory of reinforcement learning.

Markov decision process: *A markov decision process is defined by a 4-tuples <S, A, R, P>, where S is a set of possible state, A is a set of possible action,*

R is the reward function (R: S×A→$\mathcal{R}$), and P is the state transition function (P:

S×A→PD (S)).R(s, a, s') is the immediate reward after transition to state s' from

state s by performing action a. P(s, a, s') is the probability that action a in state s

will lead to state s'. The task of the agent is to learn a policy, π:S → A, for

selecting its next action at based on current observed state st, that is, π(st)=at.

The nature of Markov property is: given the state of the MDP at time t is known, transition probabilities to the state at time t + 1 are independent of all previous states or actions. If transition function P and reward function R are known, dynamic programming could be used to acquire the optimal policy. However, RL focuses on the solution of optimal policy when P and R are unknown.

Fig. 10.2. Four components of RL

To solve this problem, Figure 10.2 shows the relationship of the four basic components of RL: policy π, state transition function (value function) P, reward function R and environment model. The bottom-up relations of the four elements of are the pyramid structure. In any given moment, the policy defines the main method of choice and action of the agent. This policy can be adopted by a group of production rules, or a simple table to find it. As pointed out earlier, under specific circumstances, the policy may need extensive search for a model or plan to process the results. It can also be random. The policy is the main component part of learning agents, as it is sufficient to produce action at any time.

The policy is the decision-making function of the agent, specifying what action it takes in each of the situations that it might encounter. In psychology, this would correspond to the set of stimulus-response rules or associations. This is the core of a reinforcement agent, as suggested by Figure 10.2, because it alone is sufficient to define a full, behaving agent. The other components serve only to change and improve the policy. The policy itself is the ultimate determinant of behavior and performance. In general it may be stochastic.

The reward function defines the goal of the RL agent. The agent's objective is to maximize the reward that it receives over the long run. The reward function thus defines what are good and bad events for the agent. Rewards are the immediate and defining features of the problem faced by the agent. As such, the reward function must necessarily be fixed. It may, however, be used as a basis for changing the policy. For example, if an action selected by the policy is followed by low reward then the policy may be changed to select some other action in that situation in the future.

Whereas reward indicates what is good in an immediate sense, the transition function specifies what is good in the long run, that is, because it predicts reward. The difference between value and reward is critical to RL. For example, when playing chess, checkmating your opponent is associated with high reward, but winning his queen is associated with high value. The former defines the true goal of the task – winning the game – whereas the latter just predicts this true goal. Learning the value of states, or of state-action pairs, is the critical step in the RL methods.

The fourth and final major component of a RL agent is a model of its environment or external world. This is something that mimics the behavior of the environment in some sense. Not every RL agent uses model of the environment. Methods that never learn or use a model are called model-free RL methods. Model-free methods are very simple and, perhaps surprisingly, are still generally able to find optimal behavior. Model-based methods just find it faster. The most interesting case is that in which the agent does not have a perfect model of the environment a priori, but must use learning methods to align it with reality.

The system environment is defined by the environment model. Because the model of P and R function are unknown, the system can only rely on the immediate reward received by each trial and error to choose policies. The objective is to find a policy that, roughly speaking, maximizes the total reward received. In the simplest formulation, the tradeoff between immediate and delayed reward is handled by a discount rate $0 \leq \gamma < 1$. The value of following a policy π from a state s is defined as the expectation of the sum of the subsequent rewards, r_1, r_2 . . ., each discounted geometrically by its delay as follows:

$$R_t = r_{t+1} + \gamma r_{t+2} + \gamma^2 r_{t+3} + \cdots = r_{t+1} + \gamma R_{t+1} \qquad (10.2)$$

$$V^\pi(s) = E_\pi\{R_t | s_t = s\} = E_\pi\{r_{t+1} + \gamma V(s_{t+1}) | s_t = s\} = \sum_a \pi(s,a) \sum_{s'} P_{ss'}^a \left[R_{ss'}^a + \gamma V^\pi(s')\right] \qquad (10.3)$$

Values determine a partial ordering over policies, whereby $\pi_1 \geq \pi_2$ if and only if $V_{\pi 1}(s) \geq V_{\pi 2}(s)$, $\forall s$. Ideally, we seek an optimal policy π^*, one that is great or equal than all others. All such policies share the same optimal value function. According to Bellman optimality equations, the value function $V^*(s)$ of optimal policy π^* at state s could be defined as follows.

$$V^*(s) = \max_{a \in A(s)} E\{r_{t+1} + \gamma V^*(s_{t+1}) | s_t = s, a_t = a\}$$

$$= \max_{a \in A(s)} \sum_{s'} P_{ss'}^a \left[R_{ss'}^a + \gamma V^*(s')\right] \qquad (10.4)$$

Dynamic programming methods involve iteratively updating an approximation to the optimal value function. If the state-transition function P and the expected rewards R are known, a typical example is value iteration, which starts with an arbitrary policy π_0, and then

$$\pi_k(s) = \arg\max_a \sum_{s'} P_{ss'}^a \left[R_{ss'}^a + \gamma V^{\pi_{k-1}}(s')\right] \qquad (10.5)$$

$$V^{\pi_k}(s) \leftarrow \sum_a \pi_{k-1}(s,a) \sum_{s'} P_{ss'}^a \left[R_{ss'}^a + \gamma V^{\pi_{k-1}}(s')\right] \qquad (10.6)$$

In RL, without knowledge of the system's dynamics, we cannot compute the expected value by Equation (10.5) and (10.6). It is necessary to estimate the value by iteratively updating an approximation to the optimal value function, and Monte Carlo sampling is one of the basic methods. Keeping policy π, iteratively using Equation (10.7) to obtain approximate solutions.

$$V(s_t) \leftarrow V(s_t) + \alpha \left[R_t - V(s_t)\right] \qquad (10.7)$$

Combining Monte Carlo method and dynamic programming method, equation (10.8) gives the iterative equation of Temporal-difference learning (TD).

$$V(s_t) \leftarrow V(s_t) + \alpha \left[r_{t+1} + \gamma V(s_{t+1}) - V(s_t)\right] \qquad (10.8)$$

10.3 Dynamic Programming

The term dynamic programming (DP) refers to a collection of algorithms that can be used to compute optimal policies given a perfect model of the environment as a Markov decision process (MDP). Classical DP algorithms are of limited utility in RL because of their assumption of a perfect model and their great computational expense, but they are still important theoretically. DP provides an essential foundation for the understanding of the methods presented in the rest of this book. In fact, all of these methods can be viewed as attempts to achieve the same effect as DP, with less computation and without assuming a perfect model of the environment.

First we consider how to compute the state-value function V^{π} for an arbitrary policy π. This is called policy evaluation in the DP literature. We also refer to it as the prediction problem. For all s in S,

$$V^{\pi}(s) = \sum_a \pi(a \mid s) \times \sum_{s'} \pi(s \to s' \mid a) \times (R^a(s \to s') + \gamma(V^{\pi}(s'))) \tag{10.9}$$

where $\pi(a \mid s)$ is the probability of taking action a in state s under policy π, and the expectations are subscripted by π to indicate that they are conditional on π being followed. The existence and uniqueness of V^{π} are guaranteed as long as either $\gamma < 1$ or eventual termination is guaranteed from all states under the policy π. Fig. 10.3 illustrates the first step of the computing process, and the three subsequence state of s_t are all known. As for policy π, the probability of the action a is $\pi(a \mid s)$. For each state, the environment may respond to one of the states to s' with a reward r. Bellman equation is adopted to average the probability of these, without weight. It is noted that the value of starting state must look forward to the discount value of the next state, γ, and the reward obtained with the path. In dynamic programming, if n and m are the number of states and action, although the total number of the policy is nm, a dynamic planning method can be guaranteed in polynomial time to find the optimal strategy. In this sense, dynamic programming strategy is faster than any of the direct search index-class, and has polynomial time of action and states. However, if the state is based on the exponential growth of certain variables, of course, it will also appear dimensions of the disaster.

In dynamic programming iterative equation (10.10) can be derived from equation (10.4) :

$$V_{t+1}(s) \leftarrow \underset{a}{\text{MAX}} \sum_{s'} P^a_{ss'} [\mathfrak{R}^a_{ss'} + \gamma V_t(s')] \tag{10.10}$$

$V_t(s) \rightarrow V^*(s)$ When $t \rightarrow \infty$. The award evaluation will be acquired until $|\Delta V|$ less than a small positive number if repeat and make iteration to each state.

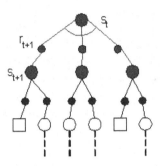

Fig. 10.3. Dynamic programming method

The typical model of dynamic programming model has limited usage, as many problems are difficult to give the integral model of the environment. For example, simulation robot soccer is such a problem, which can be solved by real-time dynamic programming methods. In real-time dynamic programming, the environment model is not required to give first, but get the environment model by testing in a real environment. The use of anti-nerve-state network can be used for generalization of states. The input unit of the network is the state of the environment s. The output of the network is the evaluation of the state V(s).

DP methods update estimates of the values of states based on estimates of the values of successor states. That is, they update estimates on the basis of other estimates. We call this general idea bootstrapping. Many reinforcement learning methods perform bootstrapping, even those that do not require, as DP requires, a complete and accurate model of the environment. In the next chapter we explore reinforcement learning methods that do not require a model and do not bootstrap. In the chapter after that we explore methods that do not require a model but do bootstrap. These key features and properties are separable, yet can be mixed in interesting combinations.

10.4 Monte Carlo Methods

Monte Carlo methods are a class of computational algorithms that rely on repeated random sampling to compute their results. Monte Carlo methods are often used when simulating physical and mathematical systems. Because of their reliance on repeated computation and random or pseudo-random numbers, Monte Carlo methods are most suited to calculation by a computer. Monte Carlo methods tend to be used when it is infeasible or impossible to compute an exact result with a deterministic algorithm. Unlike DP, the Monte Carlo methods do not assume complete knowledge of the environment. Monte Carlo methods require only experience--sample sequences of states, actions, and rewards from on-line or simulated interaction with an environment. Although a model is required, the model need only generate sample transitions, not the complete probability distributions of all possible transitions that are required by dynamic programming (DP) methods. The term Monte Carlo method was coined in the 1940s by physicists working on nuclear weapon projects in the Los Alamos National Laboratory.

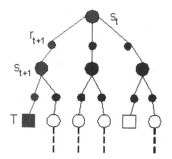

Fig. 10.4. Monte Carlo Methods

Monte Carlo methods are ways of solving the reinforcement learning problem based on averaging sample returns. There is no single Monte Carlo method; instead, the term describes a large and widely-used class of approaches. However, these approaches tend to follow a particular pattern:

(1) Define a domain of possible inputs.
(2) Generate inputs randomly from the domain, and perform a deterministic computation on them.
(3) Aggregate the results of the individual computations into the final result.

Here we use it specifically for methods based on averaging complete returns (as opposed to methods that learn from partial returns, considered in the next chapter). Fig. 10.4 gives the return reward by Monte Carlo sampling for one step during learning. Then through iterative learning, the actual obtained rewards are used to approximate the real value function.

Monte Carlo methods do not assume complete knowledge of the environment, but learn from on-line experience. Monte Carlo methods are ways of solving the reinforcement learning problem based on averaging sample returns. Given policy π, compute V^{π}: subsequence state s_t under policyπ, $R_t(s_t)$ is the long reward return, add $R_t(s_t)$ to the list R_{si}, $V(s_t) \leftarrow average(R_{si})$.

The list could use incremental implementation,

$$V(s_t) \leftarrow V(s_t) + \frac{R_t(s_t) - V(s_t)}{N_{s_t} + 1}$$

$$N_{s_t} \leftarrow N_{s_t} + 1$$

(10.11)

Under Monte Carlo control, policy evaluation and improvement use the same random policy as.

$$a^* \leftarrow \arg\max_a Q(s,a)$$

$$\pi(s,a) \leftarrow \begin{cases} 1 - e + \dfrac{e}{|A(s)|}, & a = a^* \\[3mm] \dfrac{e}{|A(s)|}, & a \neq a^* \end{cases}$$

(10.12)

In learning, if some actions are found to be good, then what action should the agent select in the next decision-making? One consideration is making full use of existing knowledge, select the current best action. But it has a drawback: maybe some better actions are not found; in contrast, if the agent always tests new actions, it will lead to no progress. The agent faces a tradeoff in choosing whether to favor exploration of unknown actions (to gather new information), or exploitation of existing actions that it has already learned will yield high reward (to maximize its cumulative reward). These are two main methods: e-greedy method and genetic simulated annealing. The selection probability of each action is related to its Q value:

$$p(a\mid s)=\frac{e^{Q(s,a)/T}}{\sum_{a'}e^{Q(s,a')/T}} \qquad (10.13)$$

10.5 Temporal-Difference Learning

Temporal-difference (TD) learning is a combination of Monte Carlo ideas and dynamic programming (DP) ideas. Like Monte Carlo methods, TD methods can learn directly from raw experience without a model of the environment's dynamics. TD resembles a Monte Carlo method because it learns by sampling the environment according to some policy. TD is related to dynamic programming techniques because it approximates its current estimate based on previously learned estimates (a process known as bootstrapping). TD learning algorithm is related to the Temporal difference model of animal learning.

As a prediction method, TD learning takes into account the fact that subsequent predictions are often correlated in some sense. In standard supervised predictive learning, one only learns from actually observed values: a prediction is made, and when the observation is available, the prediction is adjusted to better match the observation. TD(0) is the simplest case of temporal-difference learning as described as follows.

Algorithm 10.1 TD(0) learning algorithm.

Initialize $V(s)$ arbitrarily, π to the policy to be evaluated
Repeat (for each episode)
   Initialize s
   Repeat (for each step of episode)
   Choose a from s using policy π derived from V(e.g., ε-greedy)
   Take action a, observer r, s'
   $V(s)\leftarrow V(s)+\alpha\left[r+\gamma V(s')-V(s)\right]$
   $s\leftarrow s'$
  Until s is terminal

TD(0) learning algorithm contains two steps: determine the new action policy according to the current value function, and evaluate the action policy by the immediate reward under the new action policy. The learning process is as follows:

$$v_0 \rightarrow \pi_1 \rightarrow v_1 \rightarrow \pi_2 \rightarrow \cdots \rightarrow v^* \rightarrow \pi^* \rightarrow v^*$$

Until the value function and the policy reach the stable value. In TD learning, the computation of value function is shown in Figure 10.5.

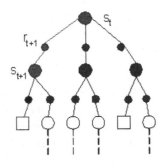

Fig. 10.5. Temporal-difference Learning Method

To illustrate the general idea of reinforcement learning and contrast it with other approaches, we consider the familiar child's game of tic-tac-toe. Two players take turns playing on a three-by-three board. One player plays ◇s and the other Os until one player wins by placing three marks in a row, horizontally, vertically, or diagonally.

If the board fills up with neither player getting three in a row, the game is a draw. Because a skilled player can play so as never to lose, let us assume that we are playing against an imperfect player, one whose play is sometimes incorrect and allows us to win. For the moment, in fact, let us consider draws and losses to be equally bad for us. How might we construct a player that will find the imperfections in its opponent's play and learn to maximize its chances of winning?

An evolutionary approach to this problem would directly search the space of possible policies for one with a high probability of winning against the opponent. Here, a policy is a rule that tells the player what move to make for every state of the game--every possible configuration of ◇s and Os on the three-by-three board. For each policy considered, an estimate of its winning probability would be obtained by playing some number of games against the opponent. This evaluation would then direct which policy or policies were considered next. A typical evolutionary method would hill-climb in policy space, successively generating and evaluating policies in an attempt to obtain incremental improvements. Or, perhaps, a genetic-style algorithm could be used that would maintain and evaluate a population of policies. Literally hundreds of different optimization methods could be applied. By directly searching the policy space we mean that entire policies are proposed and compared on the basis of scalar evaluations.

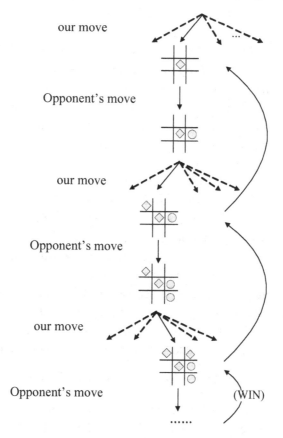

Fig. 10.6. A sequence of tic-tac-toe moves. The solid lines represent the moves taken during a game; the dashed lines represent moves that we (our RL player) considered but did not make.

Here is how the tic-tac-toe problem would be approached using reinforcement learning and approximate value functions. First we set up a table of numbers, one for each possible state of the game. Each number will be the latest estimate of the probability of our winning from that state. We treat this estimate as the state's value, and the whole table is the learned value function. State A has higher value than state B, or is considered "better" than state B, if the current estimate of the probability of our winning from A is higher than it is from B. Assuming we always play ◇s, then for all states with three ◇s in a row the probability of winning is 1, because we have already won. Similarly, for all states with three Os in a row, or that are "filled up," the correct probability is 0, as we cannot win from them. We set the initial values of all the other states to 0.5, representing a guess that we have a 50% chance of winning.

We play many games against the opponent. To select our moves we examine the states that would result from each of our possible moves (one for each blank space on the board) and look up their current values in the table. Most of the time, we move greedily, selecting the move that leads to the state with the greatest value, that is, with the highest estimated probability of winning. Occasionally, however, we select randomly from among the other moves instead. These are called exploratory moves because they make us to experience states that we might otherwise never see. A sequence of moves made and considered during a game can be diagrammed as in Figure 10.6.

While we are playing, we change the values of the states in which we find ourselves during the game. We attempt to make more accurate estimates of the probabilities of winning. To do this, we "back up" the value of the state after each greedy move to the state before the move, as suggested by the arrows in Figure 10.6. More precisely, the current value of the earlier state is adjusted to be closer to the value of the later state. This can be done by moving the earlier state's value a fraction of the way toward the value of the later state. If we let s_n denote the state before the greedy move, and s_{n+1} the state after the move, then the update to the estimated value of s, denoted $V(s)$, can be written as,

$$V(s_n) = S(s_n) + c(V(s_{n+1}) - V(s_n)) \tag{10.14}$$

where c is a small positive fraction called the step-size parameter, which influences the rate of learning. This update rule is an example of a temporal-difference learning method, so called because its changes are based on a difference, $V(s_{n+1})-V(s_n)$, between estimates at two different times.

The method described above performs quite well on this task. For example, if the step-size parameter is reduced properly over time, this method converges, for any fixed opponent, to the true probabilities of winning from each state given optimal play by our player. Furthermore, the moves then taken (except on exploratory moves) are in fact the optimal moves against the opponent. In other words, the method converges to an optimal policy for playing the game. If the step-size parameter is not reduced all the way to zero over time, then this player also plays well against opponents that slowly change their way of playing.

This example illustrates the differences between evolutionary methods and methods that learn value functions. To evaluate a policy, an evolutionary method must hold it fixed and play many games against the opponent, or simulate many games using a model of the opponent. The frequency of wins gives an unbiased estimate of the probability of winning with that policy, and can be used to direct the next policy selection. But each policy change is made only after many games, and only the final outcome of each game is used: what happens during the games is ignored. For example, if the player wins, then all of its behavior in the game is given credit, independently of how specific moves might have been critical to the win. Credit is even given to moves that never occurred! Value function methods, in contrast, allow individual states to be evaluated. In the end, both evolutionary and value function methods search the space of policies, but learning a value function takes advantage of information available during the course of play.

This simple example illustrates some of the key features of reinforcement learning methods. First, there is the emphasis on learning while interacting with an environment, in this case with an opponent player. Second, there is a clear goal, and correct behavior requires planning or foresight that takes into account delayed effects of one's choices. For example, the simple reinforcement learning player would learn to set up multi-move traps for a shortsighted opponent. It is a striking feature of the reinforcement learning solution that it can achieve the effects of planning and looking ahead without using a model of the opponent or conducting an explicit search over possible sequences of future states and actions.

While this example illustrates some of the key features of reinforcement learning, it is so simple that it might give the impression that reinforcement learning is more limited than it really is. Although tic-tac-toe is a two-person game, reinforcement learning also applies in the case in which there is no external adversary, that is, in the case of a "game against nature." Reinforcement learning also is not restricted to problems in which behavior breaks down into separate episodes, like the separate games of tic-tac-toe, with reward only at the end of each episode. It is just as applicable when behavior continues indefinitely and when rewards of various magnitudes can be received at any time.

Finally, the tic-tac-toe player was able to look ahead and know the states that would result from each of its possible moves. To do this, it had to have a model of the game that allowed it to "think about" how its environment would change in response to moves that it might never make. Many problems are like this, but in others even a short-term model of the effects of actions are lack. Reinforcement learning can be applied in either case. No model is required, but models can easily be used if they are available or can be learned.

10.6 Q-Learning

One of the most important breakthroughs in reinforcement learning was the development of an off-policy TD control algorithm known as Q-learning. Q-learning is a reinforcement learning technique that works by learning an action-value function that gives the expected utility of taking a given action in a given state and following a fixed policy thereafter. A strength with Q-learning is that it is able to compare the expected utility of the available actions without requiring a model of the environment.

The core of the algorithm is a simple value iteration update. For each state, s, from the state set S, and for each action, a, from the action set A, we can calculate an update to its expected discounted reward with the following expression:

$$Q(s_t, a_t) \leftarrow (1-c) \times Q(s_t, a_t) + c \times [r_{t+1} + \gamma \underset{a}{MAX} Q(s_{t+1}, a) - Q(s_t, a_t)] \quad (10.15)$$

where r_t is an observed real reward at time t, c are the learning rates such that $0 \leq c \leq 1$, and γ is the discount factor such that $0 \leq \gamma < 1$. Figure 10.7 illustrates the learning trace of V* and Q*.

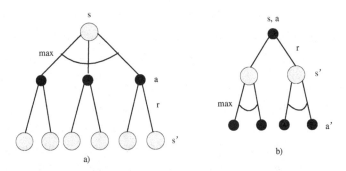

Fig. 10.7. a)V* and b)Q* Learning Trace

Q-Learning uses tables to store data. This quickly loses viability with increasing levels of complexity of the system it is monitoring/controlling. One answer to this problem is to use an (adapted) Artificial Neural Network as a function approximation, as demonstrated by Tesauro in his Backgammon playing Temporal Difference Learning research. An adaptation of the standard neural network is required because the required result (from which the error signal is generated) is itself generated at run-time.

Monte Carlo methods perform a backup for each state based on the entire sequence of observed rewards from that state until the end of the episode. The backup of Q-learning, on the other hand, is based on just the next reward, using the value of the state one step later as a proxy for the remaining rewards (Bootstrapping method). Thus RL need repeated learning to reach optimal policies. We construct a λ-reward function Rt′ by rewriting (10.8) as Equation (10.16) shown. If the system reaches the end state at T step, the value function conforms to Equation (10.17). The theoretical meaning of λ-reward function is illustrated in Fig. 10.8.

$$R'_t = r_{t+1} + \lambda r_{t+2} + \lambda^2 r_{t+3} + \cdots + \lambda^{T-1} r_{t+T} \tag{10.16}$$

$$V(s_t) \leftarrow V(s_t) + \alpha \left[R'_t - V(s_t) \right] \tag{10.17}$$

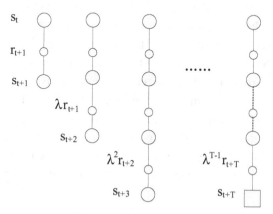

Fig. 10.8. λ-reward Function

The TD(λ) algorithm can be understood as one particular way of averaging n-step backups. According to Equation (10.17), TD(λ) could be designed. In

TD(λ), the value function will be updated by Equation (10.17) through e(s). An complete algorithm for on-line TD(λ) is given in Algorithm 10.2.

Algorithm 10.2   TD(λ) Algorithm.

Initialize $V(s)$ arbitrarily and $e(s)=0$ for all $s \in S$
Repeat (for each episode)
Initialize s
Repeat (for each step of episode)
$a \leftarrow$ action given by π for s(e.g., ε-greedy)
Take action a, observer r, s'
$\delta \leftarrow r + \gamma V(s') - V(s)$
$e(s) \leftarrow e(s) + 1$

for all s
$V(s) \leftarrow V(s) + \alpha \delta e(s)$
$e(s) \leftarrow \gamma \lambda e(s)$

$s \leftarrow s'$

Until s is terminal

We could combine the two steps of estimate and evaluation of value function to construct value function of state-action pair, Q function. In Q-learning, the learned action-value function Q, directly approximates Q*, the optimal action-value function, independent of the policy being followed. The policy still has an effect in that it determines which state-action pairs are visited and updated. However, all that are required for correct convergence is that all pairs continue to be updated. This is the minimal requirement in the sense that any method guaranteed to find optimal behavior in the general case must require it. Under this assumption and a variant of the usual stochastic approximation conditions on the sequence of step-size parameters, Q_t has been shown to converge with probability 1 to Q*. The Q-learning algorithm is shown in procedural form in Algorithm 10.3.

Algorithm 10.3 Q-Learning Algorithm

Initialize $Q(s, a)$ arbitrarily
Repeat (for each episode)
Initialize s

Repeat (for each step of episode)

    Choose a from s using policy derived from Q (e.g., ε-greedy)

    Take action a, observer r, s'

$$Q(s,a) \leftarrow Q(s,a) + \alpha \left[r + \gamma \max_{a'} Q(s',a') - Q(s,a) \right]$$

    $s \leftarrow s'$

Until s is terminal

10.7 Function Approximation

RL is a broad class of optimal control methods based on estimating value functions from experience, simulation, or search. Most of the theoretical convergence results for RL algorithms assume a tabular representation of the value function, in which the value of each state is stored in a separate memory location. However, most practical applications have continuous state spaces, or very large discrete state spaces, for which such a representation is not feasible. Thus generalization is crucial to scaling RL algorithms to real world problems. The kind of generalization we require is often called function approximation because it takes examples from a desired function (e.g., a value function) and attempts to generalize from them to construct an approximation of the entire function. The mapping relations in RL include S→A、S→R、S×A→R、S×A→S and so on. The nature of function approximation in RL is to estimate these mapping relations by parameterized functions.

Assuming the starting value of value function is V0, then the sequence of value functions during learning are:

$$V_0, \Gamma(V_0), \Gamma(\Gamma(V_0)), \Gamma(\Gamma(\Gamma(V_0))), \ldots\ldots$$

where Γ represent equation (10.8).

Most of the traditional RL algorithms adopt lookup-table to save the value functions. And function approximation adopts parameterized functions to replace lookup-table. The model of RL with function approximation is shown in Fig. 10.9. In the model, value function V is the objective function, function V' is the estimated function, and M : V→V' is the estimated operator. Assuming the starting value of value function is V_0, then the sequence of value functions during learning are:

$$V_0, M(V_0), \Gamma(M(V_0)), M(\Gamma(M(V_0))), \Gamma(M(\Gamma(M(V_0)))), \ldots$$

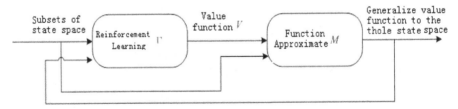

Fig. 10.9. RL model with function approximation

Like Q-learning, the equations of RL with function approximation are as follows.

$$Q(s,a) \leftarrow (1-\alpha)V'(s,a) + \alpha \left(r(s,a,s') + \max_{a'} V'(s',a') \right) \qquad (10.19)$$

$$V'(s,a) = M\big(Q(s,a)\big) \qquad (10.20)$$

In RL learning with function approximation, two iterative processes work simultaneously. One is the iterative process of value function Γ. The other is the approximation process of value function M. The correctness and convergence of the approximation process M play the key role in RL. Function approximation is an instance of supervised learning, the primary topic studied in machine learning, artificial neural networks, pattern recognition, and statistical curve fitting, such as state aggregation, function interpolation and artificial neural networks, etc.

Aggregation is an intuitive and applicable technique to solve large scale problems. In state aggregation, the state space of the Markov chain is partitioned, and the states belonging to the same partition subset are aggregated into one meta-state. The Markov chain is said to be lumpable if the transition process among meta-states is Markovian for every probability distribution of the initial state of the original Markov chain, and weak lumpable if the transition process among meta-states is Markovian only for some initial probability distributions. It is proved that the function approximation with state aggregation is convergent. However, it is possible that the convergent value is not the optimal value. To reach the optimal value, the step could be too long. Thus, it also suffers from the dimension tragedy for large MDP problems.

Function approximation with artificial neural networks has attracted much research currently. Though these new methods could accelerate the speed largely, the convergence could not be ensured. Therefore, the new methods of function approximation which have both convergence and high speed, is still one of the most important research in reinforcement learning.

10.8 Reinforcement Learning Applications

Reinforcement Learning addresses the question how an autonomous agent that senses and acts in its environment can learn to choose optimal actions to achieve its goals. In a Markov decision process (MDP) the agent can perceive a set S of distinct states of its environment and has a set A of actions that it can perform. At each discrete time step t, the agent senses the current state s_t, chooses a current action at, and performs it. The environment responds by giving the agent a reward $r_t = Q(s_t, a_t)$ and by producing the succeeding state $s_{t+1} = P(s_t, a_t)$. Here the functions P and Q are part of the environment and are not necessarily known to the agent. In an MDP, the functions P and Q depend only on the current state and action, and not on earlier states or actions. Reinforcement learning is a useful way to solve MDP problems. Reinforcement Learning reaches its goal by learning reward function $r_t = Q(s_t, a_t)$ and state transition function $P(s_t, a_t)$. Q-learning acquires the optimal policy by learning $r_t = Q(s_t, a_t)$.

RoboCup is an international robotics competition founded in 1993. The aim is to develop autonomous robots with the intention of promoting research and education in the field of artificial intelligence. The name RoboCup is a contraction of the competition's full name, "Robot Soccer World Cup". The following is the application of Q-learning algorithm to simulate robot soccer with three members (2 to 1). The training is aimed at trying to get to the main strategy of awareness in the attack when running. In Figure 10.10, striker A controls the ball in the shoot region. But A has no angle to shoot; teammate B also is in the shoot region, and B has a good shot angle. Thus A pass ball to B, and B complete the shot. Then the cooperation is very successful. Through Q-learning approach in the training, the action A pass ball to B is the best action in this state after training a large number of examples.

Figure 10.11 illustrates the description of states. The attack region is divided into 20*8 small regions. Each small region is a square with the length of 2m. A two-dimensional array $A_{i,j}(0 \leq i \leq 19, 0 \leq j \leq 7)$ can be used to describe the region. The attack state can be described by the location of three Agents. Fig. 10.11 shows the generalization of the state. The state in the same region can be considered as the similar states. Though the description of the state is not precise, it is a description of the strategic level that agent can be running in the same strategic region actively. So, (S_A, S_B, S_G) describes a particular state, which SA is the regional code of offensive team member A, S_B is the regional code of offensive team member B, and , S_G is the regional code of offensive team member G. The regional code is calculated as follows: $S = i * 8 + j$. And the states are preserved by triples of the three regional code.

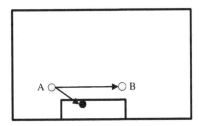

Fig. 10.10. Robot soccer world cup training, 2 to 1

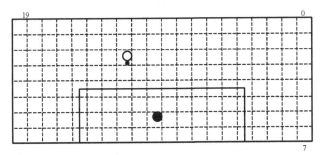

Fig. 10.11. Position Partition

The optional actions have {Shoot, Pass, Dribble}, described as follows.

Shoot: the strategy is obtained by learning through a strategy based on the probability of shot.

Dribble: the strategy is always to reduce threat, and pass ball to regions with a high probability to shoot the goal. In order to achieve this strategic objective, the offensive region can be divided into a number of strategic areas. In each strategic area, shot evaluation is recorded with the shooting success rate.

Pass: strategy is very simple, just passing ball between any two agents, and do not need to choose the target agent. If the pass fails, then that the state of adoption of this strategy is unsuccessful; through this training, impossible path of passing ball can not be adopted.

All states in training include four absorption states. Assume that the offensive in the left half, according to specifications of the standard Soccer server, the four state are play on, goal left, goal kick right and free kick right. If taking the action and the state reaching the four absorption states, the agent will be given the ultimate reward r. For other actions, the agent will be given the procedure rewards as immediate rewards. For example, the maximum reward value of goal left is 1, which means shooting the ball to the goal region.

The agent will obtain the ultimate reward by taking several actions through corresponding states. At this time, the state-action pair will get the reward value. The core of Q-learning algorithm is that every state-action pair has its Q-value. And the Q-values will be updated when getting the ultimate rewards. As Robocup simulation platform add a smaller random noise in the design of the state transition, the model is non-deterministic MDP. The Q value is updated by the following equation.

$$Q(s,a) = (1-\alpha)Q(s,a) + \alpha\left(r + \gamma \max Q\left(s_{t+1}, a_{t+1}\right)\right) \quad (10.21)$$

where $\alpha = 0.1$, $\gamma = 0.95$.

In actual training, the initial Q is 1. After about 20,000 of the training (to reach a state of absorption), the majority of items in Q value has changed, and has separated. Table 10.1 is the updated scene of Q-values with different training numbers.

Table 10.1 Q value

	initial value	5,000	10,000	20,000
Shoot	1	0.7342	0.6248	0.5311
Pass	1	0.9743	0.9851	0.993
Dribble	1	0.9012	0.8104	0.7242

Reinforcement Learning has received much attention in the past decade. Its incremental nature and adaptive capabilities make it suitable for use in various domains, such as automatic control, mobile robotics and multi-agent system. A critical problem in conventional reinforcement learning is the slow convergence of the learning process. However, in most learning systems there usually exists prior knowledge in the form of human expertise or previously learned experience. Therefore, how to integrate other machine learning techniques, such as neural networks, symbol learning technology, to help accelerate the learning speed is an important directions of RL. At present, the main technical difficulty is: how to prove and guarantee the convergence of learning algorithm from theoretical aspects. The development of effective models for complex MDP will also be important direction in the future.

Exercises

1. Given a brief description for the main branches of reinforcement learning and its research history.
2. Explain the similarities and differences between reinforcement learning models and other machine learning methods.
3. Explain the decision process of MDP and its essence.
4. Given the basic ideas of Monte Carlo methods and its applications in reinforcement learning.
5. Given the basic ideas of Temporal-difference (TD) learning and illustrate its process considering playing the game of tic-tac-toe.
6. Consider the deterministic grid world shown below with the absorbing goal-state G. Here the immediate rewards are in the figure for the labeled transitions and 0 for all unlabeled transitions. Given the V^* value for every state in this grid world. Given the $Q(s, a)$ value for every transition. Finally, show an optimal policy using $\gamma = 0.8$.

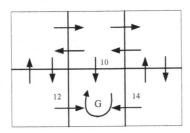

Chapter 11

Rough Set

11.1 Introduction

In classical logic, there are only two values: true and false. However, in reality, some ambiguous phenomena can not be briefly represented by true and false. Thus, how to describe and deal with these phenomena becomes a research topic. A lot of logicians and philosophers have been devoted to studying the vague concept for a long time. Since 1904, the founder of predication logic G. Frege proposed the word—Vague. He considered the concept on the boundary line. That is to say, some individuals in universe can be classified neither into a subset nor into the supplementary of the subset.

The term "fuzzy set" was proposed by Zadeh in 1965, which was later used by computer scientists and logicians in attempt to explain Frege's definition of "vague". However, fuzzy set is incomputable, that is, there is neither mathematic formula to describe this ambiguous concept nor practical approach to calculate the exact number of its vague elements, such as the membership function μ in fuzzy sets and the operator λ in fuzzy logics. Twenty years later, in early 80s, according to Frege's idea of boundary region, Rough Set was first proposed by Pawlak in Poland (Pawlak, 1982). He concluded that individual elements that can't be determined should be incorporated into the boundary region which is defined as the difference of the upper approximate set and the lower approximate set.

Based on its concrete description of mathematic formula, the number of vague elements is computable, which in terms makes the degree of vagueness between the values of true and false computable. Rough set theory provides an ordinary rough set approach for processing ambiguous problems, that is, the ability to handle uncertainty based on incomplete information or knowledge as well as the ability to distinguish data based on inaccurate observation and measurement.

Rough set was widely studied by computer scientists and mathematicians since the 1980s and has grown more and more mature in its theory. Its successful application in the area of knowledge discovery during the later 1980s and early 1990s brought pervasive international attention to this subject. Compared to other theoretical tools handling uncertainty and fuzziness, rough set theory has many unique desirable features. In recent years, it has been successfully applied to information system analysis, artificial intelligence and application, decision support system, knowledge and data discovery, pattern recognition and classification, and fault diagnosis, etc.

In some extent, the concept of rough set is similar to many other mathematical tools that aim to handle vague and inaccurate problems, especially the evidence theory proposed by Dempster-Shafer (Shafer, 1976). The major difference between them is that the main tool used by Dempster-Shafer's theory is credibility function whereas rough set uses upper approximate and lower approximate sets as its main tool. Another relationship exists between rough set theory and fuzzy set theory. Rough set theory is related to fuzzy set theory in many aspects, and it tries not to compete with the later but to supplement it. In general, for incomplete knowledge, rough set theory and fuzzy set theory are two independent methodologies. Moreover, there're also relations between rough set theory and discriminant analysis, Boolean inference method and decision analysis.

One of the major advantages of rough set theory is that it does not require any preliminary or additional information about the data such as: probability distribution in statistic, basic probability assignment in Dempster-Shafer theory or membership/probability in fuzzy set theory.

In the 1980s, intensive study on the rough set theory is done by Polish scholars, including extensive analysis on the mathematical characteristics of rough set theory and its logic systems. Most of these findings are published on "Bulletin of The Polish Academic of Science: Mathematics" and "Bulletin of The Polish Academic of Science: Technical Science". Application systems were also developed by them.

Professor Z. Pawlak published the first monograph on rough set theory in 1991, and R. Slowinski chief-edited the symposium on applications and comparative studies on rough set in 1992. More and more researchers began to study the applications and theoretical research on rough set theory. The first international seminar on rough set was held in Kiekrz Poland in 1991. The conference focused on basic ideas of approximate definitions of set and its applications, whereas fundamental research on machine learning in the context of rough set was one of the four special topics of the conference. However, the number of attendees to this conference and its impact was limited. 15 papers were selected from the conference and were published on "Foundation of Computing and Decision Sciences", vol. 18, 1993. Hereafter, the international seminar on rough set theory has been held regularly annually.

The second International seminar on rough set and knowledge discovery was held in Banff Canada, 1993. The main topics of this conference are rough set, fuzzy set and knowledge discovery. Since KDD was a popular research topic at that time, some famous scholars in KDD attended the conference and introduced many knowledge discovery methods and systems based on extended rough sets. The third international conference on rough set and soft-computing was held in San Jose USA in 1994. The syncretizing of rough set, fuzzy logics, neural network and evolution theory is extensively discussed at this conference.

Advocators of rough set theory and its applications published a brief introduction of rough set theory, one of the latest technologies in artificial intelligence, on ACM transactions, vol. 11, 1995. Basic concepts and project applications on knowledge acquisition, machine learning, decision analysis, and knowledge discovery are introduced. Rough set seminar was held in Willmington USA in 1995. The fourth international conference on fuzzy theory and technology (Fuzzy Theory & Technology'95) is worth mentioning, since the intense debate on the basic view points and relationship between rough set and fuzzy set greatly enhanced the research on rough set. The first extensive seminar on rough set in Asia is the fifth international rough set conference held in Tokyo Japan, 1996. The Seventh International Workshop on Rough Sets, Fuzzy Sets, Data Mining and Granular-Soft Computing (RSFDGRC'99) discussed contemporary status and future trends of rough set and fuzzy set, and pointed out that future development should focus on applications of soft-computing, database, artificial intelligence and approximate reasoning, etc.

The second conference on current trends of rough set and computing was held in Canada in October 2000. Currently literatures on rough set can be easily found in many international conferences on AI, fuzzy set theory, information management and knowledge discovery.

We must point out that rough set theory is not omnipotent. For modeling, though rough set theory is effective for the handling of incomplete knowledge, it does not include the mechanism to handle raw data that is inaccurate or uncertain. Thus, it does not guarantee to give an effective description of inaccurate or uncertain practical problems, and supplementary methods are required. Generally speaking, evidence theory and fuzzy set theory are natural complements of rough set theory because they provide alternative approaches to handle inaccurate and uncertain data (though it is somewhat difficult to describe).

In order to have a better understanding of the essence and characteristics of rough set theory, basic definitions are introduced here to explain the essential idea of rough set theory and its difference compared to other mathematics tools in handling uncertainty and fuzziness.

11.1.1 *Categorized View of Knowledge*

Basic rough set theory concludes that knowledge is the ability of human and other species to distinguish and categorize. For example, in real world knowledge about environments mainly refers to a creature's ability to distinguish different situations according to its sense of existence. Every creature forms a complex classification mode according to its sensor signals, that is, its basic mechanism. Classification is the crucial problem of inference, learning, and decision making. Thus, rough set theory assumes that knowledge is the ability to classify specific objects. Here the term "Object" refers to almost anything we can think of, such as matter, status, abstract concept, process, and time point, etc. Moreover, knowledge must be related to the classification modes of specific parts of the concrete or abstract world. This specific part is called the universe of discussion. There is no special assumption about the characteristics of the universe and knowledge. In fact, knowledge constitutes a family of classification modes in a specific area of interests which provides dominant facts about the reality and the ability to deduct recessive facts based on these dominant facts.

For mathematical convenience, equivalent relation is used to replace classification in the following definition.

Definition 11.1 *A approximate space is defined as a relationship system*

$$K=(U, R), \qquad (11.1)$$

where U, called as universe, is the set of all discussed objects, and R is a family set of equivalence relation on U.

Definition 11.2   *Suppose $P \subseteq R$ and $P \neq \varnothing$, the intersection set of all equivalence relation on P is called as indiscernibility relation on P, denoted as IND(P). That is,*

$$[x]_{IND(P)} = \bigcap_{R \in P} [x]_R \qquad (11.2)$$

Note, IND(P) is an equivalence relation, and it is unique.

Definition 11.3   *Given approximate space K=(U, R), subset $X \subseteq U$ is called as a concept on U. Formally, empty set can also be viewed as a concept. The indiscernibility relation IND(P) generated from non-empty family subset $P \subseteq R$, denoted as U/IND(P), is called as basic knowledge, and its corresponding equivalence class is called as basic concept. Specially, if relation $Q \in R$, then Q is called as elementary knowledge, and its corresponding equivalence classes are called as elementary concepts.*

Capitalized letters such as P, Q and R usually denote relations whereas bolded *P*, *Q* and *R* denote the family set of relations respectively; $[x]_R$ or $R(x)$ denotes that relation R contains the concept or equivalent class of element x which satisfies $x \in U$. For simplicity, sometimes *P* is used to replace *IND(P)*.

According to above definition, concept is the set of objects whereas family of concepts is called knowledge on U. Classified family sets on U can be viewed as knowledge base on U, or to put it differently, knowledge base is the assembly of classification methods.

11.1.2 A New Type of Membership Relations

The rough set theory has some similarity compared with traditional set theory, whereas they have totally different motivations. An element must either belong to or be excluded from a set, that is, the membership function is $X(x) \in \{0,1\}$. Fuzzy set theory extended this definition by giving a membership to elements in fuzzy set, i.e. $\mu X(x) \in [0,1]$, which enables the fuzzy set ability to handle some fuzzy and uncertain data. However, usually the membership functions are manually defined which hinders its application in real life. Moreover, traditional set theory and fuzzy set theory treat membership relations as basic concepts, and the union and intersection of sets are based on min/max operations on the membership of their elements. This is because the memberships are predefined, and for a traditional set the default membership is 1 or 0. In rough set theory, the membership relation is no longer a basic concept thus there's no need to manually assign a membership to an element. This can avoid any possible individual bias. Moreover, uncertainty is considered to be relative to membership relation instead of the set itself (as defined in fuzzy set). To describe uncertainty clearly, we have the following definition of membership relation:

Definition 11.4 *Suppose $X \subseteq U$ and $x \in U$, the membership function of set X (or called as rough membership function) is defined as*

$$\mu_x^R(x) = \frac{card(X \cap R(x))}{card(R(x))} \tag{11.3}$$

where R is an indiscernibility relation, and $R(x)=[x]_R=\{y:(y \in U) \wedge (y\ R\ x)\}$.

In this chapter, we use card to represent the cardinal number of a set. According to above definition, some properties can be got as follows:

(1) $m_X^R(x)=1$ iff $[x]_R \subseteq X$;

(2) $m_X^R(x)>0$ iff $[x]_R \cap X \neq \emptyset$;

(3) $m_X^R(x)=0$ iff $[x]_R \cap X = \emptyset$.

Obviously, we have $m_X(x) \in [0,1]$. Note that the membership relation here is calculated based on classification of knowledge which is already known, thus it can be explained as some kind of conditional probability which can be calculated for individuals on the universe instead of predefined manually.

11.1.3 *The View of Concept's Boundary*

The granularity of knowledge is the reason that known knowledge can not explicitly express some concepts. This is the origin of the idea of "boundary" to describe inaccuracy. Frege concludes that "concepts must have an explicit boundary. The concept without explicit boundary will result in an area without clear borders." The fuzziness in rough set theory is a concept based on boundary, that is, an inaccurate concept has an ambiguous boundary that can't be explicitly classified. To describe fuzziness, every inaccurate concept is expressed by a pair of accurate concepts namely the upper approximation and lower approximation. They can be defined by membership function as follows:

Definition 11.5 *Suppose set $X \subseteq U$, we call $R_*(X)=\{x:(x \in U) \wedge (m_X (x)=1)\}$ as lower approximation, $R^*(X)=\{x:(x \in U) \wedge (m_X (x)>0)\}$ as upper approximation, and $BNR(X)=R^*(X)-R_*(X)$ as boundary.*

Apparently, if $BN_R(X) \neq \varnothing$ or $R^*(X) \neq R_*(X)$, then set X is a rough concept. Lower approximation includes all the elements that can be assigned to set X explicitly by using knowledge R, whereas upper approximation includes all the elements that are possible members of set X. The difference between upper and lower approximation composes the boundary area of the concept.

We can see that a relationship between fuzziness and uncertainty can be established, that is, fuzziness is defined by uncertainty. In general, not all object sets can be represented as concepts by given knowledge (the so called rough concept, inaccurate or similar concepts) for a certain approximation space. However, a rough concept can be roughly defined by two concepts (upper approximation and lower approximation) which enables us accurately describe inaccurate concepts. Moreover, the membership function, upper approximate and lower approximate can be used to define the inclusion relation and equivalence relation, etc.

11.2 Reduction of Knowledge

This section focus on two basic questions in rough set theory: reduction and dependency of knowledge. Reduction of knowledge is to investigate the necessary of every equivalence relation in the approximation space and the method to delete unnecessary knowledge. Knowledge reduction is of vital practical importance in information system analysis and data mining. Dependency among knowledge determines whether knowledge reduction is needed and knowledge dependency provides important heuristic information for knowledge reduction.

11.2.1 General Reduction

In the application of rough set theory, reduction and core are two of the most important basic concepts. Intuitively, the so-called reduction of knowledge is the essence of knowledge which is enough to define all basic concepts within the concerned knowledge, whereas the core is its most important component.

Definition 11.6 *Suppose R is a family set of equivalence relation, and let $R \in R$. If IND(R)=IND(R–R) then relation R is dispensable in R, or indispensable otherwise. If every relation R in family set R is indispensable then R is called as independent, or dependent otherwise.*

Definition 11.7 *If $Q \subseteq P$ is independent, and IND(Q)=IND(P), then Q is a reduct of relation family set P. The set of all indispensable relations is called as the core of P, denoted as CORE(P).*

Apparently, a family set P has more than one reduct.

The following theorem is an important property of the relationship between core and reduct.

Theorem 11.1 *The core of family set P is equal to the intersection of all reducts, that is*

$$CORE(P) = \cap RED(P) \tag{11.4}$$

where RED(P) is the family set of all reducts of P.

We can observe from above theorem that the concept of core has two aspects of meanings: first, it can be viewed as the basis of calculation for all reducts. This is because the core is incorporated in every reduct and its calculation is indirect; second, the core can be explained as the assembly of the most important components of knowledge, which can not be deleted in the reduction process.

The most common method to generate reduction is to add relations that can be reduced one by one and check them. Note that the number of ways to add relations is equal to the base number of the power set of reducible relation sets. In the best case, all irreducible relation sets are the unique reduct. So how to calculate all reducts and to calculate an optimal reduct (such as minimal relations) are NP problems.

11.2.2 Relative Reduction

This section extends the concepts of reduction and core. Before that, let's define the concept of positive region of a classification related with another classification.

Definition 11.8 *Suppose P and Q are the family set of equivalence relations on U. The so-called P-positive region of Q, denoted as POSP(Q), is defined as*

$$POSP(Q) = \bigcup_{X \in U / Q} P^*(X) \tag{11.5}$$

P-positive region of Q is the knowledge expressed by U/P in universe U, and a set composed by the objects which can be correctly classified into the equivalence classes of U/Q. The positive region of a set X relative to an equivalence relation P is the lower approximate of $X - P^*(X)$. The concept of P-positive region of Q is to deal with the problem, and the objects in the equivalence classes of Q (viewed as decision attributes) can be classified by the equivalence classes of P (viewed as condition attributes).

Definition 11.9 *Suppose P and Q are the family set of equivalence relations on U, and $R \in P$. If*

$$POS_{IND(P)}(IND(Q)) = POS_{IND(P-\{R\})}(IND(Q))$$

then relation R is called as Q-reducible in family set P, or Q-irreducible otherwise. If every relation R in family set P is Q-irreducible, then P is called as independent relative to Q, or dependent otherwise.

Definition 11.10 *$S \subseteq P$ is called as Q-reduct of P, iff S is the Q-independent family subset of P, and $POS_S(Q) = POS_P(Q)$; The set of all the Q-irreducible elementary relations in P is called as Q-core of P, denoted as $CORE_Q(P)$.*

It is easy to see that, when P=Q, above definition is same as the definition introduced in section 11.2.1.

The following theorem is the extension of theorem 11.1.

Thoerem 11.12 *The Q-core of family set P is equal to the intersection of all Q-reducts, that is*

$$COREQ(P) = \cap REDQ(P) \qquad\qquad (11.4)$$

where REDQ(P) is the family set of all Q-reducts of P.

Assume that P and Q are family sets of equivalent relations (knowledge), the P-positive region of Q is the set of all objects that can be classified into the concept of knowledge Q using knowledge P. If the whole knowledge P is necessary to categorize objects into the concept of Q, then knowledge P is called Q-independent. The Q-core of knowledge P is the essence of knowledge P, which cannot be removed, to maintain the ability of categorizing objects to the concept of Q. That is, removing any part of the Q-core knowledge will affect the ability of categorizing objects to the concept of Q. The Q-reduct of knowledge P is some kind of minimal subset of knowledge P which has the same ability as knowledge P to categorize objects to the concept of Q. Note that, knowledge P may have several reducts. In some sense, if there is only one Q-reduct of knowledge P, then knowledge P is determined, that is, there is only one approach to categorize objects to the concept of Q. When there are multiple Q-reducts of knowledge P, there are multiple approaches to categorize objects to the concept of Q. When the core is empty, it will aggravate this uncertainty.

11.2.3 Dependency of Knowledge

The dependency of knowledge can be formally defined as follows.

Definition 11.11 *Suppose $K=(U, R)$ is an approximate space, and P、$Q \subseteq R$.*

(1) Knowledge Q is dependent on knowledge P, or knowledge P can deduct to knowledge Q, iff $IND(P) \subseteq IND(Q)$, denoted as $P \Rightarrow Q$;
(2) Knowledge P and Q are equivalent, iff $P \Rightarrow Q$ and $Q \Rightarrow P$, that is, $IND(P)=IND(Q)$, denoted as $P = Q$. Apparently, $P=Q$ iff $IND(P)=IND(Q)$;
(3) Knowledge P and Q are independent, iff $P \Rightarrow Q$ or $Q \Rightarrow P$ neither holds, denoted as $P \neq Q$.

The dependency of knowledge can hold partly. That is to say, knowledge P can deduct a part of knowledge of Q, or knowledge Q is only partly dependent on knowledge P. Partial dependency (partial deducible) can be defined by the positive region of knowledge. In the following, we formally define partial dependency.

Definition 11.12 *Suppose $K=(U, R)$ is a knowledge base, and P、$Q \subset R$, we call knowledge Q is dependent on P with the dependency degree k ($0 \le k \le 1$), denoted as $P \Rightarrow_k Q$, iff*

$$k = \gamma_P(Q)=card(POS_P(Q))/card(U) \qquad (11.8)$$

(1) if $k=1$, then knowledge Q is called totally dependent on knowledge Q, denoted as $P \Rightarrow_1 Q$ or $P \Rightarrow Q$;
(2) if $0<k<1$, then knowledge Q is called partly dependent on knowledge Q;
(3) if $k=0$, then knowledge Q is called totally independent on knowledge Q.

Above idea can be explained as the ability to categorize objects. More specifically, if $k = 1$, then all elements on the universe can be used to categorize objects to the concept of Q using knowledge P. If $k \neq 1$, only the elements within the positive region of the universe can be used to categorize objects to the concept of Q using knowledge P. Thus the parameter $P(Q)$ can be viewed as the degree of dependency between knowledge P and Q.

11.3 Decision Logic

Rough set theory defines a basic framework to understand and handle knowledge using the concept of approximation space. Considering the implementation of algorithms, it is especially suitable to handle information presented in the form of data tables, which is called information systems or knowledge representation systems. This representation systems have many advantages, such as its vivacity. It can also be viewed as an assembly of propositions about reality and consequences, thus can be processed by logic tools. This is the motivation of this section.

11.3.1 *Formal Definition of Decision Table*

The formal definition of knowledge representation system is $S=(U, A)$, where U is the finite set universe of discussion and A denotes the attribute set which is non-empty and finite.

This definition of knowledge representation systems can easily be implemented using tables. The tabular representation of knowledge can be viewed as a special formal language which uses symbols to represent equivalence relations. In the data table of a knowledge representation system, columns denote attributes and rows denote objects (such as states or processes), whereas each row denotes a piece of information about the object. Data tables can be obtained through observation and measurement.

For each attribute subset $B \subseteq A$, we can define an indiscernible binary relation IND(B), that is

$$\text{IND}(B)=\{(x,y) \in U^2, \text{ for each } b \in B, b(x)=b(y)\}. \tag{11.9}$$

Apparently, IND(B) is an equivalence relation, $b \in$ B, and IND(B)$=\cap$IND(b).

Each subset $B \subseteq A$ is called as an attribute. When there is only one element in B, B is called to be original, or complex otherwise. Attribute B can be viewed as a name of knowledge expressed by equivalence relations, called as marked attribute. The elementary category including object x and attribute $B \subseteq A$ is expressed by a set pair (attribute, value), denoted as $\{b, b(x)\}_{b \in B}$.

There is a one to one relation between knowledge base and knowledge representation system, which is determined by the isomorphic of attribute and its name. Thus, for a knowledge base $K=(U, R)$ and a knowledge representation system $S=(U, A)$, the relation between them is: if $r \in R$ and $U|r=\{x_1, x_2, \cdots, x_n\}$, then for attribute set A and each attribute $a_r:U \Rightarrow V_a$, we have $V_a=\{1,2, \cdots,k\}$, and $a_r(x)=i$ iff $x \in X_i$, $(i=1,2, \cdots,k)$. Therefore, all the notions about knowledge base can be described by the definition of knowledge representation systems.

Thus, any equivalence relation within the knowledge base can be represented by an equivalence class of relations expressed by attributes and attribute values in the data table of the knowledge system. The columns in the table can be viewed as names of some categories, and the whole table includes the description of all categories within the corresponding knowledge base and all possible rules that can be deducted from the data in the table. Thus, data table of knowledge representation system is the description of valid facts and rules in the knowledge base.

A decision table can be seen as a special and important knowledge representation system. It shows that, when some conditions are satisfied, how decisions, actions, operations, or controls can be made. Most of decision problems can be expressed by decision tables, thus the tools plays an important role in the application of decision.

Decision tables can be defined as follows according to the definition of knowledge representation systems.

$S=(U, A)$ is a knowledge representation system, and $C \setminus D \subset A$ are two attribute subsets, which are called condition attribute subset and decision attribute subset respectively. The knowledge representation systems having condition attributes and decision attributes can be expressed by decision tables, denoted as $T=(U, A, C, D)$ and called as CD decision tables for short. The equivalence classes of relation $IND(C)$ and $IND(D)$ are called condition classes and decision classes respectively.

11.3.2 Decision Logic Language

In this chapter, we view data tables as special logic models, called as decision logic. They infer conclusions according to the knowledge acquiring from knowledge representation systems. And, we will use symbol tools of logic deduction to discover knowledge dependency and to reduce knowledge.

Although algorithms are usually a series of statements, we still use the term "decision algorithms" to represent a set of decision rules, because decision logic is our main focus. Moreover, as a set of formulas, the decision algorithms do not have the property of being true or false, which is different with ordinary formulas. The basic property of decision algorithm is consistent or inconsistent, so we mainly consider the consistency of data. Computational methods are used to infer rules from data.

In this chapter, the decision logic languages defined and discussed are composed by atomic formulas. Formulas are described by a pair with the form "attribute-data". Using some classical methods, formulas can construct complex formulas with propositional connectives: "and", "or", "not", etc.

First, we define the basic representation of decision logic language as follows:

(1) A — the set of attributes;
(2) $V = \cup V_a$, $a \in A$, V — the set of attribute values;
(3) The set of propositional connectives $\{\sim, \vee, \wedge, \rightarrow, \equiv\}$ representing negative, disjunction, conjunction, implication and equivalence respectively.

Note, propositional connectives can be viewed as logic connectors: "not", "or", "and", "if ……, then ……", "if and only if".

Basic representations do not include variables, and it is composed by symbols for attributes and attribute values, propositional connectives, assistant symbols (for example, bracket), and etc.

The formula set of decision logic language is the minimal set satisfying the following conditions:

(1) Formula (a, v) (or a_v for short) is an elementary atomic formula, and it is a formula of decision logic language for each $a \in A$ and $v \in V_a$;
(2) If θ and ψ are formulas of decision logic language, $\sim \theta$, $\theta' \vee \psi$, $\theta \wedge \psi$, $\theta \rightarrow \psi$, $\theta \equiv \psi$ are also formulas of decision logic language.

11.3.3 Semantics of Decision Logic Language

Formulas are used as the tools to describe the objects in universe. It can also be applied into the description of the object sets satisfying some properties. For example, in atomic formula, ordered pair (a, v) can be explained as the expression of objects with value v on attribute a.

To describe decision logic language explicitly, we can use the concepts of models and satisfiability to define the Tarski semantics of decision logic language, that is, use models to express knowledge representation system $S = (U, A)$. Model S describes the meaning of predication symbol (a, v) in universe U and expresses the properties of some objects. The concept of satisfiability is used to define decision logic language, that is:

If S is understandable, an object $x \in$ U satisfies formula θ in S=(U, A), denoted as $x|=_S\theta$ (written as $x|=\theta$ for short), if and only if the following conditions are satisfied:

(1) If and only if f(a, x)=v, $x|=(a, v)$;
(2) If and only if $x|=\theta$, $x|=\sim\theta$;
(3) If and only if $x|=\theta$ or $x|=\psi$, $x|=\theta\vee\psi$;
(4) If and only if $x|=\theta$ and $x|=\psi$, $x|=\theta\wedge\psi$;

As corollaries of above conditions, we can get:

(1) If and only if $x|=\sim\theta\vee\psi$, $x|=\theta\rightarrow\psi$;
(2) If and only if $x|=\theta\rightarrow\psi$ and $x|=\psi\rightarrow\theta$, $x|=\psi\equiv\theta$.
(3) If θ is a formula, set $|\theta|S$ is defined as: $|\theta|S=\{x\in$ U, $x|=S\theta\}$, and it is called as the meaning of formular θ in S . The independent variable with the meaning is a formula of language, and its value is a subset of objects in system.

The following proposition explains the meaning of formulas.

Proposition 11.1

(1) $|(a, v)|_S=\{x\in U: a(x)=v\}$;
(2) $|\sim\theta|_S=-|\theta|_S$;
(3) $|\theta\vee\psi|_S=|\theta|_S\cup|\psi|_S$;
(4) $|\theta\wedge\psi|_S=|\theta|_S\cap|\psi|_S$;
(5) $|\theta\rightarrow\psi|_S=-|\theta|_S\cup|\psi|_S$;
(6) $|\theta\equiv\psi|_S=(|\theta|_S\cap|\psi|_S)\cup(-|\theta|_S\cup|\psi|_S)$.

From the proposition, it is easy to know that the meaning of formulas is the object set expressed by formula θ, or we can say, it is the description of object set $|\theta|S$ with knowledge representation language.

In the logic, we also use the concept "true". If and only if $|\theta|S=U$, that is, all objects in universe satisfy formula θ, the formula is called as "true" in knowledge representation system S.

If and only if $|\theta|_S=|\psi|_S$, formula θ and ψ are equivalent in S.

The following proposition proposes some simple properties related with above concepts.

Proposition 11.2

(1) *If and only if* $|\theta|_S = U, |=_S \theta$;

(2) *If and only if* $|\theta|_S = \varnothing, |=_{S\sim} \theta$;

(3) *If and only if* $|\theta|_S \unlhd |\varphi|_S, |=_S \theta \rightarrow \varphi$;

(4) *If and only if* $|\theta|_S = |\varphi|_S, |=S \equiv \varphi$.

At last, we should emphasize that the meaning of formulas depends on the understanding of the knowledge in universe, that is, depends on the knowledge representation systems. Especially, although a formula can be true in a knowledge representation system, it can be false in another knowledge representation system. In our research, they make special sense.

11.3.4 *Deduction of Decision Logic*

In above sections, we use language to describe the knowledge included in a special knowledge representation system. Although for many knowledge representation systems, different object sets can be used to the common language processing, but we still use the coordinate sets of attributes and their values to process. From the viewpoints of Semeiology, all the languages of these systems are coordinate. However, according to the sets of different objects, their semantics are diverse and the properties expressed by their appointed knowledge representation systems are also different.

All axiom sets of decision logic are constructed by proposition repetition logic and some special theorems. Before presenting the axioms of knowledge representation systems, we first introducing some assistant concepts, which are written as follows for short:

$$\theta \wedge \varnothing =_{df} 0$$
$$\theta \vee \varnothing =_{df} 1$$

Apparently, $|=1$ and $|=\sim 0$. Thus, 1 and 0 represent true or false respectively. Usually, a formalized formula is defined as follows:

$$(a_1, v_1) \wedge (a_2, v_2) \wedge \cdots \wedge (a_n, v_n)$$

Here, $v_i \bullet v_{a_i}$, $\{a_1, a_2, \cdots, a_n\} \subseteq P$ and $P \subseteq A$. Above formalized formula is called as P basic formula. For attribute set A, above formalized formula is called as A-basic formula.

Given that $P \subseteq A$, a P-formula θ and $x \in U$, if $x| = \theta$, θ is called as the P-expression of x in S. This is similar with the introduction in previous section, which uses condition attribute sets to describe objects.

In a knowledge representation system $S = (U, A)$, all sets satisfying A-basic formula are called as basic knowledge in S.

$\sum(P)$ denotes the decompositions in S that satisfying P-formula. If $P = A$ and the eigenformula of $S = (U, A)$ is defined as $\sum(A)$, then $\sum(A)$ represents the decompositions in S that satisfying A-formula, and it is a token of all the knowledge in S. Specifically, each row in our language table can be expressed by a given A-basic formula, and the whole table is described by all this kind of formulas.

In the following, we give some axioms of decision logics:

(1) For each $a \in A$, v, $u \in V_a$, and $v \neq u$, $(a, v) \wedge (a, u) \equiv 0$;
(2) For each $a \in A$ and $v \in V_a$, $\vee(a, v) \equiv 1$;
(3) For each $a \in A$, $u \in V_a$ and $v \neq u$, $\sim(a, v) \equiv \vee(a, u)$.

Axiom (1) *is based on the assumption: for each attribute, each object only has an exact value on it. For example, if a material is red, it cannot be blue or green.*

Axiom (2) *is based on the assumption: for each attribute, each object in system must have a value field on it. For example, if an attribute is a description of color, then an object with the attribute must have a color. The color is the value of this attribute.*

Axiom (3) *is to show that negative words can be omitted. If an object has some property, then we cannot say it does not have other properties. For example, we can say a material is green or blue, but we cannot say it is not red.*

Proposition 11.3 *For each $P \subseteq A$, $|=S$ $\sum S(P) \equiv 1$.*

Proposition 11.3 shows that the knowledge in knowledge representation system is all that can be acquired currently. It corresponds to the so called closed word assumption.

If and only if formula θ can be inferred from the axioms and formulas of formula Ω, we call θ as a formula inferred from Ω, denoted as $\Omega | - \theta$. If θ can be inferred from axioms uniquely, θ is called a theorem of decision logic, written as $\vdash\theta$ for short.

If and only if formula $\theta \wedge \sim\theta$ cannot be inferred from formula Ω, the set of Ω is called as consistent.

11.3.5 Standard Expression

The formulas in knowledge representation language can be expressed by a kind of standard expressions, which are similar with classical propositions.

Let $P{\subseteq}A$ be an attribute subset and θ be a formula in knowledge representation language. If and only if $\theta=\varnothing$ or $\theta=1$, or θ is a decomposition of a non-empty P-basic formula in S, we call θ as a P-standardized form in S. A-standardized expressions are called standardized formulas.

Proposition 11.4 *Given θ which is a formula in decision logic language, and P which includes all attributes of θ, if axioms (1) to (3) and formula $\sum S(A)$ are satisfied, then there is only one formula ψ in P form of criterion satisfying $\vdash \theta{\equiv}\psi$.*

It is obvious that, we can calculate a formula's form of criterions by inferring propositions and transforming some axioms of knowledge representation systems.

11.3.6 Decision Rules and Algorithms

In logic language, $\theta{\rightarrow}\Psi$ is called as a decision rule in knowledge representation languages. Here, θ and Ψ are named as the premise and consequence of the decision rule respectively, which is similar with the condition attributes and decision attributes we used to describe objects. Decision rule is to express a kind of cause-and-effect relations.

If $\theta{\rightarrow}\Psi$ is true in S, we say the rule is consistent in S, otherwise inconsistent. If a decision rule is consistent in S, identical premises must infer to identical consequences; but identical consequences may not be inferred by identical premises.

Given P and Q, if $\theta{\rightarrow}\Psi$ is a decision rule, and θ, Ψ are P-basic formula and Q-basic formula respectively, then $\theta{\rightarrow}\Psi$ is called as a *PQ-basic decision rule* or *PQ rule* for short. Here, P-attributes and Q-attributes can be viewed as the condition attributes and decision attributes we explored before.

If $\theta_1 \to \Psi$, $\theta_2 \to \Psi$, $\cdots$, $\theta_n \to \Psi$ are all basic decision rule, $\theta_1 \vee \theta_2 \vee \cdots \vee \theta_n \to \Psi$ is called as the composition of $\theta_1 \to \Psi$, $\theta_2 \to \Psi, \cdots$, $\theta_n \to \Psi$ or compositional decision rule for short.

To explore the value of PQ rule (consistent or inconsistent), we can use following proposition.

Proposition 11.5 *If and only if all {P∨Q}-basic formulas appear in {P∨Q}-formal expressions of PQ rule's premise and consequence, the PQ-rule is true (consistent) in S, otherwise false (inconsistent).*

Any finite decision rule set in decision logic language is called as a decision algorithm, and any finite decision rule is called as a basic decision algorithm.

If the decision rules in a basic decision algorithm are all *PQ*-decision rules, the algorithm is called as *PQ*-decision algorithm or *PQ*-algorithm for short (denoted as (P, Q)). If and only if all decision rules in S are consistent, *PQ* algorithm in *S* is consistent, otherwise inconsistent.

If for each $x \in U$, there exists a *PQ*-rule $\theta \to \Psi$ in an algorithm that $x|=\theta \wedge \Psi$, the *PQ*-algorithm is complete, otherwise incomplete.

Given a knowledge representation system, the non-empty subset of attribute *P*, *Q* can determine a *PQ*-decision algorithm uniquely. That is to say, *PQ*-algorithm and *PQ*-decision table can be viewed as equivalent.

11.3.7 *Inconsistent and Indiscernibility of Decision Rule*

To test the consistency of a decision algorithm, we must consider the values of all its decision rules. We can use proposition 11.5 to test it, while the following proposition gives a simpler method.

Proposition 11.6 *For any PQ-decision rule $\theta_1 \to \varphi_1$ in a PQ-decision algorithm, if and only if $\theta = \theta_1$ implicates $\varphi = \varphi_1$, decision rule $\theta \to \varphi$ in the PQ decision algorithm is consistent in S.*

Note that, to test the values of decision rule $\theta \to \Psi$, we must prove that the premise of decision rule (formula θ) can distinguish the decision class Ψ with other classes. That means the concept true can be replaced by the concept —

indiscernibility. Apparently, if identical premises have different consequences, the rule is inconsistent.

11.4 Reduction of Decision Tables

Before decision making, we usually face a problem: whether are all condition attributed necessary? Or, whether can decision table be reduced? The decision tables after reduction has the same functions with the tables before reduction, but the tables after reduction has less attributes. Therefore, the reduction of attributes is very important in real applications. With the reduction, we can make decisions based on fewer conditions, that is, same results can be acquired by simpler methods. Strictly speaking, although decision algorithm and decision table are different concepts, the decision algorithms expressed by decision tables are more compact, more understandable and simpler than those expressed by decision logic language. Decision algorithms can describe decision tables with the methods of logics, thus some properties of them can be used mutually.

11.4.1 *Dependency of Attributes*

To process data and make decisions, the internal relations of data and the dependency of attributes must be analyzed. The dependency of attributes is relative to the dependency of knowledge we introduced before. If there exists a consistent PQ-decision algorithm in S, we say attribute set Q is totally dependent (or dependent for short) on attribute set P, denoted as $P{\Rightarrow}Q$; if there exists some inconsistent PQ-decision algorithm, we say attribute set Q is partly dependent on attribute set P.

Similar with the definition of knowledge dependency, we can also use the concept of positive region to define the dependency among attribute sets.

If (P, Q) is a PQ-algorithm in S, the set of all consistent PQ-rules in the algorithm is called as the positive region of the algorithm, denoted as $POS(P, Q)$. $POS(P, Q)$ is the consistent part of an inconsistent algorithm. Apparently, if and only if $POS(P, Q){\neq}(P, Q)$ or $card(POS(P, Q)){\neq}card((P, Q))$, the algorithm is inconsistent.

For a PQ-algorithm, the degree of inconsistency is expressed by dependency degree k, and it is defined as:

$$k=card(POS(P, Q))/card(P, Q)$$

Obviously, $0 \leq k \leq 1$. If $k=1$, the algorithm is consistent; if $k \neq 1$, the algorithm is inconsistent. If the PQ-algorithm has a dependency degree k, we call the dependency degree of Q on P is k, denoted as $P \Rightarrow_k Q$.

11.4.2 Reduction of Consistent Decision Tables

We know that the property of indiscernibility can be used to the reduction of knowledge. Given an attribute set $C \subseteq A$ in knowledge representation system S, A is redundant if and only if $\text{IND}(A-C)=\text{IND}(A)$. If $A-C$ is redundant in A and C is dependent in S, C is the reduct of A.

Here, the problem discussed is expressed by logic form, and we use the consistency of algorithm to determine and reduce.

Given a consistent algorithm (P, Q) and $a \in P$, if and only if $((P-\{a\}), Q)$ is consistent, we call a is omissible in (P, Q), otherwise it is not omissible.

If all attributes of P are not omissible in algorithm (P, Q), (P, Q) is independent. Given attribute subset $R \subseteq P$, if (R, Q) is independent and consistent, then R is the P reduct of algorithm (P, Q). If attribute subset R is the P reduct of algorithm (P, Q), (R, Q) is the reduct of (P, Q). The reduction of algorithm is to reduce unnecessary condition attributes, and it is the reduction of the dimensions of knowledge representation spaces.

In algorithm (P, Q), the set of all attributes that are not omissible is called as the core of algorithm (P, Q), denoted as $\text{CORE}(P, Q)$.

Proposition 11.7 $CORE(P, Q)= RED(P, Q)$

Here, RED(P, Q) is the set of all reducts of algorithm (P, Q).

Besides, we introduce some properties of attributes in decision tables.

Proposition 11.8 *Decision table $T=(U, A, C, D)$ is consistent, if and only if $C \Rightarrow D$.*

From proposition 11.8, we can easily test the consistency by calculating the dependency of condition attributes to decision attribute. If the degree of dependency is equal to 1, we say the decision table is consistent, otherwise inconsistent.

Proposition 11.9 *Each decision table $T=(U, A, C, D)$ can be uniquely decomposed to two decision tables $T_1=(U_1, A, C, D)$ and $T_2=(U_2, A, C, D)$, where $C \Rightarrow_1 D$ in T_1 and $C \Rightarrow_0 D$ in T_2. Here, $U_1=POS_C(D)$, $U_2= \cup BN_C(X)$ and $X \in U|IND(D)$*

If the dependency degrees of condition attributes are known and the decision table is inconsistent (the degree of dependency is less than 1), then the table can be decomposed to two tables according to proposition 11.9: one table is totally inconsistent, whose dependency degree is 0; the other table is totally consistent, whose dependency degree is 1. Certainly, only when the dependency degree is more than 0 and less than 1, the decomposition can be processed.

The steps of reduction are as follows:

(1) Reduce a condition attribute in the decision table, that is, delete a column from the decision table;
(2) Delete the reduplicate rows;
(3) Delete the redundant values in each decision rule.

Note, comparing with the description of knowledge representation system, the rows here do not represent any real objects. Therefore, if two rows represent the same decision, one of them can be deleted.

The decision table after reduction is an incomplete decision table. It only contains the values of condition attributes that are necessary in decision making. However, it possesses all the knowledge of original knowledge system.

1. Reduction of Condition Attributes

With the form of discernibility matrix, A. Skowron proposed a knowledge representation method. Because the calculation of cores, reducts and etc with the method is simple, the method has a lot of merits. The main idea of the method is as follows.

Suppose $S=(U, A)$ is a knowledge representation system, $U =\{x_1,x_2,...,x_n\}$ and $A =\{a_1, a_2, ..., a_m\}$, where x_i is the discussed object ($i=1, 2, ..., n$) and a_j is the attribute of objects ($j=1,2,..., m$).

The discernibility matrix of knowledge representation system S is denoted as $M(S)=[c_{ij}]_{n\times n}$, and the elements of the matrix are defined as:

$c_{ij}=\{a\in A: a(x_i)\neq a(x_j), i,j=1,2,...,n\}$.

Thus, c_{ij} is the set of attributes that x_i or x_j do not have. Using discernibility matrix, it is easy to calculate the core and reduction of attribute set A.

In discernibility matrix, core is the set of elements that have only one attribute, that is

$CORE(A)=\{a\in A: c_{ij}=(a), \text{ for some } i, j\}$

Attribute set B is a reduct of A, if B is the minimal attribute subset that satisfies the following condition:

$B \cap c_{ij} \neq \varnothing$, for each non-empty element $c_{ij} \neq \varnothing$ in M(S).

In other words, reducts are the minimal attribute subsets, which can discern all objects that are distinguished by the whole attribute set A.

Because M(S) is symmetrical and $c_{ii} = \varnothing$ for each i=1,2,...,n, M(S) can be expressed by its lower triangle part $(1 \leq j < i \leq n)$.

Each discernibility matrix M(S) corresponds to only one discernibility function. The function is defined as follows:

The discernibility function of information system S is a boolean function with m-dimension variables $a_1,...,a_m (a_i \in A, i=1,...,m)$. It is the conjunction of $\vee c_{ij}$, where $\vee c_{ij}$ is the disjunction of elements in c_{ij} $(1 \leq j < i \leq n$ and $c_{ij} \neq \varnothing)$.

According to the correspondence between functions and reductions, A.Skowron proposed a method for calculating the reduction RED(S) of information system S. Its steps are as follows.

(1) Calculate the discernibility matrix M(S) of information system S;
(2) Calculate the discernibility function $f_{M(S)}$ corresponding to M(S);
(3) Calculate the minimal disjunction paradigm of $f_{M(S)}$, where each element in the disjunction paradigm is a reduct.

Note, all reducts can be computed with the method. However, the method is only propitious to very small data set.

Table 11.1 Information table

A\U	a	b	c	d	e
u_1	1	0	2	1	0
u_2	0	0	1	2	1
u_3	2	0	2	1	0
u_4	0	0	2	2	2
u_5	1	1	2	1	0

To reduce a decision table, we can use the discernibility matrix based method to reduce condition attributes. We use the decision attributes to generate equivalent classes, and disregard the objects with same decision attribute values. The table in Table 11.1 is a decision table, where a, b, c, d are its condition attributes and e is its decision attribute. Then, the discernibility matrix of it is illustrated as Table 11.2.

With the discernibility matrix, we know that the core is $\{c\}$ and the discernibility function is $c \wedge (a \vee d)$ or $(a \wedge c) \vee (c \wedge d)$. Thus, we can get the two reducts $\{a, c\}$ and $\{c, d\}$.

Table 11.2 Discernibility matrix

u	u_1	u_2	u_3	u_4	u_5
u_1					
u_2	a, c, d				
u_3		a, c, d			
u4	a, d	c	a, d		
u5		a, b, c, d		a, b, d	

When the number of objects and attributes are huge, the matrix will be very space-consumed. However, discernibility matrix is intuitionistic, and it can explain the reduction process. The essence of discernibility matrix based reduction method is that using the absorption law and other principles in logic operations to reduce data. Thus, the steps generating discernibility matrixes can be omitted. Applying the interpretation algorithm of generalized decision logic formulas, logic formulas related with attributes can be extracted from decision tables directly. Then the formulas are reduced in logic deduction system. That is, extract the discernible attributes of objects first (the objects with the same decision attribute values are not compared) and then generate formulas. At the same time, he formulas are reduced. At last, the formulas are transformed to disjunction paradigms, and each element of the disjunction paradigm is a reduct.

The attribute values of u_1 and u_2, u_3, u_4, u_5 are expressed by discernible conjunction paradigm:

$$(a \vee c \vee d) \wedge (a \vee d)$$

With some logic operations like absorption law to get simpler formula ①:

$$a \vee d$$

The attribute values of u_2, u_3, u_4, u_5 are expressed by the addition of discernible conjunction paradigm and ①:

$$(a \vee d) \wedge (a \vee c \vee d) \wedge c \wedge (a \vee b \vee c \vee d)$$

With some logic operations like absorption law to get simpler formula ②:

$$(a \vee d) \wedge c$$

The attribute values of u_3, u_4, u_5 are expressed by the addition of discernible conjunction paradigm and ②:

$$(a \lor d) \land c \land (a \lor d)$$

With some logic operations like absorption law to get simpler formula ③:

$$(a \lor d) \land c$$

The attribute values of u_4, u_5 are expressed by the addition of discernible conjunction paradigm and ③:

$$(a \lor d) \land c \land (a \lor b \lor d)$$

With some logic operations like absorption law to get simpler formula ④:

$$(a \lor d) \land c$$

Process formula ④ with distributive law from $\land$ to $\lor$, and generate the discernible disjunction paradigm:

$$(a \land c) \lor (c \land d)$$

Thus, Table 11.1 can be reduced to the two tables in Table 11.3 and 11.4.

Table 11.3 A reduced decision table of Table 11.1

A \ U	a	c	e
u_1	1	2	0
u_2	0	1	1
u_3	2	2	0
u_4	0	2	2
u_5	1	2	0

Table 11.4 A reduced decision table of Table 11.1

A \ U	c	d	e
u_1	2	1	0
u_2	1	2	1
u_3	2	1	0
u_4	2	2	2
u_5	2	1	0

2. Reduction of Rows

The reduplicate rows in decision tables should be deleted, because their values of condition attributes and decision attributes are equal and they represent the same decision rule. Besides, the order of decision rules is not essential, so the rows in

Table 11.3 and 11.4 can be reduced. For example, Table 11.3 can be reduced to a Table 11.5 as follows.

Table 11.5 The Reduction of Table 11.3

A \ U	a	c	e
u_1	1	2	0
u_2	0	1	1
u_3	2	2	0
u_4	0	2	2

3. Reduction of Attribute Values

For decision tables, the reduction of attribute values is processed on decision rules. It is to reduce the unnecessary conditions of each decision rules in decision algorithms respectively with decision logic. The reduction is not the unitary attribute reduction. It is a reduction on each decision rule. The redundant attribute values in a decision rule are reduced, which make the decision algorithm smaller.

In previous sections, we have defined that, if θ is a P-basic formula and $R \subseteq P$, then θR denotes a R-basic formula that is generated by deleting all elementary formulas from θ.

$\theta \rightarrow \Psi$ is a PQ-rule and $a \in P$, if and only if $\models_s \theta \rightarrow \Psi$ implicates $\models_s \theta (P - \{a\}) \rightarrow \Psi$. At this time, we call that attribute a is omissible in $\theta \rightarrow \Psi$. Otherwise, attribute a is not omissible in $\theta \rightarrow \Psi$.

In rule $\theta \rightarrow \Psi$, if all attributes are not omissible, then $\theta \rightarrow \Psi$ is independent. If $\theta \rightarrow \Psi$ is independent, and $\models_s \theta \rightarrow \Psi$ implicates $\models_s \theta (P - \{a\}) \rightarrow \Psi$, then attribute subset $R \subseteq P$ is called as the reduct of $\theta \rightarrow \Psi$. If R is the reduct of $\theta \rightarrow \Psi$, $\theta R \rightarrow \Psi$ is called as reduced.

The set of all attributes in $\theta \rightarrow \Psi$ that are not omissible is called as the core of $\theta \rightarrow \Psi$, and it is denoted as CORE($\theta \rightarrow \Psi$).

Proposition 11.10 $CORE(P \rightarrow Q) = \cap RED(P \rightarrow Q)$,

Here, $RED(P \rightarrow Q)$ is the reduction set of $P \rightarrow Q$.

As we said, the reduction of decision rules is that using decision logic to reduce the unnecessary conditions of each decision rule in decision algorithms. That is, calculate the core and reducts of each decision rule.

The reduction of attribute values in decision tables (the reduction of decision rules) is actually processed on condition attributes. Each row of decision table corresponds to a decision rule. Thus for calculating the core of a decision rule's condition attributes, we should first delete the values of condition attributes in the row from the table, and then add some condition attribute values to the core. The resulting condition attribute values can ensure the consistency of tables, and each condition attribute values are not omissible. If there exist reduplicate rows in the reduced tables, the rows should be deleted also, because they represent the same decision rule.

For example, considering the first decision rule $a_1c_2 \rightarrow e_0$ in Table 11.5, a_1 is the core value. Because rule $a_1 \rightarrow e_0$ (after deleting c_2) is true and rule $c_2 \rightarrow e_0$ (after deleting a_1) is false, a_1 cannot be reduced. With this method, all core values of every decision rules in Table 11.5 are illustrated as Table 11.6.

Table 11.6 The Core Vlues of Table 11.5

A \ U	a	c	e
u_1	1	—	0
u_2	—	1	1
u_3	2	—	0
u_4	0	2	2

After calculating all core values, each decision rule is reduced. For example, the first decision rule has a reduct a1→e0, because the decision rule can ensure the consistency of table. Thus, we can get the reduced table of Table 11.5.

Table 11.7 Reduced table of Table 11.5

A \ U	a	c	e
u_1	1	×	0
u_2	×	1	1
u_3	2	×	0
u_4	0	2	2

The corresponding decision algorithm is: $a_1 \lor a_2 \rightarrow e_0$, $c_1 \rightarrow e_1$, $a_0c_2 \rightarrow e_2$

4. Importance of Attributes

As mentioned before, reduction is an important concept in rough set theory, which can be used for data analysis. However, the calculation of all reducts is an

NP-hard problem, thus it is necessary to simplify the calculation process and find the optimal or suboptimal reduct with the help of heuristic information.

Existing reduction algorithms usually use core as the start to calculate reducts, and then compute the best or the minimal reduct (defined by users). Employing attribute importance degrees as heuristic information, the algorithms add attributes to a set one by one according to their importance degrees. Once the attribute set is a reduct, the algorithm stops. For different algorithms, the measures of attribute importance are different. Current researchers mainly focus on the following measures.

(1) Measure based on the movement of dependency

Suppose S is a decision table, C and D are condition attribute set and decision attribute set respectively. Let $R \subset C$, then for each attribute $a \in C{-}R$, the importance degree is defined as follows:

$$SGF(a,R,D)=k(R \cup \{a\}, D)-k(R,D)$$

where $k(R,D)=card(POS_R(D))/card(POS_C(D))$.

The degree can also be defined as follows:

$$SGF(a,R,D)=\gamma_{R \cup \{a\}}-\gamma_R$$

where $\gamma_R=card(POS_R(D))/card(U)$.

Basic ideas of the two definitions are same. If a decision table is given, $card(POS_C(D))$ and $card(U)$ are both constant. Although the values of importance degrees are different, the order of attributes arranged by their importance degrees is same.

(2) Measure based on information entropy

Suppose $H(D/R)$ is the condition entropy of R related with D, the importance degree of attribute a is defined as:

$$SGF(a,R,D)= H(D/R)- H(D/ R \cup \{a\})$$

(3) Measure based on the frequency of attributes in discernibility matrix

Assume M is a discernibility matrix generated from decision table S, and let $p(a)$ be the frequency of attribute a in M, which defines the frequency of a in M. Thus, the importance degree of attribute a is defined as:

$$SGF(a,R,D)= p(a)$$

11.4.3 *Reduction of Inconsistent Decision Tables*

If all decision rules generated from a decision table are consistent, the table is consistent, otherwise it is inconsistent. It is easy to reduce a consistent decision table. The main idea is to test whether there exists some inconsistent rules after an attribute or an attribute value is reduced. However, for inconsistent decision table, the methods based on this idea are not effective. Therefore, we introduce two reduction methods for inconsistent tables in this section: one is based on the movement of positive region, and the other is based on the decomposition of an inconsistent table which results in two sub-tables — a totally consistent table and a totally inconsistent table.

The steps of reducing an inconsistent decision table are similar with those of reducing a consistent table. Note, in the process of reducing consistent tables, reduplicate rows are deleted. That is, the same decision rules are deleted. However, for inconsistent tables, the deletion of reduplicate rows depends on the consistency of decision rules. If a decision rule is consistent, it can be deleted; otherwise, it cannot be deleted. In the following subsections, we will give a detail explanation.

1. *The Method Based on the Movement of Positive Regions*

For the inconsistency during knowledge representation, similar methods as consistent cases can be proposed. The main idea is to test whether the positive regions before and after the reduction of attributes are different. Give an inconsistent algorithm (P, Q) and $a \in P$, if $POS(P, Q) = POS(P - \{a\}, Q)$, attribute a is omissible in algorithm (P, Q), otherwise a can not be omitted.

If all attributes in algorithm (P, Q) can not be omitted, (P, Q) is called to be independent. Given attribute set $R \subseteq P$, if algorithm (R, Q) is independent and $POS(P, Q) = POS(R, Q)$, R is called as a reduct of (P, Q).

The set of all attributes that are not omissible in algorithm (P, Q) is called as the core of (P, Q), denoted as $CORE(P, Q)$.

It is obvious that reducing consistent algorithms is a special case of reducing inconsistent algorithms. However, the processes of reducing decision rules, that is, the processes of reducing condition attribute values are different for consistent and inconsistent decision rules

If a decision rule is consistent, we should first calculate the core value of its condition attributes. That is to say, delete a condition attribute value from the rule, and then test whether the remaining attribute values can determine the decision attribute. If not, the value is a core value. After the generation of core values, the second step is to get the reduct of the condition attribute values. Then, some condition attribute values are combined with the core values, and the resulting values are tested whether they can ensure the consistency of the decision rule and whether each condition attribute value can be omitted.

If a decision rule is inconsistent, we should first calculate the core value of its condition attributes. That is to say, delete a value of attribute value from the table and test whether the decision attribute values determined by the values of condition attributes are same before and after deletion. If not, the value is a core value. After the calculation of core values, the second step is to get the reduct of the condition attribute values. Then, some condition attribute values are combined with the core values, and the decision attribute values determined by the resulting condition attribute values are tested whether they are different with the original set of decision attribute values and whether each condition attribute value can be omitted.

In the following, we will illustrate how to use the method to reduce an inconsistent decision table.

Consider a knowledge representation system illustrated by Table 11.8.

Table 11.8 A knowledge representation system

U	a	b	c	d	e
1	1	0	2	2	0
2	0	1	1	1	2
3	2	0	0	1	1
4	1	1	0	2	2
5	1	0	2	0	1
6	2	2	0	1	1
7	2	1	1	1	2
8	0	1	1	0	1

Here, $C=\{a, b, c\}$ and $D=\{d, e\}$ are condition attribute set and decision attribute set respectively. Because $U|C=\{\{1,5\}, \{2,8\}, \{3\}, \{4\}, \{6\}, \{7\}\}$, $U|D=\{\{1\}, \{2,7\}, \{3,6\}, \{4\}, \{5,8\}\}$, $POSC(D)=\{\{3\}, \{4\}, \{6\}, \{7\}\}$ and $rC(D)=4/8\neq 1$, table 11.8 is inconsistent.

After deleting attribute a, $U|(C-\{a\})=\{\{1,5\}, \{2,7,8\}, \{3\}, \{4\}, \{6\}\}$, $POSC-\{a\}(D) =\{\{3\}, \{4\}, \{6\}\}$ POSC(D), so attribute a can not be omitted; after deleting attribute b, $U|(C-\{b\})=\{\{1,5\}, \{2,8\}, \{3,6\}, \{4\}, \{7\}\}$, $POSC-\{b\}(D)=\{\{3\}, \{4\}, \{6\},\{7\}\}=POSC(D)$, so attribute b is not omissible; after deleting attribute c, $U|(C-\{c\})=\{\{1,5\}, \{2,8\}, \{3\}, \{4\}, \{6\}, \{7\}\}$, $POSC-\{c\}(D) =\{\{3\}, \{4\}, \{6\},\{7\}\}=POSC(D)$, so attribute c is not omissible.

From these results, we can get the condition attribute core of table 11.8 is a, and there are two reducts $\{a, b\}$ and $\{a, c\}$. Table 11.9 is the table after reducing attribute c from the original decision table.

Table 11.9 Decision table after reducing attribute c

U	a b d e
1	1 0 2 0
2	0 1 1 2
3	2 0 1 1
4	1 1 2 2
5	1 0 0 1
6	2 2 1 1
7	2 1 1 2
8	0 1 0 1

Then, we reduce the attribute values in Table 11.9. For the third decision rule $a_2b_0 \rightarrow d_1e_1$, it is a consistent decision rule. a_2, b_0 are core values, because $a_2 \rightarrow d_1e_1$ (after deleting b_0) and $b_0 \rightarrow d_1e_1$ (after deleting a_2) are both inconsistent rule. For the second decision rule $a_0b_1 \rightarrow d_1e_2$, it is an inconsistent decision rule and a_0 is its core value. The reason is that, the decision attribute values determined by a_0b_1 are $\{d_1e_2, d_0e_1\}$, and after deleting b_1, the decision attribute values determined by a_0 are also $\{d_1e_2, d_0e_1\}$. However, if a_0 is deleted, the decision attribute values determined by b_1 are also $\{d_1e_2, d_2e_2, d_0e_1\}$. So, a_0 cannot be reduced. With this method, the resulting core values of each decision rule are showed in Table 11.10.

Table 11.10 Core values of the decision rules in Table 11.9

U	a	b	d	e
1	1	0	2	0
2	0	—	1	2
3	2	0	1	1
4	1	1	2	2
5	1	0	0	1
6	—	2	1	1
7	2	1	1	2
8	0	—	0	1

Therefore, we get the reducts of all attribute values as Table 11.11.

Suppose θ and Ψ are the logic formulas for conditions and decisions respectively, and $\theta \rightarrow \Psi$ is a decision rule. We use $|\Psi|$ to represent the object set satisfying formula Ψ in S. We can attach a value to each decision rule, which is called rough operator of the rule. The operator is defined as: $\mu(\theta, \Psi)=K(|\theta \wedge \Psi|)/K(|\theta|)$, and the form of the operator's rule is: $\theta \rightarrow m\Psi$, $m=\mu(\theta, \Psi)$. In the definition, K(S) represents the cardinal number of S, which has the same meaning with symbol |S| (the number of the elements in S) in mathematical language. If rule $\theta \rightarrow \Psi$ is totally consistent, the rough operator can be omitted.

Table 11.11 The reducts of all attribute values in Table 11.9

U	a	b	d	e
1	1	0	2	0
2	0	×	1	2
3	2	0	1	1
4	1	1	2	2
5	1	0	0	1
6	×	2	1	1
7	2	1	1	2
8	0	×	0	1

Thus, the decision algorithm generated from Table 11.11 is:

$a_1 b_0 \rightarrow_{0.5} d_2 e_0,$

$a_0 \rightarrow_{0.5} d_1 e_2,$

$a_2 b_1 \rightarrow d_1 e_2,$

$a_2 b_0 \vee b_2 \rightarrow d_1 e_1,$

$a_0 \rightarrow_{0.5} d_0 e_1,$

$a_1 b_1 \rightarrow d_2 e_2,$

$a_1 b_0 \rightarrow_{0.5} d_0 e_1.$

2. The Method Based on The Decomposition of Inconsistent Tables

Each decision table T=(U, A, C, D) can be split into two decision tables T_1=(U_1, A, C, D) and T_2=(U_2, A, C, D). Thus, we have $C \Rightarrow_1 D$ in table T_1 and $C \Rightarrow_0 D$ in table T_2. Here, $U_1 = POS_C(D)$, $U_2 = \cup BN_C(X)$, and $X \in U/IND(D)$.

From this proposition we know, if the dependency degrees of condition attributes are known and a decision table is inconsistent (its dependency degree is less than 1), the table can be decomposed to two sub-tables. One table is totally inconsistent whose dependency degree is 0, and the other table is totally consistent whose dependency degree is 1. Of course, only when the dependency degree is more than 0 and not equal to 1, the decomposition can be processed. The totally consistent table can be reduced with the method introduced in Chapter 4. The totally inconsistent table needs not to be processed, and the decision rules with rough operators can be generated directly from it.

In example 11.1, the decision table illustrated by Table 11.1 can be decomposed to the following two sub-tables:

Table 11.12 Totally consistent decision table

U	a	b	c	d	e
3	2	0	0	1	1
4	1	1	0	2	2
6	2	2	0	1	1
7	2	1	1	1	2

Table 11.13 Totally inconsistent decision table

U	a	b	c	d	e
1	1	0	2	2	0
2	0	1	1	1	2
5	1	0	2	0	1
8	0	1	1	0	1

For Table 11.12, $U|C=\{\{3\}, \{4\}, \{6\}, \{7\}\}$, $U|D=\{\{3,6\}, \{4\}, \{7\}\}$, $POS_C(D)=\{\{3\}, \{4\}, \{6\}, \{7\}\}$ and $r_C(D)=4/4=1$, so Table 11.12 is totally consistent and the decision rules in this table are all consistent.

For Table 11.13, $U|C=\{\{1, 5\}, \{2,8\}\}$, $U|D=\{\{1\}, \{2\}, \{5,8\}\}$, $r_C(D)=0/4=0$, so Table 11.6 is totally inconsistent and the decision rules in this table are all inconsistent.

For Table 11.12, we reduce it and the resulting reducts of condition attributes are $\{a, b\}$, $\{a, c\}$ and $\{b, c\}$. Suppose the final reduct is $\{a, b\}$, then its corresponding decision table is as Table 11.14.

Table 11.14 Decision table after reducing attribute c from Table 11.11

U	a	b	d	e
3	2	0	1	1
4	1	1	2	2
6	2	2	1	1
7	2	1	1	2

After reducing the condition attribute values in Table 11.13, the resulting decision algorithm is:

$b_0 \vee b_2 \rightarrow d_1 e_1$

$a_1 \rightarrow d_2 e_2$

$a_2 b_1 \rightarrow d_1 e_2$

For Table 11.12, we can generate its decision rules attached with rough operators directly as follows.

$a_1 b_0 c_2 \rightarrow_{0.5} d_2 e_0$

$a_0 b_1 c_1 \rightarrow_{0.5} d_1 e_2$

$a_1 b_0 c_2 \rightarrow_{0.5} d_0 e_1$

$a_0 b_1 c_1 \rightarrow_{0.5} d_0 e_1$

At last, combine the decision algorithms generated from totally consistent and totally inconsistent decision tables, and then the decision algorithm corresponding to the original inconsistent decision table is got.

11.5 Extended Model of Rough Sets

Comparing with other method processing imprecise or uncertain information, basic rough set theory has its advantages. However, it still has some shortages. At present, most of the successful applications are based on the extension of basic rough set theory from various aspects. Under the assumption that known objects in universe have all necessary knowledge, basic rough set theory is a tool processing fuzziness and uncertainty. It is in essence a kind of tri-value logic (positive region, boundary region and negative region).

The main problems in basic rough set theory can be summarized as follows:

(1) Poor ability in processing the fuzziness of original data;
(2) Too simple description of rough set's boundary region;
(3) With basic rough set based methods, when the information is incomplete, objects are classified into a special class, and usually the class is determined. However, in real applications, a mass of objects need to be classified with given error ratios. Basic rough set theory cannot deal with these cases.

In the research of rough set theory, researchers have already proposed many extended models, such as variable precision rough set (VPRS) models, some rough set based nonmonotonic models, and the models integrating rough set theory and evidence theory. In the following, we will focus on some of them.

11.5.1 *Variable Precision Rough Set Model*

In original rough set model, universe U is assumed to be known, and the resulting conclusions are only tenable for the objects in U. However, in real applications, the assumptions are very difficult to be satisfied. To solve the problem, some new methods are needed to be developed, so that conclusions can be made from fewer objects and used to more applications. Besides, the conclusions are hoped to be tenable only for known objects, and for the whole universe, the conclusions should be viewed as uncertain or fuzzy. Based on the idea, W.Ziarko proposed an extended rough set model called as variable precision rough set model, which provides a classification strategy whose error rate is less a given value. Under the given error rate, new definitions of positive region, boundary region and negative region are presented, and related properties are discussed. Furthermore, J.D. Katzberg and W. Ziarko developed a VPRS model with asymmetry boundaries. The work generalized VPRS models and extended the application fields of VPRS. In the following, we will introduce the main idea of VPRS in brief.

In general, the fact that set X is included by Y does not give a degree measuring how much X belongs to Y. Considering this, VPRS define the degree:

$$C(X, Y)=1-card(X\cap Y)/card(X), \text{ if } card(x)>0$$
$$C(X, Y)=0 \qquad\qquad \text{ if } card(x)=0$$

$C(X, Y)$ is the rate that set X is falsely classified into set Y, that is, there are $C(X, Y)\times 100\%$ objects that are classified with mistake. Given a false classifying rate $\beta(0\leq\beta<0.5)$, according to above definition, we have $X\subseteq^{\beta}Y$, if and only if $C(X, Y)\leq\beta$.

Based on these, suppose U is a universe, R is an equivalence relation on U, and $U/R=A=\{X_1, X_2, \cdots, X_k \}$. Thus, the β-lower approximate set of definable set X is defined as

$$R_{\beta}X=\cup X_i \quad (X_i\subseteq^{\beta}X, i=1, 2, \cdots, k)$$

or

$$R_{\beta}X=\cup X_i \quad (C(X_i, X)\leq\beta, i=1, 2, \cdots, k).$$

Here, $R_{\beta}X$ is called as the β-positive region of X. The β-lower approximate set of X is defined as $R_{\beta}X=\cup X_i \quad (C(X_i, X)<1-\beta, i=1, 2, \cdots, k)$.

Thus, the β-boundary region is

$$BNR_{\beta}X=\cup X_i \quad (\beta<C(X_i, X)<1-\beta).$$

β-negative region is

$$NEGR_{\beta}X=\cup X_i \quad (C(X_i, X)\geq 1-\beta).$$

Furthermore, we can define β-dependency degrees, β-reducts and many concepts related with traditional rough set models.

It is obvious that, when β=0, VPRS models are transformed to traditional rough set models, so classical rough sets are special cases of VPRS. Moreover, VPRS is a directly extension of rough set, so it inherits the properties and advantages of rough sets. Consequently, it extends the application fields of rough set theory.

11.5.2 *Similarity Based Model*

In the case that there are lost attribute values in data set (the cases are very popular in databases), indiscernibility relations or equivalence relations cannot deal with these cases. To extend the ability of rough set, a lot of researchers use similarity relations but not indiscernibility relations as the foundation of rough set theory.

After replacing indiscernibility relations with similarity relations in rough set theory, the generated similar classes are not a partition of a set, because they are overlapped. Similar with equivalence classes, we can define a set $SIM_b(x)$ that includes all elements that are similar with x in attribute set B. Note, the elements in $SIM_b(x)$ may belong to different decision classes, so the definition of similar decision classes is needed. Similar decision classes are the decision classes corresponding to similar sets.

Because the elements in a similar set may not belong to identical decision class, thus the relative-absorption term set is defined. Subset $Y \subseteq U$ is called as relative-absorption term set, if for each $x \in U$, there exists $y \in Y$ that is similar with x and has the same decision value with x. Obviously, relative-absorption term set can be used to reduce data. With the help of relative-absorption term set, positive region can be easily defined. Positive region is the union of similar sets included by decision classes. Dependency degrees and reducts can be defined similarly with classical sets.

In practice, similarity models have better performances than traditional rough set models. In the case that there is lost data in databases, a simple similar relation can be defined as follows (symbol "? " represents that the value is unknown or unconcerned.):

$$\tau_C(x, y) = \{x \in U, y \in U | \forall a \in C, a(x) = a(y) \text{ or } a(x) = ? \text{ or } a(y) = ?\}$$

11.5.3 *Rough Set Based Nonmonotonic Logic*

Since the development of rough set theory, its researchers thought much of its logic, and they attempted to construct rough logic with the help of rough sets. A lot of papers in this field were published. For example, Z. Pawlak published a paper titled by "Rough Logic" in 1987. In this paper, he gave the semantic explanation of rough logic formulas: true, false, rough true, rough false and rough negative. The five values can be viewed as different degrees of similarity, but they are lack of mathematical description. Z. Pawlak and etc regarded rough logic—rough set based imprecise inference logic—as the most important topic in their review paper published by Communication of The ACM (Pawlak,1995).

T. Y. Lin, Q. Liu and etc defined rough lower approximate operator L and rough upper approximate operator H based on topology. Semantic properties of the two operators are very similar with the necessity operator □ and possibility operator ◇ in modal logic. Therefore, the logic formulas with L and H operators are called as rough logic formulas. Moreover, they constructed the axiomatized rough logic deductive system, which is similar with mode logic, and parallel deductive rules. However, because for L and H, the rough logic defined is vague, it cannot be explained by mathematic language. Although the work had some shortages, it gave a research direction "*Approximation Proof*", which is giving the mathematical meanings of L and H. So that, the logic formulas constructed by L and H can have mathematical meanings. Furthermore, Q. Liu and etc defined similar degrees λ_* and λ^* based on rough set theory. The degrees were composed with professional fields based imprecise numbers and experiential numbers, and then rough numbers were generated. They also discussed the properties of rough logic and the values of $\lambda \in [\lambda_*, \lambda^*]$ in the explanation of logic formulas. Besides, Q. Liu proposed an accuracy operators based rough logic (AORL) in the fifth international conference of rough set held in Japan in 1996, and presented the process of resolution reasoning.

A. Nakamura and etc proposed incomplete information system based rough mode logic R_1 and R_2. The main idea of R_1 is based on some equivalence relation of incomplete information systems. The work presented some properties and the decision process of R_1 and an axiomatized deduction system. The completeness and correctness of R_1 were proved. R_2 is mainly based on algebraic structure of interval sets. The work proposed the definitions of incomplete information system's mode operations and the decision process of R_2, which was different with those of R_1. Moreover, the reduction of R_2 axoimatized system was explored.

11.5.4 *Integration with Other Mathematical Tools*

Rough set theory and fuzzy set theory are not opposite. They are different, but they can complement each other. Basically, rough sets show the indiscerniblity among objects in sets, that is, the rough property caused by the granularity of knowledge; fuzzy sets construct models for the unclear definition of subsets' boundaries, and it shows the fuzziness of membership boundaries. They deal with two different kinds of fuzziness and uncertainness. It is sure that combination of them can process uncertain knowledge better. Based on the idea, D. Dudios and H. Prade presented the concept of rough fuzzy set and fuzzy rough set. The main idea is to define the lower approximate set and upper approximate set of fuzzy sets when equivalence relations make the universes of fuzzy sets rough. That is to say, the equivalence relations are transformed to fuzzy similar relations, so that a more expressive rough model is got. D. Dudios and H. Prade also had a detailed research on the properties of fuzzy sets' lower and upper approximate sets, and pointed that in the case that indiscernibility and fuzzy predications are both existent, the concept of fuzzy rough sets has potential applications in logic inference.

D. Dudios and H. Prade also indicated that, evidence theory of Shafer and rough set theory of Z. Pawlak are the same model under different glossaries. A. Skowron and J. Grazymala-Buss gave more special conclusion. They pointed out that rough set can be viewed as the basis of evidence theory. In the frame of rough set theory, their work explained the basic concepts of evidence theory. Especially, lower and upper approximate sets are used to explain belief and plausibility functions, and then their complementarity is discussed.

11.6 Experimental Systems of Rough Sets

Rough set theory is proved to be very useful in practice. Plentiful applications in our real lives also support the viewpoints. The theory is regarded as an important one for AI and cognitive sciences. It made a lot of important applications on decision supporting, experts systems, inductive inferences, and switch circuits.

In these years, rough set theory has a great progress in the applications on knowledge discovery (KDD). Rough set theory based methods gradually becomes those of main KDD methods. Knowledge discovery or data mining on databases is a new subfield of AI, and it deals with uncommon knowledge mined from increased information databases of enterprises. The main tasks of it are to discover the associations and relations of internal data. However, although rough set theory plays a good role on the processing of fuzzy and incomplete knowledge, it has poor ability to deal with original fuzzy data. Therefore, the integration between rough set theory and others, such as fuzzy set theory, neural network theory and etc, will benefit its applications.

Rough set based KDD systems are usually composed by some parts, such as data preprocessing, rough set or other extended theory based data reduction, decision algorithms and etc. The general idea is that: first preprocess data and prepare for data reduction, and then calculate reducts or approximate reducts; at last, extract rules by value reduction algorithm (reduce the numbers of attributes and objects) and apply the rules to new objects.

In the past few years, a lot of rough set based KDD systems are developed. The most representative ones are LERS, ROSE, KDD-R, Rough Enough and etc.

1. LERS

LERS(Learning from examples based on Rough Set) system was developed by Kansas university of USA, which is a rough set based case learning system (Grzyrnala-busse, 1997). It is implemented on VAX9000 with Common Lisp. LERS has been used in Johnson space center as an experts systems developing tool for two years. Most of the developed experts systems can be used to the iatric decision of space station. Moreover, LERS was also applied to the research on environment protection, weather predictions and medical treatments.

2. ROSE

Poznan science and technology university of Poland developed ROSE (Rough Set Data Explorer) system to have decision analysis. It is the new version of Rough Das & Rough Class system, where Rough Das is to analyze information of system data and Rough Class is to support the classification of objects. Rough Das and Rough Class have been applied to many application fields. ROSE is an interactive software system implemented on PC compatible machine and Windows/NT system. The calculation modules of ROSE have the following features: Data verification and preprocessing
• Automatic discretization of continuous values with Fayyad and Irani discretization algorithms
• Qualitative estimation of condition attributes with traditional rough set models or variable precision rough set models
• Attribute core calculation and information table reduction with thealgorithms developed by Romanski, Skowron and etc.

- Exploring the relative importance of attribute to objective classes;
- Choosing the most important attributes to classify objects, and delete redundant attributes;
- Extracting decision rules with LEM2 algorithm or Explore algorithm;
- Post-processing after acquiring rules;
- Classifying new objects with decision rules;
- Evaluating decision rule sets with k-cross validation method.

3. KDD—R

KDD—R is a variable precision rough set model based KDD system developed by Regina university of Canada. It used the decision matrix based method in knowledge discovery field. The system was used to analyze medicinal data, and generate new relations between symptoms and states of illness. Besides, it also supported the market exploration of telecommunication industry. The system is composed by four parts:

- Data preprocessing;
- VPRS model based attribute dependency analysis, and redundant attribute reducing;
- Rule extraction;
- Decision making.

4. Rough Enough

Based on rough set theory, Troll Data Inc. company of Norway developed a data mining tool —Rough Enough. Readers can download the software from the Website http://www.trolldata.no/renough.

Rough Enough can calculate discernibility matrix from information systems. It provided many tools to process approximate sets, such as equivalence classes, decision classes, lower approximate sets, upper approximate sets, boundary fields, rough membership values, extensive decision rules and etc. The reducts are generated by genetic algorithms.

11.7 Granular Computing

Broadly speaking, granular computing may be considered as a label of a new field of multi-disciplinary study, dealing with theories, methodologies, techniques, and tools that make use of granules (i.e., groups, classes, and clusters) in the process of problem solving. A granule is usually composed by elements, which are indiscernible, similar, adjacent or functional. The essence of information granulation is approximation.

Suppose $K=(U, R)$ is an approximate space, and R is a partition of U, then the granularity of knowledge R can be defined as:

$$GK(R) = (1/|U|^2) * (|R_1|^2 + |R_2|^2 + \ldots \ldots + |R_m|^2) \qquad (11.10)$$

Granular computing is an umbrella term which covers any theories, methodologies, techniques related with granularities. In brief, granular computing is the superset of fuzzy granular theory, while rough set theory and interval computing theory are the subsets of granular mathematics. When a problem involves incomplete, uncertain or fuzzy information, the distinguishing of objects are very difficult. Thus, granularities are needed to deal with these cases.

The concept of granular computing was first presented by Prof. Zadeh in his paper "Fuzzy sets and information granularity" (Zadeh, 1979). Pawlak and etc related granular computing with rough set theory, and did many researches on them (Peter, 2002). In Yao' work, he uses decision logic language (DL-language) to describe the granularities of sets (that is, use the sets of objects satisfying formula ϕ to define equivalence classes $m(\phi)$), and then utilize the lattices constructed by all partitions to solve consistent classification problems. Moreover, Yao pointed out that researchers can make use of multilayer granulation to explore the approximation of hierarchical rough sets. Lin and Yao researched on granular computing with the help of neighbor systems.

L. Zhang and B. Zhang indicated that concepts with different granularities can be represented by subsets, and concepts with different granularities can be expressed by subsets with different granularities. A cluster of concepts can constitute a partition of universe – quotient space (knowledge base). Different concept clusters can construct different quotient spaces. Therefore, given some knowledge bases, the research on granular computing is to find the relations and transformations among various subsets. The model of quotient spaces can be described by a triplet (X, F, T), where X denotes a universe, F denotes a attribute set, and T denotes the topology structure on X. When choosing coarse granularities, that is, giving an equivalence relation R (or a partition), we say that a quotient set is related with R is generated, which is denoted by $[X]$. The corresponding triplet of $[X]$ is $([X], [F], [T])$, called as the quotient space related with R. The research on Quotient space theory is to explore the relations, composition, synthesis, decomposition of quotient spaces and also the inference on quotient spaces(Zhang et al, 2005).

In 1962, Zeeman proposed that cognitive activities can be viewed as some kind tolerance spaces in a function space. The tolerance spaces, which are constructed by distance functions based tolerance relations, is used for stability analysis of dynamic system by Zeeman. In our work, tolerance spaces based on distance functions are developed for the modeling and analysis of information granulation, which is defined as tolerance relation granulation in the following part.

The aim of describing a problem on different granularities is to enable the computer to solve the same problem at different granule sizes hierarchically. We can use a tolerance space to describe a problem (Zheng et al, 2005). A tolerance granular space model $TGSM$ can be formalized as a 4-tuple (OS, TR, FG, NTC), where OS denotes an object set system and is composed by the objects processed and granulated in tolerance granular space, which can be viewed as the object field; TR denotes a tolerance relation system and is a (parameterized) relation structure. It is composed by a set of tolerance relations. It includes the relations or coefficients that the granular spaces base on; FG denotes transformation function between tolerance granules; NTC denotes a nested tolerance covering system. It is a (parameterized) granular structure, which denotes different levels granules and the granulation process based on above object system and tolerance relation system. It denotes a nested granular structure to express the relationships among granules and objects. NTC defines a nested granular structure to represent:

- Relations among granules and objects;
- The composition and decomposition of granules.

11.8 Future Trends of Rough Set Theory

Rough set theory is proved to be complete and very useful in real applications. It provides some effective methods which can be applied into many fields. Rough set theory based rough logic seems to be a worthy topic, because the logic can make monotone logic be nonmonotonized so that it can play a great role in the approximation of AI or uncertainty inference. From these viewpoints, it is obvious that the research on rough set theory based rough logic is promising.

Another important topic of rough set theory is the research on theory and applications of rough functions, which includes various approximate operations of rough functions, the basic properties of rough functions (such as rough continuity, rough derivative, rough integral and rough stability, control of rough functions) and the construction of discrete dynamic systems controlled by rough real functions. These topics need to be formalized under the model of rough function theory. The research on these topics will make contributions to the exploration on qualitative inference methods. The essence of these researches is to discrete continuous mathematics. Thus, continuous mathematics can also be processed by modern computers.

Control based on rough set theory seems to be another promising application field. Besides, the development of new neural network algorithms and genetic algorithms with the help of rough set theory is also very important. How to construct a uniform logic model to explain uncertainty theories, such as rough set theory, fuzzy set theory, evidence theory, probability theory and etc, is also worth to be researched. At present, there are still a few noticeable fields not mentioned. They are introduced in brief as follows.

(1) Based on the inheritance of original rough set models' basic mathematical properties, research on how to extend the models so that they can be applied to data compression and information system analysis better;
(2) In the distributed environments, research on the expression of incomplete or uncertain knowledge and the knowledge transformation among multi-agents;
(3) Research on how to introduce the concepts of upper and lower approximate sets, and their mathematical properties to some special algebraic structures. For example, research on the definition and relations of rough set operations defined on concept lattices;
(4) Research on the relations between rough set theory and formalized languages.

From the viewpoints of knowledge discovery, we list some possible research topics and application fields as follows.

Efficient reduction algorithms Efficient reduction algorithms are the basis of rough set theory applied to knowledge discovery. At present, there is not a very efficient method. Therefore, develop a fast reduction algorithm and its incremental version is still one of the main topics.

Huge data problems In practice, the sizes in databases are increased. For rough set theory, how to deal with the challenge is still a problem. Although exists a lot of helpful explorations, there are not satisfactory methods. Possible solving methods can be sampling, parallelizing, and etc.

Integration of various methods There are a lot of data mining methods. Experiments showed that, there is not a method that exceeds all of others.

Therefore, integrating various methods can be a possible way to enhance classification efficiency.

Readers can review the Website of Electronic Bulletin of the Rough Set Community (http://www.cs.uregina.ca/~roughset) to see current fruits of rough set theory.

Exercises

1. What is the basis of rough set theory?
2. What are decision tables and decision logic? Write the basic expression of decision logic language.
3. Explain knowledge reduction and knowledge dependency.
4. Why can attributes be reduced based on rough sets? Give an example to illustrate the reduction methods of inconsistent decision tables.
5. What is the meaning of minimal attribute set?
6. Describe the main problem and classical extended models of rough set theory in brief.
7. What is granular computing? Try to compare the features of the three granular computing models.

Chapter 12

Association Rules

12.1 Introduction

The purpose of the association rules mining is to find out a hidden associated relation between different sets of data fields in a database. It is one of the most widely used and more studied data mining methods. The association rule model is an important model among knowledge models in data mining. The concept of the association rule was proposed by Agrawal, Imielinski, Swami(Agrawal, 1993). It is a kind of simple but very practical rule about data relations. The model of association rule belongs to description pattern and the algorithm which discovers the association rule belongs to nonsupervised learning.

At the present, the trends of the research on association rules are as follows:

(1) Discover association rules from the concept with single layer to multiple layers. That is, the mining rule should effect on different layers of database. For example, in the analysis of sell database of a supermarket, if only the original fields of table, such as "bread", "milk" were mined, it will be difficult to discovery interesting rules. When some abstract concept about original fields, such as "food" were considered for mining meantime, some new and abstract rules will be probably found. So the mining on different abstract layers in database to discovery rules and metarules is a new research direction.

(2) Improve the efficiency of mining algorithm. Usually large quantities of data were processed in association rule mining and database may be scanned for many times. So it is important to improve the efficiency of mining algorithm. There exist three methods: one is to reduce the times of scanning database and it would

430

improve the efficiency greatly. Another is sampling technology, which selects the data sets for data mining. This method is efficient in the applications which pay attention to efficiency. The other method is parallel data mining. Because data in large scale of database are often located in different nodes in network and the parallel data mining can improve the efficiency apparently. This method is often used in Web mining on Internet.

(3) Besides of the above, key research topics also contain how to control the total scale of association rules, how to select and deal with the acquired rules, and how to discover fuzzy association rules and the mining algorithm with high efficiency. From the point of view of mining object, it is a valuable problemthat how to extend rule mining from relation database to text and Web data in the future.

Association rules mine mainly from transaction database, such as sales data in supermarkets, also called basket data. A transaction typically includes a unique transaction identity number and a list of the items making up the transaction. In transaction databases, we will investigate transactions with many items. Suppose product A appears in transaction 1, product B appears in transaction 2, we want to know how about product A and B appear in a transaction. In the knowledge discovery of database, association rule is a knowledge pattern which describes some products appear meantime in a transaction. Association rule learners are used to discover elements that co-occur frequently within a data set consisting of multiple independent selections of elements (such as purchasing transactions), and to discover rules, such as implication or correlation, which relate co-occurring elements. Questions such as "if a customer purchases product A, how likely is he to purchase product B?" and "What products will a customer buy if he buys products C and D?" are answered by association-finding algorithms. This application of association rule learners is also known as market basket analysis. As with most data mining techniques, the task is to reduce a potentially huge amount of information to a small, understandable set of statistically supported statements.

Let $R=\{I_1, I_2, \cdots, I_m\}$ be a itemset, W is a set of transactions. Each transaction T which is in W is a itemset, $T \subseteq R$. Suppose A is a itemset, T is a transaction and $A \subseteq T$, we call transaction T supports set A. A_n association rule is an implication of the form $A \Rightarrow B$, where A, B are two itemsets, $A \subset R$, $B \subset R$, and $A \cap B = \varnothing$.

Usually the following four parameters are applied to describe the attributes of rules

(1) Confidence

Suppose c% transactions which support itemset A in W also support itemset B at the same time, then c% is the confidence of association rule $A \Rightarrow B$. That is, confidence stands for the probability which a itemse A occurs in the transaction T and a itemset B also occurs in transaction T. The rule $A \Rightarrow B$ has confidence c in the transaction set W, where c is the percentage of transactions in W containing A that also contain B. This is taken to be the conditional probability, $P(B|A)$. That is,

$$\text{confidence}(A \Rightarrow B) = P(B|A). \tag{12.1}$$

For example, suppose 70% consummer who bought bread also bought butter, then the confidence is 70%.

(2) Support

Suppose s% transactions in W supporting both the itemset A and B, s% is called the support of rule $A \Rightarrow B$. The rule $A \Rightarrow B$ holds in the transaction set W with support s, where s is the percentage of transactions in W that contain $A \cup B$, that is, the union of set A and B. This is taken to be the probability, $P(A \cup B)$ which indicates a transaction contains the union of set A and set B.

For example, suppose there are 1000 customers in a supermarket someday and among them 100 customers purchased both bread and butter, then the support of $A \Rightarrow B$ is 10%(100/1000).

(3) Expected Confidence

Suppose e% transactions in W support the itemset B, then e% is called the expected confidence of rule $A \Rightarrow B$. Expected confidence reflects the probability of the itemset B occurs in all transactions when there are no other restrictions. For example, suppose there are 1000 customersr in a supermarket and 200 customers purchased butter, then the expected confidence of $A \Rightarrow B$ is 20%.

(4) Lift

Lift is the ratio of confidence to the expected confidence. Lift reflects the influence which the occurrence of itemsets A to the occurrence of itemset B.

Beacause the expected confidence is the probability of the occurrence of set B in all transactions and the confidence is the probability of the occurrence of set B in the transactions which set A is presented. Then the ratio of confidence to the expected confidence reflects the change of probability of the occurrence of set B when the precondition "the occurrence of set A" is added. The lift between the occurrence of A and B can be measured by computing

$$lift(A, B) = \frac{P(A \cup B)}{P(A)P(B)}$$ (12.2)

In the above example, the lift is 70%/20%=3.5.

Let $P(A)$ be the probability of the occurrence of itemset A, $P(B|A)$ be the probability of the occurrence of itemset B when itemset A occurs, then the above four parameters can be expressed as Table 12.1.

Confidence is a precise measure for an association rule. Support is an measure for the importance of a association rule. Support stands for the importance of a rule and the more the support is, the more important the rule is. There are rules which are with high confidence but low support, which means that the rule is neither important nor practical.

Table 12.1. Formula of the four parameters

Name	Description	Formula
Confidence	the probability of the occurrence of itemset B when itemset A is occurred	$P(B|A)$
Support	the probability of the occurrence of both itemset A and itemset B	$P(A \cup B)$
Expected Confidence	the probability of the occurrence of itemset B	$P(B)$
Lift	the ratio of confidence to the expected confidence	$P(B|A)/P(B)$

Expected confidence describes the support of itemset B where there is no influence from itemset A. Lift describes the influence of itemset A on itemset B. A great lift shows a great influence of itemset A on itemset B. Generally, the lift is often greater than 1 when the rule is practical for applications. Only when the confidence is greater than expected confidence, then the presence of A has promoted effect on the presence of B and it shows itemsets A and B are related on some grade. If the lift is less than 1, it shows that the rule has no meaning.

Note that among the four parameters confidence and support are used frequently.

12.2 The Apriori Algorithm

The association rule mining is to discover the rules with the minium support (minsup) and the minium confidence (minconf) defined by users from transaction databases. The problem of association rule mining can be decomposed into the following two subproblem.

(1) Find all large itemsets (or frequent itemsets) in a transaction database. The large itemset is defined as the itemset X with support(X) no less than the minsup defined by user.

(2) Generate association rules from large itemset. For every large itemset A, if $B \subset A$, $B \neq \spadesuit$, and confidence($B \Rightarrow (A-B)) \geq$ minconf, then constuct the rule $B \Rightarrow (A-B)$.

The second subproblem is easier than the first one. Most research works focus on the first subproblem. So we introduce the algorithm which is concerned with the first subproblem.

The famous Apriori algorithm is concentrate on mining frequent itemsets for Boolean association rules(Agrawal 1993, Agrawal, 1994). The name of the algorithm is based on the fact that the algorithm uses prior knowledge of frequent itermset properties. Apriori employs breadth-first search, where k-itemsets are used to explore $(k+1)$-itemsets. First, the set of frequent 1-itemsets is found by scanning the database to accumulate the count for each item, and collecting those items that satisfy minimum support. The resulting set is denoted L_1. Next, L_1 is used to find L_2, the set of frequent 2-itemsets, which is used to find L_3, and so on, until no more frequent k-itemsets can be found. We give the classical Apriori algorithm as follows.

Algorithm 12.1 Apriori Algorithm(Agrawal, 1994).

Input: DB, a database of transactions;
      minsup, the minimum support count threshold.
Output: L, frequent itemsets in DB
Method:

(1) L_1 = find_frequent_1-itemsets(DB);

(2) for $(k=2; L_{k-1} \neq \emptyset; k++)$\{

(3)　　C_k = apriori_gen(L_{k-1});

(4)　　for each transaction $T \in$DB\{ //scan DB for counts

(5)　　　　C_T = subset(C_k,T); //get the subsets of T that are candidates

(6)　　　　for each candidate $c \in C_T$

(7)　　　　　　c.count++

(8)　　　　\}

(9)　　　　L_k = \{ $c \in C_k$| c.count$\geq$minsup\}

(10)　\}

(11) return $L = \cup_k L_k$

Procedure apriori_gen(L_{k-1}: frequent(k-1)-itemsets)

(1) for each itemset $l_1 \in L_{k-1}$

(2)　　for each itemset $l_2 \in L_{k-1}$

(3) if($l_1[1]= l_2[1]$)$\wedge$($l_1[2] = l_2[2]$)$\wedge \cdots \wedge$($l_1[k-2]= l_2[k-2]$) $\wedge$($l_1[k-1]= l_2[k-1]$)then\{

(4)　　　　　　　$c = l_1 \bowtie l_2$; //join step: generate candidates

(5)　　　　　　if has_infrenquent_subset(c, L_{k-1}) then

(6)　　　　　　　　delete c; //prune step: remove unfruitful candidate

(7)　　　　　　else add c to C_k;

(8)　　　　\}

(9) return C_k.

Procedure has_infrequent_subset(c: candidate$k$-itemset;

　　　　　　L_{k-1}: frequent(k-1)-itemsets; //use prior knowledge

(1)　for each (k-1)-subset s of c

(2)　　if $s \notin L_{k+1}$ then

(3)　　return TRUE;

(4)　return FALSE.

Apriori algorithm scans DB several times and calculates k-itemsets in the k times. If the number of element in the top itemset is k at most, then the algorithm will scan DB k times, or $k+1$ time. Hash approach was used to improve Apriori algorithm. It minus the verified record T to support the calculation of C_k by the means of reducing the number of candidate item sets, reducing the length of record and reduceing the total number of record. There is the concept of negative boundary in sampling algorithm. It utilizes the downward closeness of frequent item sets. Suppose there is a downward close power set of an itemset SI, if all subset of the itemset s are subsumed by S and the set is not subsumed by S itself, then the set will be an element of the negative boundary. All elements with these attributes form negative boundary, which marked as Bd(S). For example, if $I=\{A,B,C,D,E\}$, $S=\{\{A\},\{B\},\{C\},\{E\},\{A,B\},\{A,C\},\{A,E\},\{C,E\},\{A,C,E\}\}$, then Bd($S$)=$\{\{B,C\},\{B,E\},\{D\}\}$. S is the superset of itemsets with high frequency if none of the sets in Bd(S) with high frequency.

For database DB in Figure 12.1, we can get the candidate itemsets C_1 when we count the number of every item by scanning the whole sets of transaction in the first scanning of database. If the minum support is 2, then the single dimension of itemsets L_1 is produced. Because there is the minium support of any subset of large itemsets, Apriori calculates the L_2 using L_1*L_1. The operation * is defined as

$$L_1*L_2=\{X\cup Y|X,Y\in L_{k,} |X\cap Y|=k-1\}$$

Then the candidate itemsets C_2 is produce and L_2 is produced from the minium support. From L_2 to C_3, the two itemsets which have the same head item: $\{BC\}$ and $\{BE\}$ will be confirmed. Then the rear itemsets $\{BC\}$ and $\{BE\}$, which are defined as $\{CE\}$ are tested if they are satisfied with the minium support. Because they are satisfied with the minium support, all the two dimension subsets of $\{BCE\}$ are large itemsets, so $\{BCE\}$ is a candidate itemset. Because there isn't any three dimension candidate itemsets from L_2, C_3 is confirmed and L_3 is gained. Then there are no higher dimension itemsets any more. So the whole large itemsets are confirmed.

Except Apriori algorithm, sampling algorithm and DIC algorithm also are classical association rules mining algorithm. The main idea of sampling algorithm is to define a value lowsup which is less than minsup and to calculate the itemsets which Support(db(X))>lowsup on sampling data with the help of algorithm of sampling. This itemsets is marked as S. Suppose S is the super set of frequent itemsets. Negative boundary Bd(S) is calculated. Scanning DB and S and the support of Bd(S) are calculated. If no set in Bd(S) is frequent itemsets, then S is the super set of frenquent itemsets. Otherwise failure is reported and frequent itemsets in Bd(S) are added into S. The negatice boundary of Bd(S) is calculated and DB is scanned and so on until no frequent   itemsets can be added into S.

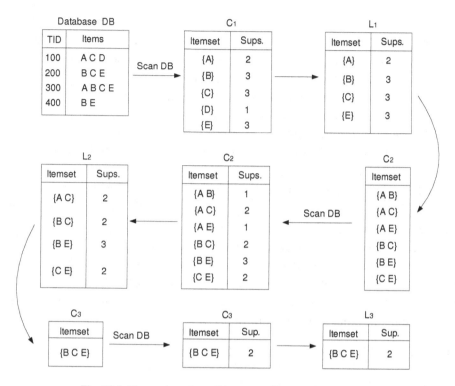

Fig. 12.1. Generation of candidate sets of items and sets of items

A DB is devided by M blocks in DIC algorithm. The first around of Apriori algorithm is executed in the first block. The first and the second around of Apriori algorithm is executed in the second block. The first, the second and the third around of Apriori algorithm is executed in the third block and so on till the end of the DB. Return to the head of DB, the second and after around is executed in the first block. the third and after around is executed in the second block and so on till all frequent itemsets are confirmed. There is a dynamic adjusting procedure on frequent itemsets and candidate itemsets. Another version of DIC algorithm is executed with random sampling.

12.3 FP-Growth Algorithm

Apriori algorithm or Apriori-like approach, which is based on an anti-monotone Apriori heuristic: if any length k pattern is not frequent in the database, its length

(k +1) super-pattern can never be frequent. The essential idea is to iteratively generate the set of candidate patterns of length (k + 1) from the set of frequent patterns of length k, and check their corresponding occurrence frequencies in the database. The bottleneck of the Apriori method is at the candidate set generation and test. If one can avoid generating a huge set of candidates, the mining performance can be substantially improved.

A frequent pattern tree (FP-tree in short) is a tree structure which consists of one root labeled as "null", a set of item prefix subtrees as the children of the root, and a frequent-item header table.

Each node in the item prefix subtree consists of three fields: item-name, count, and node-link, where item-name registers which item this node represents, count registers the number of transactions represented by the portion of the path reaching this node, and node-link links to the next node in the FP-tree carrying the same item-name, or null if there is none. Each entry in the frequent-item header table consists of two fields, item-name and head of node-link, which points to the first node in the FP-tree carrying the item-name. FP-tree construction algorithm shows as follows.

Algorithm 12.2 FP-tree construction (Han et al, 2000)

Input: DB, a database of transactions;
         minsup, the minimum support count threshold.
Output: FP-tree, frequent pattern tree.
Method:

1.   Scan the transaction database DB once. Collectthe set of frequent items F and their support s. Sort F in support descending order as L, the list of frequent items.
2.   Create the root of an FP-tree, T, and label it as "null". For each transaction T in DB do thefollowing. Select and sort the frequent items in T according to the order of L. Let the sorted frequent item list in T be [$p|P$], where p is the first element and P is the remaining list. Call insert_tree([$p|P$], T).

Procedure: insert_tree([$p|P$], T)

1.   If T has a child N and N.item-name= p.item-name, then increment N's count by 1;

2.   else create a new node N, and let its count be 1, its parent link be linked to T,

and its node-link be linked to the nodes with the same item-name via the node-link structure.

3. If P is nonempty, call Insert_tree(P, N) recursively.

Table 12.1 Transaction Database (Han et al, 2000)

TID	Items Bought	(Ordered) Frequent Items
100	*f, a, c, d, g, i, m,p*	*f, c, a, m, p*
200	*a, b, c, f, l, m, o*	*f, c, a, b,m*
300	*b, f, h, j, o*	*f, b*
400	*b, c, k, s, p*	*c, b, p*
500	*a, f, c, e, l, p, m, n*	*f, c, a, m, p*

Table 12.1 lists a transaction database. We can use Algorithm 12.2 to construct a FP-Tree shown in Figure 12.2. First, a scan of DB derives a list of frequent items, $\{(f{:}4), (c{:}4), (a{:}3), (b{:}3), (m{:}3), (p{:}3)\}$, in which items ordered in frequency descending order. This ordering is important since each path of a tree will follow this order. Second, one may create the root of a tree, labeled with "null". Scan the DB the second time. The scan of the first transaction leads to the construction of the first branch of the tree: $\{(f{:}1), (c{:}1), (a{:}1), (m{:}1), (p{:}1)\}$. For the second transaction, since its (ordered) frequent item list $\{f, c, a, b,m\}$ shares a common prefix $\{f, c, a\}$ with the existing path $\{f, c, a, m, p\}$, the count of each node along the prefix is incremented by 1, and one new node $\{b{:}1\}$ is created and linked as a child of $\{a{:}2\}$ and another new node $\{m{:}1\}$ is created and linked as the child of $\{b{:}1\}$. For the third transaction, since its frequent item list $\{f, b\}$ shares only the node $\{f\}$ with the f-prefix subtree, f's count is incremented by 1, and a new node $\{b{:}1\}$ is created and linked as a child of $\{f{:}3\}$. The scan of the fourth transaction leads to the construction of the second branch of the tree, $\{(c{:}1), (b{:}1), (p{:}1)\}$. For the last transaction, since its frequent item list $\{f, c, a, m, p\}$ is identical to the first one, the path is shared with the count of each node along the path incremented by 1. To facilitate tree traversal, an item header table is built in which each item points to its occurrence in the tree via a head of node-link. Nodes with the same item-name are linked in sequence via such node-links. After scanning all the transactions, the tree with the associated node-links is built and shown in Figure 12.2.

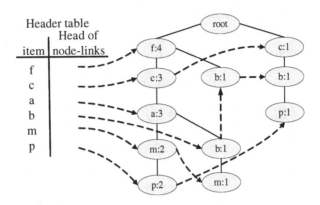

Fig. 12.2. A FP-tree in Table 12.1(Han et al, 2000)

FP-tree based association rules mining method transforms the problem of fiding long frequent patterns to searching for shorter ones recursively and then concateneting the suffix. It uses the least frequent items as suffix, offering good selectivity. FP-growth algorithm is summarized as follows.

Algorithm 12.3 FP-growth algorithm

Input: FP-tree, constructed based on Algorithm 12.2;
            minsup, the minimum support count threshold.
    Output: The complete set of frequent patterns.
    Method: FP-growth (FP-tree, α).
1.   if FP-tree contains a single path P then
2.   for each combination (denoted as β) of the nodes in the path P
3.   generate pattern β∪α with support_count = minimum support count
                of   nodes in β;
4.   else for each ai in the header of FP- tree {
5.   generate pattern β= a_i∪α with support_count = a_i.support_count;
6.   construct β's conditional pattern base and then β's conditional FP-tree;
7.   if FP-tree$_β$ ≠♠ then
8.   call FP-growth (FP-tree$_β$, β);
9.   }
    The FP-growth method shows that it is efficent and scalable for mining frequent patterns. The method substantially reduces the search cost and is about an order of magnitude faster than the Apriori algorithm.

12.4 CFP-Tree Algorithm

In FP-growth algorithm there are 6 fields in a FP-tree node, containing item-name, count, parent-link, child-link, sibling-link and next-link (a pointer to next node that has same item-name). However, child-link and sibling-link are only used in the FP-tree constructing process, parent-link and next-link are only used in the mining process. So we can reduce the number of fields by joining child-link with parent-link as cp-link which is first pointing to its child-node and after construction pointing to its parent node, and joining sibling-link with next-link as sn-link which is first pointing to its sibling-node and finally pointing to next node(Qin,2004).

The compact FP-tree (CFP-tree) has similar structure as FP-tree, but several differences btween them:

(1) Each node in CFP-tree has 4 fields, item-no (which is the sequential number of an item in frequent 1-itemsets according frequency descending order), count, cp-link and sn-link. Therefore, CFP-tree requires only 2/3 memory spaces of FP-tree.

(2) FP-tree is bi-directional, but CFP-tree is single directional. After the construction, CFP-tree only exists paths from leaves to the root.

The CFP-tree is constructed by Algorithm 12.4.

Algorithm 12.4 CFP-tree construction.

Input: DB, a database of transactions;
          minsup, the minimum support count threshold.
Output: CFP-tree, compact frequent pattern tree..
Method:

1. Scan the transaction database DB once. Collect the set of frequent items F and their supports. Sort F in support descending order as L, the list of frequent items.
2. Create the root of an FP-tree, T, and label it as "null". For each transaction in DB do the following. Select the frequent items and replace them with their order in L, and sort them as Is. Let the sorted Is be $[p|P]$, where p is the first element and P is the remaining list. Call insert tree($[p|P]$, T).

Procedure: insert_tree($[p|P]$, T).

1. If T has no child or can not find a child which its item-no=p, then create a new node N. N.item-no=p, N.count=1, N.cp-link=T; Insert N before the first node which item-no is greater than p.

2. If *T* has a child *N* such that *N*.item-no=*p*, then increment *N*.count by 1.

3. If *P* is not empty, then call insert_tree(*P, N*) recursively.

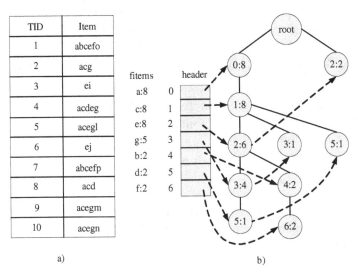

a)   b)

Fig. 12.3. CFP-tree (minsup=20%)

After the construction of CFP-tree, we should change the sn-link from sibling-link to next-link and reverse the cp-link. The processing procedure is as follows: Traverse the tree from the root. Add current node CN to the link of header[CN.item-no] as the last node. If CN has no child or all of its children and siblings have been processed then let CN.cp-link=CN's parent, else process its children and its siblings recursively.

Figure 12.3 (a) shows an example of a database and Figure 12.3 (b) is the CFP-tree for that database.

Here give a CFP-tree mining algorithm based on constrained subtree and array-based technique(Grahne, 2003). The following is the pseudocode of CFP-tree mining algorithm.

Algorithm 12.5 CFP-tree mining algorithm

Input: A CFP-tree T

Output: The complete set of FI's corresponding to T

Method:

1.   patlen=1;

2.   for (k=flen-1; k>=0; k--)   {   // flen is the length of frequent itemset
3.   pat[0]=fitem[k];
4.   output { pat[0]} with support count[k];
5.   generate ST(k).EndArray[];
6.   mine(ST(k));
7.   }

Procedure mine(ST($i_k,...,i_2,i_1$)) {
1. generate ST($i_k,...,i_2,i_1$).fitem[] and ST($i_k,...,i_2,i_1$).count[], let the length be listlen;
2. if (listlen==0) then return;
3. if (listlen==1) then {pat[patlen]= ST($i_k,...,i_2,i_1$).fitem[0];
                 output pat with support ST($i_k,...,i_2,i_1$).count[0]; return}
4. if   ST($i_k,...,i_2,i_1$) has only single path then
           {   output pat $\cup$ all the combination of   ST($i_k,...,i_2,i_1$).fitem[];
               return;   }
5. patlen++;
6. for (k=listlen-1; k>=0; k--)   {
7.   generate array;
8.   generate ST($i_k,...,i_2,i_1,k$).EndArray[];
9.   if ST($i_k,...,i_2,i_1,k$).EndArray[]   is   not   NULL   then
10.   mine(ST($i_k,...,i_2,i_1,k$));
11.   }
12.   patlen--;
13.   }

In mine procedure, line 1 generate frequent itemset in the constrained subtree ST($i_k,...,i_2,i_1$). Line 2~3 process the condition while listlen is 0 or 1. Line 4 process the condition while constrained subtree has only single path. Line 6~11 generate new array and constrained subtree, then mine the new subtree.

Because the CFP-tree could have millions of nodes, thus, it takes plenty of time for allocating and deallocating the nodes. Just like (Grahne, 2003), we also implement unified memory management for CFPmine algorithm. In the recursively mining process, the memory used in it is not frequently allocated and freed. It allocating a large chunk before the first recursion, and when a recursion ends, it doesn't really free the memory, only changes the available size of chunk. If the chunk is used up, it allocates more memory. And it frees the memory only when all the recursions have been finished.

12.5 Mining General Fuzzy Association Rules

The main method of mining association rules about digital attributes to disperse continuous data, which transform the mining association rules about digital attibutes into the mining association rules about boolean attibutes. One method is dividing the universe of discourse about attributes into nonoverlapping intervals, and then mapping the discreted data into these intervals. Nonoverlapping interval may ignore elements which are nearby the boundery of some intervals. This may lead to the ignorance of meaningful interval. The other method is dividing the universe of discourse about attibutes into overlapping intervals, and then the elements nearby boundary may be located in two inservals meanwhile. This may lead to over-emphasized on some inservals because the contribution of elements nearby boundery. The main weak point of the above two methods is that the boundary is too rigid. A solution proposed by Jianjiang Lu is to vague the boundary with fuzzy set which is defined on the domain of attributes (Lu, 2000), beacause fuzzy set can supply a smooth transition between elements in set and elements not in set. With this transition, all elements nearby boundary will not be excluded and will not be over emphasized. The degree of membership of the elements of fuzzy set in the domain of attributes is language value. The language value is expressed as closed positive fuzzy number and zero fuzzy number with boundary. So the problem of mining association rules about digit attibutes is transformed into the problem of mining association rules about fuzzy association rules.

Definition 12.1 *Suppose R is real number field, the closed interval [a,b] is called the number of closed interval, and a,b∈R, a≤b.*

Definition 12.2 *Suppose* $[a,b]$, $[c,d]$ *are two closed intervals, and* $0 \notin [c,d]$, *then:*

$$[a,b]+[c,d]=[a+c,b+d];$$

$$[a,b]-[c,d]=[a-d,b-c];$$

$$[a,b]\times[c,d]=[ac \wedge ad \wedge bc \wedge bd, ac \vee ad \vee bc \vee bd];$$

$$[a,b] \div [c,d]=[\frac{a}{c} \wedge \frac{a}{d} \wedge \frac{b}{c} \wedge \frac{b}{d}, \frac{a}{c} \vee \frac{a}{d} \vee \frac{b}{c} \vee \frac{b}{d}], \quad \mathbf{0} \notin [a,b].$$

Definition 12.3 *Suppose A is a fuzzy set on R*

(1) A is called closed convex fuzzy set on R if and only if $\forall \lambda \in (0,1]$, $A\lambda$ is a closed convex set, that is to say, $A\lambda$ is a closed interval.

(2) A is called regular fuzzy set on R if and only if $\exists x0 \in R$ then $A(x0)=1$, $x0$ is called regular   point of A

(3) If $\forall \lambda \in (0,1]$, and $A\lambda$ is a set with boundary, A is called fuzzy set with boundary.

(4) A regular convex fuzzy set on R is called a fuzzy number, a regular closed convex fuzzy set is called a closed fuzzy number and a regular closed convex fuzzy set with boundary is called a closed fuzzy number with boundary. $\tilde{\theta}$ is a zero fuzzy number and $\tilde{\theta} = \begin{cases} 1, x = 0 \\ 0, x \neq 0 \end{cases}$

(5) Suppose A is a fuzzy number, if all numbers in supp A= $\{x \in R \mid A(x) > 0\}$ is positive real number, then A is called positive fuzzy number. All the positive fuzzy number with boundary is marked as G, $\tilde{G} = G \cup \{\tilde{\theta}\}$.

Definition 12.4 *"$\leq$" in $\tilde{G}$ is defined as: $\forall A, B \in \tilde{G}$, $A \leq B$ if and only if for $\forall \lambda \in (0,1]$, $a_1^\lambda \leq b_1^\lambda$ and $a_2^\lambda \leq b_2^\lambda$. $A_\lambda = [a_1^\lambda, a_2^\lambda]$, $B_\lambda = [b_1^\lambda, b_2^\lambda]$.*

"$\leq$" is partial order in $\tilde{G}$.

Definition 12.5 *Suppose $A, B \in \tilde{G}$, then:*

$$(A+B)(z) = \bigvee_{x+y=z} (A(x)) \wedge B(y)), \forall z \in R$$

$$(A-B)(z) = \bigvee_{x-y=z} (A(x)) \wedge B(y)), \forall z \in R$$

$$(A \times B)(z) = \bigvee_{x+y=z} (A(x)) \wedge B(y)), \forall z \in R$$

$$(A \div B)(z) = \bigvee_{x+y=z} (A(x)) \wedge B(y)), \forall z \in \mathbf{R}$$

$$(kA)(z) = A(\frac{z}{k}), k \neq 0, \forall z \in \mathbf{R}$$

Theorem 12.1 *Suppose* $A, B \in \tilde{G}$, *for* $\forall \lambda \in (0,1]$, *then* $(A \pm B)_\lambda = A_\lambda \pm B_\lambda$;

$(A \times B)_\lambda = A_\lambda \times B_\lambda$; $A / B_\lambda = A_\lambda / B_\lambda$, $B \neq \bar{\theta}$, $(kA)_\lambda = kA_\lambda, k \neq 0$.

Note 1: From Theorem 12.1 and Definition 12.2, it is clear that suppose

$A, B \in \tilde{G}$ then $A + B \in \tilde{G}$, $A \times B \in \tilde{G}$, $A / B \in \tilde{G}(B \neq \bar{\theta})$, $kA \in \tilde{G}(k > 0)$.

We will discuss the calculation about fuzzy association rules in general sense. If there is a database $T = \{t_1, t_2, \ldots, t_n\}$, ti denotes the ith tuple $I = (i_1, i_2, \ldots, i_n)$ is the set of attributes, $t_j [i_k]$ denotes the value of the attribute ik on the jth tuple. Suppose $X = \{x_1, x_2, \ldots, x_p\}$, $Y = \{y_1, y_2, \ldots, y_q\}$ are the subsets of I, and $X \cap Y = \spadesuit$, $D = \{f_{x1}, f_{x2}, \ldots, f_{xp}\}$, $E = \{f_{y1}, f_{y2}, \ldots, f_{yq}\}$, $f_{xi}(i = 1, 2, \ldots, p)$ is the fuzzy set in the domain of attribute xi and $f_{yj}(j = 1, 2, \ldots, q)$ is the fuzzy set in the domain of attribute y_j. The degree of membership of elements of these fuzzy sets is language value. The language value is expressed as closed positive fuzzy number with boundary or zero fuzzy number. Suppose ε' is a valve value, α' is the minium rate of support. β' is the minium confidence, α', β', ε' are closed positive fuzzy number with boundary. The form of fuzzy association rules in general sense is "if X is D then Y is E".

Suppose $f_{xj}(t_i [x_j]) = x_y'$, $i = 1, 2, \ldots, n$; $j = 1, 2, \ldots, p$; $f_{yj}(t_i [y_j]) = y_{ij}'$, $i = 1, 2, \ldots, n$; $j = 1, 2, \ldots, q$; both x'_{ij} and y'_{ij} are closed positive fuzzy number with boundary or zero fuzzy number. Suppose

$$\overline{x'_{ij}} = \max\{x \in R \mid x'_{ij}(x) = 1\} \qquad i = 1, 2, \cdots, n; j = 1, 2, \cdots p;$$

$$\overline{y'_{ij}} = \max\{x \in R \mid y'_{ij}(x) = 1\} \qquad i = 1, 2, \cdots, n; j = 1, 2, \cdots q;$$

$$\overline{\alpha'} = \max\{x \in R \mid \alpha'(x) = 1\} \qquad \overline{\beta'} = \max\{x \in R \mid \beta'(x) = 1\}$$

$$\bar{\varepsilon}' = \max\{x \in R \mid \varepsilon'(x) = 1\} \qquad M = \max\{\bar{x}'_{ij}, \bar{y}'_{ij}, \bar{\alpha}', \bar{\beta}', \bar{\varepsilon}'\}$$

$$x_{ij} = \frac{x'_{ij}}{M}, i = 1, 2, \cdots, n; \, j = 1, 2, \cdots p$$

$$y_{ij} = \frac{y'_{ij}}{M}, i = 1, 2, \cdots, n; \, j = 1, 2, \cdots q$$

$$\alpha = \frac{\alpha'}{M}, \beta = \frac{\beta'}{M}, \gamma = \frac{\gamma'}{M}$$

x_{ij}, y_{ij}, α, β, ε are closed positive fuzzy numbers with boundaries or zero fuzzy numbers, their regular points are in the interval of $[0,1]$.

Definitions 12.6   *The general support rate S about the general fuzzy association rules in general sense "if X is D then Y is E" is defined as*

$$S = \frac{\sum\limits_{i=1}^{n}[\prod\limits_{j=1}^{p}\bar{a}(x_{ij}) \times \prod\limits_{j=1}^{q}\bar{a}(y_{ij})]}{n}, \quad \bar{a}(x) = \begin{cases} x, & x \geq \varepsilon'; \\ \tilde{\theta}, & \text{others.} \end{cases} \quad (12.3)$$

Definitions 12.7 *The general confidence C about about the general fuzzy association rules "if X is D then Y is E" isdefined as*

$$C = \frac{S}{\dfrac{1}{n}\sum\limits_{i=1}^{n}[\prod\limits_{j=1}^{p}\bar{a}(x_{ij})]}, \quad \bar{a}(x_{ij}) = \begin{cases} x_{ij}, & x_{ij} \geq \varepsilon' \\ \tilde{\theta}, & \text{others} \end{cases} \quad (12.4)$$

When $\dfrac{1}{n}\sum\limits_{i=1}^{n}[\prod\limits_{j=1}^{p}\bar{a}(x_{ij})] = \tilde{\theta}$, then $S = \tilde{\theta}$, and the rule will not be adopted.

Supposed $\dfrac{1}{n}\sum\limits_{i=1}^{n}[\prod\limits_{j=1}^{p}\bar{a}(x_{ij})] \neq \tilde{\theta}$, it is easy to find that S in definition 12.6 and C in definition 12.7 belong to $\tilde{G}$. Meanwhile, all regular points of x_{ij} are in $[0,1]$. So the regular points of $\dfrac{1}{n}\sum_{i=1}^{n}[\prod_{j=1}^{p}\overline{a}(x_{ij})]$ are in [0,1] also. That is, the maxium regular point of C will not be less than the maxium regular point of S, so C will not be less than S. Because S, C, α, β are in $\tilde{G}$, S can be compared with α, C and β. When S≥α and S≥β, the rule "if X is D then Y is E" will be suitable.

12.6 Distributed Mining Algorithm For Association Rules

The typical application of asociation rules mining is market-basket analysis, where the items represent products, and the records represent point-of-sales data at large grocery stores or department stores. Other application domains for asociation rules mining include customer segmentation, catalog design, store layout, and telecommunication alarm prediction. Because data is increasing in terms of both the dimensions and size, asociation rules mining algorithm should handle massive data stores. Sequential algorithms cannot provide scalability, in terms of the data dimension, size, or runtime performance, for such large databases. Therefore, we must rely on high-performance parallel and distributed computing.

Two dominant approaches for using multiple processors have emerged: distributed memory and shared memory. A shared-memory architecture has many desirable properties. Each processor has direct and equal access to all the system's memory. Parallel programs are easy to implement on such a system. In a distributed-memory architecture, each processor has its own local memory, which only that processor can access directly. For a processor to access data in the local memory of another processor, message passing must send a copy of the desired data elements from one processor to the other. Although a shared memory architecture offers programming simplicity, a common bus's finite bandwidth can limit scalability. A distributed memory, message-passing architecture cures the scalability problem by eliminating the bus, but at the expense of programming simplicity. A very popular paradigm combines the best of the distributed- and shared-memory approaches. Included in this paradigm are hardware or software distributed shared-memory systems. These systems distribute the physical memory among the nodes but provide a shared global address space on each processor.

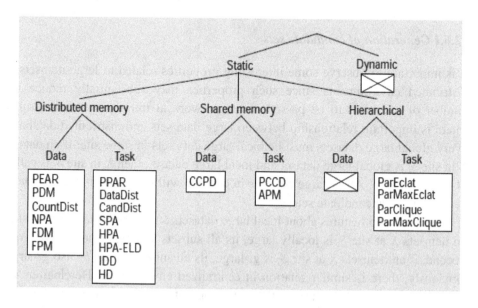

Fig. 12.4. Parallel and distributed association rules mining algoithms(Zaki, 1999)

Figure 12.4 shows where each parallel association rules mining methods fall in the design space(Zaki, 1999). Distributed memory methods form the dominant platform, and a mix of data- and task- parallel approaches have been explored. However, all schemes use static load balancing, or very limited dynamic load balancing. The main design issues in distributed memory methods are minimizing communication and evenly distributing data for good load balancing.

David Cheung and his colleagues proposed the Fast Distributed Mining (FDM) algorithm for association rules (Cheung et al, 1996). The main difference between parallel and distributed data mining is the interconnection network latency and bandwidth. David Cheung and his colleagues discover that there exist valuable properties between local and global large data sets. One should maximally take advantages of such properties to reduce the number of messages to be passed and confine the substantial amount of processing to local sites. Fast Distributed Mining is developed three editions: FDM-LP, FDM-LUP, FDM-LPP. They all had similar structure, but different pruning algorithms. FDM-LP only discussed local pruning; FDM-LUP discussed local pruning and upperbound pruning; FDM-LPP discussed local pruning and step by step pruning.

12.6.1 *Generation of candidate sets*

It is important to observe some interesting properties related to large itemsets in distributed environments since such properties may substantially reduce the number of messages to be passed across network at mining association rules. There is important relationship between large data sets and distributed database: every global large datasets must be local large data sets in some site. If an dataset X in site S_i is global large dataset and local large dataset, then X in site S_i is called gl-large at site S_i. All gl-large datasets in one site will form a basis for the site to generate its own candidate sets.

There are two features about local large datasets and gl-large datasets: First, if an itemsets X at site S_i is locally large, its all subsets at site S_i also locally large. Second, if an itemsets X at site S_i is gl-large, its all subsets at site S_i also gl-large. Obviously, there is similar relation in centralized environment. Hereinafter, we show important results, adopting the technology of effectively creating candidate sets in distributed environment.

Let GLi denote the set of gl-large itemsets at site S_i, and $GL_i(k)$ denote the set of gl-large k-itemsets at site S_i. If $X \in L_{(k)}$, then there exists a site S_i, such that all its size-$(k - 1)$ subsets are gl-large at site S_i, i.e., they belong to $GL_i(k-1)$. In a straightforward adaptation of Apriori, the set of candidate sets at the k-th iteration, denoted by $CA_{(k)}$, which stands for size-k candidate sets from Apriori, would be generated by applying the Apriori_gen function on $L(k-1)$. That is,

$$CA_{(k)} = \text{Apriori\_gen}(L_{(k-1)}).$$

At each sites S_i, let $CGi(k)$ be the set of candidates sets generated by applying Apriori_gen on $GL_{i(k-1)}$, i.e.,

$$CG_{i(k)} = \text{Ariori\_gen}(GL_{i(k-1)}),$$

where, CG stands for candidate sets generated from gl-large itemsets. Therefore $CG_{i(k)}$ is generated from $GL_{i(k-1)}$. Since $GL_{i(k-1)} \subseteq L_{(k-1)}$, $CG_{i(k)}$ is a subset of $CA_{(k)}$. In following discuss, let $CG_{(k)}$ denote the sets $\bigcup_{i=1}^{n} CG_{i(k)}$

For every $k > 1$, the set of all large k-itemsets $L_{(k)}$ is a subset of $CG(k)$ $=\bigcup_{i=1}^{n} CG_{i(k)}$, where $CG_{i(k)} = \text{Ariori\_gen}(GL_{i(k-1)})$. Therefore,

$$L_{(k)} \subseteq CG_{(k)} = \bigcup_{i=1}^{n} CG_{i(k)} = \bigcup_{i=1}^{n} \text{Ariori\_gen}(GL_{(k-1)}). \tag{12.5}$$

It indicates that $CG_{(k)}$ is a subset of $CA_{(k)}$, and may be much smaller than $CA_{(k)}$, and then can be candidate sets for the size-k large itemsets. The differences between $CG_{(k)}$ and $CA_{(k)}$ depends on distributing degree of the itemsets. The set of candidate sets $CG_{i(k)}$ can be generated locally at each site S_i at the k-th iteration. After the exchange of support counts, the gl-large itemsets $GL_{i(k)}$ in $CG_i(k)$ can be found at the end of that iteration. Based on $GL_{i(k)}$, the candidate sets at S_i for the $(k + 1)$-st iteration can then be generated. By using this approach, the number of candidate sets generated can be substantially reduced to about 10 - 25% of that generated in Count Distribution.

12.6.2 *Local pruning of candidate sets*

When the set of candidate set $C'G_{(k)}$ is generated, to find the globally large itemsets, the support counts of the candidate sets must be exchainged among all the sites. Notice that some candidate sets in $CG_{(k)}$ can be pruned by a local pruning technique before count exchange starts. The general idea is that at each site S_i, if a candidate set $X \in CG_{i(k)}$ is not locally large at site S_i, there is no need for S_i, to find out its global support count to determine whether it is gllobally large. This is because in this case, either X is small, or it will be locally large at some other site, and hence only the site(s) at which X is locally large need to be responsible to find the global support count of X . Therefore, in order to compute all the large k-itemsets, at each site Si, the candidate sets can be confined to only the sets $X \in CG_{i(k)}$ which are locally large at site Si. For clarity, the notations used in this section are listed in Table 12.2.

Table 12.2 Notation list

D	number of transaction in DB
s	minimum support *minsup*
$L(k)$	Globally large k-itemsets
$CA(k)$	candidate sets generated from $L_{(k)}$
$X.sup$	global support total count of X
DI	number of transactions in DB_i
$GLi\ (k)$	Gl-large k-itemsets at site S_i
$CGi\ (k)$	candidate sets generated from $GL_{i(k-1)}$
$LLi\ (k)$	local large k-itemsets in $CG_{i(k)}$
$X.supi$	local support total count at site S_i

Following shows the local pruning procedure of candidate sets.

1. Candidate sets generation: Generate the candidate sets $CG_{i\ (k)}$ according to global large itemsets found at $(k-1)$-st iteration at site Si using formula $CG_{i\ (k)}$ = Ariori_gen（$GL_{(k-1)}$）.

2. Local pruning: For each $X \in CG_{i\ (k)}$, scan each local database DB_i to compute local support total count $X.sup_i$. If X at site S_i isn't local large, it will be deleted from candidate data sets $LL_{i\ (k)}$. This pruning only deletes X from candidate data sets of site S_i, X may present at candidate data sets of other sites).

3. Support count exchange: Broadcast the candidate sets in $LL_{i\ (k)}$ toward other sites, to collect support count. Compute global support count, and obtain all global large k-data sets in site S_i.

4. Broadcast the results of mining: Broadcast all global large k-itemsets computed toward other sites.

In the above processes for finding globally large candidate itemsets, step 2 "local pruning" and step 3 "support count exchange", each site S_i should has two support count sets. For local pruning, S_i should find out the local support counts of its local candidate sets $CG_{i(k)}$. For support count exchange, S_i should find out different local support count with global support count sets in other sites. A simple approach would be to scan two times, firstly find out local support count basing on local candidate $CG_{i(k)}$; secondly respond to quests of support count from other sites. However, this would substantially degrade the performance.

In fact, it is unnecessary to scan database two times. At site S_i, before k-th iteration, $CG_{i(k)}$ was obtained, some other relative sets also could be obtained. For example, $CG_{j(k)}(j=1,\ldots,n, j \neq i)$. Because all $GL_{i\ (k-1)}$ $(i=1,\ldots,n)$ were broadcasted toward each site, and candidate $GL_{i\ (k-1)}$ $(i=1,\ldots,n)$ could be computed from corresponding $GL_{i\ (k-1)}$, after $(k-1)$-st iteration. That is, because all global large data sets created by previous iteration were broadcast toward all sites, at the beginning of iteration.each site could compute candidate itemsets in other sites.Therefore, local support count of all candidate itemsets could be obtained in a scan, and be stored in structure similar to Apriori algorithm Hash-tree. Two different support count sets, can be searched in this structure, in the exchange of local pruning and support count.

12.6.3 *Global pruning of candidate sets*

The local pruning at site S_i, only makes use of the local support counts in DB_i to prune the candidate sets. In fact, local support counts in other sites are also pruned, adopting global pruning technology to realize prune. The main technology is to obtain all local and global support count of candidate itemsets X after each iteration. after confirming one candidate data set to be global and large, local and global support count can be broadcasted toward all sites. Using this information, candidate itemsets can be pruned in the process of iteration.

After finishing each iteration, if one candidate itemset is globally large, system automatic broadcast local support count of each candidate elements toward other sites. Suppose X is a size-k candidate itemset. Therefore, the local support counts of all the size-$(k-1)$ subsets of X are available at every site. For a partition database DB_i $(1 \le i \le n)$, maxsup$_i(X)$ stands for minimum local support count of all size-$(k-1)$ subsets fo X, that is, maxsup$_i(X)$=min$\{Y.\text{sup}_i | Y \subset X$ 且 $|Y|=k-1\}$. According to the relation of superset and subset, maxsup$_i(X)$ is upper bound of local support count $X.\text{sup}_i$. Therefore, maxsup(X) stands for the sum of these upper boundary functions in distributed database, namely, the upper boundary of $X.\text{sup}$. $X.\text{sup} \le$maxsup$(X)= \sum_{i=1}^{n}$ maxsup$_i(X)$. Note that maxsup(X) can be computed in each sites, at the beginning of one iteration. Because maxsup(X) is upper boundary of its global support count, it can be pruned globally. That is, if maxsup$(X) < s \times D$, X is impossible to be one candidate data set. This technology goes by name of global pruning.

Global pruning can be combined with local pruning to form different pruning strategies. Two particular variations of this strategy will be adopted when we introduce several versions of FDM. The first method is called upper-bound-pruning and the second one is called polling-site-pruning. A possible upper bound of the global support count of a candidate set X is the sum

$$X.sup_i + \sum_{j=1, j \ne i}^{n} maxsup_j (X) \tag{12.6}$$

where $X.sup_i$ is found already iin the local pruning. Therefore, this upper bound can be computed to prune the candidate set X at site S_i.

12.6.4 *Count polling*

In general, few candidate itemsets are locally large at all the sites. Therefore, the FDM algorithm will usually require much less than $O(n^2)$ messages for computing each candidate itemset. To ensure that FDM requires only $O(n)$ messages for every candidate itemset in all the cases, a count polling technique is introduced.

This technology uses an assignment function to the candidate itemset X, which acts on X's Hash function that maps X to a polling site (Suppose that this function can be quoted in any sites). There is no relation to X's polling site and the sites of X being locally large. The polling site of each candidate itemset X is used to compute if X is globally large. To realize the purpose, corresponding X's polling site should broadcast X's polling request toward all the other sites, and collect local support counts, and compute global support counts. Because there is only one polling site for each candidate item X, the number of X's total exchange information can be reduced to $O(n)$.

At the k-th iteration, after the pruning phase, (both local and global pruning), has been completed, FDM uses the following procedure at each site S_i to do the count polling.

(1) Send candidate sets to polling sites: At site S_i, find out candidate elements of belonging   to set $LL_{i\,(k)}$ and polling site S_j for each polling site S_j, which will be stored in $LL_{i,j(k)}$(That is, store candidate elements according to group of their polling site). Each local support count of candidate itemsets also is stored in corresponding $LL_{i,j(k)}$. Send each $LL_{i,j(k)}$ to the corresponding polling site S_j.

(2) Poll and collect support count: if S_i is a polling site, S_i will receive all $LL_{i,j(k)}$ from other sites. S_i firstly find out original address l_{ist}, whose X is sent, for each candidate itemset X, then broadcast polling request to other sites, which is not in the original site list, to collect support count.

(3) Compute global large itemsets: S_i accepts support count from other sites, and computes global support count for each candidate elements, then find out globally large itemsets. Eventually, S_i broadcasts gl-large itemsets with their global support count to other sites.

12.6.5 *Distributed mining algorithm of association rules*

Here we first introduce distributed mining algorithm FDM-LP which is a FDM with local pruning, including candidate set reduction and local pruning.

Algorithm 12.6 FDM-LP algorithm(Cheung, Han et al, 1996).

Input: $DB_i(i=1,\ldots,n)$, the database partition at each site S_i

Output: L, all global large data sets

Method:

1. if k = 1 then

2. $T_{i(1)}$ = get_local_count($DB_i, \varnothing, 1$)

3. else {

4. $CG_{(k)} = \bigcup_{i=1}^{n} CG_{i(k)}$
                $= \bigcup_{i=1}^{n}$ Apriori_gen($GL_{i(k-1)}$);

5. $T_{i(k)}$ = get_local_count($DB_i, CG_{(k)}, i$);}

6. for_all $X \in T_{i(k)}$ do

7.   If $X.sup_i \geq s \times D_i$ then

8.   for j = 1 to n do

9.   if polling_site(X) = S_j then
                         insert $<X, X.sup_i>$ into $LL_{i,j(k)}$;

10. for j = 1,...,n do send $LL_{i,j(k)}$ to site S_j;

11. for j = 1,...,n do {

12.   receive $LL_{j,i(k)}$;

13. for_all $X \in LL_{j,i(k)}$ do {

14.   if $X \notin LP_{i(k)}$ then
                    insert X into $LP_{i(k)}$;

15.   update $X.large\_sites$; }}

16. for_all $X \in LP_{i(k)}$ do

17.   send_polling_request(X);

18. reply_polling_request($T_{i(k)}$);

19. for_all $X \in LP_{i(k)}$ do {

20.   receive $X.sup_j$ from the sites S_j,

                where $S_j \notin X.large\_sites$;

21. $X.sup = \sum_{i=1}^{n} X.sup_i$;

22.   if $X.sup \geqq s \times D_i$ then

                    insert X into $G_{i(k)}$; }

23. broadcast $G_{i(k)}$;

24. receive $G_{j(k)}$ from all other sites S_j , $(j{\neq}i)$;

25. $L_{(k)} = \bigcup_{i=1}^{n} G_{i(k)}$.

26. divide $L_{(k)}$ into $GL_{i(k)}$, $(i = 1,...,n)$;

27.return $L_{(k)}$.

In FDM-LP algorithm, firstly, every S_i is initially a "home site" of the candidate sets, then as polling site to respond the request from other sites. Finally, S_i is transformed into remote site to support local support count to other polling site. We explain the above procedure according to different roles and activities of steps in FDM-LP algorithm as follows.

(1) Home site: generate candidate itemsets and submit to polling sites (lines 1-10).
(2) Polling site: receive candidate itemsets and send poll requests (lines 11-17).
(3) Remote site: return support count to polling site (line 18).
(4) Polling site: receive support count and find out large itemsets (lines19 –23)
(5) Home site: receive large itemsets (lines 24 – 27)
     In the following discuss, by using two different global pruning technologies, shows two more refined editions of FDM-LP algorithm.

Algorithm 12.7 FDM-LUP algorithm, FDM algorithm of local and upper bound pruning

Method:

The program fragment of FDM-LUP is obtained from FDM-LP by inserting the following condition (line 7.1) after line 7 of Algorithm 12.6.

(7.1)   if $g\_upper\_bound(X) \geq s \times D_i$ then

Alone update of FDM-LUP algorithm is that append upper bound pruning (line 7.1). Function g_upper_bound computes upper bound for each candidate itemsets. In other words, g-upper-bound returns an upper bound of X as the sum:

$$X.sup_i + \sum_{j=1, j \neq i}^{n} maxsup_j\ (X)$$

$X.sup_i$ was computed in the process of local pruning, and $maxsup_j(X)$ $(j=1,...,n, j \neq i)$ can be computed by local support count after $(k-1)$-st iteration. If upper bound is a smaller number than global minsup, it is used to prune X. Comparing with FDM-LP algorithm, FDMLUP should usually have a smaller number of candidate sets for count exchange.

Algorithm 12.8 FDM-LPP, FDM algorithm of local and poll address pruning

Method: The program fragment of FDM-LPP is obtained from Algorithm 12.6 by replacing its line 17 with the following two lines.

(16.1)   if $p\_upper\_bound(X) \geq s \times D_i$ then

(17) $end\_polling\_request(X)$;

FDM-LPP algorithm appends a new step, which is polling site pruning. In this step, polling site S_i accepts requests from other sites to perform polling. Each requestes includes local large itemset X and its local support count $X.sup_j$. S_j is site from which delivers itemset X to S_i,. Note that X.large_sites is the set of all the originating sites from which the requests for polling X are being sent to the polling site (line 15). For every site $S_j \in X$.large_sites, the local support count $X.sup_j$ has been delivered to S_i. For a site $S_q \notin X$.large_sites, because X in S_q is not locally large, $X.sup_q$ is smaller than $s \times D_q$. $X.sup_q$ is bounded by the value $\min(maxsup_q(X), s \times D_{q-1})$. Therefore, an upper bound of $X.sup_q$ can be computed by following formula:

$$\sum_{j \in X.large\_Sites} X.sup_j + \sum_{q=1, q \neq X.large\_sites}^{n} \min(maxsup_a(X), s * D_q - 1) \qquad (12.7)$$

In FDM-LPP algorithm, S_i uses function p_upper_bound and above formula, to compute upper bound for X.sup. This upper bound will be pruned, when it issmaller than global support count.

Similar to above discuss, FDM-LUP and FDM-LPP all can obtain candidate itemset less than FDM-LP. However, they request more storage and communication messages for local support counts. Their efficiency mainly depen on the data distribution.

12.7 Parallel Mining of Association Rules

Data mining researchers expect parallelism to relieve mining methods from the sequential bottleneck, providing scalability to massive data sets and improving response time. The main challenges include synchronization and communication minimization, workload balancing, finding good data layout and data decomposition, and disk I/O minimization The parallel design space spans three main components: the hardware platform, the type of parallelism, and the load-balancing strategy.

Table 12.3 Parallel algorithm for association rules (Zaki, 1999)

ALGORITHM S	CHARACTERISTIC
Count Distribution(CD)	**Apriori-base**
PEAR	**Candidate prefix tree**
PDM	Hash table for 2-itemsets, parallel candidate **generation**
NPA	Only master does sum reduction
FDM	Local and global pruning, count polling
FPM	Local and global pruning, skewness handling
CCPD	Shared memory
Data Distribution	Exchange full database per iteration
SPA	Same as Data Distribution
IDD	Ring-based broadcast, item-based candidate partitioning
PCCD	Shared memory (logical database exchange)
Hybrid Distribution	Combines Count and Data Distribution
Candidate Distribution	Selectively replicated database, asynchronous
HPA	No database replication, exchange itemsets
HPA-ELD	Replicate frequent itemsets
ParEclat	Eclat-based, asynchronous, hierarchical
ParMaxEclat	MaxEclat-based, asynchronous, hierarchical
ParClique	Clique-based, asynchronous, hierarchical
ParMaxClique	MaxClique-based, asynchronous, hierarchical
APM	DIC-based, shared memory, asynchronous
PPAR	Partition-based, horizontal database

Table 12.3 shows the essential differences among the different methods and groups together related algorithms. As you can see, there are only a handful of distinct paradigms. The other algorithms propose optimizations over these basic cases. For example, PEAR, PDM, NPA, FDM, FPM, and CCPD are all similar to Count Distribution. Likewise, SPA, IDD, and PCCD are similar to Data Distribution, whereas HPA and HPAELD are similar to Candidate Distribution. Hybrid Distribution combines Count and Data Distribution techniques. ParEclat, ParMaxEclat, ParClique, and ParMaxClique are all based on their sequential counterparts. Finally, APM is based on the sequential DIC method, and PPAR is based on Partition.

12.7.1 *Count Distribution Algorithm*

Count Distribution(CD) is a parallel version of Apriori. It is one of the earliest proposed and representative parallel algorithms for mining of association rules(Agrawal et al, 1996) . We describe here briefly its steps. The database D is partitioned into D_1, D_2,..., D_n and distributed across n processors. The program fragment of CD at processor p_i, $1 \le i \le n$, for the k-th iteration is outlined. For convenience, we use $X.sup_{(i)}$ to represent the local support count of an itemset X in partition D_i. In step 1, every processor computes the same candidate set C_k by applying the aprior_gen function on L_{k-1}, which is the set of large itemsets found at the $(k-1)$-th iteration. In step 2, local support counts (support in D_i) of candidates in C_k are found. In steps 3 and 4, local support counts are exchanged with all other processors to get global support counts (support in D) and globally large itemsets (large with respect to D) L_k are computed independently by each processor. CD repeats steps 1-4 until no more candidate is found.

Algorithm 12.9 Count Distribution algorithm

1. C_k = apriori_gen(L_{k-1});
2. scan partition D_i to find the local support count $X.sup(i)$ for all $X \in C_k$;
3. exchange { $X.sup(i) | X \in C_k$ } with all other processors to get global support counts $X.sup(i)$
    for all $X \in C_k$;
4. L_k = { $X \in C_k | X.sup(i) \ge minsup \times |D|$}.

12.7.2 *Fast Parallel Mining Algorithm*

David Cheung and Yongqiao Xiao recently proposed a parallel version of FDM, called Fast Parallel Mining (Chenug, 1999). The problem with FDM's polling mechanism is that it requires two rounds of messages in each iteration: one for computing the global supports and one for broadcasting the frequent itemsets. This two-round scheme can degrade performance in a parallel setting. FPM generates fewer candidates and retains the local and global pruning steps. But instead of count polling and subsequent broadcast of frequent itemsets, it simply broadcasts local supports to all processors. The more interesting aspect of this work is a metric Cheung and Xiao define for data skewness (the distribution of itemsets among the various partitions). For an itemset X, let pX(i) denote the probability that X occurs in partition i. The entropy of X is given as

$$H(X) = -\sum_{i}^{n} pX(i) \log(pX(i)) \tag{12.8}$$

The entropy easures the distribution of the local support counts of X among all partitions. FPM is an enhancement of CD. The simple support counts exchange scheme in CD is retained in FPM. The main difference is the incorporation of both the distributed and global prunings in FPM to reduce the candidate set size. In FPM the first iteration is the same as CD. Each processor scans its partition to find out local support counts of all size-1 itemsets and use one round of count exchange to compute the global support counts. At the end of the 1-st iteration, in addition to L_1 , each processor also finds out the gl-large itemsets $GL_1(i)$, for $1 \le i \le n$. For the k-th iteration of FPM, $k>1$, the program fragment executed at processor i, $1 \le i \le n$, is described as Algorithm 12.10.

Algorithm 12.10 FPM algorithm.

1. compute candidate sets $CG_k = \bigcup_{i=1}^{n} \texttt{apriori\_gen}(GL_{k-1(i)})$; (distributed pruning)

2. prune candidates in CGk by global pruning

3. scan partition D_i to find the local support count $X.\text{sup}(i)$ for all remaining candidates $X \in$ CGk

4. exchange   { $X.\text{sup}(i)$| $X \in$ CGk } with all other processors to get global support counts $X.\text{sup}(i)$ for all $X \in$ CGk

5. $GL_{k(i)} = \{ X \in CG_k \mid X_{.sup} \geq minsup \times \mid D \mid, X_{.sup(i)} \geq minsup \times \mid D_i \mid \}$ compute

for all i, $1 \leq i \leq n$

6. return $L_k = \bigcup_{i=1}^{n} GL_{k(i)}$

12.7.3 DIC-based algorithm

The DIC algorithm proposed by Sergey Brin and others is a generalization of Apriori (Sergey, 1997). The database is divided into p equal-sized partitions so that each partition fits in memory. For partition 1, DIC gathers the supports of single items. Items found to be locally frequent (only in this partition) generate candidate 2-itemsets. Then DIC reads partition 2 and obtains supports for all current candidates. That is, the single items and the candidate 2-itemsets. This process repeats for the remaining partitions. DIC starts counting candidate k-itemsets while processing partition k in the first database scan. After the last partition p has been processed, the processing wraps around to partition 1 again. A candidate's global support is known once the processing wraps around the database and reaches the partition where it was first generated.

DIC is effective in reducing the number of database scans if most partitions are homogeneous. If data is not homogeneous, DIC might generate many false positives (itemsets that are locally frequent but not globally frequent) and scan the database more than Apriori does. DIC proposes a random partitioning technique to reduce the data–partition skew.

Cheung and colleagues have proposed the Asynchronous Parallel Mining algorithm, which is based on DIC(Cheung et al, 1998). APM uses FDM's global-pruning technique to decrease the size of candidate 2-itemsets. This pruning is most effective when there is high data skew among the partitions.

However, DIC requires that the partitions be homogeneous.

APM addresses this problem by treating the first iteration separately. APM logically divides the database into many small, equal-sized virtual partitions. The number of virtual partitions l is independent of the number of processors p, but usually $l \geq$ p. Let m be the number of   items. APM gathers the local counts of the mitems in each partition. This forms an $l \times m$ data set, with l item support vectors in an m-dimensional space. APM groups these l vectors into k clusters, maximizing intercluster distance and minimizing intracluster distance. Thus, the k clusters or partitions are as skewed as possible, and they are used to generate a small set of candidate 2-itemsets. APM now prepares to apply DIC in parallel. The idea is to divide the database into p homogeneous partitions. Each processor independently applies DIC to its local partition.

However, there is a shared prefix tree among all processors, which is built asynchronously. APM stops when all processors have processed all candidates, whether generated by themselves or others, and when no new candidates are generated. To apply DIC on its partitions, each processor must divide its local partition into r subpartitions. Furthermore, DIC requires that both the p interprocessor   partitions and the r intraprocessor partitions be as homogeneous as possible. APM ensures that the p partitions are homogeneous by assigning the virtual partitions from each of the k clusters of the first pass in a round-robin manner among the p processors. Thus, each processor gets an equal mix of virtual partitions from separate clusters, resulting in homogeneous processor partitions. To get intraprocessor partition homogeneity, APM performs a secondary kclustering. That is, they group the r partitions into k clusters, and again assign elements from each of the k clusters to the r partitions in a round-robin manner.

In the APM Algorithm, preprocessing contains: all processors scan their partitions to compute local supports of size-l itemsets in their intervals; compute L_1 and generate C_2 = Apriori_gen(L_1); perform a k-clustering on the intervals and a virtual partition pruning on C_2;   initialize the shared trie with the remaining size-2 candidates; perform inter-partition interval configuration and intra-partition interval configuration to prepare a homogeneous distribution. The preprocessing is to serve two purposes : (1) reduce the number of size-2 candidates by a virtual partition pruning and initialize the trie with the remaining size-2 candidates; (2) perform interpartition and intra-partition interval configurations to increase the homogeneity of the itemset distribution.

Algorithm 12.11 APM Algorithm (Cheung et al, 1998).

// Parallel execution: every processor i runs the following fragment on its partition D_i

1. while (some processor has not finished the counting of all the itemsets on the trie on its
   partition)

2.   {while (processor i has not finished the counting of all the itemsets on the trie on
      D_i)

3.   {scan one more interval on D_i and count the supports of the itemsets on the

         trie;

4. found out the locally large itemsets among the itemsets on the trie for the interval

    scanned;

5. generate new candidates from these locally large itemsets;

6. perform pruning on these candidates and insert the survivors into the trie;

7. remove globally small itemsets on the trie;

8.   }

9.   }

Every processor in APM performs the dynamic generation and counting. The new candidates generated by each process go through a pruning similar to the partition pruning before the survivors are inserted into the trie. Before a processor starts a new round of counting on the next interval,it traverses the trie to remove itemsets which are found to be globally small. This will keep the size of the trie minimum. If all the processors have counted all the itemsets on the trie, then APM terminates.

12.7.4 Data skewness and workload balance

In a database partition, two data distribution characteristics, data skewness and workload balance, have orthogonal effects on prunings and hence performance of FPM. Intuitively, the data skewness of a partitioned database is high if the supports of most large itemsets are clustered in a few partitions. It is low if the supports of most large itemsets are distributed evenly across the processors.

David Cheung and Yongqiao Xiao have developed a skewness metric based on the well established notion of entropy. Given a random variable X, it's entropy is a measurement on how even or uneven its probability distribution is over its values. If a database is partitioned over n processors, the value $px(i) = \dfrac{X.sup(i)}{X.sup}$

can be regarded as the probability of occurrence of an itemset X in partition D_i, $1 \le i \le n$. The entropy $H(X) = -\sum_{i=1}^{n}(px(i) \times \log(px(i)))$ is a measurement of the distribution of the local supports of X over the partitions For example, if X is skewed completely into a single partition D_k, $(1 \le k \le n)$, i.e., it only occurs in Dk, then $p_x(k) = 1$ and $p_x(i) = 0$, $\forall i \ne k$. The value of H(X) = 0 is the minimal in this case. On the other hand, if X is evenly distributed among all the partitions, then $px(i) = 1/n$, $1 \leq i \leq n$, and the value of $H(X) = \log(n)$ is themaximal in this case. Therefore the following metric can be used to measure the skewness of a data partition.

Definition 12.8 *Given a database partition D_i, $(1 \leq i \leq n)$, the skewness $S(X)$ of an itemset is defined by*

$$S(X) = \frac{H_{max} - H(X)}{H_{max}} \tag{12.9}$$

where $H(X) = -\sum_{i=1}^{n}(px(i) \times \log(px(i)))$ and $H_{max} = \log(n)$

The skewness $S(X)$ has the following properties:
(1) $S(X) = 0$, when all $p_x(i)$, $1 \leq i \leq n$, are equal. So the skewness is at its lowest value when X is distributed evenly in all partitions.
(2) $S(X) = 1$, if $\exists k \in [1,n]$ such that $p_x(k) = 1$, and $p_x(i) = 0$ for $\forall i \neq k$, $1 \leq i \leq n$. So the skewness is at its highest value when X occurs only in one partition.
(3) $0 < S(X) < 1$, in all the other cases.

Workload balance is a measurement of the distribution of the support clusterings of the large itemsets over the partitions at the processors. We define $W_i = \sum_{x \in L_s} w(X) \times px(i)$ to be the itemset workload in a partition D_i, where Ls is the set of all the large itemsets. Intuitively, the workload W_i in partition Di is the ratio of the total supports of the large itemsets in D_i over all the partitions. Note that $\sum_{i=1}^{n} W_i = 1$

Definition 12.9 *For a database partition D_i, $(1 \leq i \leq n)$, of a database D, the workload balance factor TB(D) of the partition is given by*

$$TB(D) = \frac{-\sum_{i=1}^{n} W_i \log(W_i)}{\log(n)} \tag{12.10}$$

The metric $TB(D)$ has the following properties:

(1) $TB(D) = 1$, when the workload across all processors are the same.

(2) $TB(D) = 0$, when the workload is concentrated on one processor.

(3) $0 < TB(D) < 1$,   in all the other case.

The data skewness metric and workload balance factor are not independent. Theoretically, each one of them could have values range from 0 and 1. However, some combinations of their values are not admissable.

Association rules mining has become a mature field of research with diverse branches of specialization. The fundamentals of association mining are now well established and, with some important exceptions. Current research appears to focus on the specialization of fundamental association mining algorithms, many areas of which are still emerging. These include fields such as, measures of interest, the inclusion of domain knowledge and semantics, quantitative mining, disassociation mining, privacy mining, incremental mining, iterative and interactive or guided mining, and higher order mining.

Exercises

1. Illustrate what the support, confidence, minsup, minconf and large item set are.

2. The following table shows four transactions with the misup being 60%, please find out one frequent item set

TID	Date	Items_bought
1	01/05/2005	I_1, I_2, I_4, I_6
2	02/05/2005	I_1, I_2, I_3, I_4, I_5
3	03/05/2005	I_1, I_2, I_3, I_5
4	04/05/2005	I_1, I_2, I_4

3. Try to describe classical Apriori algorithm.

4. Try to do association rule mining based on the distributed system.

5. What are the positive and negative relations? Can you give an example?

6. Summarize how to effectively mine the following rule, "A free commodity possibly triggers 200 total shopping in identical transaction" (agrees the price of each kind of commodity not negative)

7. The following table includes nine transactions. Suppose the minsup is 20%, please give all the frequent item sets.

TID	Items
1	I_1,I_2,I_5
2	I_2,I_4
3	I_2,I_3,I_6
4	I_1,I_2,I_4
5	I_1,I_3
6	I_2,I_3
7	I_1,I_3
8	I_1,I_2,I_3,I_5
9	I_1,I_2,I_3

8. Develop an incremental algorithm for association rule mining.

Chapter 13

Evolutionary Computation

13.1 Introduction

Evolutionary computation is a computing system which applies natural evolution and adaptive thought(Yao,2006). Darwin's evolutionism is a robust mechanism for searching and optimization, which has great impacts on the development of computer science, in particular artificial intelligence. The majority of organisms evolve by natural selection and sexual reproduction. Natural selection determines which individuals in population can survive and reproduce, while sexual reproduction is the guarantee of gene mixture and recombination in the next generation. The principle of natural selection is "to select the superior and eliminate the inferior, survival of the fittest".

Early in the 1960s, the above features of natural evolution had drawn Holland's great interest. In those years, he and his students were studying on how to establish a machine learning system. He found that machine learning can be realized not only by an individual's adaptation, but also by plurivoltine evolutions of a population. By inspiration of Darwin's evolution thought, Holland realized that in order to obtain an excellent learning algorithm, a reproduction of a population with multiple candidate strategies, instead of only one strategy, should be built and improved. As this idea originated from genetic evolution, Holland called this research field genetic algorithm. Genetic algorithm was not well known until his currently famous monograph "Adaptation in Natural and Artificial Systems "(Holland, 1975) was published in 1975. His monograph systematically introduces the basic theory of genetic algorithm, and forms a foundation for genetic algorithm. In the same year, De Jong finished his doctoral dissertation "An Analysis of the Behavior of a Class of Genetic Adaptive Systems". In this doctoral dissertation, De Jong applied Holland's schema theory to his experiments, and drew some important conclusions and presented some effective methods, which has produced prodigious influence on the application and development of genetic algorithm.

The idea of genetic algorithm originates from biological evolution process. It is essentially a class of stochastic search algorithm based on information genetic mechanism and the principle of natural selection, including the principle of adaptation, struggling for existence, in evolution process. In genetic algorithm, a state space is expressed as a set of character strings. It is by applying probability search process that genetic algorithm searches in state space and generates new individuals. Comparison of genetic algorithm and natural evolution is presented in Table 13.1.

Table 13.1 Comparison of genetic algorithm and natural evolution

natural evolution	genetic algorithm
Chromosome	character string
gene	character, feature
allele	feather value
locus	location in a string
genotype	structure
phenotype	parameter set, decoding Structure

The adaptation process is pivotal to artificial genetic systems. It generates a new structure by a population's structures and genetic operations, such as crossover and mutation, not by a simple structure. In a population, every structure has its own fitness value, which is used to determine which structures can generate new structures.

The most simple learning system based on genetic algorithm is shown in Fig. 13.1. The system consists of two subsystems. One is genetic algorithm-based learning subsystem, which leads to proper change of structures. The other is executive subsystem, which results in improvement of system's behaviors.

In 1988, Mayr had proposed neo-Darwinism, whose major viewpoints are as follows (Mayr, 1988):

(1) An individual is a basic goal of selection;
(2) Stochastic process plays a great role in evolution, while most genetic variations are accidental phenomena;
(3) Most genotypic variations, especially mutations, are the products of recombination;

(4) Gradual evolution is possibly related to uncontinuous phenotype;

(5) Not all the changes of phenotype are the inevitable result of natural selection;

(6) Evolution varies with diversified forms, including changing genes.

(7) Nature selection is based on probability model, not on deterministic model.

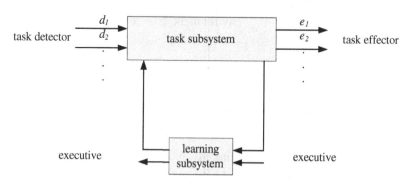

Fig. 13.1. Execution-oriented learning system

At present, evolutionary computation mainly includes genetic algorithm, evolutionary strategy and evolutionary programming, which are introduced as follows.

13.2 Formal Model of Evolution System Theory

Evolution plays its roles in population. Waddington showed the importance of relationship between genotype and phenotype(Waddinton, 1974). Population rejects heterogeneous environment. And "epigenetic environment" is a multidimensional space. The interaction of genotype with environment determines the phenotype, which then acts through heterogeneously selecting environment. Note that, this multidimensional space is different from "epigenetic environment". At this time, adaptability is the product of phenotype space and selected environment space. It usually is an one-dimensional function, denoting the contribution of many offspring to next generation.

Based on the above idea, Muhlenbein and Kindermann presented a model which was called formal model of evolution system theory(Muhlenbein 1989). Fig.13.2 shows the relationship of this model. Genotype space(GS) and phenotype space(PS) are defined by genotype and phenotype, respectively.

$$GS = \{g = (a_1, \ \dots, \ a_n), \ a_i \in A_i\} \qquad (13.1)$$

$$PS = \{p = (p_1, \ \dots, \ p_m), \ p_i \in IR\} \qquad (13.2)$$

where g denotes genotype and p denotes phenotype. The possible value of gene g_i is called allele. In Mendel's genetics, it is assumed that there are finite alleles in each gene.

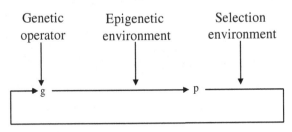

Fig. 13.2. Major processes of evolution

Given a set of epigenetic environment:
$$EP = \{EP_1, ..., EP_k\}$$
and transformation function:
$$f: GS \times EP \rightarrow PS$$
$$p = f(g, EP). \tag{13.3}$$

In fact, the transformation function presents a model, which shows that the change of phenotype is due to the interaction of gene with environment and this change is higher-order nonlinear. The final phenotype has all the characteristics, while the initial one just has a simple one-to-one correspondence. Quality function q expresses the quality of phenotype in a given selection environment ES_i, and it is defined as follows:
$$q(p, ES_i, t) \rightarrow IR^+ \tag{13.4}$$

This quality function is in fact a fitness function, which is used for Darwinian selection. So far, there are three general models:

(1) Mendel's genetics;
(2) Genecology;
(3) Evolutionary gamete;

In Mendel's genetics, genotype is modeled detailed, but phenotype and environment are almost left in the basket. In genecology, the case is just the opposite. The theory of evolutionary gamete is a model induced from sociobiology.

Let's first discuss the selection model in Mendel's genetics. For simplicity, assume that there are n alleles $a_1, \cdots, a_n$ in a gene. Double-genotype is expressed as a 2-tuple (a_i, a_j), and $p_{i,j}$ is defined as the frequency of genotype (a_i, a_j) in population. Suppose that genotype is equal to phenotype. Quality function is used to assign a value to each phenotype:

$$q(a_i, a_j) = q_{i,j}$$

where $q_{i,j}$ can be explained as the difference between birthrate and death rate.

Suppose that $p'_{i,j}$ is the frequency of the next generation's phenotype. Then, Darwin's selection adjusts the distribution of phenotype according to selection equations:

$$p'_{i,j} = p'_{i,j} \frac{q_{i,j}}{\overline{Q}} \qquad (13.5)$$

$$\overline{Q} = \sum_{i,j} q_{i,j} p_{i,j} \qquad (13.6)$$

where $\overline{Q}$ is the average fitness of population. Assume that p_i is the frequency of alleles of population. If

$$p_{i,j} = p_i p_j$$

then a selection equation in GS is obtained as follows:

$$p'_i = p_i Q_i / \overline{Q} \qquad (13.7)$$

$$Q_i = \sum_j q_{i,j} p_j \qquad (13.8)$$

The above discrete selection equation can be approximated with the following continuous equation:

$$\frac{dp_i}{dt} = p_i (Q_i - \overline{Q}) / \overline{Q} \qquad (13.9)$$

If $q_{i,j} = q_{j,i}$, then

$$\frac{dp_i}{dt} = p_i (Q_i - \overline{Q}) \qquad (13.10)$$

It is easy to verify that:

$$\frac{d\overline{Q}}{dt} = 2(E(Q^2) - \overline{Q}^2) = 2\text{Var}(Q) \geq 0 \qquad (13.11)$$

This result is called Fisher's fundamental theorem, which shows that average fitness is proportional to the difference of fitness. In fact, only some of all possible genotypes are realized. This is the task of genetic operations to search genotype space with small number of individuals. These genetic operations are the main origin of the genetic variation of population. And the most important genetic operations are mutation and recombination.

In genecology, it is usually supposed that dominance is inherited by interaction of gene locus. At each gene locus, two alleles are separated, and dominant value increases by one, while the other decreases by one.

Individual's phenotypic value is expressed as:

$$P_{i,j} = \mu + G_i + E_{i,j} + (GE)_{i,j}$$

where μ is the average of dominant value, G_i denotes the i-th phenotype, $E_{i,j}$ is the i-th gene in the j-th individual, GE denotes the interaction of genotype and environment.

The complex relationship prevents population directly accessing some "best phenotypes". This relationship constrains the selection. The important constraint has no genetic variation, interaction of genes and nonlinear transformation from genotype to phenotype.

In the theory of evolutionary gamete, each individual can suit N strategies. Suppose that p_i is the frequency of strategy i in the next generations, $E_{i,j}$ is the profit of strategy i resisting strategy j. The quality of strategy i is

$$Q_i = \sum_j p_i E(i, j)$$

The average fitness of population is

$$\overline{Q} = \sum_i p_i Q_i$$

Suppose that the number of asexual reproduction individuals is proportional to their fitness. This can be expressed by the familiar selection equation:

$$p_i' = p_i \frac{Q_i}{\overline{Q}} \tag{13.12}$$

Evolution gamete theory requires dynamical attractors, which are called evolutionarily stable strategy(ESS). For p_i, $p_j \neq 0$, ESS is characterized by $Q_i = Q_j$.

13.3 Darwin's Evolutionary Algorithm

According to quantitative genetics, Darwin's evolutionary algorithm uses simple mutation/selection kinetics. Darwin's algorithm can be formalized as follows:

$$(\mu/\rho, \ \lambda) \ \ (\mu/\rho + \lambda) \tag{13.13}$$

where μ is the number of the parents, λ is the number of offspring. Integer ρ is called "hybrid" number. If two parents' genes are mixed, then $\rho = 2$. Individuals are allowed to generate offspring only if μ is the best. The comma denotes that parents have no choice while plus sign denotes that the parents have.

An important part of Darwin's algorithm is that the range of mutation is not fixed, but is inherited. It adapts itself to environment by way of evolutionary process. Darwin's algorithm is described as follows.

Algorithm 13.1 Darwin's evolutionary algorithm.

1. Construct an initial population;
2. Generate offspring by mutation:

$$s'_1 = sg_1$$
$$x'_1 = x + s'_1 Z_1$$
$$\cdots$$
$$s'_\lambda = sg_\lambda$$
$$x'_\lambda = x + s'_\lambda Z_\lambda$$

3. Selection:

$$Q(x) = \max_{1 \le i \le \lambda} \{Q(x')\}$$

4. Goto step 1.

In Darwin's evolutionary algorithm, random vector Z_i usually has distributed components, and $g_i s$ comes from distributed normative logs. Therefore, the algorithm generates λ offspring near the parents. By inheriting and adaptive neighbour's property, model can be extended to one with $2n$ genes, while the whole individual mutation is limited in n-dimensional space.

13.4 Classifier System

Holland and his colleagues had proposed a cognitive model of classifier system, where rules in it are not expressed as a rule set, but internal entity manipulated by genetic algorithm. Fig. 13.3 presents a general structure for classifier system. From Fig. 13.3, a classifier system consists of three parts: executive subsystem, credit assignment subsystem and discovery subsystem.

Executive subsystem is at the lowest level in the general structure, and reacts directly with environment. It is the same as expert system, which consists of production rules. However, they are based on message passing. This kind of rules is called classifier.

For classifier system-based learning, environment is required to be capable of providing feedback and affirming whether the wanted state arrives or not. The system will validate these rules' effectiveness. These activities are usually called credit assignment, such as barrel chain algorithm.

The last level is discovery subsystem, which generates new rules and substitutes some rules of little usefulness. The system generates rules by cumulative experiences, and performs genetic selection, recombination and substituting rules according to fitness.

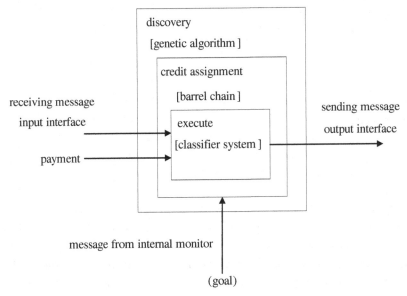

Fig.13.3. General structure of classifier system

Classifier system is a system which is executed concurrently and based on message passing and rules. In a simple way, a message is expressed with a given character set and fixed length. All the rules are expressed in the form of "condition/action". Each condition defines all the required information, and then each action defines related message to be sent when the condition is satisfied. For simplicity，suppose that a message is expressed with a binary character string whose length is 1 and character set is {1,0,#}, where # means that it can match both 1 and 0. For example, the character string 11···1# defines a subset consisting

#, then m_j can be either 1 or 0.

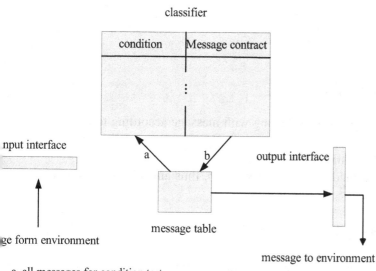

a. all messages for condition test
b. the selected messages from classifier

Fig. 13.4. Basic structure of classifier system

ssages meeting the above requirement constitute a subset, which is a
e in message space. A classifier system consists of a set of classifiers
·,C_N}, a message table, input interface, output interface. Fig. 13.4
he basic structure of a classifier system. Each of its part's function is
as follows.

rrent environment state is transformed into standard message through
iterface.

(2) Classifier defines the process of dealing with message according to the given rules.

(3) Message table contains all current messages.

(4) Messages are transformed into effector's action, thus amending environment state.

Algorithm 13.2 Classifier's Basic Algorithm.

1. Put all messages from input interface into message table;

2. Compare all messages in message table with all conditions in classifiers and record all matching;

3. For all matching that satisfying classifier's condition, put the message that is defined by its action into message table;

4. Let all messages in message table be replace with newly generated messages;

5. Standardize messages in message table so that they satisfy output interface, forming current system's output;

6. Go to step 1.

In order to show the interaction of classifiers and the influence of rule-based learning, we introduce a simple visual classifier system in this section, presented in Fig.13.5. Every object in receptive field generates message in input interface. Detectors and their values are defined according to practical needs. There are three kinds of effectors in the system, which determine the actions in environment. One is to control visual vector, which denotes position of object in receptive field. Visual vector can increasingly rotate by time-step(V-LEFT or V-RIGHT, 15 degrees at a time). The system also have motion vector, which denotes its motion direction. In general, visual direction is independent. The second vector then is to control the rotation of motion vector(M-LEFT or M-RIGHT). The second effector can also align motion vector and visual vector, or oppose them(ALIGN or OPPOSE). The third effector is used to set up movement rate(FAST, CRUISE, SLOW, STOP) in a given direction. Classifiers are used to deal with the information that is generated by detector, and provide effector with command sequences so as to get a given target. Detector defines the right 6 bits in the message from the input interface(Fig.13.5). Property detector defines the following values:

$$d_1 = \begin{cases} 1, & \text{if object is moved} \\ 0, & \text{other} \end{cases}$$

$$(d_2,d_3)=\begin{cases}(0,0), & \text{if object is at the center of receptive field} \\ (1,0), & \text{if object is on the left of the center} \\ (0,1), & \text{if object is on the right of the center}\end{cases}$$

$$d_4=\begin{cases}1, & \text{if system is near to objects} \\ 0, & \text{other}\end{cases}$$

$$d_5=\begin{cases}1, & \text{object is large} \\ 0, & \text{other}\end{cases}$$

$$d_6=\begin{cases}1, & \text{object is flat and long} \\ 0, & \text{other}\end{cases}$$

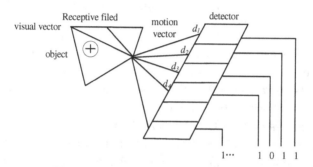

Fig. 13.5. A simple visual classifier system

Consider an irritation-reaction classifier, which has the following rules:

IF a prey(small, moving, nonstriped object) is centered and nonadjacent
THEN quickly move toward the object (ALIGN),(FAST).

In order to realize this rule, detection value is used as condition, which is expressed in the form of #'s. The 2- triple (0, 0) denotes the message generated in input interface. According to above definition, the classifier has the following condition:

00########000001

where the leftmost 2 bits are label, # is irrelevent to bits, and the rightmost 6 bits are the values of prescriptive detectors. If the condition is satisfied, the following message is sent out by classifier:

0100000000000000

where the prefix 01 shows that this message does not come from input interface. This message can be used to set the condition of effector of output interface. The whole rule is as follows:

00########000001 / 0100000000000000，ALIGN，FAST.

In a warning system, the following rule can be used to determine whether or not the system is in a warning state:

IF	there is a moving object in the visual field,
THEN	set up warning timer and send out a warning message.
IF	the warning timer is not zero,
THEN	send out a warning message.
IF	there is no a moving object in the visual field and the

timer is not zero,

THEN	cancel the warning timer.

There are two effectors used to build a classifier by using the above rules. The effectors include SET ALERT,DECREMENT ALERT as well as a detector:

$$d_9 = \left\{ \begin{array}{ll} 1, & \textit{if the timer is not zero} \\ 0, & \textit{other} \end{array} \right\}$$

The classifier can realize the following three kinds of rules, which have the following forms:

00#############1 / 0100000000000011，SET ALERT

00#####1######## / 0100000000000011

00#####1#######0 /DECREMENT ALERT.

A classifier system can be expressed as a network. The most direct method is to use each node in network to denote related classification. Fig. 13.6 gives such a network chart. If a moving object appears in the visual field, then ALERT node is labeled. If the nodes ALERT, SMALL and NOT STRIPED are labeled, then TARGET node is labeled. In order to make this network become a classifier, every node is associated with an identification-tag. In Fig 13.6, the five prefix bits are used as tags.

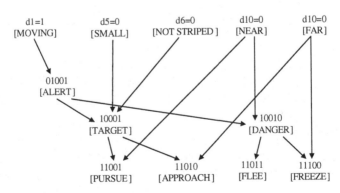

Fig. 13.6. A network chart

From Fig. 13.6, if a MOVING node is labeled by detector d_1, then the directed arc from MOVING to ALERT can be built by the following classifier:

00##############1 / 01001###########,

The directed arc from SMALL, NOT STRIPED and ALERT to TARGET then can be built by a single classifier:

00#########00####, 01001########### /
10001###########.

The other part in the network can be similarly accomplished.

13.5 Bucket Brigade Algorithm

A classifier system is a highly time-parallel learning system based on rules. It can continuously build and improve its environmental model, which is built by using obtained experience. The basic units of classifier system consists of message and classifier(rules). However, the combination of the two units and default classifier can generate very complex knowledge structure.

Two kinds of learning mechanism are used in classifier system:

(1) Bucket brigade algorithm. According to the contribution to the system, every rule is assigned with a credit value.
(2) Algorithm for discovering rules. This kind of algorithm may include genetic algorithm, which can discover new rules, so as to improve system's knowledge database.

Based on the whole availability of classifier system, bucket brigade algorithm endows the classifier with a credit value. By modifying executing cycle, competition mechanism is used in bucket brigade algorithm. In the working cycle, each classifier scans all messages in global message table. Each message satisfying condition can generate new messages. By modifying this process, the satisfied classifier must use competition mechanism to obtain messages from message table. Each classifier bids based on intensity, and only the classifier with higher bidding scale will obtain message from message table. Bidding scale is related not only to the intensity of classifier but also to its characteristics. More precisely, bidding scale is directly proportional to the product of the intensity and the characteristic. If condition part of classifier C is satisfied, bidding scale can be expressed in the following form:

$$Bid(C, t) = cR(C)S(C, t) \tag{13.14}$$

where $R(C)$ denotes characteristic, equaling to the ratio of the number of bits which are not equal to # with the number of all bits in condition part; $S(C, t)$ denotes the intensity of C at moment t; c is a constant small than 1, such as 1/8 or 1/16.

Victorious bidders put message in message table, and at the same time their intensities reduces bidding scale. Take classifier C for example:

$$S(C, t+1) = S(C, t) - B(C, t) \qquad (13.15)$$

while classifier $\{C'\}$ for matching message sent by victorious bidders increase their intensities, their values are equal to bidding scale:

$$S(\underline{C}', t+1) = S(C', t) + aBid(C, t) \qquad (13.16)$$

where $a=1/($the cardinality of $\{C'\})$.

Fig. 13.7 presents two purposes of bid: supporting service and shift of bid by message flow. In addition, bid is used to modify provider's intensity.

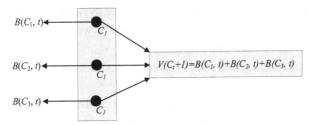

Fig. 13.7. Intensity of classifier is modified by bid

If the system can learn effectively and work steadily, and related results are acceptable, then the decentralization of rule intensity can be reduced. If the decentralization can not be controlled, system may adopt the rules with high intensity, such leading to loss of useful rules with low intensity. For changes of bidding competition and that of mechanism of message generation, some of them require "parasitic" rules to be controlled, while some require finite message table be utilized effectively.

13.6 Genetic Algorithm

Holland had abstractly analyzed adaptive process of natural system, and had designed artificial system having adaptive features of natural system. In this kind of artificial system, an adaptive process is described as a search process in changing structural space. He pointed out: ① Many complex structures can be coded in the simple form of bit strings; ② These bit strings can gradually improved by some simple transforms, so that they transform toward good direction. Based on the above ideas, he proposed genetic algorithm to simulate evolution process of structures.

In genetic algorithm, structure is first coded in the form of character string, and each character string is called an individual. Then a set of character strings, which is called a population, are iteratively operated. Each iteration is called a generation, which contains the process of keeping superior structure in population and that of information transform among structural and stochastic character strings. Similar to natural evolution, genetic algorithm gets good chromosome by operating gene in chromosome, so as to solve related problem. Similar to nature, genetic algorithm knows nothing about the problem to be solved. It just needs to evaluate each chromosome, and selects chromosome according to evaluation value, so that the chromosome with higher value has more chances to propagate. In genetic algorithm, a bit string serves as a chromosome, while single bit serves as a gene. Population is randomly generated, and each individual in population is a bit string. Each individual is endowed with a numerical value, which is called fitness. An individual with low fitness is deleted while one with high fitness then is selected for further operations. The common genetic operators mainly include reproduction, crossover, mutation and inversion.

Comparing with traditional optimization algorithm, genetic algorithm has the following features:

(1) Genetic algorithm does not directly operate parametric variables, but utilizes related codes of parametric variables;
(2) Genetic algorithm's searching starts with one point which is from population but not from problem space;
(3) Genetic algorithm utilizes fitness value, not differential coefficient or other information;
(4) Genetic algorithm utilizes probabilistic transition rules, not deterministic rules.

Genetic algorithm can solve the hard problem through coding technique and breed mechanism to simulate the complex phenomenon. In particular, it is not constrained by the restriction hypothesis of search space and does not require the searching space to be continuous and derivative; it can get global optimal solution with high probability from discrete, multiple-extremum and noising high-dimensional problem. In addition, genetic algorithm's inherent parallelism makes it very suitable for massively parallel computing. At present, genetic algorithm is widely applied to various domains, such as optimization, machine learning, parallel processing.

13.6.1 *Major steps of genetic algorithm*

In order to use genetic algorithm to solve problem, the preparation is divided into the following four steps:

(1) Confirm the expression scheme;
(2) Confirm method to measure fitness value;
(3) Confirm parameters and variables controlling the algorithm;
(4) Confirm method to get results and criterion of how to terminate the algorithm.

In additional genetic algorithm, expression scheme is to express every possible point in search space as a string with fixed length. Confirming expression scheme needs to select character string's length l and alphabet's size k. Binary bit string is usually used to express chromosome in genetic algorithm. The measurement of fitness associates a fixed length string with a fitness value. The main parameters that are used to control genetic algorithm include the size N of population, the maximum generation number M and other parameters including selection probability p_r, crossover probability p_c, mutation probability p_c, etc. The criterion of algorithm termination is determined by concrete problems. Once after these preparation steps are finished, we can utilize genetic algorithm.

Algorithm 13.3 Basic genetic algorithm

1. Randomly generate a population which consists of fixed length strings;
2. Iteratively the following steps on the population until selected criterion is satisfied:
   ① Calculate the fitness value for every individual in population;
   ② Use the following three operators(first two operators at least) to generate new population:
      · Reproduction: reproduce the existing individual string to a new population.
      · Crossover: generate new strings by randomly choosing and recombining two existing individual strings.
      · Mutation: randomly select a gene in a string and variate this gene.

3. The individual string with the highest fitness value is used as the operation result of genetic algorithm, which is regarded as the solution to the problem(or approximate solution).

Fig. 13.8 presents the flow chart of basic genetic algorithm, where variable GEN is currently evolution generation number.

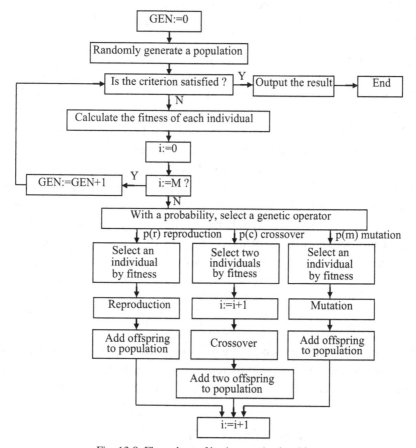

Fig. 13.8. Flow chart of basic genetic algorithm

13.6.2 Representation schema

For genetic algorithm, let's consider an alphabet $V_+ = \{0,1,*\}$ and use it to express schema. So called schema is a structure, which is used to describe a subset of strings. All strings in this subset take the same values at some positions. Symbol " * " denotes uncertain letter; that is, the symbol "*" match both "0" and

"1" at given position. For example, consider a schema H = *11*0** with length of 7. Let string A=0111000, then A is a representation of H; H can match A at the 2,3,5-th positions.

There are 3^l schemas with length of l. In general, if alphabet contains k letters, there are totally $(k+1)^l$ schemas with length of l. The order of a schema is defined as the number of the symbol which is not equal to "*" in the schema, denoted by o(H). For a binary string, its order is equal to the number of 1 and 0. For example, the order of schema 011*1** is equal to 4, denoted by o(011*1**) = 4; o(0*****) =1.

As the number of the symbol which is not equal to "*" in the schema, denoted by o(H). For a binary string, its order is equal to the number of 1 and 0. For example, the order of schema 011*1** is equal to 4, denoted by o(011*1**) = 4; o(0*****) =1.

Definition length of a schema is the distance between the first determining position and the last determining position in the schema, denoted by delta(H). For example, Let H=011*1**, then delta(H)=4. This is because that the first determining position in this schema is 1, while the last determining position is 5, and then the distance between them is 5-1=4.

Suppose at the moment t, schema H has M representations, which are contained in population B(t), denoted by $M = M(H, t)$. At reproduction stage, every string is reproduced according to its fitness value. String B_i's reproduction probability is

$$p_i = \frac{f_i}{\sum_{j=1}^{n} f_j} \tag{13.17}$$

After population B(t) is replaced with population consisting of n strings which are not superposed, we hope that there are M(H, t+1) representations of schema H in population B(t+1) at the moment t. This can be calculated by the following equation:

$$M(H, t+1) = M(H, t) \cdot n \cdot \frac{f(H)}{\sum_{j=1}^{n} f_j} \tag{13.18}$$

where $f(H)$ denotes average fitness value of strings of schema H at the moment t. Because the average fitness value of the whole population can be written as

$$\overline{f} = \sum_{j=1}^{n} \frac{f_j}{n}, \tag{13.19}$$

the reproduction growth equation of schema can be expressed by

$$M(H, t+1) = M(H, t) \frac{f(H)}{\bar{f}} \tag{13.20}$$

This shows that the size of a particular schema is directly proportional to the ratio of the average fitness of the schema to that of population. In other words, the schema whose average fitness value is higher than that of population can generate more representation strings in next generation, while the representation strings of a schema with lower average fitness will reduce in next generation. Suppose that schema H's average fitness value is greater than that of population by value $c\bar{f}$, where c is constant, then growth equation of a schema is

$$M(H, t+1) = M(H, t) \frac{\bar{f}+c\bar{f}}{\bar{f}} = (1+c) \cdot M(H, t) \tag{13.21}$$

Further, we can conclude that

$$m(H, t) = m(H, 0) \cdot (1+c)^t \tag{13.22}$$

Expression (13.22) shows that the representation strings of a schema whose average fitness is higher than that of population will grow exponentially with generation; on the contrary, for the schema whose average fitness is lower than that of population, its representation strings will reduce at an exponentially decaying rate.

13.6.3 Crossover operation

Crossover operation is a process of information exchange among structural random strings. Suppose that population $B(t)$ is a set of schemas, where historical information is expressed in the form of instances, which are saved in B(t). Crossover operation is to generate new instances of the existing schemas. At the same time, new schemas are also generated. A simple crossover operation can be divided into three steps:

(1) Select two strings from population $B(t)$: $a = s_1 s_2 \cdots s_l$, $a' = s'_1 s'_2 \cdots s'_l$
(2) Randomly select a integer $x \in \{1, 2, \cdots l\text{-}1\}$
(3) Exchange the elements on the left of the position x in a and a', and then generate two pieces of new strings: $s_1 \cdots s_x s'_{x+1} \cdots s'_l$ and $s'_1 \cdots s'_x s_{x+1} \cdots s_l$

If each string is endowed with intensity $S(C_j, T)$, then genetic algorithm is described as follows:

Algorithm 13.4 Genetic algorithm with Intensity

1. At the moment t, randomly generate population $B(t)$ with the number of M. Calculate the average fitness of this population, denoted by $v(t)$, and then endow each string in $B(t)$ with the standardizing value $S(C_j, t)/v(t)$.
2. Endow each string in $B(t)$ with a probability value, which is directly proportional to the standardizing value. Then, select n pairs of strings from $B(t)$ based on probability, where $n \ll M$, and reproduce them.
3. For every pair of replicated strings, cross one string with the other, such forming 2n new strings.
4. Use newly generated 2n strings in step (3) to replace 2n strings with the smallest intensities in $B(t)$.
5. Let $t=t+1$, goto step (1).

To show how the above genetic algorithm works, we give a simple example as follows(Fig. 13.9). In this example, there are 8 strings which constitute a population.

$$
\begin{array}{l}
C_1 \;\; 111011101 \cdots \leftarrow 1 \\
C_2 \;\; 110011110 \cdots \leftarrow 0 \\
C_3 \;\; 000111110 \cdots \leftarrow 2 \\
C_4 \;\; 011010011 \cdots \leftarrow 0 \\
C_5 \;\; 100011101 \cdots \leftarrow 2 \\
C_6 \;\; 011001100 \cdots \leftarrow 2 \\
C_7 \;\; 100100101 \cdots \leftarrow 0 \\
C_8 \;\; 100010010 \cdots \leftarrow 1
\end{array}
$$

where the value on the right of arrowhead is intensity of corresponding string C_i in $B(t)$. The strings C_2, C_3, C_6 are all the instances of schema ******1*0*...*, denoted by H_1; the strings C_3, C_5, C_8 are the instances of schema *00*1**...*, denoted by H_2. Calculate each schema's average intensity:

$$
v(H_1) = \frac{0+2+2}{3} = 1.33
$$

$$
v(H_2) = \frac{2+2+1}{3} = 1.67
$$

Then, we endow each string C_i with the standardizing value $S(C)/v(H)$ and then with a probability value according to the standardizing value. Select 3 pairs of strings for crossover based on probability distribution. When crossing, select a position at random and then exchange the elements on the left of the position. This simple operation may lead to subtle influence. Fig. 13.9 shows the whole influences on schema, where C_2, C_3, C_6 are the instances of schema ******1*#. The average intensity of this schema is as follows:

$$v(******1*\#) = \frac{0+2+2}{3} = 1.33$$

C_3, C_5, C_8 is the instances of schema *00*#*****. Its average intensity is as follows:

$$v(*00*\#*****) = \frac{2+2+1}{3} = 1.67$$

In genetic algorithm, if only simple crossover operator is applied, then after a generation, the average proportion of each schema H from $B(t)$ in population changes as follows:

$$P(H,\ t+1) \geq (1 - p_c \frac{\delta(H)}{l-1}(1 - P(H,\ t)))\frac{f(H,t)}{\overline{f}(t)}P(H,\ t) \qquad (13.23)$$

where p_c denotes crossover probability. It can be concluded that as long as $f(H,t) \geq [1 + \frac{\delta(H)}{l-1}]\overline{f}(t)$, the number of the instances of schema H will increase.

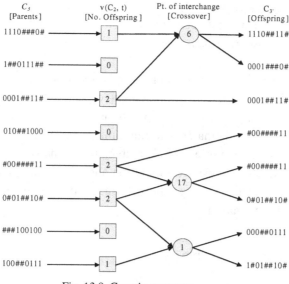

Fig. 13.9. Genetic operators

13.6.4 Mutation operation

For each individual $a = s_1 s_2 \ldots s_l$ in pupolation $B(t)$, the simple mutation operation is described as follows:

(1) There is a mutation probability for each character in a string(individual), and they are independent of each other. Randomly select several locations: x_1, x_2 , $\cdots$, x_l.

(2) Create a new string $a'=s_1\cdots s_{x1-1}s'_{x1}s\ _{x1+1}\cdots s\ _{x2-1}s'\ _{x2}s\ _{x2+1}\cdots s_l$, where s'_{x1} is randomly generated from the domain corresponding to location x_1. And s'_{x2}, $\cdots$, s'_{xk} are generated in the same way.

If mutation probability of each location in schema H is less than or equal to p_m, then the mutation probability of the schema H, whose order is supposed to be o(H), is as follows:

$$1-(1-p_m)^{o(H)} \approx o(H)p_m, \quad (p_m << 1/l) \tag{13.24}$$

13.6.5 Inversion operation

A simple inversion operation can be described through three steps:

(1) Randomly select a string from current population: $a= s_1s_2\cdots s_l$;

(2) Randomly select two numbers i' and j' from $\{0, 1, \cdots, l+1\}$, and let $i = \min\{i',j'\}, j = \max\{i',j'\}$;

(3) Inverse the elements between locations i and j, and then a new string is obtained: $s_1s_2\cdots s_is_{j-1}s_{j-2}\cdots s_{i+1}s_j\cdots s_l$

Inversion operation can change the location of character in a string(individual). Any kind of arrangement of characters in a string can be obtained by using related inversion operations in turn. The main influence of inversion operation on schema H is to randomly change the length of schema H and the relationship among effective characters in schema H.

Besides reproduction, crossover, mutation and inversion operations, there are other genetic operations, such as intrachromosomal duplication, elimination, translocation and segregation.

13.7 Parallel Genetic Algorithm

Discrete Mandl's model-based genetic algorithm consists of the following five parts:

(1) Chromosome representation for a given problem solving;

(2) Original species for problem solving;

(3) Quality function serving as environment;
(4) Selection process for generating offspring;
(5) Genetic operators, such as mutation, recombination;
(6) Parameters for controlling algorithm itself.

In natural world, selection operation in individual's environment is accomplished locally. Natural selection equation which is abstracted from environment may lead to the risk of repetition. Parallel genetic algorithm has been successfully applied to solve many combinatorial problems. Each species is simulated on a processor. A parallel genetic algorithm can be described as follows:

1. Given N individuals with different initial phenotype;
2. Calculate local maximum value of each individual;
3. Selection: select near-neighbour individuals for mating;
4. Create offspring by recombination and mutation;
5. Goto step 2.

There are two differences between parallel genetic algorithm and classical genetic algorithm. One is that individual mating is locally finished; the other is that individual utilizes hill climbing method.

Therefore, parallel genetic algorithm utilizes genotype learning and phenotype learning. Further, each individual survives in a certain environment, and crossover and selection are accomplished in such environment, such as 2-D grid. Individual's neighbor does not connect to the grid of genotype and phenotype space. Parallel genetic algorithm originates mainly from classical genetic algorithm. In genetic algorithm, individual is regarded as the result of selecting "the best behavior". On the contrary, parallel genetic algorithm is based on internal driver. Parallel genetic algorithm has more differences over general genetic algorithm. Its evolution is based on driver of internal self-Organization.

13.8 Classifier System Boole

In 1987, Wilson developed a classifier system for solving boolean problem: Boole(Wilson, 1987). A boolean function is a mapping from strings with length of L to {0,1}. Learning function means that the ability to correctly map any input(a string) to 0 or 1 is obtained.

Every Boole classifier consists of a class name and an action. For an input string with L-bit, the length of its class name is L; action is simply a bit of 0 or 1, which denotes one of the possible two values of boolean function. If class name matches the current input string, the system will make a decision. Classifier population [P] is initialized with 0,1 or # based on a certain random rules. Action is initialized in the similar way. For example, the classifier with length of L=6 is:

$$1\ 0\ \#\ 0\ \#\ 1\ /\ 1$$

In Boole, [P] contains 400 classifiers, which are initialized based on uniform distribution. Initial intensity is 100.

During executing cycle, when a string is input, the system will output 0 or 1. Its executing cycle can divided into two steps:

(1) Match input strings and form matching set [M].
(2) Probability distribution is used in the intensity of [M] classifier. A classifier is selected from [M]; that is, a particular classifier's selection probability is equal to the ratio of its intensity to the sum of all intensity of classifier in [M]. The action of selected classifier is used as the system's decision.

After executing cycle, enhanced components adjust the intensity of classifier according to the profit obtained from environment. Wilson used the following algorithm to do this:

Algorithm 13.5 An algorithm for adjusting intensity of classifier(Wilson, 1987).

1. Create a set of classifiers which have the same selected actions, called action set [A]. And the set of all classifiers which are not in [M] is denoted by MOT[A].
2. For each classifier in [A], its intensity is reduced by a fraction e.
3. If the system decides correctly, the profit R is assigned to intensity of [A].
4. If the system decides incorrectly, the profit $R'(0 \leq R' \leq R)$ is assigned to intensity of [A], and [A]'s intensity is reduced by a fraction p, where one of R' and p is equal to 0.
5. NOT[A]'s intensity is reduced by a fraction t.

If the system makes a correct decision in step 3, intensity of [A] can be calculated by the following formula:

$$S'_A = S_A - eS_A + R \tag{13.25}$$

Where S_A is the sum of intensity of [A] before profit is obtained, and S'_A is the sum of profit. Suppose that R of [A] is the same for all time, it can be proved that S_A is gradually closed to R/e. It is suggested that S_A is function of estimated value of classical profit under relatively stable profit condition. Step 4 defines three kinds of different profit mechanism: profit-punishment, $p \neq 0$; just considering profit, p and R' are all equal to 0; profit-profit, $R' \neq 0$. The first situation reflects the environment, showing that the result of the system is incorrect. The second situation responds to the environment, and there is no difference before correct action is generated. The third situation then reflects a general case, where there is an action getting the maximal profit and the others get the same profit. In step 2, e is regarded as the cost of each classifier in [A] in order to obtain the profit. The total profit of [A] is assigned by distribution function D, and the simplest method is to share R with each classifier.

The discovery component is based on Holland's genetic algorithm, using reproduction, crossover and elimination. Boole's genetic algorithm is presented as follows.

Algorithm 13.6 Boole's genetic algorithm

1. Select a classifier C_1 from [P] according to probability and intensity.
2. Similar to step 1, select classifier C_2 according to probability χ, and then cross C_2 with C_1; then select one result as offspring, and the other one is discarded.
3. If step 2 is not finished, reproduce C_1 so as to generate offspring.
4. Apply mutation operation to generated offspring, that is, change allele of each individual with probability μ.
5. If each parent's intensity is reduced by one third through mutation operation, then let offspring's initial intensity is equal to the sum of the reduced intensity of parents, else that of C_1 is reduced by one half and initial intensity of offspring is equal to the reduced scale.
6. Add offspring to [P].
7. Delete the classifier with the minimal intensity from [P].

In each executing circle, the algorithm is called with probability p. This algorithm is basically the same as the normative genetic algorithm. The difference between this algorithm and the normative genetic algorithm lies in the fact that the former can generate only one offspring when it is called at a time, while the latter usually generates many offspring.

In addition, discovery component also uses another mechanism---creation. Namely, if [M] is empty in executing circle, then a new classifier is created. The name of the created classifier is a replication of currently input string. The probability of inserting # is equal to the proportion of # in [P]. In order to get related location in [P], we may apply the method in step 7 to delete a classifier. Then, [M] is recalculated.

For example, let's consider learning 6-path multiplexer. For every integer $k>0$, the length of multiplexer of binary character string is $L = k + 2k$. For every input string, there are k address bits a_i and data bits d_i. Related string is expressed in the following form:

$$a_0a_1... \ a_{k-1}d_0d_1... \ d_{2^{k-1}}$$

Table 13.1 Learning results of 6-path multiplexer

Instance NO.	Concept (class name)						(action)		intensity
56	0	1	#	0	#	#	/	0	7655
52	0	1	#	1	#	#	/	1	7541
48	0	0	0	#	#	#	/	0	7056
46	1	0	#	#	0	#	/	0	7095
45	0	0	1	#	#	#	/	1	6665
41	1	1	#	#	#	0	/	0	5964
39	1	1	#	#	#	1	/	1	6323
35	1	0	#	#	1	#	/	1	5145
7	#	1	#	1	#	1	/	1	1044
4	1	1	#	#	#	#	/	1	522
3	#	0	#	#	1	#	/	1	293
3	1	1	#	#	0	#	/	0	210
2	#	0	1	#	#	#	/	1	330
2	0	1	1	#	#	#	/	1	212
2	1	0	0	#	0	#	/	0	150
2	0	0	#	#	#	#	/	1	219
2	1	#	#	#	1	#	/	0	326
2	1	0	#	0	#	#	/	0	238
1	#	1	#	0	#	#	/	0	129
1	1	0	#	#	#	#	/	0	168
1	1	1	#	#	#	#	/	0	97
1	1	0	#	#	0	0	/	0	100
1	0	0	#	#	1	#	/	1	81
1	1	#	#	#	#	0	/	0	212
1	1	0	#	#	0	1	/	1	56
1	0	1	#	#	#	#	/	1	116

Function value is given by data bits(0 or 1). For example, the following are the 6-path multiplexer's input string and correct output value, where $L = 6$, $k = 2$:

$$0\ 0\ 0\ 1\ 0\ 1 \quad 0$$
$$1\ 1\ 0\ 0\ 0\ 1 \quad 1$$
$$1\ 0\ 1\ 1\ 0\ 1 \quad 0$$

Because $k=2$, the first two address bits in the first example are 00, showing that the output value of the data bits is 0. For the second example, its data bits are 11, so the bit 3 must be considered and the output value is 1. The disjunctive normal form of the function is expressed in the following form:

$$F_6 = a'_0 a'_1 d_0 + a'_0 a_1 d_1 + a_0 a'_1 d_2 + a_0 a_1 d_3$$

The 6-path multiplexer is as follows:

$$0\ 0\ 0\ \#\ \#\ \#\ /\ 0$$
$$0\ 0\ 1\ \#\ \#\ \#\ /\ 1$$
$$0\ 1\ \#\ 0\ \#\ \#\ /\ 0$$
$$0\ 1\ \#\ 1\ \#\ \#\ /\ 1$$
$$1\ 0\ \#\ \#\ 0\ \#\ /\ 0$$
$$1\ 0\ \#\ \#\ 1\ \#\ /\ 1$$
$$1\ 1\ \#\ \#\ \#\ 0\ /\ 0$$
$$1\ 1\ \#\ \#\ \#\ 1\ /\ 1$$

This set is denoted by $[S_6]$. Boole can find multiple members of a particular classifier. On trial, profit-punishment policy is adopted, where $e = 0.1$, $R = 1000$, $R' = 0$, $p = 0.8$, $G = 4.0$, $\mu = 0.001$, $\chi = 0.12$, $\rho = 1.0$, $t = 0.1$. The results of 13,000 tests are presented in Table 13.1. The top 8 classifiers in Table 13.1 are the members of $[S_6]$.

13.9 Rule Discovery System

In rule discovery system, the first task is to evaluate the quality of the existing rules in the system, and then improve them. Grefenstette had developed a rule discovery system: RUDI(Grefenstette,1988). Figure 13.10 presents its control structure. The levels of problem solving consist of simplified classifier system. In learning level, genetic operators are used to operate population of knowledge structure, which is expressed as a set of rule table. The whole behavior of knowledge structure is used to control these structures' reproduction.

In RUDI, credit-valuating method, profit-sharing plan(PSP) and bucket brigade algorithm(BBA) are used to provide each rule with mutually complementary effective information. According to expected exterior reward, PSP-intensity provides rule effectiveness with even more accurate evaluation. During problem solving, it is used to solve confliction. On the contrary, BBA-intensity evaluates the dynamic correlations between rules. This kind of measure can be used to assist clustering rules.

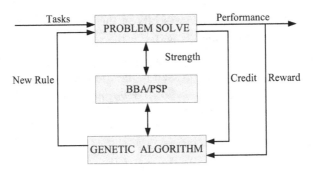

Fig. 13.10. Control structure of RUDI (Picture from Grefenstette, 1988)

Grefenstette had proposed a method to modify intensity, called profit-sharing plan(PSP). In this method, problem solving plan is divided into a series of plots, which are differentiated based on received exterior reward. If a plot wins in bidding competition, related rule is considered to be active in this plot. In the plot t, PSP can modify the intensity $S_i(t)$ of each active rule:

$$S_i(t+1) = S_i(t) - bS_i(t) + bp(t), \tag{13.26}$$

where $p(t)$ is the obtained exterior reward when the plot is finished; that is, when exterior reward is obtained, each active rule collects the bids and offers a part of exterior reward. PSP's influence on a given rule R_i can be calculated by the following equation:

$$S_i(t) = (1-b)^t S_i(0) + b \sum_{i=1}^{t} (i-b)^{t-i} p(i-1) \tag{13.27}$$

where t is a plot in which rule R_i is active, namely, $S_i(t)$ is basically the average of exterior reward; $(1-b)$ is exponential attenuation factor. If b is small enough, $S(t)$ is equal to the average of $p(t)$. If exterior reward $p(t)$ is a constant p_*, S_i will converge to an equilibrium value S_i^*:

$$S_i^* = \lim_{t \to \infty} [(1-b)^t S_i(0) + b \sum_{i=1}^{t} (i-b)^{t-i} p^*] = p^* \tag{13.28}$$

Under the case of constant profit, it is in accord with equation (13.27), and the error $E_i(t) = p^* - S_i(t)$ is reduced by the following rate $E_i(t) = p^* - S_i(t)$:

$$\Delta E_i = E_i(t+1) - E_i(t)$$
$$= S_i(t) - S_i(t+1)$$
$$= -b(p^* - S_i(t))$$
$$= -bE_i(t).$$
(13.29)

The difference between current intensity and equilibrium intensity is reduced by factor b every time the intensity is changed. For example, assume that $p^* = 500$, $b = 0.1$ and $S_i(t) = 100$, then $S_i(t+1) = 100 - 10 + 50 = 140$. Note that the error $p^* - S_i$ is reduced from 400 to 360; that is, this error is reduced by 10%.

We can find that under the case of constant reward, each rule's intensity can quickly converge to equilibrium intensity, and reward can be evaluated when the plot is over. A possible restriction of PSP is that credit must be assigned in the interval corresponding to the plot differentiated by exterior reward. It is very important to select such a plot.

Suppose that rule R_i is ignited at step τ while rule R_j at step $\tau + 1$. Then BBA uses the following formula to modify the intensity S_i of rule R_i:

$$S_i(\tau+1) = S_i(\tau) - bS_i(\tau) + bS_j(\tau)$$
(13.30)

Except that plot index t is replaced with step index τ and exterior reward $p(t)$ is replaced with the intensity S_j of rule R_j, this formula is the same as (13.26). The first change means that the number of modifying rule's intensity in a given plot is larger than one. The second modification leads to the basic difference between PSP and BBA. Consider two pieces of rule R_i and R_j. Rule R_i is ignited after rule R_j. Assume that R_i and R_j are ignited in a plot no more than one time, then we have:

$$S_i^* = \lim_{t\to\infty}[(1-b)^t S_i(0) + b \sum_{i=1}^{t} (i-b)^{t-i} p^*] = p^*$$

$$S_i(t) = (1-b)^t S_i(0) + \sum_{i=1}^{t} b(1-b)^{t-i} S_j(i-1)$$
(13.31)

where the range of t is the whole plot and the two activity. In other words, the intensity of R_i follows that of R_j. If S_j can converge to a constant S_j^*, then S_i can also converge.

$$S_i^* = \lim_{t\to\infty} S_i(t) = \lim_{t\to\infty}[(1-b)^t S_i(0) + \sum_{i=1}^{t} (1-b)^{t-i} S_j(i-1)] = S_j^*$$
(13.32)

Similarly, formula (13.29) shows that S_j can converge to S_j^* (the internal payoff for R_i). This kind of analysis can be extended to any rule chain. For example, when $<R_1, R_2, \dots, R_n>$ are ignited in turn, only rule R_n can receive exterior reward. At the balance condition, all rules in the chain have the same intensity. At the unbalance condition, all rules in the chain are described by (13.31), not by (13.32). In any case, if expected reward received by rule chain is well consistent, then the intensity of the rules in the chain will converge to general level.

Table 13.2 Different methods to modify intensity

Ruel	PSP's intensity	BBA's intensity
R_1	1000	648
R_2	299	567
R_3	1000	645
R_4	4	644
R_5	300	300
R_6	999	531
R_7	300	300

To compare PSP with BBA, let's consider Figure 13.11. This figure presents 10 states, including initial states A and B, terminal states H, I and J. The exterior rewards generated in states H, I and J are 1000, 0 and 300, respectively.

In this example, classifier system uses PSP or BBA to modify the intensity of rule. All initial intensities are set to be 100, and bidding rate b is 0.1. In addition, interior rewards are distributed to 1000 plots. This means that each classifier system consists of 3000 steps. The obtained intensities of rules are presented in Table 13.2.

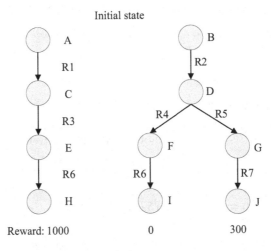

Fig. 13.11. Comparison of PSP and BBA

13.10 Evolutionary Strategy

Evolutionary strategy(ES) is a method to solve parameter optimization problems by simulating natural evolution process. Early evolution treatment is based on a population consisting of many individuals and an operator: mutation. Evolutionary strategy operates mainly on individual-level. It can be simply described as follows:

1. The defined problem is to find a n-dimensional real vector x, such that the maximum value of function $F(x)$: $R^n \to R$ is obtained.
2. The initial population of parental vector is randomly selected from the feasible range of each dimension.
3. Offspring vector is created by adding parental vector with Gaussian random variable with mean square deviation of zero.
4. Create next generation's parents by selecting vectors according to minimum error principle.
5. The process terminates, if the standard deviation of vectors keeps unchanged, or there is no effective calculation method.

13.11 Evolutionary Programming

Evolutionary programming(EP) is to search a computer program, which is coded as an individual, with high fitness in the space consisting of all possible computer programs. In evolutionary programming, there are several thousands computer programs used to evolve. Evolutionary programming is first proposed in 1962 by L.J. Fogel, A.J. Owens and M.J. Walsh.

Evolutionary programming focuses on the change of behaviors of species. The representation of evolutionary programming is naturally oriented to task-level. Once a representation of fitness is determined, mutation operation can be defined based on such a representation and related offspring are created based on concrete parental behaviors.

Evolutionary programming starts with an initial population consisting of randomly generated computer programs, which consist of the functions suitable for problem space. Thus functions can be normal arithmetic function, normal programming operation, logic function or particular function. Each individual(computer program) in population is evaluated by fitness value, which is related to particular field.

Evolutionary programming is capable of reproducing new computer programs so as to solve problems. It consists of three steps:

1. Generate initial population, which randomly consists of the functions(programs) related to the problem.
2. Repeat the following sub-steps, until selection criterion is satisfied:
    ① Perform each program in population and endow it with a fitness value according to its ability to solve problem.
    ② Use related operations, such as mutation, to generate new computer programs, and then form a new population. Probabilistically select a computer program from population based on fitness value and then use a related operation to deal with this program. Replicate existing computer program to a new population. Create new computer programs by randomly recombining two computer programs
3. In the final population, the computer program with the highest fitness value is regarded as the result of evolutionary programming. This result is possibly the optimal or approximate solution to the problem.

Exercises

1. Describe the theoretical model of evolution systems.
2. Give Darwin's evolutionary algorithm.
3. Expatiate the definition of classical genetic algorithm and explain its basic elements.
4. Genetic algorithm attempts to keep genetic diversity as well as some important features(genetic schemas). Please design a different genetic operator, so that genetic algorithm can reach the both targets.
5. What is simple mutation? Please give its brief description.
6. What is simple inversion operation? Please give its brief description.
7. For TSP problem, discuss the problem of its effective coding and design related genetic operations and fitness function.
8. Design a genetic algorithm for solving TSP problem.
9. Please explain how to express chromosomes and genes in genetic algorithm.
10. For two parent individuals 1110###0# and 1##0111##, suppose that crossover location is 6. Please use alone point crossing operator to create their offspring.
11. Please use a programming language to develop a program for parallel genetic algorithm.

Chapter 14

Distributed Intelligence

Distributed intelligence mainly researches how to solve the problem by physically or logically distributed system. Agent computing is not only the hot topic of artificial intelligence, but also an important breakpoint for next-generation software development.

14.1 Introduction

Solving large and complex problems usually needs many professional persons or social groups to work together. Since 1970s distributed intelligence became a hot research topic gradually with the development of computer networks, communication and parallel program design technology. From 1990s, the rapid development of Internet provides great conditions for novel information systems and decision support systems. They greatly increase in scale, scope and complex degree. Distributed intelligence become the key point of these systems which has following characteristic:

(1) The data, knowledge and control is distributed not only on logic but also on physical. It has no control for the whole system and
(2) Each problem solver is connected by computer network. The cost of communication is much less than the problem solution cost.
(3) Every component collaborates with each other to solve the problem which one component can not solve it singly.

The implementation of distributed artificial intelligence can remedy the shortage of traditional expert system and greatly improve the performance of knowledge system. The main advantages are as follows:

(1) Improve problem solving capacity. Because of the distributed characteristics of the intelligent system, its problem solving capacity increases substantially. First of all, once high reliability, communications path, processing nodes, as well as knowledge of the redundancy are failure, the whole system just reduces the response time or solving accuracy and will not completely paralyzed; Second, the system is easy to expand. To increase processing units, it can expand the system's scale and increase problem solving ability. Thirdly, modules characteristics will enable the design of the whole system very flexible.

(2) Improve the efficiency of problem solving. Because the nodes of the distributed intelligent system can be parallel to solve problems, we can develop parallelization to solve problems and increase the efficiency of problem solving.

(3) Expand the scope of application. Distribution of intelligent technology can break the restriction of current knowledge engineering field through only using an expert. In distributed intelligent systems, different areas, and even different experts from the same field can collaborate to solve a problem that particular experts can not. At the same time, many non experts can cooperate to solve the problem which may also meet or exceed an expert level.

(4) Reduce the complexity of the software. Distributed intelligent system will broke down a task into sub tasks to solve a number of relatively independent of the sub tasks. The result is to reduce the complexity of the problem solving.

Distributed intelligent research can be traced back to the late 1970s. Early distributed intelligent research focuses on distributed problem solving (DPS). Their goal is to create large size of the cooperative groups to work together to solve a problem. In distributed problem solving systems, data, knowledge, control systems are distributed in the various nodes. There is no overall control and knowledge of the overall data and storage. Because no system in the node has enough data and knowledge to solve the whole problem, each node needs to exchange information, knowledge, and problem solving state. They are through mutual cooperation for solving complex problems of collaboration. In a pure DPS system, the problem is broken down into tasks. For solving these tasks, we need to design a specific task execution system for the problem. All the interactive strategies have been integrated for part of the overall system design. This is a top-down design of the system, because the system is designed to meet the needs of top requirements.

Hewitt and his colleagues developed an ACTOR model based concurrent programming design system (Hewitt,1983). ACTOR model provides parallel computing theory in distributed system, a group of experts and the ability for ACTOR to acquire intelligence. Hewitt in 1991 proposed open information systems semantics (Hewitt,1991). He pointed that competitiveness, commitment, cooperation and negotiation should be scientific basis of distributed intelligent system. He attempted to provide a new basis for distributed artificial intelligence. In 1980, Davis and Smith proposed contract net (CNET) (Smith,1980). CNET use the bid - contract ways to implement task distribution in multi nodes. Contract Net system provides an important contribution to distributed tasks by mutual agreement and negotiation.

Distributed vehicle test monitoring (DVMT) system is also one of the earliest and most influential researches in distributed artificial intelligence field. Lesser, Corkill and Durfee from University of Massachusetts were responsible for this project (Lesser, 1980). The system could track to monitor the travelling vehicles of the urban area. Under this environment, they took many kinds of research on distributed problem solving (Durfee, 1987). DVMT used the distributed sensor network data as background to research on complex interaction problem solving of blackboard to provide a method of abstracting and modeling distributed system.

In 1987, Gasser developed a system named MACE which is an experimental environment of distributed artificial intelligence system development (Gasser, 1987).Every computing unit in MACE was named an agent. They have knowledge and reasoning ability. The agents communicate through message transmission. MACE is similar to object-oriented environment, but avoiding the complicated inherits issue in object-oriented system. Every component in MACE can compute in parallel and provide the description language, the demons tracking mechanism. The research focused on the implementation of distributed intelligent system and maintained the clarity of the concepts.

Zhongzhi Shi and his colleagues in Institute of Computing Technology, Chinese Academy of Sciences developed a distributed knowledge processing system DKPS. The system uses logic - object knowledge model and research on knowledge sharing and collaboration solving problems (Shi, 1990b). ACTOR-based model, Ferber developed a reflection ACTOR Mering IV language in 1991 (Ferber,1991). In this model, actor is active object to interact through asynchronous transmission. Mering IV is a reflection language that can represent itself from structure and operation. Reflective of the system makes use of different sizes and the size of the agent can interact in a uniform manner.

In the 1990s, multi-agent system (MAS) became a hot research topic in distributed intelligence. Multi-agent system mainly research on intelligent behaviors coordination between multi agents. For a common global goal or their different goals, they share the knowledge of problem and solving approaches and collaborate for problem solving. Based on the concept of agent, people proposed a new definition of artificial intelligence: "Artificial intelligence is a branch of computer science. Its goal is to construct an intelligent agent with showing certain intelligent behaviors." Therefore, the research on intelligent agent is the core problem of artificial intelligence. Hayes-Roth from computer science department of Stanford University said in the special report of the IJCAI'95: "intelligent computer is the first goal and ultimate goal of the artificial intelligence". Now, the research on intelligent agent not only attracts the concern of artificial intelligence researchers, but also attract researchers from data communications, human-computer interface design, robotics, concurrent engineering.

14.2 The Essence of Agent

14.2.1 *The concept of agent*

In English, term "agent", there are three main meanings: First, referring to the people accountable for their actions; Second, agent is defined an article to produce a certain effect, the physical, chemical or biological significance of the active things; Thirdly, the delegate that a person receiving the commission and do actions on behalf of other persons. In computer sciences and artificial intelligence field, an agent can be viewed as an entity which perceives its environment through sensors and acts upon that environment through effectors. If the agent is a person, the sensors have eyes, ears and other organs, hand, legs, mouth and other parts of the body is the effector. If it is the robot, cameras are sensor and all moving parts is the effector. Generally, agent has structure as Figure 14.1.

Generally, agent needs to have part or all of the following characteristics:

(1) Autonomy. This is a basic characteristic of the agent, that is, it can control its own behavior. The autonomy of the agent is reflected in: the acts of agent should be active and spontaneous; agent should have its own goals or intentions. According to the requirements of the goal, and environmental, the

agent should plan for their own short-term acts.

(2) Interactive. That is the awareness and influence to environment. Whether the agent survival in the real world (such as robots, Internet services on the agent, etc.) or the virtual world (such as the agents in virtual shopping malls, etc.). They are able to sense the environment and can change environment through behaviors. An agent can not called "Agent" if it can not affect the environment.

(3) Collaborative. Usually the agent is not alone there, but survival in a lot of the agent world. The good and effective cooperation among agents can greatly enhance the multi-agent system performance.

(4) Communication. This is also the fundamental characteristics of an agent. The so-called communications, means of information exchange between the agents. Furthermore, the agents and people should be able to carry out a certain sense of "conversation." To undertake the task, agents' collaboration and negotiation is based on communication.

(5) Longevity (or coherence time). Traditional procedures are activated when needed, be stopped when the operator end. The agent is different. It should at least "fairly long" for the time to run. Although not the indispensable characteristics of agents, it is generally believed that is the important characteristics of agents.

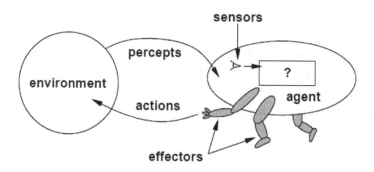

Figure 14.1. the agent entity (Russell et al., 1995)

In addition, some scholars also raised the agent should be adaptive, personality and other characteristics. In practical applications, the agent needs take actions under certain restrictions of time and resources. Therefore, the agents in real world should have real-time characteristics besides the general natures.

At present, the research on multi agent system is very active. Multi-agent systems are trying to use the agents to simulate the human behaviors. Agents are used in the real world and the community simulation, robots and intelligent machinery, and other fields. In the real world survival, the agents need to face a changing environment. In such an environment, agents not only maintain a timely response to emergency situations, but also plan for the use of certain short-term strategy. And then they are through the world and the other main modeling to predict the future of the state, as well as through communication language to realize cooperation or negotiation with other agents.

14.2.1 *Rational agent*

Bratman's Research on intention from philosophy generates broad impact to artificial intelligence. He believes the balance between belief, desire and intention can solve the problem effectively. In the open world, rational agents can not be driven by intention; desire and their combination since there is belief based intention exist between desire and planning. The reason is as follows:

(1) Agent actions are restricted limited resources. Once agents decide what to do, they build a limited format commitment.
(2) In multi agent environment, agents need commitment to coordinate the actions of agents. If there is no commitment, no actions are existent. Intention is the choice of commitment.

In open and distributed environment, the actions of a rational agent are restricted by intention. The intention is represented:

(1) If an agent wants to change its intention, it need reasons to do so;
(2) An agent can not insist on its unimportant intention without considering the change of environment.

The main purpose of rational balance is to make a rational act in conformity with the characteristics of the environment. The so-called characteristics of the environment not only refers to the objective conditions, but also include environmental factors in the social groups, such as social groups on the rational judgement of the law. Bratman presented the intention - action principle: If A take action B under the current intention is reasonable, then Agent A changes intention to action. Action B is reasonable.

In the specific time, agent is show as follows:

(1) Performance test provides performance measure the degree of success.
(2) Agents can percept all things, we will call this sense of history as the perception sequence.
(3) Agents know the environment.
(4) Agents can perform the actions.

An ideal agent can be defined: for each sequence may be the perception, the ideal rational agents, on the basis of the evidence provided by the perception sequence and the agent inner knowledge, should do the desired actions to make its performance largest.

14.2.3 *BDI model*

BDI agent model can be described by the following elements:

(1) A group of belief about the world
(2) A group of goals that agents want to achieve
(3) A plan base to describe how to reach the goal and change the belief
(4) A intention structure to describe currently how the agent to achieve the goal and change the believes.

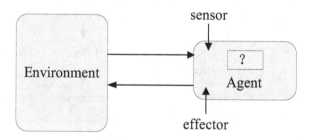

Fig. 14.2. Agents interact with environments

14.3 Agent Architecture

14.3.1 *Agent basic architecture*

Agent can be seen a black box. It perceives the environment through the sensor and effect the environment with the actor. Human being, if we see it an agent, perceives environment with eyes, ear, nose, etc. It affects the environment using hands, legs etc. Robot agent usually holds some cameras for getting environment information and the motor is their actor. Software agent uses codes as their sensor and actor (Figure 14.2).

Besides communication with environment, most agents need to deal with the received information to achieve their goals. Figure 14.3 shows the work process of intelligent agent. After receiving the information, the first step for agents is syncretizing the information to make it acceptable by knowledge base of agents. Information syncretizing is very important because the results from different communication components are often heterogeneous and the representation is different. For example, for the same thing, the information provided by human being and received by agents may be different. So, Information syncretizing must identify and differentiate correctly this kind of variance.

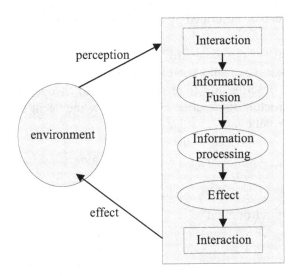

Intelligent agent

Fig. 14.3. The work process of intelligent agent

Once the agents received the outer information, the information process becomes the key tasks of agents since it reflect the real function of every agent. The purpose of information processing is explaining the useful data and form the concrete plan. Because every agent has its own goal, the impact of inner goal must be considered as a part of whole impact. If agents know the impact, they need to adopt actions to realize the goal. To form plan, agents may prescribe knowledge, including new conditions to reflect the concrete actions. However, this is not obligatory since sometimes agents need not plans when take actions。

If communicating with environmental objects, action model will adopt the proper communication component. The control task is also part of action component.

From the discussion above, the agents can be defined as a map from perceptive knowledge to actions. Suppose O is the perceptive set, A is the possible actions which can be achieved by agents. The agent function $f: O^* \rightarrow A$ define the actions of all agents. The task of artificial intelligence is to design agent programs which can realize the map from perceptive knowledge to actions. The Skeleton of agent program is as follows:

Algorithm 14.1 Skeleton-Agent(percept) return action

Input static: memory
Method:
1. *memory* ← Update-Memory(*memory,percept*);
2. *action* ← Choose-Best-Action(*memory*);
3. *memory* ← Update-Memory(*memory,action*);
4. return *action*.

The agents will change its memory to reflect the new percept after every function call. An ideal rational agent hopes to achieve the best performance for every percept.

Not every agent's action is the reflection of new conditions. Agents can also create their new plan. In this condition, the knowledge of information provider is useful only in specific time. This is the main difference between reactive agents and deliberative agents.

14.3.2 *Deliberative agent*

Deliberative agent (or cognitive agent) is a distinct symbol model which includes the reasoning ability about the environment and intelligent actions. It keeps the tradition of classical artificial intelligence. It is a knowledge based system. Environmental model is implemented in advance to form main knowledge base. There are two problems of this architecture:

Conversion problem: how to translate the real world to correct symbol description?

Representation/reasoning problem: how to represent the real entity and process. How to let the agents in possession of the ability to make decision according to reasoning the information at a limited time.

The first problem results in the research of computer vision and natural language processing. The second problem induces the research on knowledge representation, autonomic reasoning and planning. In the real world, these problems are a bit difficult since the representation is very complex. So, the deliberative agents have its limitation in dynamic environment. Without necessary knowledge and resource, it is difficult to add the new information and knowledge about environment into existent model.

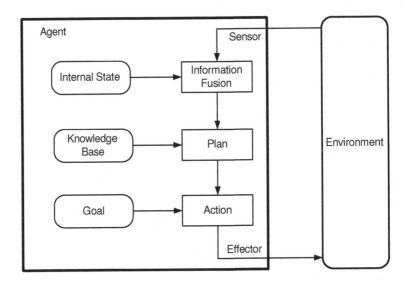

Fig. 14.4. the architecture of deliberative agent

Deliberative agent is a kind of active software. Different with concrete domain knowledge, it has the knowledge representation, problem solution representation, and environment representation and communication protocol. According to the way of thinking, deliberative agents can be divided into abstract thinking agents and visual thinking agents. Abstract thinking agents have abstract concepts. They think through the symbol information processing. However, visual thinking agents think using the visual material. It adapts the connection theory of nerve mechanism.

Figure 14.4 give the architecture of deliberative agent. Agent gets outer information through the sensors. After then, the agents syncretize the information according to the inner states and generate the description of current state. They create the plan with the support of knowledge base then. After then, agents can form a series of actions which is taken by actors to affect the environment.

Algorithm 14.2 Deliberate-Agent algorithm.

Input: static: *environment,* //describing the current world environment
            Kb,   //knowledge base
            plan   // Plan
Method:

1. *environment* ← Update-World-Model(*environment,percept*)
2. *state* ← Update-Mental-State(*environment,state*)
3. *plan* ← Decision-Making(*state,kb,action*)
4. *environment* ← Update-World-Model(*environment,action*)
5. return *action*

In the program above, Update-World-Model function generate the abstract description of current world environment from percept. Update-Mental-State funcation revises the agent's inner mental state according to the percept environment. The knowledge base includes the general knowledge and real knowledge. Agents apply the knowledge to make decision with the Decision-Making function.

BDI model which is a core of typical deliberative agent can be described with the following elements:

· a group of beliefs about the world;
· current goals;
· a plan base which describe how to achieve the goal and revise the belief;
· an intention structure to describe how to achieve the current goals and revise the current beliefs.

According to BDI Architecture，Rao and Georgeff proposed a simple BDI interpreter (Rao et al,1992).

Algorithm 14.3 BDI-Interpreter

1. BDI-Interpreter（）{
2. initialize-state()；
3. do
4.   options := option-generator(event-queue, B, G, I)；
5.   selected-options := deliberate(options, B, G, I)；
6.   update-intentions(selected-options, I)；
7.   execute(I)；

8.   get-new-external-events();
9.   drop-successful-attitudes(B,G,I);
10.   drop-impossible-attitudes(B,G,I);
11.   until quit

14.3.3 *Reactive agent*

The problems in traditional artificial intelligence are reflected in deliberative agent without any change. The main criticism focuses on the rock-bound architecture. The agents work in dynamic environment. So, they need to make a decision according to the current conditions. However, their intention and plan were developed on the symbol model of past specific time. There is little change about that. Rule-based rock-bound extends the disadvantage since the conversion between planer, scheduler and executor is time cost. The implementation of condition of scheduler changes more or less. The symbol algorithms of deliberative agents are often ideal and decidable which cause the high complication. In dynamic environment, it is more important to meet the requirement than the plan optimization. On other way around, deliberative agents are good at mathematics proof of plans.

Different with the deliberative agents, Reactive agents include no world model. They have not complex symbol reasoning (Wooldridge, 1995). Figure 14.8 give the architecture of reactive agents. The condition-action rules connect the cognition and actions. The rectangle in the figure represents the current inner states of decision process. The ellipse shows the background knowledge which is used in the process.

Algorithm 14.4 Reactive-agent algorithm.

Reactive-agent (percept) returns action
        static: state, describe the current world state
                rules, a group of condition-actions rule
1. state ← Interpret-Input(percept)
2. rule ← Rule-Match(state, rules)
3. action ← Rule-Action[rule]
4. return action

In the program, Interpret-Input function generates the abstract description of current states from the percept. Rule-Match function returns a rule which is matched with the description of current states.

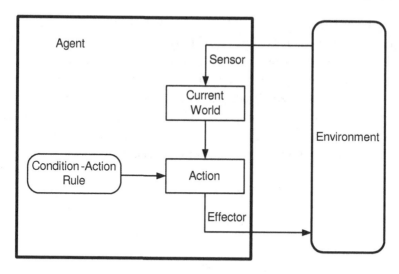

Figure 14.5. the architecture of reactive agent

Reactive agents are related with Professor Brooks in MIT who proposed the behavior-based artificial intelligence (Brooks, 1991). He think intelligent behaviors are result of communication between agents and the environment. Brooks is not only a critic, but also a practice expert. He implemented some of Robots without symbol reasoning. These Robots is a subsumption architecture system. Subsumption architecture is a hierarchical behaviors which can finish the tasks. Every behavior try to control the robot which cause the competition between them. The behaviors in base layer represent the relative original behaviors which have high priority. As a result, the implementation of this kind of architecture is relative simple. Brooks alleged the agent with this kind of architecture can finish the tasks by symbol based artificial intelligence.

14.3.4 *Hybrid Agent*

We have discussed the architecture of reactive agent and deliberative agent. They reflect the characteristics of behavior based artificial intelligence. However, both pure reactive agent and deliberative agent architecture are best way to build agent. People begin to propose the hybrid agent which to connect the classic and non-classic artificial intelligence.

The obvious architecture is that an agent includes two sub system. The one is deliberative agent which has the symbol based world model and can generate the plan and decision. The other is reactive agent which can react to the environment without reasoning. Generally speaking, reactive agent has higher priority than the deliberative agent since this can make the reactive agent to quickly react to the important events happening in the environment.

MAPE(Multi-Agent Processing Environment) is a parallel programming environment with special language(Shi et al, 1994). The agent architecture is hybrid style shown in Figure 14.6. Each agent contains perception, action, reflection, mdel, planning, communication, decision making and so on modules.

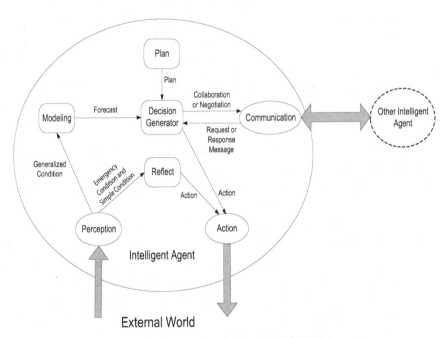

Figure 14.6. Hybrid architecture of MAPE Agent

In 1998 Agent-Oriented Software Development Environment (AOSDE) has been constructed at Intelligence Science Laboratory (Shi et al,1998). Figure 14.7 shows you the agent model which consists of three layers, that is virtual machine layer, logic layer and resource layer.

Virtual machine layer is intended to be a general interface to environment which provides the agent's communicative, sensoric and actoric links to outside world. The communicative part provides the functionality of sending message to and receiving message from other agents using Software Agent Communication Language (SACL) or other language. Agent can sense its environment through sensoric part. Actors will carry out the physical actions the agent may perform.

This layer   provides a set of primitives to the upper layer, and so hide the difference of real machines. Through this layer the upper layers can run successfully without concerning the network, operating system, or hardware configuration. Resource layer is a set of resources, such as knowledge base, database, model base, image base and so on, which will be used by a special agent.

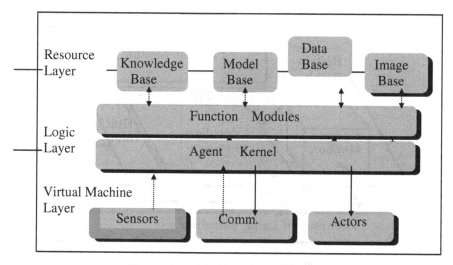

Figure 14.7. The agent model of AOSDE

Virtual machine layer is intended to be a general interface to environment which provides the agent's communicative, sensoric and actoric links to outside world. The communicative part provides the functionality of sending message to and receiving message from other agents using Software Agent Communication Language (SACL) or other language. Agent can sense its environment through sensoric part. Actors will carry out the physical actions the agent may perform. This layer   provides a set of primitives to the upper layer, and so hide the difference of real machines. Through this layer the upper layers can run successfully without concerning the network, operating system, or hardware configuration. Resource layer is a set of resources, such as knowledge base, database, model base, image base and so on, which will be used by a special agent.

Logic layer is core of agent model. We defined agent as an entity that can execute some specific actions and communicate with its environment. Although agents may differ in many aspects to each other, they do have many features in common. For examples, their communication method, execution engine, and representation of mental states, can be the same. The differences are only in the decision making strategies, actions they may perform, and representation of knowledge. By separating these parts, we can get a kernel of agents that is same for all agents. We make some slots on the kernel, so the decision making methods, and domain related function modules can be inserted to the kernel very conveniently.

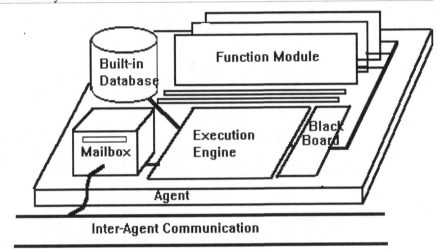

Figure 14.8. Illustration of agent kernel

The agent kernel is like the main frame of a computer, while the function modules are just like some functional cards inserted to the slots. The mailbox is a device used to perform inter-agent communication, and the blackboard is for the communication within the agent, that is, between function modules, or function module and execution engine. The agent kernel also has a built-in database, where it records useful information of itself and other agents.

14.4 Agent Communication Language ACL

FIPA (Foundation for Intelligent Physical Agents) is an IEEE Computer Society standards organization that promotes agent-based technology and the interoperability of its standards with other technologies. FIPA, the standards organization for agents and multi-agent systems was officially accepted by the IEEE as its eleventh standards committee on 8 June 2005.

FIPA was originally formed as a Swiss based organization in 1996 to produce software standards specifications for heterogeneous and interacting agents and agent based systems. Since its foundations, FIPA has played a crucial role in the development of agents standards and has promoted a number of initiatives and events that contributed to the development and uptake of agent technology. Furthermore, many of the ideas originated and developed in FIPA are now coming into sharp focus in new generations of Web/Internet technology and related specifications.

FIPA defines a language and support tool. For example, the protocol is used for communication each other. Software agent technology adopts a high view for this kind of agent. Many of its ideas root in other way of social interaction, e.g. the communication between people. The specification is not to define a communication related basic and mid layer's service, for example network service and transmission service. In fact, the bit series for agent interaction is supposed to be existent.

For software agent, there is single, general definition. However, the characteristic of agent actions is broadly accepted. FIPA defines the communication language to support and facilitate the behaviors. These traits includes but not limited to the following:

• Goal driven activity
• Self decision for act process
• Interaction through the negotiation and delegation
• Mental state model, for example intention belief desire plan and promise
• The adaptation to environment and requirement

14.4.1 *Agent Communication introduction*

The abstract characteristics can be described by agent's mental states:

(1) Belief a group of facts which the agent think them true. If agent accepts a false proposition, it indicates the agent think the proposition is false
(2) Indetermination. It shows the agent can not determine the true or false of the proposition. Worth the whistle, indetermination do not impede proposition to adopt some support proposition format, for example, probability. To be more accurate, indetermination provides a smallest promise mechanism for different representation methods.
(3) Intention indicates a choice, or a group of characteristics that the desire is true or current is not true. To accept this intention, the agent will form a

series of actions. These actions will cause the generation of specific society state.

For a proposition P, believe P, not believe P, the determination of P and indetermination of P is inconsistent.

Besides, agents understand and can execute some actions. In distributed system, an agent can realize its intention through affecting other agent's actions.

Affecting other agents' behaviors is realized by a kind of specific class named communication action behavior. The communication action is taken from one agent to other agents. To execute a communication action, the agent needs the mechanism to send codes action message. So, communication action initiator and acceptor are message's sender and receiver.

The message of the FIPA definition is gathered by a core sets. It means a correspondence action, but this correspondence action tries the general balance definition, express ability and simplicity, and the relation with the understand of agent developer. The correspondence action that the message type defined to be carries out. The one who combines appropriate realm knowledge, correspond by letter the language and can make accept makes sure the news contents of meaning.

About the mental state and from the sender' view to accepter's mental state generating the expectation is expressed by precondition. However, because the sender and receiver are independent, the expectation result can not be guaranteed.

If two agents want to interaction through communication, they need a common point for message transmit. The message transmission service attribute discussion is taken by FIPA committee 1- agent management to take charge of.

If two agents want to interaction through communication, they need a common point for message transmission. The message transmission service attribute discussion is taken by FIPA committee 1- agent management to charge of.

The contribution of agent technology to complex system action and interaction process manifests on the high interaction. The ACL in FIPA is based on this view. For example, the communication action described by the book is used to inform the facts, request complex action and negotiate protocol. The mechanism mentioned can not compete with the basic network protocol for example TCP/IP, OSI seven protocols and can not compare with them. They are also not substitute of CORBA. JAVA RMI and Unix RPC. However, their functions are the same with some of the above examples. At least, the ACL message is transmitted by this mechanism.

After considering the goal of FIPA general open agent system, the function of ACL is clearer. Other mechanism for example CORBA has the same goal. However, some constraints are added to object interface when implementation. Historical experience tell us: the agent and agent system can be implemented by diversified interface mechanism; the existent examples include using the TCP/IP socket, HTTP, SMTP and GSM short message for agents. ACL try to decrease to the smallest to respect the diversification. Especially, the smallest message transmission is defined: the text through the small bit stream. This is the method adopted by KQML. This broad method is used high performance. This system's message is very high. FIPA is defined substitute transmission method, including other transmission expression. They satisfy the high performance of request.

At the same time, ACL is transmitted a group request:

Message service can transmit a bit series to the message to the destination. Through the message service interface, the agent can find whether it can deal with the 8 bit stream.

Under normal circumstances, the message service is a reliable (the message package can reach its destination) and accurate (the forms of received is the same with the sent), and orderly (from the agent A sent to a agent b when the message arrived b And send it from a different order). Unless specified, an agent will be considered to have these three characteristics.

If the messaging services can not guarantee that one or all of the above characteristics, it will represent through the message transmission services interface that in some way out.

The agents will be able to choose whether to pause and wait for the results of news or to continue to other unrelated tasks when wait for reply information. This effectiveness of action is implementation details, but whether or not to support such actions must be clear.

Impart information of the parameters of action, for example, if there is no response time beyond, not in the message that at this level, but it is messaging services as part of the interface.

Message transmission services will find and report errors and return to agents, e.g. the form of an error message, not transmission, could not find agents. Based on the errors circumstances, it will return a value of message send interface, or through an error message related to return to.

A principal will have a name makes messaging services can the news reached the right destination. Messaging services can determine the correct transmission mechanism (TCP / IP, SMTP, HTTP, etc.), allowing the main location of the change.

14.4.2 *FIPA ACL message*

FIPA has defined the types of information, especially information on the format and types of information meaning. Message type is a reference to grammar rules; these types give a meaning for the entire message and information content.

For example, if i notices j "Bonn in Germany." The content of the message from i to j is "Bonn in Germany", and action is to inform this act. "Bonn in Germany" has a certain significance, but also to the two symbols "Bonn" and "Germany" of any reasonable explanation of the circumstances it is true, but the significance of information includes the principal role of i and j. Decision on the nature of these roles i and j is a private matter, but as a result of this meaningful communication imminent, the role of these will be the reasonable expectations are met.

Clearly, the news content in the areas of knowledge will be unrestricted. ACL is not mandatory that the content of the message to be any formal way. The agent itself must be able to correctly interpret any of the known the content of the message. The ontology share issues will be discussed later since this version did not discuss. This was announced by the specification regulating the content independent of the meaning of the rules. A set of standard communication movements and their implications are defined in detail.

It is worth noting that there is a balance between action capacity and norms. A group action type conveying subtle differences and a group of small amounts of more common type of action may effect the same, but this group acts type will be the agent types of action are different and that the implementation of restrictions. This type of action group targets can be expressed as: a) cover all large-scale communications; b) not to allow the burden of agent design is too heavy; c) for the agent action to provide communications services using the choice, reduce redundancy and fuzzy. In short, the objectives of ACL language definition are: integrity, simple and concise.

The basic viewpoints of ACL are that message is expressed as a communication action. In order to elegance and consistency in the dialogue, dealing with communications and actions should be handled as the same; a known communication action is one of actions an agent can complete. Terminology messages in this paper have two different meaning: message can be a synonym for communications action, or refer to computing structure speech to the messaging service.

ACL communication language specification is based on a precise form of semantics. It gives a clear meaning to the communication action. In fact, this formal base also added effective interactive communication. On this foundation, the message parameters below are defined by describing the form of information to be defined. Similarly, the norms agents used, such as information exchange protocol is only a description of the operational semantics.

1. The agent requirement

Here introduces some pre-defined message types and protocols for agents. However, not all messages require implementation of all agents. The following is a list of minimum requirements for the FIPA ACL compatible agent:

(1) If agents receive message that they do not know or could not address the content of the message, they send "not-understood". The agents must receive and address "not-understood" messages from other agents.
(2) The agents can choose to implement all the pre-defined type and source of any protocols or a subset. The implementation of the information provided by the action must be consistent to definition of semantics.
(3) The agent that uses the communication act defined in the article must be in line with the definition.
(4) The agent can use the other definition of communication act this article did not define. It has the responsibility to ensure that the agent understand the meaning of action. But the agent should not define new matching with standard actions.
(5) The agent will be able to correct grammatical form of good message and generate consistent form of transmission. Similarly, the agent must also be able to transfer the good form of grammar translated into a sequence of characters related messages.

2. Message Structure

Figure 14.9 show the main elements of message.

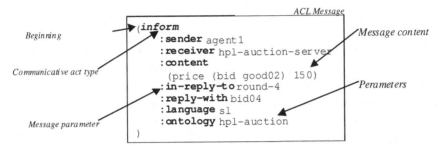

Figure 14.9. Message Structure

In transmission, messages are represented as s-form. The first element of message determines the communication act and main meaning of the message. Followed are message keyword parameters by a colon to guide, no space between the colon keyword parameters. One parameter contains message content using some form of coding. Other parameters are used to help messaging services to correctly transmit information (such as the sender, receiver), or to help the recipient to explain implications of information (such as language, ontology), or help the receiver to reply more cooperatively (such as reply-with, reply-by).

The transmission form is the serial bit stream transferred by messaging service. The receiver agent is responsible for bit stream decoder, decoding elements of messages and correctly handles it.

Communication act of message is corresponding to performative in KQML.

3. Message Parameter

As mentioned earlier, message includes a group of one or more parameters. These parameters in the message can be any chronological order. Only one of the parameters: receiver is indispensible with which such messaging service can correctly transmit message. Obviously, the message is useless if it has not the recipient of the message. However, parameters for effective communication are different under different circumstances.

Pre-defined message parameter:

Message Parameter	Meaning
:sender	message sender
:receiver	message receiver
:content	message content
:reply-with	reply the original message
:in-reply-to	the message act reply
:envelope	message service content
:language	act content decode
:ontology	The meaning of symbols as expressions
:reply-by	the time and date of sending message
:protocol	use protocol
:originator	delegate agent requested information
:reply-to	the agent answer to which agent
:protocol " ("<protocol name>+")")	use protocol nested
:conversation-id " ("<id>+") ")	the communications action sequences the table is sub protocol
:conversation-id	the communications action sequence

4. The message content

The message content represents what the communication act applies for. If the communication act believes the message is sentence, the content is grammatical elements. Generally, content is encoded in one language. The language is defined in the language parameter. The requirements for Language content are that it should have the following characteristics:

A content language must represent proposition, objects and actions. While any language can have more characteristics, here do not need other features. Language content must represent data structure of act: the proposition notice, requesting action, and so on.

Proposition: representing the sentence is true or false. Object: A confirming structure representative of discussion in the area (may be abstract or concrete). Object does not necessarily mean the object-oriented languages such as C + + and Java programming in the professional programming structure. Action: An agent explanation of the grounds will be completed some of the agent structure.

The most common situation is the agent content of a joint consultation language. However, the agent must be overcome content difficulty of the first step to begin a dialogue. So there must be the common reference point in advance that both sides know. To register a directory service and the implementation of other key agent management functions. This specification includes the following language definition:

(1) FIPA specification the management of the agent content of language is the s-expressions that are used to the concept of life-cycle management of the agent proposition, objects and actions. Expressions are defined in the first part of the specification.
(2) The agent needs to execute standard agent management capacity through the agent management content language and message in ontology. Language and ontology is represented in the corresponding parameters fipa-agent-management field.

5. The representation of message content

The contents of a message refer field expression of communications action. It is encoded in the message with content parameters. FIPA specification does not require a standardized content language.

In order to provide a simple language coding services, ACL grammar, including the s-expression forms allow arbitrary length and complexity of the s-expression structure. Therefore, universal s-expression syntax language could be modified to accept for effective ACL language. However, the agents usually need to embed a coded with a symbol of expression, and not for the news itself a simple form of s-expression. ACL syntax provides two mechanisms. They should avoid the need ACL interpreter explained the expression of any language problem:

(1) Using double quotes to include expressions makes it into a string of ACL. With a backslash symbol, it distinguishes difference between double quotes in double quotes. Note contents of expression in the backslash character also need to distinguish. Example:
   (inform :content "owner (agent1 ,\"Ian\")"
       :language Prolog
   ...)
(2) Before the appropriate expression in a long string of code, expressions are processed to ensure that its structure has nothing to do with the vocabulary symbols. Example:
   (inform :content #22 "owner (agent1, "Ian")"
       :language Prolog
   ...)

Therefore, ACL interpreter will generate a language that all embedded in the vocabulary of symbols, a string. Once the message was explained, the content of expression through symbols: language coding schemes based on parameters can be explained.

Table 14.1 shows you the Communicative act directory

Table 14.1 Communicative act directory

Communicative act	Information passing	Requesting information	Negotiation	Action performing	Error handling
accept-proposal			✓		
Agree				✓	
Cancel				✓	
Cfp			✓		
Confirm	✓				
Disconfirm	✓				
Failure					✓
Inform	✓				
Inform-if (macro act)	✓				
Inform-ref (macro act)	✓				
Not-understood					✓
Propagate				✓	
Propose			✓		
Proxy				✓	
Query-if		✓			
Query-ref		✓			
Refuse				✓	
Reject-proposal			✓		
Request				✓	
Request-when				✓	
Request-whenever				✓	
Subscribe		✓			

14.5 Coordination and Cooperation

14.5.1 *Introduction*

In computer sciences, one of the most challenge goals is to build a computer system which can cooperate with each other (Kraus,1997). Computer system becomes more and more complex. To integrate the intelligent agents is more challenge. The cooperation between agents is the key point for cooperative work. Besides, the multi-agent cooperation is an important concept for distinguishing multi-agent system with other distributed computing, object-oriented system and expert system(Doran, 1997). Coordination and cooperation is the core problem of multi-agent research since based the intelligent agent. Coordinating the knowledge, desire, intention, plan and action to implement the cooperation is the main goal of multi-agent system.

Coordination is a kind of character that multi-agents interact to finish a group of activities. Coordination is the adaptation to the environment. Coordination is to change the intention of agents. The reason for multi agent to coordinate is that the agents have intention. Cooperation is special example of multi-agent coordination. Multi-agent research is based on the human being society. In human being society, the communication is indispensable. The communication is between the conflict and non-conflict. At the same time, in open, dynamic multi-agent environment, agents with different goals and resources must coordinate with each other. For example, there will generate dead lock when resource conflict without coordination. In other side, if one agent can not finish the goal independently, it needs the cooperation with other agents.

In multi-agent system, cooperation can not only improve the ability of single agent but the performance of multi-agent system and increase the agent's ability to solve the problem which makes the system more agile. Through the cooperation, multi-agents can solve more real problems and extend application. Although for the single agent, it only cares its own requirement and goal. Its design and implementation can be independent to other agents. However, in the multi-agent system, agents are not existent alone. The agents' actions must meet the society rules although they are complied agents. The relationship between the multi agent systems makes the interaction and cooperation has great conditionality to agent's implementation and design.

In current phase, the research on multi agent cooperation has two species. The one is borrowing the approach from the research on multi entities' behaviors (Kraus, 1997).The other is from the view of intention, goal and plan to research the multi agent cooperation, e.g. FA/C model (Leeser, 1991), the Joint Intention Framework (Levesque, 1990) and share plan (Grosz, 1996).The later method has bigger application scope. Each theory is only adapted to some specific coordination environments. Once the environment changes, for example, the number of agent, type and interaction relationship disagree with theory, the cooperation based on this theory lost its superiority. The later approach focuses on the planning and solution of problems and assumes the process of coordination different. Some agents find the cooperative partners firstly and then generate the plans. Some may generate plan for the problem first and then take cooperative actions. Some may generate the partial global planning; PGP to regulate its actions for the cooperative goals (Lesser, 1991).The later two cooperative methods seems relaxed and lack the necessary disposal mechanism. They require the shared cooperative plan between agents. The first approach has bigger uncertainty and the cooperative plans are influenced by the cooperative team.

In multi-agent system, agent is autonomic. The knowledge, desire, intension and behavior of agents are different. To coordinate the cooperative work is the necessary condition for problem solution and keeping the efficiency. Many researches on organization theory, politics, sociology, social psychology, anthropology, jurisprudence and economics are applied in multi agent system. Multi-agent coordination is the process that multi agent interact with each other for the consistent work way. Coordination can avoid the deadlock and livelock of multi agents. Deadlock means multi-agent can not take the next action; the livelock is the state that multi-agent consecutive work but there is no result. There are many coordination methods:

- Organizational Structuring
- Contracting
- Multi-agent Planning
- Negotiation

From the point of social psychology, multi agent cooperation has following types:

(1) Cooperation: put its own interest at the second place
(2) Selfish: put the cooperation at the second place
(3) Completely selfish: do not consider any cooperation
(4) Completely cooperation: do not consider its own interest
(5) The hybrid of cooperation and selfish

The interaction between agents has two kind of relationship: negative and positive relationship. Negative relationship causes the conflict. The resolution of conflicts constructs coordination. Positive relationship represent the plan of multi-agent has overlap or some agent has the excluded ability. Every agent can get help through the cooperation.

Before mid of 1980s, research on coordination and cooperation in distributed intelligence mainly focus on the help each other to realize the goal without conflicts. This kind of research is used in distributed problem solution. In the mid of 1980s, Rosenschein did a deep research in his doctor thesis on multi agent interaction when agents had the goals conflicts. He applied the game theory to build the static model for rational agent interaction (Rosenschein,1986).It then become the theory foundation for the multi agent coordination and cooperation. After then, many researchers used the game theory to formalize the multi agent cooperation. All of these researches are to build model to coordinate the actions or through the cooperation to realize the goal with the inconsistent goals condition. Some of research considered time preference. Some of research is open environment oriented.

MIT's research adopted the meta-communication to coordinate multi agent computing under the foundation of intensifying FA/C and PGP approaches. MacIntosh applied the heuristic approach to introduce the cooperation to machine theorem proof. Sycara researched the negotiation based the labor and capital problem (Sycara, 1996). The approach applied the heuristic and constraint satisfaction technology to solve the distributed search problems. It adopted the asynchrony trace to resume the inconsistent search policies. The disadvantage is this approach need an arbitrage machine to solve the conflicts. Conry research multi steps negotiation under the multi goal and resources. Hewitt proposed the distributed artificial intelligence approach which challenges Rosenschein's static interaction model. The real world is open and dynamic. The coordination and cooperation is also open and dynamic. Computing bionomics argue that the agents need not have the strong reasoning ability in the open and dynamic environment. They can gradually coordinate the relationship with the environment through the consecutive interaction to make the whole system having the evolution ability. That is similar to ecosystem. In BDI model, it emphasizes the agent intention, desire and intention's rational balance in interaction process.

Shohan proposed the artificial agent society need a law to regulate the agents' actions. Every agent must follow the law and believe that other agents also abide the law. This law can regulate the agents' behaviors on one side. On the other side, it can insure other agents' action style. This guarantees the realization of agents' behaviors. Decker proposed a dynamic coordination algorithm in distributed sensor network (Decker, 1995). The agent can revise the sensor domain according to the unified standard which can automatically reach the coordination. This dynamic reconstruction domain can realize the system load balance in the whole system. Its performance is better than static sub area algorithm. Especially, this approach can decrease the fluctuation of performance which is more adapted to dynamic real condition.

In the multi agent planning, agents can regulate the pertinence of goals of to realize the autonomic behaviors coordination. German Wei□ proposes approach to form action and goal's correlation value for specific problem through the distributed learning. The other autonomic coordination approach is Markov process proposed by Kosoresow. Markov process is a quick probability coordination approach when the agent's goal and preference is consistent. If Markov process is applied as the agent's reasoning mechanism, it can analyze the astringency of multi agent interaction and average astringency time. When the agent's goal and preference is not consistent, it can check the inconsistence at specific time point and solve the conflict by submitting it to higher coordination protocol. In order to describe a group of agent actions, we need a common intention to connect the member's behavior. Jennings adopts common duty concept to emphasize the function of intention as the action controller. It prescribes how the agents to action in the cooperative problem solution. This common duty can provide function instruction for architecture design, provide standard for inspecting problem solution and exception dispose. They realized this common duty in GRATE system.

14.5.2 *Contract net protocol*

In 1980, Smith proposed the contract net protocol in distributed problem solution (Smith, 1980). This protocol was widely applied in the multi agent coordination. The communication among agents has the same message format. The real contract net system provides a contract protocol based the contract net protocol. It prescribes the task assignment and the roles of agents. Figure 14.10 shows the architecture of node in contract net protocol.

The locale database includes the knowledge base related to the node which is used to negotiate the information in current state and problem solution process.

The other three components execute their tasks according to local knowledge base. The communicator is in charge of communicating with other nodes. The node can only connect the network through the communicator. Especially, the communicator should understand the message send and receive.

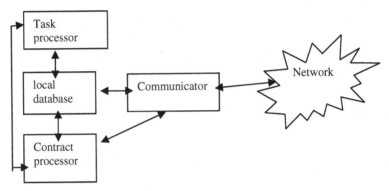

Figure 14.10. architecture of node in contract net protocol

The contract processor judges the tasks, send the application and finish the contract. It can also analyze the reached information. Finally, the contract processor executes the coordination for whole nodes. The task of task processor is dealing with the tasks. It receives the tasks from the contract processor and applies the local database for solution and return the result to contract processor.

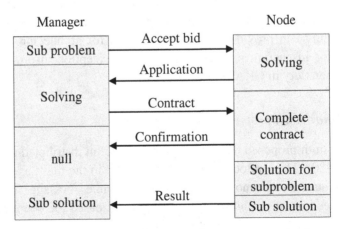

Figure 14.11. the negotiation process in contract net protocol

Contract net protocol partitions the task into sub tasks. It designates a node as the manager node. The manger node is familiar with the sub tasks (Figure 14.11).

The Manager node provides the bids. Those are unsolved sub problems contract. The message format in contract net protocol:

For example:

TO:	All nodes
FROM:	Manager
TYPE:	Task bid announcement
ContractID:	xx-yy-zz
Task Abstraction:	<description of the problem>
Eligibility Specification:	<list of the minimum requirements>
Bid Specification:	<description of the required application information>
Expiration time	<latest possible application time>

The bids are open for all agents. They solve the bids through the contract processor. They apply the local database to solve the current resources and agent knowledge. The contract processor decides which tasks are worth to do. If they want to do, they need inform the manager using the following message format.

TO:	Manager
FROM:	Node X
TYPE:	Application
ContractID:	xx-yy-zz
Node Abstraction:	<description of the node's capabilities>

The manager must select nodes to give the contract to the most proper node in the whole application. It visits the concrete knowledge solution and approach to select the best performance and assign the sub problem to the node. According to the message, the assignment contract is as follows:

TO:	Node X
FROM:	Manager
TYPE:	Cntract
ContractID:	xx-yy-xx
Task Specification:	<description of the subproblem>

The communicator send the confirm message for accepting the contract to the Manager. Once the problem finished, the solved problem is sent to the Manger. The promising node is in charge of the solution of the problem. The contract net protocol is for task allocation. The node can not accept other agents' current state information. If the node can not finish the task because of the resource or ability limitation, it can divide the task to some sub tasks and allocate the sub tasks to other nodes. In this condition, the node is a manager role and provides the bids. Every node can be a manager, bid applicant or contract member.

The traditional contract net protocol is extended to inference the negotiation process. One of these extensions is publicizing the bid file. All the nodes can join the bid process. This requires the communication and abundant resources. Manager must evaluate many lot of bid files and use lot of resources. The big load of manager is caused by the publicizing the bid files. Firstly, manger needs the ability to inform part of the nodes. You can image that if the manager knows the knowledge of every node, it can estimate the candidate nodes for dealing with the sub problems. Secondly, the common bid request can be cancelled. If the unsolved problems can use the previous methods, the manager can contact the previous solution nodes. Once the resource can be used, the manager and the node write down the contract. Besides, the node can self bid. In this condition, many open bids only investigate the new tasks. The bid request is only needed when can not find the proper bids.

The second side of contract net system extension is influencing the real contract assignment. In the traditional protocol, manager needs to wait the node's information after the assignment. Before the coming of the information, manager do not know whether the node accept the contract. The node can not form contract and build the constraint of contract after bid. Some suggestion for the extension is build the contract constraint in an early time. For example, when a node bid, it can provide the possible clause of accepting promise. The acceptance is not the easy acceptant or refuse. It can hold some reference and conditions. The biggest time limit for contract confirmation is extending farther. If there is no confirmation for the contract in the limited time, the manager will stop the contract. The contract process can send the information and avoid manager for waiting long time. The managers can assignment the contract again before the longest time interval.

14.5.3 *Partial global planning*

The most important trait of Partial Global Planning （PGP） approach is the ability of each agent is determined in multi-agent system(Durfee,1991). That is collecting the current states to reach the goals. The agents can optimize their tasks with knowledge. PGP provides a flexible concept and coordinate the distributed problem solution component.

The basic condition to apply the PGP is there are several agents for the whole problem to work. An agent is as part of PGP and considers the other agents' action and relation to reach their own conclusion. This knowledge is seemed as partial global planning. Figure 14.12 gives an example to explain the basic work principle. Two agents work for two sub problems (A or B). Each agent sends information to their cooperative agent. Agent 1 informs agent 2 its current sub problem A. At the same time, agent 2 inform its sub problem B. Every agent can know the cooperative agent's condition according to the information. For example, agent 1 knows its sub problem A2 is determined by agent 2's sub problem B. It can inform agent 2. PGP's process can be divided into four steps:

Communication

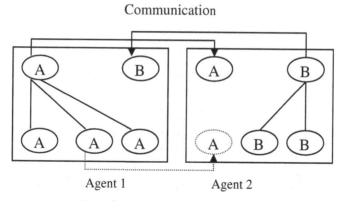

Agent 1   Agent 2

Figure 14.12. Partial Global Planning

（1） Each agent create partial planning
（2） Communication and exchange rules between agents
（3） Create partial planning
（4） Revise and optimize the partial global planning

At the beginning of the coordination, each agent must crate partial planning and solve the assigned tasks. Every partial planning at least has two different layers. The whole structure includes the important steps for solving the problem which reflects the long planning for solving the problem. It includes the detailed information about every sub problem.

Once finish the partial plan, agents exchange the knowledge between each other. Each agent need to have some specific organization knowledge. It can determine other agents' roles and which information is interest. Meta organization determines the layers of agents. Once agents received the plan information from other agents, it must organize the information with the PGP format. It also needs to check if there is new information including the dependence to the inner plan. After then, they form logic components with the sub plans. PGP consists of the following components:

(1) Goal. Goal includes the basic information, the reason for existent, long goal and the comparable priority.
(2) Plan activity diagram. It includes other agents' tasks and their current states, detailed plan, expected result and some experiments.
(3) Solution construction diagram. This diagram includes how the agents to communicate and cooperate among agents. The size and time of the sent plan are very important.
(4) State. State includes reporting PGP's whole important information, e.g. other agents' plan and time mark.

PGP core planer is to analyze the information sent by other agents and determine if they work for a same goal. PGP planer integrates the knowledge through planning the activity diagram. It can forecast the behavior and result of other agents. Plan activity diagram form the foundation of future work. Plan activity compares the partial plan and new knowledge to create revised partial plan. In this time, they create the solution construction diagram. PGP planner generate revised partial plan as the final result. After the concrete plan is sent to the specific agents, planer use the current knowledge about the whole system to optimize and enrich the minutia.

There are many advantages to use the partial planner. The most important advantage is high dynamic system behavior. All plans can adapt the environment solution at any time and the whole system has high ability and effect. PGP can identify the change of old plan. The system must send the revision to the node as soon as possible since revision can inference their work. If any small revision needs to send to the node, the whole system will be high load. In this condition, PGP agree small inconsistent and only inform the big revisions. The system developers must develop the fault tolerance system and designate a threshold to indicate the revision is important. The second advantage is effective and avoiding the redundancy. Two and more agents have the similar problems and register their PGP, and reassign and construction. The work assignment is very effective.

The old PGP model has many constraints especially in the heterogeneous agents' different problems solution. How to deal with dynamic agents change solution policy again? How to finish the concrete tasks in the limited time? How to negotiation between agents? There are some methods to extend the PGP model. For example, using the general partial global planning, GPGP provides new components to meet the need(Decker,1995).

Osawa proposed an approach to construct cooperative plan in open environment based on robots' collaboration (Osawa,1993). In the approach, rational agent used the "multi world model" construct incomplete single agent plan and then according to the effect-based model to balance the cost. This process can be described as following:

(1) Requestor sends RFP to call-board
(2) Leisure agent apply a RFP from call-board
(3) Call-board sends RFP to leisure agents
(4) Leisure agent generate the plan
(5) Leisure agent sends it to requestor
(6) Requestor investigates the possibility of cooperation
(7) Requestor sends cooperation rewards
(8) Applicants form cooperative plan

The utility is computed using the following formula
$$\text{utility}(a,g)=\text{worth}(a,g)-\text{cost}(\text{plan}(a,g))$$
The average utility is the principal of cooperation. Although Osawa solved the cooperative problems in open environment, it is not a good way to add the utility to be divided for average value since the utility is only the order relation of agent to goal. We can not compare the utilities between different kind of agents.

14.5.4 *The Planning based on constraint propagation*

In multi-agent System, The coordination work of agents can be realized by situated action and planning. The Method based situated action emphasized the interaction between agents and environment, and the effects of perception——action looping upon agent actions. The planning decides the sequence of agent actions which will be executed, and the sequence will be decided by some searching way. Compared with situated action, planning can make the agent actions more correct and more rational, therefore planning is applied generally in deliberative agent.

Because of the lack of considering coordination、cooperation among agents in Multi-Agent System, generally planning algorithms, as UCPOP, GraphPlan, SNLP, can not be applied directly. In Multi-Agent environment, the actions among agents are concurrent, which is not controlled by a single agent. A agent can make system more coordinate by communication and protocol to try to change the actions of other agents, and to complete the work which can not be complicated itself by requesting the cooperation of other agents. Classical planning algorithms assure that a agent is the only one who can change the environment, therefore the planning result can not ensure that there is no conflict with other agents, and the solution capability of agent is limited. The distributed planning in dynamic environment hypothesizes that the paroxysm in environment is not foreseeable, and the planning and executing are handled alternately. This method can not ensure the reliability and completeness of planning.

A planning, especially partial order planning can be assured by the constraints in planning steps as follows: Using temporal constrains to designate the time sequence of executing steps; using codesignation constraints to designate the executing steps. Planning solving is a process which adds and refines constraints gradually. The conflict of coordination and cooperation among agents can be accomplished by designating the temporal constraints and codesignation constraints. The resource confliction of agent actions and the services which are offered by one agent for other agents can be presented by causal link, and can be solved by adding temporal constraints to agent actions. At the same time, the cooperation actions among agents, as two agents cooperating to take up a desk, must be described by single action description. The correctness of a agent planning is assured by truth criterion in multi-agent System. We propose a multi-agent concurrent partial order planning algorithm(Shi et al, 2002). Each agent is planning for the target to be accomplished parallel. When an agent decides to add a new action, it accomplishes the coordination of multi-agent System by the constraint propagation with other agents.

1. Planning representation

To describe the planning action, there are too many constraints in the accomplishment of practical scheduler using STRIPS, and it is too difficult to use situated checking computations.

In 1989 Pednault proposed a kind of action described language ADL (Pednault, 1989). We expand ADL to describe the planning actions in Multi-Agent System(Shi et al, 2002). The represent capability of it is more powerful than STRIPS, but less powerful than First-order logic.

The semantic of ADL is based on the mathematics structure which describes the world statements. A action a is represented by a statement couple<s,t> in ADL, and action a produces a statement "t" when it is executed at statement s. The relations between a statement s and a statement description ϕ are represented by a symbol $\models$, denote as s ϕ.

The action template in ADL represents a set of possible actions, which is described by four selectable clauses: Precond, prerequisite; Add and Delete, the set of formulas added or deleted in relation R on statement t; Update, a set of relations which describe the functions how to transform from s to t.

The Multi-agent Planning means that one or more concurrent process of agent search their respective targets in their respective planning space simultaneously. In order to coordinate actions of different agents, we have to add partial constraint between actions which may conflict with each other. The partial constraint distributes in different agents, so there should be problem on judging consistency in the partial constraint.

Algorithm 14.5 Consistency Checking of distributed partial order constraint.

calculate_transition_closure(α, A_i)

Input: planning $\langle S, B, O, L \rangle$, constraint $A_i \prec A_j$,

Output: transitive closure $T_<(A_i)$.

1. send information to all agents to set temporal constraint O in its planning to read only mode;
2. compute of local transitive closure $T_<^\alpha(A_i)$ of action A_i in agent α;
3. $T_<(A_i) = T_<^\alpha(A_i)$;
4. let SET(agentn) be actions of the agent in $T_<(A_i)$.
5. start a new thread for every nonempty SET(agentn)
6. {
7. $T_<(A_i) = T_<(A_i)$ + request (calculate_transition_closure(agentn, SET(agentn)));
8. return.
9. }
10. after all subthreads return, return $T_<(A_i)$;
11. demand of all agents to disable the read-only mode of constraint.

In algorithm 14.6, the cooperation between agents involves two phases: task assignment for every agent and subgoal planning of agent. Task assignment means that global goal of multi-agent system is decomposed and is assigned to one or a group of agents in the system so as to accomplish the target. Here we emphasize the later problem, or say, in the beginning of planning every agent has its own goal, which may be assigned to the agent or be formed to meet its own interest. Furthermore, for multi-agent system and agents in the system we assume:

(1) Any effect of all actions is a deterministic function of system status when the job and action is being preformed.
(2) Agent posses all the knowledge of its own action, actions of other agents and the initial states of the system.
(3) The change of system can only be caused by actions of agents.
(4) No matter whether a agent could make planning successfully, it will keep the promise of actions with other agents in the planning phase so as to enable other agents to accomplish their planning.

Communication between agents is accord with message transmission protocol in communication language ACL. Specification. In particular, the communication should be without delay, and the message sent to the same target will arrive according to the sequence of the message sending.

The architecture of agents is given in Figure 14.13. Due to requirements of negotiation between agents and judging consistency in constraint, in every agent there are three independent threads, which are:

Planning thread: responsible for executing algorithm 14.6 for solving its own planning problems.

Constraints maintenance thread: calculating the local transitive closure of the action on its own actions set S, and judging consistency in the distributed partial order planning

Communication and Negotiation thread: responsible for sending action constraints and accomplishing cooperation and coordination of actions between agents.

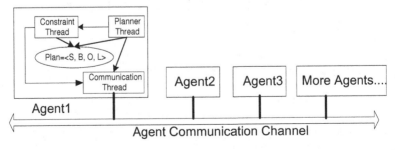

Figure 14.13. The architecture of planning agents

Every agent could solve its own subgoal planning according to algorithm 14.6. In algorithm 14.6, agents construct and maintain planning according to the UCPOP framework; when need for requesting services from and cooperating with other agents to judge consistency in the distributed partial order constraint, agents communicate with each other.

Algorithm 14.6 Planning algorithm.

planning $\left(\langle S, B, O, L\rangle, G, \Lambda\right)$

1. Termination conditions: if G is empty, return $\langle S, B, O, L\rangle$;

2. Targets resolution: get a target $\langle Q, A_c\rangle$ from G,

   ① If Q is a conjunction of Q_i, add every $\langle Q_i, A_c\rangle$ into G, and go to step 2;

   ② If Q is a disjunction of Q_i, randomly choose a Q_k, and add it into G, and go to step 2;

   ③ If Q is a character and $A_p \xrightarrow{\neg Q} A_c$ exists in L, return failure.

3. Select operator: randomly choose an action existing in S, or from Λ choose a new action A_p, which has effection e and an universal clause p, where $p \in T(\theta_\ell)$ and $MGU(Q, p) \neq \perp$ (Q and p have a general resolution); if there is not any action satisfying conditions in Λ and there is a agent β whose action $A_{\beta j}$ satisfies conditions, send a request to β; if there are joint-actions satisfying conditions, send requests to all executors of joint-actions; the agent which receives a request executes the step 7 and 8 in its planning P_b, if it succeeds, β returns Comm($A_{\beta j}$) and add joint-actions or Comm($A_{\beta j}$) into S, and go to 2; otherwise, β returns failure.

4. Enabling new action: Let $S' = S$, $G' = G$. If $A_p \notin S$, add A_p into A', and add $\langle preconds(A_p) \backslash MGU(Q, R, B), A_p\rangle$ into G', and add non-cd-constraints(A_p) into B'.

5. Protection of Causal Link: for every causal link $l = A_i \xrightarrow{p} A_j$ and every action A_t which may be a threat to l, choose one from following three solutions (if do not choose any solution, return failure)

   ① Upgrade: for O judge consistency in the distributed partial order constraint, if constraint is consistent, $O' = O' \cup \{A_j < A_t\}$

   ② Degrade: for O judge consistency in the distributed partial order constraint, if constraint is consistent, $O' = O' \cup \{A_t < A_j\}$

③ Facing: if l which A_t becomes a threat to is a conditional conclusion, let condition be S and conclusion be R, and add $\langle \neg S \setminus MGU(P,R), A_t \rangle$ into G'.

6. Recursive call: if **B** is inconsistent, return failure; otherwise, call $\left(\langle S', B', O', L' \rangle, G, \Lambda \right)$.

Algorithm 14.6 is sound but not complete. Soundness means that for a planning problem if an agent found a planning using a planning algorithm, the planning is the solution for the problem. Algorithm 14.6 is not complete, because there is temporal and equivalent constraint relationship when an agent and other agents search in planning space, which means that planning space of agents has been limited. In particular, in order to does not cause parallel planning to be too complex and prolix, we do not provide a mechanism that when an agent can not find a solution after backtracking process the agent could ask other agents to adopt backtracking process or to relax constraints, which will expand its current solution space and the agent could continue searching.

14.5.5 *Ecological based cooperation*

In the end of 1980s, a new subject—the ecology of computation is presented. It is a subject to research the behavior and resource application. It spurns the traditional closed, static algorithm for solving the problem. It thinks the world is an open, evolved, concurrent ecosystem which solves the problem with the collaboration. Its development is related with the research of open information system.

The distributed system is similar to the society and biologic organization. This kind of open system is different with the current computer system. It computes the tasks asynchronously. Its nodes can generate the process in other machines. These nodes can make decision according to incomplete and late knowledge. There is no center control node. It solves the problem according to the communication and cooperation of many nodes. These characteristics consist of a concurrent combination. Its communication, policy and competition are similar to ecosystem. Hewitt proposed open information system concept (Hewitt, 1991). He argued that the incomplete knowledge, asynchronous computing and inconsistent data are inevitable in open computing system. Human society, especially the problems in sciences can be solved by cooperation.

The computing bionomics considers the computing system as ecosystem. It introduces make biologic mechanism, e.g. mutation in computing system. This revision causes the change of life gene which forms the diversity to improve the ability to adapt the environment. This mutation policy becomes a method to improve its own ability in artificial intelligence system. Miller and Drexler discussed a series of evolution model, for example the ecosystem, commerce market and pointed the difference with the ecosystem. They think a direct computing market is the most ideal system model.

Because of the incomplete knowledge and late information is the inner characteristic of computing ecosystem. The dynamic activities research under these constraints is important. Huberman and Hogg proposed and analyzed the process of dynamic games(Huberman et al,1987). They pointed that if there are many choices when the processes to finish the tasks, dynamic graduate process may become non-linear fluctuation and chaos. This indicates the stable policy for computing biologic system is not existent. They also discussed possible common rules and the importance of cooperation and compared with the biologic ecosystem and human organization. Similar to dynamic theory, Rosenschein and Geneserth proposed static policy theory to solve the conflicts in nodes with different goals.

Famous ecosystem models include biologic ecosystem model, species evolution model, economic model, sciences group's society model. Large ecosystem's intelligence surpasses any single intelligence.

1. Biologic ecosystem model

It is the most famous ecosystem which has typical evolution characteristic and hierarchical traits. This trait reflects in food chain. For complex biologic ecosystem, all the species consist of closely network- food chain. This system's main roles are catchers and preys. The life is dependant on life. The large ecosystem consists of small ecosystem.

2. Species evolution model

Species evolution is depending on gene. From the plant heredity to model genetics, researchers indicate the combination of gene's importance in the species evolution. The gene pool consists of a group of gene from a species. The biologic organization is the carrier of gene. If environment change, the selection mechanism will change. This change inevitably causes the change of gene pool. The change of specific species is named gene stream. A species is always experience isolation, gene flow and change circle.   At the beginning, a geographically isolated group develops lonely and the gene is quickly flow in the inner structure. Because of the open, the system can communicate and compete to realize the survival of the fittest.

3. Economics model

Economic system is similar to biologic ecosystem. In commerce market and ideal market, evolution determines economic entities' decision. The choices mechanism is market encouragement mechanism. The evolution is rapid. The relationship between the enterprise and consumer and the inter-enterprise is dependant with each other. Decision maker can adopt the effective approaches in order to purse the long interest, especially sustain losses in business in short time.

14.5.6 Game theory based negotiation

In multi-agent system, negotiation has many understanding. A point of view is that negotiation is about allocation of resource and sub problem. Another view thinks the negotiation is peer to peer direct negotiation. The goal of negotiation is to build cooperation among a group of agents. Agents have their owe goal. Negotiation protocol provides the possible basic rules and the negotiation process and the foundation of communication. The policy of negotiation is decided by the concrete agents. Although the agent developers provide different extent ability of negotiation, it must guarantee the match between protocol and policy. That is to say the policy can run in the protocol.

From single agent, the goal of negotiation is improve their states and support other agents without affecting themselves. The agents must make a tradeoff to maintain the ability of whole system. From this view, the negotiation communication can be divided into some types:

(1) Symmetry cooperation. The result of negotiation is better that the past result and the inference by other agents is positive.
(2) Symmetry tradeoff. Agents would like to achieve their goals. Negotiation means the tradeoff of participants which will decrease the effects. However, the negotiation can not ignore the existence of other agents. They can only take the policy of tradeoff and make the participants to accept the result.
(3) Asymmetry cooperation/tradeoff. The effect to one agent cooperation is positive, but to the other agent, the tradeoff is required.
(4) Conflict. Because of the conflicts of goals of multi-agents, they can not reach an acceptable result. The negotiation must stop before the result.

14.5.7 *Intention based negotiation*

Grosz applied the belief, desire and intention theory to the agent negotiation (Grosz et al,1996). This method does not use the sub plan, while use the intention for negotiation to decrease the communication. BDI theory thinks that the agents' actions were not the desire and plan but the result of combination of belief and desire. The sub plan to realize the intension is generated by this intension. One intension is correspondence with some sub plans. Agents' communication need not to exchange the sub plans and only exchange the intentions. However, Grosz's approach assumes the agents are completely cooperative.

Zlotkin's work greatly improves the static negotiation theory of two agents. However, to open multi-agent system, his approach is not applicable. Current BDI team approaches lack tools for quantitative performance analysis under uncertainty. Distributed partially observable Markov decision problems (POMDPs) are well suited for such analysis, but the complexity of finding optimal policies in such models is highly intractable. Nair and Tambe have proposed a hybrid BDI-POMDP approach, where BDI team plans are exploited to improve POMDP tractability and POMDP analysis improves BDI team plan performance (Nair et al,2005).

14.5.8 *Team-oriented collaboration*

Coordination between large teams of highly heterogeneous entities will change the way complex goals are pursued in real world environments. Scerri and his colleagues proposed a Machinetta approach which combines Team Oriented Programming and proxy architecture to overcome the limitations of effective coordination between very large teams of highly heterogeneous agents (Scerri, 2003). The main advantages to Machinetta approach display one or a combination of the characteristics: large scale, dynamic environment, and integration of humans. By connecting the Machinetta proxies with the graphical development tool for constructing team plans, the Team Oriented Programming programmer gains a good idea of what is going on in the plan and how to make effective changes in it.

Token-based coordination is a process by which agents attempt to maximize the overall team reward by moving tokens around the team. If an agent were to know the exact state of the team, it could use an Markov Decision Process (MDP) to determine the expected utility maximizing way to move tokens. Unfortunately, it is infeasible for an agent to know the complete state, however, it is illustrative to look at how tokens would be passed if it were feasible. Then, by dividing the monolithic joint activity into a set of actions that can be taken by individual agents, we can decentralize the token routing process where distributed agents, in parallel, make independent decisions of where to pass the tokens they currently hold. Thus, we effectively break a large coordination problem into many small ones.

Algorithm 14.7 Token pass local model which makes decision process for agent α to pass incoming tokens (Xu et al,2005).

Method:
(1) while true do
(2) $Tokens(\alpha) \leftarrow getT\,oken(sender)$;
(3)   for all $\Delta \in Tokens(\in)$ do
(4)   if $Acceptable(\Delta, \alpha)$ then
(5)   if $\Delta.type == Res$ then
(6) $Increase(\Delta,threshold)$;
(7)   end if
(8)   else
(9) $Append(self, \Delta.path)$;
(10)   for all $\Delta_i \in H_\alpha$ do
(11) $Update(P_\alpha[\Delta],\Delta_i)$;
(12)   end for
(13)   if $(\Delta.type == Res)\|(\Delta.type == Role)$ then
(14) $Decrease(\Delta.threshold)$;
(15)   end if
(16) $acquaintance \leftarrow Choose(P_\alpha[\Delta])$
(17) $Send(acquaintance,\Delta)$;
(18) $AddtoHistory(\Delta)$;
(19)   end if
(20)   end for
(21) end while

In above model $P\alpha$ is the decision matrix agent α uses to decide where to move tokens. Initially, agents do not know where to send tokens, but as tokens are received, a model can be developed and better routing decisions made. That is, the model, $P\alpha$ is based on the accumulated information provided by the receipt of previous tokens. Algorithm 14.8 shows the reasoning of agent α when it receives incoming tokens from its acquaintances via function getToken(sender) (line 2). For each incoming token Δ, function Acceptable(α, Δ) determines whether the token will be kept by α (line 4). When a resource is kept, its threshold is raised (line 6). If α decides to pass Δ, it will add itself to the path of Δ (Line 9) and Update($P\alpha[\Delta],\Delta_i$) will update how to send Δ according to each previously received token Δ_i in α's history (line 11). If Δ is a resource or role token, its threshold will be decreased (line 14). Then α will choose to the best acquaintance to pass the token to according to $P\alpha[\Delta]$ (line 16) and record Δ in its history, $H\alpha$ (line 18).

14.6 Mobile Agent

Along with the development of Internet application, especially the information retrieval, distributed computing and electronic commerce, the people hope to acquire the best service within the scope of the whole Internet, to build the network as a whole, to make the software agent moved freely in the whole network. The concept of mobile agent conceives gradually at this time.

At the beginning of 1990's, the General Magic proposed mobile agent concept for the first time in industry when released its business system Telescript. Mobile agent was defined as a kind of agent which can independently move from one host to another in the heterogeneous network environment. Mobile agent is a special software agent who can communicate with other agents and resources. Besides the basic characteristic: autonomy, active and reasoning, it has the mobility function. It can delegate the users to finish the task through moving from one host to another host. The mobility can reduce the network load, increase the efficiency of communication. It can adapt the dynamic environment and has good security and fault tolerance ability.

Mobile agent can be seen as a combination of agent technology and distributed computing technology. It is not similar with the traditional computing model. Different with Remote Procedure Call (RPC), mobile agent can move from one node to another. This mobility can be selected according to the requirement. Mobile agent is also different with the common process move because common process can not allow the process to select when and where to move. However, mobile agent can decide where and when to move at any time. Mobile agent is also different with the Applet in Java Language. Applet can only move from server to client machine. Mobile agent can move both from server and client.

Although the architecture of mobile agent is different, almost all mobile agent systems include Mobile Agent (MA) and Mobile Agent Environment (MAE) which build the correct and security environment for mobile agents to run. It also provides basic services (including create, transmit and execute),constraint mechanism, fault tolerance policy, security control and communication mechanism. MA's mobility and problem solution ability is decided by the MAE's services. Generally speaking, MAE includes the following services:

(1) Transaction service: realizing the creation, mobility, persistence and environment allocation for mobile agents.
(2) Event service: including agent transfer and communication protocol, realizing events move in mobile agents.
(3) Directory service: providing locating and routing services
(4) Security service: providing secure run-environment
(5) Application service: providing service interface for special task

In general, a MAE can only locate at one machine. However, a MAE can run in multi machines if the hosts are connected by fast network. MAE uses agent transfer protocol to realize the mobility and allocate the run-time environment and service interface. MA runs in MAE which communicates with each other by Agent Communication Language (ACL) and access the services provided by MAE.

In architecture of mobile agent, MA can be divided into two types: user agent(UA) and server agent(SA).UA can move from a MAE to anther MAE. It runs in MAE and communicates with other MA through ACL. It can access the services provided by MAE. SA can not move whose main function is to provide services for local and visit MA. A MAE holds several SAs which provide different services. Because SA can not move and can only be controlled by local MAE administrator, it ensures that SA can not be vicious. A can not directly access the system resource. It can only through the SA's interfaces to access the restrictive resources which can avoid the hostile agents to attack the hosts. This is the common security policy in mobile agent system.

Mobile agent is a novel concept which has not unified definition. However, almost all mobile agent has the following characteristics:

(1) Unique Identification Mobile agents must hole the specifically identification which can delegate the willing of users.
(2) Autonomic mobility Mobile agents can automatically move from one node to anther. This is the basic characteristics of mobile agent which distinguishes it with other kinds of agents.

(3) Continuous run Mobile agents must keep the ability to run consecutively at different addresses. Specifically, mobile agents can hang the state when they begin to move another node and run again at the hang state when they reach the destination.

Currently, mobile agents have already come into practical applications from the theory research. Researchers have built a series of mature development platforms and run environments. Theoretically speaking, mobile agents can be coded by any languages (such as C/ C++, Java, Perl, Tcl and Python etc.) and can run on any machines. However, since mobile agents need to support different software and hardware environment, it is better to choose an expositive, platform-independent language to develop mobile agents. Java is an ideal development language for mobile agent currently, since Java binary code after compiling can run on any system that has the Java Virtual Machine (JVM), having good cross-platform characteristic.

Although mobile agent has been a hot topic in academic research for many years, the first really applicable mobile agent system was created until 1996. Currently, the mobile system can be divided into three types: traditional expositive language based, Java language based and CORBA platform based. We introduce several typical mobile agent systems which represent the direction and trend of mobile agents.

1. General Magic's Odysses

As the early exploration, the Telescript developed by General Magic Company has been widely adopted in last years. Telescript is a kind of object-oriented expositive language. The mobile agents coded by Telescript have two formats in communications. Firstly, one agent can call other agents' methods if they are in the same place. Secondly, mobile agents can build the connection to transfer the computable mobile objects if they are in different places. Telescript is a relative successful mobile agent system since its emergence. It was secure and robust. The performance is also excellent. Telescript's three basic concepts (agent, place and go) gave a clear description for mobile agents: agent go place.

As the development of Java language and cross-platform technology, Telescript lost its superiority and attraction. Under this condition, General Magic began to change its policy. They developed a Java-based system called Odyssey which can support Java RMI, Microsoft DCOM and CORBA IIOP. Odyssey inherited many characteristics of Telescript and become a widely used mobile agent development platform.

2. IBM's Aglet

Aglet is one of the earliest mobile agent systems based on Java. Its name is the combination of agent and applet. It can be seen as an applet object which has agent characteristics. Aglet was produced as a thread on one machine. It can stop running work at any time and transfer the unfinished work to another machine. From concept, an aglet is a mobile object. It supports autonomic running and can be moved from a machine to another machine which has the aglet running environment.

Aglet build a simply but all-sided mobile agent programming framework. It provides dynamic and effective communication mechanism for mobile agent communication. It also hold a detailed and easy-to-use security mechanism. These simplified the mobile agent development.

3. Recursion's Voyager

Voyager can be seen as an improved object request broker. Comparing with other mobile agent systems, Voyager has deeper relation with Java language. It can be used to develop mobile agent systems and create distributed systems. Voyager is a pure Java distributed computing platform which can quickly generate high performance distributed application programs. It is a good mobile agent development platform which represents the current technology level.

14.7 Multi-Agent Environment MAGE

Multi-Agent Environment (MAGE) is an agent-oriented software development, integration and run environment developed by Intelligence Science Laboratory, Institute of Computing Technology, Chinese Academy of Sciences(Shi et al,2003). It provides users a software deployment and system integration mode which includes requirement analysis, system design and agent generation. It also provides multi software reuse mode which is beneficial for agent software. It can also wrapper other legacy systems to quickly integrate as a new software.

14.7.1 *The architecture of MAGE*

MAGE System framework includes requirement analysis and modeling toolkit AUMP, visual agent studio and multi agent run-time environment MAGE. The structure of MAGE is as figure 14.14. AUMP support agent-oriented analysis and design. Vastudio can realize the model to programs, including different agent behaviors. Finally, agents can run in the agent supporting environment.

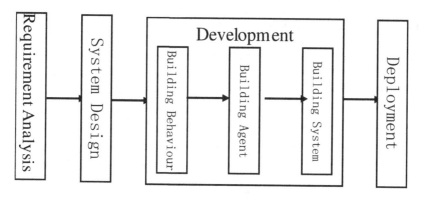

Figure 14.14. MAGE Architecture

14.7.2 *Agent Unified Modeling Language*

Agent Unified Modeling Language (AUML) is an agent-oriented modeling language. Its main function is help the software designers and programmers to model the software, describe the software development process from the beginning to the end. AUML unify the agent-oriented and object-oriented methods.

AUMP is multi-window application software which runs on the Windows platform. It provides the Graphic User Interface for users to edit and revise the models.

14.7.3 *Visual agent development tool*

On the agent-oriented distributed platform, we combine the common object request broker agent and internet to build the common agent request broker architecture (CARBA) (Cao et al, 1998). As figure 14.15, CABAR consists of agent request broker (ARB),agent application facilities (AppFacilities),agent domain pattern(appPattern) and agent services.

CARBA is a distributed management mechanism which uses the ARB as its core component. It defines the way distributed agents send request and receive the response. AppFacilities provides the agent components from horizontal and vertical directions. AppPattern build the templates according to the domain requirement, e.g. agent life circle, agent library, name etc. CARBA can realize the following objectives:

(1) Decompose the system according to the function in heterogeneous and distributed environment
(2) Integrate the components according to requirement

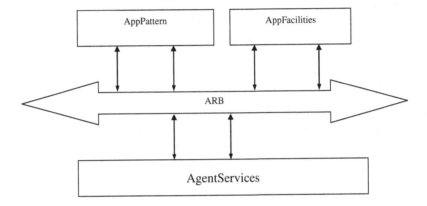

Figure 14.15. CARBA Architecture

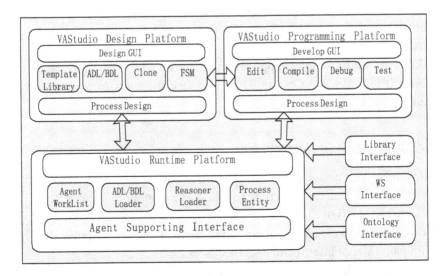

Figure 14.16. VAStudio structure

Based the above method, we developed a visual development toolkit named VAStudio (Visual Agent Studio).The objective for designing this toolkit is providing a user-friendly GUI to support the agent-oriented development. It is not just a programming editor but a design and coding environment. It can use GUI to step-by-step generate the agents. It also provides a series basic tool, e.g. components management tool, behavior library, agent library, etc.(Figure 14.16).

14.7.4 *MAGE running platform*

MAGE platform follows the rule of FIPA. It is a realization of FIPA standard. It provides agent generation, localization, registration, communication services, and mobility and exit services (Figure 14.17).

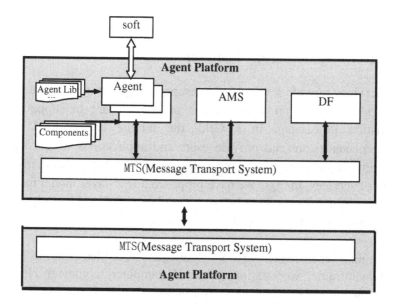

Figure 14.17 MAGE running platform

(1) Agent Management System (AMS): It is an indispensable component in MAGE platform. AMS controls the agent access and use in the platform. One platform has only one AMS which records the agent directory, including agent name and address. AMS also provides white-page services for other agents. Every agent must register on AMS to get an effective Agent ID.

(2) Directory Facilitator (DF): it also indispensable in the platform. DF provides yellow-page service for other agents. Agents can register their services on DF and can search services provided by other agents. One platform can exist several DF.

(3) Message Transport Service (MTS): it provides communication service for agent from different platform.

(4) Agent: it is a basic component in the platform. It is an unified and whole component to provide one or more services. It can access outer resources, user interface and communication infrastructure. Every agent has unique AID.

(5) Agent platform(AP)： it provides physic infrastructure for agents which includes machine, operation system, agent support software, agent management components(DF,AMS,MTS) and agents.

(6) Software: it includes all non-agent software. Agent can access them, e.g. adding new service, acquiring new service protocol and new security protocol/ algorithm, new negotiation protocol and access supporting toolkits.

(7) Agent librar

14.8 Agent Grid Intelligence Platform

Web Services provide a means of interoperability that was essential to achieve large-scale computation with a focus on middleware to support large scale information processing. In a Grid, the middleware is used to hide the heterogeneous nature and provide users and applications with a homogeneous and seamless environment by providing a set of standardized interfaces to a variety of services. In 2002 we have proposed a four-layer model for agent-based grid computing to combine agent computing with grid computing through middleware concept shown in Figure 14.18 (Shi et al., 2002):

(1) Common resources: consist of various resources distributed in Internet, such as mainframe, workstation, personal computer, computer cluster, storage equipment, databases or datasets, or others, which run on Unix and other operating systems.

(2) MAGE environment: it is the kernel of Grid computing which is responsible to resources location and allocation, authentication, unified information access, communication, task assignment, agent developing tools and others.

(3) Developing toolkit: provide developing toolskitx, containing distributed computing, data mining applications, collaborative applications, image and video processing, global search engine, semantic Web services, negotiation support, to let users effectively use middelware resources.

(4) Application service: organize certain agents automatically for specific purpose application, such as power supply, oil supply e-business, distance education, e-government.

In terms of the model of AGEGC we have developed Agent Grid Intelligence Platfrom(AGrIP) which is a powerful developing environment for complex and large distributed intelleigent systems. AGrIP has been applied to develop many group intelligent decision support systems, such as GEIS (Agent Grid-Based City Emergency Interactive Response System), RSMAS (Residential Power Demand Simulatior Based on MAS) and so on.

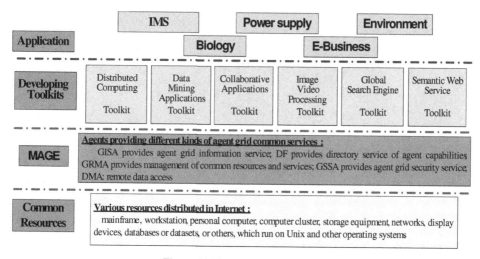

Figure 14.18. Model of AGEGC

Exercises

1. Describe briefly the solution process of distributed problem solving.
2. Explain briefly the concept of agent and its basic structures.
3. What is deliberative agent? What is the reactive agent? Compare the difference between them.
4. What is the BDI model? Please explain the algorithm.
5. Describe the communication between the agents. Compare the KQML and FIPA' s ACL.
6. What is the principle of the contract net protocol in distributed problem solving?
7. How to realize the collaborative work of multi-agent systems?
8. Explain the concept and characteristic of mobile agent and the difference between mobile agent technology and traditional network computing.
9. Investigate several typical mobile agent systems.

10. What components constitute the multi-agent environment MAGE? Please describe the main functions of each component.
11. Explain which aspect for AUML to extend the functions of UML?
12. Draw the architecture of visual agent development environment VAStudio and explain why it can realize the software reuse.

Chapter 15

Artificial Life

Artificial life is the study of simulation or model systems created using computers and precision mechanisms, which exhibit the behavior characteristics of natural living systems. The behavior characteristics of natural living systems are represented not only by the basic properties including self-organizing, self-repairing, and self-replicating, but also by the principles of property formation including chaos dynamics, environment adaptation, and evolution.

15.1 Introduction

In the real world, there exist all kinds of complicated systems, such as human body system, nervous system, immune system, psychological system, cognitive system, etc. It is generally considered that the origins of complexity are non-linearity, instability, and uncertainty.

The "prevalence" in daily life is the following phenomenon: Each member of a group wears a dress in accord with his (or her) individuality. But one day when a dress type shows its superiority, it will influence the dressing inclination of the whole group. And then the inclination of the whole group changes the state of each member, which conversely has an influence on the whole group. In this way, the microscopic behavior determines the macroscopic order, and the macroscopic order also influences the microscopic behavior. Similarly, the information processing in the nervous system can also be regarded as the functioning process between the macrocosm and the microcosm. The nerve cell and the neural network take role of the member and the society respectively. When receiving new information from the outside, the brain generates new information structure by itself, through absorbing the new information as well as utilizing existing information. Every nerve cell influences the neural network, and the neural network conversely controls the behavior of each nerve cell. The way of understanding new knowledge is like this. From the viewpoint that the course of information processing is dynamically changing, "prevalence" and the nervous system are in essence the same. The research on complexity can not adopt the existing element-based reduction method, in which each thing is divided into its constituent elements for analyzing and researching. The complex thing can only be understood as a whole.

C. G. Langton in the non-linear research group of Santa Fe Institute in USA, proposes the concept of artificial life in 1987(Langton, 1989). The position of artificial life as an independent research field has been admitted by the international academia. The international journal Artificial Life, which started publication in 1994 with the MIT Press as its publisher, is the authoritative publication in this field. The following are the brief comments of the international academic workshops and conferences held by the academia of artificial life:

(1) "Artificial Life: The Interdisciplinary Workshop on the Synthesis and Simulation of Living Systems". This workshop was held in Los Alamos, New Mexico, USA in September 1987. There are totally 24 papers in the proceedings of this workshop, the content of which mainly includes: theories of artificial life research, simulation of life phenomena, cellular automata (CA), genetic algorithm, and evolution simulation. Langton published the paper entitled "Artificial Life", in which he proposed the concept of artificial life and discussed the meaning of its existence as an emerging research field or discipline. Langton is recognized as the founder of artificial life research. This workshop symbolizes the birth of the artificial life research field.

(2) "Artificial Life II: The 2nd Interdisciplinary Workshop on the Synthesis and Simulation of Living Systems". This workshop was held in Santa Fe, New Mexico, USA in February 1990. There are totally 31 papers in the paper collection of this workshop, the content of which can be divided into 8 parts including the overview, self-organization, evolution dynamics, development, learning and evolution, computing, philosophy and emergence, and the future. In this collection, Langton's "Life at the Edge of Chaos", and John Koza's "Genetic Evolution and Co-evolution of Computer Programs" are classic papers.

(3) "Artificial Life III: The 3rd Interdisciplinary Workshop on the Synthesis and Simulation of Living Systems". This workshop was held in Santa Fe, New

Mexico, USA in June 1992. The paper collection of this workshop includes 26 papers. Besides the classic content of artificial life, such as genetic algorithm, evolution simulation, emergence behavior, the overview of adaptive degree, group dynamics, and chaos mechanism, the application problem of robot planning is also discussed. Koza's "Artificial Life: Spontaneous Emergence of Self-replicating and Evolutionary Self-improving Computer Programs" can be rated as the masterpiece, which discusses the key emergence mechanism of artificial life research in respect of genetic algorithm programming.

(4) "Artificial Life IV: The 4th International Workshop on the Synthesis and Simulation of Living Systems". This workshop was held at MIT, USA in July 1994. There are 56 papers in the paper collection of this workshop, the content of which can be divided into 3 parts including invited talks, regular papers, and short papers. Its content covers a wide range of directions, such as co-evolution, genetic operators, the synthesis of evolution and other methods (e.g., the neural network), AL algorithm, research on bifurcation and the edge of chaos, AL modeling, learning capabilities, evolution dynamics, cellular automata, research on non-balance theory of DNA, the application of artificial life in character recognition and robotics, etc.

(5) "Artificial Life V: The 5th International Workshop on the Synthesis and Simulation of Living Systems". This workshop was held in Nara, Japan on May 16-18, 1996, in which more than 500 scholars from around the world participated. This is the first time that the international workshop on artificial life is held in Asia. The newly proposed concept of artificial life drew the attention of Japanese scholars, and many of them participated in the workshop. This workshop symbolizes that Japan has become the center of artificial life research in Asian.

(6) "Artificial Life VI: The 6th International Conference on Artificial Life". This conference with the theme "Life and Computation: The Boundaries are Changing", was held at UCLA, USA on June 26-29, 1998. About 100 submitted papers were received on this conference. Among these papers, 39 papers were accepted as regular papers and introduced in the paper collection of this conference. Besides, 9 papers were considered to be new work with high quality in artificial life area. Some important papers were related to the molecular and cell biology in computation. On this conference, lots of new ideas were proposed, mainly about development process, the mechanism of molecular differentiation, and the creation of immune reaction models. These

papers showed the exciting new directions in artificial life research.

(7) "Artificial Life VII: The 7th International Conference on Artificial Life". This conference, the theme of which is "Looking Backward, Looking Forward", was held at Reed College, Portland, USA on August 1-6, 2000. The papers of this conference are divided into 7 broad topic areas: ① the origin of life, self-organization, and self-replication, including artificial chemical evolution, autocatalytic systems, virtual metabolism, etc; ② development and differentiation, including artificial and natural morphogenesis, multi-cellular differentiation and biological evolution, gene-regulation networks, etc; ③ evolutionary and adaptive dynamics, including the ecology of artificial evolution, evolvability and its influence on organisms, evolution computing, etc; ④ robots and autonomous agents, including evolutionary robots, autonomous and adaptive robots, software agents, etc; ⑤ communication, cooperation and collective behavior, including collective behavior of emergence, evolution of linguistic, social, economic, and technical systems, etc; ⑥ methodological and technological applications, including the applications in industry, commerce, finance, economy, medicine, and education (e.g., evolvable hardware, self-repairing hardware, molecular computing, computer games, etc); ⑦ the basic problems of epistemology and methodology in this area, including ontology, epistemology, ethics, social influence, etc.

(8) "Artificial Life VIII: The 8th International Conference on Artificial Life". This conference was held at the University of New South Wales, Sydney, Australia on December 9-13, 2002. The problems discussed on this conference include: the origin of life, development and differentiation, evolutionary and adaptive dynamics, robots and intelligent agents, communication, cooperation and collective behavior, technological application of artificial life, the tools and methodology of simulation and synthesis, etc.

The 9th International Conference on Artificial Life was held in Boston, USA on September 12-15, 2004. International Society of Artificial Life (ISAL) was established in 2001 (http://www.alife.org/). The 8th European Conference on Artificial Life was held at the University of Kent, UK in September, 2005. Please refer to the Website: http://www.ecal2005.org/.

Why do we research on artificial life? What does the research in this area support? We can find its applications in ecological environment engineering, and a wide range of other fields provided for us by the nature.

The research on artificial life can make us understand the emerging characteristics better. The set of low-grade elements can often bring out characteristics through our interaction. Each characteristic is not only the overlay of elements, but also a newly emerging characteristic on the whole. Such a phenomenon can be seen in all the domains of the nature, but it is most obvious in life system. The life itself has emerging characteristics indeed. If the whole is divided into constituent elements, all of the emerging characteristics produced by interaction will disappear. The research approaches in reduction science can be regarded as the most serious ones today, the majority of which are analytical approaches. Reduction science has succeeded in all kinds of fields. But there are still many characteristics of the natural which are neglected. It is not because these characteristics are meaningless or unimportant, but on the contrary, there is a shortage of appropriate tools and effective methods in researching on these characteristics. The research in artificial life field must be comprehensive, in which all factors should be considered for life creation.

There are many methods of making new characteristics emerge, although the evolution of natural selection has increased the complexity, and made it difficult to get and employ these methods. The common tools and methods in artificial life research are probably useful for other fields. The fact that a lot of remarkable physicists study on emerging characteristics has drawn the attention of artificial life field. For studying the emerging characteristics of the nature, artificial life has provided a kind of non-traditional approach.

Artificial life will become a very useful tool of researching living beings. To study the abstract subjects, such as entropy condition, can support the research on life problems. For a long time, certain achievements have been made in biological research, ranging from simple organism models to complex phenomena.

On the one hand, artificial life provides short life cycles for the experiments (e.g., 20 years for people, 10 days for the fruit bats, and 1 second for Hillis classification algorithms). On the other hand, artificial life systems give the chance of non-parallel running to both of control and reproduction. Artificial life has also provided the chance for people to see the interesting, but unpredictable emerging characteristics, and return to the past time to study their heredity.

As the basic research tools of the living nature, artificial life is capable of making organisms and the society simple. It is useful although it is artificial.

For developing new technologies and strengthening our capability of controlling the natural, artificial life systems have great potential. Take automatic programming as an example, which uses the specification language to describe a task, produces codes explicitly from the task specification, and then refines the program to improve the performance of the programming system. In addition, we can also do research on machine learning, through offering the expected input and output data, training the computer, and obtaining the needed knowledge.

In the program developing of artificial life, firstly choose a kind of computer system architecture, and then offer a series of environments to make the program evolve and complete the designated task.

By now, the academia of genetic algorithm has already provided and the parameter set of evolution. For many tasks, this parameter set can provide good, but possibly not the best solutions.

The engineering of these capabilities depends on the tasks and modern technologies of computer system architecture undoubtedly. Exactly like the artificial neural network, through learning to obtain new capabilities, parallel in essence. Some large-scale parallel computer systems in dealing with problems that are highly parallel have made the good result.

Another notable application of artificial life is the genetic engineering. As to the place that the traditional life can not inhabit, the new life of evolution has the ability to live in these places. Through molecular biological technology, the possibility to have such ability is very exciting.

To develop the new education tools seldom drew attention in the past, but draw attention around now. It is the needs of the times to make the future generation grasp more science and mathematics knowledge. Through synthesizing the new life forms, make students understand and study the emerging characteristics of the living beings more easily. This kind of phenomenon also exists in social science extensively.

It is already mentioned above that life model is available in ecology simulation and evolution. There are millions of children died at insects ' infectious disease every year. A lot of grain in the world has a poor harvest because of plague of insects. If there is no useful chemical pesticide, great losses will be caused. Excessively using pesticide can also cause the ecosystem of the world to present very serious problem. It is urgent to find out the method of using pesticide more effectively and cleverly, which requires that better simulation technology should be used. The artificial life software has already been developed in the world, which can simulate insect's reproduction in order to control the number of mosquitoes for agricultural production. The insects in different reproducing place, considered as different sub insect colonies, can reproduce themselves, interact with other insect colonies through moving, and disappear for various reasons (such as droughts and floods). We can regenerate the past colony cycle of these insects, and could control them by different methods.

15.2 Exploration of Artificial Life

For a long time, the mankind has been attempting to simulate the work of the nature using new technologies, and understand the essence of the nature by artificial methods. Early mechanical technologies offered tools, expanded the capabilities of manual labor of people, and lightened the manual labor greatly. At the beginning of the 20th century, the application of logic in arithmetic and mechanical operations caused the abstract formalization of the procedure. Church, Kleen, Turing, and Post formalized the concept of the logic sequence step, which formed the foundation of realizing the mechanical processing. In the symposium on brain and computer in Princeton Institute on January 6, 1945, it was considered that the engineering and neural network were the foundations. Later, Wiener put forward cybernetics. McCullouch and Pitts proposed M-P neural network model. The interest of von Neumann was the research on the similarity of brain and computer in organization, and how to represent the brain with formal logics. On the conference on cybernetics in March, 1946, two groups formed, in which one was the formal theory group headed by von Neumann, and the other was the cybernetics group headed by Wiener. Von Neumann's method turned all representations and mathematical calculations to basic logic world, and realized the symbols with explicit logic process. The computer system architecture proposed by von Neumann was the typical representative. Wiener began to use the concept of information, feedback, control, etc, to study on the biological and mechanical problems under the unified scientific concepts, which formed the cybernetics school.

In the end of the 1940s and the beginning of the 1950s, von Neumann put forward the possibility theory of machine self-growth. Using the computers as tools, we welcomed the development of information science. On the summer conference in Dartmouth in 1956, McCarthy proposed the term of artificial intelligence, which formed the research of artificial intelligence discipline. A lot of early work of artificial life came from artificial intelligence. In the 1960s, Rosenblatt drew specially study on the perceptron, and in the meantime Stahl set up several models of cellular activities, by using the Turing machine as the "enzyme of the algorithm", and representing biochemistry by strings. On later stage of the 1960s, Lindenmayer put forward the mathematical model of the cell interaction in growing and developing, which is called L-system now. These relatively simple models can obviously reveal the complex developing history, and support the communication and the difference of cells.

Since the 1970s, Conrad and his colleagues researched on self-adaptation, evolution and colony dynamics of artificial bionic systems, and proposed "artificial world" model which was improved repeatedly. Later, the research emphasis was put on the individual adaptability of system emergence. Chomsky's formal language theory was applied to the specification of programming language and the development of compiling program. The cellular automata were applied to image processing. Conway proposed the game theory of life cellular automata. In this theory, a cell will be open, if there are 3 open cells among the 8 cells around it. And a cell will keep open, if there are 2 or 3 open cells in the cells around it. Otherwise, it will shut off. Such cellular automaton systems were tested extensively.

The areas related to artificial intelligence, such as classical logic, search algorithm, heuristic searching, reasoning, neural network, genetic algorithm, fuzzy mathematics, etc, had made great progress. And the most important thing was the proposition of knowledge based reasoning, i.e., knowledge engineering and expert system, which applied artificial intelligence to practice and caused the emerging of various expert systems. But there existed many problems of expert system in the application, such as knowledge representation, commonsense reasoning, non-monotonic reasoning, framework issue, knowledge acquisition, validity of problem solving, etc.

In the eighties, the artificial neural network rose again. Many neural network models and learning algorithms emerged. In the meantime, the research of artificial life also rose gradually. The 1st International Workshop on Artificial Life was held in 1987.

15.3 Artificial Life Model

The development of the research in artificial life is similar to the early history of artificial intelligence. At present, there are many examples of artificial life programs. The famous ones are as follows:

1. Computer viruses

Computer viruses can be taken as vivid examples of artificial life, which describe the inherent characteristics of life systems including reproduction, organism-integration, unpredictablity, etc. The programs like viruses may be useful to the computer network.

2. Computer processes

Like computer viruses, computer processes are regarded as life bodies, which can reproduce in space and time, draw information from environment, and revise the environment they are located in. It should be distinguished that processes rather than computers are life bodies. Processes interact with the supporting physical media (such as processors, memory, and disks if virtual storage exists), so it is considered that the processes have life characteristics.

Obviously, there are essential differences between the computer process and the natural life. It because that there are little inner link between the processes and the supporting physical media. For example, the computer process which occupies the CPU can be interpreted and sent to the memory or the disk, and in the meantime another process is executed by the CPU.

Some seeds have kept hibernating for thousands of years, without metabolism or stimulation, but undoubtedly they are living and can sprout in appropriate condition. Similarly, computer processes can also live in a certain place outside the memory, and wait for the appearance of appropriate condition to go into active state again.

3. Biostatistics and individual embryology

The life systems can evolve and are capable of generating the forms of complex integrated modes. This kind of capability seems to be nearly the only, complex, and beautiful mode in the nature, which often has some geometric figures appearing by the simple action repeats and comprehensive result of life cells.

At present, the evolution technologies and self-producing capabilities are different in the systems which are similar to the life form. The application of the computer image will become more extensive, so there is the potential to produce the beautiful, life-like, and unpredictable modes and behavior. Someone has programmed the evolving neural network, in which the individuals having behavior can move and send messages to other individuals. It is emphasized that the event chains between gene and the whole organism need to be studied. The genotype is just the bit strings, the parameters of which are exactly like the weight values or thresholds in the artificial neural network.

4. Robots

The robots offer the approaches totally different from life-like systems. With respect to the form they are similar to living beings, but they have no reproduction capability. They can predict the future through deducing. The robots have a lot of properties related to life—complexity, organism-integration, stimulation, and movablity.

5. Autocatalytic network

In contrast to high-technology robots, the autocatalytic network is designed and constructed by people, which produces simple life-like systems with the reproducing (or self-evolving) capabilities in the simulating chemical test tube. This kind of systems have two active research phrases—autocatalytic network and cellular automata.

Autocatalytic network has some transformation, the most complete one of which is the theory of hypercycle. It is linked to the response component (RNA) network, which allows the consistent function coupled evolution, and self-replicating entity. Herein, the hypercycle network is taken as an example to describe all the natural life systems. Eigen has already developed the theory of deducing on hypercycle network, which can increase its complexity spontaneously, and know when collapses. Its mathematics processing is based on continuous reaction kinematics. Suppose there is no structure of space in the complete mixing of the element, it is superior to the model of cellular automata.

6. Cellular automata

It is a cell array, each cell of which is in discrete structure. According to the rules given in advance, the states can change with time. The transfer rules are to compute the present state of a cell and states of its neighbors by the array, all cells are updated spontaneously. Both of autocatalytic networks and cellular automata produce the modes of self-organization and self-replication, which do not change with time, but the mathematical modes of processing them are different.

The history of cellular automata is brilliant. Cellular automata are invented by von Neumann in 1940, which can be regarded as not only an important method of understanding the natural systems (natural automata) in the forms of mathematics and logics, but also a systematical theory of understanding the simulation and digital computers (artificial automata). With the development of large-scale parallel single instruction multiple data (SIMD) computers, it is very easy to obtain the color image at low price, which benefits the research of cellular automata. Langton's work, which can not only distinguish the rule set of cellular automata, but also support self-organization and the bit change in natural system, takes one step forward in realizing the vision of von Neumann's computer. In the former Soviet Union, Vladimir kuz'min and his colleagues are using the cellular automata to simulate life in another direction. Because of the close relation between cellular automata and computers, there exist bridges between Turing machine and some chemical system or life cell, which benefit the studies on their equivalence.

Boerlijst and Hogeweg combine hypercycle and cellular automata methods together to produce the self-reproducing process, which offers satisfactory solution for the problems of hypercycle theory, and explains how the natural system is organized and how it increases the complexity spontaneously.

7. Artificial nucleotides

The artificial life is not confined to the computer, which is very important to be recognized. A lot of substances, on which enzymes have effects, can support life. Based on this, various lives generated from chemical systems are being developed.

In 1960, based on the minimum set of molecules known at that time, Sol Spiegelhe and his colleagues realize RNA self-replicating in a test tube—nucleotide forebody, inorganic matter molecule, energy, replicating enzyme, and RNA embryonic form from the αβ bacteriophage. After meeting these needs, the RNA molecules of bacteriophage no longer needs the infected bacterium host, and can quickly replicate it in order to keep the suitable frequency, a series of figures of transferring to RNA molecules increase fast, but meanwhile RNA molecule diminished instead, until reach minimum measurement. The molecule colony turns from the massive and infective form into the small and anti-infective form, possibly because it can come off the nucleotide of bacterium. It is clear that these replicating and evolving RNA molecules are similar to the original forms of artificial life.

The new development of biology has become more interesting, which makes the artificial molecules evolve. Cech and Allman discovered that RNA acts as an enzyme in some cases and has the replication capability. This discovery is very important, which allows single RNA molecule to evolve. Another meaningful development is expanding the polymerase chain reaction of DNA.

15.4 Research Approach of Artificial Life

According to the organization of artificial life, its content can be roughly divided into two classes:

(1) The internal systems which construct an organism, including brain and nervous system, endocrine system, immune system, hereditary system, enzyme system, metabolic system, etc.
(2) The external systems of organisms and their colony, such as environmental adaptation system, genetic evolution system, etc.

The information received from internal and external systems of the organism constitutes the research approaches of artificial life, which mainly include two kinds:

(1) Modeling approaches. According to the life behavior of internal and external systems, build the information models.
(2) Working principle approaches. The life behavior is self-disciplined, dispersing and non-linear. Its working principles are chaos and differentiation, according to which we can research on its mechanism.

For example, it is currently considered that artificial neural network is the model system of internal systems, and genetic algorithm is the model system of external systems. Information processing in neural network shows the characteristics of chaos, but in genetic algorithm it is regarded as parallel processing which is self-disciplined and dispersing. From such a model system, we can see all kinds of organism behavior.

The research of artificial life must combine information science and life science together to form life information science. It can adopt the following strategies:

(1) Use the hardware, which takes information processing machines such as computers as the center, to produce the life behavior. Generally, there are two kinds of approaches: One is adopting the existing information processing machines and execution devices to implement the systems which have

artificial life behavior. The other is using the biological devices to construct life systems. All of them are called bio-computers, which can be regarded as a method to approach the artificial life.

(2) Use computer simulation technologies to study and develop the software model, which can exhibit the behavior characteristics of life bodies. In short, both of neural network and genetic algorithm adopt the mathematical model of information to simulate the creation of artificial life.

(3) Based on working principles, use computer simulation technologies to generate the life bodies. The foundation of the life phenomena is becoming disorderly and unsystematic with increasing of physical entropy. The principles of this phenomenon are chaos fractal, dissipative structure, concerted reaction, etc.

(4) Through computer simulation, analyze the characterized behavior producing of life, set up new theory. Utilize the 3 strategies above to get the general properties of the life behavior. By summarizing, set up the basic theories of life. This strategy forms the theories of self-organization, hyper-parallel processing, etc.

The above 4 research strategies of artificial life, accept a lot of concepts and inspiration from the real biological information processing systems, which construct life using artificial media such as computers, etc. The life concept of real true living beings is abstracted, generalized, and extended. The achievements of artificial life research take the molecular biology of reductionism as the center, which can be regarded as the supplement of modern biology. The mechanisms of life behavioral information processing, such as abstract, generalization, and extending, can be applied to the fields of precision mechanisms, control engineering, computer science, etc. The artificial life is the great force for forming the new information processing system.

One of the goals of artificial life is to extend experience database used in establishing theories. One kind of methods is to create processes in computer. While other artificial media which can represent life-like behavior, have no explicit simulation and concrete known organism model.

Von Neumann researched on construction related self-reproduction. He found there are two different ways can be used to describe organism heredity:

(1) Interpret the commands and construct descendants,
(2) Do not explain the data, but only replicate it to the created description copy, and then hand it down to the descendants.

Watson and Crick uncovered the working mechanism of DNA, which was regarded as the organism heredity.

Von Neumann provided the constructive proof of the possibility of machine self-replication, which requires that the self-replicating machine should have computation and construction universality. Smith also provided the proof of replication universality. His proof gracefully uses the recursive theorem in recursive function theory.

Another life form in computer is the computer virus, which has existed for 10 years. More and more computer viruses are developed rapidly, which will become infective in near future. The biologists are arguing about whether biological virus has life. Though they can reproduce themselves, they do not have their own metabolism to replicate the part needed, and must take over the metabolism of the parents to reproduce the offspring. Because the media are different, computer viruses seem a bit more active than biological viruses.

The goal of studying artificial life is to attempt to pursue the goals of supreme science and intelligence, but if keep carelessly and let them creep into the computer network or the biosphere, it will cause the crushing consequence to the real world. At present, it is known that artificial life can bring a small amount of dangers. As we have more and more knowledge of biosynthesis phenomenon, this kind of danger will increase. When the robots can reproduce themselves, just as easy as the computers do, we do not know what the world will be like.

Artificial life has offered a new forum for discussing many philosophy problems, which are the classical and modern problems about essence, intelligence and existence of life. There are many arguments about the possibility of artificial intelligence, in which it seems to fall into the hopeless mire as to the concepts such as "thinking" and "consciousness".

The arguments about artificial life are more or less similar to that about machine intelligence. Both of artificial intelligence and artificial life attempt to realize in the computer. When the scientists are thinking what "intelligence" is, artificial intelligence has totally changed its direction. Though artificial intelligence has not reached its total goal, it has already made many contributions to scientific field.

Similar to artificial intelligence, artificial life can also impel us to think what "living" means. In fact, there is no generally acknowledged definition of the "life state". When being asked about what life is, biologists will often enumerate the main behavior and characteristics of most life systems, such as self-reproduction, metabolism, death, complex organization and behavior, etc. It is true that the behavior listed above has constituted the strict behavioral standard, but the computers also have the above behavior. As to this, we have two kinds of choices.

(1) Admit the behavior of the computer is alive,
(2) Change the behavior standard listed above to make computer process become not alive.

The reason, why artificial intelligence fails in reaching "intelligence", is that it attempts to pursue an active goal. It is generally considered that playing chess needs real intelligence, but when computers can defeat most people in playing chess, someone thinks that the capability of playing chess should not be taken as the symbol of intelligence.

Just as the situation of artificial intelligence, there are two kinds of opinions on the substantial state of artificial life model: On one hand there is the weak explanation: The computer process is nothing but the simulation of life. Of course, it is clear that it is useful when discussing some concrete science issues of the "real" life, but the processes has never been regarded as the examples of life itself. On the other hand there is a strong explanation: The behavior listed above can describe all the known biological life as well as some computer processes, therefore it should be considered that the processes are "alive" in fact.

At first, the quality and the simple characteristics of life must be defined in different ways. Many concepts are useful for thinking and daily talking, but it is impossible to accurately define them, for example, the well known "machine", "game", and "love", but "alive" is another matter.

According to the vigor theory, there are essential differences between living systems and non-living systems. This makes biologists make great efforts to distinguish living and non-living life bodies. Today, a few biologists still think this is a problem which is worth paying attention to. Though nearly all the characteristics of natural life systems can be recognized, there is no satisfactory formal definition of the life. Some of the most important characteristics in life systems are:

The complexity and organization of life bodies;
The uniqueness of the chemical structures of their constituent molecules;
The uniqueness and variation of the single life body;
Having genetic programs which will form the genetic phenotype finally;

The formation through the natural selection;
The obvious uncertainty of behavior.

The above really facilitates understanding what makes a life body unique.

The key problem is self-reproduction, which is not only the most important characteristic of the naturally generated organisms, but also the most important characteristic to distinguish the life and non-life bodies. However, not all the natural life bodies are capable of reproducing themselves, so it is still considered that the boundaries of life exist. For example, the prions contain the protein, but not the ribonucleic acid. Take the AIDS retroviruses as another example, which contain RNA, but not DNA. They can not reproduce themselves, but replace the metabolic system of the host. The relation between the definitions of reproduction and life is not clear. For example, mules and castrated persons can walk, talk, and think, but not reproduce themselves, which shows they are alive by all the standards. Therefore, reproduction is not the defined characteristic of life.

The fundamental theories of artificial life research include the cellular automata theory, morphogenesis theory, chaos theory, genetic theory, information complexity theory, etc. In the following sections, the introductions will be given respectively.

15.5 Cellular Automata

Cellular automata (CA) provide another example of recursively applying a simple set of rules to a structure. In a CA, the structure that is being updated is the entire lattice of finite-automata. In this case, the local rule set is the transition function obeyed homogeneously by every automaton in the lattice. The local context considered in updating the state of each automaton is the state of the automata in its neighborhood. The transition function of automata constructs a kind of local physical components in a simple, discrete space/time universe. The universe is updated by applying the local physics to each "cell" of its structure again and again. Although the physical structure itself does not develop in this process, its state does.

In such universes, all processing methods can be embedded to propagate information in the universe meaningfully, depending on the rule context-sensitivity of local neighborhood conditions. In particular, the general purpose computers can be embedded. Since these computers are simply particular configurations of states within the lattice of automata, they can compute over the very set of symbols out of which they are constructed.

In the following part, we will discuss the growth of cellular automata in the 2-dimensional space. Let V be the cell state set, in which there is an element v_0 taken as the static state. Let f be the function of $V*V* \cdots *V \rightarrow V$, which satisfies that $f(v_0, v_0, \cdots, v_0)= v_0$. Then, we call (V, v_0, f) and f the cellular automaton of m neighbors, and the transformation function of this cellular automaton, respectively.

Because any complete cellular automaton is always an infinite set, the cellular automaton discussed here is embedded to 2-dimensional plane. The cells in this cellular automaton have 8 states, i.e., 0, 1, 2, 3, 4, 5, 6, and 7. In these states, 0, 1, 2, and 3 constitute the basic structure of the cellular automaton, and then 04, 05, 06, and 07 are the signals. The cells in state 1 are called the nuclear cells, and the cells in state 2 are called the shell cells. In the figures below, both of the symbol * and the blank space represent the cells in state 0.

The process of signal propagation can be explained with the following example:

```
2 2 2 2 2 2          2 2 2 2 2 2

1 1 0 s 1 1    →     1 1 1 0 s 1

2 2 2 2 2 2          2 2 2 2 2 2
```

The above example shows the propagation process of the signal 0s. Herein, $s=$ 4, 5, 6, 7, so it is called the data path. As its name suggests, it can propagate data in the "signal" form. A signal contains two state cells which move together. The signal (4, 5, 6, 7) itself has the state 0, and the data path can branch and fan out. At the branch point, the signal can replicate itself. The following figure shows the process of signal replication at time t, $t+1$, and $t+2$.

```
2 2 2 2 2 2          2 2 2 2 2 2          2 2 2 2 2 2

1 0 s 1 1 1    →     1 1 0 s 1 1    →     1 1 1 0 s 1

2 2 1 2 2 2          2 2 s 2 2 2          2 2 0 2 2 2

* 2 1 2 * *          * 2 1 2 * *          * 2 1 2 * *

* 2 1 2 * *          * 2 1 2 * *          * 2 1 2 * *

   time t               time t+1             time t+2
```

The combination change of signal 06 at the joint point is as follows, from which we can see the expansion of data path.

```
2  2  2  2  2  2  2  2            2  2  2  2  2  2  2  2

1  1  0  6  1  1  1  1     →      1  1  1  0  7  1  1  1

2  2  2  2  6  2  2  2            2  2  2  2  0  2  2  2

*  *  *  2  0  2  *  *            *  *  *  2  1  2  *  *

*  *  *  2  1  2  *  *            *  *  *  2  1  2  *  *

*  *  *  2  1  2  *  *            *  *  *  2  1  2  *  *
```

Our construct the following transformation rule table, based on which the growth of cellular automaton in the two-dimensional space can be given.

f(0,1,2,7,6)=1	f(7,0,0,0,2)=3	f(2,0,0,2,3)=7	f(1,0,2,3,2)=6
f(0,1,2,3,2)=1	f(3,0,2,2,1)=0	f(7,0,2,1,2)=0	f(1,0,7,2,2)=3
f(4,0,2,0,2)=2	f(2,0,0,2,4)=0	f(2,0,2,6,2)=4	f(2,0,0,1,4)=2
f(4,0,2,6,2)=2	f(2,0,4,6,2)=4	f(1,2,4,2,6)=4	f(4,1,2,2,2)=0
f(2,0,0,4,2)=0	f(2,0,2,4,2)=0	f(2,0,1,2,4)=2	f(6,0,2,4,2)=4
f(7,0,0,2,1)=0	f(0,1,2,7,2)=4		

In the table above, the first independent variable of the function f is the state of the center cell. And the following 4 independent variables are the states of 4 neighbors, which rotate clockwise in order to generate the minimum 4-digit number.

The concept of cellular automata can be established in the following ways: At first, we have a cellular space which constitutes the N-dimensional Euclidean space, as well as the neighbor relation defined in the cellular space. Because of the neighbor relation, each cell must have a limited number of cells as its neighbors. A cellular automaton system ("cellular system" for short) is defined as follows: In this system, each cell is given a limited number of states, a distinguishing state (called the "empty state"), and a rule. The rule is a function of the states of the cell itself and its neighbors at time t, which provides the state of each cell at time $t+1$. All the possible states of a cell together with the rules of its state transformation are called the transformation function. So a cellular automaton system is made up by a cellular space and the transformation function defined in this space. The state of a cellular automaton is determined by a limited number of cells together with their states. And it can be considered that all of the other cells are in the empty state.

In the following part, we will discuss the problems of cellular automata.

In order to avoid discussing the boundary problem, we consider an infinite space, which is the N-dimensional Euclidean space divided into square cells of the same size. We call this space the tessellation. The neighbor of a given cell is the cell the coordinate of which differs from the given cell's coordinate by 1 at the most. The tessellated structure can be formally defined as a five-element group (N, T, S, q, f). Herein, N is a positive integer, and T is the subdivision of N-dimensional Euclidean space, i.e., the set of cells. Each cell of T is the N-dimensional hypercube (line segment, square, or cube in low-dimensional spaces) the side length of which is 1. The center of T is a positive integer coordinate. S is a finite set of states, in which q is the distinguishing state called static state. Herein, f is the mapping function, which maps the set of all the states of cell x and its neighbors at time t-1 onto the set of the states of cell x at time t.

The limited square of trellis cells is named the array, the state or configuration of this kind of array is the function related to the state of each cell. That is to say, the state of an array is determined by the state of each cell of the array at time t. If there is a surjective map from array C' onto array C in which each cell and its image have the same state, the state of C' will be a copy of the state of C. Given an array C^* with n subsets, if any two of these subsets do not intersect with each other and each subset is a copy of C, the state of C^* will contain n copies of the state of C.

15.6 Morphogenesis Theory

The typical morphogenesis theory is the L-Systems proposed by Lindenmayer in 1968. L-Systems consist of sets of rules for rewriting symbol strings, and are closely related to the Chomsky formal grammars. In the following, "$X \rightarrow Y$" means that each occurrence of symbol "X" in the structure is replaced with string "Y". Since the symbol "X" may appear on the right as well as the left sides of rules, the set of rules can be used recursively to rewrite new structures.

Here is a simple example of L-system. The rules are context free, which means that when a particular part changes, its context need not to be considered. Take the following rules as an example:

(1) A $\rightarrow$ CB

(2) B → A

(3) C → DA

(4) D → C

If apply these rules to the initial seed structure "A", we can get the structural sequence as shown below:

time	structure	rules applied
0	A	initial "seed"
1	C B	rule 1, replaces A with CB
2	D A A	rule 3, replaces C with DA; rule 2, replaces B with A
3	C C B C B	rule 4, replaces D with C; rule 1 twice, replaces A with CB
4	...	...

L-Systems combine with meta-symbols to represent branching points, allowing a new line of symbols to branch off from the main "stem". The symbols "( )" and "[ ]" indicate left and right branches, respectively. Suppose there are the following rules:

(1) A → C[B]D

(2) B → A

(3) C → C

(4) D → C(E)A

(5) E → D

If apply these rules to the initial seed structure "A", we can get the structural sequence as shown below:

time	structure	rules applied
0	A	initial "seed"
1	C[B]D	rule 1.
2	C[A]C(E)A	rules 3,2,4.
3	C[C[B]D]C(D)C[B]D	rules 3,1,3,5,1.
4	C[C[A]C(E)A]C(C(E)A)C[A]C(E)A	rules 3,3,2,4,3,4,3,2,4.

In order to propagate signals along a structure, there should be more than one symbol on the left-hand side of a rule. In this case, the rules become context-sensitive. In the following example, the symbol in "{ }" is the symbol (or string of symbols) to be replaced, the rest of the left-hand side is the context, and the symbols "[" and "]" indicate the left and right ends of the string, respectively. Take the rule set as an example, which contains the following rules:

(1) [{C} → C   a "C" at the left-end of the string remains a "C".
(2) C{C} → C   a "C" with a "C" to its left remains a "C".
(3) *{C} → *   a "C" with an "*" to its left becomes an "*".
(4) {*}C → C   an "*" with a "C" to its right becomes a "C".
(5) {*}] → *   an "*" at the right end of the string remains an "*".

Under these rules, the "*" in the initial structure "*CCCCCCC" will be propagated to the right as shown below:

The capability of signal propagation is extremely important, because it allows any computational process to be embedded within the structure, which may directly influence the structure's development.

time	structure
0	*CCCCCCC
1	C*CCCCCC
2	CC*CCCCC
3	CCC*CCCC
4	CCCC*CCC
5	CCCCC*CC
6	CCCCCC*C
7	CCCCCCC*

15.7 Chaos Theories

From the perspective of the system, life behavior can be defined as the non-linear, non-equilibrium open system in physics at first. So, the special behavior of this kind of systems is natural oscillation, i.e., limited period and chaos. The particular behavior of life is concerned by ontologism and advanced information processing. In artificial life, its formation principles are most important. The limited periods can be divided into stable ones and unstable ones. The natural oscillation is called the stable limited period. Limited oscillation and chaos are the two respects of structure stability. The only thing can distinguish between them is that the difference of initial conditions of limited period greatly influences the future movements. In chaos, the difference of the initial conditions is expanded with time quickly, so it is difficult to reproduce it approximately. This kind of property is called orbit instability, which forms obvious contrast to the ordering of the orbit stability based on limited period. The dynamics of the nature can be divided into order and chaos. The regular behavior of order is the periodic solution. Other chaos systems are complex, with unpredictable behavior in the long term. From the perspective of time development, both of them are basically the dynamics systems. Therefore, life bodies are the compositions of chaos and order.

What is it about the computation capabilities of order and chaos, which are taken as the formation principles of characteristic phenomena emerging from life behavior? At first, ordered systems have the periodic complexity, so it is impossible to implement the highly complicated computation. There are strict rules in the chaos systems. Because of this, it is difficult to compute the unstable behavior of their orbits theoretically. Thus, we only consider the life behavior seen at the edge of chaos. In this way, the basic operations of information, such as storage, transmission, transformation, etc, can be implemented in the mixed systems of order and chaos:

(1) The information storage is obtained from stable period dynamics of ordered systems.
(2) The transmission and transformation of information can be realized using unstable dynamics of chaos systems.

Langton found that people could make the one-dimensional cellular automaton continuously change its state as "fixed-value type → periodic type →

complicated type → chaos type", through adjusting the parameter λ of rules which describe the cellular automata. Thus, he proposed that the state of complicated cellular automaton was between order (fixed-value type, periodic type) and chaos, which he named "the edge of chaos". Besides, it is not difficult to find that, all the complicated phenomena of the nature, including life, intelligence, and society, are at the edge between order and chaos in fact. If a system needs to be complicated enough, it can neither be too ordered to become ossified, nor be too chaotic to become disordered. So these systems should skillfully keep the balance between the states of order and chaos.

15.8 Experimental Systems of Artificial Life

The goal of the research platforms of artificial life is to simulate the behavioral characteristics of life using computers, which can form the life computing theory finally. That is to say, the computer will not become the life body, but can be regarded as a strong tool for studying artificial life. These platforms can display some basic behavior of life, as well as some special behavior of life, such as self-organizing, self-learning, etc. On the one hand, to study these platforms facilitate explaining the overall picture of life and exploring the origin and evolution of life. On the other hand, they also provide the new approaches for biological research, and offer the beneficial tools for the research on artificial life.

15.8.1 *Digital life evolutionary model Tierra*

In 1991, Thomas S. Ray, who is a biologist of the University of Oklahoma in USA, implemented a computer simulation program called Tierra (in Spanish, which means the earth). Thomas S. Ray researches on the evolution of tropical rain forests and the ecological problems. In Tierra system, a virtual life world is constituted by many digital living beings which are capable of self-replicating. The evolving process goes on in the physical environment made up of the CPU and the memory of computer. The time of CPU represents quantity, while the space of memory represents resource. These digital living beings or self-replicating programs change their evolution strategies repeatedly, and compete to survive in Tierra world. Those programs, which obtain more time and memory space, can leave more copies for the future generation. On the contrary, those having less time and space will be eliminated. The running of this system exhibits many characteristics of evolution and variation, as well as all sorts of behaviors similar to life on earth. In the beginning, there is only a simple ancestor "living being" in Tierra model. After the computation of 5,260,000 commands, 366 kinds of digital living beings in different sizes appear in Tierra model. After 2,560 million commands, 1180 kinds of different digital living beings appear. Among these living beings, some live in the bodies of other digital living beings, and some are immune to the parasites. Tierra also generates the punctuated equilibrium phenomenon, in which the social organization even appears. In a word, nearly all the characteristics in the process of natural evolving, and all kinds of functional and behavioral organizations similar to the life on earth, will appear in Tierra. The homepage of Tierra is http://www.his.atr.jp/~ray/tierra/index.html.

The most exciting achievement of Tierra is proving that the machine codes can evolve. This means that machine codes can have variation or reorganization, and the generated codes keep enough functions in order to change at times through the natural selection. In addition, the natural environment also evolves with the evolving of organisms. This is one of the basic factors of promoting the evolution of biological species and complexity on the earth.

Another achievement of Tierra is adding a digital multi-cellular analog into Tierra. Thomas S. Ray thought that it was the natural analogy of parallel computation, as well as the characteristic of increasing the variety of evolution. The characteristics in multi-cellular Tierra model include:

(1) The cellular organism originates in the single-cellular form, and develops into the multi-cellular form through a binary cell division process;
(2) Each cell of an individual has the same genetic materials, because all of them come from one initial cell;
(3) There are potential differences among sufficiently developed cells, so that they can represent different parts of the genome.

However, the multi-cellular evolution has increased the quantity of cells, but not the number of cell types.

In order to cause the growth of cell types in the evolving multi-cellular digital organisms, Tierra runs on the distributed computer network. Thomas S. Ray utilizes a new observation tool called Beagle to observe and control the running Tierra in the network. The digital life designed by Thomas S. Ray, takes numbers as carriers to explore various phenomena, laws and emergence behavior of complex systems in the evolving process.

15.8.2 *Avida*

Avida is an adaptive genetic system, the concepts of which are similar to the concepts of Tierra. Avida is obviously different from the traditional genetic algorithm. The selection in Avida approaches the natural selection more closely than most genetic algorithm mechanisms.

Avida system creates an artificial (virtual) environment inside the computer. This system has implemented a virtual two-dimensional grid processor, which runs a limited assembly language. The programs are stored in system memory as consecutive strings of the commands. Each program (organism) is related to a grid.

This program and its derivatives are influenced by various random mutations subsequently. Any mutation, which results in the improvement of reproduction capability in an appointed environment, is considered beneficial. Most mutations are unfavorable (which typically make the organisms unable to reproduce themselves completely) or neutral. Only a few beneficial mutations make the organisms reproduce themselves more effectively and grow up stronger in the environment. Through a period of time, the organisms which are more adaptive to the environment appear. The important concepts of Avida system are as follows:

1. Timesharing

Timesharing is the method of allocating the time to grid living beings, in which they can occupy the processor and run their codes. Some living beings have the processors faster than others, so the timesharing codes should confirm that they run at the (relatively) appropriate speed. Each living being has an index which determines its processor speed. Time allocator will adjust the indexes repeatedly until the living beings are satisfied with task execution in the environment they are located in. The timesharing mechanism has a far-reaching influence on the overall behavior of the biological colony.

2. Adaptive degree

Adaptive degree is an unit-free measuring method, by which a particular organism in some environment can measure its replication capability. Only in comparison with others, can the adaptive degree of an organism make sense, which provides the ratio of the replication rate of the organism to that of another one. In order to compute the adaptive degree, divide the organism index by the preparative time. If the adaptive degree of an organism is twice that of another one, it will reproduce twice as many offspring as another one per unit time. The representation of adaptive degree makes programs be capable of showing useful behavior rather than simply self-reproducing.

3. Reproduction

It means self-replicating and producing the offspring. The reproduction in Avida is accomplished through the four processes shown below:

(1) Allocate new memory to the subprogram;
(2) Copy father program into new memory by copying the commands one by one;
(3) Divide the program into father program and subprogram;
(4) Place the subprogram in the grid.

4. The selection of placing methods

After the birth of an offspring, which grid should be chosen to place it around the father?   We have the following options:

(1) Choose the empty position: This is a highly limited method of reproduction, but when dying is started, it is a generally effective method. In this mode, cells are forbidden to kill each other, and only the newly born living beings are allowed to move into empty cells.
(2) Choose the oldest one: This is the default method in Avida. The living beings around the father body (including the father body itself) will be assessed, and the oldest one among them will be deleted. If there exist several living beings with the same degree, choose and delete one in the oldest units at random, and then wait for the arrival of new living beings.
(3) Choose the maximum age/index: This placing method relatively benefits the living beings with higher indexes, and helps to stimulate the living beings to study the extra special skills as an encouraging method.
(4) Choose at random: Choose the son living being from the father and its eight neighbors at random. Because before they have any offspring, about half of these living beings will be substituted, so this kind of method is bad for evolving.

5. Mutation

The types of mutation implemented in Avida include:

(1) Copy mutation: the mutation taking place when copying.
(2) Point mutation: the mutation taking place at random.
(3) Division mutation: the mutation taking place when father and son are dividing.
(4) Division insert, division delete: the mutation of deliberately inserting or deleting a certain character when the cell is dividing.

Generally speaking, all the mutation rates must be under a determinate value to avoid killing the colony. But if the mutation rate is too low, the evolution will become very slow. Some parameter variables in Avida system can be revised, which makes Avida system approach the Darwin biological evolution process of natural selection and survival of the fittest.

15.8.3 *Ecosystem for biological breed Terrarium*

In order to show some important features in the .NET frame and stimulate study interests of the programmers, Microsoft Corporation introduces the demonstration program of an ecosystem named Terrarium. Terrarium is in fact a teaching game to exhibit the application and development technologies of .NET frame to software developers. And in the meanwhile it is also a modeling tool for studying evolutionary biology and artificial intelligence. In the Terrarium game, the developers can create plant-eating animal, carnivore or plant, and put them into the ecosystem which is based on the model of "survival of the fittest" and peer-to-peer network structure. This game provides not only a competitive environment for testing developer abilities in software development and strategy design, but also an nearly real model of evolutionary biology and artificial intelligence for testing the adaptive capacities of the living beings with different behavior and attributes in the struggle of surviving.

The URL address of Microsoft ecosystem named Terrarium, which is used for raising living beings, is http://www.terrariumgame.net/terrarium/. A Microsoft server is responsible for running the whole ecosphere, and uses the manageable container manner to let all living beings live in it. There is an environment program on the server side, which has some basic parameters of biological world including: time, energy, resource, space, etc. There is also a seed program on the client side, which is the code set of bottom rules, and has the DNA code of growing into a complete digital creature in the environment program. Users can revise the source code of the seed program to make the generated digital living beings have special capabilities and habits. The seed program is divided 3 classes including plant, animal, and microorganism programs, which can grow into three kinds of digital living beings respectively by revising. The produced digital living beings make up the food chain, and launch the struggle for existence. In order to survive, digital living beings can unite to live, showing the phenomena such as symbiosis, parasitics, etc. Finally, population scales of all kinds of living beings reach the relative equilibrium state. If new species are joined in, the equilibrium may be broken, and then the competition of new round is launched. Because the competition is endless, users must generate new species repeatedly to face the challenge for existence. The programmers of the environment programs can also introduce the disasters such as aerolite, flood, drought, etc to do destructive experiments on the survival capability of each species. The seed program must be upgraded repeatedly, for example, if the definition of water is added into the environment, the seed must take water as one of its key surviving elements accordingly. Therefore, users must follow to upgrade repeatedly as well, otherwise they will be extinct on the annual disaster day.

15.8.4 Artificial fish

Xiaoyuan Tu's thesis for the PhD degree at the University of Toronto, entitled "Artificial Animals for Computer Animation: Biomechanics, Locomotion, Perception, and Behavior", won her the ACM Doctoral Dissertation Award in 1996. The main work of this thesis is researching on and developing the artificial fish(Tu,1996).

The "artificial fish" created by Xiaoyuan Tu is a society of artificial shoal which perch in the virtual sea world. Each artificial fish is an autonomous agent, which can act independently as well as interact with each other. The "artificial fish" have the "intention generator" corresponding to fish brain, and the virtual perceptive organ corresponding to fish eyes based on computer vision. So it can discern and perceive other artificial fish and the virtual marine environment around. Each fish lives in the "sensing-acting" mode, and has intelligent characteristics such as self-stimulating, self-learning, self-adaptation, etc. Based on these characteristics, the corresponding intelligent behavior is generated, such as seeking and eating food because of hunger, learning the bitter lessons of other fish, not going to eat the bait with hook, adapting to the social environment with sharks, and escaping the danger of being preyed on, etc. The colony of artificial fish is a typical multi-agent distributed intelligent system. The society of artificial fish of fish shows the capabilities of self-organization and intelligent collective behavior, for example, when the colony of artificial fish meets barriers in roaming, it can discern the obstacle, changes the formation, and reforms the formation to continue advancing again after winding the obstacle.

15.8.5 Autolife

The Autolife model developed by Jiang Zhang is an artificial life system with the "openly evolving" capability [Li et al., 2006]. Each agent model is constructed using the finite automaton model the rule table length of which is alterable. On one hand agent can reproduce itself, on the other hand the selection mechanism in the model has not adopted the simple models of the energy consumption emerges spontaneously rather than explicit adaptive degree functions. Thus agent model can be regarded as a Tierra-like system. But different from the digital life models such as Tierra, Avida, etc, Autolife model has been simplified greatly, which has friendly interface and direct operation. Though has not assembled a virtual computer for each agent, the coupling of agent and environment can be regarded as a Turing machine model. So the agent can "arbitrarily" program by variation. Using the Autolife model, people can see the phenomenon coexisting in general ecosystem at first: great biological explosion, great extinction, and the agent evolving to be more cleverly; Secondly, users can explore the relation between agent and environment through changing the food adding rules; Finally, if allow to change the environment and produce the food automatically through seeding in agent, the organization emergence is an unavoidable result. The organization constituted by agents has characteristics of independently moving and self-repairing. We can say that the organization in Autolife is real "living bodies".

(1) Internal structure: There is a group of parameters including energy value, life-span, current coordinate, current direction, etc. There also exists a rule table with variable length. This rule table can be regarded as the genetic data (i.e., the chromosome) used in heredity and variation, as well as the program rules which can instruct the movement of life bodies.

(2) How to take action: In each simulation cycle, the life body only reads the states of the three squares in front of it. If 0 and 1 denote the blank square and the square with food respectively, what the life body reads each time is the 3-bit binary string such as 010, 001, etc. The life body also has the internal state which is encoded into 0, 1, 2, 3, or 4... In this case, according to the binary string it reads and the internal state, the life body searches its rule table, finds out the matching rule, and gets the output actions (0, 1, 2, 3, 4) and the next state. Herein, (0, 1, 2, 3, 4) are the action codes, which denote moving ahead, turning left, turning right, reproducing, and seeding, respectively. That is to say, the actions which the life body takes in each cycle are totally determined by its rules. Reproduction means that a new life body is born in current location, which inherits all the states of its father.

(3) Environmental rules: If there exists some food in the world which the life body is located in, eat up the food to increase its energy value. In addition, each kind of actions of the life body corresponds to a certain energy consumption value. A newly-born life body will receive some energy from its father. If the energy has been totally consumed or the life-span exceeds the maximal life-span, the life body will die. In order to limit the reproduction of life bodies, each life body is given the upper limit of its reproductive number.

(4) Genetic rules: In the process of heredity, the father passes the complete rule table down to its offspring. But at the same time, the variation is caused with probability muteP, and the length of rule table also changes with the probability lenP (which may increase or decrease). The living agents can write programs for themselves by means of heredity and variation.

With respect to artificial life, the essence of life is information. The change of information symbolizes the life. The research and breakthroughs of artificial life show that information, algorithm, and computation have become important concepts in understanding the essence of life. People can not only create artificial life by artificial means in the natural environment, but also create digital life in the virtual environment of computer. The artificial creatures can have variation as well as replicate themselves. They can even struggle for the living resources, in order to make their offspring use these resources more efficiently.

Exercises

1. Give a sketch of the basic meaning of artificial life.

2. Try to discuss the necessity of the research on artificial life.
3. Based on the state of art of research on artificial life, give some examples of artificial life programs.
4. What is cellular automaton? What is the transform function of cellular automata?
5. Explain the morphogenesis theory using a concrete system as an example.
6. Each agent model is modeled using the finite automata which can change the length of rule table. Design an artificial life system, and research on the relation between an agent and the environment through changing the rules of adding food.
7. Design the artificial fish which can avoid obstacles.
8. Considering the state in figure (a), there are only two squares (denoted by X) with just three neighbors which have been taken up. In figure (b) produced in the next life cycle, there are also only two squares (denoted by Y) with just three neighbors which have been taken up. Obviously, the state of this society circulates between figure (a) and figure (b), producing the neighborhood set of the flashing phenomenon. Please design a program to realize this life game.

(a)   (b)

Neighborhood set of the flashing phenomenon

9. With the development of biotechnology, the further integration of genetics and computer will become a reality. On the one hand, computer will enter the human body and become a part of it. On the other hand, the development of artificial intelligence probably means that mankind will give up the supreme status in intelligence to the thinking machine. Thus, someone predict that computer will be the next life form. Do you agree to this point of view? What is your opinion?

References

Adamatzky, A. and Maciej Komosinski. (2009) *Artificial Life Models in Hardware*. New York: Springer.

Agrawal, R, Imieliski T., and Swami A. (1993) Mining association rules between sets of items in large database. *In Proceedings of ACM SIGMOD International Conference on Management of Data(SIGMOD'93)*, 207-216, May.

Agrawal, R., and Srikant. R. 1994. Fast Algorithms for Mining Association Rules. In: *Proc. 20th Int'l Conference on Very Large Data Bases (VLDB'94)*. Santiago, Chile, 487~499.

Agrawal, R. and J.C. Shafer. (1996) Parallel mining of association rules: Design, implementation and experience. Special Issue in Data Mining. *IEEE Trans. on Knowledge and Data Engineering*, 8(6): 962-969.

Aha, D.A. (1990) Study of Instance-Based Algorithms for Supervised Learning Tasks: Mathematical, Empirical, and Psychological Evaluations. Ph.D. thesis. Aha, D. (1997) *Lazy Learning*. Kluver Academic Pub.

Aha, D., Kibler, G. and Albert, M. K. (1991) Instance-Based Learning Algorithms. *Machine Learning*, 6(1): 37-66.

Aleksander, I. (editor), (1989) *Neural computing architectures*. North Oxford Academic.

Ali, K.M. (1989) Augmenting domain theory for explanation-based generalization. In *Proceedings of IWML-89*, Cornell University, Ithaca, New York.

Allen, J.F. (1984) Towards a general theory of action and time, Artificial Intelligence, 23: 123-154.

Amarel, S. (1986) Program synthesis as a theory formation task: problem representations and solution methods. In R.S. Michalski, J.G. Carbonell and T.M. Mitchell (editors), *Machine Learning: An Artificial Intelligence Approach*, Vol. II, Morgan Kaufmann.

Amari, S. (1985) *Differential Geometrical Methods in Statistics*, Springer Lecture Notes in Statistic, 28, Springer.

Amsterdam, J. (1988) Extending the Valiant Learning Model. In *Proceedings of ICML-88*, San Mateo, CA.

Amsterdam, J. (1988) Some philosophical problems with formal learning theory, In *Proceedings of AAAI-88*, Saint Paul, Minnesota.

Anderson, J.R. (1989) A theory of the origins of human knowledge, Artificial Intelligence, 40(1): 313-351.

585

Angluin, D. and C.H. Smith. (1983) Inductive Inference: Theory and Methods, *ACM Computing Survey*, 15(3): 237-70.

Angluin, D. (1988) Queries and concept learning. *Machine Learning*, 2(3): 319.[13]

Ashley, K. D., and Rissland, E. L., 1988. Compare and Contrast: A Test of Expertise, in J.L. Kolodner, editor, Proceedings of a DARPA Workshop on Case-based Reasoning, Florida, May.

Baader, F., Calvanese, D., McGuinness, D., Nardi, D., Patel-Schneider, P. (eds.), (2003) *The Description Logic Handbook. Theory, Implementation and Applications.* Cambridge.

Bakker, R.R., F. Dikker, F. Tempelman and P. M. Wognum. (1993) Diagnosing and solving over-determined constraint satisfaction problems, IJCAI-93, 276-281.

Banerji, R.B. (1985) The logic of learning: a basis for pattern recognition and for improvement of performance, Advances in Computers.

Bareiss, R. (1988) PROTOS: a unified approach to concept representation, classification and learning, Ph.D. Dissertation, University of Texas at Austin, Dept. of Comp. Sci.

Barletta, R. and W. Mark. (1988) Explanation-Based Indexing of Cases. In *Proceedings of AAAI-88*, Saint Paul, Minnesota.

Barletta, R. and R. Kerber. (1989) Improving explanation-based indexing with empirical learning. In *Proceedings of IWML-89*, Cornell University, Ithaca, New York.

Belew, R.K. and S. Forrest. (1988) Learning and programming in classifier systems. *Machine learning*, 3(2): 193-223.

Bellman, R. (1957) *Dynamic Programming*. Princeton Press.

Benferhat, S., C. Cayrol, D. Dubois, J. Lang and H. Prade. (1993) Inconsistency management and prioritized syntax-based entailment. *IJCAI-93*, 640-647.

Bergadano, F. and A. Giordana. (1988) A knowledge intensive approach to concept induction. In *Proceedings of ICML-88*, San Mateo, CA.

Biberman, Y. (1994) A Context Similarity Measure. *Machine Learning: ECML-94*, Springer-Verlag, Berlin Heidelberg.

Bies, Robert R, Muldoon, Matthew F., Pollock, Bruce G., Manuck, Steven, Smith, Gwenn and Sale, Mark E. (2006) A Genetic Algorithm-Based, Hybrid Machine Learning Approach to Model Selection. *Journal of Pharmacokinetics and Pharmacodynamics* (Netherlands: Springer): 196–221.

Blumer, A., A. Ehrenfeucht, D. Haussler and A. Warmuth. (1986) Classifying learnable geometric concepts with the Vapnik-Chervonenkis dimension, In Proceedings of 18th Annual ACM Symposium on Theory of Computation, Berkeley, CA.

Boden, M.A. (1988) *Computer Models of Mind*. Cambridge University Press.

Booker, L.B. (1982) Intelligent behavior as an adaptation to the task environment. Dissertation Abstracts International, 43(2), 469B. (University Microfilms No. 8214966).

Booker, L.B. (1988) Classifier Systems that Learn Internal World Models. *Machine Learning,* 3(2): 161-192.

Booker, L.B., D.E. Goldberg and J.H. Holland. (1989) Classifier Systems and Genetic Algorithms. *Artificial Intelligence*, 40(1): 235-282.

Bradshaw, G.L., P.W. Langley and H.A. Simon. (1980) BACON.4: the discovery of intrinsic properties. In *Proceedings of the Canadian Society for Computational Studies of Intelligence*, Victoria, B.C.

Bratman, M. E., Israel, D. J. and Pollack, M. E. (1987) Toward an architecture for resource-bounded agents. *Technique report CSLI-87-104*, Center of Study of Language and Information, SRI and Stanford University.

Braverman, M.S. and S.J. Russell. (1988) Boundaries of operationality. In *Proceedings of ICML-88*, San Mateo, CA.

Brin S. et al. (1997) Dynamic Itemset Counting and Implication Rules for Market Basket Data. *Proc. ACM SIGMOD Conf. Managementof Data*, ACM Press, New York, pp. 255–264.

Brooks, R.A. (1991a) Intelligent without representation. *Artificial Intelligence*, Vol. 47, 139-159.

Brooks, R.A. (1991b) Intelligence without reasoning. In *Proceedings of IJCAI'91*, Sydney.

Buchanan, B.G. and T.M. Mitchell. (1978) Model-directed learning of production rules. In D.A. Waterman and F. Hayes-Roth, (editors), *Pattern-Directed Inference Systems*, Academic Press.

Buchanan, B.G., T.M. Mitchell, R.G. Smith and C.R.Jr. Johnson. (1979) Models of learning systems. Dept. of Computer Science, Stanford University.

Buchanan, B.G., J. Sullivan, T. Cheng and S.H. Clearwater. (1988) Simulation-assisted inductive learning, In *Proceedings of AAAI-88*, Saint Paul, Minnesota.

Buggleton, S.H. and W. Buntine. (1988) Towards constructive induction in first-order predicate calculus. Working paper, Turing Institute.

Bundy, A. (1983) *The computer modelling of mathematics reasoning*. Academic Press.

Bunt, Harry, Zhongzhi Shi (Eds.) (1994) *International Workshop on Knowledge Engineering and Applications*.

Buntine, W. (1989) A critique of the Valiant model. In *Proceedings of IJCAI-89*, Detroit, Michigan, USA.

Buntine, W. (1991) Classifiers: A theoretical and empirical study. In *Proceedings of IJCAI-91*, 638-644.

Burges, J. C. J. (1998) A tutorial on support vector machines for pattern recognition. *Data Mining and Knowledge Discovery*, 2(2): -167

Burke, R. and Kass, A. (1996) Retrieving Stories for Case-Based Teaching. *Case-Based Reasoning (Experiences, lessons, &Future Directions)*, AAAI/MIT Press, 93-110

Burstein, M.H. (1986) A model of learning by incremental analogical reasoning and debugging. In *Machine Learning: An Artificial Intelligence Approach*, Los Altos, Calif.

Callan, J.P., Fawcett, T.E., and Rissland, E.L. (1991) CABOT: An Adaptive Approach to Case-based Search. in *IJCAI-91*, Australia.

Cao, Hu, Zhongzhi Shi. (1998) CARBA: Common Agent Request Broker Architecture. *PRICAI'98*, Singapore.

Carbonell, J.G. (1981) A computational model of problem solving by analogy, In *Proceedings of the Seventh IJCAI*, Vancouver, B.C.

Carbonell, J.G. (1983) Derivational analogy and its role in problem solving. In *Proceedings of AAAI83*, Washington, D.C.

Carbonell, J.G., R.S. Michalski and T.M. Mitchell. (1983) Machine learning: a historical and methodological analysis, *AI Magazine*, 4(3): 69-79.

Carbonell, J.G. (1983) Learning by analogy: formulating and generalizing plans from past experience. In R.S. Michalski, J.G. Carbonell and T.M. Mitchell (editors), *Machine Learning: An Artificial Intelligence Approach*, Tioga.

Carbonell, J.G. (1986) Analogy in problem solving. In R.S. Michalski, J.G. Carbonell and T.M. Mitchell (editors), *Machine Learning: An Artificial Intelligence Approach*, Morgan Kaufmann.

Carbonell, J.G. (1989) Introduction: paradigms for machine learning. Artificial Intelligence, 40(1): 1-9.

Carnap. R. (1950) *Logical foundations of probability*. The University of Chicago Press.

Caruana, R. A., L.J. Eshelman and J.D. Schaffer. (1989) Representation and hidden bias II: eliminating defining length bias in genetic search. In *Proceedings of IJCAI-89*, Detroit, Michigan, USA.

Catlett, J. (1991) Overpruning large decision trees. In *Proceedings of IJCAI-91*, 764-769.

Chang, C.L. and R.C. Lee. (1973) *Symbolic Logic and Mechanical Theorem Proving*. Academic Press.

Chen H., P. Tino and X. Yao (2009) Probabilistic Classification Vector Machines. *IEEE Transactions on Neural Networks*, **20**(6):901-914.

Chen W., K.S. Decker. (2006) Analyzing characteristics of task structures to develop GPGP coordination mechanisms. *AAMAS 2006*: 662-669.

Cheung D.W., J. Han, V. Ng, A. Fu, and Y. Fu. (1996) A Fast Distributed Algorithm for Mining Association Rules. *Fourth Int'l Conf. Parallel and Distributed Information Systems*, Dec. pp31-42.

Cheung D. W., V. T. Ng, A. W. Fu, and Y. Fu. (1996) Efficient Mining of Association Rules in Distributed Databases. *IEEE Transactions On Knowledge And Data Engineering*, 8:911-922.

Cheung, D., K. Hu, and S. Xia. (1998) Asynchronous Parallel Algorithm for Mining Association Rules on Shared-Memory Multi-Processors. *Proc. 10th ACM Symp. Parallel Algorithms and Architectures*, ACM Press, New York, 1998, pp. 279–288.

Cheung D.W. and Y. Xiao. (1999) Effect of Data Distribution in Parallel Mining of Association, *Data Mining and Knowledge Discovery*, Kluwer Academic Publishers, 3, 291-314.

Chien, S.A. (1989) Using and refining simplifications: explanation-based learning of plans in intractable domains. In *Proceedings of IJCAI-89*, Detroit, Michigan, USA.

Chickering, D and Heckerman, D. (1996) Efficient approximations for the marginal likelihood of incomplete data given a Bayesian network. *Technical Report MSR-TR-96-08*, Microsoft Research, Redmond, WA.

Clark, P. and T. Niblett. (1989) The CN2 induction algorithm. *Machine Learning*, 3(4): 261.

Cohen, W.W. (1988) Generalizing number and learning from multiples in explanation based learning. In *Proceedings of ICML-88*, San Mateo, CA.

Cook, D.J. (1991) The base selection task in analogical learning. In *Proceedings of IJCAI-91*, 790-795.

Cooper, M.C. (1989) An optimal k-consistency algorithm. *Artificial Intelligence*, 41: 89-95.

Cooper, Greg F. and Herskovits, E. (1992) A Bayesian Method for the Induction of Probabilistic Networks from Data. *Machine Learning*, 1992(9): 309-347

Cui, Z., A.G. Cohn, D.A. Randell. (1992) Qualitative simulation based on a logical formalism of space and time. *AAAI-92*, 679-684.

DARPA. (1989) *Case-based reasoning*. In Proceedings of Case-based Reasoning Workshop.

Danyluk, A.P. (1987) The use of explanations for similarity-based learning. In *Proceedings of IJCAI-87*, Milan, Italy.

Dasarathy, B.V. (1991) Nearest Neighbor (NN) Norms: NN Pattern Classification Techniques. IEEE Computer Society Press, Los Alamitos, CA.

Davies, S. (1997) Multidimensional triangulation and interpolation for reinforcement learning. In: Michael C Mozer, Michael I Jordan, Thomas Petsche, eds. *Advances in Neural Information Processing Systems 9*, NY: MIT Press, 1005-1010.

Davies, T.R. and S.J. Russell. (1987) A logical approach to reasoning by analogy. In *Proceedings of IJCAI-87*, Milan, Italy.

Davis, A.L. and A. Rosenfeld. (1981) Cooperating Process for low-level vision: A survey. *Artificial Intelligence*, 17:245-263.

Davis, D. (1987) Constraint propagation with interval labels. *Artificial Intelligence*, 32: 281-331.

Davis, L. (editor) (1987) *Genetic algorithms and simulated annealing*. Pitman.

Davis, R. (1984) Diagnosis reasoning from structure and behavior. *Artificial Intelligence*, 24: 347-410.

Davis, R. (1983) Diagnosis via Causal Reasoning: Paths of Interaction and the Locality Principles, in: *Proceedings AAAI-83*, Washington, D.C., 88-92.

de Kleer, J. (1984) How circuits work. *Artificial Intelligence*, 24: 205-280.

de Kleer, J. (1986) An assumption-based TMS. *Artificial Intelligence*, 28: 127-162.

de Kleer, J. (1989) A comparison of ATMS and CSP techniques. In *Proceedings of IJCAI-89*, Menlo Park, 290-296.

de Kleer, J. (1993) A view on qualitative physics. *Artificial Intelligence*, 59: 105-114.

de Kleer, J. and J. Brown. (1984) A qualitative physics based on confluences. *Artificial Intelligence*, 24: 205-280.

de Roure, D., N. R. Jennings, N. Shadbolt (2005) The Semantic Grid: Past, Present and Future. *Proc. of the IEEE* **93** (3) 669-681.

Dechter, R. and J. Pearl. (1987) Network-based heuristics for constraint network. *Artificial Intelligence*, 34: 1-38.

Dechter, R. and J. Pearl. (1987) The cycle-cutset method for improving search performance in AI applications. in *Proceedings 3rd IEEE on AI Applications*, Orlando, FL.

Dechter, R. and J. Pearl. (1987) Tree clustering for constraint networks. *Artificial Intelligence*, 28: 342-403.

Dechter, R. (1989/90) Enhancement for Constraint Processing: Backjumping, Learning, and Cutset Decomposition. *Artificial Intelligence*, 41: 273-312.

Decker, K. and V. Lesser. (1993) An approach to analyzing the need for meta-level communication, *IJCAI-93*, 360-366.

Decker, K. Environment Centered Analysis and Design of Coordination Mechanisms. *PhD thesis*, University of Massachusetts,1995.

Deerwester, S., Dumais, S. T., Furnas, G W., Landauer, T. K., Harshman, R. (1990) Indexing by latent semantic analysis, *Journal of the American Society for Information Science, 41.*

DeJong, G. (1979) Skimming stories in real time: an experiment in integrated understanding. Dept. of Computer Science, Yale University.

DeJong, G. (1981) Generalizations based on explanations. In *Proceedings of IJCAI-81,* Vancouver, B.C.

DeJong, G. (1982) Automatic schema acquisition in a natural language environment. In ***Proceedings of AAAI-82,*** Pittsburgh, Pa.

DeJong, G. (1983) Acquiring schemata through understanding and generalizing plans. In Proceedings of IJCAI-83, Karlsruhe, W. Ger.

DeJong, G. (1986) An approach to learning from observation. In Michalski, R.S., J.G. Carbonell and T.M. Mitchell (editors), *Machine Learning: An Artificial Intelligence Approach,* Morgan Kaufmann.

DeJong, G. and R. Mooney. (1986) Explanation-based learning: an alternative view, *Machine Learning,* 1(2): 145.

DeJong, G. (1988) Some thoughts on the present and future of explanation-based learning. In Proceedings of the ECAI-88.

De Jong, K. (1988) Learning with genetic algorithms: an overview. *Machine Learning,* 3(2): 121.

De Jong, K.A. (2006) Evolutionary computation: a unified approach. MIT Press, Cambridge MA.

Delahaye, J.P. (1987) *Formal methods in artificial intelligence.* North Oxford Academic Pub. Ltd.

Dershowitz, N. (1986) Programming by analogy. In Michalski, R.S., J.G. Carbonell and T.M. Mitchell (editors), *Machine Learning: An Artificial Intelligence Approach,* Morgan Kaufmann.

Dietterich, T.G. (1984) Constraint propagation techniques for theory-driven data interpretation, Dept. of Computer Science, Stanford University.

Dietterich, T.G. (1989) Limitations on inductive learning. In *Proceedings of IWML-89,* Cornell University, Ithaca, New York.

Dietterich, T.G. and R.S. Michalski. (1981) Inductive learning of structural descriptions: evaluation criteria and comparative review of selected methods, *Artificial Intelligence,* 16(3): 257-94.

Dietterich, T.G., B. London, K. Clarkson and G. Dromey. (1982) Learning and inductive inference. In Cohen, P.R. and E.A. Feigenbaum (editors), *The Handbook of Artificial Intelligence,* Kaufmann.

Dietterich, T.G. and R.S. Michalski. (1983) A comparative review of selected methods for learning from examples, In Michalski, R.S. and J.G. Carbonell and T.M. Mitchell (editors), *Machine Learning: An Artificial Intelligence Approach,* Tioga.

Dietterich, T.G. and R.S. Michalski. (1986) Learning to predict sequences, In Michalski, R.S. and J.G. Carbonell and T.M. Mitchell (editors), *Machine Learning: An Artificial Intelligence Approach,* Morgan Kaufmann.

Dietzen, S. and F. Pfenning. (1989) Higher-order and model logic as a framework for explanation-based generalization. In *Proceedings of IWML-89,* Cornell University, Ithaca, New York.

Domeshek, E., Kolodner, J. and Zimring, C. (1994) The Design of a Tool Kit for Case-Based Design Aids. In *Artificial Intelligence in Design, Norwell*, Ma., Kluwer.

Doran J. E., S. Franklin, N. R. Jennings, T. J. Norman. (1997) On cooperation in multi-agent systems. *The Knowledge Engineering Revue*, 12(3): 309-314.

Doyle, J. (1979) A truth maintenance system. *Artificial Intelligence*, 12(3): 231-72.

Durfee, E.H., V.R. Lesser and D.D. Corkill. (1987) Cooperation through communication in a distributed problem solving network. in *Distributed Artificial Intelligence*, Pitman Publishing.

Durfee, E. H. and Lesser, V. R. (1991) Partial Global Planning: A Coordination Framework for Distributed Hypothesis Formation. IEEE *Transactions on Systems, Man, and Cybernetics*, Special Issue on Distributed Sensor Networks, SMC-21(5):1167--1183.

Ebbinghaus, H-D. (1985) Extended logics: The general framework. in *Model-Theoretic Logic*, Spriger-Verlag.

Edward R. Omiecinski. (2003) Alternative interest measures for mining associations in databases. *IEEE Transactions on Knowledge and Data Engineering,* 15(1):57-69.

Ellman, T. (1988) Approximate theory formation: an explanation-based approach, In *Proceedings of AAAI-88*, Saint Paul, Minnesota.

Ellman, T. (1989) Explanation-based learning: programs and perspectives, *ACM Computing Surveys*, 21(2): 163-221.

Epstein, S.L. (1987) On the discovery of mathematical theorems. In *Proceedings of IJCAI-87*, Milan, Italy.

Ernst, G.W. and M.M. Goldstein. (1982) Mechanical discovery of classes of problem-solving strategies. *Journal of the ACM*, 29(1): 1-23.

Etzioni, O. (1988) Hypothesis filtering: a practical approach to reliable learning. In *Proceedings of ICML-88*, San Mateo, CA.

Falkenhainer, B. (1985) Proportionality graphs, units analysis, and domain constraints: improving the power and efficiency of the scientific discovery process. In *Proceedings of IJCAI85*, Los Angeles, Calif.

Falkenhainer, B. (1987) Scientific theory formation through analogical inference. In *Proceedings of the 4WML,* University of California, Irvine.

Falkenhainer, B.C. and R.S. Michalski. (1986) Integrating quantitative and qualitative discovery: the ABACUS system. *Machine Learning*, 1(4): 367.

Fayyad, U., G. Piatetsky-Shapiro, and P. Smyth. (1996) From data mining to knowledge discovery in databases. *AI Magazine*, Fall, 37-54.

Fayyad U, Piatetsky-Shapiro, Smyth, and Uthurusamy. (1996a) *Advances in Knowledge Discovery and Data Mining*, MIT Press.

Feigenbaum, E.A. and J. Feldman. (1963) *Computers and Thought*. McGraw-Hill.

Feigenbaum, E A. (2003) Some challenges and grand challenges for computational intelligence. *Journal of the ACM*, 2003(1).

Ferber, J. (1991) Actors and agents as reflective concurrent objects: a merging IV perspective. *SMC-21*: 991.

Ferguson, I. A. (1991) Towards an architecture for adaptive, rational, mobile agents. In Werner and Demazeau(eds.) *Decentralised AI 3* --Proc. of the 3rd European Workshop on Mod.

FIPA. (1996) FIPA Application Types. http://www.cselt.stet.it/fipa/yorktown/

Fisher, D.H. and P. Langley. (1985) Approaches to conceptual clustering. In *Proceedings of IJCAI-85*, Los Angeles, Calif.

Fisher, D.H. (1987a) Improving inference through conceptual clustering. In *Proceedings of AAAI-87*, Seattle, Washington.

Fisher, D.H. (1987b) Knowledge acquisition via incremental conceptual clustering. *Machine Learning*, 2: 139-172.

Fisher, D.H. and K.B. McKusick. (1989) An empirical comparison of ID3 and back-propagation. In *Proceedings of IJCAI-89*, Detroit, Michigan USA.

Fisher, D.H. (1989) Noise-tolerant conceptual clustering. In *Proceedings of IJCAI-89*, Detroit, Michigan USA.

Fitzpatrick, J.M. and J.J. Grefenstette. (1988) Genetic algorithms in noisy environments. *Machine Learning*, 3(2): 101.

Flach, P.A. (1987) Second-order inductive learning. In Jantke, K.P., (editors), *Analogical and Inductive Inference*, Springer-Verlag.

Forbus, K.D. (1984) Qualitative Process Theory. *Artificial Intelligence*, Vol. 24,96-168, 1984.

Forbus, K.D. and D. Gentner. (1986) Learning physical domains: toward a theoretic framework. In Michalski, R.S. and J.G. Carbonell and T.M. Mitchell (editors), *Machine Learning: An Artificial Intelligence*, Morgan Kaufmann.

Forbus, K.D., P. Nielsen and B. Faltings. (1991) Qualitative spatial reasoning: the CLOCK project. *Artificial Intelligence*, Vol. 51, 417-471.

Forbus, K.D. (1993) Qualitative Process Theory: twelve years after. *Artificial Intelligence*, 59, 115-123.

Forsyth, R. (1984) Machine learning systems. In *Proceedings of the Association for Library and Information Management*, London.

Freeman-Benson, B. and A. Borning. (1992) Integrating Constraints with an object-Oriented language, In *Proceedings of the 1992 European Conference on Object-Oriented Programming*, 268-286.

Freund, Y. Schapire, R. E. (1995) A decision-theoretic generalization of on-line learning and an application to boosting. *Proc. Of the Second European Conference on Computational Learning*

Freuder, E.L. (1982) A sufficient condition of backtracking-free search. *J. ACM*, 29(1): 24-32.

Freuder, E.L. (1988) Backtrack-Free and backtrack bound Search. In *Search in Artificial Intelligence*, L. Kanal and V. Kumar (eds.), 343-369,New York: Springer-Verlag.

Freuder, E.L. (1989) Partial constraint satisfaction, in *Proceedings of IJCAI-89*, 278-283.

Fu, Wai-Tat, John R. Anderson. (2006) From Recurrent Choice to Skill Learning: A Reinforcement-Learning Model. Journal of Experimental Psychology: General **135** (2): 184 –206.

Gallier, J.H. (1986) *Logic for Computer Science*. Harper and Row.

Galton, A. (1993) Towards an integrated logic of space, time and motion. *IJCAI-93*, 1550-1555.

Genello, R. and F. Mana. (1991) Rigel: an inductive learning system. *Machine Learning*, 6(1): 7-35.

Gasser, L., C. Bragaza and N. Herman. (1987) MACE: A flexible testbed for distributed AI research, in *Distributed Artificial Intelligence*, Pitman Publishing.

Genesereth, M.R. and N.J. Nilsson. (1987) *Logical Foundation of Artificial Intelligence.* Morgan Kaufmann.

Gennari, J.H., Pat. Langley and Doug Fisher. (1989) Models of incremental concept formation. *Artificial Intelligence*, 40(1): 11-61.

Gennari, J.H. (1989) Focused concept formation. In *Proceedings of IWML-89*, Cornell University, Ithaca, New York.

Gentner, D. (1983) Structure-mapping: A theoretical framework for analogy. *Cognitive Science*, 7(2): 155-170.

Gerwin, D.G. (1974) Information processing, data inferences, and scientific generalization. *Behav. Sci.,* 19: 314-325.

Gick, M.L. and K.J. Holyoak, (1983) Schema induction and analogical transfer. *Cognitive Psychology*, 15: 1-38.

Ginsberg, A. (1988) Theory revision via prior operationalization. In *Proceedings of AAAI-88*, Saint Paul, Minnesota.

Ginsberg, M. L. (1986) Counterfactuals. *Artificial Intelligence*, 30: 35-79.

Goebel, R. (1987) A sketch of analogy as reasoning with equality hypotheses. In Jantke, K.P. (editors), *Analogical and Inductive Inference*, Springer-Verlag.

Gold, E.M. (1967) Language identification in the limit. *Information and Control*, 10: 447-74.

Goldberg, D.E. (1985) Dynamic system control using rule learning and genetic algorithm. in *Proceedings of IJCAI-85*, Los Angeles, Calif.

Goldberg, D.E. and H. Holland. (1988) Genetic algorithms and machine learning. *Machine Learning*, 3(2): 95.

Goldberg, D.E. (1989) *Genetic Algorithms in Search, Optimization, and Machine Learning.* Addison-Wesley Publishing Com., Inc.

Golding, A., P.S. Rosenbloom and J.E. Laird. (1987) Learning general search control from outside guidance. In *Proceedings of IJCAI-87*, Milan, Italy.

Grahne, G., Zhu, J. (2003) Efficiently using prefix-trees in mining frequent itemsets. In: *First Workshop on Frequent Itemset Mining Implementation (FIMI'03).* Melbourne, FL

Greco, Salvatore, Matarazzo, Benedetto and Słowiński, Roman. (2001) Rough sets theory for multicriteria decision analysis. *European Journal of Operational Research* **129** (1): 1–47.

Green, C. (1969) Theorem proving by resolution as a basis for question answering systems. In Michie, D. and B. Meltzer (editors), *Machine Intelligence 4*, Edinburgh University Press.

Grefenstette, J.J. (1988a) Credit assignment in rule discovery systems based on genetic algorithms. *Machine Learning*, 3(2): 225-246.

Grefenstette, J.J. (1988b) Credit assignment in genetic learning systems. in *Proceedings of AAAI-88*, Saint Paul, Minnesota.

Grefenstette, J.J. (1989) Incremental learning of control strategies with genetic algorithms. In *Proceedings of IWML-89*, Cornell University, Ithaca, New York.

Greiner, R. (1989) Learning by Understanding Analogies. *Artificial Intelligence*, Vol. 35, No. 1.

Grosz, B. and Sarit Kraus. (1996) Collaborative plans for complex group actions. *Artificial Intelligence*, 86(2): 269-357.

Grzymala-Busse, Jerzy W. (1997) A New Version of the Rule Induction System LERS. *Fundam. Inform.* 31(1): 27-39.

Grzymala-Busse, Jerzy W., Yiyu Yao. (2008) A Comparison of the LERS Classification System and Rule Management in PRSM. *RSCTC 2008*: 202-210

Gu, J. (1992) Efficient local search for very large-scale satisfiability problems. *Sigart Bulletin*, 3(1): 8-12.

Guha, R.V. and D.B. Lenat. (1990) Cyc: A midterm report. *AI Magazine*, Fall,32-59.

Hadzikadic, M. and D.Y.Y. Yun. (1989) Concept formation by incremental conceptual clustering. In *Proceedings of IJCAI-89*, Detroit, Michigan USA.

Hall, R. (1988) Learning by failing to explain using partial explanations to learn in incomplete or intractable domain. *Machine Learning*, 3(1): 45.

Hall, R.P. (1989) Computational approaches to analogical reasoning: a comparative analysis. *Artificial intelligence*, 39(1): 39-120.

Hammond, K.J. (1986) CHEF: A model of case-based planning. in *Proceedings of AAAI-86*, Philadelphia, PA.

Hammond, K.J. (1990) Explaining and Repairing Plans That Fail. in *Artificial Intelligence* 45.

Harmelen, F. van and A. Bundy (1988) Explanation-based generalization = partial evaluation. *Artificial Intelligence*, 36, 401-412.

Han J. and M. Kamber. (2006) *Data Mining: Concepts and Techniques (2nd edition)*. Morgan Kaufmann.

Han J., J. Pei, and Y.Yin. Mining. (2000) Frequent patterns without candidate generation. In *Proc. 2000 ACM-SIGMOD Int. Conf. Management of Data (SIGMOD'00)*, pp. 1-12.

Han, Jiawei, Jian Pei, Yiwen Yin, and Runying Mao. (2004) Mining frequent patterns without candidate generation. *Data Mining and Knowledge Discovery* 8:53-87.

Haussler, D. (1987) Learning conjunctive concepts in structural domains, In *Proceedings of AAAI-87*, Seattle, Washington.

Haussler, D. (1988) New theoretical directions in machine learning. *Machine Leaning*, 2(4): 281.

Haussler, D. (1988) Quantifying inductive bias: AI learning algorithms and Valiant's learning framework. *Artificial Intelligence*, 36, 177-221.

Haussler, D. (1989) Generalizing the PAC model: sample size bounds from metric dimension-based uniform convergence results. in *Proceedings of the Second Annual Workshop on Computational Learning Theory*, Santa Cruz, CA.

Hayes-Roth, F. and D.J. Mostow. (1981) Machine transformation of advice into a heuristic search procedure. In J.R. Anderson (editor), *Cognitive Skills and Their Acquisition*, Erlbaum, Hillsdale, NJ.

Hayes-Roth, F. (1983) Using proofs and refutations to learn from experience. In R.S. Michalski, J.G. Carbonell and T.M. Mitchell (editors), *Machine Learning: An Artificial Intelligence Approach*, Tigoa.

Hayes-Roth, F., D.A. Waterman and D.B. Lenat. (1983) *Building Expert Systems*. Addison Wesley.

Hebb, D.O. (1949) *The organization of behavior*. Wiley.

Heckerman, D. (1997) Bayesian Networks for Data Mining. *Data Mining and Knowledge Discovery*, 1:79-119.

Hewitt, C. and DeJong, P. (1983) Analyzing the roles of descriptions and actions in open systems, In *AAAI*.

Hewitt, C. (1991) Open systems semantics for distributed artificial intelligence. *Artificial Intelligence*, 47: 79-106.

Hinton, G.E. (1989) Connectionist learning procedures. *Artificial Intelligence*, 40(1): 185-234.

Hirsh, H. (1987) Explanation-based generalization in a logic-programming environment. in *Proceedings of IJCAI-87*, Milan, Italy, 221-227.

Hirsh, H. (1988) Reasoning about operationality for explanation-based learning. in *Proceedings of ICML-88*, San Mateo, CA.

Hirsh, H. (1989) Combining empirical and analytical learning with version spaces. in *Proceedings of IWML-89*, Cornell University, Ithaca, New York.

Hofstadter, D. (1985) Analogies and roles in human and machine thinking. In Hofstadter, D. (editors), *Metamagical Themas*, Basic Books.

Holland, J.H. (1971) Proceeding and processors for schemata. In E.L. Jacks, (editors), *Associative Information Processing*, American Elsevier.

Holland, J.H. (1975) *Adaptation in Natural and Artificial Systems*. University of Michigan Press.

Holland, J.H. (1985) Properties of the bucket brigade algorithm. In *Proceedings of an International Conference on Genetic Algorithms and Their Applications*, Pittsburg, PA.

Holland, J.H. (1986) Escaping brittleness: The possibilities of general-purpose learning algorithms applied to parallel rule-based systems. in Michalski, R.S. and J.G. Carbonell and T.M. Mitchell (editors), *Machine Learning: An Artificial Intelligence Approach*, Morgan Kaufmann.

Holland, J.H., K.J. Holyoak, R.E. Nisbett and P.R. Thagard. (1986). *Induction: Processes of Inference, Learning, and Discovery*, The MIT Press.

Holyoak, K.J. and P. Thagard. (1989) Analogical mapping by constraint satisfaction. *Cognitive Science*, 13, 295-355.

Hu, Xiaohua. (1995) *Knowledge discovery in database: an attribute-oriented rough set approach.* Dissertation, Regina.

Huberman, B. A., Tad Hogg. (1987) Phase Transitions in Artificial Intelligence Systems. *Artif. Intell.* 33(2): 155-171.

Hunt, E.B., J. Marin and P.T. Stone. (1966) *Experiments in Induction*. Academic Press.

Iba, G.A. (1979) *Learning disjunctive concepts from examples*. Master's thesis, MIT.

Inmon, W. H. (1992) *Building the Data Warehouse*. QED Technical Publishing Group

Inmon, W.H. (1996) The data warehouse and data mining. *CACM*, No. 11.

Iwasaki, Y., H. A. Simon. (1986) Causality in Device Behavior. *Artif. Intell.* 29(1): 3-32

Jennings, N.R. (1993). Commitments and Conventions: The foundation of Coordination in Multi-Agent System. *The Knowledge Engineering Review*, 8(3): 233-250

Jennings N.R. (2000) On Agent-Based Software Engineering. *Artificial Intelligence Journal* **117** (2) 277-296.

Jennings N. R., A. G. Cohn, M. Fox, D. Long, M. Luck, D. T. Michaelides, S. Munroe and M. J. Weal (2006) Interaction, planning and motivation. in *Cognitive systems: Information processing meets brain science* (eds R. Morris, L. Taressenko and M. Kenward) Elsevier, 163-188.

Jiao, Wenpin, Zhongzhi SHI. (2000) Methodology for Agent-Oriented Software Analysis and Design and its Software-Supporting Environment. In *the 16th IFIP World Computer Congress: ICS2000 - Software - Theory and Practice*, Beijing, China.

Jin L., Keith Decker. (2006) KDMAS: A Multi-Agent System for Knowledge Discovery via Planning. *AAAI 2006*, 1877-1878.

Johnson-Laird, P.N. (1988) *The computer and the mind: an introduction to cognitive science*. Harvard University Press.

Kaelbling, Leslie P., Michael L. Littman, Andrew W. Moore (1996). Reinforcement Learning: A Survey. *Journal of Artificial Intelligence Research* 4: 237–285.

Kally, K.T. (1988) Theory discovery and the hypothesis language. in *Proceedings of ICML-88*, San Mateo, CA.

Keane, M. T. (1988) *Analogical Problem-Solving*. Ellis Horwood Limited.

Kearns, M., Ming Li, L. Pitt and L. G. Valiant. (1987) Recent results on Boolean concept learning. in *4WML*.

Kearns, M. and L. Pitt. (1989) A polynomial-time algorithm for learning k-variable pattern languages from examples. in *Proceedings of the Second Annual Workshop on Computational Learning Theory*, Santa Cruz, CA.

Kedar-Cabelli, S. (1987) Formulating concepts according to purpose. in *Proceedings of AAAI-87*.

Kedar-Cabelli, S.T. (1985) Purpose-directed analogy. in *Proceedings of the Cognitive Science Society*, Irvine, Calif.

Kedar-Cabelli, S.T. (1988) Analogy: from a unified perspective. in D.H. Helman, (editor), *Analogical Reasoning: Perspectives of Artificial Intelligence*, Cognitive Science, and Philosophy.

Keller, R.M. (1987) Defining operationality for explanation-based learning, in *Proceedings of AAAI-87*.

Kephart, J.O. and D. Chess. (2003) The Vision of Autonomic Computing. Computer, 36(1): 41–50.

Kerber, M. (1987) Some aspects of analogy in mathematical reasoning, in K.P. Jantke (editor), *Analogical and Inductive Inference*, Springer-Verlag.

Kerber, R.G. (1988) Using a generalization hierarchy to learn from examples. in *Proceedings of ICML-88*, San Mateo, CA.

Kirsh, D. (1991) Foundations of AI: the big issues. *Artificial Intelligence*, 47: 3-30.

Kodratoff, Y. (1988) *Introduction to machine learning*. Pitman.

Kohonen, T. (1984) *Self Organization and Associate Memory*. Springer-Verlag.

Kokar, M. M. (1986) Determining arguments of invariant functional descriptions. *Machine Learning*, 1, 403-422.

Kolodner, J. L., R. L. Simpson and K. Sycara. (1985) A process model of case-based reasoning in problem solving. in *Proceedings of IJCAI-85*, Los Angeles, Calif.

Kolodner, J. L. (1987) Extending problem solver capabilities through case-based inference. in *Proceedings of the Fourth International Workshop on Machine Learning*, University of California, Irvine.

Kolodner, J.L. (1988) Retrieving events from a case memory: a parallel implementation. in *Proceedings of Case-based Reasoning Workshop*.

Kolodner, J. L. (1993) *Case-Based Reasoning*. Morgan Kaufmann.

Maciej Komosinski and Andrew Adamatzky. (2009) *Artificial Life Models in Software.* New York: Springer.

Kota R., N. M. Gibbins and N. R. Jennings. (2009) Self-organising agent organisations. *Proc. 8th Int. Conf on Autonomous Agents and Multi-Agent Systems*, Budapest, Hungary, 797-804.

Koulichev, V. N. (1990) *Generalization in Case-based Machine Learning.* master thesis, University of Trondheim, Norway, February.

Koza, J.R. (1989) Hierarchical genetic algorithms operating on populationist learning algorithms. in *Proceedings of IJCAI-89*, Detroit, Michigan USA.

Kraus, S. Negotiation and Cooperation in Multi-Agent Environments. *Artificial Intelligence Journal*, Special Issue on Economic Principles of Multi-Agent Syste.

Kuipers, B.J. (1984) Common sense reasoning about causality. *Artificial Intelligence*, Vol. 24,169-203.

Kuipers, B.J. (1986) Qualitative simulation. *Artificial Intelligence*, Vol. 29, 289-338.

Kuipers, B.J. (1993) Reasoning with qualitative models. *Artificial Intelligence*, Vol. 59, 125-132.

Kulis, Brian, Sugato Basu, Inderjit Dhillon. (2009) Semi-supervised graph clustering: a kernel approach. *Mach Learn* 74: 1–22.

Kurtzberg, J. M. (1987) Feature analysis for symbol recognition by elastic matching, in: *int' l Business Machines J. of Research and Development*, 31:91- 9.

Kumar, V. (1992) Algorithms for constraint satisfaction problems: a survey. *AI magazine*, 13 (1): 32-44.

Laird, J. (1988) Recovery from incorrect knowledge in SOAR. in *Proceedings of AAAI-88*, Saint Paul, Minnesota.

Laird, J.E, P.S. Rosenbloom and A. Newell. (1986) Chunking in SOAR: The anatomy of a general learning mechanism, *Machine Learning*, 1(1): 11.

Laird, J.E. and A. Newell. (1983) A universal weak method: summary of results. in *Proceedings of IJCAI-83*, Karlsruhe, W. Ger.

Laird, J.E. and P.S. Rosebbloom. (1984) Toward chunking as a general learning mechanism. in *Proceedings of AAAI-84*, Austin, Tex.

Laird, P.D. (1988) *Learning from good and bad data.* Kluwer Academic Publishers.

Langley, P.W. (1978) BACON. 1: A general discovery system. in *Proceedings of the Canadian Society for Computational Studies of Intelligence*, Toronto.

Langley, P.W. (1986) On machine learning. *Machine Learning*, 1(1): 5.

Langley, P.W. and J.M. Zytkow. (1989) Data-driven approaches to empirical discovery. *Artificial Intelligence*, 40(1): 283-312.

Langton, C.G. (ed.) (1989) *Artificial Life.* Redwood City, CA: Addison-Wesley.

Langton, C.G., Taylor, C., Farmer, J.D., Rasmussen, S. (eds.) (1992) *Artificial Life II.* Redwood City, CA: Addison-Wesley.

Langton, C.G. (Ed.) (2000) *Artificial life: An overview.* Cambridge: MIT Press.

Lee S.-I., V. Ganapathi, and D. Koller. (2007) Efficient Structure Learning of Markov Networks using L1-Regularization. *Advances in Neural Information Processing Systems.*

Leech, G., Garside, R., Bryant, M. (1994) CLAWS: the tagging of the British national corpus. In *Proc of 15th Int' l Conf on Cimputation Linguistics*, Kyoto, Japan

Leler, W. (1988) *Constraint programming languages:Their Specification and generation*. Addison-Wesley Publishing Company.

Lenat, D.B. (1976) AM: An artificial intelligence approach to discovery in mathematics as heuristic search. Dept. of Computer Science, Stanford University.

Lenat, D. B. (1995) CYC: A Large-Scale investment in knowledge infrastructure. *Commun. ACM*, 38(11): 32-38.

Lenat, D. B. (2005) Applied ontology issues. *Applied Ontology*, 1(1): 9-12.

Lenat, D.B., R.V. Guha, K. Pittman, D. Pratt and M. Shepherd. (1990) CYC: toward programs with common sense. *CACM*, 33(8) .

Lesser, V.R. (1991) A retrospective view of fa/c distributed problem solving. *IEEE Transactions on Systems, Man, and Cybernetics*, Special Issue on Distributed Artificia.

Levesque, H.J. (1990) All I know: a study in autoepistemic logic. *Artificial Intelligence*, 42: 263-309.

Lhomme, O. (1993) Consistency techniques for numeric CSPs. IJCAI-93, 232-238.

Lesser, V.R., L.D. Erman. (1980) Distributed interpretation: a model and experiment. *IEEE Transaction on Computer*, C-29: 1144-1163.

Lesser, V.R. (1991) A retrospective view of FA/C distributed problem solving. *IEEE Trans. SMC*, SMC-21.

Li, Jianhui and Jiang Zhang. (2006) *Digit create century—artificial life*(in Chinese). Beijing: Science Press.

Liao, Lejian and Zhongzhi Shi. (1992) Default reasoning in constraint network. *Proceedings of the International Workshop on Automated Reasoning*, Zhongzhi Shi (ed.), 35-39.

Liao, Lejian, Zhongzhi Shi, Shijun Wang. (1994) Influence-based Backjumping Combined with Most-Constrained-First and Domain Filtering. *DKSME-94*, pp. 657-662.

Liao, Lejian, Zhongzhi Shi. (1995) Minimal Model Semantics for Sorted Constraint Representation. *J. of Computer Science and Technology*, 10(5): 439-446, 1995.

Liepins, G.E., M.R. Hilliard, M. Palmer and G. Rangarajan. (1989) Alternatives for classifier system credit assignment. in *Proceedings of IJCAI-89*, Detroit, Michigan USA.

Lin, Fangzhen and Reiter, R. (1994) How to progress a database (and why) I: logic foundations. *4th International Conference on Principles of Knowledge Representation and Reasoning*.

Littlestone, N. (1988) Learning quickly when irrelevant attributes abound: A new linear-threshold algorithm. Machine Learning, 2(4): 285.

Lloyd, J.W. (1987) *Foundations of Logic Programming*. Springer-Verlag.

Lu, Jianjiang and Liu Haifeng. (2000) General fuzzy association rules mining in databases. *Journal of Engineering Mathematics*. 17(1): 117-120.

Luger, George E. (2005) *Artificial Intelligence—Structures and Strategies for Complex Problem Solving (5th Edition)*. Addison-Wesley, Inc.

Lutz, C. and M. Milicic. (2007) A Tableau Algorithm for DLs with Concrete Domains and GCIs. *Journal of Automated Reasoning*, 38(1–3):227–259.

Lutz, C., Frank Wolter, and Michael Zakharyaschev. (2008) Temporal Description Logics: A Survey. In *Proceedings of the Fifteenth International Symposium on Temporal Representation and Reasoning*. IEEE Computer Society Press, 2008.

Lv, Cuiying. (1994). Explanation-based learning for touble diagnosis in petroleum distillation process. Ph.D. Dissertation, Graduate School of University of Petroleum.

Lynne, K.J. (1988) Competitive reinforcement learning. In *Proceedings of ICML-88*, San Mateo, CA.

Ma, Haibo. (1990) Eaplanation-based learning. Master Thesis, Institute of Computing Technology, Chinese Academy of Sciences.

Mackworth, A.K. (1977) Consistency in networks of relations. *Artificial Intelligence*, 8(1): 99-118.

Mahadevan, S. and P. Tadepalli. (1988) On the tractability of learning from incomplete theories, in Proceedings of ICML-88, San Mateo, CA.

Mahadevan, S. (1985) Verification-based learning: A generalized strategy for inferring problem-reduction methods, in *Proceedings of IJCAI-85*, Los Angeles, Calif.

Maes, P. (1989) The dynamics of action selection. In: *Proceedings of IJCAI-89*, PG991-997. Detroit, Michigan.

Manna, Z. and R. Waldinger. (1985) *The Logical basis for computer programming.* Addison-Wesley.

Mark, W., Simoudis, E., and Hinkle, D. (1996) Case-Based Expectations and Results. *Case-Based Reasoning* (Experiences, lessons, &Future Directions), AAAI/MIT Press, 269-294

Matheus, C.J. and L.A. Rendell. (1989) Constructive induction on decision trees, in *Proceedings of IJCAI-89*, Detroit, Michigan USA.

Mauldin, M.L. (1984) Maintaining diversity in genetic search. In *Proceedings of AAAI-84*, Austin, Tex.

Mayr, E 1988. *One Long Argument: Charles Darwin and the genesis of modern evolutionary thought*, Harvard University Press.

McCarthy, J. (1958) Programs with common sense. in *Proceedings of the Symposium on the mechanization of Thought Processes.*

McCarthy, J. (1968) Programs with Common Sense. in M. Minsky (editor), *Semantic Information Processing*, MIT Press.

McCarthy, J. (1980) Circumscription ---a form of non-monotonic reasoning. *Artificial Intelligence*, 13(1-2): 27-39.

McCarthy, J. (1986) Applications of circumscription to formalizing commonsense knowledge. *Artificial Intelligence*, 28: 89-116.

McCarthy, J. (2005) The future of AI-A manifesto. *AI Magazine*, 26(4): 39.

McDermott, D. and Doyle J. (1980) Non-monotonic logic I. *Artificial intelligence*, 13(1-2): 41-72.

McClelland, J.L. and Rumelhart, D.E. (1987) *Explorations in Parallel Distributed Processing: A Handbook of Models, Programs, and Exercises.* The MIT Press.

McDermott, D. (1982) Non-monotonic logic II: non-monotonic modal theories. *JACM*, 29(1): 33-57.

McGraw, K.L. and K. Harbison-Briggs. (1989) *Knowledge Acquisition: Principles and Guideline.* Prentice Hall.

Meng, Zuqiang, Zhongzhi Shi. (2009) A fast approach to attribute reduction in incomplete decision systems with tolerance relation-based rough sets. *Information Sciences.* 179 2774–2793.

Menascé Daniel A., Jeffrey O. Kephart, (2007) Autonomic computing. *IEEE Internet Computing*, Jan.-Feb.:18-21.

Michael L. (2009) Ant-Based Computing. *Artificial Life* Summer, Vol. 15, No. 3: 337–349.

Michalski, R.S. (1973) Discovering classification rules using variable-valued logic system VL1. in *Proceedings of IJCAI-73*, Stanford, Calif.

Michalski, R.S. (1975) Variable-valued logic and its applications to pattern recognition and machine learning. in D.C. Rine (editor), *Computer science and multiple-valued logic theory and applications*, North-Holland.

Michalski, R.S. (1980) Knowledge acquisition through conceptual clustering: A theoretical framework and an algorithm for partitioning data into conjunctive concepts. *Policy Analysis and Information Systems*, 4(3): 219-44.

Michalski, R.S. and R. E. Stepp. (1981) An application of AI techniques to structuring objects into an optimal conceptual hierarchy. in *Proceedings of IJCAI-81*, Vancouver, B.C.

Michalski, R.S. and R. Stepp and E. Diday. (1981) A recent advance in data analysis: Clustering objects into classes characterized by conjunctive concepts. in Kanal, L. and A. Rosenfeld (editors), *Pattern Recognition*, North-Holland.

Michalski, R.S. (1983) A theory and methodology of inductive learning. in R.S.

Michalski, J.G. Carbonell and T.M. Mitchell (editors), *Machine Learning: An Artificial Intelligence Approach*, Tioga.

Michalski, R.S. (1986) Understanding the nature of learning, in Michalski, R.S. and J.G. Carbonell and T.M. Mitchell (editors), *Machine Learning: An Artificial Intelligence Approach*, Morgan Kaufmann.

Michalski, R.S. and R. Stepp. (1983) Learning from observation: Conceptual clustering. in R.S. Michalski, J.G. Carbonell and T.M. Mitchell (editors), *Machine Learning: An Artificial Intelligence Approach*, Tioga.

Michalski, R.S., J.G. Carbonell and T.M. Mitchell. (1983) *Machine Learning: An Artificial Intelligence Approach*. Tioga.

Michalski, R.S. (1984) Inductive learning as rule-guided generalization of symbolic descriptions: A theory and implementation. in A.W. Bierman, G. Guiho and Y. Kodratoff (editors), *Automatic Program Techniques*, Macmillan.

Michalski, R.S., J.G. Carbonell and T.M. Mitchell. (1986) *Machine Learning: An Artificial Intelligence Approach*. Morgan Kaufmann.

Michalski, R.S., S. Amarel, D.B. Lenat, D. Michie and P.H. Winston. (1986) Machine learning: Challenges of the eighties. in R.S. Michalski, J.G. Carbonell and T.M. Mitchell (editors), *Machine Learning: An Artificial Intelligence Approach*, Morgan Kaufmann.

Michalski, R.S. (1989) Evolving Research in Machine Learning. *Summer School on Machine Learning*.

Michie, D. (1983) Inductive rule generation in the context of the fifth generation, in Proceedings of the International Machine Learning Workshop, Allerton House.

Mingers, J. (1989) An empirical comparison of selection measure for decision-tree induction, *Machine Learning*, 3(4), 319.

Minsky, M.L. (1954) *Theory of neural-analog reinforcement systems and its application to the brain-model problem.* Princeton University, Princeton, NJ.

Minsky, M. (1961) Steps Toward Artificial Intelligence. *Proceedings of the IRE*, vol. 49, No. 1., 8–30.

Minsky, M. (1975) A framework for representing knowledge. in Winston, P.H. (editor), *Psychology of Computer Vision*, McGraw-Hill.

Minsky, M. (1985) *The Society of Mind*. Simon and Schuster Inc.

Minsky, M. (1989) *Semantic Information Processing*. Cambridge, MA. : MIT Press, Hall.

Minsky, M. (2006) *The Emotion Machine: Commonsense Thinking, Artificial Intelligence,*
and the Future of the Human Mind. Simon & Schuster.

Minsky, M. and S. Papert. (1969, 1988) *Perceptrons*. MIT Press.

Minton, S. (1984) Constraint-based generalization: Learning game-playing plans from single examples. in *Proceedings of AAAI-84*, Austin, Tex.

Minton, S. (1985) Selectively generalizing plans for problem-solving. in *Proceedings of IJCAI-85*, Los Angeles, Calif.

Minton, S. and J.G. Carbonell. (1987) Strategies for learning search control rules: An explanation-based approach. in *Proceedings of IJCAI-87*, Milan, Italy.

Minton, S. (1988) Quantitative results concerning the utility of explanation-based learning. in *Proceedings of AAAI-88*, Saint Paul, Minnesota.

Minton, S. (1988) *Learning Search Control Knowledge: An Explanation-Based Approach*. Kluwer Academic Publishers.

Minton, S., J.G. Carbonell, C.A. Knoblock, D.R. Kuokka, O. Etzioni, Y. Gil. (1989) Explanation-based learning: A problem solving perspective. *Artificial Intelligence*, 40(1): 63-118.

Minton, S., A. B. Philips, P. Laird. (1992) Minimizing conflicts: a heuristic repair method for constraint satisfaction and scheduling problems. *Artificial Intelligence*, 58, 161-205.

Mitchell, T.M. (1977) Version spaces: A candidate elimination approach to rule learning. in *Proceedings of IJCAI-87*, Cambridge, Mass..

Mitchell, T.M. (1980) The need for biases in learning generalizations. *Technical Report CBM-TR-117*, Rutgers University.

Mitchell, T.M., P.E. Utgoff, B. Nudel and R. Banerji. (1981) Learning problem ---solving heuristics through practice. in *Proceedings of IJCAI-81*, Vancouver, B.C.

Mitchell, T.M. (1982) Generalization as Search. Artificial Intelligence,18(2): 203-26.

Mitchell, T.M., P.E. Utgoff and R.B. Banerji (1983) Learning by experimentation: Acquiring and refining problem —solving heuristics. in R.S. Michalski, J.G. Carbonell and T.M. Mitchell (editors), *Machine Learning: An Artificial Intelligence Approach*, Tioga.

Mitchell, T.M. (1983) Learning and problem solving. in *Proceedings of IJCAI-83*, Karlsruhe, W. Ger.

Mitchell, T.M. (1984) Toward combining empirical and analytic methods for learning heuristics. in A. Elithorn and R. Banerji (editors), *Human and Artificial Intelligence*, North-Holland.

Mitchell, T.M. (1997) *Machine Learning*. McGraw Hill.

Mitchell T., R. Hutchinson, M. Just, R.S. Niculescu, F. Pereira, X. Wang. (2003) Classifying Instantaneous Cognitive States from fMRI Data. *American Medical Informatics Association Symposium*.

Mitchell, T.M., S. Mahadevan and L.I. Steinberg. (1985) LEAP: A learning apprentice for VLSI design. in *Proceedings of IJCAI-85*, Los Angeles, Calif.

Mitchell, T.M., R.M. Keller and S.T. Kedar-Cabelli. (1986) Explanation-based generalization: A unifying view. *Machine Learning*, 1(1): 47.

Mo, Chunhua, Zhongzhi Shi. (1995) Artificial Animate: Sensor and Behavior, *ICCADG-95*.

Mohr, R. and Henderson, T.C. (1986) Arc and path consistency revisited. *Artificial Intelligence*, 28: 225-233.

Montana, D.J. and L. Davis. (1989) Training feedforward neural networks using genetic algorithms. in *Proceedings of IJCAI-89*, Detroit, Michigan USA.

Mooney, R. and G. DeJong. (1985) Learning schemata for natural language processing. in *Proceedings of IJCAI-85*.

Mooney, R., J. Shavlik, G. Towell and A. Gove. (1989) An experimental comparison of symbolic and connectionist learning algorithms. in *Proceedings of IJCAI-89*, Detroit, Michigan USA.

Mooney, R.J. (1988) Generalizing the order of operators in macro-operators. in *Proceedings of ICML-88*, San Mateo, CA.

Mooney, R.J. (1989) The effect of rule use on the utility of explanation-based learning. in *Proceedings of IJCAI'89*, Detroit.

Moore, A.W. (1994) The parti-game algorithm for variable resolution reinforcement learning in multidimensional state spa ces. In : Jack D Cowan, Gerald Tesauro, Joshua Alspector, eds. *Advances in Neural Information Processing Systems*, 6: Morgan Kaufmann Publishers, 711-718.

Moore, R.C. (1985) Semantical considerations on nonmonotonic logic. *Artificial Intelligence*, 25(1): 75-94.

Moore, R.C. (1993) Autoepistemic logic revisited. *Artificial Intelligence*, 59(1-2): 27-30.

Mostow, J. and N. Bhatnagar. (1987) Failsafe ---a floor planner that uses EBG to learn from its failures. in *Proceedings of IJCAI-87*, Milan, Italy.

Mostow, J. (1989) Design by derivational analogy: Issues in the automated replay of design plans. *Artificial Intelligence*, 40(1): 119-184.

Muggleton, S.H. and W. Buntine. (1988) Machine invention of first-order predicates by inverting resolution. in *Proceedings of IWML*.

Muhlenbein, H. and J. Kindermann. (1989) The dynamics of evolution and learning -- towards genetic neural networks. in R. Pfeifer and Z. Schreter and F. Fogelman-Soulie and L. Steels (editors), *Connectionism in Perspective*, North-Holland.

Muller, B. and J. Reinhardt. (1990) *Neural networks—an introduction*. Springer -Verlag.

Muller, J.P. and Pischel, M. (1994) Modelling interacting agents in dynamic environments. In: *Proceedings of the 11th European Conference on Artificial Intelligence (ECAI-94)*, 1994, 709-713.

Nadel, B.A. (1989) Constraint Satisfaction algorithms. *Computational Intelligence*, 5(4): 188-224.

Nadel, B. (1990) Tree search and arc consistency in constraint satisfaction algorithms. In *Search in Artificial Intelligence*, eds. L. Kanal and V. Kumar, 287-342. New York, Springer-Verlag.

Nair R., Milind Tambe. (2005) Hybrid BDI-POMDP Framework for Multiagent Teaming. *J. Artif. Intell. Res. (JAIR)* 23: 367-420.

Natarajan, B.K. and P. Tadepalli (1988) Two new frameworks for learning. in *Proceedings of ICML-88*, San Mateo, CA.

Nelwamondo, Vincent, Marwala, Tshilidzi. (2007) Rough sets: Rough Set Theory for the Treatment of Incomplete Data. *Proceedings of the IEEE Conference on Fuzzy Systems*.: 338–343.

Newell, A. (1990) *Unified Theories of Cognition*. Cambridge, Mass.: Harvard University Press.

Newell, A. (1992). Unified theories of cognition and the role of Soar. In *Soar: A Cognitive Architecture in Perspective*, eds. J. A. Michon and A. Anureyk. Dordrecht: Kluwer Academic Publishers.

Newell, A. and H.A. Simon. (1972) Human Problem Solving. Prentice-Hall.

Newell, A., & Simon, H.A. (1976). Computer science as empirical inquiry: Symbols and search. *Communications of the Association for Computing Machinery*, 19(3), 113-126.

Newell, A. and P. Rosenbloom. (1981) Mechanisms of skill acquisition and the law of practice. In Anderson, J.R., (editor), *Cognitive Skills and Their Acquisition*, Erlbaum.

Nickles, T. (1980) *Scientific discovery, logic, and rationality*. D. Reidel Publishing Company.

Niculescu, R.S., T.M. Mitchell, R.B. Rao. (2006) Bayesian Network Learning with Parameter Constraints. *Journal of Machine Learning Research,* 7, pp. 1357–1383, July.

Nigam, K., McCallum, A., Thrun, S. and Mitchell, T. (1998) Learning to Classify Text from Labeled and Unlabeled Documents. In *Proceedings of the Fifteenth National Conference on Artificial Intelligence (AAAI-98)*,792-799.

Nilsson, N.J. (1980) *Principles of Artificial Intelligence*. Tioga.

Nilsson, N.J. (2005) Human-Level Artificial Intelligence? Be Serious!. *The AI Magazine*, 26(4): 68-75.

Nilsson, N.J. (2007) The Physical Symbol System Hypothesis: Status and Prospects. in M. Lungarella, *et al.*, (eds.), *50 Years of AI, Festschrift*, LNAI 4850, pp. 9-17.

Nilsson, N.J., (2009) *The Quest for Artificial Intelligence: A History of Ideas and Achievements*. Cambridge University Press.

Norton, S.W. (1989) Generating better decision trees. in Proceedings of IJCAI-89, Detroit, Michigan USA.

O'Rorke, P. (1984) Generalization for explanation-based schema acquisition. in *Proceedings of AAAI-84*, Austin, Tex.

Osawa, E.I. (1993) A Schema for Agent Collaboration in Open Multiagent Environments. IJCAI-93, 352-359.

Padgham, L. and T. Zhang. (1993) A terminological Logic with defaults: A definition and an application. IJCAI-93, 662-668.

Pagallo, G. (1989) Learning DNF by decision trees. in *Proceedings of IJCAI-89*, Detroit, Michigan USA.

Pagallo, G. and D. Haussler. (1989) Two algorithms that learn DNF by discovering relevant features. in *Proceedings of IWML-89*, Cornell University, Ithaca, New York.

Paredis, J. (1993) Genetic state-space search for constrained optimization problems. *JCAI-93*, 952-959.

Pate J. l, W. T. L. Teacy, N. R. Jennings, M. Luck, S. Chalmers, N. Oren, T. J. Norman, A. Preece, P. M. D. Gray, G. Shercliff, P. J. Stockreisser, J. Shao, W. A. Gray, N. J.

Fiddian, S. Thompson. 2005) Agent-based virtual organisations for the Grid. *Int J. Multiagent and Grid Systems* **1** (4) 237-249.

Pawlak, Z. (1982) Rough sets. *International Journal of Information and Computer Science,* 11(5): 341-356.

Pawlak, Z. (1991) Rough Sets: Theoretical Aspects of Reasoning About Data. Kluwer Academic Publishers.

Pawlak, Z., Grzymala-Busse, J., Slowinski, R. and Ziarko, W. (1995) Rough sets. *CACM* 38(11): 89–95.

Pazzani, M.J. (1988) Integrated learning with incorrect and incomplete theories. in *Proceedings of ICML-88*, San Mateo, CA.

Pazzani, M.J. (1989) Explanation-based learning with weak domain theories. in Proceedings of IWML-89, Cornell University, Ithaca, New York.

Pednault, E. P. D. (1989) ADL: exploring the middle ground between STRIPS and the situation calculus. *Proceedings of the first international conference on Principles of knowledge representation and reasoning,* pp. 324 – 332.

Peters, Jan, Sethu Vijayakumar, Stefan Schaal. (2003) Reinforcement Learning for Humanoid Robotics. IEEE-RAS International Conference on Humanoid Robots.

Peters, J.F., Pawlak, Z. and Skowron, A. (2002) A rough set approach to measuring information granules, *Proceedings of COMPSAC 2002*, 1135-1139.

Pettit, E. and K.M. Swigger. (1983) An analysis of genetic-based pattern tracking and cognitive-based component tracking models of adapta tion. in *Proceedings of AAAI-83*, Washington, D.C.

Pitt, L. (1987) Inductive reference, DFAs, and computational complexity. in Jantke, K.P. (editor), *Analogical and Inductive Inference*, Springer-Verlag.

Poetschke, D. (1987) Analogical reasoning for second generation expert systems. in Jantke, K.P. (editor), *Analogical and Inductive Inference*, Springer-Verlag.

Politakis, P. and S.M. Weiss. (1984) Using empirical analysis to refine expert system knowledge bases. *Artificial Intelligence*, 22(1): 23-48.

Popper, K. (1968) *The Logic of Scientific Discovery.* Harper and Row.

Porat, S. (1991) Learning automata from ordered examples. *Machine Learning*, 7(2-3): 109-138.

Porter, B. and D. Kibler. (1984) Learning operator transformations. in *Proceedings of AAAI-84*, Austin, Tex.

Porter, B. (1984) *Learning problem solving.* Department of Computer and Information Science, University of California, Irvine.

Porter, B.W. and D.F. Kibler. (1986) Experimental goal regression: A method for learning problem-solving heuristics. *Machine Learning*, 1(3), 249.

Prieditis, A.E. and J. Mostow. (1987) PROLEARN: Towards a prolog interpreter that learns. in *Proceedings of AAAI-87*.

Prosser, P. (1991) Hybrid Algorithms for the constraint satisfaction problem. Research report, AISL-46-91, Computer Science Dept., Univ. of Strathclyde.

Prosser, P. (1993) Domain filtering can degrade intelligent backtracking search. In *Proceedings IJCAI-93*, 262-267.

Prosser, P. (1993) BM + BJ =BMJ. *Proceedings of CAIA- 93*, 257-262.

Purdom, P.W. Jr., C.A. Brown. (1983) An Analysis of Backtracking with Search Rearrangement. SIAM J. Comput. 12(4): 717-733.

Qian, Xuesheng. (1986) *On Noetic Science* (in Chinese). Shanghai: Shanghai People Press.

Qin, Liangxi, Ping Luo, Zhongzhi Shi. (2004) Efficiently mining frequent itemsets with compact FP-tree. *Intelligent Information Processing* 2004: 397-406

Quinlan, J.R. (1979) Discovering rules from large collections of examples: A case study. in Michie, D. (editor), *Expert Systems in the Micro Electronic Age*, Edinburgh University Press.

Quinlan, J.R. (1983) Learning efficient classification procedures and their application to chess end-games. in R.S. Michalski, J.G. Carbonell and T.M. Mitchell (editors), *Machine Learning: An Artificial Intelligence Approach*, Tioga.

Quinlan, J.R. (1986a) Induction of decision trees. *Machine Learning*, 1(1): 81.

Quinlan, J.R. (1986b) The effect of noise on concept learning. in R.S. Michalski, J.G. Carbonell and T.M. Mitchell (editors), *Machine Learning: An Artificial Intelligence Approach*, Morgan Kaufmann.

Quinlan, J.R. (1987) Generating production rules from decision trees. in *Proceedings of IJCAI-87*, Milan, Italy.

Quinlan, J.R. (1988) An empirical comparison of genetic and decision-tree classifiers. In *Proceedings of ICML-88*, San Mateo, CA.

Quinlan, J. R. (1993) *C4.5: Programs for Machine Learning*. Morgan Kaufmann Publishers Inc.

Rajamoney, S.A. (1988) Experimentation-based theory revision. in *Proceedings of the AAAI Spring Symposium on EBL*, Menlo Park, Calif.

Randall, D.A., Z. Cui and A.G. Cohn. (1992) A spatial logic based on regions and connection. *ICKRR'92*, 165-175.

Rao, A.S. and Georgeff, M. P. An Abstract Architecture for Rational Agents. In *Proc.of the 3rd International Conference on Principles of Knowledge Representation and Reasoning*, Morgan Kaufmann,1992

Redmond, M. (1989) Combining case-based reasoning, explanation-based learning, and learning from instruction. in *Proceedings of IWML-89*, Cornell University, Ithaca, New York.

Reinke, L.P. (1988) Criteria for polynomial-time(conceptual) clustering. *Machine Learning*, 2(4): 371.

Reiter, R. (1978) On closed world data bases. in H. Gallaire and J. Minker, (editors), *Logic and Data Bases*, Plenum Press.

Reiter, R. (1980) A logic for default reasoning. *Artificial Intelligence*, 13(1-2): 81-132.

Reiter, R. and G. Criscuolo. (1983) Some representational issues in default reasoning. *International Journal of Computers and Mathematics*, 9(1): 15-27.

Reiter, R. and J. de Kleer. (1987) Foundation of assumption based truth maintenance systems: Preliminary report. in *Proceedings AAAI-87*, Seattle WA.

Richie, G.D. and F.K. Hanna, 1984. AM: A case study in AI methodology. Artificial Intelligence, 23(3): 249-68.

Rieger, C., and Grinberg, M. (1977) The declarative representation and procedural simulation of causality in physical mechanisms. *IJCAI-97*, 250-256.

Riesbeck, C.K., and Schank, R.C. (1989) *Inside Case-based Reasoning*. Lawrence Erlbaum Associates, Inc., Publishers, Hillsdale, New Jersey.

Robertson, G.G. (1988) Population size in classifier systems. in *Proceedings of ICML-88*, San Mateo, CA.

Robertson, G.G. and R.L. Riolo. (1988) A tale of two classifier systems. *Machine Learning*, 3(2): 139.

Robinson, J.A. (1965) A machine-oriented logic based on the resolution principle. *JACM*, 12(1), 23-41.

Rogers A., D. D. Corkill and N. R. Jennings. (2009) Agent technologies for sensor networks. *IEEE Intelligent Systems* **24** (2) 13-17.

Rose, D. and P. Langley. (1986) Chemical discovery as belief revision. *Machine Learning*, 1(4), 423.

Rosenbloom, P.S. and A. Newell. (1982) Learning by chunking: summary of a task and a model, in *Proceedings of AAAI-82*, Pittsburgh, Pa.

Rosenbloom, P.S. (1983) The chunking of goal hierarchies: A model of practice and stimulus-response compatibility, Department of Psychology, Carnegie-Mellon University.

Rosenbloom, P.S. and A. Newell. (1986) The chunking of goal hierarchies, in R.S. Michalski, J.G. Carbonell and T.M. Mitchell (editors), *Machine Learning: An Artificial Intelligence Approach*, Morgan Kaufmann.

Rosenbloom, P.S. and J.E. Laird. (1986) Mapping explanation-based generalization onto SOAR. in *Proceedings of the AAAI-86*, Los Altos, Calif.

Rosenbloom, P.S., J.E. Laird and A. Newell. (1987) Knowledge Level Learning in SOAR. in *Proceedings of AAAI-87*.

Rosenschein, J.S. (1986) *Rational Interaction Cooperation Among Intelligent Agents*, Ph.D. Disertation, Stanfont University.

Roy, S. and J. Mostow. (1988) Parsing to learn fine grained rules. in *Proceedings of AAAI-88*, Saint Paul, Minnesota.

Rumelhart, D.E. and D. Zipser. (1985) Competitive Learning, *Cognitive Science*, 9, 75-112.

Rumelhart, D.E. and J.L. McClelland. (1986) *Parallel Distributed Processing*. The MIT Press.

Rumelhart, D.E., G.E. Hinton and R.J. Williams. (1986) Learning internal representations by error propagation, in Rumelhart, D.E. and J.L. McClelland and the PDP Res. Group (editors), *Parallel Distributed Processing: Explorations in the Microstructure of Cognition*, I: Foundations, MIT Press.

Russell, S.J., P. Norvig. (1995, 2003) *Artificial Intelligence: A Modern Approach*. Prentice Hall.

Russell, S.J. and B.N. Grosof. (1987) A declarative approach to bias in concept learning, in *Proceedings of AAAI-87*.

Sakama Chiaki, Katsumi Inoue. (2009) Brave induction: a logical framework for learningfrom incomplete information. *Mach Learn* 76: 3–35.

Salzberg, S. (1983) Generating hypotheses to explain prediction failures, in *Proceedings of AAAI-83*, Washington, D.C.

Salzberg, S. (1985) Heuristics for inductive learning, in *Proceedings of IJCAI-85*, Los Angeles, Calif.

Shanahan, Murray. (1997) *Solving the Frame Problem*. The MIT Press.

Sarrett, W.E. and M.J. Pazzani. (1989) One-sided algorithms for integrating empirical and explanation-based learning, in *Proceedings of IWML-89*, Cornell University, Ithaca, New York.

Scerri, P., Pynadath, D., Schurr, N., Farinelli, A., Gandhe, S. and Tambe, M. (2004) Team Oriented Programming and Proxy Agents. The Next Generation. *PROMAS 2003*: 131-148.

P. Scerri, Y. Xu, E. Liao, J. Lai, and K. Sycara. (2004) Scaling Teamwork to Very Large Teams. in *AAMAS'04*.

Schaffer, J.D. and J.J. Grefenstette. (1985) Multi-objective learning via genetic algorithms, in *Proceedings og IJCAI-85*, Los Angeles, Calif.

Schank, R.C. (1972) Conceptual dependency: a theory of natural language understanding. *Cognitive Psychology*, Vol. 3,No. 4.

Schank, R.C. (1982) *Dynamic Memory*. Cambridge University Press, Cambridge.

Schank, R.C. (1992) Story-Based Memory. in R.Morelli, et al,(eds). *Minds, brains, and computers*, Ablex, 134-151.

Schank, R.C. and David B.L. (1989) Creativity and learning in a case-based explainer. *Artificial Intelligence*, 40(1),353-385.

Schapire, R.E. (1989) The strength of weak learnability. in *Proceedings of the Second Annual Workshop on Computational Learning Theory*, Santa Cruz, CA.

Schlimmer, J.C. and D. Fisher. (1986) A case study of incremental concept induction, in *Proceedings of AAAI-86*.

Schlimmer, J.C. and R.H. Granger, Jr. (1987) Incremental learning from noisy data. *Machine Learning*, 1(3), 317.

Schreiber, Guus. (2000) *Knowledge Engineering and Management*. MIT Press.

Segre, A.M. (1987) On the operationality/generality trade-off in explanation-based learning. in *Proceedings of IJCAI-87*, Milan, Italy.

Segre, A.M. (1988) Operationality and real world plans. in *Proceedings of AAAI-88*,Menlo Park, Calif.

Shapiro, E.Y. (1981) Inductive inference of theories from facts. *Research Report 192*, Department of Computer Science, Yale University, New Haven, CT.

Shapiro, E.Y. (1983) *Algorithmic Program Debugging*. MIT Press.

Shavlik, J.W. and G.F. DeJong. (1987) An explanation-based approach to generalizing number, in *Proceedings of IJCAI-87*, Milan, Italy.

Shavlik, J.W. and G.F. DeJong. (1987) BAGGER: An EBL system that extends and generalizes explanations, in *Proceedings of AAAI-87*.

Shavlik, J.W. and G.G. Towell. (1989) Combining explanation-based learning and artificial neural networks. in *Proceedings of IWML-89*,Cornell University, Ithaca, New York.

Shi, Zhiwei, Zhongzhi Shi, Xi Liu, Zhiping Shi. (2008) A Computational Model for Feature Binding. *Science Press, C-Life Sciences*, Vol. 51 No. 5, pp. 470-478.

Shi, Zhongzhi. (1984) Design and Implementation of FORMS. *Proceedings of International Conference on Computer and Applications*, Beijing.

Shi, Zhongzhi. (1987) Intelligent Scheduling Architecture in KSS. *The Second International Conference on Computers and Applications*, Beijing.

Shi, Zhongzhi. (1988a) On Knowledge Base System Architecture. *Proceedings of Knowledge-Based Systems and Models of Logical Reasoning*, Cairo.

Shi, Zhongzhi. (1988b) *Knowledge Engineering* (In Chinese). Tsinghua University Press.

Shi, Zhongzhi. (1989) Distributed Artificial Intelligence. *Proceedings on the Future of Research in AI.*

Shi, Zhongzhi. (1990a) Hierarchical model of mind. Invited Speaker. *Chinese Joint Conference on Artificial Intelligence.*

Shi, Zhongzhi. (1990b) Logic —object based knowledge model. *Chinese Journal of Computer*, No. 10.

Zhongzhi Shi. (1990c) Neural Computer. *Proceedings of National Conference on Neural Network.*

Shi, Zhongzhi. (1992a) Hierarchical model of human mind. invited talk, *PRICAI-92*, Seoul.

Shi, Zhongzhi. (1992b) *Principles of Machine Learning.* International Academic Publishers.

Shi, Zhongzhi (Ed.) (1992c) *Automated Reasoning.* IFIP Transactions A-19, North-Holland.

Shi, Zhongzhi. (1993) *Neural Computing* (In Chinese). Electronic Industry Press.

Shi, Zhongzhi. (1994) Artificial thought and intelligent systems, AI Summer School'94, 1994.

Shi, Zhongzhi. (2000) *Intelligent Agent and Application* (In Chinese). Science Press.

Shi, Zhongzhi. (2001a) *Knowledge Discovery* (In Chinese). Tsinghua University Press.

Shi, Zhongzhi. (2001b) *Advanced Computer Network* (In Chinese). Electronic Industry Press.

Shi, Zhongzhi. (2006a) *Intelligence Science* (In Chinese). Tsinghua University Press.

Shi, Zhongzhi. (1998, 2006b) *Advanced Artificial Intelligence* (In Chinese). Science Press.

Shi Zhongzhi. (2006c) Agent Grid Intelligence Platform for Collaborative Working Environment. Keynote Speaker, SELMAS2006 (ICSE 2006), Shanghai, May 22-23.

Shi, Zhongzhi. (2007) *Artificial Intelligence* (In Chinese). Defence Industry Press.

Shi, Zhongzhi. (2008) *Cognitive Science* (In Chinese). University of Science and Technology of China Press.

Shi, Zhongzhi. (2009a) *Neural Networks* (In Chinese). High Education Press.

Shi, Zhongzhi. (2009b) On Intelligence Science. To be appeared in *International Journal on Advanced Intelligence.*

Shi, Zhongzhi. (2010) *Intelligence Science.* Will be published by World Scientific Publishers.

Shi, Zhongzhi, Hu Cao, Yunfeng Li, Wenjie Wang, Tao Jiang. (1998). A Building Tool for Multiagent Systems: AOSDE. IT & Knows, IFIP WCC '98.

Shi, Zhongzhi, Yuan Chen, Lejian Liao. (1996) Constraint reasoning system COPS. The Progress of Artificial Intelligence 1996, pp. 69-73.

Shi, Zhongzhi, Mingkai Dong, Haijun Zhang, Qiujian Sheng. (2002) Agent-based Grid Computing. Keynote Speech, *International Symposium on Distributed Computing and Applications to Business, Engineering and Science*, Wuxi, Dec. 16-20.

Shi, Zhongzhi, Mingkai Dong, Yuncheng Jiang, Haijun Zhang. (2005) A Logic Foundation for the Semantic Web. *Science in China, Series F Information Sciences*, 48(2): 161-178.

Shi, Zhongzhi and J. Han. (1990) Attribute Theory in Learning System, *Future Generation Computer Systems*, North Holland Publishers, No.6.

Shi, Zhongzhi, Hong Hu, Shiwei Ye. (1993) Neural Approximate Logic, *Chinese Journal Of Electronics*, Vol. 2, No. 2.

Shi, Zhongzhi, He Huang, Jiewen Luo, Fen Lin, Haijun Zhang. (2006) Agent-based Grid Computing. Applied Mathematical Modeling, 30: 629-640.

Shi Zhongzhi, Youping Huang, Qing He, Lida Xu, Shaohui Liu, Liangxi Qin, Ziyan Jia, Jiayou Li. (2007) MSMiner-A Developing Platform for OLAP. *Decision Support Systems*, 42(4): 2016-2028.

Shi, Zhongzhi, Chunhuan Mo. (1995) Artificial Life (In Chinese). *Journal of Computer Research and Development*, Vol. 32, No. 12.

Shi, Zhongzhi, Qijia Tian, Wenjie Wang, Tao Wang, (1996) Epistemic Reasoning About Knowledge and Belief Based on Dependence Relation. *Advanced Software Research*, Vol. 3, No. 2.

Shi, Zhongzhi, Qijia TIAN, Yunfeng LI. (1999) RAO Logic for Multiagent Framework. *Journal of Computer Science and Technology*, 14(4): 393-400.

Shi, Zhongzhi, Jun Wang, Applying Case-Based Reasoning to Engine Oil Design. *AI in Engineering*, 11 (1997),167-172.

Shi, Zhongzhi, Tao Wang, Wenjie Wang, Qijia Tian, Meng Ye. (1995) A Flexible Architecture for Multi-Agent System, *PACES-95*.

Shi, Zhongzhi and J. Wu, H. Sun, J. Xu. (1990) OKBMS, An Object-Oriented Knowledge Base Management System. *International Conference on TAI*, Washington.

Shi, Zhongzhi and Zhihua Yu. (1990) *Cognitive Science and Computer*. Scientific Popularization Press.

Shi, Zhongzhi, Haijun Zhang, Mingkai Dong. (2003) MAGE: Multi-Agent Environment. *ICCNMC-03*, IEEE CS Press, pp. 181-188.

Shi, Zhongzhi, Zhang Jian, Liu Jimin. (1998) Neural Field Theory-A Framework of neural Information Processing. *Neural Network and Brain Proceedings*, 421-424.

Shi, Zhongzhi, Zhikun Zhao, Hu Cao. (2002) A Planning Algorithm Based on Constraints Propagation. *International Conference on Intelligent Information Technology (ICIIT2002)*, Sep 22-25, Beijing, China, P410-416.

Shi, Zhongzhi and Zheng Zheng. (2007) Tolerance granular space model (In Chinese). In Miao Teqian etc. (Eds.) *Granular Computing: Past, Present and Future*. Science Press, 42-82.

Shivakumar, V., Byron Dom. (1998) Model-Based Hierarchical Clustering. *PRICAI Workshop on Text and Web Mining*.

Shoham, Y. (1992) On the synthesis of useful social laws for artificial agent societies. *AAAI-92*.

Shoham, Y. (1993) Agent-oriented programming. Artificial Intelligence, 60: 51-92.

Shoham Yoav and Kevin Leyton-Brown, (2008) *Multiagent Systems: Algorithmic, Game-Theoretic, and Logical Foundations*, Cambridge University Press.

Shoham,Y., Moshe Tennenholtz. (1995) On social laws for artificial agent societies: off-line design. *Artificial Intelligence*, 73: 231-252.

Siekmann, J. and P. Szabo. (1982) *Universal Unification*. Springer-Verlag.

Sierra C., C. Castelfranchi, K. S. Decker, J.S. Sichman. (2009) *AAMAS 2009*. Budapest, Hungary, May 10-15, 2009, IFAAMAS 2009.

Silver, B. (1986) Precondition analysis: learning control information,in R.S. Michalski, J.G. Carbonell and T.M. Mitchell (editors), *Machine Learning: An Artificial Intelligence Approach*, Morgan Kaufmann.

Silver, Daniel L., Ryan Poirier, Duane Currie. (2008) Inductive transfer with context-sensitive neural networks. *Mach Learn* 73: 313–336.

Simon, H.A. (1982) *The Sciences of the Artificial*. MIT Press.

Simon, H.A. (1983) Why should machines learning?, in R.S. Michalski, J.G. Carbonell and T.M. Mitchell (editors), *Machine Learning: An Artificial Intelligence Approach*, Tioga.

Simon, H.A. (1986) *Human Cognition: Information Processing Theory of Thinking*. Beijing: Science Press.

Simon, H.A. (1998) Discovering explanations. Minds and Machines, 8(1), 7-37.

Simon H.A. (2001) Creativity in the arts and sciences. In Cultures of creativity: The centennial celebrations of the Nobel Prizes. The Kenyon Review, Spring, 23(2), 203-220.

Simpson, R.L. (1985) *A computer model of case-based reasoning in problem solving*. School of ICS, Georgia inst. of Tech., Atlanta, GA.

Singh, S., T. Jaakkola, M.I. Jordan. (1995) Reinforcement learning with soft state aggregation. In: G Tesauro, D Touretzky, eds. *Advances in Neural Information Processing Systems*, 7. Morgan Kaufmann: MIT Press, 361-368.

Sleeman, D.H., P. Langley and T.M. Mitchell. (1982) Learning from solution paths: An approach to the credit assignment problem. *AI Magazine*, 3(2),48-52.

Smith, R. (1980) *A learning system based on genetic algorithms*. Department of Computer Science, University of Pittsburgh.

Smith, R.G. (1980) The contract-net protocol: high-level communication and control in a distributed problem solver. *IEEE Transaction on Computers*, C-29(12): 1104-1113.

Stepp, R.E. and R.S. Michalski. (1986) Conceptual clustering: inventing goal-oriented classifications of structured objects,in R.S. Michalski, J.G. Carbonell and T.M. Mitchell (editors), *Machine Learning: An Artificial Intelligence Approach*, Morgan Kaufmann.

Stepp, R.E. (1987) Concepts in conceptual clustering. In *Proceedings of IJCAI-87*, Milan, Italy.

Song, Zhiwei, Xiaoping Chen. (2003) Reinforcement learning in the robot soccer. *Robot*, 24 (7S): 761-766.

Stone, P., Veloso, M. (1999) Task decomposition, dynamic role assignment, and low-bandwidth communication for real time strategic teamwork. *Artificial Intelligence*, 110(2): 241-273

Sutton, R. S. (1996) Generalization in reinforcement learning: successful examples using sparse coarse coding. In: D Touretzky, M. Mozer, M. Hasselmo, eds. *Advances in Neural Information Processing Systems*, 8, NY: MIT Press, 1038-1044.

Sycara, K., K. Decker, A. Pannu, M. Williamson, D. Zeng. (1996) Distributed Artificial Agents. URL: http://www.cs.cmu.edu/~softagents/.

Tadepalli, P. (1989) Lazy explanation-based learning: A solution to the intractable theory problem, in *Proceedings of IJCAI-89*, Detroit, Michigan USA.

Tadepalli, P. (1991) A formalization of explanation-based macro-operator learning, in *Proceedings of IJCAI-91*, 616-622.

Tambe, M. and P. Rosenbloom. (1989) Eliminating expensive chunks by restricting expressiveness. in *Proceedings of IJCAI-89*, Detroit, Michigan USA.

Tesauro, G.J. (1992) Practical Issues in Temporal Difference Learning. *Machine Learning*, Vol. 8, pp. 257-277.

Thagard, P. and D.M. Cohen and K.J. Holyoak. (1989) Chemical analogies: Two kinds of explanation. in *Proceedings of IJCAI-89*, Detroit, Michigan USA.

Thagard, P., Holyoak, K. J., Nelson, G. and Gochfeld, D. (1990) Analogy Retrieval by Constraint Satisfaction. in *Artificial Intelligence*, 46.

Thornton, C.J. (1987) Analogical inference as generalized inductive inference, In Jantke, K.P. (editors), *Analogical and Inductive Inference*, Springer-Verlag.

Tian, Qijia, Zhongzhi Shi, Wenjie Wang, Tao Wang. (1995) An Approach to Autoepistemic Logic, *ICYCS-95*.

Tian, Qijia, Zhongzhi Shi. (1996) A Model-Theoretical Approach to Action and Progression, *SMC-96*, 1996.

Tian, Qijia, Zhongzhi Shi. (1997) Model-theoretical foundation of action and progression. *Science Press*, Series E-Technological Sciences. Vol. 40 (4): 430-438.

Tsitsiklis, John N. (1994) Asynchronous stochastic approximation and Q-learning. *Machine Learning*, 16(3): 185-202.

Tu, Xiaoyuan. (1996) *Artificial Animals for Computer Animation*. Ph.D. Dissertation, University of Toronto.

Utgoff, P.E. (1984) *Shift of bias for inductive concept learning*. Department of Computer Science, Rutgers University.

Utgoff, P.E. (1986) *Machine Learning of Inductive Bias*. Kluwer Academic Publishers.

Utgoff, P.E. (1988a) Perceptron trees: A case study in hybrid concept representations. in *Proceedings of AAAI-88*, Saint Paul, Minnesota.

Utgoff, P.E. (1988b) ID5: An incremental ID3. in *Proceedings of ICML-88*, San Mateo, CA.

Utgoff, P.E. and T.M. Mitchell. (1982) Acquisition of appropriate bias for inductive concept learning. in *Proceedings of AAAI-82*, Pittsburgh, Pa.

Vaculín R., K. Sycara. (2008) Semantic Web Services Monitoring: An OWL-S based Approach. in *Proceedings of 41st HICSS conference*, Hawai.

Vaithyanathan, S., Byron Dom. (1998) Model-Based Hierarchical Clustering. *PRICAI Workshop on Text and Web Mining*.

Valiant, L.G. (1984) A theory of the learnable. *Communications of the ACM*, 27(11), 1134-42.

Valiant, L.G. (1985) Learning disjunction of conjunction. in *Proceedings of IJCAI-85*, Los Angeles, Calif.

VanLehn, K. and W. Ball. (1987) A version sapce approach to learning context-free grammars. *Machine Learning*, 2(1), 39.

Vapnik, V. N. (1995) *The Nature of Statistical Learning Theory*. Springer-Verlag, New York.

Vapnik, V.N. (1998) *Statistical Learning Theory*. Wiley-Interscience Publication, John Wiley&Sons, Inc.

Vapnik, V.N. A. Ja. Chervonenkis. (1991) A Necessary and Sufficient Conditions for Consistency in the Empirical Risk Minimization Method. *Pattern Recognition and Image Analysis,* 1(3): 284-305.

Vapnik, V., Golowich S, Smola A. (1997) Support Vector Method for Function Approximation, Regression Estimation, and Signal Processing. in *Advances in Neural Information Processing Systems 9*.

Waddington, C.H. (1974) A catastrophic theory of evolution. *Annals of the New York Academy of Science*, 231, 32-42.

Waltz, D. (1975) Understanding line drawings of scenes with shadows. *In The Psychology of Computer Vision*, P.H. Winston (ed.), 19-91, McGraw Hill.

Warmuth, M.K. (1987) Towards representation independence in PAC learning. In K.P. Jantke, (editor), *Analogical and Inductive Inference*, Springer-Verlag.

Watkins, C., Peter Dayan. (1989) Q-learning. Machine Learning, 8, 279-292.

Werbos, P.J. (1974) *Beyond regression: New tools for prediction and analysis in the behavioral sciences*. Harvard University, Cambridge, MA.

Widmer, G. (1989) A tight integration of deductive and inductive learning. in *Proceedings of IWML-89*,Cornell University, Ithaca, New York.

Wilkins, D.C. (1988) Knowledge base refinement using apprenticeship learning techniques. in *Proceedings of the AAAI-88*, Los Altos, Calif.

Williams, B. C. (1988) MINIMA: A symbolic approach to qualitative reasoning, *AAAI1988*, 105-112.

Williams, B.C. and de Kleer, J. (1991) Qualitative reasoning about physical systems: a return to roots. *Artificial Intelligence*, 51 (1-3) pp. 1-9.

Wilson, S.W. (1987) Classifier systems and the animat problem. *Machine Leanring*, 2(3), 199.

Wooldridge, M. (2002) *An Introduction to MultiAgent Systems*, John Wiley & Sons Ltd.

Wooldridge, M., N. R. Jennings. (1995). Intelligent Agents: Theory and Practice. *Knowledge Engineering*, 10(2)

Xu, Y., Scerri, P., Yu, B., Okamoto, S., Lewis, M., Sycara, K. (2005) An integrated token-based algorithm for scalable coordination. In: *Proceedings of the fourth international joint conference on Autonomous agents and multiagent systems (AAMAS)*, Utrecht, NL 407–414.

Xu, Y., Scerri, P., Lewis, M., and Sycara, K. (2008) Token-Based Approach for Scalable Team. In *Cooperative Networks: Control and Optimization*, Edward Elgar Publishing.

Yao, Xin, Yong Xu. (2006) Recent Advances in Evolutionary Computation. *Journal of Computer Science and Technology*, 21(1): 1-18.

Yao, Y. Y. (2001) Information granulation and rough set approximation. *International Journal of Intelligent Systems*, 16: 87-104.

Yao, Y.Y. (2008) A Unified Framework of Granular Computing, in: Pedrycz, W., Skowron, A. and Kreinovich, V. (Eds.), *Handbook of Granular Computing,* Wiley, pp. 401-410.

Ye, Shiren. (2001) *Massive Data Reduction and Classification*. Ph D. Dessertation, Institute of Computing Technology, Chinese Academy of Sciences.

Ye, Shiwei, Zhongzhi Shi. (1995) Generalized K-means Clustering Algorithm and Frequency Sensitive Competitive Learning. *Journal of Computer Science and Technology*, Vol. 10, No. 6.

Yoon, Sungwook, Alan Fern. (2008) Robert Givan, Learning Control Knowledge for Forward Search Planning, *The Journal of Machine Learning Research*, 9: 683-718.

Zadeh, L.A., Fuzzy sets and information granularity, in Gupta, M.M., Ragade, R.K. and Yager, R.R. (eds.) (1979) *Advances in Fuzzy Set Theory and Applications*, Amsterdam: North-Holland.

Zadeh, L.A. (1997) Towards a theory of fuzzy information granulation and its centrality in human reasoning and fuzzy log ic. *Fuzzy Sets and Systems.* 19: 111-127.

Zadeh, L.A. (2005) Toward a generalized theory of uncertainty (GTU)—an outline. *Information Sciences* 172: 1–40.

Zaki M.J. (1999) Parallel and Distributed Association Mining: A Survey. *IEEE Concurrency*, 7(4): 14-25.

Zaki M.J. (2000) Scalable Algorithms for Association Mining. *IEEE Trans. Knowl. Data Eng.* 12(3): 372-390.

Zaki M.J. (2005) Efficiently Mining Frequent Trees in a Forest: Algorithms and Applications. *IEEE Trans. Knowl. Data Eng.* 17(8): 1021-1035.

Zhang, Bo, Ling Zhang. (1992) *Theory and Applications of Problem Solving*, Elsevier Science Publishers B. V., North-Holland.

Zhang, Lin. and Bo Zhang. (2005) Fuzzy Reasoning Model under Quotient Space Structure, *Information Sciences*, vol. 173, issue 4, pp. 353-364.

Zheng, Zheng, Hong Hu, Zhongzhi Shi. (2005) Tolerance Relation Based Information Granular Space, *Lecture Notes in Computer Science*, Vol. 3641, pp. 682-691.